PUBLICATIONS OF THE NORTH CAROLINA HISTORICAL COMMISSION

Christoph Von Graffenried's Account of the Founding of New Bern

EDITED WITH AN HISTORICAL INTRODUCTION AND AN ENGLISH TRANSLATION

BY
VINCENT H. TODD, PH.D.
UNIVERSITY OF ILLINOIS

IN COOPERATION WITH
JULIUS GOEBEL, PH.D.
PROFESSOR OF GERMANIC LANGUAGES
UNIVERSITY OF ILLINOIS

HERITAGE BOOKS
2009

HERITAGE BOOKS
AN IMPRINT OF HERITAGE BOOKS, INC.

Books, CDs, and more—Worldwide

For our listing of thousands of titles see our website
at
www.HeritageBooks.com

A Facsimile Reprint
Published 2009 by
HERITAGE BOOKS, INC.
Publishing Division
100 Railroad Ave. #104
Westminster, Maryland 21157

Copyright © 1920 Vincent H. Todd, Ph.D.

THE NORTH CAROLINA HISTORICAL COMMISSION

J. Bryan Grimes, Chairman
W. J. Peele   D. H. Hill
M. C. S. Noble   Thomas M. Pittman
R. D. W. Connor, Secretary, Raleigh

— Publisher's Notice —
In reprints such as this, it is often not possible to remove blemishes from the original. We feel the contents of this book warrant its reissue despite these blemishes and hope you will agree and read it with pleasure.

International Standard Book Numbers
Paperbound: 978-0-7884-1390-2
Clothbound: 978-0-7884-8129-1

CONTENTS

PREFACE	5
HISTORICAL INTRODUCTION	7
BIBLIOGRAPHY	112
GERMAN VERSION	115
ENGLISH TRANSLATION OF THE GERMAN VERSION	219
FRENCH VERSION	321
ENGLISH TRANSLATION OF THE FRENCH VERSION	357
VOCABULARY	393
INDEX	419

PREFACE

A carefully prepared and conservative computation made within the last ten years gives the surprising result that, of our white population there are at least twenty-seven per cent of German birth or extraction, while those of English origin number but thirty per cent. With such a proportion of Germans, is it not strange that almost nothing is said in our histories about this great element of our population; about the causes that induced them to leave their homes; about the circumstances of their first settlements; about their influence upon the growth of our common culture?

The reason of this lies, partly in the undeveloped provincial character of American historiography, partly in the fact that American History was first written by men from New England. They wrote of the things with which they were most familiar, their own Puritan commonwealths and the institutions developed from them. Biased by provincial prejudices they overlooked other events of equally great importance, so that their histories read like a one-sided glorification of their ancestors. A very powerful contributory cause for this discrimination is the fact that the Germans made their settlements comparatively late, and for the most part avoided New England. By the time the first permanent settlements were made at Germantown, near Philadelphia (1683) New England had passed through some of its most epoch-making experiences. The colonies about Massachusetts Bay, Connecticut and Rhode Island had been settled and their characteristic institutions, which have come down to our own time, were becoming fixed in laws and customs of the people. American historiography as first conceived by the New England historians has since followed the same or similar lines, and until recently when the German-Americans themselves took up the work, very little, in general, was known about the early life of this portion of our population.

It is to be hoped that this regrettable division in matters of historical truth will be done away with, and since no one nationality can rightfully claim all the honor of having made America what it is, Germans as well as Puritans and Cavaliers will come to be recognized for what they are or have done, and not be excluded from consideration for what they have not done.[1] To illustrate: It was not a German woman's pig to which we traced the bicameral system of

---

[1] There is some assurance that this hoped for change of attitude will come, when a historian like Channing in his History of the United States (vol. II, pages 116, 395, 404 ff) gives a rather extended and appreciative notice of the Germans in Pennsylvania. In a foot note on page 405 he mentions the manuscripts on which this paper has been based.

Government in Massachusetts; but it is to the German settlers at Schoharie that we, in a large measure, owe the fortunate outcome of the French and Indian war, for it was they who kept the Six Nations from joining the French, when such an event would have spelled disaster to the New York and New England colonies; they did not give us theocracies from which a doubtful ideal of the state eventually evolved; but they helped to give us freedom of conscience, the very corner-stone of modern politics, and it is to the German printer in New York that we owe an untrammeled public press. Who shall say which is the worthier?

It is not sufficient then to know that in the seventeenth and eighteenth centuries a large number of Germans came to America, and made or tried to make certain settlements. We want to go further and learn about their life and work and be able to appreciate them as we do the other pioneers. It is for this reason that a study of Baron Christoph von Graffenried's settlements may be considered worth while.

This colony in North Carolina would have consisted of only a few Swiss adventurers but for the events of the year 1709. These enlarged the scope, increased the prestige of the undertaking, gave the leadership to one of the few ever to possess a title of nobility in Locke's new American order, made this pioneer of several Swiss undertakings the nearest approach to Locke's ideal that ever existed in America, and taking it out of its isolation, made it a part of the great German migration of 1709; a consideration of which may properly precede the study of Graffenried's own adventures.

Since a man should be judged by his intentions and by the times in which he lived, as well as by the actual results of his efforts, it has seemed well to quote from or make references to the writings of contemporaries wherever possible.[1] For instance, his expectation of becoming rich from silver mines in Maryland or Virginia seemed to us absurd because we know there is no silver in those parts in paying quantities; but if we find, that in his day, everyone believed that there was silver to be found there, and if we remember that the Secretary of the London Royal Society in 1669 urged Governor John Winthrop to look for mines in Connecticut and if necessary to "employ dogs of the best scent"[2] for this purpose, Graffenried's persistency in searching for silver takes on a different aspect.

[2]Proceedings Mass. Hist. Society, 1878, pages 229-240.

PART I

THE PALATINATE MOVEMENT

CHAPTER I

THE GENERALLY ACCEPTED CAUSES OF THE PALATINE MIGRATION

The great stream of emigration from Germany to England and from thence to America, beginning rather feebly in the latter part of the seventeenth century, then suddenly swelling to such enormous proportions that more Germans had come to New York, Pennsylvania, and North Carolina in one year than had come to New England in the first ten years of the settlements about Massachusetts Bay, has as its fundamental cause the great intellectual movement of the Reformation, and the equally intense Counter Reformation which began in the latter part of the sixteenth century and extended far into the seventeenth century.

Since the Protestant Reformation in England had come rather later than in Germany, and had not been so radical at the start, English reformers long looked upon Germany as the fatherland of the Reformation, and during the persecutions which accompanied the reaction under Mary (1553-1558) those who escaped over seas found refuge in Holland, Germany and Switzerland. Under Elizabeth protestantism was again gradually restored, but there was no place for any who disagreed with the church as established by the state and dissenters were severely punished, but still the sentiment of protest grew until after the revolution of 1642, when Cromwell, having finally become a dictator, was able to introduce a second reformation, which led to a wider separation from Rome. He hoped to secure the ground gained, by a union of the protestant states against the Catholic Spanish world. He conceived England to be the champion protector of protestantism, and by such a union, he hoped to make it a world power. During the reigns of Charles II and James II there was another reaction which, however, was not so violent as that in the reign of Mary. When William of Orange became King of England protestantism was again fully restored and there was even some relief given dissenters. It was Queen Anne, however, who took up Cromwell's work, and to the best of her ability carried out his program of national and protestant expansion. Public opinion, moreover, was, to a large degree, with her in this matter.

Interest in the German protestant situation was kept alive by pamphlets which gave information about the conditions of the Reformation in Germany and particularly in the Palatinate to which they felt related because of the marriage of Elizabeth, daughter of James I of England, to the Elector Frederick, better known as the Winter King. This interest was further increased since the cause had been compelled to fight for its life in Germany as well as in England.

Not only the wars which came in Luther's time and immediately following his death were caused by the Reformation; but the Thirty Years' War and the wars in which the French King, Louis XIV, involved Europe during his long reign were also very largely incited by the same spirit of enmity that animated the earlier Counter Reformation.

In all these struggles no portion of Germany suffered so much as that part called the Lower Palatinate.[1] Lying as it does on the eastern boundary of France, it was easily accessible to the French soldiery; a fertile country, it offered excellent opportunity for maintaining an army; and being protestant it was an especial object of resentment to the French King. Turenne in 1674 thoroughly ravaged the province in accordance with his policy of making the enemy support his army. Then in the wars of 1688-89, while the rest of Germany which might have given aid was busy warding off the Turks, Louis XIV took the opportunity of weakening the enemy, venting his malice against the protestants, and doing a pleasure to Madame de Maintenon by devastating the province in a way unparalleled in modern history. He purposed to make the country as nearly a desert as possible, and to do so wantonly burned cities and towns as well as isolated dwellings, cut down orchards and uprooted vines. Many of the inhabitants were butchered, others died of exposure, others fled, and the few who remained were left in a most miserable condition. The treaty of Ryswick gave a temporary relief and many refugees returned to their homes. But in 1700 the wars of the Spanish Succession broke out, and the Palatinate was again overrun with troops. The destruction seems not to have been so severe as in the previous war, but the new Elector, now a Catholic, subjected the Protestants to a system of persecution which was very annoying and disquieting; for the persecutions which had long accompanied the Reformation throughout Europe were still fresh in men's memories and they dreaded the worst.

---
[1] Eccl. Rec. vol. III, page 1453 ff.

By the Peace of Westphalia (1648) the Lutheran and Reformed religions had been established in the Palatinate and the Catholic religion was allowed only on sufferance of the Elector. But now under John William (1690-1716) religious toleration was announced, and the Roman Catholic religion thereby put upon a theoretical equality with the other two. As a matter of fact, he went further and took revenues, churches, and schools belonging to the Protestants, whether or not they had been Catholic property, and turned them to Catholic uses, or else arranged for Catholics and Protestants to have joint possession of the church edifices. He refused to allow Protestant clergymen to sit in the Ecclesiastical Council; and when the people protested, he said that the "ministers were seditious rebels." Soldiers, moreover, were quartered on the peasants to harass them. The persecution, also, often took the form of bodily injury and death was frequently the result. No wonder, then, the poorer subjects became alarmed.

In Switzerland the Anabaptists having no legal status had always been exposed to the doubtful mercies of the bigoted Reformed Church.[2] The martyrdom of many of the leaders was a recent memory and at this very time (1708-9) the prisons were full of those whose greatest crime was obedience to the scriptural injunction "swear not at all," and a disagreement with the Reformed Church as to the time in the candidate's life when baptism is to be administered.

In other provinces of Germany, as well as in the Palatinate, there was great suffering among the poorer classes because of the oppressions of the petty princes who fashioned their courts after the model of Versailles, plunged into extravagance and excess of all kinds, the burden of which fell upon the laboring classes who suffered severely from the exorbitant taxes and tolls demanded to defray these expenses.

This widespread poverty, and the religious persecutions had for years been producing a general unrest, and those who saw no hope of better conditions at home began to look to America as a place where they could go and be safe. A rather small colony had gone to Pennsylvania with Pastorius as early as 1683, and a few families or single persons had gone every year since. Another small company, 50 persons in all, under the Lutheran pastor, Kocherthal, came to England in 1780 and were sent to New York.[3]

In 1709 a further cause was given in an exceedingly hard winter.[4] The cold was so intense that birds and animals succumbed to its severity and the loss of life among the very poor was considerable. Such an experience would doubtless make Kocherthal's description

[2] E. Mueller, Bernische Taeufer.
[3] E. Mueller, Penn. Ger. Soc. vol. VII, page 263.
[4] Penn. Ger. Soc. vol. VII, page 283.

of Carolina more attractive than ever. That same spring and summer great numbers of Germans came through Holland to England and were given all possible care by public and private philanthropy. This is generally spoken of as the Palatine Migration, but the name is misleading because there were many other German-speaking people in the movement. The majority of these immigrants did, however, come from the Palatinate; and as the English people were interested in that province, they gave the name without distinction to all who came.

CHAPTER II

THE DECISIVE CAUSE OF THE PALATINE MIGRATION

The causes mentioned, together with the so-called German *Wanderlust* and the attraction which America had for Europeans, have been considered sufficient to explain this migration. But are they sufficient? Is there not a more important problem still unsolved? When one considers that all these contributing causes, political oppression, religious persecution, devastation of property, and poverty had existed for years in Germany and Switzerland; that the passion for travel had always been characteristic of this people; that the advantages of America had been well set forth by the preaching of William Penn and other Quakers before this colony was founded; that over 50 books,[1] broadsides, and pamphlets had been circulated over Germany, all in the interest of inducing emigration to Pennsylvania, resulting in only one small settlement at Germantown in Pennsylvania in 1683; his conclusion must be that there must have been something more than the severe winter added to the above causes which increased the numbers of the emigrants from a small flock of 50 under Kocherthal's leadership in 1708, to a mass of over 10,000 persons without a leader in 1709. How does it happen that they all expected to be taken to America, despite the fact that the Walloons who preceded them had had no such hopes?

The truth is Queen Anne was attempting to continue Cromwell's plan of expansion, and in this program there was need of increasing her subjects at home and in the colonies, by inviting, and even subsidizing, people to settle in British America. At the same time also the Proprietors of the Provinces were quite as anxious as the Queen to have their territories settled; and no one was more industrious than Penn in advertising his province. Yet the subject is difficult to treat, because direct evidence is not plentiful, since no one wished to take the responsibility of tempting the subjects to leave their rightful lord. But there was one document which had great, perhaps the greatest, influence in persuading people to go to America; and that was a small volume printed first in 1706, by the Reverend Mr. Kocherthal.

The Reverend Mr. Kocherthal, just mentioned, had not been to America at the time he published his book, but had been in England to make inquiries about the colonies. Having become convinced of the advantages of South Carolina, he wrote a handbook for Germans,

[1] Penn. Ger. Soc. vol. VII, page 175.

describing the province, with directions how to go there. This book was so eagerly read that in 1709 it had reached its fourth edition. Graffenried and several of his settlers mention Kocherthal's book, indeed this is the only book the settlers do mention; and from the nature of their allusions to it one must conclude they were strongly influenced by it. In fact, the book continued to have such an effect, even after Kocherthal had gone to New York (1708) that Anton Wilhelm Boehme,[2] pastor of the German Court Chapel of St. James, felt called upon to issue a series of tracts in book form, under the title "Das verlangte nicht erlangte Canaan," directed specifically against Kocherthal's description of South Carolina.

An investigation, detailed mention of which will be made later, brings out the additional fact that another great cause of the emigration was the so-called Golden Book, so named because the Queen's picture adorned one of the front pages, and the title page was printed in gilt letters. This was evidently a very special and expensive edition, and was probably published with the Queen's permission some time after she had ascended the throne in 1702, the evident intention being to impress German readers. From the language in the report of the investigating committee it is clear that the book was written chiefly in praise of Carolina.

Absolute proof cannot be given; but judging from the coincidence of the date at which the books appeared, Kocherthal's in 1706, the Golden Book between 1702 and 1709, from the similarity of the subject matter, both treating of Carolina in particular, and from the effect, one may conclude that Kocherthal's book and the Golden Book are identical. The following passages occur in the fourth edition undoubtedly reprinted from the first, and are among the directions to prospective colonists:

8. Nachdem aber die Fracht selbsten zu bezahlen sehr theuer/ und solche abzuverdienen sehr beschwehrlich—als hat der Author auff alle Weise sich angelegen seyn lassen/ ob dißfals andere Mittel außzufinden seyn möchten; worauff endlich der Vorschlag geschehen/ daß die Königin mit einer Supplication müszte ersucht werden/ ob selbige die Schiffe zur Überfahrt hergeben wolte/ da dann vielleicht geschehen könte/ daß man auch mit Königl. Schiffen von Holland abgeholet würde/ und also auch diese Ueberfahrts=Kosten erspahren könte: doch müsten auff solchen Fall eine gute Anzahl Leute miteinander kommen/ weilen widrigenfals der Mühe nicht werth seyn würde/ die Königin zu bemühen viel weniger so viel Kosten anzuwenden/ als bei diesen zu den Schiffen und Convoy erfordert wird.

9. Weilen auch bey diesen Zeiten an dem Königl. Hoff so wol wegen des schwehren Kriegs/ als auch wegen der immerfort währenden vielen Collecten=

---
[2] Penn. Ger. Soc. vol. VII, page 47 ff.

Gelder die Außgaben unbeschreiblich groß als hat man hierinnen mehrere Vorschläge gethan/ wie die Sache anzugreiffen/ damit die Königin der anderwärtigen schwehren Unkosten ungeachtet/ die Schiffe zur Ueberfahrt hergeben möchte; es seyn aber diese Vorschläge zu weitläufftig hier zu beschreiben; doch hoffet man/ daß vermittelst derselben die Bemühung nicht umsonst seyn werde wiewol niemand hierinnen etwas gewisses versprechen kan/ sondern erwarten muß wasz die Göttliche Schickung hierinnen verfügen werde.³

No very definite hopes are held out in these passages, but it would not require the Queen's picture and the gilded title page to give the impression to the poor people into whose hands the book would come, that they might expect help from her, both in crossing the Channel and after their arrival in England, in going to the Colonies. The effect could be no better with a direct and unequivocal statement, and there would be no danger of serious complications with the German princes, while, likewise, such a procedure would be quite in harmony with her diplomatic methods.

The Queen's policy of relieving the distressed Protestants met with considerable approval by the English people at first, for not only could they congratulate themselves on doing a charitable act to members of their own faith, but they could enjoy the prospect of turning the recipients of their charity to the material advantage of England. Simon Beaumont (July 18, 1709) expresses this mixture of motives in a letter too long to quote in full. "But these arguments aside. Receiving and succoring these poor Palatines seems to me but the payment of a just debt for the kind entertainment that gave many of our learned divines and others who were forced to take shelter beyond seas in the time of Queen Mary's persecution, and met with a hospitable reception at Frankfort in Germany, in the Palatinate, the Netherlands, Switzerland and other places; and shall we now suffer any of the posterity of our quondam benefacts to perish for want of bread that Providence has thrown into our arms for relief?" To the objection that England has enough poor of her own, he admits

---

³"But since it is very expensive to pay the freight one's self, and very difficult to work it out, the author has been very much concerned to find out whether in this case other means might not be found. Whereupon finally the proposal was made that the Queen be presented with a supplication to see whether she herself would not grant the ships, since it then might be that the people would be brought from Holland in the royal ships and thus this expense of passage could be saved; but yet in such a case a goodly number of people would have to come together, because if not, it would not be worth while to trouble the Queen, much less to go to so much expense as would be demanded for the ships and convoy.

"Because in these times the outlays at the Royal Court are indescribably great on account of the heavy war as well as because of the continual money collections, several proposals of how to attack the matter were made, in order that the Queen, regardless of other great expenses, might grant the ships for the passage. But these proposals are too extensive to describe here, and yet it is hoped that through them the effort will not be in vain, although in this matter no one can promise anything certain, but must wait and see what dispensation Divine Providence will make in this regard,"—*Kocherthal*, page 28.

she has beggars enough and suggests that they go to work and there
will be enough food for all; he then advances the generally accepted
economic principle that "multiplying the number of inhabitants con-
duces to the strength, grandeur, and wealth of the kingdom, since
its people are the Riches, Honor, and Strength of a nation and that
wealth increases in an equal proportion to the additional number of
the inhabitants." He also cites the fact that "the Palatines who went
to Magdeburg in 1689 are worth 100,000 crowns a year to the King
of Prussia. . . . That Holland by giving refuge to distressed
Protestants was enabled to beat off the Spanish" and concludes that
"10,000 Palatines is about 8,000£ without detriment to the nation."
Beaumont would have had them retained in England, then, in place
of letting them go to the colonies.[4]

The encouragement, however, was not limited to mere expressions
of good will on the part of private and public individuals, but, as will
be shown, official help, to which Queen Anne, the Duke of Sunderland,
and probably the Duke of Marlborough were parties, was given in
secret.

A bill to naturalize foreign Protestants, which had long been discussed, was now passed (March 3, 1709),[5] if not for the sake of the
immigrants, at least very opportunely for them. The result of the
encouragement given was very flattering, for within a few months
between 10,000 and 15,000 Germans were in England and had to be
cared for. The people and the government rose to the emergency;
tents and barns were assigned to these people for shelter;[6] private
charity was invoked for their relief; and the Queen authorized a daily
expenditure at first of £16, but later increased the amount to £100.[7]
Meanwhile their spiritual welfare was attended to. Ministers were
appointed for that particular service,[8] Bibles were distributed freely
among them,[9] and as soon as possible plans for settlement were made.
About 3,000 were settled in Ireland on what was intended to be advantageous terms, but of these, 232 families returned to London.[10]
Many enlisted,[11] and provision was made to send great numbers to
America at the expense of the government.

The phenomenal success of this scheme proved to be its undoing,
for so many Germans took advantage of the opportunity that London
was embarrassed with the expense and labor of supporting them.
Soon complaints were made, not only by the poor of England who
might be expected to look askance at this expenditure on these for-

---
[4]Eccl. Rec., vol III, page 1774 ff.
[5]Luttrel, vol. VI, page 413.
[6]Eccl. Rec., vol. III, page1750.
[7]Eccl. Rec., vol. III, page 1753, 1786.
[8]Eccl. Rec., vol. III, page 1742, 1785.
[9]Eccl. Rec., vol. III, page 1786.
[10]Eccl. Rec., vol. III, page 1836.
[11]Pennsylvanien im 17ten Jahrhundret, page 71.

eigners, when it could be so well employed by the needy folks at home, but also by persons in higher stations who did not all look upon such expenditures with favor. This opposition grew and in consequence a petition was presented to the House of Commons. This resulted in the appointment of a committee (January 15, 1710) to inquire, among other things "upon what invitation or encouragement the Palatines came over, and what moneys were expended in bringing them here and by whom." A bill was also ordered prepared to repeal the act for naturalizing foreign Protestants. But the important thing to notice is that the investigation assumes that these Protestants were invited or encouraged to come by some one, for otherwise such language would hardly have been used in the bill authorizing the investigation.

April 14, 1711, the committee made its report, of which the following extracts directly concern our discussion: "And upon the examination of several of them (Palatines) what were the motives which induced them to leave their native country, it appears to the committee that there were books and papers dispersed in the Palatinate with the Queen's picture before the book (and the title pages in letters of gold which from thence was called the Golden Book) to encourage them to come to England in order to be sent to Carolina or other of her Majesty's Plantations to be settled there. The book is chiefly a commendation of that country.

"What further encouraged them to leave their native country was the ravages the French had made and the damages the hard frost had done to their vines, and accordingly, one Joshua Kocherthal, a Lutheran Minister with some other Palatines to the number of 61 persons applied to Mr. Davenant at Frankfort for passes, but he refused them passes, moneys and recommendations for fear of disgusting the Elector Palatinate and desired to know her Majesty's pleasure therein, how to behave himself, in which Mr. Boyle signifies her Majesty's commands that, though the desire of the poor people to settle in the plantations is very acceptable and would be for the public good, yet she can by no means consent to Mr. Davenant giving in any public way encouragement, either by money or passes to the Elector Palatine's subjects to leave their country without his consent. . . . The next year an act for naturalizing Protestants being passed a great number of Palatines and some from other parts of Germany came into Holland, and from thence into England at several times, being upon their first arrival in Holland subsisted by the charity of Rotterdam, but afterwards at the Queen's expense and transports and other ships at her Majesty's charges provided to bring them thither, as also all sorts of necessaries during this voyage by Mr. Dayralle, her Majesty's Secretary at the Hague, who had received instructions from Mr. Secretary Boyle (in her Majesty's name) to that purpose, pursuant to my Lord Duke of Marlborough's desire. . . .

"Palatines still continued to come till the middle of October, 1709, although the orders to Mr. Dayralle to hinder their coming were often repeated; and the States General had been applied to by the English to send instructions to their minister in Germany, to discourage the coming of any more of the Elector Palatine's subjects in this manner since the Elector was highly offended by their desertion. Upon this Mr. Dayralle informed Mr. Secretary Boyle that these people (20 in August, 1709) were encouraged to emigrate by somebody in England, and that since the Prohibition, a Gentleman with a servant who came over in the Packet boat had gone amongst the Palatines at the Brill and distributed money and printed Tickets to encourage them to come over, and that many of these tickets were sent to their friends in Germany to persuade them to do the like.

"Mr. Dayralle could never discover who this gentleman was though he endeavored it all he could, and the committee could come to no certain knowledge therein, but find by two letters that Mr. Henry Torne a Quaker at Rotterdam, who in all this matter acted under Mr. Dayralle, forced a great many to embark for England after they had provided themselves a passage to go back to their own country, which the Palatines owned upon their arrival, was the only reason that induced them to come."[12]

A report of the various attempted settlements follows, and then is given the results of an investigation into the expenses incurred. The total is 135,775£ 18s 0½d. Of this there had been paid in two different transactions a total of 6,289£ 1s 9d in bringing Palatines to England. The report closes with the following resolutions:

Resolved, that the House doth agree with the Committee that the petitioners have fully proved the allegations of their petition and had just reason to complain.

Resolved, that the inviting and bringing over into this kingdom of the poor Palatines of all religions at the public expense was an extravagant and miserable charge to the kingdom, and a scandalous misapplication of the public money to the increase and oppression of the poor of this kingdom and of dangerous consequences to the constitution in church and state.

Resolved, that whosoever advised the bringing over of the poor Palatines into this kingdom was an enemy to the Queen and to this Kingdom.

This investigation after all did not lead to any definite conclusion, the reason for which may perhaps be inferred from a few sentences taken from a pamphlet which was styled *A Letter to a Gentleman in*

---

[12] Eccl. Rec., vol. III, page 1724 ff.

*the Country*¹³ in which it is written that "the committee having sate die in diam for a considerable time and searched into papers from the Commissioners of Trade, etc., among which there is said to be a letter from the E. of S. (Earl of Sunderland) that lets them into the whole mystery of the affair, they made their report to the House and their resolutions in manner and form following which was agreed to by those noble patriots." (The records omit the report which had been given before.) The author then quotes the resolutions which have been given in the preceding paragraphs.

The inference is, of course, that the Earl of Sunderland's letter involved persons whom it would have been impolitic to expose, and that, as a result, the committees chose to save their own reputations by launching brave sounding resolutions at no one in particular, even though they left the matter in a state of official uncertainty. And this was, perhaps, the wisest, if not the most courageous course.

The following extract from a letter which was written from London, July 13, 1708, and which appears as the third appendix to Kocherthal's 1709 edition of his *Berichte* shows that there was official help given in transporting Germans from the Continent to England. . . .

"Wir haben aller Orthen/ durch Gottes Gnade/ überauß gutthätige und hülffreiche Leuthe angetroffen. Auff dem Rheinstrohm haben uns unterschiedliche Leuthe etwas an Geld und Brod/ zum theil auch Fleisch/ Butter/ Käse/ und einigemal etwas an Kleidungen verehrt/ in Roterdam schenkte uns ein Mann allein 40. Holländische Gülden/ etliche andere gute Leuthe gaben uns auch unterschiedliches an Geld. Der Stadt-Rath in Rotterdam verehrte uns 25 fl. und ließ uns auf ihren Kosten/ in einem der Stadt zugehörigen Schiff nach Hellevotschluiß bringen. Im Haag haben wir von dem Engelländischen Envoys erhalten/ daß uns freyer Paß biß Engelland gegeben wurde/ und also seynd wir auß Hellevotschluiß in Holland/ biß nach Harwich in Engelland/ ohne einigen Hellers Kosten gebracht worden."¹⁴

Another statement written after the great movement had subsided shows the same thing. This is quoted from Sauer in the *Pennsylvanische Berichte* of December 1, 1754—not so long after the event but that he could get the accurate information. "Als im Jahre 1704 die frantzösische Völker ins Reich eingezogen, und die Reichs-Fürsten die Anna Königin in England um Hülff anrieffen, und diese den Duc de Malborough

---

¹³Eccl. Rec., vol. III, page 1754.

¹⁴"Through God's grace we have found everywhere exceedingly benevolent and helpful people. Upon the Rhine different people presented us with something in the way of money and bread, in part also with meat, butter, and cheese, and a few times with some clothing. In Rotterdam one man alone gave us 40 Holland Guldens; some other good people also gave us varying amounts of money. The city council in Rotterdam gave us 25 florins and had us brought to Hellevotschluiss at their own cost in a ship belonging to the city. At the Hague we obtained from the English envoy that a free pass was given us to England and so we were brought from Hellevotschluiss in Holland clear to Harwich in England without a penny's cost."—Kocherthal, page 77.

mit einer großen Armee englischer Völker ins Reich gesandt, durch deren Tapferkeit am 2. Juli die Frantzosen bey Schellenberg geschlagen worden, hatte er der Kayser und die Reichs-Fürsten die Königin Anna fragen lassen, was sie ihr zur Danckbarkeit vor diesen großen Dienst thun können? Darauff hat die Königin Anna sagen lassen, daß sie von ihren Offizieren und Soldaten erfahren habe, daß sie so viele Arme Leuthe im Reich angetroffen, die ihr Brodt und nötigen unterhalt nicht haben; es sollen die Reichs-Fürsten, ihren armen Leuthen erlauben, nach America zu ziehen, wo Land genug ist, worauf sie sich ernehren konnten. Dieses haben sie nebst großer Ehr-Bezeugung und Danckbarkeit eingewilliget, und weil das arme Volk keine möglichkeit gesehen dahin zu kommen, so hat die Königin auf ihren eignen Kosten viele Tausende nach Engelland bringen lassen, und die da wollten nach America ziehen, die wurden Frachtfrey herübergebracht und mit Proviant, Werkzeug und Geräthschaften versehen.,,[15]

[15] When in the year 1704 the French people invaded the Empire and the princes of the realm appealed to Queen Anne in England for help, and she had sent the Duke of Marlborough with a great army of English people into the Empire, through the bravery of whom the French were defeated on July 2, at Schellenberg, he, the Kaiser and the princes of the realm, had a request presented to Queen Anne to know what they could do for her out of gratitude for this great service. Thereupon the Queen sent word that she had learned from her officers and soldiers that they had met so many poor people in the Empire who cannot get their bread and necessary support, that the princes of the realm ought to let their poor people go to America, where there is plenty of land upon which they could support themselves. To this they agreed, evidencing great respect and gratitude, and because the poor people saw no possibility of getting there, the Queen had many thousands brought to England at her own cost and whosoever wished to go to America was brought over, passage free, and provided with provisions, tools, and utensils.—Der Deutsche Pionier, XIV Jahrgang, page 295.

CHAPTER III

Survey of the Final Disposal of the Palatines—The English Settle Great Numbers of Them in America under Conditions Which Reveal Such Mercenary Motives as to Rob the Act of Most of its Claim to Charity—Contempt for the Germans Shown to be Characteristic Both in England and in America

Whoever may have been responsible for the coming of the Palatines, there is no doubt about their welcome during the first year of the movement. Besides the public expenditure of 135,775£,[1] private persons contributed freely both of their time and money for the relief of these poor strangers, and in fact it became the correct thing to have one's name on a subscription list, and the camps at Blackheath and Camberwell became popular promenades for the élite of London. When the Mohawk chiefs visited London, the Palatines were shown them among other sights. Their evident wretchedness touched the hearts of these red men and afforded them an opportunity later to show what true generosity is.

But this charity, excited partly by gratitude for kindnesses shown the English reformers by the Germans,[2] partly by religious sympathy[3] and political ties, partly by the warm feelings of an impulsive woman and in the case of some, probably, by a desire[4] to be on the popular side, soon began to be burdensome and annoying when the first pleasure and the novelty of it passed. The Palatines could not camp indefinitely in Camberwell and Blackheath, or live in the barns provided for them, and various were the schemes proposed for permanently settling them. Beaumont in his letter, which has a very sensible and a kindly tone, would keep them in England and allow them to settle on land that was lacking in tenants, and thus retain them in England to the advantage of all. His plan, however, was never successfully carried out.

About 3000 were settled in one body in Ireland and these for the most part stayed; others were scattered about over England wherever any parish was willing to receive them for 5£ per head. But after the 5£ was received, the refugees were left to shift for themselves among a people who considered them intruders; and most of them came back to London, more wretched if anything than before.[5] The best plan, after all, seemed to be to settle them in America.

[1] Eccl. Rec., vol. III, page 1732.
[2] Eccl. Rec., vol. III, page 1777.
[3] Eccl. Rec., vol. III, 1620.
[4] Eccl. Rec., vol. III, page 1753.
[5] Penn. Ger. Soc., vol. VII, page 314.

The English colonies in America at this time occupied a narrow strip along the Atlantic coast from Massachusetts to the Spanish settlements in Florida, while the interior from the St. Lawrence river to the Gulf of Mexico was claimed, and to some extent settled, by the French, who came closest to the English in New York and New England, and there offered a real menace. The French, moreover, being mostly traders, were on better terms with the Indians; they also intermarried with them and adopted many of their habits, while the English held themselves more aloof and as fast as they acquired land cleared it and so spoiled the hunting. But while the Indians beyond the Great Lakes and in the Mississippi favored the French, the Iroquois of the New York colony, an important exception in this, were friendly with the English. The French traders, however, were among the Iroquois; their allegiance could not, therefore, be counted on, and one of the most heartless proposals [6] for disposing of the Palatines was "to settle them along the Hudson river in the province of New York where they may be useful to this Kingdom, particularly in the production of naval stores and as a frontier against the French and their Indians." There can be no possible offense taken to the statement that "Her Majesty was convinced that it would be more for the advantage of Her Kingdom if a method could be found to settle them here (in America) in such a manner that they might get a comfortable livelihood instead of sending them to the West Indies; that it would be a great encouragement to others to follow their example; that the addition to the number of her subjects would in all probability produce a proportional increase of their trade and manufactures." [7] But the proposal made by the council to take these protestant refugees, who could have no choice in the matter, and use them as a buffer against the savages, certainly robs the act of much of its claim to generosity.

The Reverend Mr. Kocherthal went first with a small party. He was followed in 1710 by over 3000 under Governor Hunter. They were treated more like slaves than fellow Christians, for they were forced to sign a contract by which they were put under a sort of military discipline and set at the fruitless task of trying to make tar in commercial quantities from northern pines. Their whole time was to be devoted to this industry and they were to be fed and maintained at the Queen's expense. The well meaning but incompetent Governor Hunter had the supervision of the colony. Compelled to work under task masters, who themselves knew nothing of the business, defrauded of their provisions by the contractors, when petition and resistance failed, like the brick makers of Egypt, some of them remembered a promised land, and in the depth of winter (1711-12)

[6]Eccl. Rec., vol. III, page 1703.
[7]Eccl. Rec., vol. III, page 1733, 1818.

CHAPTER III

Survey of the Final Disposal of the Palatines—The English Settle Great Numbers of Them in America under Conditions Which Reveal Such Mercenary Motives as to Rob the Act of Most of its Claim to Charity—Contempt for the Germans Shown to be Characteristic Both in England and in America

Whoever may have been responsible for the coming of the Palatines, there is no doubt about their welcome during the first year of the movement. Besides the public expenditure of 135,775£,[1] private persons contributed freely both of their time and money for the relief of these poor strangers, and in fact it became the correct thing to have one's name on a subscription list, and the camps at Blackheath and Camberwell became popular promenades for the élite of London. When the Mohawk chiefs visited London, the Palatines were shown them among other sights. Their evident wretchedness touched the hearts of these red men and afforded them an opportunity later to show what true generosity is.

But this charity, excited partly by gratitude for kindnesses shown the English reformers by the Germans,[2] partly by religious sympathy[3] and political ties, partly by the warm feelings of an impulsive woman and in the case of some, probably, by a desire[4] to be on the popular side, soon began to be burdensome and annoying when the first pleasure and the novelty of it passed. The Palatines could not camp indefinitely in Camberwell and Blackheath, or live in the barns provided for them, and various were the schemes proposed for permanently settling them. Beaumont in his letter, which has a very sensible and a kindly tone, would keep them in England and allow them to settle on land that was lacking in tenants, and thus retain them in England to the advantage of all. His plan, however, was never successfully carried out.

About 3000 were settled in one body in Ireland and these for the most part stayed; others were scattered about over England wherever any parish was willing to receive them for 5£ per head. But after the 5£ was received, the refugees were left to shift for themselves among a people who considered them intruders; and most of them came back to London, more wretched if anything than before.[5] The best plan, after all, seemed to be to settle them in America.

[1]Eccl. Rec., vol. III, page 1732.
[2]Eccl. Rec., vol. III, page 1777.
[3]Eccl. Rec., vol. III, 1620.
[4]Eccl. Rec., vol. III, page 1753.
[5]Penn. Ger. Soc., vol. VII, page 314.

and subjects of Great Britain, than to have our Frontiers secured by a Warlike People, and our Friends, as the Switzers are; especially when we have more Indians than we can civilize, and so many Christian Enemies lying on the back of us, that we do not know how long or short a time it may be, before they visit us."

Even as late as 1733 according to William Byrd, the Indians were a real menace in Virginia; and one of the reasons he gives for encouraging a Swiss colony to settle in his "Land of Eden" was the protection they would afford against the Indians and the French. Moreover, he preferred for his purpose the honest Swiss to the settlers who were coming in from Pennsylvania.[12]

Whether or not such use was made of the particular colony in which we are at present interested let the following extracts show.

"The Governor acquainting the Council that Sundry Germans to the number of forty-two men women and children who were invited hither by the Baron de Graffenried are now arrived but that the said Baron not being here to take care of this Settlement the Governor therefore proposed to settle them above the falls of Rappahannock River to serve as a barrier to the inhabitants of that part of the Country against the Incursions of the Indians and desiring the opinion of the Council whether in consideration of their usefulness for that purpose the Charge of building them a Fort, and clearing a road to their settlement and carrying thither two pieces of Canon and some ammunition may not properly be defrayed by the publick.

"It is the unanimous opinion of the Board that the settlement, tending so much to the security of that part of the Frontiers, it is reasonable that the expense proposed by the Governor in making thereof should be defrayed at the public charge of the Government, and that a quantity of powder and ball be delivered for their use out of her Majestie's magazine. And because the Sd Germans, arriving so late cannot possibly this year cultivate any ground for the(ir) Subsistance, much less be able to pay the public Services of the Government. It is the opinion of this Board that they be put under the denomination of Rangers to exempt them from that charge, and for the better enabling the Sd Germans to supply by hunting the want of other provisions. It is also ordered that all other persons be restrained from hunting on unpatented Lands near the Settlement."[13]

July 21st, 1714.

To the L'ds Comm'rs of Trade.
My Lords:
Since my last of the 9th of March, (whereof the enclosed is a Duplicate) I have had the hon'r to receive y'r Lo'ps of the 6th of April, with the Treatys of

[12] The Writings of Colonel William Byrd, pages 300, 302, 390 ff.
[13] Virginia Magazine, vol. XIII, page 362.

Peace and Comerce, which I have accordingly made public. It is with great satisfaction that I can acquaint y'r Lo'ps that this Country enjoys a perfect Peace and that even the Indians, since the last Treaty made with them, have not offered the least disturbance, notwithstanding the Tuscaros, induced thereto, (as they say) by the people of Carolina, have departed from their agreements with this Governm't, and gon(e) to settle once more upon that Province, I continue, all resolv'd, to settle out our Tributary Indians as a guard to ye Frontiers, and in order to supply that part, w'ch was to have been covered by the Tuscaros, I have placed here a number of Protestant Germans, built them a fort and furnished it with two pieces of cannon and some ammunition, which will awe the Stragling partys of Northern Indians, and be a good Barrier for all that part of the Country. These Germans were invited over, some years ago, by the Baron de Graffenreed, who has her Majesty's Letter to ye Governor of Virginia to furnish them with Land upon their arrival. They are generally such as have been employed in their own country as Miners, and say they are satisfied. There are divers kinds of minerals in those upper parts of the Country where they are settled, and even a good appearance of Silver Oar, . . .[14]

Virginia, Feb'ry 7, 1715.

To the L'ds Comm'rs of Trade and Plantation:

. . . As to the other Settlement, named Germanna, there are about forty Germans, Men, Women, and Children, who, having quitted their native Country upon the invitation of the Herr Graffenriedt, and being grievously dissapointed by his failure to perform his Engagements to them, and they arriving also here just at a time when the Tuscaruro Indians departed from the Treaty they had made with this Government to settle upon its Northern Frontiers, I did both in Compassion to those poor Strangers and in regard to the safety of the Country, place them together upon a piece of Land, several Miles without the Inhabitants, where I built them Habitations, and subsisted them until they were able, by their own Labour, to provide for themselves, and I presume I may, without a Crime or Misdemeanor, endeavor to put them in an honest way of paying their Just Debts. . .[15]

This policy, pursued so consistently in New York, Virginia, and Carolina, while doubtless a compliment to German courage and honesty, points to a contempt for them which has continued, in a more or less marked degree, down to the present time. The writer of the history of the Germans in Maine found in the state archives that those documents relating to the German colony of Waldo alone were unprinted, although this colony had had a history as interesting and as tragic as Deerfield or Schenectady, and no one can imagine documents relating to these two settlements remaining long unprinted in the public archives. Happily this attitude is changing, due largely to the efforts of the German-Americans themselves, and new chapters are constantly being added to the story of their part in the making of our country.

[14] Spotswood, vol. II, page 70.
[15] Spotswood, vol. II, page 196. This refers to his employment of them in building and operating his iron furnace.

PART II

THE NEW BERN ADVENTURES

CHAPTER I

Graffenried's Early Life

Christoph von Graffenried, the eldest of several children, was born at Bern, Switzerland, about the first of November, 1661. His father, Anton von Graffenried, was a member of the patrician family of that name, and while not rich in his younger days, he had claims on profitable political position, but, what is more important, he possessed the ability to succeed and to keep his wealth on a solid and conservative foundation. He was frugal in his expenditures, honest in his business relations, but unaffectionate in his family life. He could never understand or sympathize with Christoph, who had an adventuresome disposition even as a child, and father and son were always more or less estranged. Moreover, Christoph's mother died when the boy was only a few years old, but her place was soon after taken by a stepmother.

At seven years of age Christoph was one of five little boys sent to a Latin teacher who insisted that the pupils speak Latin, and punished infractions of the rule with fines. Judging from the Latin in the German version of his account, the school was not a success in his case, and Anton found the fines he was called upon to pay a grievous hardship. Other offenses brought punishments so severe that the boy ran away to one of his relatives for protection, through whose intercession, however, he was shortly afterwards allowed to return home to stay.

In 1676 Anton von Graffenried went into partnership with the foreman and purchased a salt works at Roche. The families were so friendly at the start that the plan was made, very agreeably to the young people, that Christoph should marry the foreman's daughter. But a quarrel arising over the claims of the two fathers in the salt works, the relation was broken off, never to be renewed.

Not long after this, Sir William Waller, a relative of one of the regicides, who had come to Bern for protection, saw the boy and was so impressed by his appearance and manners, that he encouraged him to go to England to try his fortune there, and the father was so far persuaded that he was making plans to send him to England when a better way seemed to present itself. One of Anton's brothers was a chamberlain and captain in the bodyguard of the Elector of Saxony, and it was hoped that Christoph would be able to get a place at that court through his influence. But the captain died at just this time and the hope was shattered. Christoph then went to school in Geneva. He was still restless, however, and wanted to travel on the 20,000£ which fell to him from his mother. Anton did not approve of the plan, but after a violent argument gave his consent for the lad to go under the conduct of a theological student who was to supervise the expenditures as well. The two went first to Heidelberg, where Christoph was soon in the politest society, thanks to his family name and his own engaging appearance. His intercourse in the Elector's social circle progressed better than his university studies; and when the story of a duel came to Bern, Anton concluded it was time for his son to change his location. In Leyden, where he next went to study, his law, history and mathematics progressed better, and he stayed two years.

Through Sir William Waller's influence Anton now allowed his son to go to England, where he was promised a position with Mr. Roux, secretary to the Duke of Carlyle, on his embassy to Constantinople. Since the father expected Sir William to advance what money Christoph would need, no money accompanied the letter of introduction; and when the young Switzer landed in London, ten ducats was all he had in his pockets. At this time he did not speak English, and it was only by chance that he found a German porter who could understand him. With such directions as this man could give him, he found Sir William Waller's house. Lady Waller met him and from her manner he could guess that nothing was to be expected from Sir William, who was at that time in the Fleet for debt.[1] Through the porter Graffenried learned that the Duke had already gone to Constantinople, and all hopes of an appointment disappeared. This same porter also introduced him to a Swiss locksmith by the name of Engel, with whom he stayed until money arrived from Bern. Thereupon he took lodging with Pastor Horneg, chaplain to the Duke of Marlborough, and not long after was introduced into the society of the Duke by a German friend, a trumpet major in the army; and from this time he moved in the society of courtiers and was even presented to King Charles II himself.

In 1682, the Duke of Albemarle, chancellor of Cambridge University, was not able to be present at the conferring of degrees and sent

[1]Luttrell, vol. I, pp. 84 and 91. This was between the 11th and 25th of May, 1681.

two of his friends, Farwel and Graffenried, to represent him. And we may judge of the favor and popularity of the latter when we learn that to his astonishment the doctorate was offered him. He refused, however, saying that he was not worthy, since he had not studied for such a degree, but that he would accept a degree of Master of Arts, according to the proverb, *In omnibus aliquid, in toto nihil.*

Meanwhile Graffenried had fallen in love with a niece of the Duke of Buckingham, a lady of good birth but poor family. Money and station were, nevertheless, necessary to succeed in the courtship of a lady of rank; and so he planned to buy a vacant commission as cornet in the British army. This would cost a thousand pounds, but would pay well when secured and would enable him to pursue his courtship with some prospect of success. A letter to Bern asking for money and for permission to take this place was answered by a summons to start for home immediately, with the penalty of losing his prerogatives and right to act as his grandfather's substitute in the government at Worb, in case he refused. Not even money for the whole journey was allowed him, but his way was paid stage by stage through designated persons. All this was caused by a false report spread by one of his own countrymen, to the effect that he was acting the spendthrift, and Anton learned the truth too late to repair the injury entirely. It was no use to go back to England now, and with his father's permission, Christoph stayed a year in France. His social success was as great here as it had been in England. Reports of him reached Louis XIV and Graffenried had the pleasure of meeting both the Dauphin and the great king. After this he spent some time in Lyons and finally reached home some time about 1683. Reproaches for the wasted time and money were not lacking, and Anton decided it was time for the son to marry, and settle down in an office. Christoph showed no enthusiasm for marriage and left the choice largely to his relatives, with the result that he married Regine Tscharner in 1684. On this occasion Anton showed himself so niggardly that the groom had to lend him money with which to buy presents and hire the carriage himself.

It was hoped that the grandfather would now assist Christoph to an office, but the old gentleman died too soon and it was several years before Christoph obtained even a minor appointment. At length, however, he became bailiff of Iferton in Neuchatel in 1702. This had the reputation of being a lucrative position, but the festivities which custom compelled him to give on his induction into office, reduced the profits of the first year; and the next year, during the religious troubles, Iferton had to support a garrison. The bailiff had to keep open house for officers; other officials and friends

came to pay him their respects, and these merry, but expensive
occasions were a heavy drain upon his resources, for out of 200
doubloons spent, only 50 were repaid him by the state. Graffenried
also had a feeling for the peasants, and did not wring as much from
them as he might have done, and as was the usual practice of bailiffs.
Meanwhile his family was increasing. He made bad speculations,
gave securities, and contracted debts until prospects of a catastrophe
began to loom up before him when his term of office should end in
1708. The strife over Neuchatel, the violation of the peace by the
war of the Spanish succession, the troubles between the Protestant
and the Catholic cantons, and the continual persecutions of the
Anabaptists made his home distasteful to him; the ambitions of his
youth returned with a renewed force, and now he determined to seek
in America the fortune which was denied him at home.

The account of his life thus far, taken mostly from papers in the
Graffenried family,[2] by one of his descendants, shows that Christoph
von Graffenried was no ordinary man. He had the ability of making
friends, and inspired confidence in people. He had an acute mind
and above all, possessed the love of adventure necessary to the success
of such an undertaking as that on which he was embarking. The
failure of his plans must be laid, not to him, but to circumstances
over which he had no control, and which he could not, by any possibility, have foreseen.

---

[2] Neujahrsblatt, page 4 ff.

CHAPTER II

LITERATURE WHICH GRAFFENRIED STUDIED BEFORE DECIDING TO GO TO AMERICA:—BLOME, HENNEPIN, KOCHERTHAL

Graffenried, we know, had long been considering the bettering of his fortune in America. He had made extensive inquiries about mines, agriculture, and the best means of settling there, and the authors he read certainly included Blome, Hennepin, and Kocherthal. Blome gives a brief description of all the English colonies, and speaks favorably of them. Hennepin, among other things, has this to say of Carolina: "So that the Providence of the Almighty God seems to have reserved this country for the English, a Patent whereof was granted Fifty years ago to the Lords Proprietors of Carolina, who have made great discoveries therein, seven hundred Miles Westerly from the Mountains, which separate between it Carolina and Virginia, and Six hundred Miles from North to South, from the Gulf of Mexico to the great Inland Lakes, which are situated behind the Mountains of Carolina and Virginia. Besides, they have an account of all the Coast, from the Cape of Florida to the River Panuco, the Northerly Bounds of the Spaniards on the Gulf of Mexico, together with most of the chief Harbours, Rivers, and Islands thereunto appertaining; and are about to establish a very considerable Colony on some part of the Great River, as soon as they have agreed upon the Boundaries, or Limits, which Lords Proprietors of Carolina, who claim by a Patent procured long after that of Carolina. But there being space enough for both, and the Proprietors generally inclin'd to an amicable conclusion, the Success of this undertaking is impatiently expected, For considering the Benignity of the Climate, the Healthfulness of the Country, the Fruitfulness of the Soil, Ingenuity and Tractableness of the Inhabitants, Variety of Productions, if prudently manag'd, it cannot, humanely speaking, fail of proving one of the most considerable Colonies on the North-Continent of America, profitable to the Publick and to the Undertakers." [1]

Other accounts of Carolina, [2] all favorable, but less entertainingly written, by Horne, Smith, by one T. A., probably Thomas Ashe, and by Archdale had appeared before this; and Graffenried may have been acquainted with some or all of these. Kocherthal's *Bericht* was undoubtedly the most influential book among German-speaking people, having reached the fourth edition in 1709. It contains a

---
[1] A continuation of the New Discovery of a vast Country in America. Reprinted by Thwaites, page 678.
[2] Carrol's Collections, vol. II.

rather detailed description of the country, plants, animals, and products, and has little but praise for the new country. On the subject of greatest concern, the danger from the Indians, it reads as follows:

> Mit denen Indianern leben auch die Englische allda in vollkommener Freundschaft und guter Vernehmen in dem sie beiderseits einander gar nützlich und zuträglich seyn: und tragen die Lords/ so Eigenthums Herrn dieses Landes sind/ gute Sorgfalt/ daß ihnen nichts unbilliges zugefüget werde. Sie haben zu solchem Ende ein sonderliches Gerichte angeordnet und bestellet/ welches aus denen Bescheidensten und dem Eigen-Nutz am wenigsten ergebenen Einwohnern bestehet: worinnen denn all die Streitigkeiten beigeleget werden sollen/ so sich etwa zwischen denen Englischen und irgend einem von den Indianern zutragen möchten welches sie bloß auß einer Christlichen und vernünftig billichen Bewegung gethan/ keineweges aber darum/ als ob man sich etwa einiger Gefahr von ihnen zu besorgen hätte.
>
> Es sind nemlich die Indianer bißanhero stetig untereinander so im Kriege verwickelt gewesen . . . daß selbige diesem Volk nicht zugelassen haben, sich sonderlich zu vermehren aber zuzunehmen . . . Dieses verursachet demnach/ daß sie an Mannschafft so schwach/ auch über diß so zerteilet bleiben/ daß die Englischen von ihnen nicht die allergeringste Forcht haben/ oder sich einiger Gefahr besorgen dörffen/ . . . [3]

---

[3] "The English also live with the Indians there in complete friendship and good understanding, since they are mutually useful and agreeable. And the Lords who are the owners of this land take good care that no ill treatment is given them. They have, to this end, arranged and established for them an especial court which consists of the most modest inhabitants and those least given to selfishness, in which, then, all disputes which may come up between the English and any of the Indians are settled. This they have done merely out of a Christian and reasonably proper impulse, but not at all as though one had to fear any danger from them.

"That is to say, the Indians up until now have been engaged so continually in war with each other that the same has not allowed this race to increase or grow very much. This brings it about, accordingly, that they are so weak in numbers of warriors, and, besides this, remain so divided that the English have not the slightest fear of them or need allow themselves to have anxiety about any danger whatever."—Kocherthal, page 57.

CHAPTER III

ANOTHER COLONIZATION PROJECT—GRAFFENRIED MEETS THE AGENT —FRANZ LOUIS MICHEL—FULLY PERSUADED TO GO TO AMERICA— GRAFFENRIED LEAVES FOR ENGLAND AND MEETS JOHN LAWSON

While Graffenried was still in Switzerland the Canton of Bern had begun to negotiate through a former citizen of Bern, Franz Louis Michel, for land in North Carolina[1] and Virginia.[2] They requested to be allowed to hold whatever tract they should buy independently of either the Proprietors of Carolina or the Governor of Virginia.[3] Since such a request could not, of course, be granted, nothing definite was done concerning purchase. An independent colonization project was started, however, the chief member of which was a man named Ritter.[4]

In 1708 Michel was back in Bern[5] again and from him Graffenried informed himself more fully about conditions in America, and Michel's favorable reports fully persuaded him to go to the New World. His plan had no connection as yet with the colonization schemes of the Canton of Bern or the Ritter Company, as will be shown later. All he had in mind was to go over to America, and following Michel's directions and maps, to find the deposits of silver ore, which he, together with Michel, expected to work for their own profit, using for this purpose miners from Germany, who should be engaged before he left, but who were not to emigrate until he sent for them.[6] Accordingly, when his term of office ended in 1708,[7] Graffenried left Switzerland secretly, not even telling his friends of his plans, and went first to Holland and then to England. While in Holland, or on his way there, he engaged twelve miners to come to him when he should send for them.[8]

During his stay in England Graffenried became acquainted with Michel's friend John Lawson, who was having the account of his travels in Carolina printed. None of the descriptions with which Graffenried was acquainted, except Hennepin's, compare in interest and freshness with Lawson's Journal. He had been eight years in Carolina, and had taken a thousand-mile journey from Charleston to a point near the present site of New Bern, making, however, a wide circuit in which he ascended the Santee River to its sources,

---
[1]Lawson's Journal, page 205 ff.
[2]French Version.
[3]French Version.
[4]Neujahrsblatt, page 21. Bernische Taeufer, page 258.
[5]French Version, German Version.
[6]French Version, German Version.
[7]Neujahrsblatt, page 17.
[8]French Version, German Version.

and then turned northward, crossing the upper waters of the Congaree, Wateree, and Yadkin Rivers, then bearing more to the east until he reached the Moratok, now the Roanoke River, some 120 miles above its mouth. From this point he went southward, almost to Chatoka, now New Bern. This trip gave him a good idea of the country and its inhabitants, at least Graffenried must have thought so, and furthermore, he confirmed Michel's reports about the presence of silver ore.[1]

The passages and abstracts from Lawson's book which follow will give an idea of his style and the kind of arguments that doubtless influenced Graffenried to go to Carolina rather than to Virginia, as he intended at first to do. As copies of the book are very rare and not easily accessible, and Lawson was from this time on so intimately associated with Graffenried, I have made the quotations and extracts rather full.

---

[1] The influence of Lawson and his description of Carolina is attested further by the fact that his book was printed so soon in German and published in an edition that was evidently an expensive one, as shown by the gilt lettering. The title of the German edition was as follows:

Allerneuste Beschreibung der Provintz Carolina in West-Indien sammt einem Reise-Journal von mehr als Tausend Meilen unter allerhand Indianischen Nationen, auch einer Accuraten Land-Carte und andern Kupfer-Stichen. Aus dem Englischen übersetzt durch M. Vischer.

HAMBURG.

Gedruckt und verlegt/ durch seel. Thomas von Wierings Erben bey der Börse/ in güldenen A, B, C, Anno 1712 sind auch zu Frankfurt und Leipsig/ bey Zacharias Herlteln zu bekommen.

Most Recent Description of the Province Carolina in the West Indies, along with a Travel-Journal of more than a Thousand Miles among all sorts of Indian Nations, with an Accurate Map and other Copper Plates also. Translated out of the English by Mr. Vischer.

HAMBURG.

Printed and published by the heirs of the late Thomas von Wiering at the Exchange in golden A, B, C, Anno 1712, are also to be had in Frankfort and Leipsig at Zacharias Herldn's.

CHAPTER IV

John Lawson and His Journal

Lawson began his journey of exploration December 28, 1700. There were six Englishmen, three Indian men and an Indian woman, the wife of one of the guides in the party. They canoed from Charlestown to the Santee River, up which they rowed several days, and as occasion required enjoyed the hospitality of the French settlers along the river. The following extracts will show how he livened up his description.

"Monday. The next Morning very early we ferry'd over a Creek that runs near the House; and, after an Hour's Travel in the Woods, we came to the River-side, where we stay'd for the Indian, who was our Guide, and was gone around by Water in a small Canoe, to meet us at the Place we rested at. He came after a small time and ferry'd us in that little Vessel over Santee River 4 miles, and 84 Miles in the Woods, which the overflowing of the Freshes, which then came down, had made a perfect Sea of, there running an incredible Current in the River, which had cast our small Craft and us away, had we not had this Sewee Indian with us; who are excellent Artists in managing these small Canoes.

"Santee River, at this time, (from the usual Depth of Water) was risen perpendicular 36 Foot, always making a Breach from her Banks, about this Season of the Year. The general Opinion of the cause thereof, is suppos'd to proceed from the overflowing of fresh Water-Lakes that lie near the Head of this River, and other upon the same Continent; But my Opinion is, that these vast Inundations proceed from the great and repeated Quantities of Snow that falls upon the Mountains, which lie at so great a Distance from the Sea, therefore they have no Help of being dissolv'd by those saline, piercing Particles, as other adjacent Parts near the Ocean receive: and therefore lies and increases to a vast Bulk, until some mild Southerly Breezes coming on a sudden, continue to unlock these frozen Bodies, congeal'd by the North-West Wind: dissipating them in Liquids: and coming down with Impetuosity, fills those branches that feed these Rivers, and causes this strange Deluge, which oft-times lays under Water for Miles distant from the Banks: tho' the French and Indians affirmed to me they never knew such extraordinary Floods there before.

"We all by God's Blessing and the Endeavours of our Indian-Pilot, pass'd safe over the River, but was lost in the Woods which seem'd like some great Lake, except here and there a Knowl of high Land, which appear'd above water.

"We intended for Mons. Galliar's, jun; but was lost, none of us knowing the Way at that Time, altho' the Indian was born in the Country, it having receiv'd so strange a Metamorphosis. We were in several Opinions concerning the right way, the Indian and myself, suppos'd the House to bear one Way, the rest thought to the contrary; we differing, it was agreed amongst us that one half should go with the Indian to find the House and the other part to stay upon one of these dry Spots, until some of them returned to us, and inform'd us where it lay.

"Myself and two more were left behind, by Reason the Canoe would not carry us all; we had but one Gun amongst us, one Load of Ammunition, and no Provision. Had our Men in the Canoe miscarry'd, we must (in all Probability) there have perish'd.

"In about six Hour's Time, from our Mens Departure, the Indian came back to us in the Same Canoe he went in, being half drunk, which assur'd us they had found some Place of Refreshment. He took us three into the canoe, telling us all was well: Paddling our Vessel several Miles thro' the Woods, being often half full of water; but at length we got safe to the Place we sought for, which prov'd to lie the same Way the Indian and I guess'd it did." [1]

Another short extract speaking of the Indians:

"Amongst Women it seems impossible to find a scold; if they are provok'd, or affronted, by their Husbands, or some other, they resent the Indignity offer'd them in silent Tears, or by refusing their Meat. Would some of our European Daughters of Thunder set these Indians for a Pattern, there might be more quiet Families found amongst them, occasion'd by that unruly Member, the Tongue. [2]

"A Second Settlement of this Country was made about fifty years ago, in that part we now call Albemarl County and chiefly in Chuwon Precinct, by several substantial Planters from Virginia and other Plantations; Who finding mild winters, and a fertile Soil beyond expectation, producing that which was planted to a prodigious Increase, their Cattle, Horses, Sheep and Swine breeding very fast, and passing the Winter without any assistance from the Planter: so that everything seem'd to come by Nature, the Husbandman living almost devoid of Care, and free from those Fatigues which are absolutely requisite in Winter-Countries, for providing Fodder and other Necessaries; these Encouragements induced them to stand their Ground altho' but a handful of People, seated at great Distances one from

---
[1]Lawson's Journal, page 4 ff.
[2]Lawson's Journal, page 37.

another, and amidst a vast number of Indians of different Nations, who were then in Carolina. Nevertheless, I say, the Fame of this new discovered Summer-Country spread through the neighbouring Colonies, and in a few Years, drew a considerable number of Families thereto, who all found Land enough to settle themselves in (had they been many Thousands more) and that which was very good and commodiously seated, both for Profit and Pleasure. And indeed, most of the Plantations in Carolina naturally enjoy a noble Prospect of large and spacious Rivers, pleasant Savannas and fine Meadows with their green Liveries, interwoven with beautiful Flowers, of most glorious Colours, which the several Seasons afford; hedged in with pleasant Groves of the ever-famous Tulip-tree, the stately Laurel, and Bays, equalizing the Oak in Bigness and Growth; Myrtles, Jessamines, Woodbines, Honeysuckles, and several other fragrant Vines and Ever-Greens, whose aspiring Branches shadow and interweave themselves with the Loftiest Timbers, yielding a pleasant Prospect, Shade and Smell, proper Habitations for the Sweet-singing Birds, that melodiously entertain such as travel thro' the Woods of Carolina.

"The Planters possessing all these Blessings, and the Produce of great Quantities of Wheat and Indian Corn in which this Country is very fruitful as likewise in Beef, Pork, Tallow, Hides, Deer-Skins and Furs; for these Commodities the New-England-Men and Bermudians visited Carolina in their Barks and Sloops, and carry'd out what they made, bringing them in exchange Rum, Sugar, Salt, Molasses and some Wearing Apparel, tho' the last at very extravagant Prices.

"As the land is very fruitful, so are the Planters kind and hospitable to all that come to visit them; there being very few Housekeepers, but what live very nobly, and give away more provisions to Coasters and Guests who come to see them, than they expend amongst their own Families. [3]

"When we consider the Latitude and convenient Situation of Carolina, had we no farther Confirmation thereof, our Reason would inform us, that such a Place lay fairly to be a delicious Country, being placed in that Girdle of the World which affords Wine, Oil, Fruit, Grain, Silk with other rich Commodities, besides a sweet Air, moderate Climate, and fertile Soil; these are the Blessings (under Heaven's Protection) that spin out the Thread of life to its utmost Extent, and Crown our Days with the Sweets of Health and Plenty, which, when join'd with Content, renders the Possessors the happiest Race of Men upon Earth.

---
[3] Lawson's Journal, page 62 ff.

"The Inhabitants of Carolina, thro' the Richness of the Soil, live an easy and pleasant life. The Land being of several sorts of Compost, some stiff, others light, some marl, others rich black Mould; here barren of Pine, but affording Pitch, Tar and Masts; there vastly rich, especially on the Freshes of the Rivers, one part bearing great Timbers, others being Savannas or natural Meads, where no trees grow for several Miles, adorn'd by Nature with a pleasant Verdure, and beautiful Flowers, frequent in no other Places, yielding abundance of Herbage for Cattle, Sheep and Horse. The Country in general affords pleasant Seats, the Land (except in some few Places) being dry and high Banks, parcell'd out into most convenient Necks, (by the Creeks) easy to be fenced in for securing their Stocks to more strict Boundaries, whereby, with a small trouble of fencing, almost every man may enjoy, to himself, an entire Plantation, or rather Park. These with the other Conveniences which the Summer-Country naturally furnishes, has induc'd a great many families to leave the more Northerly Plantations, and sit down under one of the mildest Governments in the world; in a Country that, with moderate Industry, will afford all the Necessaries of Life. We have yearly abundance of Strangers come among us, who chiefly strive to the Southerly to settle because there is a vast Tract of rich Land betwixt the Place we are seated on, and Cape-Fair, and upon that River, and more Southerly, which is inhabited by none but a few Indians, who are at this time well affected to the English, and very desirous of their coming to live among them. The more Southerly, the milder Winters, with the advantage of purchasing the Lords Land at the most easy and moderate Rate of any Lands in America, nay (allowing all advantages thereto annex'd) I may say, the Universe does not afford such another; Besides, Men have a great advantage of choosing good and commodious Tracts of Land at the first Seating of a Country or River, whereas the later Settlers are forced to purchase smaller Dividends of the old Standers, and sometimes at very considerable Rates; as now in Virginia and Maryland, where a thousand Acres of good Land cannot be bought under twenty Schillings an Acre, besides two Schillings yearly Acknowledgement for every hundred Acres; which Sum, be it more or less, will serve to put the Merchant or Planter here into a good Posture of Buildings, Slaves, and other Necessaries, where the Purchase of his Land comes to him on such easy Terms. And as our Grain and pulse thrives with us to admiration, no less do our Stocks of Cattle, Horses, Sheep, and Swine multiply. [4]

"The Christian Natives of Carolina are a straight, clean-limb'd People; the Children being seldom or never troubled with Ricketts,

[4]Lawson's Journal, page 79 ff.

or those other Distempers, that the Europeans are visited withal. 'Tis next to a miracle to see one of them deformed in Body. The Vicinity of the Sun makes Impression on the Men, who labour out of doors, or use the Water. As for those Women, that do not expose themselves to the Weather, they are often very fair, and generally as well featur'd, as you shall see anywhere, and have very brisk charming Eyes, which sets them off to Advantage. They marry very young; Some at Thirteen or Fourteen; and She that stays 'till Twenty is reckoned a stale Maid; which is a very indifferent Character in that warm Country. The Women are very fruitful; most Houses being full of Little Ones. It has been observ'd that Women long marry'd and without Children, in other Places, have remov'd to Carolina and become joyful Mothers. They have very easy Travail in their Childbearing, in which they are so happy, as seldom to miscarry. Both Sexes are generally spare of Body, and not Cholerick, nor easily cast down at Disappointments and Losses, seldom immoderately grieving at Misfortunes, unless for the Loss of their nearest Relations and Friends, which seems to make a more than ordinary Impression upon them. Many of the Women are very handy in Canoes, and will manage them with great Dexterity and Skill, which they become accustomed to in this Watery Country. They are ready to help their Husbands in any servile Work, as Planting, when the Season of the Weather requires Expedition; Pride seldom banishing good Houswifery. The Girls are not bred up to the Wheel and Sewing only; but the Dairy and affairs of the House they are very well acquainted withal; so that you shall see them, whilst very young, manage their Business with a great deal of Conduct and Alacrity. The Children of both Sexes are very docile, and learn anything with a great deal of Ease and Method; and those that have the Advantages of Education, write good Hands, and prove good accountants, which is most coveted, and indeed most necessary in these Parts. The young Men are commonly of a bashful, sober Behaviour; few proving Prodigals, to consume what the Industry of their Parents has left them, but commonly improve it. [5]

"I shall add this: That with prudent Management, I can affirm, by experience, not by Hear-say, that any Person, with a small Beginning, may live very comfortably, and not only provide for the Necessaries of Life but likewise for those that are to succeed him. [6]

"Moreover it is remarkable, that no place on the Continent of America has seated an English Colony so free from Bloodshed as Carolina; but all the others, have been more damag'd and disturb'd

---

[5] Lawson's Journal, page 84.
[6] Lawson's Journal, page 86.

by the Indians than they have, which is worthy Notice, when one considers how oddly it was first planted with Inhabitants. [7]

"Great Plenty is generally the Ruin of Industry. Thus our Merchants are not many, nor have those few there be, apply'd themselves to the European Trade. The Planter sits contented at home, whilst his Oxen thrive and grow fat, and his Stocks daily increase; the fatted Porkets and Poultry are easily raised to his Table, and his Orchard affords him Liquor so that he eats, and drinks away the Cares of the World and desires no greater Happiness, than that which he daily enjoys. Whereas, not only the European, but also the Indian-Trade might be carried on to great profit, because we lie as fairly for the Body of Indians, as any Settlement in English-America; and for the small trade that has been carried on in the Way, the Dealers therein have throve as fast as any Men, and the soonest raised themselves of any People I have known in Carolina. [8]

"One great Advantage of North-Carolina is that we are not a Frontier, and near the Enemy; which proves very chargeable and troublesome, in time of War, to those Colonies that are so seated. Another great Advantage comes from its being near Virginia, where we come often to a good Market, at the Return of the Guinea-Ships for Negro's, and the Remnant of their Stores, which is very commodious for the Indian trade. [9]

"Therefore as my Intent was, I proceed to what remains of the Present State of Carolina, having already accounted for the Animals, and Vegetables, as far as this Volume, would allow of; whereby the Remainder, though not exactly known, may yet be guess'd at, if we consider what Latitude Carolina lies in, which reaches from 29 to 36 degrees, 30 minutes, Northern Latitude, as I have before observ'd. Which Latitude is as fertile and pleasant, as any in the World, as well as for the Produce of Minerals, Fruit, Grain, and Wine, as other rich Commodities. And indeed, all the Experiments that have been made in Carolina, of the Fertility and natural Advantages of the Country, have exceeded all Expectation, as affording some Commodities, which other Places, in the same Latitude, do not. As for Minerals, as they are subterraneous Products, so, in all new Countries, they are the Species that are last discover'd; and especially in Carolina, where the Indians never look for any thing lower than the Superficies of the Earth, being a Race of Men the least addicted to delving of any People that inhabit so fine a Country as Carolina is. As good if not better Mines than those of the Spaniards in America, lie full West from us; and I am certain, we have Mountainous Land, and as great Probability of

[7] Lawson's Journal, page 86.
[8] Lawson's Journal, page 86 ff.
[9] Lawson's Journal, page 88 ff.

having rich Minerals in Carolina, as any of those Parts that are already found to be so rich therein. But, waving this subject, till some other Opportunity, I shall now give you some Observations in general, concerning Carolina; which are, first, that it lies as convenient for trade as any of the Plantations in America." [10]

The Healthfulness of the Country is lauded next. He says that gout is rare and consumption they are wholly strangers to. [11]

"The trade with Virginia is good, for ships visiting there provision themselves from the products of Carolina and give bills of exchange for England which are as good as Sterling money, and while Tobacco may be very cheap at times provisions are always in demand. Besides the Carolinians can get to market when the northern colonies are frozen up. The Sand banks protect the coast from enemies, yet allow trading vessels to approach.

"If a Man be a Botanist, here is a plentiful Field of Plants to divert him in; if he be a Gardner, and delight in that pleasant and happy Life, he will meet with a Climate and Soil, that will further and promote his Designs, in as great a Measure, as any Man can wish for; and as for the Constitution of this Government, it is so mild and easy, in respect to the Properties and Liberties of a Subject, that without rehearsing the Particulars, I say once for all, it is the mildest and best established Government in the World, and the Place where any Man may peaceably enjoy his Justice and Equity which is the Golden Rule that every Government ought to be built upon, and regulated by. Besides, it is worthy our Notice, that this Province has been settled, and continued the most free from the Insults and Barbarities of the Indians, of any Colony that was ever yet seated in America; which must be esteemed as a particular Providence of God handed down from Heaven, to these People; especially when we consider, how irregularly they settled North Carolina, and yet how undisturb'd they have ever remain'd, free from any Foreign Danger or Loss, even to this very Day. And what may well be looked upon for as great a Miracle, this is a Place, where no Malefactors are found, deserving Death, or even a Prison for Debtors; there being no more than two Persons, that, so far as I have been able to learn, ever suffer'd as Criminals, although it has been a Settlement near sixty years; One of whom was a Turk that committed Murder; the other, an old woman, for Witchcraft. These, 'tis true were on the Stage and acted many Years, before I knew the Place; but as for the last, I wish it had been undone to this Day; although they give a great many Arguments to justifie the Deed, which I should rather they should have a hand

---
[10] Lawson's Journal, page 163.
[11] Lawson's Journal, page 164. A summary.

in, than myself; feeling I could never approve of taking Life away upon such Accusations, the Justice whereof I could never yet understand.[12]

"But to return to the Subject in Hand; we there make extraordinary good Bricks throughout the Settlement. All sorts of Handicrafts, as Carpenters, Joiners, Masons, Plaisterers, Shooemakers, Tanners, Taylors, Weavers, and most others may, with small Beginnings, and God's Blessing, thrive very well in this Place, and provide Estates for their Children, Land being sold at a much cheaper Rate there, than in any other Place in America, and may, as I suppose, be purchased of the Lords-Proprietors here in England, or of the Governor there for the time being, by any that shall have a mind to transport themselves to that Country. The Farmers that go thither (for which sort of men it is a very thriving place) should take some particular Seeds of Grass, as Trefoil, Clover-grass all sort, Sanfoin, and Common Grass . . . Hoes of all sorts, Axes, Saws, Wedges, Augurs, Nails, Hammers, Tools for Brick and Stonework."[13]

He compares the price of land which is 1–50 in Carolina of what it is in Virginia with a lower quit rent.

"And as there is a free Exercise of all Persuasions amongst Christians, the Lords Proprietors, to encourage Ministers of the Church of England, have given free Land towards the Maintenance of a Church, and especially, for the Parish of S. Thomas in Pampticough, over against the Town, is already laid out for a Glebe of two hundred and twenty-three Acres of rich well-situated Land, that a Parsonage House may be built upon."[14]

It is noticeable, in view of what followed that none of the accounts referred to show any apprehension of immediate danger from the Indians, though Spotswood's correspondance and Byrd's writings prove that they recognized that such a menace existed, and one cannot but believe that these accounts glossed over the danger in the attempt to attract settlers.

This is sufficient to show why Graffenried decided to turn towards North Carolina when occasion afforded him the chance. As yet he had no other colonists engaged than his few miners and their families. It was not long, though, before he had prospect of a considerable increase in the size and dignity of his undertaking.

---
[12]Lawson's Journal, page 166.
[13]Lawson's Journal, page 167 ff.
[14]Lawson's Journal, page 167 ff. In part, a summary.

CHAPTER V

GRAFFENRIED AND MICHEL UNITE THEIR MINING PROJECT TO THE BERN–RITTER COLONIZATION COMPANY, OF WHICH MICHEL IS AGENT—GRAFFENREID MADE LANDGRAVE—NEGOTIATIONS FOR LAND AND SETTLERS—650 PALATINES SECURED—THEY START IN JANUARY, 1710—DIFFICULTIES IN GETTING THE BERN CONVICTS THROUGH HOLLAND—GRAFFENRIED AND MICHEL SECURE MINING CONCESSIONS—DISCUSSION OF THE CONTRACT WITH THE GEORG RITTER COMPANY—ASSISTANCE PROMISED BY THE PROPRIETORS—SWISS COLONY STARTS IN THE SUMMER OF 1710

The early part of the year 1709 found Graffenried in London, waiting to see what could be done about his intended mines. To a man of active temperament, burdened with debts, and anxious to get something started that would enable him to clear them, the delays of this year must have been most exasperating. His plans so far were only tentative and he was waiting for any better offer that might be made him by any of his friends in England.

His partner, Franz Louis Michel, as has been stated in Chapter III, was meanwhile conducting negotiations for the Ritter Company. This company was also to bring over religious convicts for the Canton of Bern; and so had a semi-official character.[1] On the 28th of April, 1709 "Mr. Mitchells Proposals in the name of some of the Swiss Cantons of Bern were read (at Craven House) and it was then agreed that 10,000 Acres of Land on or betwixt News or Cape Fear or their branches in North Carolina should be set out for the Proposers or their heirs they paying to the Lords Proprietors £10 purchase money for each thousand acres to the Lords Proprietors and their Heirs forever.

"Agreed further that 100,000 Acres be reserved to the proposers for 12 years during which term no other person shall purchase any of the same, which said 100,000 Acres are to be set out by the Surveyor General and may be purchased by any of the Proposers at the rate above mentioned during the term of seven years but after that time is expired they are to pay according to the custome of that part of the Province.

"And lastly that one of their number be made a Landgrave he paying for 5000 acres the usuall purchase money for each 1000 acres the customary quitrent for every 100 acres to the Lords Proprietors for the same."[2]

[1] E. Mueller, Bernische Taeufer, page 258.
[2] Col. Rec., vol. I, page 707.

Meanwhile the influx of Germans into England, treated of in Chapters I and II, was beginning. On the 28th of April, the day that Michel's proposals were read, Luttrell mentions that, "the elector Palatine, upon many protestant families leaving his domains, and gone for England to be transported to Pennsylvania, has publish'd an order, making it death and confiscation of goods for any of his subjects to quit their native country."[3] Some time after this they arrived in England. From this passage, as well as from the encouragement the people themselves received, it is clear that the general notion was that these Germans were to be sent to America. But now a greater number of people on their hands than they expected, there was difficulty in executing the plan. Schemes were proposed; some suggested Reya de la Plata, Jamaica, the sugar islands, the Canary Islands, New England, Pennsylvania, Virginia, the Jerseys, Maryland, and England itself.[4] The Proprietors also wanted to share in any advantage that might be reaped from the foreigners; and on July 11 "detailed proposals were made for the encouragement of the palatinate's transportation into the province of Carolina."[5] What these proposals were is given in part by Luttrell, July 16, 1709. "The Lords Proprietors of Carolina have made proposals to a committee of council to take all the Palatines here from 15 to 45 years old, and send them to their plantations; but her majestie to be at the charge of transporting them, which will be above 10£, a head."[6]

While this was under consideration, the proprietors, apparently fully confident of the success of their plan, wished the persons immediately concerned to know about it and on July 28, they "ordered, that the advertisement printed in the gazette for the palatinates' transportation, be printed in High Dutch, for the use of the poor palatines and the rest of the Germans."[7]

Graffenried could hardly have been a member of the Swiss colonization company at the time the proposals were made [April 28] or his name would have been given. He was then in London, and well known from his previous life in the court circles of Charles II. The proprietors were, as ever, anxious to sell an extra 5000 acres of land; and if they could persuade any of the company to buy with such an inducement as a title thrown in, they would gladly do so. It is not strange, then, that shortly after this Graffenried did become a member of the company, for Michel who was interested with him in the mining project, was also interested in the Bern-Ritter colonization scheme; and a community of interests in one direction would natur-

[3]Luttrell, vol. VI, page 435.
[4]Eccl. Rec., vol. 3, page 1790.
[5]Hist. Soc. S. Carolina, vol. I, page 179.
[6]Luttrell, vol. VI, page 465.
[7]Hist. Soc. S. Carolina, vol. I, page 179.

ally bring the two men together in any other scheme where one was involved. Thus, before anything definite about the Proprietors' proposals for settling the Germans on their land had been made by the committee, Graffenried paid 50£ for 5000 acres [August 4, 1709] and was made a Landgrave.[8] Of the 5000 acres, 1250 had belonged to Lawson, but what arrangements Lawson had with the Proprietors is nowhere given. But the important thing is that from this time on Graffenried, who had not been mentioned in the preceding proposals, is the most prominent member in the company.

The committee, having considered the proposals made on July 11th were still unable to make any decision; and on the 11th of August the Proprietors gave a few more details of their plan. At that time they had decided to give the poor Palatines who should have a mind to settle in Carolina, whether man, woman, or child, 100 acres of land each, free from quitrent for ten years, after which they were to pay one penny per acre yearly; or if they should settle in towns, they were to have lands to build upon for three lives, or 99 years, with opportunity for renewal.[9]

These proposals from the Proprietors had not borne any fruit as yet, when arrangements were made between Graffenried, Michel, and the Proprietors to take the place of Michel's arrangement of April 28. On the 3rd of September, 100,000 acres were granted to Graffenried and his heirs, and it was agreed to sell Michel 3500 acres.[10] From the contract with Georg Ritter and Company we know, however, that the 10,000, mentioned on page 43, paragraph 2, were for the society and Graffenried himself owned but 5,000 acres in his own private right.

On the 22 of September, 1709, a warrant was signed at Craven House for only 2,500 acres to Michel,[11] and this is the amount he is credited with in the contract. In the French version Graffenried claims to have paid for 15,000 acres on the Neuse and Trent Rivers and 2,500 on the Weetock. The delays Michel's negotiations had suffered, and the statement in the contract that Ritter had advanced considerable sums,[12] along with Graffenried's statement above, make it seem probable that Ritter advanced the money to Graffenried for all but Graffenried's own 5,000 acres, and that Graffenried actually paid it over to the Duke of Beaufort at Craven House. However this may be, he appears to have been responsible for the full 17,500 after the settlement was made.

Later in the year the propositions of the Proprietors to take charge of the Palatines found a better reception, for on the 10th of October it

[8] Col. Rec., vol. I, page 717.
[9] Hist. Soc. S. Carolina, vol. I, page 157.
[10] Col. Rec., vol. I, page 718.
[11] Col. Rec., vol. I, page 718 ff.
[12] German Version, Contract.

was allowed to Graffenried and Michel to take 600 of them, making about 92 families. Eleven days later 50 more persons were added.[13] Graffenried had the choosing of these and he picked out young, healthy, and industrious persons of various trades. The only lack, then, was a minister, and Graffenried was empowered by the Bishop of London to exercise the two important functions for a young colony, marriage and baptism.[14] The Queen promised 5£ 10 shillings for each emigrant to pay for their passage and gave each 20 shillings worth of clothes as a present.[15]

The colonists were secured against fraud by a bond for 5,000£ which Graffenried was required to give to the commissioners for the faithful performance of his obligations.[16] But for some reason there was a long delay in sending the colony after the contract with the committee had been signed, and it was not until January, 1710, that they finally departed for America.[17]

Things were not moving any more rapidly for the Swiss portion of the settlers. The first company of these, numbering about one hundred persons, left Bern, March 8, 1710.[18] To them there was to have been added at some stage of the journey, the 56 convicts, men who had been in prison now two years because of their Anabaptist views. Passes through England had already been secured, but it was not until March 12 that the Swiss Ambassador to Holland, St. Saphorin, was instructed to get the consent and assistance of the Dutch authorities in bringing the prisoners on their way.[19] On March 18 the little band of convicts started by boat from Bern under Michel's care. The States General had not yet given their consent and showed no signs of doing so, as they had no sympathy with the Anabaptist persecutions, for in Holland people of this sect were welcomed on account of their industry and orderly lives.

Difficulties arose, however, to prevent the execution of the design. On the way down the Rhine just one half of the number became too sick to proceed further, and had to be left in the Palatinate. The most tactful diplomacy the Ambassador could use failed to effect aid from the States General, for by the laws of Holland these prisoners on reaching Dutch territory would thereby become free. And the Dutch authorities determined to see the law enforced. If these people of their free will wished to go to America, nothing would be laid in the way, but they could not be brought through Holland as prisoners. An attempt to have the English Ambassador Townshend use

[13] Col. Rec., vol. I, 986.
[14] German Version, French Version.
[15] Col. Rec., vol. I, page 986.
[16] German Version, Report.
[17] French Version, German Version.
[18] German Version, Letters.
[19] Bernische Taeufer, page 259.

his influence in favor of the deportation failed also, for he asserted the Queen wished to have only voluntary colonists in her provinces.

Michel, who had this expedition in charge, finally got his twenty-eight remaining prisoners as far as Nimwegen, a town a short distance across the border of Holland, and hoped to be able to send them the rest of the way to England. But the vigilance of the Dutch Anabaptists discovered the prisoners; complaint was made; and they were immediately released and allowed to go back to their friends in the Palatinate, or wherever they would, in search of their families from whom they had been so long separated.[20] From one of the letters in which the writer claims to have started from Bern March 18[21] it would appear that one, at least, kept on to America.

On May 18, 1710, while the Swiss were on the way, Graffenried and Michel signed the contract with Georg Ritter and Peter Isot, by which they became, legally, members of the Georg Ritter Company. The foundation of the enterprise was the 17,000 acres actually purchased and the twelve years' option on the 100,000 acres.[22] They also had permission to take up land above the falls of the Potomac, which would, however, be held of the Crown, subject to the Governor of Virginia. The amount actually paid for land was 175£. Besides these land grants they had mining rights in Carolina, Virginia, Maryland, and Pennsylvania.[23] Those rights in Carolina are defined as follows:

"Agreed that Baron de Graffenried and Mr. Lewis Michel shall have a lease of all royal mines and minerals in the Province of Carolina that they shall discover and work for a term of 30 years, they being at the entire charge. The produce of it to be divided into eight parts whereof four eights are to be paid to the Lords Proprietors the other four eights to the said Baron de Graffenried and Mr. Lewis Michel for the term of 5 years after any such Mines shall be found and opened. But after the aforesaid term of five years then the Lords to have five eights, the said Baron de Graffenried and Mr. Lewis Michel three eights the Lords being to pay the Crown the fourth part according to the Words of the Charter."[24] [Apparently this was to be the fourth part of the half which for the first five years should go to the two operators, or one eighth of the whole.]

In their contracts with the Georg Ritter Company, however, Michel, who had done all of the exploration and claimed to have found mines, was to have all the product for three years after the opening of the mines, except what belonged to the Proprietors. In the fourth year

---
[20] Bernische Taeufer, page 258 ff.
[21] German Version. Letters.
[22] German Version, Contract.
[23] German Version, Contract.
[24] Col. Rec., vol. I, page 728.

Ritter and Graffenried were to draw from the produce according to the amount they had subscribed, and the surplus, for the seventeen years the society was to continue, was to go to the members, and they were to pay Ritter for the capltal he advanced out of the production of the first year of the mine in case it turned out well.[25] The contract between the Company and the other provinces is not given; in fact the claims of the Crown were not settled as far as Virginia was concerned, and a year or two later the uncertainty caused Spotswood considerable anxiety.[26]

The stock of the company consisted of 7,200£ divided into twenty-four shares of 300£, no one person holding more than one share; but it was not all paid in, for Michel was credited with a share to pay him for his discoveries which he claimed to have made and for the 2,500 acres which he turned into the society. Graffenried had a share credited to him for his 5,000 acres and his labors with the Palatines; and Georg Ritter had a share for expenses already incurred, leaving only 6,300£ to be paid in. Albrecht von Graffenried had paid in his share, but when the contarct was signed others had not contributed their amounts; and since they had until September, 1711, to do so,[27] it is impossible to tell how much Graffenried had on hand to support himself and his colonists. The report written months afterwards [in May, 1711] indicates a lack of 2,400£ which should have been raised in some way. At that time he had spent 2,228£, a part or all of which he had borrowed;[28] and the 2,400£ would have paid this and left a little besides, and so very likely the keeping of the contract would have saved the colony.

The amount of help he might expect from the Proprietors is not definitely stated. But from the following resolutions passed at Craven House September 3, 1709, at the time the 10,000 acres were bought, it would appear that there was a possibility of Graffenried's being disappointed, even if the promise had been kept, for "To the 2nd Proposal relating to the poor Palatines that shall be transported into North Carolina, It was resolv'd that their Lordships will not undertake to provide them with all provisions they shall want but they will give directions to their Receiver General to supply the Palatines with such provisions as may be spared from the necessary use of the government at the same rates he received them the sd Christopher de Graffenried and Lewis Michel paying their Lordships for the same in Sterling money in London at the end of two years after the arrivals of the Palatines in North Carolina at £50 per Cent discount."[29] In

---
[25]German Version, Contract.
[26]Spotswood, vol. I, page 161. June 11, 1712.
[27]German Versionm Contract.
[28]German Version.
[29]Col. Rec., vol. I, page 718.

a letter by Urmstone, quoted in part, in Chapter X, it is stated that Graffenried was to expect 1,500£ colonial money. This statement may be somewhat exaggerated as are other statements in the letter; but taken in connection with the fact that Cary, as we shall see, promised to give him 500£ on the proprietors' account, it showed conclusively that Graffenried had reason to expect substantial assistance from them. And yet as it turned out (see Chapters VIII and X) this provision saved the Lords Proprietors from giving any assistance to the colony and became a powerful contributing cause to the ruin of the enterprise, a circumstance which Graffenried could not be expected to have forseen from the glowing accounts he had received, of the land and its government, in London.

After a pleasant voyage Graffenried and his Switzers came in sight of land September 10th, and the 11th they came ashore.[30] The news which he then received of his first shiploads must have been a terrible disappointment, for despite the fact that he had had the Royal Commissioners inspect the ships and had sent the emigrants under the care of Surveyor General Lawson, Receiver General Gale, and another official going to Carolina, many of them had died on the voyage because of the overcrowding of the ships and the salt food which did not agree with them.

[30]German Version, Letters; French Version.

CHAPTER VI

Discussion of the Transportation Facilities Provided for the Palatines by the Commissioners—The Colony Plundered by a French Privateer—Graffenried and his Colony Arrive September 10; They Learn of the Distress of the First Shiploads—Graffenried and His Swiss Start for North Carolina as Soon as Possible After Landing

It was certainly not to the credit of the commissioners that these people endured such hardships. Graffenried had them make a particular inspection before the ships started to be sure all was right, for his own experience in shipping was limited; but since the same crowding of the passengers, the same bad food, and the same appalling mortality prevailed on the ships which were carrying the Palatines to New York, the only conclusion is that the commissioners were either shamefully careless of the lives of these people, or totally unfitted by their ignorance to have charge of the transportation of so many. When the proprietors first asked to have some of the Palatines sent to their colonies at the government's expense, Luttrell[1] estimated that it would require over 10£ for each person. In the case of Graffenried's colonists this figure was cut down to 5£ 10 shillings by the commissioners. Graffenried himself, later, estimated that 100 persons could be carried on a ship of 120 tons burden from Holland to America for 700£ at 7£ per person. Boehme[2] in 1711 estimated the cost of transportation from England to America as 7£ for adults and half of that for children.

The committee fixed on the lowest amount possible and paid the ship captains in advance for each passenger. The following passage written at the time of the emigration to New York shows how wretched the management really was, though, of course, the ship captains must bear their share in this disgrace.

"Man hat zwar den Kapitänen, die die Uberführung dahin übernahmen, auf den Kopf einen gewissen Betrag vergütet, aber bei der großen Menge mußten die Leute dermaßen eingepfercht werden, daß viele davon, noch ehe die englische Küste außer Sicht kam, sehr unter Gestank und Ungeziefer gelitten haben, ganz abgesehen davon, daß die zu unterst Liegenden weder frische Luft schöpfen konnten, noch das Tageslicht sahen. Namentlich sind unter diesen Umständen die Kinder zahlreich dahingestorben, vollends bey stürmischer See.

[1] Luttrell, page 465.
[2] Pennsylvanien im 17. Jahrhundert, page 67.

Ja von mehreren Familien blieb niemand übrig, weder Kinder, noch die Eltern selbst. In Briefen von Portsmouth, wo die Einschiffung statt fand, ist im April 1710 hierher nach London mitgeteilt worden, daß auf einem einzigen der Schiffe noch vor der Abfahrt achtzig der Auswanderer gestorben sind. Hundert andere lägen noch krank darin und schienen den Gestorbenen nachfolgen zu wollen. Die Ursache der Sterblichkeit wäre teils in der engen Einpferchung, teils darin zu suchen, daß der Schiffsherr die Menschen nicht mit guter und gesunder Nahrung versehe. Aber eben der Tod der Auswanderer bedeute Gewinn für den Schiffsherrn, da er dann auf der Fahrt weniger Leute zu verköstigen brauche.„ [3]

"They had, to be sure, granted the captains who undertook the transport a certain amount per head, but because of the great number the people had to be packed in so that many of them, even before they got out of sight of the English coast suffered from the foul odor and vermin, entirely apart from the fact that those lying below could neither get fresh air nor see the light of day. And so under these circumstances many children died, especially with a stormy sea. Indeed, of many families no one survived, neither children nor the parents themselves. In letters from Portsmouth, where the embarkation took place, it was reported to London that upon one single ship even before the departure eighty of the emigrants died. Hundreds of the others lay sick therein and seemed to want to follow the dead. The cause of the mortality could be sought partly in the close crowding and partly in the fact that the shipmaster did not provide the people with good and wholesome food. But even the death of the emigrants meant gain for the shipmaster, for then upon the voyage he had to feed less people."

Sickness and death was not all the Palatines had to endure; for just at the mouth of the James River in full view of shore and of an English warship, they were overhauled by a French privateer and one of the ships plundered. The people on board were deprived of even their clothes, and when they came ashore several more died from eating fruit and drinking water. In all, the losses amounted to about half the number which set out. Those who had finally recovered and were left alive had now been in their new home in Carolina several months, when Graffenried and the Switzers landed on September 10th.

He had doubtless been informed immediately of the disasters which had attended his first shiploads of colonists on their voyage and after landing; and their urgent letters were not needed to make him see that his presence was required in Carolina at once. As a Landgrave and head of an important colony he had some obligations to the Governor of Virginia, and therefore could not go immediately into Carolina, but had first to call and pay his respects to the head of the colony. As Spotswood himself was not at home, he called upon the Lieutenant-Governor, and also met Edward Hyde, who had been sent by the Proprietors to be governor of North Carolina; and through them he was made acquainted with the political situation in Carolina. He made his visit as short as he decently could and before long he

[3] Pennsylvanien im 17. Jahrundert, page 66 ff. The author is here quoting a German writer, Hoen, but with orthographic changes and modern expressions in the German where the original is not easily understood.

and his people set out over land for the Chowan River, where they expected to find boats to take them to their tract on the Neuse and Trent.

Leaving them at this point for a time we must now recall some of the events of the years preceding, in order better to appreciate what Graffenried encountered on his arrival in America.

CHAPTER VII

THE EARLIEST SETTLEMENT—EARLY GOVERNMENT—DEVELOPMENT OF SELF-GOVERNMENT—IMPOSITION OF LOCKE'S FUNDAMENTALS—CONFUSIONS RESULTING FROM ATTEMPTS TO ENFORCE CERTAIN PROVISIONS AND NAVIGATION LAWS—TROUBLE GROWING OUT OF TEST OATHS—CARY IN OPEN OPPOSITION TO EDWARD HYDE, THE PROPRIETORS' APPOINTEE—GRAFFENRIED MET BY A DELEGATION AND OFFERED THE PRESIDENCY OF THE COUNCIL—HE REFUSES A TEMPTING OFFER FOR THE SAKE OF HIS COLONY

The first immigrants into the Carolinas were wealthy Virginians who were attracted by the opportunity to better their condition, and not religious refugees as has generally been supposed. They purchased land of the Indians and settled themselves about Albemarle Sound as early as 1659,[1] without asking permission of anyone. In 1662 Governor Berkeley of Virginia gave them patents and required of them the quit rents usual in Virginia, that is one farthing per acre. They did not form compact towns, but each planter had his own wharf to which trading vessels came. No very serious Indian troubles drove them to continuously concerted action; and as they had no ministers for a long time, although many of them doubtless belonged to the established church, there grew up a reckless sort of independence which was strengthened by the arrival of new colonists, from the attempted settlements of New Englanders at Cape Fear, which had failed, partly because the colonists had stubbornly resisted the purpose of the proprietors to appoint governors over them rather than let them elect their own.

These proprietors were eight favorites of Charles II whom he wished to reward for their assistance in helping him to his throne after the downfall of the Protectorate. They were given almost absolute power, holding all the rights which the Bishop of Durham held. Besides they had the power to create an order of nobility among the inhabitants of their domains, but the titles were not to be the same as those used in England and the laws they should make were not to be opposed to those of England. The grant took in a strip from ocean to ocean between 31° and 36° north latitude, the same grant which Charles I had made to Robert Heath in 1629.

Later, in 1665, the grant made to Robert Heath was formally set aside and the proprietors were given an increase, the new grant extending from 29° to 36° 30', north latitude. They were allowed also

[1] Johns Hopkins Historical Studies, May-June, 1892; Ashe, vol. I, page 59.

discretionary powers with regard to freedom of conscience, and could grant religious liberty and toleration as they chose.

Another provision of the charter is so important in this later history that I shall quote verbatim so much of it as applies. "And also to ordain, make and enact, and under their seals, to publish any laws and constitutions whatsoever, either appertaining to the publick state of the said whole province or territory, or of any district or particular county, barony or colony, of or within the same, or to the private utility of particular persons, according to their best discretion, *by and with the advice, assent and approbation of the freemen of the said province or territory, or of the freemen of the county, barony or colony, for which such law or constitution shall be made, or the greater part of them, or their delegation or deputies, whom for enacting of the said laws, when, and as often as need shall require,* [2] we will that the said Edward Earle of Clarendon, George Duke of Albemarle, William Earl of Craven, John Lord Berkeley, Anthony Lord Ashley, Sir George Cartaret, Sir John Colleton, and Sir William Berkeley, and their heirs or assigns, *shall from time to time* assemble in such manner and form as to them shall seem best; etc."[3] A saving clause permitted laws to be passed on an emergency, which had not received the sanction of the people.

In 1664 a man named Drummond was sent out with six councilors to be governor of the province. With them was sent the Concessions, under which all this territory of Carolina was to be governed. By this document the freemen were either to meet in one body or to elect twelve representatives to act with the six councilors. The first assembly which met not later than 1665 was composed of all the freemen, and was in this respect a democratic body. Full liberty of conscience was established with this exception that the General Assembly might appoint as many ministers as it pleased, thus giving a preference to the Church of England. Officers were either to swear allegiance or to sign a declaration in a book, and no tax was to be levied without the consent of the Assembly. The Assembly might choose a president in place of an absent governor or deputy governor. Quit rents were made a halfpenny per acre. Until 1667 the governor, six councilors, and the twelve deputies (for the meeting of all the freemen was not continued) sat in one body. In the general meeting of 1665 a petition had been sent to the proprietors that the quit rent be reduced to the rate which prevailed in Virginia of one farthing per acre payable in commodities. In 1668 this was granted in an instrument called ever since the "Great Deed," and any encroachments upon its provisions by the proprietors were bitterly resented.

[2]The italics are mine, V. H. T.
[3]Carrol's Collections, vol. II, page 43 ff.

After these years of self-government there came an unwelcome change, which in Carolina marks the beginning of that unrest which finally ended with the Revolution, for never after this was there any extended period of satisfaction with the government from England, whether administered by the proprietors or the royal governors. One of the proprietors, the Earl of Shaftesbury, had his friend, the philosopher John Locke, draw up a system of government for the colony; and in 1669, what was considered the most perfect system ever devised was sent out to be tried on the few scattered settlers in this vast woods. No stretch of the imagination can make this seem like emergency legislation, and there is not the slightest ground for thinking the proprietors considered it as such; the freemen never unqualifiedly sanctioned it; and therefore, by the provision of the charter above quoted, this Grand Model of government was not legally binding upon the people. The resistance, however, was not entirely consistent. For example, they objected to the requirement of an oath to support the constitution, and in this degree, they may be said to have objected to the whole plan; but nevertheless they accepted the provision for regularly holding elections for their representatives, and for having meetings every two years whether the governor called one or not. There is no evidence that they were opposed to the theoretical founding of high sounding courts, or an actual establishing of a hereditary nobility. Their great complaint was against a raise of the quit rents from a farthing to a penny per acre, payable in silver.

Further trouble was caused by attempts to enforce the navigation laws. In 1673 Carteret tired of trying to enforce the enactments, resigned the governorship, and from that time till 1707 there were six open revolts leading to the deposition or suspension of governors and collectors. The people had never been trained in the obedience presupposed in the constitutions, and resisted every attempt to invade their previous liberties.

To these economic and political disturbances were added religious difficulties. The proprietors had allowed people of dissenting opinions to settle in their dominions and practice their religious worship as they wished, so long as they refrained from disturbing others. But the idea, nevertheless, had always been to establish the Church of England in the colonies in Carolina. The first missionaries sent out by the Society for the Propagation of the Gospel were unfortunate choices. They antagonized many of their own faith as well as the dissenters, for the very idea of having a church supported by the state was repugnant to many of them. After the visit of Edmundson and Fox in 1672 the Quakers, too, had become rather numerous; and, of course, they objected to being compelled to pay for the support of other ministers than their own, and in particular, to the support of Church of England ministers.

In 1698, by act of Parliament, oaths of office were required of the governors of colonies; and in 1701, Governor Walker had the Assembly pass an act to establish parishes and churches and maintain ministers. The Quakers, Presbyterians, and some members of the Established Church objected very strongly to this. But the trouble calmed down without being finally settled when the bill was vetoed by the proprietors because they considered it inadequate. In 1704 Daniel became governor, and he required the oath of allegiance to Queen Anne, in accordance with an act of Parliament, and denied the right of any to sign a declaration in a book, in lieu of the oath, a privilege which had been expressly granted in the instructions of 1670.[4] The governor was technically in the right in his demand, for such oaths were required very strictly in England at this time and for years afterwards; but the laws had always been dead letters in Carolina, and might just as well have been treated as such at this time if Governor Daniel had desired to have it so. The measure seems to have been aimed at the Quakers, since this effectually excluded them from the Assembly, weakened the opposition to the strict Church party to this degree and allowed the establishing of the Church of England by law, as Lord Granville, the most influential of the proprietors, desired. This was so distasteful to the Presbyterians and other dissenters who might ordinarily be expected to favor the exclusion of the Quakers, that they united with them and secured Daniel's removal by order of the proprietors. This compliance of the proprietors shows that there was no need of applying the act of Parliament regarding oaths very rigidly in the colonies.

Thomas Cary, who before this had been a merchant in South Carolina, was next appointed. He shared the general feeling against the Quakers, and not only had them excluded by this same test oath, but also imposed a fine upon those who should enter upon an office without first taking the oath. He also secured the passage of another law by which the election of any one who promoted his own candidacy was declared void. By the application of this measure he could keep out anyone he chose, by merely having it shown that the person in question had in some way promoted his own interests in the election. These enactments gave him control over Presbyterians as well as Quakers, but the measures were too thorough, and Mr. John Porter was sent to England to petition the proprietors for relief; and in 1707 he returned bringing an instrument by which the laws regarding oaths were suspended and Cary removed from the government. At the

[4] Col. Rec., vol I, page 181.

time of his arrival, however, Cary was absent, and William Glover, President of the Council, was acting in his place. Porter, therefore, did not at once enforce his new instrument; but left Glover in power, and held in abeyance the action against Cary. Yet, since Glover was still keeping the Quakers out by the test oaths, discontent grew until Cary, Porter, Pollock and Foster, heads of various factions, in 1708 unitedly issued a proclamation to the people to obey the existing government. But the coming of two Church of England missionaries, Adams and Gordon, at this time, was the signal for another outbreak on the part of the different dissenting bodies, who saw in the actions of the government a menace to their religious liberty, and an attempt to saddle the established church on the colony.

Porter next broke with Glover, and Cary was elected. Since Lord Granville was now dead, there was no need for Cary to still hold high church views; and while there is no record of such an agreement, it appears that Cary promised to give up the requirement of the test oaths and other restrictions. And it was probably for this reason that he was chosen president of the council. Glover also claimed to be president since his incumbency had not been disturbed by Porter's instructions from the proprietors, while they had said specifically that Cary should be removed. Glover certainly had some right on his side as well as did Cary, for by the Constitutions and by precedent the president of the council was to be governor in the absence of a governor or his deputy, approved by the proprietors. Thus we find two governors, and the country in turmoil. The principals agreed to leave the decision to an assembly, and each issued writs for an election. Cary had the majority of votes if the Quakers were admitted. Glover, however, insisted upon the exclusion of the Quakers, but without avail, and he with Pollock and Gale, went over into Virginia, leaving Cary in charge. But still a large faction, composed of those who had been trained in public affairs during the time that the others had been kept out by the exclusion laws, was dissatisfied, and the government was not very efficient.

In 1708 Tynte had been appointed governor of South Carolina with instructions to deputize Edward Hyde over the northern colony, and until Hyde should come Tynte left Cary in charge. Unfortunately for affairs in North Carolina, Tynte died during the summer of 1710 without signing Hyde's commission and administering the oath, and since under the circumstances Hyde did not care to come into the colony, he was still in Virginia when Graffenried landed with his Switzers in September, 1710, and after a short delay started for Carolina.

At Somerton a delegation of Quakers and other persons met him, and desired him by virtue of his title of Landgrave to take the presidency of the council, which, in the absence of the governor, as had been noticed, carried with it the executive function. If Graffenried had been ambitious for himself he might well have been tempted by the offer. He was the friend of Hyde, whose appointment lacked only a signature and an oath to make it valid, and as such might have felt sure of the support of Hyde's adherents and of many of Cary's dissenters. Moreover, since Glover's departure for Virginia, his followers were looking forward to Hyde's coming, and these men, too, would probably have supported him. His favor with the Queen and the proprietors, which must have been well known in the colony, since he had been made Landgrave and his Palatines had been provided for over a year before, might have led him to hope that a goodly number from the contending parties could be brought to recognize him as their executive officer, for Hyde had no patents and was, in addition, afraid to trust himself in the province. If Graffenried had been acquainted with the previous history of the colony at all, he would have known that there was not much to fear from the proprietors, so long as he could keep the factions united. Their weakness in dealing with their colonies was well recognized,[5] and just as in the case of Cary, they could be expected to leave the matter in *statu quo* so long as no complaint was made to them. That the factions were tiring of the struggle is shown by the fact that after Graffenried refused to be led astray by such brilliant prospects, they united in an address to Hyde to take the presidency until his commission should arrive. Cary himself was one of the signers,[6] persuaded, to be sure, by Graffenried.[7] For Graffenried, although his refusal was not accepted by the delegation, had resolved to devote his time and energies to his settlement, and to avoid the difficulties of politics.

[5]Col. Rec., vol. I, page 725.
[6]Col. Rec., vol. I, page 725.
[7]German Version.

CHAPTER VIII

GRAFFENRIED'S PRECARIOUS POSITION—THE PALATINES' PITIFUL CONDITION—GRAFFENRIED DEFRAUDED—NO HELP TO BE OBTAINED FROM THE PROPRIETORS—MAKES PEACE WITH THE INDIANS—LAWSON'S HUMANE SENTIMENTS NOT BORNE OUT IN HIS TREATMENT OF THE INDIANS—MICHEL DISTURBS THE PROCEEDINGS—GRAFFENRIED COMPELLED BY CIRCUMSTANCES AS WELL AS INCLINATION TO JOIN HYDE'S FACTION

Graffenried's position was now a peculiar one. On the one hand, he had, immediately on his arrival, become one of the most influential men in the province. His title of Landgrave, the fame of his undertaking, and his friendship with eminent persons in England made him very much respected, and yet of the actual necessaries of life he had almost nothing with which to support his dignity. When he reached the settlement he found conditions worse than he expected. Lawson had not sold all the land on the point between the Neuse and the Trent Rivers to Graffenried, and in order to further his own interests, he had settled those under his charge on his own land to gain the benefit of any clearing they might do. Thus when Graffenried came, the Palatines found their summer's work had gone for nothing. The directors had also exploited them by taking their goods in return for their services in looking after them on the way over, and what was left after this had gone to the English settlers in return for food to keep them alive. Moreover, the place where Lawson had settled them was on a southern exposure where the heat was very oppressive, and as a result, sickness was added to starvation. To make matters worse, instead of finding the land free of Indians as he had been led to believe it was, he discovered that King Taylor with a small tribe of twenty families was still living there, and that they were none too well pleased to have their lands taken up in this way, for they had never as yet been paid for the tract. If in this situation the Germans did not supply their wants by hunting, supposing they had the strength and equipment, one cannot blame them. As for living on fish, oysters, and crabs, such a diet in the heat of summer after they had been weakened by their illness on the long voyage across the Atlantic and after landing in Virginia would have been almost impossible.

But Graffenried's coming changed all this, for he brought supplies for their present needs, and began immediately to see what could be done on the account of the Lords Proprietors with the province. His treatment of the Indians on this and later occasions is more a

credit to his heart than to his business sagacity, perhaps, if one may
judge his actions by the standard set by most of the whites who have
had dealings with the Indians. The result justified him in his peculiar
notions, however, when it came to be a life and death matter with
him. He had previously paid for the particular piece of ground
where the settlement was then being made, supposing that the original
owners had been satisfied for it and had moved off leaving it perfectly free for white settlers. Likewise it was scarcely to be expected
that Lawson would work a fraud on him and an injustice to the
Indians after such generous expressions as the following, chosen from
several such to be found in his book:

"These are them that wear the English Dress. Whether they have
Cattle now or no, I am not certain; but I am of the Opinion that such
Inclinations in the Savages should meet with Encouragement, and
every Englishman ought to do them Justice and not defraud them
of their Land, which has been allotted them formerly by the Government; for if we do not shew them Examples of Justice and Vertue,
we can never bring them to believe us to be a worthier Race of Men
than themselves.

"They are really better to us than we are to them; they always
give us Victuals at their Quarters, and take Care we are armed
against Hunger and Thirst; we do not so by them (generally speaking) but let them walk by our Doors hungry, and do not often relieve
them. We look upon them with Scorn and Disdain and think them
little better than Beasts in humane Shape, though if well examined,
we shall find that for all our Religion and Education, we possess more
moral Deformities and Evils than these Savages do, or are acquainted
withal."[1]

It appears, though, that an opportunity to enrich himself overcame
his scruples and he did as others had done before him, disposed
of land which by rights was not yet his to dispose of. When Graffenried came and found the savages still claimed the land, rightfully
as he looked at it, Lawson's advice to chase them off did not appeal
to him, although it would have been possible, perhaps, to do so.
Rather, he paid them for the tract and established friendly relations
with them. Then finding that his people and the Indians were not
likely to live together harmoniously, he had a very solemn pow-wow
with the red-men, paid them again for the land where the first settlement had been made, probably bought what other land he needed
to parcel out to his settlers and made the Indians satisfied to move
out of the neighborhood of his people. His influence over the Indians
and their confidence in him comes out indirectly in this conference.

[1]Lawson's Journal, pages 192 ff.

The Indians, seventeen heads of families and their chief, took their places in a circle on the ground, dressed in their finery, the chief looking to Graffenried more like an ape than a man. Graffenried sat on a chair and also wore whatever ornaments he had that would glitter most. He could not help but be convinced that their arguments for staying were better than any he could present to induce them to leave, but yet they finally agreed to go. Michel, his business partner, was not far away during the conference, making himself drunk with some English friends. In this condition he suddenly broke in on the assembly, snatched off the king's headdress and threw it as far as he could, then seizing the orator beat him and dragged him out of the circle. Graffenried had difficulty restoring order and peace; finally, however, Michel was taken away and put in charge of his friends, and the negotiations went on to a happy termination for Graffenried. That night, Michel, still under the influence of liquor, broke into the Indian camp while Graffenried was asleep, and again beat and insulted the orator; and again Graffenried had to be peacemaker. [2] The fact that he succeeded at all is sufficient evidence of the regard in which he was held by the savages.

The need of separating the Indians from the settlers is illustrated by the story he tells of one of his workmen. This man, a Berner, coming home from wood chopping happened to pass by an idol representing the evil divinity. This image was painted red and black, the colors of the wood chopper's native city. He could not endure seeing these colors misused in such a manner, and destroyed the ugly representation of the Devil with his ax. On reaching home he boasted that he had split the Devil with one blow. [3] The Indians were horrified at such a sacrilege and peace was with difficulty restored. Nevertheless they were finally persuaded to forego hostilities when Graffenried promised to see that no further injury was done them. Partly for their sake he sent Michel on surveying expeditions and into Pennsylvania to look for silver. [4] The settlers, thus, could not appreciate the Indians' point of view although they speak kindly of them in their letters, wherever they mention them at all, and so, it was better to keep them apart. [5]

Having reached the province and provided for the immediate needs of his people, Graffenried now felt his next duty to be the securing of the continuation of supplies. As a landgrave he would be compelled to take sides in the political quarrel in the colony, and the question was with whom should he cast in his fortune. He and his

---

[2] French Version.
[3] French and German Versions.
[4] French Version.
[5] German Version, Letters.

colony were dependent upon the favor of the Proprietors for their very existence, and he could not hope for their favor while supporting one who was defying their authority. Yet the principles for which the dissenting faction had contended in the beginning, before Cary took sides with them—freedom from the domination of the Church of England—must have appealed to him, even though he and his colonists were under the spiritual protection of the Bishop of London and had become members of that church.[6] Moreover, among 650 Palatines there must have been a goodly number of Anabaptists, and some of the letters of his settlers which he copied for the German version seem to have been written by people of this sect. One of their fundamental tenets was freedom of conscience, and both in framing the contract for the society and in the agreement with the settlers, Graffenried and the company did not depend upon the charter of Carolina nor upon the Fundamental Constitutions alone, but made special provision for religious liberty. The distractions produced in the province in the efforts to secure it, however, could not have impressed the colonists favorably, and as a matter of self-defense Graffenried had to espouse Hyde's cause. And yet Hyde was not technically governor, lacking Tynte's signature, and was afraid to come into the province.

The very numbers of people Graffenried brought with him was a disadvantage, because whichever side he joined, he would be sure to gain the ill-will of the opposition. But as Cary, who had been deposed once, was governing a second time with a legality which was questioned by the first people with whom Graffenried had become acquainted,[7] and as it was the will of the Lords Proprietors that Hyde should be governor, he did not hesitate to declare himself against Cary. And again the situation was complicated, for Cary had in his possession all the funds of the province, and it was necessary for Graffenried to look to him for what the Proprietors had promised on their account with the province. When the demand was made of him, he promised well, but kept evading fulfillment until Graffenried lost hope at last and sent to Virginia where he had made arrangements for flour before leaving England. Only thus were the people enabled to proceed with the building of their town.

[6]Col. Rec., vol. I, pp. 756, 734. French Version.
[7]Col. Rec., vol. I, page 731.

CHAPTER IX

FOUNDING OF THE CITY—LEET COURT SYSTEM—ARTICLES IN THE FUNDAMENTALS RELATING TO LEET COURTS—DISCUSSION OF BARONIES AND MANORS, SHOWING IRREGULARITIES IN APPOINTMENTS—ARTICLES IN FUNDAMENTALS REFERRING TO BARONIES, MANORS, ETC.—IDEAL ONCE GIVEN UP REVIVED IN MODIFIED FORM FOR GRAFFENRIED'S COLONY—REASONS FOR THIS—CONTRACTS WITH PROPRIETORS AND COLONISTS—EVIDENCES FROM MANUSCRIPTS—EVIDENCES OF A PATERNAL GOVERNMENT—EVIDENCES OF POPULAR ASSEMBLIES

The little city was placed on a point of land between the Neuse River and the Trent, and was laid out in the form of a cross, one arm extending from river to river, and the other, from the point, back indefinitely. At a reasonable distance Graffenried built a line of fortifications from one river to the other and had his coast line well defended also. These fortifications were doubtless frail enough, but would have been of service in case of an Indian attack if all the people were inside and acted in concert. He planned to have a church at the four corners. Market was to be held once a week, and a fair yearly. His best contribution was his water mill for grinding grain. There was only one other mill in the whole province and it was a poor one, and the only way the people had of getting flour or meal was to beat their grain in a wooden mortar with a wooden pestle and sift it through a basket. When the little town was completed, a solemn assembly gave it the name of New Bern. It had such a favorable beginning that people in Virginia and Pennsylvania bought lots there, and Graffenried could say that his town made more progress in a year than some other towns had made in several.[1] A plan to live at one common expense, but in separate households was formulated, but was given up as impracticable.[2]

The form of government at New Bern is nowhere definitely given, yet we can get some general idea of it from the few references in the writings Graffenried left. One is tempted to see in it the attempt to introduce the leet court system of the Fundamental Constitution, though in a modified form, despite the fact that the revised fundamentals of 1698 had omitted the provision relating to such courts. If this is the case, we have the only such attempt so far as I am able to discover, to put the system into practice in the province. The

---
[1]German Version; French Version.
[2]German Version, Report.

omission of many of the articles in the revised Constitution need not imply a change of conviction on the part of the proprietors, but only a concession to the conditions in America. In Graffenried's case, also, such a system would, perhaps, seem more practicable and thus the old idea would, naturally, be revived.

The following articles of the Fundamentals refer to this sort of serfdom, and show the ideals which the proprietors had.

"16th. In every signiory, barony, and manor, the respective Lord shall have power in his own name to hold court leet there, for trying of all causes, both civil and criminal; but where it shall concern any person being no inhabitant, vassal, or leet man, of the said signiory, barony or manor, he upon paying down of forty shillings, for the Lords Proprietors' use, shall have an appeal from the signiory, or barony court, to the county court, and from the manor court to the precinct court.

"19th. Any Lord of a manor, may alienate, sell, or dispose to any other person and his heirs forever, his manor all intirely together, with all the priviledges and leet men, thereunto belonging, so far forth as any colony lands; but no grant of any part thereof, either in fee or for any longer term than three lives, or for one and twenty years, shall be good against the next heir.

"22d. In every signiory, barony and manor, all the leet men shall be under the jurisdiction of the respective Lords of the said signiory, barony or manor, without appeal from him. Nor shall any leet man, or leet woman have liberty to go off from the land of their particular Lord and live anywhere else without license obtained from their said Lord, under hand and seal.

"23d. All the children of leet men, shall be leet men, and so to all generations.

"24th. No man shall be capable of having a court leet, or leet men, but a Proprietor, Landgrave, Casique, or Lord of a manor.

"25th. Whoever shall voluntarily enter himself a leet man, in the registry of the county court, shall be a leet man.

"26th. Whoever is Lord of Leet men, shall upon the marriage of a leet man, or leet woman of his, give them ten acres of land for their lives, they paying to him therefore, not more than one eighth part of all the yearly produce and growth of the said ten acres. [3]

In the application of their "unalterable Constitutions" relative to the German colony, as in other matters, the proprietors allowed themselves a considerable latitude, and so we find several variations from their ideals expressed in the articles quoted above. In the first place, the appointment of landgraves had always been irregular. According

[3]Col. Rec., vol. I, page 187 ff.

to their charter they could confer their title "upon such of the inhabitants of the said province as they shall think do or shall merit the same," [4] and yet of twenty-five appointees eleven never lived in America, and several of those who did live in America were appointed before they ever came to this country. [5] Locke was the first to receive the title, and in his case it appears to have been merely honorary, and if the four baronies of 12,000 acres each was ever assigned to him there is no record of it left. Nevertheless it was intended at first to have the title always associated with land and in the amounts presented in the articles, as an act passed by the Assembly of Albemarle and approved by the proprietors in 1669 shows. By this act it is decreed that "noe person or persons whatsoever he be within this County under the degree of Proprietor, Landgrave or Cassique shall have Liberty for the space of five yeares next ensueing to survey or lay out above six hundred and sixty acres of Land in one devidend that soe the County may be the speedier seated, without express leave obtained from the Lords Proprietors.

"And it is hereby further enacted that there shall not be granted in any warrent any quantity of Land but what is allowed according to the Quality of the right and is exprest in the Proprietors Instructions, concessions or Fundamental Constitutions or forms of Government." [6]

This intention on the part of the assembly was not always carried out, for it was ordered by the Proprietors near the beginning of this new form of government that the Proprietors should have but three signiories, and each landgrave and cacique but one barony. [7] Nevertheless, John Price, [8] another of those who never lived in America, was made a landgrave in 1687 and "four baronies of 12,000 acres" were annexed to the title. In 1698 a new plan was hit upon, [9] and instead of conferring the title and the domains which belonged to it as a mark of the high regard in which the person was held by the Proprietors, blanks were sent out for six landgraves and eight caciques. These were to be sold to whomsoever would buy, provided they were considered worthy by Major Robert Daniel and Landgrave Morton, who had the disposal of them. The sale was not very rapid, for only two purchased. One of these, Captain Edmund Bellinger, was in England at the time of the purchase but paid in America, and John Bayley took another but paid in Ireland. After this another change was allowed, for in 1709 Abel Ketelby, who also became a nonresident

[4] Col. Rec., vol. I, page 29.
[5] McCrady, page 717.
[6] Col. Rec., vol. I, page 186.
[7] McCrady, page 141.
[8] McCrady, page 719.
[9] McCrady, page 292.

landgrave, purchased 5,000 acres.[10] And after this fashion the title had lost in dignity until it was offered for sale with few takers, while the amount of land which went with it was reduced from a vast tract to a moderate-sized manor, the lords of which strips were originally intended to be of the lowest order of nobility.

Graffenried's appointment was no exception to the others in irregularities. He was a foreigner, but probably naturalized,[11] for he was in England when the naturalization laws were made and in his Memorial he advises it. He was required to buy and actually did buy but 5,000 acres to secure the title, and the 10,000 additional which he purchased for the company and Michel's 2,500 acres over which he appears to have had the disposal for the company had nothing to do with the bestowal of the highest dignity in the power of the Proprietors.

Fortunately, the Carolinians seem not to have been disturbed by all these irregularities in his appointment and he thought the title an advantage to him, as it seemed to help him keep the respect of his own settlers and the other colonists.

The following articles relate to the order of nobility which was to be established.

"4th. Each signory, barony, and colony, shall consist of twelve thousand acres, the eight signories being the share of the eight proprietors, and the eight baronies of the nobility; both which shares, being each of them one fifth of the whole, are to be perpetually annexed, the one to the proprietors and the other to the hereditary nobility; leaving the colonies, being three fifths, amongst the people; so that in setting out and planting the lands, the balance of the government may be preserved.

"9th. There shall be just as many Landgraves as there are counties, and twice as many Casiques, and no more. These shall be the hereditary nobility of the Province, and by right of their dignity be members of parliament. Each Landgrave shall have four baronies, and each Casique two baronies, hereditarily and unalterably annexed to and settled upon the said dignity.

"17th. Every manor shall consist of not less than three thousand, and not above twelve thousand acres in one piece and colony; but any three thousand acres or more in one piece and the possession of one man, shall not be a manor, unless it be constituted a manor by the grant of the Palatine's court.

"21st. Every Lord of a manor, within his own manor, shall have all the powers, jurisdictions and privileges which a Landgrave or Casique hath in his baronies."[12]

---
[10]Col. Rec., vol. I, page 705.
[11]German Version, Memorial.
[12]Col. Rec., vol. I, page 187.

In the provisions for a continuance of the proprietary government with its almost regal powers in the hands of a hereditary and self-perpetuating body of eight persons; and a limited proportion of landgraves and casiques, with lords of manors below them, and last of all leet men—four classes likewise hereditary—the proprietors attempted to establish a feudal system more perfect in its working than any in Europe. For the systems with which they were familiar were the results of development or accident, while this was to be carefully thought out and the results calculated beforehand with almost mathematical accuracy, and applied arbitrarily to a new state which was just forming.

In the new nobility the amount of land belonging to a certain title had been fixed with the exception of manors, the size of which might vary from 3,000 to 12,000 acres. The obligations of the leet men, whether subject to lords of manors, caciques, or landgraves, were to be the same in all parts of the province. As has been shown, the theory could not be put into practice as originally intended in the case of the nobility, and it turned out to be even more impracticable to put the articles relating to leetmen into operation. There is not the slightest evidence that the offer of ten acres with its feudal acknowledgment, which might amount to an eighth of the proceeds therefrom yearly, tempted any one to put himself and his children into bondage to an overlord, when land was in abundance near by and free from burdensome obligations. It was so manifestly impossible to carry out these promises, that in the instructions to Colonel Philip Ludwell sent out in 1791, which were in reality a revision of the Fundamentals from 120 to 43 articles,[13] there is no mention of leetmen or leetcourts, although landgraves and caciques are mentioned as if they were still to exist as before. In place of leetcourts there were to be representatives chosen by the freemen, and the criminal courts were to be administered by the governor or by commissioners appointed by him.

But when Graffenried brought out his colony, the old idea seems to have been revived for him and his settlers, for he would hardly have made an arrangement which removed his colonists from the jurisdiction of the officers of the province without the advice of the proprietors. The conditions under which the settlement was being made would favor such a government as they had originally planned, but would not make it essential. His people were coming out together, all spoke the same langauge and would naturally be somewhat cut off from the rest of the inhabitants of the province because of this; but since the French colonists,[14] though living somewhat segregated from the rest, held their lands just as did the English settlers and were subject to the

[13]Col. Rec., vol. I, page 373 ff.
[14]McCrady, page 319 ff.

same government, Graffenried's arrangement was not made necessary by the fact that his people spoke a different language from those about them. By his contract with the Swiss and Palatines they were to pay a higher quit-rent than was charged elsewhere in the province, but in return for it they were to receive material help in getting settled, which would offset the disadvantage of the higher rate. The proprietors had trouble over quit-rents continually. Penn in Pennsylvania complained that the people did not appreciate what he was doing for them and that his revenues were not as large as they should be, and it was perhaps in hopes that if the people could be brought into a modified feudal relation with the proprietors there would be less trouble over quit-rents than if they were allowed to live as free as the English colonists, a condition which could be more easily maintained with a group of people speaking a different language from the main body of inhabitants.

The agreement which Graffenried and Michel entered into with the Commissioners has only an indication of some such arrangement in the words, "that some number of the said poor Palatines may be disposed of and settled in the said tract in North Carolina aforesaid, *as well for the benefit of the said Christopher de Graffenried and Lewis Michel* as for the relief and support of the poor Palatines."[15]

In the abstract of the treaty[16] with the proprietors we find, furthermore, that Graffenried was to be the judge of all disputes arising among the Germans, but in cases where the English were involved the jurisdiction was in the hands of the courts. But all cases of capital crimes were reserved for the proprietors themselves. This is not as complete

---

[15]Col. Rec., vol. I, page 937 ff. The italics are mine. V. H. T.

[16]1. Ils m'ont vendu 15000 arpents terre choisie que j'ay fait arpenter Sur la Riviere de News et Trent et 2500 acres Sur Weetock River, à 10 livres Sterlins le 1000, ou une livre Sterl: p cent acres, et 6 Sols par 100 arpendts. cen ce fonciere, ce qui fait la Somme de 175£ Sterl: ce que j'ay d'abord paye content. 2. Il y a eu une reserve de 100 mille acres a choisir entre ces Rivieres cy nomees et Clarendon R. pour le meme prix, et pour cela j'ay eu 7 ans de terme pour faire le premier payement et des la 7e: jusques a la 12e: le tout devoit être payé. 3e. Les differents qu'auroient mon Peuple avec les Anglois ce devoient terminer devant les juges Anglois mais ce que mes Colonists auroient de dificulté entre Eux cela ce termineroit entre Eux ou par devant moy: La haute Jurisdiction au faits criminels a mort reservez zux Seigrs. Prop: 4e. Liberte de Religion, et d'avoir un ministre de notre Pays qui pourroit precher en notre langue—. 5e. Droit de Ville et marche ou faire a Neuberne. 6e. francs de toutee taille et impots dimes et Cences hormi les 6 Sols p 100 acres annullement come susdit. 7e. Les Seigrs Prop: ou la Province par leurs ordres me devoint fournir pour 2 ou 3 ans de provision de vivres et betail pour moy et toutte la Colonie moyenant restitution apres le terme prescrit.

"1st. They sold me 15,000 acres of choice land which I had surveyed upon the River Neuse and the River Trent and 2,500 acres upon the Weetock River at 10 pounds sterling per 1,000, or one pound sterling per hundred acres, and six pence per 100 acres, quit-rent rent, which makes the sum of 175£ sterling which I payed down. 2d. There was a reserve of 100 thousand acres to choose between these rivers here named and Clarendon River for the same price, and for that I had a period of seven years for the first payment and between the 7th and 12th the whole was to be paid. 3d. The differences which my people might have with the English were to be settled before the English judges, but the difficulties which my colonists might have among themselves were to be settled either among themselves or before me, the final jurisdiction in capital crimes reserved to the Lords Proprietors. 4th. Religious liberty and the right to have a minister of our own country to preach in our language. 5th. Rights of cite, and market or fair at New Bern. 6th. Freedom from all taxes and imposts, tithes and hundredths except the 6 pence per 100 acres annually as above said. 7th. The Lords Proprietors or the province by their orders were to furnish me and all my colony with food and live stock for 2 or 3 years with reimbursement after the prescribed time."

a jurisdiction as the Fundamental Constitutions had originally given to Landgraves and others who should have leetmen; but it nevertheless put a very considerable authority into Graffenried's hands and where his own settlers alone were concerned in any but capital crimes is just as great. That he actually exercised authority is proved by the fact that he incurred the enmity of the Palatine blacksmith by sentencing him to a day's log sawing for using foul language.

In the abstract of his treaty [17] with the Palatines he was to give each family 300 acres of land, for which they should pay a quit rent of two-pence per acre, while he took for himself the payment of the Lords Proprietors' six pence per 100 acres. Thus, as has been said before, the colonists paid a higher rent than was customary in the other provinces and dealt with Graffenried and not with the officers of the province who usually attended to the collection of quit-rents. The Swiss who wrote the letters home, when referring to their farms, used the word "Lechen" (Lehen) which carries with it the idea of an estate held of another, while "Gut," which is used but once, usually has the meaning of a freehold, but not necessarily so. The frequency of the use of Lechen indicates that the colonists themselves recognized a sort of feudal relationship. His own language in characterizing the actions of his colonists in following Brice, when he speaks of them as abtruennig (disloyal), verraeterisch (traitorous) would not have been used except in the case of subjects; and later when the distress became more pressing he exercised one of the rights expressly given in the Constitution to landgraves, caciques, and lords of manor, when he gave his people *permission* to leave their farms. In this case he gave them leave to go away for two years to look for work, the implication being at the end of that time they should come back. Referring again to the articles on leetmen, we find that they were not allowed to leave their land without the express permission of their lord. And lastly, his agreement with the colonists says that they owed him fidelity, obedience and respect, and that he owed them protection—certainly a rather feudal-like expression. This is the relationship

---

[17] J'avois aussi un Traitte particulier et bien exact avec les Palatins lequell fust projecte examine et arrete, devant et par la Commission Royale trop ample a inserrer icy, seulement en Substance ce qui suit le. mes Colonistes me devoient fidelite obeysance et Respect, et moi la Protection. au 2e. Je devois fournir chaque famille de provision pour la premiere annee, d'une Vache de deux Cochons et de quelques utensils, moyenant restitution apres 3 ans. 3e. Je devois doner a chaque famille 300 arp: de Terre et ils devoient me livrer pour Cence fonciere 2 Sols par acre, en contre ie devois Supporter les 6 sols p 100 acres de reconnoissance envers les Seigrs. Prop. come desia Susdit.

"I also had a private and very exact treaty with the Palatines which was projected, examined and agreed upon before and by the Royal Commission, too ample to be inserted here more than in substance, as follows. 1st. My colonists owed me fidelity, obedience and respect, and I owed them protection. 2d. I was to furnish each family for the first year a cow and two swine and some utensils, reimbursement to be made after 3 years. 3d. I was to give to each family 300 acres of land and they were to give me for quit-rent two pence per acre, and I on the other hand was to be responsible for the 6 pence per 100 acres acknowledgment toward the Lords Proprietors as already mentioned above."

planned for at least one generation. How far the system might have been planned to extend cannot be determined. We only know that the landgraveship was hereditary, and, that these estates may have been planned to descend likewise in the same family from father to son. From these considerations, then, it seems to me that this colony was the nearest approach to Locke's ideal ever established in this country—the only one founded on the Grand Model.

In the report to the Georg Ritter Company, also, it is expressly stated that purchasers of land shall have the right to sell their holdings; but under the proprietary government buying and selling of land did not alter the fact that each acre of ground owed its half penny quit-rent to the proprietors, and it is to be supposed that if any one should buy one of these farms owned by a Palatine, he would assume the responisbilities of rent, obedience, and respect to the landgrave. In the end when the scheme failed, we find that Graffenried made over the whole tract to Colonel Pollock and the people lost their holdings; a result which could not have happened had they held of the proprietors as others did, for the system of registration of deeds was very perfect in Carolina at this time, and there could have been no mistake about ownership.

It would be too much to expect Graffenried, a member of one of the few patrician families of Bern, an ex-bailiff of an important city, coming to America as the head of the colonizing project, to show an entirely democratic spirit or to be very favorable to such democracy as he saw in those around him. The disorders attendant upon Cary's and Glover's rivalry; and Cary's refusal to submit to Governor Hyde, were menacing the very existence of the colony, and one might expect a stronger expression of what must have been his sentiments, when, in speaking of the help asked for from Spotswood, he says, "Seeing that these Virginians were not disposed to help us, perhaps themselves having a little of that free and democratic spirit."[18] All the assistance from the proprietors and from the company in Bern on which the continuance of the colony depended, were to come through him, and it is natural that we should find evidences of a paternal government in the little colony at New Bern. Nevertheless, patrician though he was, Graffenried had the welfare of the colony at heart. The letters from the settlers express satisfaction with his administration and he seems to have regarded the title as of value only as it made the Carolinians respect him, and so benefited his colony and company.[19]

It is unfortunate that the colony was broken up so early in its history, before the system of government had had time to become some-

---
[18]French Version.
[19]German Version.

thing more than a mere paper scheme of the proprietors, and before it had time to develop, as it most certainly would have done, into something suited to the needs of the people. It has been seen that the modified system of leetmen actually put into operation was much more workable than the scheme as laid out in the Unalterable Constitutions. When we remember that besides the Palatines who were seeking liberty as well as freedom of conscience, there were some Swiss country people who had belonged to the religious brotherhood where they had a voice in matters that concerned the community, that in Switzerland in general there had always been a tradition of liberty, that in Bern, from whence most of them had come, popular assemblies had been held as late as 1653, and that shortly after this, assemblies were to be tried again (1713) showing that the sentiment was still strong among the common people, [20] it is not surprising to see indications of such an assembly in New Bern, when the town was to be named. [21] On later occasions his people showed a spirit which, while distressing to Graffenried and perhaps of actual harm to themselves, proves very conclusively that where they considered it necessary they showed their independence by leaving Graffenried without permission, and seeking with Brice the protection the Baron appeared unable to afford. Whatever may have been planned, it is reasonably sure that a feudal government would not have endured long with these liberty loving Germans and Swiss. As it is, there appears to have been a paternal government with indications of concerted and independent action of the people.

[20] Cambridge History, vol. VI, page 623 ff.
[21] The sentence, French Version, in which this occasion is mentioned reads as follows:
Il s'agissoit de doner un nom a la ville ce que nous fumes en grande Solemnité, et nous joignimes au nom de Neuws celuy de Berne, ainsi la ville fust baptiseé Neuberne.
Compare with the above the following passages:
. . . et je fis meme une espece d'aillance avec ce Roitelet nomé Taylor et Son Monde, cela ce fist Solennellmt.
. . . Ils commencerent de gouter mes raisons et on tient pour cela une assemblee Solenelle.
Die Indianer nun betrefend, so sind sie nicht zu befӧrchten, so man einen Bund mit Ihnen macht, welches schon Sollenisch.

"It was a question of giving a name to the city, which we did in great solemnity; and we joined to the name of Neuws that of Berne, and so the city was christened Newbern.

" . . . and I even made a sort of alliance with this kinglet named Taylor and his people. This was done solemnly.

" . . . They commenced to appreciate my reasons, and there was held for that purpose a solemn assembly.

"As far as the Indians are concerned, they are not to be feared if one makes a league with them, which we have already solemnly done."

This use of some form of the word meaning solemn in the last three cases, evidently referring to an assembly for free discussion, argues that it is used in the first case with the same connotation, especially since he does not use the word elsewhere in the manuscripts.

CHAPTER X

Hyde Comes to North Carolina in January, 1711—Graffenried Made a Colonel—Hopes to Receive Assistance from the Province—Cary Preparing for Open Rebellion—Condition of the Town—Graffenried Sends a Report to Bern—Appearance of Prosperity Deceptive—Letter by Urmstone Shows the Condition to be as Graffenried Describes—Cary's Attack and Retreat—Peace of Short Duration—The Governor of Virginia Sends Help—Effect of the War on the German Colony—An Exploring Trip—Lawson and Graffenried Captured by the Indians

Taking up the story again from where it was left in Part II, chapter VIII: Hyde entered upon his duties some time in January, 1711,[1] and shortly after sent Graffenried a Colonel's commission along with a summons to attend the assembly. Graffenried could ill afford the time from his own affairs, but hoped the opportunity had now come to obtain the needed assistance for his people. The Governor's will in the matter was good, but the treasury was empty, for Cary still held the funds of the province, and was, moreover, making preparation for active resistance. Graffenried now had to take one side or the other, for the situation was growing more tense, and the question of colonial support for the Palatines had to be brought to an issue and decided as soon as possible. His only hope was in Hyde, for Cary's promises had proved unreliable; and he threw himself into Hyde's cause with all his might, although he and his people would have preferred to stay out of the trouble. In the report[2] to the Georg Ritter Company he says that he and his people took Hyde's part, but in the accounts he says that they remained neutral, because they were intimidated by Cary. Most likely Hyde had their sympathy and half hearted support, but they took no active part in the "war." Some time during the spring the Hyde and Graffenried forces took Cary into custody, but he made his escape.

Meanwhile the colony was prospering, the settlers were contented and there were excellent prospects, for people as far away as Pennsylvania had taken lots.[3] Graffenried had expended 2,228£ in provisions of one sort or another, though not in the amount specified in the contract with the commissioners, regarding cattle for the Palatines. However, the settlers were apparently satisfied and there was

[1]Col. Rec., vol. I, page 751.
[2]German Version, Report.
[3]German Version, Report.

still time to supply them completely. There were two boats [4] belonging to the colony which he and Michel had bought to save transportation charges. Their town had one of the few schoolmasters in the province, for Graffenried had provided for this need before leaving London, and the trades were also well represented. Graffenried took charge of the ordinary religious services, which consisted in reading of prayers in the houses of his colonists, using the Episcopal forms, and vary rarely a sermon was preached to them by the Church of England missionary. During the lull in the Cary troubles, while he was preparing for his next attempt on the government, Graffenried used the occasion of one of his settler's going home to write to his Company a circumstantial account of the situation, and several of his settlers, likewise wrote to their friends or relatives, and from these letters one can gather that the future was full of hope, and they had no doubt of Graffenried's ability to continue to supply them what was needed, or even to take charge of more who might wish to come.

But in spite of the appearance of prosperity, ruin was imminent, though of all the Newbern colony Graffenried alone gives evidence of seeing it. Persons on the outside soon began to notice that something was wrong, for his difficulties were known to Missionary Urmstone who mentions them in his letter to the Secretary of the Society for the Propagation of the Gospel in Foreign Parts. This letter though evidently intended to discredit the Quaker Proprietor, Danson, and exaggerated, at any rate, as to the number of Palatines who had come to the colony, must have had some foundation in fact. The letter was written July 17, 1711, and the following postscript was added, one item of which has been alluded to before.

"P. S. As for the Rebels, I am not much concerned, but 'tis grievous to here the complaints of the poor men & families, who have been so long in arms that they have lost their crops & will want bread, the ravage & plunder of the enemies have committed has ruined others,—another instance of the Quakers Knavery I cannot omit which concerns you to Knowe as having been commissioner for the Palatines. Baron Graffenried with his people must have starved, if not supplied by others here, He had an order from the proprietors, i. e. Danson, for the rest never concern themselves, to receive 1,500£ here for which he was to pay 1,000£ sterling; a great cheat, for £1,000 sterling is worth £3,000 here in our pay. Danson in his Letter to his friends here bragged they should get an Estate by these Foreigners. Cary the late ursurper of this government, & now head of the Rebel was to pay it out of the proprietors dues which he had received he was arrested & made his escape what reason then have they to protect him

[4] French Version.

to prevent others from supplying the Baron in his great distress. Roach & the Quakers reported that the Baron had no credit in England, nor had he any money anywhere. through ill usage in their way hither & since their arrival of 900 palatines there are but 300 nowe alive, & those ready to starve. through the instigation of the English, who live near them the neighboring Indians are very troublesome to them in the beginning of this present Rebellion the Baron with the Swiss & palatines would have joined the Governor but were threatened with fire & sword. the Engld & Indians designed to destroy them & all they had such encouragement do the proprietors give people to come into their colony. I have written a very tart letter to Sir John Colleton a proprietor concerning all matters whether pleased or displeased, it matters not the proprietors promised me all friendship & favor. but as yet never shewed me any & I believe never will."[5]

With Cary and a considerable faction in active opposition to the government, something had to be done immediately in self defense, and a council was held at Colonel Pollock's. This was Cary's chance, if he ever had one, to succeed, and on June 30,[6] while the Governor, Graffenried, and Colonel Pollock were in session, consulting how to meet the emergency, the rebels as they are always called, came up in their brigantine and fired a shot which damaged the roof. The Colonel returned an answer and followed it with another. The ship then withdrew, having suffered an injury to one of her masts, and sent out a landing party, thinking the defenders were but few in number. But when they saw the yellow livery of Graffenried's servant they thought the whole Palatine colony present under arms, and this so alarmed them that they immediately steered back for the ship. The Colonel seized the strategic moment and launched a boat in pursuit. The attacking party boarded their vessel again and tried to escape. But unable to outdistance their pursuers the crew were seized with a panic, ran ashore, and took to the woods. This victory gave Hyde the advantage, for with the brigantine in his power, the Governor was able to make terms; offering a free pardon to all except the ringleaders. Graffenried used this opportunity to have the council recognize Hyde—over a year after his appointment and about seven months after his arrival in the colony.

The peace was of short duration, however. Cary fortified himself on an island; and efforts to dislodge him proving unsuccessful in what may be called the second battle of the war, Graffenried was sent to Virginia for help. After a long and tedious journey, he arrived at

---
[5]Col. Rec., vol. I, page 774.
[6]Col. Rec., vol. I, page 802.

Williamsburg and presented his petition. There was still the difficulty that Hyde lacked the signature of the Governor of South Carolina and Spotswood, therefore, scarcely dared send troops.[7] But finally in his position as Admiral of the Virginia coasts he sent a vessel with marines. He had hoped to send a fleet which was then in Virginia waters on their way home, but the Commander refused to go. The Governor also assembled militia troops on the frontier to be ready if anything serious should happen. On the 28th of July, 1711, he writes that the rebels were so alarmed that they fled at the arrival of the marines and so a third battle never took place.[8] Cary was caught and taken to England for trial, but the matter was dropped and nothing was ever done with him.

This short and bloodless war marks the beginning of the end for Graffenried's colony. Up until April and May of the year 1711, as the letters and the report show, the colony prospered and the people had enough to live on after the coming of Graffenried with the shipload of Swiss in September, 1710. Immediately after the dispersal of the rebels an assembly was held, and Hyde was received as governor. Graffenried was present and hoped to receive help, but failed again. A proposition to borrow from the province on two or three year's time was also refused, for the whole northern province of Carolina was suffering from the confusion, and crops were bad because of neglect. When, finally, Graffenried was permitted to return from the assembly, having accomplished nothing for their relief, he found his people without food, many of them sick, and several of them dead, because of their neglect of his very sensible order to boil all their drinking water. The disease which took so many of them away at this time, from Graffenried's description, seems to have been typhoid fever, and the injunction to use plenty of boiled water was the best remedy that could have been prescribed for them.

In some way or other Graffenried and his colony managed to get along till about the first of September. At that time, since the weather seemed suitable, and the Indians well disposed, he had no great fear of making a fifteen days exploring expedition up the river with Surveyor Lawson. The plan was to see how far the river was navigable, and to find out if a better road to Virginia might not be made on the higher ground and thus save the dangerous voyages by way of the Albemarle Sound, which was very treacherous on account of the numerous shoals and shifting sand bars. They went in a canoe with two negro servants and two friendly Indians, one of whom rode Graffenried's horse along the bank. On the second day from home

---
[7]Col. Rec., vol. I, page 779 ff.
[8]Col. Rec., vol. I, page 783.

the Indian who was riding the horse was halted by one of King Hancock's men, and the whole party taken before that chief. Only a few days before this Graffenried had been very hospitably used, when he had lost his way in the woods, for they kept him over night and even took some cider from a sick woman in order to give to him, and the next day guided him home. He in turn had paid their generosity with presents, not forgetting a little brandy for the invalid, and consequently he hardly expected this treatment. But since he had last seen them, the Indians had begun to plan a revenge for some of their wrongs. Graffenried gives Cary credit for having before this slandered him to them, by making them believe that he, Graffenried, intended to rob them of their lands. Other Carolinians had robbed them in trade and disturbed them in their hunting, and the exploring party, which, at least looked suspicious to them, had the misfortune to come just as the Indians were assembling for the attack.

CHAPTER XI

DOCUMENTS TO PROVE THAT THE INDIANS HAD CAUSE FOR RESENT-
MENT AT THEIR TREATMENT BY THE ENGLISH.

In view of the idea people generally have of the Indians as descending without provocation upon helpless frontier settlements and satisfying an inhuman thirst for blood on innocent victims, it has seemed well to quote a few extracts from Lawson's Journal, Spotswood's letters, the memoirs of Sir William Byrd, and the Colonial Records, to show that the Indians in Carolina had, at least, reason to be alarmed at the encroachments on their territories, and dissatisfied at their treatment by their English neighbors.

"The next day, early, came two Tuskeruru Indians to the other side of the River, but could not get over. They talked much to us, but we understood them not. In the Afternoon, Will (the Indian Guide) came with the Mare and had some discourse with them; they told him the English, to whom he was going, were very wicked People; and, That they threatened the Indians for hunting near their Plantations." [1]

"Thus you have an account of the Latitude, Soil, and Advantages of Cape Fear, or Clarendon-River, which was settled in the Year 1661, or thereabouts; and had it not been for the irregular Practices of some of that Colony against the Indians, by sending away [2] some of their Children, (as I have been told) under Pretence of instructing 'em in Learning and the Principles of the Christian Religion; which so disgusted the Indians that tho' they had then no Guns, yet they never gave over, till they rid themselves of the English by their Bows and Arrows; with which they did not only take off themselves, but also their Stocks of Cattle. And this was so much the more ruinous to them, in that they could have no Assistance from South Carolina which was not then planted; and the other Plantations were but in their Infancy. Were it not for such ill Practices, I say, it might, in all Probability have been, at this day, the best Settlement in their Lordships great Province of Carolina." [3]

The next is an extract of a letter from Governor Spotswood to the Lords Commissioners for Trade and Plantations, April 5, 1717.

"The Inhabitants of our frontiers are composed generally of such as have been transported hither as Servants, and being out of their time, and settle themselves where Land is to be taken up and that

---
[1]Lawson's Journal, page 58.
[2]He means selling them into slavery.
[3]Lawson's Journal, page 73.

will produce the necessarys of Life with little Labor. It is pretty well known what Morals such people bring with them hither, which are not like to be mended by their Scituation, remote from all places of worship; they are so little concerned about Religion, that the Children of many of the Inhabitants of those frontier Settlements are 20, and some 30 years of age before they are baptized, and some not at all.

"Those who are nearest Neighbors to the Indians, by whose principles and practices they are not like to be most improved; but this is not all, for these people, knowing the Indians to be lovers of strong liquors, make no scruple of first making them drunk and then cheating them of their skins, and even of beating them in the bargain; on the other hand, the Indians, being unacquainted with the methods of obtaining reparation by law, frequently revenge themselves by the murder of the persons who thus treated them, or, (according to their notions of Satisfaction) of the next Englishmen they could most easily cutt off. And it is a very generall observation, both here and the neighboring Provinces, that no murders or hostility have ever been committed by the Indians unless where the English have given the first provocation." [4]

Colonel Byrd has this to say with reference to the troubles under consideration: "There are generally some Carolina Traders that constantly live among the Catawbas and Pretend to Exercise a dictatorial Authority among them. These petty Rulers don't only teach the honester Savages all sorts of Debauchery, but are unfair in their dealings, and use them with all kinds of Oppression. Nor has their Behavior been at all better to the rest of the Indian Nations, among whom they reside, by abusing their Women and Evil-Entreating their Men; and, by the way, this was the true Reason of the fatal war which the Nations roundabout made upon Carolina in the year 1713. [5]

"Then it was that the Neighboring Indians grown weary of the Tyranny and Injustice with which they had been abused for many Years, resolved to endure their bondage no longer, but enter'd into General Confederacy against their Oppressors of Carolina.

"The Indians open'd the War by knocking most of those little Tyrants on the Head that dwelt amongst them under pretence of regulating their Commerce, and from thence Carry'd their Resentment so far as to endanger both North and South Carolina." [6]

An actual instance of oppression had occurred a few years before. In 1707 the Maherine Indians had been assigned lands for their use

---
[4] Spotswood, vol. II, page 227.
[5] The time of their final defeat. Their massacres were made in the fall of 1711 and the summer of 1712.
[6] Byrd, page 239.

by the government of Virginia; and since they were living in peace
with the English in both Virginia and Carolina, no complaints of
depredations were ever made against them. Their lands, however,
were the subject of dispute between the two provinces, and as the
line had not been run yet the quarrel could not be settled. Thomas
Pollock wanted these lands for his own use and attempted to drive
the Indians off with armed force. He captured 36 of them, kept
them for two days in a fort, without water, in the meantime he broke
down their cabins and threatened to destroy their corn crop if they
did not move off the reservation. As the Indians could have had
no very clear notion of the dispute between Carolina and Virginia,
and had been promised the peaceful possession of their land by the
Virginia government, this encroachment by Pollock must have shaken
their faith in the honesty of the white men. Even if the lands lay
in territory south of 36° 30' (a matter which was not settled till years
after) [7] it was unjust and impolitic to make them suffer for the mistake
of the Virginia government. The Virginians naturally expected the
Indians to call on other Indians to help them retaliate. In 1710
complaints were sent by the assembly of North Carolina to Virginia
that these Maherines were committing depredations. [8] Spotswood did
nothing about it and expressed no sympathy because, he says, the
whites had been the aggressors. [9]

---

[7] Byrd, page 3. The line was run in 1728.
[8] Col. Rec., vol. I, page 754.
[9] Col. Rec., vol. I, page 667 ff.

CHAPTER XII

GRAFFENRIED A PRISONER—LAWSON KILLED—GRAFFENRIED KEPT A PRISONER—THE INDIANS PLAN TO MASSACRE ENGLISH AND GERMANS—DISCUSSION OF THE CAUSE OF THE MASSACRE—THE BLAME LAID ON THE LATE REBELS—DOCUMENTS PROVING THAT OTHERS BESIDES GRAFFENRIED BELIEVED THEM GUILTY—GRAFFENRIED'S TRUCE—ATTACK BY THE ENGLISH AND PALATINES—GRAFFENRIED AGREES TO A RANSOM AND IS ALLOWED TO GO HOME—SPOTSWOOD APPROVES OF THE TRUCE—ENGLISH AND PALATINES DISAPPROVE AND PLOT AGAINST HIS LIFE

Had Graffenried been alone it would have been better for him on this exploring expedition, for the Indians knew he had never done them any harm, but they disliked Lawson because of his having cheated them.[1] At first the Indians were disposed to let both of them go when they found who they were. But at a second examination, Lawson could not refrain from quarreling with one of his captors, and this destroyed all possibility of a release. The Indians in anger prepared to execute both men. Bound hand and foot, the victims sat on the ground and watched the preparations, not the least frightful of which was the great heap of burning wood. Graffenried, however, managed to speak to one of the Indians who understood a little English, explained his innocence and also threatened them with the Queen's displeasure and the vengeance she would take if they harmed him, but his arguments did not seem to have much effect at first; so in expectation of immediate torture and death he fortified himself and his negro slave with prayer and exhortation and found peace of mind in these exercises. About three or four o'clock in the morning he was unbound and led away, as he supposed, to his death, but the Indian signified to him that his life was to be spared and only Lawson would have to die, and so it proved. Just what the manner of his death was Graffenried never learned, for the Indians steadfastly refused to divulge it; but he had heard them threaten to cut Lawson's throat with a razor.[2] Yet while Graffenried's life was spared, they

---
[1] Byrd, page 228.
"It was on that Provocation they resented their wrongs a little too severely upon Mr. Lawson, who under Colour of being Surveyor gen'l had encroached too much upon their territories at which they were so much enraged that they waylaid him and cut his throat from ear to ear, but at the same time released the Baron de Graffenried, whom they had seized for Company, because it appeared plainly he had done them no wrong."
[2] Col. Rec., vol. I, page 836.
From a letter of Christopher Gale, November 3, 1711:
"But the fate of Mr. Lawson (if our Indian information be true) was much more tragical, for we are informed that they stuck him full of fine small splinters of torch wood like hog's bristles and so set them gradually afire."
The following from Lawson's Journal (197) in this connection has a grewsome interest:
"Their cruelty to their Prisoners of War is what they are seemingly guilty of an error in, (I mean as to a natural Failing) because they strive to invent the most Inhumane Butcheries for them that

did not let him go home immediately, but kept him a prisoner for six weeks.

During this time the indirect consequences of the civil difficulties were felt by the Colony. The violence of the feeling in the later Cary disturbances make it manifestly impossible for the partisans of either side to be fair to the others, and unfortunately, since the record of the quarrel was written by strong partisans of Hyde, statements must be accepted with caution. Graffenried [3] occasionally, and Spotswood [4] repeatedly, state that Cary and the other opponents of Hyde tried to bring down the Indians to aid them in their resistance. Such a crime is hard to believe, and Weeks [5] does not credit these statements, because the district of Bath, which was friendly to Cary, suffered as severely as New Bern, which favored Hyde. Nevertheless, the Indians somehow had gotten the notion that Hyde was their enemy, and it does not seem unlikely that Cary and others might have gone among them to enlist help. For on July 28, 1711, Governor Spotswood writes:

"There are several affidavits sent me to prove that one Porter who is one of Cary's pretended Council was with the Tuscaruro Indians promising great Rewards to incite them to cut off all the Inhabitants of that part of Carolina that adhered to Mr. Hyde. The Indians own that the proposal was accepted by their young men, but that their old men (who bare great Sway in all their Councils) being by their own nature Suspitious of some trick or else directed by Superior providence, refused to be concerned in that barbarous design." [6] Such positive statements and the fact that Graffenried's death was determined when the Indians supposed him to be Governor Hyde, and that they let him go when they found who he really was, help to confirm the report. [7] Moreover, the crime, though great, of using the savages as allies was duplicated by the English Government as late as during the Revolution and the War of 1812, so that the mere repulsiveness of the thought does not disprove the fact.

Although at the time of the Cary troubles, the Indians did not make any moves against the white settlers, such invitations, if one may trust reports like the above, certainly showed them the colony's

---

the Devils themselves could invent, or hammer out of Hell; they exteeming Death no Punishment, but rather an Advantage to him, that is exported out of this into another World. Therefore they inflict on them Torments in which they prolong Life in that miserable state as long as they can, and never miss skulping of them, as they call it which is, to cut off the Skin from the Temples, and taking the whole Head of Hair along with it, as it were a Night-cap, Sometimes they take the Top of the Skull along with it; all which they preserve; and carefully keep by them, for a Trophy of their Conquest over their Enemies. Others keep their Enemies Teeth, which are taken in War, whilst others split the Pitch pine into Splinters and stick them into the Prisoner's Body yet alive. Thus they light them, which burn like so many torches; and in this Manner they make him dance around a great Fire, every one buffeting and deriding him till he expires, when every one strives to get a Bone or some Relick of this unfortunate Captive."
[3] German Version.
[4] Col. Rec., vol. I, page 776. Spotswood, pp. 84, 94, 108.
[5] Johns Hopkins Studies, vol. X, page 300 ff.
[6] Col. Rec., page 797; see also page 802 for statement by Hyde.
[7] German Version.

weakness. And it is but natural that they determined to profit by
it. Notwithstanding their personal friendship for Graffenried, they
were still savages and acted the part by massacring all the whites
in the Bath County they could reach, whether Swiss, Palatines or
English.

Spotswood thus describes one of these massacres: "On the 22nd of
the last month some towns of the Tuscaruro Indians and other Nations
bordering on Carolina, made an incursion upon the head of the Neuse
and Pamlico Rivers, in that province, without any previous declaration of War or show of discontent, and having divided themselves
into partys at Sun rise (which was the Signal for their bloody design)
began a barbarous Massacre on the Inhabitants of the Frontier plantations, killing without distinction of age or Sex, 60 English and upwards
of that number of Swiss and Palatines, besides a great many left
dangerously wounded. The Baron de Graffenried, Chief of the Swiss
and Palatines' Settlement there, is also fallen into their hands and
carryed away Prisoner. Since which they have continued their Ravages in burning those plantations and others deserted by the Inhabitants for fear of the like Crueltys. The Governor, Mr. Hyde, has
raised what men he can to oppose the further Invasion of the
heathen and protect the rest of the Country, but that Spirit of disobedience to which they have long been accustomed, still prevails
so much that he can hardly persuade them to unite for their common
Safety. I will not affirm that the Invitation given those Savages
some time ago by Collo. Cary and his party to cutt off their fellow
Subjects has been the only occasion of this Tragedy, tho' that heavy
charge is proved by divers Testimonys and firmly believed in Carolina.
Yet it appears very reasonable to believe that they have been greatly
encouraged in this attempt by the unnatural Divisions and Animosi-
ties among the Inhabitants, and I very much fear their mutinous
and Cowardly behavior in some late Shirmishes will Embolden the
Indians to continue their Insolences."

The plan of this massacre was perfected while Graffenried was
still a prisoner among the Indians. He knew of their design and
was in anxiety for his people, of course, but although the red men
promised that they would spare such of the Palatines as were in the
city, he was not much comforted, for he had no way of warning his
people to retire from their farms to the village. In a few days the
warriors with the prisoners and the booty returned. Among these
prisoners was a Palatine boy, and from him he learned that many
of the Palatines as well as English had been slaughtered.

Graffenried now saw no hopes of getting back home except by
making a treaty of neutrality between himself and the Indians. By

this he was to give a ransom for his own life and help neither the English nor the Indians during the war, and in return all his colonists' houses marked with a big N were to be safe from harm.

Another important clause provided that the Indians should be allowed to buy goods at reasonable rates. The colonists had not gone into the Indian trade as yet, but by the report, memorial and letters [8] we learn they were intending to do so, and in April had sent in orders for goods, knives, brass rings, and pipes, but had not yet had time to get them back, when Urmstone writes July 17 that the Indians incited by jealous traders, had been annoying the colony. [9] One cannot suppose the Germans, knowing that the Indians were unfriendly, would go among them later if their goods should have come. Graffenried himself seems to have felt that all was not well when Lawson persuaded him to go up the river to explore; and so the clause can scarcely be directed against him or his colony, but rather shows that there was dissatisfaction with the professional traders and their extortions, against which the Indians intended to secure themselves beforehand by a treaty, in case they and the Germans should have dealings together.

After Graffenried had been some time among them Spotswood wrote a letter ordering the Indians to release their prisoner, with no better result than to anger them the more. Spotswood had gone to a village called Notaway, and Graffenried meanwhile was taken to a village called Tasqui which lay in the direction of Notaway; but he was disappointed in his hopes of meeting the Governor, and soon after was taken to Catechna for security, because the Indians were afraid of losing the ransom. While he was here, the English and Palatines made an attack which angered the Indians very much in view of Graffenried's treaty, though, of course, his people knew nothing of such an agreement as yet. The attack, furthermore, hampered Graffenried's negotiations for liberty, and it was with difficulty that he deceived the Indians into believing that his people had not been among the assailants. This attack also alarmed the Indians to such an extent that they moved their wives, children and old men to their fortified stronghold near Catechna, and the Carolinians, unable to capture the position, were forced to retreat with some loss in killed and captured. When they had gone the Indians returned to Catechna and Graffenried was set at liberty under promise of sending back the ransom. After two days hard traveling and sleeping at night on the ground, in constant danger of wild beasts and hostile Indians, he reached home about October 30.

---
[8] German Version.
[9] See page 81.

Graffenried expected, as far as possible, to keep the truce he had made, and greatly angered [10] some of the English and Palatines when he refused to allow them to kill the Indian who came for the ransom. But he also delayed giving the ransom in hopes of inducing the Indians to free the other prisoners whom they still held. He also gave much valuable information concerning the situation to the English. It was on this account, he says, that a man Brice, who had estranged many of his people including a Palatine blacksmith, prepared 20 or 23 articles against him, tried to arrest him, and threatened to have him hanged.

---

[10] Spotswood, vol. I, page 142. (Extract of a letter) February 8, 1711:
"The Baron de Graffenried being obliged, while he was prisoner among the Indians, to conclude a neutrality for himself and his Palatines lives as yet undisturbed by the Heathen, *but is sufficiently persecuted by the people of Carolina for not breaking with the Indians, tho' they will afford him neither provisions of War or victuals nor Assistance from them.* He has always declared his readiness to enter into a war as soon as he should be assisted to prosecute it, but it would be madness in him to expose his handful of people to the fury of the Indians, without some better assurance of help than the present confusions in that province gives him reason to hope for, and the Indians would soon Either Entirely destroy that settlement or starve them out of the place by killing their stocks and hindering them from planting corn. In the meantime the people of Carolina receive very great advantage by this Neutrality, for by that means the Baron has an opportunity of discovering and communicating to them all the designs of the Indians, tho' he runs the Risque of paying dear for it if they ever come to know it. This makes him so apprehensive of his danger from them, and so diffident of help or even justice from the Government under which he is, that he has made some efforts to remove with the Palatines to this Colony upon some of her Majesty's Lands; and since such a number of people as he may bring with him, with what he proposes to invite over from Swisserland and Germany, will be of great advantage to this Country and prove a strong Barier against the incursions of the Indians if they were properly disposed above our inhabitants. I pray your Lord'ps' directions what encouragement ought to be given to this design." . . .
(Italics are mine. V. H. T.)

CHAPTER XIII

DISCOVERY OF THE PLOT—MEASURES TAKEN FOR THE DEFENSE OF THE TOWN—GRAFFENRIED BEGINS TO MAKE PLANS TO GO TO VIRGINIA—A LETTER OF SPOTSWOOD SHOWING THE CONDITION OF THE COLONISTS—BRICE'S THOUGHTLESS ATTACK PRECIPITATES WAR—GRAFFENRIED'S PART IN THE WAR—BARNWELL'S BREACH OF FAITH—INDIANS PREPARE FOR A NEW MASSACRE—GRAFFENRIED'S CONDITION—VISIT TO GOVERNOR HYDE—LOSS OF A BOATLOAD OF PROVISIONS—GRAFFENRIED GOES TO VIRGINIA TO PLAN FOR A NEW SETTLEMENT

Brice and his friends had plotted well, but their cause was destined to ruin by a trivial incident. While the plot was being made, a little Palatine boy was in the room, unnoticed by the conspirators. He knew something was wrong and told his mother. She, being friendly to the Baron, got word to him; and when Brice and his friends came to get him they found themselves in a trap. But because of lack of direct evidence against them, Graffenried had to let them go. At a meeting of the assembly Graffenried justified himself in an impassioned speech, answering the series of complaints which had been made against him, but could get no satisfactory decision. The truce with the Indians was acceptable to no one, because the people, Germans and English, were angered against the Indians and anxious for a revenge. It appears that Graffenried would have had the truce include the whole province, but no one would hear to such a proposition in their eagerness for retaliation. The situation among the Palatines, too, was far from favorable, for after the first massacre Brice had drawn off with him a large number of the settlers; and this not only left the outlying homes of the disaffected ones unprotected, but also materially reduced the defending force of the town. With the situation as it was on his return, Graffenried was too prudent to trust to the truce, and immediately began to fortify his town and to collect supplies and munitions of war.

In the meantime although no large marauding parties took the warpath, many smaller bands of Indians harassed the outlying districts, and kept the colonists in suspense for fear of an extensive and concerted attack. Just at this unfortunate moment the new disturbing element again asserted itself. Brice and his followers began a campaign, with most of the able-bodied men in the Palatine settlement in their following. The exact time of this unofficial expedition is uncertain, but it was probably just before the general attack in

January. Their most atrocious act of violence was the roasting alive of an innocent Indian chief, which, while not particularly barbaric compared with the Indian massacres of the autumn before, was sufficient to arouse the savage wrath. Moreover, the campaign had other and more far-reaching effects. The Indians, not only attacked and destroyed more outlying homes, but chiefly they lost confidence in Graffenried, who previously had been the one man who could act as a mediator between them and the whites.

But Graffenried was in sore straits in other ways. Added to the danger of sure attack and possible siege was the danger of starvation, for the stores were running short. One alternative was thought of only to be abandoned—it was to send away all the families whose men had followed Brice; but they begged so hard to be allowed to remain, promising valiant aid in case of need, that Graffenried was touched and acquiesced. But neither courage nor the promise of courage availed to create foodstuffs, and starvation became imminent. Possibilities of making a new settlement in Virginia were discussed, but all such plans were for the time being abandoned for they still hoped to save the settlement at New Bern. With insufficient food supplies and ammunition for an extended campaign, without forts or stockades of sufficient strength to resist attack, the province awaited war with a cunning, cruel, and savage people. It was an awful time. The situation is nowhere better described than in the following extract of a letter written by Spotswood on December 28, 1711: "The shortness of their crops, occasioned by their Civil Dissensions last Summer and an unusual Drowth that succeeded, together with the Ravages made by the Indians among their Corn and Stocks, gives a dreadful prospect of a Famine, Insomuch that the Baron de Graffenried writes he shall be constrained to abandon the Swiss and Palatines' Settlement, without speedy Succours, the people being already in such despair that they have burnt their own houses rather than be obliged to stay in a place exposed to so many hardships."

The Indians, on the other hand, were well equipped, and in addition, capable of mustering large numbers almost at their very doors. And here was Brice with a small force of English and Palatines declaring war before any preparation could be made, and thereby destroying the only thing, slight as it was, which stood between the province and the Indians—Graffenried's truce. With the truce broken thus, Graffenried realized that the only safety lay in prosecuting the war as vigorously as possible; and when 50 white men and 800 tributary Indians under Colonel Barnwell came from South Carolina, he sent 50 Palatines under Michel to assist in the attack of the Indian fort. These hostilities took place in January, 1712. In the first battle the

Indians had the advantage, and then Graffenried suggested that two small cannon belonging to the province be used. These he had slung on poles and transported to the place of battle. Two shots from them were sufficient to frighten the Indians into submission, and a truce was arranged, leading to a release of the captives which the Indians still held. Thus ended the first hostilities.

The end of the Indian troubles, however, brought the Germans little relief, and at this time Graffenried exercised one of the rights of a lord over his leetmen, in permitting such of his settlers as wished to work for the English planters, to leave their own colony for two years, during which time they should be free from their quit-rents.

Concerning Graffenried's part in this war there seems to be some difference of opinion, for Spotswood's letter previously quoted contradicts Graffenried's statement. But this is probably due to the fact that the former's letter was written before he received information concerning the battle in which the Indians were defeated through the use of the cannon which Graffenried had sent to be of assistance to the attacking party. But he was acquainted with the Baron's attitude towards the Indians and knew about his treaty with them. He knew, probably, of the unpopularity of Graffenried's truce and from such indications concluded that he was not taking part in the efforts to subdue the savages.

But the close of hostilities did not bring security. The Indians were far from subdued, even after this battle, for a piece of barbarous injustice practiced on them by Barnwell enraged them more than ever. His men were not paid the salary due them and to reimburse themselves they treacherously took a great many of the Core Indians prisoner to sell for slaves, and people with reason began to fear another outbreak.

Renewal of the war was not, however, the greatest danger to the New Bern adventurers, for not long after the treaty of peace was made, Graffenried's provisions, except one measure of wheat, were consumed, and the ammunition, too, was low, for it had now been twenty-two weeks since his return from captivity, and during this time he had been compelled to support his little garrison with what he had been able to store up during the summer preceding. Graffenried decided to appeal once again to the Province, hoping in such straits to obtain aid. To this end he undertook what proved to be a perilous journey, but only to be disappointed. For the Governor could do but little for him; he did, however, supply him with a boatload of provisions, which never reached his poor settlers, for at the mouth of the Neuse River the crew carelessly let fire get among some tobacco leaves and it spread to a cask of gunpowder. The men escaped, but the boat was lost; and with it went the last hope of relief for New Bern.

During this time Graffenried was detained at Hyde's for six weeks by governmental affairs. The principal business was how to meet and ward off the threatened attacks of the Indians. Graffenried advised that the exportation of provisions be forbidden, and that new help be secured from Virginia and South Carolina. Governor Spotswood in a letter of July 26, writes as follows: "I thereupon made extraordinary efforts to assist them with 200 white men and Indians as your Lordship will observe in the Journal of the Council the 24th, of April last and accordingly directed the Rendevouze of those forces on the 10th of May." This in answer to the petition of the assembly would fix the date of the Parliament some time before April 24, probably in March. The session lasted six weeks, before the end of which, Graffenried learned of the ill fate of his boat, and his next efforts were to secure other provisions, which he sent in a larger boat, in order that as many of his settlers as wished to, might come to him in Virginia or Maryland where he now intended to resettle. It appears that he went directly from Governor Hyde's to the Governor of Virginia after transacting this business, and petitioned for the help above mentioned, and then explored along the Potomac for a suitable location, and also attempted to find the silver mines which he had heard so much about. The results of this trip, however, could not have been very encouraging if we are to judge from contemporary comment. In a letter of Governor Spotswood written May 8, 1712, occurs this passage, "According to what I had the hon'r to write to Your Lord'ps in my last, the Baron de Graffenried is come hither with a design to settle himself and sev'll Swiss familys in the fforks of Potomack but when he expected to have held his Land there of her Majesty, he now finds Claims made to it both by the Proprietors of Maryland and the Northern Neck," (i. e. Culpepper) . . . As a result he had to choose a place more on the frontier than he hoped, and again as though fated, the Palatines were to become a forepost against the Indians.

CHAPTER XIV

THE NEW LOCATION—PROSPECTING FOR SILVER—GOVERNOR SPOTSWOOD'S LETTER DESCRIBING THE SAME EVENT—GRAFFENRIED RETURNS TO CAROLINA—GOVERNOR HYDE'S DEATH—GRAFFENRIED DISAPPOINTED IN MICHEL, MAKES ONE LAST EFFORT—GRAFFENRIED IN VIRGINIA—MOORE DEFEATS THE INDIANS, MARCH 20, 1713

The places chosen for the new start were just below the falls of the Potomac about where Washington now stands and at an island which he calls Canavest, further up the river. Graffenried went as far as the Shenandoah River, which he writes Senantona, but seems to have preferred the location nearer the English settlements, which he describes as a most charming location at the head of navigation for large vessels. The Governor gave him the necessary patents, and several gentlemen from Pennsylvania came to confer with him about mines. The soil and situation pleased him, but the best search he could give showed no signs of silver (and never has since, though a tradition to the effect that silver exists somewhere in the mountains thereabouts causes a few people to search for it even to this day). The men from Pennsylvania returned to their homes very badly satisfied, while he himself was convinced that Michel's story was a fabrication. As for Michel, he failed to appear, although Graffenried waited long and did not return to the Governor until long after his partner was due. From him he learned that the Captain whom he had sent to convoy the brigantine had waited six days, and then nothing appearing, the mate had gone out in the yawl and found the boat stuck fast, and the people gone. The Governor was naturally very much disgusted with such treatment, and at first was inclined to blame Graffenried as well as Michel, since the latter was supposed to be acting under orders. Learning, however, that Michel had been duping them both, his resentment toward Graffenried changed to pity for the chief sufferer.

A letter written by Spotswood July 26, 1712, reports Graffenried's trip up the Potomac as follows, and is self-explanatory of the Governor's attitude. "At present I cannot think of anything of greater concernment to this Country, as well as the particular Service of her Majesty, than what I hinted to Your Lord'ps in my letter of the 15th of May, for encouraging the discovery of Silver mines. I have, since the return of the Baron de Graffenried from Potomac, discoursed him concerning the probability of Mines in these parts, he says, tho' he has no doubts of finding such from the accounts he received from one Mr. Mitchell, a Swiss Gentleman who went on the like discovery some years ago, Yet he finds himself much discouraged from prosecuting his first intentions, not only because of the uncertainty of the property of the soil, whether belonging to the Queen or the proprietors, but the share which the Crown may claim in those Mines is also uncertain, and after all his trouble in the discovery he may chance to have his labour for his pains. Whereas he would gladly employ his utmost diligence in making such discoveries if it were once declared what share her Majesty would expect out of the produce of the Mines, or if her Majesty would be pleased to take the Mines into her hands, promising him the superintending of the works with a hansdome Sallary, he says it is a matter not new to him, there having been Mines of the like nature found on his father's lands in Switzerland, which were at first wrought for the benefit of the State, but turning to small account were afterward Yielded to the proprietors of the soil upon paying a share out of the produce thereof; that he has some relatives now concerned therein, and by their interest can procure skilful workmen out of Germany for carrying on the works. I shall submit to your Lor'ps better judgment, which of the alternatives proposed by the Baron will be best for her Majesty's service, and shall hope for a speedy signification of her Majesty's pleasure thereon for promoting a design which I can but believe will turn out to the advantage of her Majesty and the improvement of this Colony. The Baron has not been so far up the Potomac as to discover the head Springs of that River nor to make a true draught of their Course, so that I can't now send Your Lor'ps the Mapps I promised in my last, nor forme a Judgment of the pretentions of the sev'll proprietors."[1]

Whatever lingering hopes, as indicated by this letter, Graffenried may have had in his ability to find and develop deposits of silver ore and to found a new colony in Virginia or Maryland were dissipated by the failure of the Palatines and Swiss to come to him in Virginia. Seeing there was no hope of making a new start in a more favorable location, Graffenried went back to North Carolina and stayed some time with Governor Hyde. While there they all fell sick and on September 9 the Governor died. Graffenried stayed on two weeks longer and then returned to Newbern. Again the governorship was offered him, but he had to refuse on account of his precarious financial condition. The man sent to fix the brigantine found it too much damaged to repair, and Graffenried was allowed nothing for either of his two boats, although he considered them destroyed in the service of the province. Attempts to get satisfaction from Michel brought

[1]Spotswood, vol. I, page 168.

nothing better than proposals to settle in Mexico or along the Mississippi River, and Graffenried was persuaded that his only hope would be to take his two slaves and settle at Canavest and gradually draw a few people about him. This would be difficult because his creditors, including Pollock, were suspicious. In fact, when his two slaves, who liked him for a master, tried to cross the river to him, they were caught and held for their master's debts. In this condition, heavily in debt, almost penniless, his pet scheme demolished, his partner faithless, he retired to Virginia, September 20, 1712, where he stayed until spring among his friends, trying all the time to get help. His friends, however, could only advise him to go back to England or Bern, as it would not be safe for him to try to stay in Virginia, nor to go among the Indians, for the traders would be sure to find him out and tell his creditors. This truly disheartening situation was cheered a little perhaps by the news that on March 20, 1713, Colonel Moore administered a crushing defeat to the Tuscarora Indians with the very troops Graffenried had helped to secure.

CHAPTER XV

The Journey Home—Graffenried Meets his Miners in London—Arranges for Their Passage to America—His Own Affairs Do Not Keep Him Long in England—Discussion of the Language of His Manuscripts—Efforts to Relieve His Colony—Life as a Swiss Official—Death

Having exhausted all his resources in America, Graffenried had only two alternatives—to let the law take its course, or else to try to get assistance from abroad. He chose the latter, and on Easter day of 1713 Graffenried started for New York, traveling on horseback. After a short stay there, he left for England, landing at Bristol after a six weeks voyage. In London he met Mr. Eden, whom the proprietors were sending out to take Hyde's place. He also met Albrecht with twelve miners and their families, 40 persons altogether. These were the men whom he and Michel had originally engaged to come to America when sent for. They had, however, become tired of waiting and now were preparing to come anyway. When Graffenried found them they were in hard straits, and looked to him for the assistance he had contracted with them to furnish, entirely overlooking the fact that he had told them to stay in Germany until they should be summoned. His only suggestion, so far, of removal to America had been that in case the miners so desired, the master and one or two men might come to America to inspect the ground; but this was, clearly, no invitation or order to begin the trip. The situation was further complicated by Graffenried's financial embarrassment, for his own resources were slender, as we have seen, and he had still to live during the time that his business kept him in London, and moreover, he had to retain enough to pay his passage home. He did not desert his miners, however, but going from one acquaintance to another, he got work for a part of them on a dike which was being repaired, and secured other employment to support them through the winter. Meantime he wrote to Virginia and arranged with Governor Spotswood for their reception there. Furthermore, he persuaded them to put their money into a common fund and persuaded two merchants to forward their passage money, and about New Year's day they started, and landed in Virginia April 28, 1714, where they were first settled as rangers and later put to work in working Spotswood's iron mines.[1]

[1] Part I, chapter III.

Meanwhile Graffenried had not delayed long in England, but had traveled incognito to his home. A lack of passports was a serious hindrance to him, but finally on St. Martin's day, 1713, he reached Bern. The three accounts vary. Professor Goebel's two versions very distinctly make his return home St. Martin's day, 1714, while the one printed in the Colonial Records of North Carolina makes it a year earlier, 1713. This, however, is but one of several items which indicate that at the time Graffenried wrote his accounts the story was becoming a little confused in some of its details—a not uncommon occurrence with any one who tries to tell of events in his life a few years after they took place. His language in speaking of his stay in London is entirely misleading, as is shown by a quotation from Professor Goebel's French version, which probably was written last: "A Londre je fis Sejour de quelques Semaines (months in the Colonial Records and the German version) esperant de pouvoir presenter ma Supplication a la Reine Anne par le Duc de Beaufort, mon Patron, qui estoit le premier Lord Prop; de Caroline et Palatin de la Province, mais peu de tems avant qu'il voulust presenter ma supplication il est mort Subitement encore un coup de mon infortune bientost apres la Reine mourust elle meme, il ne faloit que cela pour m'oster tout esperance d'aucun retour. La dessus il y eust tant d'alterations a la Cour d'Angleterre que ie ne pouvois esperer aucune faveur de longtems en cette nouvelle Cour, quand meme on pouvoit conjecture qu'avec le tems ce nouveau Roy come Allemande de Nation seroit enclin pour ma Colonie allemande." [2] This certainly reads as though Graffenried were in London at the time of the death of these two personages and the accession of George I. So long a stay after his recent disasters in America leaving him almost penniless seems improbable, at least. Other sources, then, will have to be called upon to settle the matter. In the Neujahrsblatt there is a passage taken from Anton von Graffenried's Diary which says, "Den 2. December 1713 ist der alt Landvogt von Ifferten aus America durch Engelland und Frankreich wieder allhier angelangt und hat mich erst den 10. Dezember salutirt." [3] In addition to this evidence we know that Pollock received a letter from him written from Bern on April 30, 1714.

---

[2] "In London I made a sojourn of several weeks (months in the Colonial Records and the German version), hoping to be able to present my petition to Queen Anne by the Duke of Beaufort, my patron, who is the first Lord Proprietor of Carolina and Palatine of the Province. But a little while before he intended to present my petition he suddenly died. One more stroke of my misfortune: the Queen herself died soon after, and it needed only that to remove from me all hope of my return. Thereupon there were so many alterations at the English Court that I could not hope for any favor for a long time at this new court, even though one might conjecture that in time this new king, as a German, would be inclined toward my German colony."

[3] "On the 2d of December, 1913, the old bailiff of Iverton arrived here by way of England and France, but did not greet me until the 10th of December."

These two evidences taken with his own statements in the three versions prove that he made only a comparatively short stay in England, for he left Virginia at Easter-time, or April 16, 1713, and went to New York, where he stayed for about two weeks. His voyage across the Atlantic occupied six weeks, and we are told that he rested awhile at Bristol before proceeding on horseback to London. He accounts, thus, with fair accuracy for eight weeks, but this allows no time for his sojourns in New York and Bristol nor for his journeys from Virginia to New York and from Bristol to London. But even eight weeks would place his arrival in the middle of June. His actual time of arrival, however, was much later than this owing to the stops and other delays, and can be roughly estimated by the remark when he met the newly appointed Governor Eden, that had he (Graffenried) come a month earlier, the position had fallen to him. Now since Eden was not appointed until August 13, 1713, Graffenried must have come later, perhaps about a month, somewhere near September 13. [4]

His journey to Bern was also rather long, for he was beaten about by storms for three weeks in his passage across the channel; and then there was the remainder of the way to be covered by coach. Despite some further delays for passports and in finding his people when he reached Switzerland, he, nevertheless, finally reached his family St. Martin's day, November 11, 1713. This would leave him only a small part of August, if any, all of September and perhaps a part of October in England.

The most puzzling thing, however, is that any one reading any of the three versions would suppose that Graffenried had been present at the time of the deaths of the Duke of Beaufort and of Queen Anne, and the Accession of George I, and had stayed after that until he was sure nothing would be done for his colony. But since Beaufort [5] died July 25, 1714; and Queen Anne [6] August 1, 1714, and he had reached Bern in November of the year before, this is impossible, unless he made a second voyage to England, which is nowhere mentioned directly, and alluded to, if at all, in such vague terms that no one would suspect it on reading the accounts.

But his efforts for his colony did not stop even after he reached home. Yet the final chapter is brief. Too poor to sue his company for their breach of contract, he next tried to have a commission appointed to investigate and hear his proposition, but this was refused. His efforts to interest others failed, and at last,to his own regret, he had to abandon his colony.

[4] Col. Rec., vol II, page 58.
[5] McCrady, page 526.
[6] McCrady, page 527.

The story of the rest of his life is soon told. He was dependent upon his father for a support which was not cheerfully granted. And the following letter gives as much light on the father's character as on Christoph's.

"Ayez, Monsieur, la bonté de mettre en oublis le passé, et m'estant corrigé de depuis, ayez meilleure opinion de moy pour le present et advenir; Pourtant quoyque Je vous aye chagriné par mon evasion et mes debts, cependant j'ay deservis mon Balliage avec honneur au contentment du Souverain et des Ressortissants, et n'ay rien comis d'atroce qui vous aye fait deshonneur, ny ay-je jamais, que je sache, manqué anvers Vous de Respect ny de Soumission, pardonnez moy dont le passé et ne retouchez pas toujours cette corde facheuse, mais ayez moy, Monsieur et tres honorable Pere, en recommandation puisque je feray touts mes efforts pour vous contenter et vous montrer que je suis avec toutte l'obeissance Respect et Soumission *L'Enfant perdu retrouvé*, et amandez, regardez moy donc aussi en *Pere benin* et faitte moy sentir plus outre les effects de Votre Bienveillance."[7]

"Have, Sir, the kindness to forget the past, and, now that I have corrected myself since then, conceive a better opinion of me for the present and the future. But yet, although I have grieved you by my evasion and my debts, yet I have served my bailiwick with honor to the satisfaction of the Sovereign and the subjects, and have committed nothing atrocious which might have done you dishonor, nor have I, so far as I know, failed toward you in respect and submission. Pardon me, then, the past and do not keep touching again upon this disagreeable string, but take me unto favor again, Sir and honorable Father, since I shall make all effort to satisfy you and show you that I am with all obedience, Respect and Submission the Prodigal returned and amended. Look upon me, then, as the gracious Father and make me to feel further yet the effects of your benevolence."

In 1731, after the death of a brother, the Oberherr von Worb, Anton secured and sold to Christoph the management of the estate which went with the office, reserving for himself the revenues of the office. The management of the estate was not very lucrative, but the father thought he had made a rather generous expiation for his previous treatment. Next, when Anton became Mayor of Murton he wanted a representative in Iverton; and although Christoph did not relish the place, still to please his wife he ran for it and was elected. In 1730 at Anton's death the estate of Worb came to Christoph without encumbrance, and he held it till 1740, when he retired in favor of his sons. Three years later he died and was buried in the choir of the Church at Worb, ending a life the last years of which, while uneventful, were not unpleasant.

---

[7] Neujahrsblatt, page 89.

CHAPTER XVI

PROOF THAT GRAFFENRIED NEVER CAME BACK TO AMERICA TO LIVE—
DEBT TO POLLOCK UNPAID—LAST NOTICES OF THE GERMAN
SETTLERS AND END OF THE NEW BERN ADVENTURERS

It is improbable that Graffenried ever returned to America, although it has been asserted that he did. It appears that the Graffenried who lived in this country after 1714, was a *son* of, but *not* the Baron Christoph von Graffenried who founded the settlement at New Bern. According to the *Neujahrsblatt*, Christoph's eldest son came at the time of the settlement and stayed here after his father's departure, settling finally in Williamsburg, New York, where he married. The *Virginia Magazine* quotes the following from the files of the *Virginia Gazette* for February 18-25, 1736: "This is to give notice to all Gentlemen and Ladies that Mrs. Barbara de Graffenried intends to have a Ball on Tuesday the 26th of next April and an assembly on the 27th in Williamsburg: For which tickets will be delivered out at her Home." A footnote then states that "This was the wife of Christopher, Baron von Graffenried of Berne, Switzerland who brought over a colony of Swiss and Palatines to North Carolina in 1709." In the article to which the note is added in explanation, she is called "la Baronne de Graffenriedt." The statement of her being the wife of Christopher von Graffenried is made, but no proof is given, and other evidence would indicate that the *Virginia Magazine* is here in error.

Colonel William Byrd, also, in his memoirs[1] mentions meeting a certain Madame de Graffenriedt not far from Williamsburg. This lady could hardly be any other than the one named in the *Virginia Magazine* who lived at Williamsburg. According to the *Neujahrsblatt* Christoph's wife is named Regine Tscharner, while in the *Virginia Magazine* her given name is Barbara. The writer in the *Neujahrsblatt* is evidently mistaken about the son settling in Williamsburg, New York, but he would have no difficulty learning the name of Graffenried's wife if other means were lacking when he copied the inscription on the Graffenried memorial in the church at Worb.

The most plausible explanation then is this, that the writer in the *Virginia Magazine* supposed because this lady was called la Baronne she must be the wife of Christoph von Graffenried, overlooking the fact that the title was hereditary and would belong to the eldest son and his wife even during the father's lifetime. The writer in the *Neujahrsblatt* with the means at his disposal could hardly have

[1] Byrd, page 326.

gotten the name of Christoph's wife wrong, but the confusion may have arisen between the two Williamsburgs and he wrote New York when he should have written Virginia. If all these suppositions are correct, Madame de Graffenried, the lady Colonel Byrd speaks of, and the wife of the son who stayed in America are all the same person; and this evidence, which so far as I can learn, is the only evidence that the Baron ever returned to this country, is destroyed. Christoph's own statement that for 20 years no complaint had been made of his administration completes the proof if more is needed, for his official duties began in 1722 and lasted until 1742, and the notices of Madame de Graffenried's ball were printed in 1736.

One more disputed point concerning Graffenried needs to be settled. Careful searching of the Colonial Records down to Graffenried's death in 1743 make no mention of Pollock's having received more than the assignment of the Palatines' land, for the money due him on the loans. As he had lent much more than the 17,500 acres were worth, he had reason to feel misused and defrauded, although Graffenried was acting in good faith, and fully expected assistance from the Proprietors and the Company. And when these sources failed him, he had nothing to pay with. Pollock also seems to have lost confidence in his honesty because of his failure to deliver letters to the Lords Proprietors as he was returning to England.[2] But the attitude is unjust, for Graffenried complains that a box full of papers and curios was lost on the way to Europe, and these letters most likely were in it.[3] In a letter of February 10, 1715, Pollock asks him to pay 700£ at London and keep this title to the land he had taken up.[4] Graffenried's petition

---

[2]Col. Rec., page 145.

Oct. 20th, 1714.
"My first letter to you dated September 20th, 1712 (a copy whereof is enclosed) I delivered myself to Baron Graffenried, who was then (goin)g to Verginia; and he told me that the Gouvernor of Verginia took care—his letters to London with his own pacquets, and that there was no—that they would come safe to your Lordships hands. —second letters, dated April 2d, 1713 immediately after the taking the great Indian Fort I sent into Verginia an I know they came to Baron Graffenreid who was then in Verginia I would have sent (your Lord)ship copies of all, but the state of affairs being much altered, and they being long, thought it not worth while to trouble your (Lordshi)p with them. What reason Baron Graffenried had to conceal (or) keep up my letters, I know not. I took him for a man of honour and integrity, but have found the contrary to my great loss."
[3]French Version.
[4]Col. Rec., vol. II, page 166.

North Carolina, February 10th, 1715.
Hond. Sir:
Yours from Berne dated April, 30th 1714, came to hand and (am glad to) understood you got safe to your own country, and I should (be) well satisfied, (if for your advantage and to pay it? your creditors) (you) could procure a new surety. But I could never have expected Baron Graffenreid, whom I always took to be a man of honour and honesty would have proposed to me to give away the matter of 900 pounds sterling money of England for nothing. You know how readily and fully (I served) you; you cannot but remember your reiterated promises that I should be fully and honestly satisfied. And now to propose to put me off with (nothing) is what I never expected of you. Your debt to me was 612 pounds, besides some other small debts I (paid) by your desire, after making up accounts: your debt to Cap . . . and his brother was fifty-six pounds which makes 668 pounds, the bills being pro(tested) the change and re-exchange at 15 per cent is 91 pounds 4 sh(illings) makes with the charge in England for the protest near 770 pounds. To (which) will be two if not three years interest due before I can have it of you . . . at London, which with the other small debts I have paid here for (you) and trouble of taking care of what insignificant matters you (left) here, having been forced to pay Mr. Graves for the surveying your land, and the heavy charge of a Land tax, will make your debt near 1000 pounds sterling money of England, of all which have received (but) 312 pounds in our public bills for your sloops et eact., which are of no use, seeing I can purchase nothing for them, but lie dead on

7

was at this time in the Duke of Beaufort's hands, waiting for an opportunity to be presented. Graffenried, also, was doing all that could be done to extricate himself from his entanglements. As we have seen, however, the Duke died before the petition could be presented and only a little while after, the Queen also; so that he received no help from England and it is probable that Pollock was never paid the money due him, for on March 29, 1743, some Palatines led by Jacob Sheets settled by Baron de Graffenried at Neuse showing their agreement with the said Baron and praying to have Title made out to them "in order that warrants might issue to them respectively for laying out their lands to each man his several proportion or otherwise to be secure in their possession.

"Then Cullen Pollock's Council produced a patent to the said Pollock's father, Thomas Pollock Esq., deceased, for a large tract of land at Neuse which was read and it appearing to the Council that the said Patent take in the Palatine Lands," the suit was dismissed.[5]

That the Palatines in the meantime had managed somehow to live will appear from the Proclamation of the Council, November 6, 1714, where "upon petition of the poor Palatines showing that they were disappointed of the lands stock and other necessary which was to be provided for them and are reduced to great want and poverty by the late war and prays that they may have Liberty to take up four hundred Acres of land for each family at the rate of ten Pounds a thousand acres and that they may have two years day of payment for the same."[6] Apparently nothing was done at the time, for in 1747 another petition was made by the Palatines, this time, to the Right Honorable the Lords of the Committee of Council for Plantation Affairs.[7] Redress was slow but at length on March 16, 1748, His Majesty gave orders to Governor Johnston to give the settlers an equivalent of the lands of which they had been dispossessed, free of quit-rent for ten years. After that they were to pay the usual rents, "*and as the settlement of the said Palatines will be a great addition to the strength of our said Province, and be a consider-*

---

my hand. And as for your goods, if you left any of any value, your friend Mr. Mitchell, the Mayor, and others of your people had conveyed an . . . I haveing got nothing, save a little iron and some rusty nails for . . . and other small things of little value.

You know that you purchased only 15000 acres of land of the Lords Proprietors, which is but 150 pounds sterling money, whereof at Mill Creek? there is only 85000 acres surveyed; the other 5000 acres not being yet taken up, which I intend to take up at White Oak River, as you designed. As for your two or three other small tracts, you not having paid the purchase to the Lords Proprietors, they were by law made here, with all other lands in Bath County that had not been paid the purchase, lost: so I was obliged to purchase them of the Receiver General. And all the land, and what else is come to me of yours, is not really of the value of 200 pounds. And if you will pay me at London, so that I may be sure to have the money seven hundred pounds sterling money within this twelve month, you shall have what land you purchased of the Lords Proprietors, you shall have the public bills I had on your account, and what other small matter of goods I had of yours or the value as they are appraised. (From Pollock's Letter Book.)

[5]Col. Rec., vol. IV, page 632.
[6]Col. Rec., vol. II, page 146.
[7]Col. Rec., vol. IV, page 954 (which gives the text of the petition also); see also pp. 868, 873 ff.

able advantage and Security to the Inhabitants whereof[8] we do hereby direct and require you to recommend to the Assembly of our said Province to make speedy provision in such manner as they shall think proper for defraying the Charge of surveying the Land so as to be granted to the said Petitioners, and of issuing the Grants for the same and all other Charges attending such Survey and Grants."[9] Two years later they were settled in what are now Craven, Jones, Onslow, and Duplin counties.[10]

This ends the story of the German settlement at Newbern as a distinctly German colony. The town had a prosperous growth and kept its original name, but as a financial venture it was a complete failure, due not to the incompetence of the leader, but to the force of circumstances and the niggardliness of those whose duty it was to contribute to his support.

---
[8] The italics are mine, V. H. T.
[9] Col. Rec., vol. vol. IV, page 967.
[10] Ashe, page 273.

PART III

THE GRAFFENRIED MANUSCRIPTS

CHAPTER I

THE DISCOVERY OF NEW MATERIAL RELATING TO NEW BERN—COMPARISON OF MANUSCRIPTS—NEW MATERIAL IN A FRENCH VERSION—NEGOTIATIONS OF BERN FOR LAND—CONSIDERED GOING TO MARYLAND—GRAFFENRIED'S TITLES—CONTRACT WITH THE PROPRIETORS—VOYAGE ACROSS THE ATLANTIC—ILLNESS OF THE COLONISTS—TREATY WITH THE INDIANS—TROUBLES WITH MICHEL—DESCRIPTION OF THE CITY OF NEW BERN—PURCHASE OF BOATS—EXPLORATION FOR SILVER ALONG THE POTOMAC IN DETAIL—INDICATIONS OF A TREATY WITH PENN—DETAILS OF VOYAGE TO EUROPE—DETAILS OF HIS CARE FOR THE MINERS—ADDITIONAL EFFORTS TO SECURE HELP—A KEY TO A FRENCH MAP OF THE POTOMAC

When Graffenried returned from America disappointed in all his plans, he found plenty of people who blamed him for the misfortune "as though he had acted rashly and imprudently." It was to vindicate himself that he wrote of his adventures in America, and in order to allow himself to be more widely understood in Switzerland, he wrote in both French and German. For some reason he appears to have left two French versions, unless indeed, one is a copy of the other, which from comparison seems hardly probable. The French version in the library at Iverton, Switzerland, has been copied and translated for the *Colonial Records of North Carolina* where it may be found in Volume I, page 905. When Professor Goebel was writing his book on the Germans in America, (*Das Deutschtum in den Vereinigten Staaten von Nord Amerika*) he found that there were other versions, and at considerable trouble and expense he had accurate copies of these made for his own use, in hopes that if they were published, they might throw some light on this early pioneer. The three manuscripts as nearly as can be judged by the translation in the *Colonial Records* which is a literal translation into poor English, are in many places word for word translations, or copies, of each other. The importance, then, of Professor Goebel's copies is that while they contain everything that the other version has, they also have much which is entirely lacking in the *North Carolina Records*.

It may be worth while to indicate the most important differences between Professor Goebel's manuscripts and the others, especially where the former contains things not found in the latter, although most of the items have been referred to already in Part II.

The most natural comparison to make is between the two French versions, as they are most alike, being each divided into twelve *contretemps*, which may be translated misfortunes. Where they treat of the same thing, they use the same language, except that Professor Goebel's copy often has things interspersed, which the other does not have, and occasionally the marginal notes are not placed in the same position. Then, again, whole paragraphs are placed in different relative positions as regards the rest of the account. For instance, the chapter on Indian customs which comes at the end of the account in the *Colonial Records*, is placed in the body of the text in connection with the account of Graffenried's capture in Professor Goebel's French text. The omissions from, or additions to the original text must have been made by Graffenried himself or else by some one very familiar with the text; for several more attempts made to relieve the colony are mentioned in Professor Goebel's French version than appear in the other accounts and two items are added in marginal notes which do not occur elsewhere, namely, that Cary was banished to a distant island and there died, and that Michel died among the Indians. These events, if recorded after the accounts had been written, would naturally be placed in the finished version, an inference borne out by the conclusions of Professor A. B. Faust on placing the three originals side by side.[1]

However, the order in which the versions were written is of minor importance compared to the contents, since they must have appeared within a very few years of each other. The following paragraphs are intended to give what seems the most important contributions which Professor Goebel's manuscripts make to what is already accessible in the *Colonial Records of North Carolina*. Taking the French version first: this says that Bern negotiated through Stanian, the Envoy Extraordinary, for a place to found a colony which should be absolutely independent of any authority except the British sovereign, but was unsuccessful, because the Queen did not wish to work to the detriment of the colonial and proprietary governments. He received permission to take up land above the falls of the Potomac but was persuaded that conditions were more favorable in North Carolina where land was cheaper, and where, under the proprietors,

---

[1] German American Annals. New Series, Vol. XI. Nos. 5 and 6.

he would have more jurisdiction and various additional privileges. When he went to Virginia, he found that Culpepper had gotten ahead of him on a part of the land, and this would have compelled him to settle in Maryland farther from white settlers than he had hoped.

As a reward for their zeal in bringing him to the throne, Charles II gave to several gentlemen a large tract in North America with power to create hereditary titles of nobility. According to the French version, Graffenried was made Landgrave of Carolina, Baron de Bernberg, and Chevelier du Cordon Bleu, and in addition was given a medal. The regalia of his orders he wore whenever he went to the assembly, and he found it increased people's deference for him.

The amount of land he took up and the charges per acre have been given already.[1] Two other very important clauses of this agreement with the proprietors were the ones providing for religious liberty and for the furnishing of provisions and stock by the proprietors, the debts so contracted by the colony to be paid in three years. Then he says: "Je passe icy sous Silence un Traitté fait avec William Penn Proprietaire de Pennsilvanie pour des Terres et des mines." This is only one of several passages which show that such an agreement existed. Then follows a description of the town.

A description of New Castle, and the voyage across the Atlantic occupies several pages and has this of interest to us, that in connection with it he states that a box of curiosities, papers, and clothes which he had given to the ship's captain, was lost on the return voyage. This may explain Governor Pollock's grievance that the letters sent by Graffenried were not delivered.[2] The voyage over was without unpleasant accidents and has little worthy of mention here, although it makes interesting reading.

When Graffenried returned from Governor Hyde's in the summer of 1711, he found many of his people ill. This gives him opportunity to tell about the diseases the people were exposed to and the remedies to employ in such cases. In all this his good sense and care for his colonists is shown most clearly. He mentions, also, the insect and reptile pests they have to guard against, and then he discusses the building of the town.

The Colonial Records relate the troubles Graffenried had in treaty making, persuading Indians unwilling to sell their lands with rum, powder, and shot, while a drunken partner makes merry with some English friends and twice brings the negotiations to the verge of ruin by insulting and even beating the Indian orator. But they do not tell of the pains Graffenried took to keep him at a distance, at one time provisioning him to survey along the Weetock River, and again

---

[1] See Part II, chapter V.
[2] See page 97.

sending him to Philadelphia to see about the silver mines, regarding which they had an express agreement with William Penna and the head miner, Justus Albrecht. The Indians naturally supposed that he sent him away for their sake, and it helped him afterwards while he was in captivity. He also called upon the Indians at Core town and promised to be a good neighbor to them. Then he took the surveyor and the clerk, and together they made the plan of the town. "As the people in America do not like to live crowded," he gave each house three acres and the streets were arranged like a cross. His artisans, who could do better in the city, had freedom from taxation for ten years. Then he enumerates the trades represented, among which ought to be particularly noticed the schoolmaster.

Prosperity seemed so certain that people outside even from as far away as Pennsylvania, took lots. The only thing lacking was ready money. All accounts agree that this was a serious difficulty. The province could not pay him and nothing had been received from Europe; but he trusted that if he could only get a message to the Georg Ritter Company by some person, they would help him out. One of the settlers was just going and was willing to take the message. This man, Bötschi[3] by name, as the German version shows, abused the confidence placed in him by contracting debts in Graffenried's name in Philadelphia and Amsterdam. Nevertheless, he delivered his message faithfully. But the disasters of the following autumn when the Indians captured Graffenried and Lawson, discouraged the Company in Bern and the Proprietors so that, even if they had intended to assist him, which is more than doubtful, they now refused to risk their money. However, while he still believed that help would be sent him, he had bought two boats for use in trading and on one trip took a cargo of wheat to the Bermudas to exchange for salt. But the wheat was damaged in a storm and the profits consequently were lessened.

A considerable space in the book is then filled with his account of the trip to Canavest, the chief part of which, however, is a detailed description of the Indians shooting the rapids in canoes.

As an additional reason why he believed in Michel's stories of the silver mine, Graffenried states that M. M. had asked the Queen for patents, and together they had made a treaty with the miners in Europe, and Mr. Penn had made a treaty with them and had made M. M. director of minerals in Pennsylvania.

The return to Europe is enlivened with a description of the wonders by the way, such as the meeting with an iceberg and a storm which almost foundered their ship, owing to the negligence of the

[3] German Version, Report.

captain. He tells in addition of how he found work on a dike for his miners who were in London when he arrived.

Along with the account, but not an integral part of it, is a document which appears to be a key to the map of the Potomac River. It has a number of interesting comments on the country about the present site of Washington which consisted of a few plantations and had as yet no name.

These, then, are the principal items which Professor Goebel's French copy adds to what has been translated for the *Colonial Records of North Carolina*.

CHAPTER II

IMPORTANT ADDITIONS TO THE GERMAN VERSION ARE A REPORT TO THE RITTER COMPANY, THE CONTRACT WITH THE RITTER COMPANY, A MEMORIAL OR ACCOUNT OF LIFE IN THE COLONY, LETTERS FROM THE COLONISTS—CONTENTS OF THE REPORT—RELIABILITY OF THE REPORT AND LETTERS—THE CONTRACT WITH GEORG RITTER COMPANY—THE MEMORIAL

In the German account there is little that the Colonial Records do not have, though it is a satisfaction to read the man's exact language. Connected with it, however, are several documents of very great importance. The first of these is the report Graffenried sent to the company in Bern. Then follow in order the contract with the Georg Ritter Company, a *Memorial* or account, apparently written at the time of the report, describing the conditions in America, and a number of letters written by Swiss settlers to their friends and relatives in the home land.

This report and these letters do more to clear Graffenried's character than anything else which has come down to us from him or others. Taking up the report first; it was written May 6, 1711, just a short time after Cary had seized his brigantine, but before he had made the attack on the governor. At this time the prospects of making the colony succeed were bright, if only help could be secured; and as soon as Cary could be reduced to obedience he might hope for help from the province. The town had been nicely laid out by this time, the people supplied as well as possible with stock, and Graffenried was beginning to think about making exploring expeditions to find gold and silver. As yet his money affairs had not reached a serious condition; he had laid out 2228£ worth of supplies of cattle and grain, and had purchased two boats. The supplies had come for the most part from one man, Thomas Pollock. He with the rest was now becoming suspicious, and refused to sell more. The letters from the settlers express no dissatisfaction, but nevertheless it existed, for the contract with the commissioners relating to supplies for the people had not been fully kept, and there was talk of making complaint to them. As Graffenried had given a bond for 5000£, such a complaint might cause him great inconvenience and loss. He and Michel had agreed to supply each family with two cows, two calves, five sows with their young, two ewes and two lambs, with a male of each kind, within two months of their arrival.[1] Repayment was to be

[1] Col. Rec., vol. I, page 988.

made by the colonists after seven years, at which time the same number of animals would be returned with one-half the stock on hand. The first comers had been in America over a year, and the confusions in the province and the distance from other colonists had made it impossible to deliver more than ten cows, 30 swine, four horses, and eight sheep. The financial difficulties were not yet at a crisis, however, and the timely arrival of money from Switzerland would have allayed all fears and have enabled the work of colonization to go on unhindered. What he wrote then, while he was in the midst of his work, knowing the bearer of the letter, Mr. Bötschi, would be present to confirm or deny the statements contained in it, make it more than likely that the information given is reliable. The accounts written several years after some of the events occurred, at a time when he was smarting under the criticism of his acquaintances, when his plans and hopes had all been shattered and when the occurrences had become somewhat confused in his memory, are, of course, more open to question as to their accuracy. The criticism he makes of his colonists, in which he accuses them of all kinds of wickedness and makes almost no exception, was certainly inspired more by the disappointment he had suffered than the actual character of the settlers, who, to judge from their letters, were pious and well meaning people. Moreover, at the time the report was written he seems to have been perfectly satisfied with them.

The contract between Graffenried and Michel on the one hand, and other members on the other, by which they became associates in the Georg Ritter Company shows that, as far as Graffenried and Michel were concerned, the mines were what they and Ritter were basing their hopes for returns upon, and that the 17,500 acres were merely a foundation to the greater enterprise of mining.

The "*Memorial*" which follows was written while Graffenried was still in an optimistic mood, and appears to have been taken, in part, from some English author. He says it was translated from the English. This is not entirely exact, for a portion of it which deals with the purchase of a ship to be used to transport colonists from Holland to America, certainly was not translated from anything. A description of the care of swine and the manner of calling them to the house at feeding time occurs in Kocherthal in almost the same words. In general, though, the *Memorial* is filled up with the results of his own observations, arranged under heads, as the writers of such accounts were fond of doing, and some of the details were perhaps taken from similar books in English.

The letters which close the accounts prove conclusively that as late as April and May there was no serious discontent among the colonists with the treatment they had received. Not a word is said about the scarcity of cattle, and Graffenried is always mentioned with respect. A hopeful tone pervades all of the letters. The complaint which occurs oftenest is over the lack of German women folks, for all who wished home comfort, washing, and mending, could not find wives. They wished their beer also, and one of the men whose wife understood brewing, was planning to supply the deficiency by ordering the necessary utensils from home. The lack, too, of a regular minister was severely felt, and caused some anxiety lest the religious fervor should die out for want of pastoral ministrations in addition to the Sunday reading of prayers. But nowhere is there any reflection on Graffenried's character or conduct.

CHAPTER III

CRITICISM OF GRAFFENRIED MORTGAGING THE SETTLERS' LANDS

The most severe criticism has been made on Graffenried for mortgaging the settlers' land to Pollock, and then when the colony was broken up, leaving them in their distress and going to Europe. Any one reading these contemporary documents with the other accounts will certainly be compelled to take a more charitable view. He will see that what Graffenried did was not only done in good faith, but was really a good business move under the circumstances, and that the fault lay with the Company in Bern.

Referring back to Part II, Chapter V, it will be seen that Georg Ritter and Company proposed to buy 10,000 acres of land before the Palatines had come to Germany, while they had in prospect only their own 156 voluntary emigrants and exiles. Then Graffenried and Michel added their small number to that on the condition that these miners with their families, numbering about 40 persons, should come later if they were sent for. After Graffenried became connected with the company, while the proprietors were making propositions to the committee, but before anything had been done to give them any reason for believing that these Germans would be sent to their colony, the Company actually purchased 10,000 acres. Graffenried contributed 5,000 which belonged to him personally, and Michel added 2,500 acres, making 17,500 acres, to which the Company had claims before they were sure of more than 156 persons. A month and more after these negotiations were completed the committee acted favorably on the Proprietors' propositions to this extent, that 650 persons were at length allowed to them. These last came at no expense to the Georg Ritter Company, and yet the Company was to get the benefit of their quit-rents and the increased value of land in the colony which would result from the larger number of settlers.

When sickness and death reduced the 650 to about 300, there were still more than enough left to take the place of the 56 prisoners whom they were unable to bring, and the nine Swiss who died on the journey and after landing in Virginia.[1] Even the massacre of September, 1711, in which 70 or 80 fell, left more than the Company had originally planned to send and had actually purchased land for; and besides there were still about 40 persons, the miners, anxious to come over. Having had all the summer of 1709 with its delays and uncertainties, in which to think over their plans, and plenty of

[1]German Version, Letters.

opportunity to change their minds, their action after the colony was
settled is most contemptible. They never sent Graffenried anything
more than advice to go ahead on credit. The loss of part of the
Palatines was no excuse, for as we have seen, they had not reasonably
counted on them in the first place, and whatever number of them
should succeed in settling was so much gain. Having made the start,
then, they should have supported their enterprise until they had
better evidence than their own fears that nothing would come of it.
Even after the massacre, it is reasonably certain that with the money
due him, Graffenried could have held his colony together, and either
rebuilt at New Bern, or have gone to Virginia and engaged in agriculture and mining there. Silver, to be sure, would never have made
them rich, but iron was there in abundance, and Spotswood only a
short time after, as has been shown (Part I, Chapter III), engaged
Graffenried's miners in a profitable enterprise, the beginning of the
iron blast furnace industry in America. The profits of this might
just as well have gone, in part at least, to the Georg Ritter Company,
and the investment would have paid them.[2] As it was, since Graffenried had no idea they were actually abandoning him, to tide his
people over the critical periods of the first year and keep the colony
intact for the Company, he had mortgaged the land beyond all hope
of redeeming it by his own efforts. In criticising this action one
must remember that the people did not own their lands outright
as other settlers. They were *tenants* of the Company which was supposed to support them. Graffenried, therefore, did not sign away
land belonging to other people; besides, by the strict system of
recording real estate transactions in use in Carolina this would have
been impossible. Rather, he signed away a tract for which he was
agent, which was made out to him, and of which he was the owner
in the eyes of the law. His position was not an enviable one, for on
the one hand he was responsible to the company which expected him
to make the investment profitable, a task that could only be accomplished by keeping the people together and supplied with necessaries;
on the other hand the people who looked to him for support, advice,
and protection, were in danger of losing their lands if the Company
failed to send help. The latter possibility was the more remote.
Hunger was at their doors, and he chose to mortgage their lands and
wait for help from Bern. Could he reasonably be expected to have
done differently? The answer is to be found in his report. For

---

[2]Byrd, page 333ff. A Progress of the Mines in the Year 1732. This gives a detailed description of the mines which Graffenreid's workmen were operating. Spotswood was one of the several who made up the Company; the enterprise was self-supporting, in that a part of the operatives tended the farms to supply food for the laborers and the oxen and horses employed. The lack of farm laborers was a hindrance, and the furnaces could not run full time in consequence. The arrangement actually made was just such as Graffenreid would have made with his settlers if he had been assisted by his Company.

this report which was written at a time when he foresaw the impending disaster unless help should be sent, which begs with the eloquence of despair for the assistance that belonged to him, and on which the welfare of several hundred colonists depended, speaks more convincingly for the integrity of his motives than any justification he could write afterwards.

The little settlement did not, however, entirely die out with the departure of the leader and the partial disbanding of the inhabitants. For many of them continued to live in the neighborhood and other settlers were attracted by the location, until in time another flourishing town arose from the ruins of the first.

It is, too, one of the ironies of fate that one of Graffenried's darling ambitions for his town was realized only after his death. He had hoped to make New Bern the chief city in the province and to move the seat of government thither, but the disaster which attended his first efforts and forced him to abandon his first colony, destroyed this hope also. Nevertheless, although he lived to see a few sessions of the assembly held in his town, it was not till 1765, over 20 years after his death, that New Bern was officially made the capital of North Carolina, a distinction which it held for over twenty-five years. Since then, although it has experienced the vicissitudes of the Civil War and the Reconstruction, it is today one of the most prosperous towns in North Carolina, and an honor to its German founders who built better than they knew.

Two full centuries have now passed since the little colony of Germans established their settlement at New Bern and contributed their share towards the religious and political liberty we now enjoy. Graffenried's failure, for such he reckoned it, is not all a failure if we may in any way learn to appreciate better the blessings we now enjoy by considering the cost at which they have been purchased for us. Certainly coming years, with their greater fullness of knowledge, will deal more fairly with Baron von Graffenried than the past has done, and the justification he so much desired, though late, will be fully rendered.

BIBLIOGRAPHY

SOURCES

Ashe, Samuel A'Court.
  History of North Carolina, Vol. I.
    Charles L. Van Noppen, Publisher, Greensboro, N. C., 1908.
The Cambridge Modern History, Vol. VI, Cambridge, 1908.
Channing, Edward.
  A History of the United States.
    The Macmillan Company, 1908.
Collections of the Historical Society of South Carolina, Vol. I.
  Published by the South Carolina Historical Society, Charleston, S. C.
    S. G. Courtenay & Co., 1857.
The Colonial Records of North Carolina, Vols. I, II, IV.
  Saunders, William L., Editor, Raleigh, N. C.
    P. M. Hale, Printer to the State, 1886.
Der Deutsche Pionier, Vierzehnter Jahrgang.
  Herausgegeben vom "Deutschen Pionier-Verein." Cincinnati, Ohio.
Ecclesiastical Records of the State of New York, Vol. III.
  Published by the State under the supervision of Hugh Hastings, State Historian, Albany, N. Y.
    J. B. Lyon Company, State Printers, 1902.
Faust, Albert Bernhardt.
  The German Element in the United States, Vols. I, II.
    Houghton-Mifflin Company, Boston and New York, 1909.
Faust, Albert. German-American Annals. New Series, Vol. II, Nos. 5 and 6; Vol. XII, Nos. 2 and 3. September-December 1913; March-October 1914.
Goebel, Julius.
  Die Gründung von New-Bern in North-Carolina.
  Internationale Wochenschrift, Berlin, October, 1910.
Hennepin, Father Louis.
  A Continuation of the New Discovery of a Vast Country in America.
    Reprinted from the second London issue of 1698 by Reuben Gold Thwaites.
    A. C. McClurg & Co., Chicago, 1903.
Heuser, F.
  Pennsylvanien im 17ten Jahrhundert und die Ausgewanderten Pfälzer in England.
    Verlag von Ludwig Ritter, Neustadt a. d. Hardt, 1910.

Johns Hopkins Studies in Historical and Political Science, Series X.
The Johns Hopkins Press, Baltimore, Md., 1892.

Kocherthal.
Außführlich, und umständlicher Bericht von der berühmten Landschafft Carolina/ In dem Engellandischen America gelegen, Vierter Druck.
Zu finden bei Georg Heinrich Dehrlin/ Frankfurt am Mähn 1709.

Lawson, John, Gent. Surveyor General of North Carolina.
A New Voyage to Carolina; containing the exact Description and Natural History of that Country: Together with the Present State thereof. And a Journal of a Thousand Miles, Travel'd thro' several Nations of Indians. Giving a particular Account of their Customs, Manners, etc.
London, Printed in the Year 1709.

Luttrell, Narcissus.
A Brief Historical Relation of Affairs from September 1678 to April 1714, Vol. I-VI.
Oxford, At the University Press, 1857.

Manuscripts and Maps in the Possession of Professor Julius Goebel, Urbana, Ill.

McCrady, Edward.
The History of South Carolina under the Proprietary Government, 1670-1719.
The Macmillan Company, New York, 1897.

Müller, Ernst.
Geschichte der Bernischen Täufer.
J. Hubers Verlag, Frauenfeld, 1895.

Neujahrsblatt herausgegeben vom Historischen Verein des Kantons Bern für 1897.
Christoph von Graffenried Landgraf von Carolina, Gründer von Neu-Bern. Wolfgang Friedrich von Mülinen.
Druck und Verlag von K. J. Wyss, Bern, 1896.

The Official Letters of Alexander Spotswood, Lieutenant-Governor of the Colony of Virginia, 1710-1722.
Published by the Virginia Historical Society, Richmond, Va., 1882.

The Pennsylvania-German Society Proceedings and Addresses, Vol. VII, 1896, Vol. VIII, 1897.
Published by the Society.

Proceedings of the Massachusetts Historical Society, Vol. XVI.
Boston, 1878.

Virginia Magazine of History and Biography, Vol. XIII.
Published by the Virginia Historical Society.
House of the Society, Richmond, Va., 1905-6.

The Writings of Colonel William Byrd of Westover in Virginia, Esqr.
Edited by John Spencer Bassett.
Doubleday, Page & Co., New York, 1901.
The following works among others, have also been consulted:
Adams, Sir Francis Ottiwell and Cunningham, C. D.
Switzerland—Constitution and Government.
Macmillan & Co., London and New York, 1894.
Bancroft, George.
History of the United States of America, from the Discovery of the Continent.
D. Appleton & Co., New York.
Bernheim, Gotthardt Dellman.
German Settlements and the Lutheran Church in the Carolinas, from the earliest period of the colonization of Dutch, German and Swiss settlers to the close of the first half of the present Century . . .
The Lutheran Book Store, Philadelphia, 1872.
Blome, Richard.
The present state of His Majesties isles and territories in America, viz. Jamaica, Barbados, S. Christophers, Mevis, Antego, S. Vincent, Dominica, New Jersey, Pennsilvania, Monserat, Anguilla, Bermudas, Carolina, Virginia, New-England, Tobago, Newfoundland, Maryland, New-York, etc. . . . from the year 1686 to 1700.
D. Newman, London, 1687.
Carrol, B. R.
Historical Collections of South Carolina, Vols. I, II.
Harper & Bros., New York, 1836.
The American Nation, a History.
Edited by A. B. Hart.
Harper & Bros. Co., New York and London.
Raper, Charles Lee, Ph.D.
North Carolina, a study in English Colonial Government.
The Macmillan Co., New York, 1904.
Rivers, William James.
A sketch of the history of South Carolina to the close of the proprietary government by the revolution of 1719.
McCarter & Co., Charleston, 1856.
Williamson, Hugh.
The history of North Carolina.
T. Dobson, Philadelphia, 1812.

GERMAN VERSION

VORBERICHT[1]

Diese relation ist in Eyl geschrieben worden, ohne viel Nachsinnes nur bei mir meinem schwachen Gedächtniss nach, die Sachen eingefallen, so dass hier kein sonderbahrer Stilus zu observieren, und ist eygentlich eingerichtet in 12. Capl: Traverses meiner Societet und anderen die etwan widrige Gedanken gehabt, meiner Conduitte halben durch mein amerikanisches Unterfangen so ich liecht daher und unversichtig vorgenommen, und meine Zeit in Carolina in Pracht und Wohlleben zugebracht, Also hätte ich das Contra gezeigt, Der Eingang ist auch dahin gerichtet zu zeigen, dass nicht nur Liederlichkeit mich zu dieser Noth getrieben, sondern auch bedenkliche Widerwertigkeit, und unglückhaftige Zufähl. So ich bey müssiger Zeit, diese relation refidiren werde, soll ein und anders besser gestelt und eingerichtet sein.

NOTE:—The references throughout are to the French Version and show wherein that version varies from the German.

GERMAN VERSION

RELATION

Meines amerikanischen Unterfangens aufgesetzt aus Anlass etlicher Klägten, als hätte unversichtiger Wys, solches Colloney Wesen fürgnommen, zum Nachteil und untergang vieler Leuthen, welches aber liecht zu justificieren.—
Nachdeme hievor in meinen Reisen mich in Engelland bey 2 Jahren aufgehalten, an selbigem Ohrt unter Carolo dem II. solche vortheilhaftige und ansehenliche Bekanntschaft gemacht, dass so ich da selbsten verblieben, ich eine ziemliche fortun zuwegen gebracht: Da theils aus Muntlichen als schriftlichen relationen mich der americanischen Landen erkundigen, ohnlängst aber nach genauweren Bericht und inbesonders von einem Bürger hiesiger Stadt vernahmen, welcher in America 5 oder 6 Jahr sich aufgehalten, was herlichen Landes, wie wohlfeil, was freyheit, was grossen aufnehmens, gute Handlung, für riche Bergwerk, und andere gute Sachen mehr, insbesonders aber vorgeben, was schönen reichen Silber Mines er entdecket und erfunden, in betrachtung dass ich mit zimlichen Schulden behaftet, welche noch vor mein Reisen hab, theils einer Handlung so mir und etlichen andern H. übel ausgeschlagen, von Bürgschaften, grossen Ausgaben in meinen pretensionen, wohlfeillen Zeiten auf dem ambt, denne die armen Bauren nicht Schindten mögen, wegen der Neuwgemachten reformation, darzu noch die Neunburgischen Troubles geschlagen, hiemit da wenig prosperiert, zu einem bessern Ambt der weg abgeschnitten, und auch eine gar lange Zeit wegen der neugemachten reformation zu einem geringen Ambtli kein Hofnung, indessen mit grosser und starker familien bescheeret.—
So haben meine Gedanken gewaltet, was fürzunehmen, die Creditoren zu bestellen, und auch meiner Familien fortzuhelfen, da nun in dem Vaterland wenig Hofnung, einer solchen grossen Noth zu steuren: gaben mir die schönen propositionen obgemelten Bürgers, welchen zu verschonen hier keinen Nahmen gebe, vast in die Augen, mich auf meine alte und neuwe fründ, in Engelland so von hohem ansehen, tröstend und verlassen, habe entlichen eine stife resolution gefasset, mein Vaterland zu verlassen, und in Engelland zu sehen, ob die fortun da mir günstiger seyn wolte. Hab aber theils von den Creditoren, theils von denn meinigen nicht aufgehalten zu werden, ganz in geheim meine Reys vorgenommen, meinem H. Vatter, der da vermöglichst gnug, die Sorgen meiner Schulden und geschäften überlassend. [1]—

Da ich in Holland angelangt, hätten mich gewisse Persohnen schier von meinem Vorhaben abwendig gemacht, und wahren mir andre Vorschläge gethan, worbey zwar meiner Unterhaltung, und noch etwas zu prosperieren hatte, allein funde nicht dass bey diesem gnug meine Sach zu retressieren, setzte hiemit meine Reys fort nach Engelland: allwo ich alsobald meine Leuth erfahren, und mir von hohen und andren persohnen, solcher Lust gemacht worden, ihn meinem unterfangen fortzufahren, neben Versprechung allerly Assistenz, so dass ich mich in Tractaten eingelassen laut welchen mir sehr vortheilhafftige propositionen, Conditionen und Privilegien von den proprietaris absol: Carolina gethan und gegeben worden welches auch zu einem Schluss gekommen.—

Grad zur selbigen Zeit kammen über 10000 Seelen aus Teuschland in Engelland an, alle unter dem Nahmen Pfeltzer, darunter aber viel Schweitzer und aus anderen Provinzen Teuschlands zusammen gezogenes Volk, dieses verursachet den Königlichen Hof, sowohl als den Particulatoren viel bedenckens ja auch unsägliche Kösten, so dass man dieser Leuthen halben embarassiert, desswegen bald eine Edict herausgieng, womit männiglichem erlaubt, von diesen Leuthen zu nehmen und sie zu versorgen, und hatte man einen guten Theil in alle drey Königreich versendet, welche aber theils wegen ihrer trägheit, theils wegen Jalousie der armen Unterthanen dess Landes, aber nicht so wohl ankömmen wie vermeint, so hat man angefangen in America dieser Leuthen ein namhafte Zahl zu senden, und hat die Königin darzu grosse Summen ertheilen lassen.—

Bei solcher Conjunctur unterschiedliche persohnen, von hochem und mittelmässigen Standes, wurde denen mein Unterfangen bekannt, mir eingerathen ob solte ich so eine günstige Gelegenheit nicht perfallieren, mir hierbey gute Hofnung machten, dass, so ich eine zimliche Quantitet dieser Leuthen nemen wolte, die Königin mir nicht nur den Transport, sondern noch ein Considerablé Steur für diese Leuth gratificieren würde, welches auch geschächen, und ist die Summa beynachen auf 4000£. Sterlin kommen, Neben dem hatte die Königin der Königlichen Raht noch Land auf der *Coutomat* [2] rivier vergünstiget, so viel als wir gleichsam nur begehrten, neben starcken Recommandationen an H. Gobry [3] von Virginien, dieses alles und der H: Proprietarys von Carolina vortheilhaftigen Versprächung, haben diesem Unterfangen ein schönes absehen geben, und wahre nicht minder Hofnung zu einem so glücklichen Ausgang als der Anfang gut und vortheilhaftig schine.—Diese Colloney nun zu versorgen und zu versenden, habe eine unbeschreibliche Mühe genommen, 1. habe getrachet zu solchem Vorhaben, gesunde arbeitsame Leuth auszulesen, darunter von allerley Nothwenigen Handwerksleuthen. 2 Provision von allerley Nothwendigen Werkzeug und sachen. 3. Wie auch gnugsamme und gute Narrung. 4. Gute Schifen und Matrosen, auch über diss Volck gewüsse Ober und Unter-Directoren, alles in guter Ordnung zu halten. 5. Damit mir nicht einige Negligent oder unwüssenheit attribuirt, habe nichts vorgenommen, ohne Wüssen Raht und Instruction der Königlichen Comité. 6. Die Ober Directoren so wohl auf den Schifen als hernacher zu Land, wahren 3 persohnen von den Vornemsten aus Carolina selbst, so schon viel Jahr dorten sich aufgehalten, und denen alles bekannt der Enden, als da wurd der oberste Richter, Justice of beace. Der Oberste oder Generalfeltmesser Surveyor general und der oberst Einzieher Receyvers general welche grad zur selbigen Zeit, wegen ihren Geschäften zu Londen sich befunden, und von dem Königlichen Comite so wohl als von den Lords propr. Carolina ordiniert, ein exactes getreuwes und gutes aufsehen bey diesen Leuthen zu halten. Die Unteraufseher wahren über 12. von den ordentlichsten und ehrbahrsten Männern dess Volckes, dem Schein nach. 4—

Nachdem nun von den Königlichen so wohl den Lord proprietarys, mir und dem Volck alles ordentlich verglichen, geschlossen und ratificiert so hatte noch vor der Abreiss, die Königliche Comité ersucht, dass sie etliche ihrer Glider zu den Schifen senden wolten, als in der Schiffart Erfahrene die Examinierten, ob alles nach Nohtdurft wohl eingerichtet, wie dann auch dem Schifcapitain zuzusprechen, welches auch geschächen, und die relation in der Comite erstattet worden. Den Tag vor der Abfart, gieng ich mit denen zu Londen blieben Pfarher [5] nacher Gravesend allwo/: weilen die bernische nachkommende kleine Colloney neben etlichen H. Associerten erwartete:/ dess wegen nicht mitfahren könnte:/ meinen Abschied genommen, mit der nohtwendigen Vermahnung, da denn der teutsche Prediger H. Cesaar eine schöne Predig dem Volk gethan, sie hiemit alle dem Schutz des Allerhöchsten anbefählend, habe sie lassen absäglen, dennoch nicht ohne precation wegen den gefährlichen Kriegs Zeiten, wie dann von den Kronadmiral dem Grafen von Pembroke die Gunst erhalten, dass er dem Chef Noris vice Admiral befohlen, unsre Leuth oder Schif in das weite Meer oder gegen Portugal, mit seiner Escadre zu begleiten, diss geschach in dem Winter Im Januario da wegen den rauhen Winden und Stürmen diese Schif so getrieben worden, dass Sie erst nach 13. Wochen in Virginia angelanget, welches Sambt den gesaltznen Speissen, deren dise Leuth nicht gewohnt, und dass sie so eng eingethan, viel contribuieret dass viel krank worden, und auf dem Meer gestorben, andere da sie ans Land kommen, da sie ihr Glust nicht enthalten konnten, zu viel süssen Wassers getrunken und sich mit rauwen früchten überlästet, dass Sie an dem Fieber gestorben, so dass diese Colloney ehe sie sich recht gesetzt halb ausgestorben. ⁶ NB: Das Einte Schif so mit den besten Gütren angefüllt, und wo die vermöglichsten Leuth hatte das unglück in der Embousse des James Rivier im gesicht eines änglischen Kriegschifes so aber am Ancker, ⁷ von einem frechen frantzösichen Caper attaquiert und geplünderet zu werden. Hier ist das erste Unglück. da die übergebliebene Colloney sich in Virginien, wo sie sehr fründlich empfangen, erholt, haben sie sich _ _ _ bey 20. englischen Mill. nacher Carolinam verfügt, welches alles sambt den Gütern viel gekostet. ⁸ Da sie nun in der Grafschaft Albermarle auf einer Rivieren Chouan genannt bey einem Obristen N. Pollock genannt dess Rahts und der vermöglichsten in Nord Carolina, so hat er diese Leuth aber pro pecunia oder dess Werts versorget, mit Schifen dass sie durch den Sund in die Grafschaft Bath auf die rivir Neuss sind—geführet worden, mit etwas Lebens Mittlen nur zur eussersten Noth, und hat sie der generalfeldmesser da auf einen Spitz Landes, zwischen der Neuss und Trent Rivier gesetzt. Das orth gennant Chatouca woher nacher das stattliche Neuw Bern angefangen worden. Hier fangt an die andere fatalite oder traversen. dieser Generalfeldmesser mit Nahmen L _ _ _ der dann alsobald diese Leuth hätte auf ihr bestimmtes Land und ausgetheilte plantationen setzen sollen, um Zeit zu gewinnen und ihr Land alsobald auszureuten zu kommen: hat sie auf der Mittag Seiten dieser Spitzen Landes an der Trent Rivier gesetzt, grad am heissesten und ungesundesten ohrt anstatt dass gegen Nord auf der Neuss Rivier besser und gesunder gesässen wäre: Allein das that er um seines eigenen Nutzens willen, weilen diss sein Land wahre, damit es ihm zu Nutzen von diesen Leuthen ausgereutet würde: Da doch er eben das Land ⁹ sambt unsern und thür genug verkauft, ja ohne recht, dan darzu keinen Theil hatte, zudeme es noch mit Indianern besetz wahre, da er doch solches uns für frey verkauft, da haben die armen Leuth in grosser Noth sich aufhalten müssen, bis in Herbst, da ich ankommen, und hätten aus Mangel an gnugsamer provision bald ihre Kleider und was sie hatten für Nahrung den benachtbarten Einwohnern geben müssen;¹⁰ Der Jammer und Elend ward schier nüt zu beschreiben, dan ich da bey meiner ankunft sahe, meistends alle krank, ja in Extrimitet, und die gesunde gantz Deforciert; in was labirinth und gefahr, mich dazumahl befunden, ja meines Lebens nicht sicher weiss der liebe Gott.—

Lass jemand gedänken wie meine Bernerleuth, die sonsten mit mir eine glückliche Ueberfahrt gehabt, die Platz genug, wohl versehen, bey lustiger und guter Zeit, auch kein Einiche krank worden unterwex, in diss traurige Spihl gesehen, wo Krankheit, Desperation, und der Mangel am Eussersten, was aber dieses verursachet war theils die schlimme Conduite der ober-und unter-aufseher und ihre Untreuw, die vornembste Ursach aber dess gantzen Ohnheils, daraus meistens alle andern entstanden, und meiner und der Coloney Ruin, war die Vermessenheit grosse Untreuw und Lieblosigkeit dess Obristen Carys; welcher dazumahl auf Absterben dess alten Goub: Sich wider Recht und Billichkeit und der Lord Proprietarys in der Regierung eintringen wolte, ja wie vernommen gar sein Seckel machen, und mit H. Cary bezogenen Einkünfte sich darvon machen, und nach Madagascar begeben wollen, ein Ohrt da allerley Seeräuber sich aufhalten,—Dieser Colonel Cary da der neuwerwählte Goub. Hide obwohl der Königin Verwalter, ich und die obermelte 3 Directores sich anmelden wollen, und unsre Patent und gewahrsame vor dem Rath procedieren wollen, hat uns alle mit Hindansetzung der H. Proprietarys Befelchen frech abgewiesen.—So der Lord Prop. mir gethaner Versprechung, auf welche mich sondrest, und mein gantzes Unterfangen, beruht, in Nichts worden: Hiemit ich mit sambt der gantzen Coloney auf eine unversprechliche Manier dargesetzt; welches dann auf alles was widerwärtiges bis auf diese Stund widerfahren. So ist diser Cary entlich gar zum Rebell worden, und sich mit spendieren einen Anhang gemacht, dass H. Goub. Hide Es anfangs nicht wagen, darfür mit gewalt sich dess Gouver. Inpossess zu setzen: Um so viel desto minder,:/ weilen er eigendlich kein Special—Patenten in Handen:/ weilen der Goub: von Süd-Carolina denn Befelch hatte ihne zu Installieren, wahre desshalben schon Zeit gesetzt und an Rath um Carolina Nord geschrieben worden.—Das Unglück aber hat wollen, dass vermelte Goubernt: von Süd Carolina Obrist Tynte in dieser Zeit gestorben, welches diese Verwirrung verursachet, in diesem Interregno wurde mir aber nicht geholfen, und wahre in solcher grossen und dringender Noth, da wegen der entstandenen Rebellion, ein jeder für sich auch sorgende, und das seine behielte die Question ob ich mein Leben risquieren und diese gantze Colloney im Stich, ja gar sie vor Hunger verrecken lassen solte, oder ob ich mich in Schulden stecken solte, diese arme Leuth in solcher Extremitet zu retten, wie einem Christen [11] und gut Gemuth wär da nicht zu hesitiren, weil dazumahl in gantz America meine ankunft erschallet, und ich in grossem Credit wahre, so schickte alsobald in Pensilvania für mähl, da zu allem Glück schon hier Anstalt gethan gegen Virginien, und sonsten hin und her in der Prozvintz für die nothwendigen Lebensmittel:/ welches entlich mit ausertheilten Wexelbriefen:/ doch langsam genug erfolget: Indessen giengen die unsre und der armen Leuthen Gütter und Wahren auf, für das Nothwendigste/: so wir theur von den benachtbarten Einwohnern zuwegen gebracht.—Indessen liess ich das Land ausmessen, und jeder famillie Ihren bezirk Landes geben, damit sie ausreuten, ihre Hütten bauwen, und Ihr Erdrich zum pflantzen und säyen ausrüsten könnten: So langte auch mit grossen Kosten und Mühj provision, an Korn, Saltz, Schwein Fett anstatt butter, und gesaltzen Fleisch, Item, Raum-und andere Erdgewächs an. Allein mit dem Vich gieng es schwär zu, die Leuth wolten es nicht holen, wo ich es Ihnen anzeigte, und könnte ich es Ihnen auch nicht grad vor die Thüre stellen, doch accommodierte man sich nach und nach, dass diese Leuth innert 18 Monathen so wohl gesetzt und ihre Sach so wohl angestellt dass sie in dieser kurtzen Zeit mehr avanciert als englische Einwohner in 4. jahren, nur Eines, als zum Exempel da in der gantzen provintz nur eine schelchte Wasser Mühl, die da bey Mittlen haben Hand Mühlen, die armen stossen ihr Korn in einem stück in einer holen Eich; und sieben das Reinste durch ein Körblein, welches viel Zeit wegnimbt, hingegen hatten unsre Leuth bequeme Wasser Bächlin aufgesucht, und darbey nach gelegenheit und sterck dess Wassers Lauf, ordentliche Stampfe gemacht, worby das Korn gemahlt, und der gute Hausvatter Zeit gewunnen andere Werk zu thun. Ich aber hatte schon eine Mühli und Sägi an einem sehr bequemen Orth zu bauwen angefangen, aber was geschach, da wir Alle verhofen nacher grosser Mühi und Sorgen die Früchte unsrer Arbeit zu geniessen, ohngeacht aller entstandener Widerwertigkeit, und Schönes ansehen zu einem guten Etablissement, kame der bewerte Sturm des unglücks durch die wilden Indianer von etlichen Jalousen und rachgierigen Rebellen dess Carys anhang geblasen, welcher alles über den Haufen geworfen, die Ergangenheit dieser Tragedie ist in einer sonderbahren Relation hiermit unnöthig hiervon zu melden, weilen aber aus dess Obrist Carys verwegner unfründlicher und widerspenstigen procedur alles Unheil so über die provintz mich und die Colloney kommend, entstanden, so wird eben nicht aus dem weg sein, etwas mehreres von diesen Verwirrungen zu melden und zu continuieren, was weiters nach dess Goubern: Tynte tödlichen Hinscheid vergangen.—So bald an die Grentzen [12] Colloney aus Virginia angelangt, und mich in Erwartung einer bequemen Ruhe, für mich und meine Leuth, im ersten Dorf aufhaltend, kame eine Truppen der Vornemsten Quaquers daher, wie dan deren viel der Enden, und sie auch der vermöglichsten persuasiven gründen vorgaben, es gebührte mir als Landgrafen, als der allezeit in einem Interregno, und auch sonsten in absens dess Goub: presidiert: und nach dem Goub: den ersten Rang hat; Ich [13] aber bedankte mich höflich der Ehren, respondieren wir, dass H: Goub: Hide würklich in Virginien und ich einer der Zeugen seye, der da gesehen, wie dass er von den Lord prop: seye zum Goub: erwehlt worden. Ihm auch in Ihrer Rathstuben zu Londen congratuliert, zu dem seye er der Königin anverwanter, und auch von Ihr Königl. Majestet approbiert worden, [14] und obwohlen ermelter H. keine patenten dermahlen in Handen, würde alsbald eine erfolgen.— Solte also die Provintz kein Bedenken machen Ihm in einen weg zu Ihrem Goubern. anzunehmen, um so viel desto eher weil doch H. Goub. Tynte dem Rath von Carolina Solches notificiert. dieses gefiel Ihnen aber nicht [15] und replicierte mir, auf welches aber nicht refutirt, nachdeme sie mit mir gethan, nahmen Sie gantz höflich von mir Abscheid und giengen. Bald hernach mit meinen Leuthen weiter in die Provintz kam, und langte bey Obrist Pollock in Chouan an, bey welchem alsobald Rath gehalten worden, von denen so für den Goub. Hiden geneigt, und wurde ich vast pressiert selbigem beyzuwohnen, welches eben in einer so gefährlichen und delicaten sach nicht gangen thäte: So wurde mir alsobald ein plan oder bericht der Situation der Sachen gegeben, und kann ich liecht observieren, dass wegen meines Carracters so wohl als der Quantitet Volcks, sie viel auf mich sehen, in deme die gewicht geben könnte, welcher partey ich zuviele, gieng also meine Meinung dahin, dass ich ein kräftig Schreiben wolte an Obrist Cary abgehen lassen, ihme eint und andres wohl representieren, und auch entlich Ihme dreuwen, wo er sich nicht zur gebühr verstehen wolte, ich mich mit den meinigen mit allen Kräften zu H. Goub. Hide stossen wollte, diss erweckte Ihme gedanken, andere Mensuren zu nehmen.—Doch gabe er mir eine gantz stoltze und schamhafte antwort. Es schine aber bald hernach ihn zu gereuwen, und arbeiten wir unter der Hand, dass endlich ein Verglich gemacht worden, und verschrieben, nämlich dass er Obrist Cary sambt seinem Anhang sich wohl dahin verstehen wolte H. Goub. Hide zu einem President, dess Rahts biss von den Proprietarys neuwe ordre einlangte, aber nicht zum Goub: zu nehmen. Ich verfügte mich indessen eilends nach Neu Bern, von wannen mir die Pfältzer geschrieben, so wegen grossem Mangel an Victualien in eusserster Extremität währen, [16] da dann grad zur fürsorg bey Collonel Pollock etwas provision verschaffen, war aber bald viel vorhanden, fur eine solche, [17] darauf hin ward H. Goub. Hide und kame er aus Virginien in Carolinam, setzte sich ohnweit von dem Obrist Pollock in _ _ _ Duckenfields Plantation bey Salomon Creek, als wo er ein ziemlich fein Losament bekame, darumb der Obrist Cary beförchtete seinen streich wurde so ihme nicht angehen, was er im sinn hatte, worvon hier oben gemelt, so hatte er subtiler weis, getrachtet den Verglich in seine Hand zu bekommen, da er dann seinen Nahmen oder Unterschrift wohl gewusst wegzunehmen, heirauf fing er seine erste Partey widerum zu nemmen, einiche sich vermittels spendierens da er alles schlimme Gesind mit Rum oder Prantwein an seine Seite Gebracht, einen sehr starken anhang, entstunde also hieraus ein öffendliche rebellion wider Geub: Hide, indessen ward der Mann so listig, und abgeschmitzt, dass er mich zu entschläfen nacher Neuw

Bern kam unterm Pretext einer Visite, wo ich ihn zwar regalierte, mit dem wenigen, so damals vorhanden, allein da wir nach der Mahlzeit[18] in Discours gerathen, über seine ungereimbte Proceduren so wohl gegen H. Goub. Hide, als mich, ja dess ungehorsams gegen seine Oberkeit den Lord Prop: ihne scharf zusprechend, ja mit dreuwen zu verstehen geben, dass ich solche Mensuren nehmen werde, dass es ihn gereuwen dörfte. So hat er in beysein 4 seiner fründ, die er mitgebracht, mir versprochen, an Rechnung dessen, was mir von den Lord, Prop: verordnet innert 3 Wochen an Getreyd und ander Victualien. item etwas an Vich, für 500£. Wehrts zu senden, oder Zedlen dafür. H. Goub: Hide betreffend lasst er es in Statuquo. so nahme er abscheid, diss aber wahre nur mich zu verblenden, welches auch war, dann ich ihme ins gesicht gesagt, ich förchte die werk werden den worten nicht respondieren. Dieses Colonel Carys Reys wahre nicht vergebens, dan er zu seinem Zweck gelangt, weilen durch anstiftung etlicher englischer oder carolinisch H:—Einwohner, und nechstgelegen Plantationen er meine Leuthe so abgeschreckt, dass keiner von Haus oder aus der Colloney sich wagen dörfte, dan es wahre Ihnen gedreut, dass so sie nicht neutral bleiben, sie von englischen und Indianern überfallen, und zu Grund gerichtet werden.—Nicht lang hernach schickte mir H. Goub: Hide expressen, mit einem ganzen Packet patenten, Eine für mich, dass mich zum Obrist gemacht, über den Distrikt Baitz Counti und mir überlass die unter oficiers zu bestellen, ihre Nahmen in albo lassend, mich ernstlich ersucht, ihme wider die Rebellen an die Hand zugehen,: worauf geantwortet ihme bezeugend wie leid es mir wäre, dass seinen verlangen noch nicht respondieren könnte, mit bericht was Colonel Cary hier vermerkt, dass meine Leuth gar nicht disponiert einicher partey zuzufallen, sonder resolviert neutral zu bleiben, diss gefiel H. Goub: nicht gar wohl, und langte bald ein scharferer befelch ein, Ihm fahl aber nichts erheb: mich hinüber, welches drey guter Tagreisen von Neuw Bern zu begeben, dem Rath beyzuwohnen, welches ich gethan, zwar schier in forcht, weilen ich auch bedreuwet worden.[19] Da ich nun bey H. Goub: angelangt, so wahren wir im Raht stark beschäftiget, wie sich gegen diesen Cary anhang in Sicherheit zu stellen, ordoniert, allsobald eine Comp. zusammengelesener Mannschaft uns zu bewahren und sehen weiter wie etwan eint oder andere gemühter zu zwingen, es kame auch grad in dieser Zeit an ein torboulenter Gesell von London[20] welcher mit einem Schif voll Wahren einem quaker so auch ein glied der prop: zugehörend, dieser Enden Negocieren wolte, wahre alsobald von widriger parthey gewunnen, welches ihnen einen starken Mut mieche. Indeme er wohl mit geschoss bulver und bley versehen, dieser hatte H: Goub: vast injouriert und verschreit auch vorgeben, er hätte von

den Lord prop: andere Ordres aber nit zu gunsten Eduard Hides,
welches grosse Zweifel und Verrwirrung macht und uns besser Spiel [21]
mieht; dieser hatte mir insbesonders auch grossen Schaden gethan,
indem er einen Wexel von 100£. Sterling [22] mir ungültig miech, sagend
er hätte ordre solchen zu b'stellen. Da doch das gelt Hanson und
Comp., meinem Correspondent zu Londen, schon erlegt worden, könnte
hiermit in meiner grossen Noth nichts darvon bekommen: Stelten also
dieser Colonel Cary, R. Roch und ein quaquer Em. Low der sich
wider den fürnemsten articul seiner eigenen Religion oder sect zu
einem Obrist ereignet und kame wohl profiantiert in einer nacht wo
wir logiert in Obrist Pollocks Haus, und da wir meistens Raht hielten
in einem wohl bewehrt und mit stucken versehehen Briquantin vor
die Landung,[23] wir stelten uns auch bestmöglichst in Postour, und
hatten nur 2. stück und nicht mehr bey uns als etwan 60 bewährter
Männer, gegen Morgen liessen die rebellen aus dem Briquantin ein
paar stück kugeln fliegen, gegen dem Haus wo wir in wahren, wahre
aber zu hoch geschossen, striche bloss über die First, so dass es kein
Schaden hatte, hierauf liessen wir unsere Stück auch ab, gegen dem
Briquantin, that auch kein Schaden. So fiengen die Rebellen in 2
kleinen Barquen von ihrer bewehrten besten Mannschaft gegen das
Land zu senden, da wir das in Acht nahmen, ordonierten wir, unsere
Mannschaft gegen der Lente [24] zu gegenwehr, worunter meine Knecht
in einer gelben Liverey welches unser gegenpart nicht wenig er-
schrecket, verursachet in deme sie vermeinten meine gantze Colloney
halte sich da im Busch, zugleich liessen wir auch unser Stück nochmahlen los, da das einte den Mastbaum nur etwas wenigs geschärft
dieses zusamen thate einen solchen guten Effeckt dass die Barquen
zurückkehrten, und sobald sie wiederum in das Schif gestigen, zogen sie
die Segel auf, und machten sich fort.—Darauf ordinerten wir die
resolviertesten Männer ihn einer Chaloupen ihnen nachzujagen, sie
könnten aber sie nicht erreichen, allein da sie den Sond hinunter gefahren, thate das Briquantin an einem bequemen ohrt anlenden, und
mieche sich durch einen Wald, die Meisten und Vornemsten darvon,
so gewonne der kleine Haufen den grössern, und brachte die Chaloupe das Briquantin sambt etwas provision und den Stücken hinauf,
dieses zertheilte die widrige parthey, und sterckte unsere, so dass wir
hierauf gut funden, ausser den Redlisführern den übrigen eine general
pardon anzukünden, da sich ein jeder, der sich zum Gouver: bequemen
und ergeben wolte, unterschrieben, worauf dann ein parlament versammlung ausgeschrieben worden, bey welchem dann die Sachen
dieser Aufrührer betreffend, verhandlet wurden. Die besten Aufrührer, so man erdappen konnte, wurden in Verhaft gezogen, die aber
ihren Fehler erbeuten (bereuten); und nur durch Aufweisung de-

bochiert, denen wurde die amnistie: accordiert, bey diesem Handel²⁵ musst ich meistens procedieren, welches micht nicht accommodiert, aus forcht mir find zu machen, nach deme nun eint und anders so gut möglich veranstaltet, H: Goub: Hide und mich angenommen und erkennt, ging ein jeder nacher Haus, der Hofnung es würde sich alles stillen, diese Stille währte nicht lang, die Auctors des Aufruhr 3 recoligierten sich, und der obgemelte Roch setzte sich in eine Insul wohl mit Proviant, g'schoss und Munition versehen, und wiglete auf was er könnte, diesen trachtete man zwar aus seinem Nest zu treiben, allein es ward nichts zu schafen, dieses Feur der Conjurierten Verschworenen gienge nach und nach wider umb an, und vermehrte sich, dass das letste bald erger wurd, als das erste, bey so bewanten Dingen funde man das beste, sich umb andere Hilf zu bewerben, wurde ich also zu H: Alexander Spotswood Goub: in Virginien gesandt, mit 2 Rahtsglidern die man mir zugab, um ihne für assistenz zu ersuchen.²⁶ Santen aber zuvor per expressen ein Schreiben an H: Goub: Spotwood, welches er ohnedas sein Volck auf den Grentzen zu mustren hatte, vernamsete mir einen Tag in einem Dorf, so zwischen beyden Provintzen wahre, so Verreisete ich zu wasser, grad in dem abgenommen Brigantin, weilen zu Land nicht gar sicher, zudeme wir auch provision aus der Nachtbahrschaft abholen wolte, da wir etliche stund gefahren, erhub sich ein solcher Widerwind, dass wir zurück getrieben wurden, so nahmen wir eine Canou ein kleines enges Schiflein aus einem Stück eines ausgehölten Baums gemacht, und fuhren fort da sich der Wind umb etwas gestillet, kamen aber zu spaad die Mustrung wahre schon vorbey, allein H: Goub: von Virginien²⁷ besser berichtet dass wann ich ankäme ihme allsobald einen expressen gesendt wurde. So schrieb ich einen höflichen Brief, an ermelten H:—welcher den Nächsten Tag mit seinem Secretario und 2. H: sich einfanden, an bestimmtem Ohrt wo dann Conferentz gehalten wurde, und H. Goub: mich überaus fründl: empfangen, diss geschäft wahre wichtiger als ich vermeinte, nach übergebenem Credidif fing ich mein proposition an, es wurde mir aber grad ein starcker Einwurf gethan, nämlich dass die Virginischen ganz nicht geneigt währen, wider die benachtbarten Brüder zu streiten, dene sie alle gleiche der Königin Unterthanen und sie eben der Casus nicht so gar just Einmahl hat H. Goub: Hide keine patenten, so müssten wir um ander experienten,²⁸ und hatte mir H. Goub: Spotswood weilen er das erste mahl dass er mich gesehen, an welchem auch wegen den Virginischen Sachen, von der Königin selbsten Recommandiert wahre, etwas angenemeres erweisen, funden entlich er solte H. Goub: Hide, mir und der provintz so viel zugefallen thun, und zur See uns ein Kriegschif senden mit der gewohnten Soldatesca welche aus der Königin Bedienten in Ihren Rahtskleidern, neben dem dass sie gute Solldaten, viel auswürken wurden, diss wurde accordiert und nahmen mein fründl: Abscheid von einander, mit was expressiones er mich zu ihme invitiert, und was für Dienst und Erbieten, könnte ich nicht gnugsam erzeigen, ich machte mich gantz freudig nacher Haus, auf eine so glückliche Negociation, da ich meine relation erstattet, wurde mit einem general aplausu dess ganzem Volcks empfangen, und thate dis meinen Credit nicht wenig vermehren: Bald hernach langte ein brafer Captain mit seinen tapfern Marens an, nachdeme er seinen gruss abgelegt, und H: Goub: Spotwood Brief übergeben, so thaten wir ihne ersuchen, dass er vor der Versammlung wolte seine Commission darlegen, und so kreftig als möglich dem Landvolck zusprechen, mit bedeuten dass im fahl die Aufrührer nicht sich gebührend einstellen wollten, man mit ihnen auf das scherfste procedieren würde.—Auf dieses dörfte sich Niemand mehr rühren, und miechen sich die autors des aufruhrs in geheim aus der provintz und dörften sich um so viel minder bleiben lassen, weillen von Londen Briefen angelangt, mit bericht, wie dass die Lords propriet: H. Eduard Hide zum Goub: von Nord Carolina erwehlt, und seye desshalben die patenten durch eine vertraute persohn versendt, der oftgemelte Colonel Cary ist neben andren seiner mithaften in Virginien arrestiert, und in einem Schif wohl verwahrt nacher Londen versendt worden, welchem da der process gemacht worden, die Sach hatte zu Londen viel Wesens gemacht,: Allein dieser Cary wahre in seinem schlimmen Handel noch so glückhaftig, dass sich seiner 2 Milord so annahmen, die ihme sein Leben errettet, ist hiemit auf Bürgschaft losgelassen worden umb sich zu deffendieren; ihme der Richter in Carolina angewiessen worden: bleibt also die Sach noch diese Stund da hangen.²⁹

Die Verwierung hatte nicht wenig zum einfahl der wilden Indianer contribuiert, in dem Etliche der Meutinierer H: Goub: Hide so verhasst gemacht bey den Indianern, dass sie ihne für ihren find angesehen, soweit, dass ich von den Wilden gefangen worden, vermeint ich währe der Goub: Zimlich hart tractiert worden, bis durch einen Indianer der englisch reden könnte, und den ich gekannt sagen lassen, dass ich nicht Goub: Hide währe, worauf sie alsobald gelinder mit mir verfahren.—Da nun dieses auch vorbey, machte ich mich widerumb nach Neuw Bern zu meinen Leuthen, es hatte aber bald hernach H: Goub: Hide seine patenten empfangen, so liesse er widerumb eine Generalversammlung ausschreiben, damit er sich einpresentieren könnte, worbey ich mich auch befunden, welches um so viel lieber gethan, weilen dabey Gelegenheit suchte bey dem Neuwen H. Goub: zuerwerben, was bey Colonel: Cary nicht könnte, bey welchem H. Goub: Hide wohl allen guten Willen verspürte, aber da ich auf die realitäten drung, so wahren sehr wenig vorhanden, welches von selbsten übel manglete: hielte hiernach einständig bey dem Parlament an, dass weilen auf Conto der Lord prop: nicht erhalten könnte, welches doch das fondament meiner Entreprise ich nun fast mit meinem Volck dargesetzt, und wir so nicht bestehen könnten, es auch eine lange Zeit erfordert, bis aus Europa berichtet wir indessen nicht von Luft leben könnten, so die provintzen uns auf gleiche Conditiones wie wir es mit dem Lord prop: hatten, assistieren solten, nämlich auf Credit, auf 2 oder 3 Jahr mit denen nothwendigen victualien, und besonders mit Vich, uns zu versehen, dessen aber Sous pretense dieser einheimische Krieg habe sie in die Unvermöglichkeit das zu thun gesetzt, mich abgewiesen, hierauf mieche mich gantz traurig nacher Haus, meine sachen so gut als möglich anstellend, wie hier vor zu sehen. [30]

FOLGET JETZUND DER INDIANISCHE KRIEG.

Was diesen Indianischen Krieg verursachet, sind erstlich die Verlümdungen und Anstiftungen etlicher Meutinier H. Goub: Hide 2./ Allso auch wider mich indeme sie die Wilden bredt ich seye kommen ihr Land zu nemen, und hiemit werden die Indianer sich zurück gegen die Bergen machen müssen, diss hat ich ihnen ausgeret, und wahre es bewiesen, durch meine gegen sie erwiesene fründlichkeit, wie auch durch die Bezahlung dess Landes, wo ich mich anfangs gesetzt, namlich darvon das Stätlein Neu Bern angefangen: ohngeachtet der Verkäufer mir es frey hatte übergeben sollen, Item hab ich auch Frieden mit selbigen indianischen Einwohnern gemacht, so dass sie mit mir gantz zufrieden. 3./Wahre es die grosse Sorglosigkeit der Coloney. [31] 4./Das harte Tractament etlicher unwirschen und rauhen englischen Einwohner, die sie betrogen in der Handlung, selbe nicht um ihre plantationes lassen jagen, unter dem pretext ihnen ihr geschoss, Munition Ihre Beltzen oder Hüet weggenommen, ja gar ein Indianer zu Tod geschlagen, welches sie am meisten und mit Grund allarmierte. Ihren Anschlag hielten die Indianer sehr geheim, und wahre es eben darum zu thun, dass sie sich berathschlagen wolten, in einer angestelten Versammlung, zu der Zeit, da ich gefangen wurde, und da ich ungefähr die rivier hinauf fahrte vermeinte ich um so viel Sicherer zu seyn, indem erst 10 oder 14 Tag zuvor in dem Wald, da ich von Land Messen kame, verrirret und eben grad da mich die Nacht übernahm, unter die Indianer gefallen, so zuvor bey meiner ankunft in Chatalognien jetzund Neuw Bern gessessen, und sich nun an diss ort gesetzt, welche mich sehr fründlich empfangen, und am Morgen bis auf den rechten Weg begleitet, 2 Indianer mitgaben so mit mir bis nacher Haus giengen, welchen dann zur Dankbarkeit, etwas geben, und für den König Rum oder Prantenwein geschickt; Eben dieser König da es um mein Leben zu thun war, hatte nicht wenig zu meiner

Rettung nebst des aller höchsten beystand Contribuiert; wie ich nun von den Indianern gefangen, zum Tod verurtheilt und wunderlich errettet worden, was bey den Indianern vorgangen, entlichen wie nacher Haus kommen und zu Neuw Bern widerumb angelangt, ist ausser meiner an H. Goub: Hide versandten relation zu ersehen. Zu End eben dieser relation hatte angefangen, zu melden was alsobald, meiner zurückkunft mir noch widriges und vertriessliches widerfahren so dass scheint meines unglücks kein End zu seyn, weilen aber das zukönftige nicht vorsehen könnte, so will ich umb so kurz als möglich, was weiters vorgangen bis zu meiner europaischen Ab- und Heimreis melden. Erstlich wie dieser Indianische Krieg fortgesetzt und ein End genommen: 2./Was für Motifa dass die Coloney verlassen, und mich in Europa ja gar widerumb nacher Bern begeben.—Was nach meiner Zurückkunft mir unter den Christen widerfahren, wahre beynach so aus gefährlicher und vertriesslicher, als ich unter den Heyden wäre; vor dem heidnischen Tribunal hatte ich meine offendliche Kläger, alles geschache in guter Ordnung, nichts hinderrücks und im Verborgenen, noch auf eine rebellische aufrührische Manier, aber da ich nacher Haus kame, vermeinet unter fründen und Christen zu seyn, und ein wenig zu ruhen, ward es erger.—

Da wahren etliche rauwe Jalousi unwirsche planter, oder Einwohner, weilen nicht alsobald in ihre Meinung treten wolten, einen Indianer zu töten, oder ihrer Discretion zu liefern, deme doch sicher Gleit versprochen, weilen er kommen meine ratzion abzuholen, und mit den Indianern zu streiten nicht thunlich erachtende, er die 15 gefangene Pfeltzer herausgeben, und geliefert, denen noch Provision an Lebens Mitteln noch an Munition noch Volck gnug, zu dem dass der halbe theil Pfältzer in meiner absentz mein Quartier verlassen, so klagten mich dieser Gattung böser Christen erger als die Heyden, nahmen geheime Information wider mich, da wahre viel redens und treuwens nicht minder als müsste ich gehenkt werden. So solte ich von einem Heydnischen Tribunal nun vor einen christlichen Richter stuhl, ja erger als der heynischen, so es etlicher gottloser Gesellen willen nachgehen solte, erscheinen: zu welchem nicht wenig contribuiert, ein pfältzischer Huf Schmied, der sich rechen wolt, weilen ihme wegen erschrecklichen excrationen ungehorsames stählen, und gräuwlichen treuwung gestraft,[32] und das hat er auf eine sehr verrätherische weis gethan, gienge alsobald hinüber zu den Indianern, bey welchen er mich sehr suspect mieche, als gulte meine Versprechung nichts, betrüge sie, indeme anstatt Frieden und Neutralität mit ihnen zu halten gantz auf Ihrer der engl: Seiten währe, sie mit gewehren und Krieg provision versehend:[33] da ich aber seine Verätherey erfahren, und desshalben ihne abstrafen wollen, hatte er darvon Wind bekommen, und sich hinüber

zu dem William Brice einem gemeinen mann, so aber wegen seiner
Frechheit zum Haubmann erwehlt worden, und mir vast zuwider
wahre, verfügt. allwo eine Garnison zusammengelesener Gesellen und
der abtrünigen Pfelzer sein eigen Haus zubewahren, da hat obgemelter
Huf Schmied gleiches von mir, wie zuvor bey den India: gesagt, und
noch viel mehr, so dass ich für einen Verräther passierte, ward alsbald
eine Liste von etlich 20 Artikeln aufgeschrieben, deren nicht ein
Puncten wahr, hab, da dieses vernommen, schrieb ich dennoch gantz
ohnerschrocken, ich ein gutes Gewissen hätte, bey dem H. Goub: von
Virginia und Carolina zu, Sie umständlich informierend, alles dessen
so ich zugetragen, welche meine Conduite abrobiert, und alle andre
Persohnen von verstand und vernuft.—

Hierbey hat sich zugetragen, dass weilen dess Schmieden als Criminalen und ausgewichenen der da mir noch vast in Depitis ich seine
Sachen inventorisieren und in Verwahrung thun lassen, dieser obermelte H: Brice [34] den Schmied vast _ _ _ und die verwahrten Sachen
heraus haben wolte, trachtete solches mit gewalt vorzunehmen, neben
dem, dass er gerne mich als der Verrätherey schuldig, zu H: Goub:
Hide g'fangen bringen wolte, so hielte er in geheim Raht, mit den
Vornemsten seiner Rott, so wahre dieses Conclusum dass wann ich
mich weigern wolte, dieses Schmieds Sachen herauszugeben, pretextierend, sie brauchten solche zur Devension. [35] dess Lutz, sie es mit
gewalt thun wolten, undweilen ohne Zweifel mich speren werde alsdann
sie sich meiner persohn bemeistern, und mich so H: Goub: zu bringen.
Es wahre aber ohngefähr ein kleiner Pfeltzer Knab in dem Zimmer
welcher englisch verstund, dessen nicht in acht genohmmen, dieser solches hörend, wich so still er könnte aus dem Gemach, zeigte es seiner
Mutter an, alls noch Eine von meinen angehörigen, welche alsbald
sich in das Schiflein miech, und zu mir hinüberfuhre,: da sie mir diese
Conspiration erzellend, so liess ich alsbald auf der Trummel schlagen,
verschloss die Thor und stelte meine Leuth in guter Postur. Könnte
kaum fertig werden, so kame Brice mit 30 oder 40 benachtbahrten
Männern, darunter grad der gottlose Schmied, und wohl 20 der abtrünnigen Pfeltzer, nicht wüssend dass ich der sachen berichtet, vermeinten grad in den Hof [36] zu gehen, und mich übernehmend, funden
aber alles in solcher postur dessen sie nicht erwarten, da sie die unsrigen befragt, was das sein solle, gab der Corporal zur Antwort, man
sey auf guter Huet wegen den wilden Indianern und wilden Christen,
ward replicirt ob man sie dann für find hielte, widerumb dubliciert
dass fründe nicht auf solche Manier ihre benachbarten zu Visiten
pflegten, schiene als wann sie unsre find, insbesondere da solche Verräther und Abtrünnige doch so Corporal Brice sambt noch einem
herein wollen, glaubte diss wurde nicht versagt, da diss mir angezeigt,

liess ich sie unter guter Wacht hinein, so nun dieser Brice meiner procedur sich beschwärt, gabe zur Antwort mir wäre sein schöner Dessin wohl bekannt, würde aber an gebührendem Ohrt sein unverschandtes und verwegenes procedieren wüssen anzubringen, ob das die Manier gegen seine Vorgesetzten so zu Meutinieren ich als Statthalter des Ober Hauses, Landesgraf und Comandant dieses District wäre im rechten ihne gefangen senden und wäre auch geschächen [37] so ich diesers falschen desieren Gesellen mit kurzem Bescheid und starker Betreuwung wider hinaus sich für das nächste parlament cediren.—was weiters für Insolentien auf seiten dieses Cap: und abtrünnigen Pfälzern gegen mich und die meinigen verübt, zu weitläufig und verdriesslich habe von kürze wegen für nichts mehr melden wollen, doch noch etwas wenix im fürgang.—

Ist zu wissen dass die hierunden unterzeichnete Convention mit den Indianern eingangen, da ich noch in Banden, und mein Leben zu fristen, so dass eben so gar nicht wäre verobligiert worden zu halten, demnach weilen mit der meinung Quod Hereticis non Habenda Fides, wahre resolviert so viel zu halten als Lauth gewissens und Pflicht, mit deren ich der Cron Engelland zugethan, ich wohl thun konnte und hätte man mich nachen lassen, wäre es dem gantzen Land wohl kommen, und währe viel Mord und Unglück vermitten worden.—

Es wahre aber dieser Capitain Brice sambt seinem Anhang so erhitzet, dass ohne die Vernunft zu raht zu ziechen ihrer blinden passion nach ohne einich Mensur zu nemen noch auf die kleine Zahl Volck, noch die wenige provision an Krieg und Lebens-Mittlen noch auf die Gefahr der armen gefangenen Weib und Kinder, reflectierend, den proponierten Stillstand recusiert, und alsbald findlich agiert, also durch sein unverständiges Caprice, die gantze provintz in gefahr gesetzt, und meine Mensuren alle unterbrochen.—Und hätte man mich machen lassen so hätte erstlich durch diesen stillstand Zeit gewunnen, dass die ganze provinz und ich uns in guter postur setzen können, und wir innert dieser Zeit, mit Volck, Krieg and Lebens-Mittlen versehen. 2./ wahre ich schon würklich an der Arbeit, in währned diesem Stillstand die armen gefangenen Weib und Kinder zu erretten, dann den Indianern meine rention nicht ausrichten wolte, sie hatten mir dann die gefangenen übergeben, solches wahre mit grosser gefahr und Mühj in der ersten Converenz veraccordiert, N. B: hat sich wohl erwiesen, wie viel daran gelegen, nachwerts in der Historj dess Indianisch Kriegs gemelt, wie dieser gefangener Holtzmann die Indianer menagieren müssen, so sonsten im Ersten mahl man ihnen den garaus machen können. Nun weilen ich am besten mit den Indianern an diesem guten Werk, und 3./ auch, durch meiner vorgegebenen Neutralität und, Verzögerung Zeit gewinnen wolte, dass was so wohl die englischen, als

Carolinischen und Coloney ins besonders noch in Ihren plantationen und Häusern verlassen und vergraben, wiederumb abholen, wie auch in den Wäldern, so viel von Ihrem Vich, als möglich aufangen könnten, so kame diese Bricésche Rott, wilder und unvernünftiger als die Indianer und verderbten mir meine gantze Handlung, durch eine unbekannte attaque, die ganze übelzellung, diese hiervor gemelte Verrätherey des Schmieden, und diese Action nahme den Indianern alles vertrauwen von mir, so dass auf das hin, gegen meine Colonisten sie auch findlich agierten; da bis daher Ihrer Häusern und sachen verschonet, namlich nach gemachter Convention, allein nach diesem unzeitigen procedieren der Caroliner, sind die Indianer gefahren, alles zu verderben, und müssten meiner armen Leuth Heuser, ungeacht die Thür mit einem Zeichen [38] gezeichnet verbrandt werden,: das übrige an Hausgeräth obwohlen verborgen und vergraben aufgesucht, weggenommen und das Vich in den Weldern niedergeschossen, von dannen haben die Indianer hin und her in der provintz, insbesonders in Neuw Trent und pamtego Rivier eine Plantation nach der andern belägeret, geblünderet, gemort und sehr viel übels gethan.—Und welches die Indianer zu mehreren equotet veranlasset, ware des Bricen hartes procedieren, dass er etliche Indianer von der Bay Rivier [39] bekommen, ist ihr Chef der König erschröcklich tractiert worden, ja bey einem grossen feur gleichsam gebraten, und mit allerley unchristlicher Marter geblagt, und so getödet worden,: welches die Indianer so verbittret, dass sich nicht zu verwundern, wann sie die Christen auch hart tractierten, was hierin am meisten verdrossen, war dass ein abtrünniger pfeltzer an diesem Marteren das meiste gethan, und Ein wohlgefallen daran hatte, eben dieser ward der autor der abtrünnigen pfeltzeren. Es waren zwar von des Bricen anhang, Verwegene und behertze Leuth aber gar unbedacht, so die übrigen Caroliner bessere Conduiten und nicht so zaghaft, wer man den Indianern ehr Meister worden, und wäre nicht so übel gangen.—

Weilen nur mir vast angelegen, Meine Conduite zu justificieren und der Bricésch Rott Gottlos und Verwegenes Verfahren vorzustellen, so wann die grosse general Versamlung [40] gehalten, gienge hinein und fragte, wo diese falsche Klägten wahren, und solte man mir solche Verlümder vor Augen stellen, Copeyen der Klägten Communicieren damit mich gebührend Verantworten und justificieren könne, dörfte sich niemand gegen mich stellen, und wolte die Klagpunkten niemand hier vorgeben, so ward dessen ein End. Indessen hat ich viel Vertruss, und ward in grosser gefahr, und litte inzwischen nicht wenig mein Ehr und reputation, begehrte Satisfaction, weilen die Kläger und Verlümder mir wohlbekannt, miech sie auch namhaft, die autoren aber erschienen nicht, und könnte ich bey solcher Confusen Regierung und

Indianischen Krieg keine Satisfaction bekommen, der H: Goub: und Oberhaus welches von 7. Rähten und represententen der Lord: prop: Zweyen Landgrafen, Etlichen Obristen, und dem Secretario bestund; miechen zwar ihre Entschuldigungen und ein Comp: hierüber, musste darmit zufrieden seyn, über diese Matery hatte viele Memorialia und Briefen, H: Goub: versendt, worin diese Verdriessliche Historie und Proceduren weitläufig zu ersehen, sonderlich im Register meiner Brief, von A. 1711. u. 1712. auch so alles so mir widerwertiges und Vertriessliches in Carolina und Virginien widerfahren, Erzellen solte, wurde es ein gross Buch abgeben;—/./Gleich wie hier oben nur etweliche Ursachen dess Indianischen Kriegs vermeldet, so hat zu dieser Indianischer Verwegenheit und frechen Verfahren, nicht wenig Contribuiert der Caroliner sorglosigkeit, indeme sie Ihnen zu vast getrauwet, zu ihrer Sicherheit in der ganzen provintz nur nicht ein ohrt befestiget, dahin man sich hätte retirieren können; auch im fahl Einicher Corruption oder findthätigkeit gar keine anstalten noch viel minder die Benöhtigte Krieg und Lebens-Mittlen oder Provision gemacht, so weit dass mit diesen Unruhen ganze Schif voll Korn und fleisch für Zucker Malasio, Brantenwein und andern minder nöhtigen sachen weggeführet worden: Summa alles liederlich bestelt, anstatt sich in ein Corpus oder 2. wohlbestelten Mannschaft zusammenzuziechen, um den find von den Grenzen der Wohnungen abzutreiben, wolte ein jeder sein Eigen Haus verwahren, und sich deffendieren. Welches die Ursach dass endlich die Indianer oder Wilden sich einer plantation nach der andern bemeistert, bald die ganze Provintz unter sich gebracht.—Meine Gedanken wahren im fahl die Wilden der gemachten Convention nicht entsprechen würden, zu keinem guten Vergleich gebracht werden könnten, selbe mit meinem gemachten frieden zu Amusieren, Einen stillstand zu procurieren, indessen sich mit Volks Hülf, und aller Nohtwendigen Muntion und Provision versehen, zu setzen, hiemit mehreren und kräftigeren Widerstand zu thun, oder die Wilden gar zu destruiren. allein es wahre mit denen wunderlichen Carolinern nichts zu schafen, die wo etwan behärzter als die andern, nahmen die sach so unbedacht, und plump vor, und gerieten hinder die Wilden, die gar viel stärcker an der Zahl, gute Schützen und wohl versehen in allem, dass diesers kleine Häuflin der Christen alsobald das Kürzere ziechen müssen: ja ohne den pfältzern und Schweizern Hülf zu grund gangen, wie in Erster relation zu sehen. N.B: In selbiger relation aus einen Brief an H: Goub: Hide geschrieben, date mit Meldung, wie die Mannschaft so in Bath: Towe, einem kleinen Dorf an der Pamtego Rivier ohngefährt in 150. dem diesem gegebenen Wort und Zeichen nicht nachgangen, das Herz nicht gehabt über die rivier zu setzen, ihren nachtbahren zu Hilf zu kommen, in Einer so tringender Noht, sondern nachdeme sie da desselben Districts Einwohner, ihr Korn und fleisch aufgefressen, uns trüben an der Neus River im Stich lassend, nacher Haus widerumb gegangen.—

Wie ich mich zu New Bern befestiget 22 wochen lang, mich und die Coloney, aus eignen Mittlen erhalten, entlich aus Mangel Subsistenz mein Posten verlassen müssen, um nach dem Goub: zu gehen,: ist theils zu sehen in Erster relation, kann doch nicht unterlassen, zu Melden, wie es mir auf dieser Reis in die Albermarle Conti gegangen.—

Nach deme nun erfahren und gesehen, wie alles so elend hergehet, was schlechte ja gar keine assistenz, die unmöglichkeit in die länge so auszuhalten, ja gar zur extremitet gekommen, wie dass durch diese Invasion der Wilden, die ganze Coloney zu grund gangen, indeme wie obgemelt bey 70 Ermort und gefangen, alle der Collonisten Häuser verbrandt, ihr Hausraht und was sie zum besten weggenommen, das meiste Vieh Erschossen, das unsrige zur Narrung aufgebraucht. So ware auf Angeben H: Michel und andre H: aus Virginien und Marienland, resolviert andre Mensuren zu nemen, und weilen die Coloney sich vertheilt, der halbe Theil Pfältzer sich von mir gewendt, mit den übrigen sambt dem Schweizern mich nach obermelten Ohrten zu begeben: Packte hiemit ein Theil meiner Sachen ein, liess meine kleine Schloop zurüsten, der Intention, wann ich werde bey H: Goub: Hide angelanget seyn, im parlament oder Generalversammlung bessre assistenz auszuwürcken, widrigen fahls mein Dessin nach Virginien und Marienland fortzusetzen.—So verreiste ich nun in grosser perplexität, weilen meine Leuth in grösster Noht, [41] ja dass nicht mehr ein Mäss Korn mehr vorhanden ward: sondern Mussten uns dess Schweinenfleisch behelfen, und das z'war sehr genauw'. Diese Reis aber ward auch unglücklich, bey schönem Wetter und Windt fuhr ich ab, nach dem Meine Leuth versammlet, und Ihnen best möglichst zugesprochen: Sie baldiger Hülfe tröstend, dess abend da wir schier an der Ambouchinen Rivier und durch den Sond ausfahren wolten, begegnet ein bedenkliches Zeichen, zu oberst an der Spitze des Mastbaums, Kehrte sich einsmahls ein kleines feurlein und pfeifete zimlich starck, ohngefehrt eine Viertel Stund, Entlich hörte es auf, da ich den Schifpatron fragte was das sein solte, so sagte er mir nicht viel guts, Es werde bald ein grosser Sturm erfolgen, und das sey gewüss, ich aber lachte herüber und wolte meinen Weg fortfahren. Es vergienge aber kein stund, finge der Wind härter zu blasen an, und weilen es gegen Nacht getrauten wir nicht, sondern sahen umb, wo etwan wir bey Land den ancker sencken könnten.—

Kaum möchten wir ans Land pordieren überfiel uns der Wind so starck, dass ein wenig speter wir in grösster gefahr kamen, so blieben wir da bey einerm Planter einem guten Mann, [42] der da auf einem Landgut gesetzt, übernacht, Morgends da der Sturm vorbey, fuhren wir fort, so kamen wir den andern Tag abends in die Mitte dess Sonds, welcher ist ein See viel grösser als der Genfer See, da in der Mitte mann kein Land sehen könnte, allein wir auf einen Sandbanck stosste; da das Schif einen so starken Krach gethan, dass wir meinten es wäre entzwey, und währe es nicht überaus starck gewesen so hätten wir da auch Schifbruch leiden müssen, wir wahren da in grossen ängsten, und nahmen alle Erdenkliche Mittel von ab diesem gefährlichen ohrt zu kommen, die meiste forcht wahre, dass, wann schon entlichen das Schif loos, es wurde einen Spalt haben, dass wir ohnfehlbar versenken müssten, Gott war aber so gnädig, dass nachdem das Meer gestigen, und der Wind besser worden, wir mit gespannten Säglen glücklich abkammen, da wir sahen, dass kein Wasser ins Schif kame, dankten wir Gott, und setzten fort, dess dritten Tags bekamen wir einen so starken Widerwind, dass wir an Einem ort, gegen Land fahren mussten, wo eine grosse Weite mit Rohren, da Sänckten wir unsern ancker, und wahren gezwungen, wohl etliche Tag da zu bleiben, bis der Wind sich um etwas gesetzt, dass wir bey eines Seiten Windts, durch einen Canal so durch die Rohr fliesst seglen konnten. So bald wahren wir nicht aus den Rohren, wolte das Unglück dass wir auf einem vesten Felsen stecken bleiben, dass wir einen halben Tag genug zu thun, bis wir los wurden, und musste uns wiederum das Meer helfen, entlichen vermehrt sich der Wind, und kammen wir glücklich darvon, und langten nach etlicher Tagen, an bestimbten Ohrt an, und wahre es Zeit weil all unsre provision die genauw ward, an Speis und Tranck aufgebraucht: anstatt dass wir verhoften bey gutem Windt, in 2 mal 24 Stunden anzukommen, haben wir über 10 Tage zugebracht: So sicht man was das Wetter Zeichen auf der Spitze des Mastbaums bedeutet, scheint aber ein Aberglauben zu seyn, die Erfahrung aber weiss es anders.—

Da ich mich nun 6 ganzer Wochen bey H: Goub: Hide aufhielt, theils dem raht und übrigen provintzgeschäften abzuwarten, theils auch meine Leuth zu Neuw Bern, mit Nohtwendigen Lebens Mittlen und Kriegsprovision zu versehen, ist nach angewenter grosser Mühj und Viel Zeit, mein Schlop mit Korn, Pulver, bley und Taback angefült und nacher Neuw Bern versendt worden, aber ach, was vor unglück, es haben die guten Leuth in Ihrer eusserster Noht, wohl vergebens darauf gewartet,: da dann die Schlop vast über den Sond und weit der Embouchure der rivier Neuss übernahmen sich die Schifleuth mit Branntenwin, so dass sie alle entschlafen, vermeinend sie wahren nun aus der gefahr, allein weilen sie das feur in dem Kuchli nicht gantzlich gelöschen, springt ein funcken von Einem Scheit Holtz, und kam in die Tabackblätter, die nicht weit darvon wahren, welche mehr und mehr angangen, bis ein feur entstanden, und entlich der Rauch die Schifleuth erweckt, welche aus forcht das Pulver Fässlein wurde angehen, drachteten sich zu salvieren, und miechen sich in den Canou, das ist ein klein rundes Schiflein darvon, ehe Sie aber Vollentz ans Land gelangt, kombt das feur ins Pulfer, und es gieng die Schlopp in feur auf.—

Lasse gedencken was vor traurige Botschaft den armen halb ausgehungerten Colonisten, solches zu vernemen, anstatt deren so lang mit grössten verlangen, erwarteten assistenz, und wie das zu Herzen gangen. Indessen ich diese traurige Zeitung vernahm, welches lang angestanden, hatte nach eusserstem Vermögen gearbeit, dass man die grössern Schlopp oder Brigantin proviantieren, welches aber so lang vortgieng, dass ich ganz vertrüssig wurde, wohl sehend dass solche Tergiversationen, in solchen Conjuncten nicht bestehen könnten, desswegen meine Sachen dahin disponiert, dass alsobald nachdeme meine Leuth diese provision wurden empfangen haben, Sie grad in selbiger Schlop mit H: Michel nacher Virginien säglen solten, diss verzoge sich sehr lang, nachdemme nun wie schon gemelt, mich eine lange Zeit bey H: Goub: Hide aufgehalten, den Krieg und provinzen sachen abzuwarten, wo viel zu thun wahre,: verfügt ich mich nach Virginien, umb alles best möglichst zu bestellen; Eh ich aber zu dieser Reis schreite, kann nicht übergehen zu melden; was unterdessen zur sicherheit des Landes gethan worden;.—Nachdeme nun H. Goub: Hide und der General Versammlung Kreftig vorstelt, wie man bessere Anstalten als bishero geschächen thun solte, sonsten wir in gefahr alle von den wilden Indianern umgebracht zu werden, so gerieten wir an die arbeit und hatte ich den Tag meines Lebens nicht vermeint so ungeschickt und verzagte Leuth, da anzutreffen.—

Erstlich wahre zu thun vor allem aus, wo proviant zu nemen, dann ohnmöglich zu kriegen, und wahre doch diese unbedachte Caroliner so liechtsinnig dass sie dennoch getreyd und fleisch aus dem Land verkaufen, desswegen H. Goub: Hide alsbald ersuchte, ein scharfes Mandat auszuschreiben, alle ausfuhr einicher sachen zu verbieten. 2tens. zu erforschen was für getreid im Land, demnach die erforderlichen Mensuren zu nemen, ward gefunden, dass dessen bey weitem nicht gnug einen so langwierigen Krieg zu führen, hiermit anstalt aus benachtbarten Provinzen solches zu procurieren, welches auch genug hatte.—

Drittens Pulver, Bley und gewehr dessen die Provinzen ganz nicht versehen, und die particularen, gar wenig hiemit gut befunden, auch unter dessen von andren Ohrten zu beschicken: Wolte aber niemand das Gelt darzu geben, noch funden die Provinz welche damahl in schlechtem Credit, Matery, da musst ich aber bey H: Goub: in Virginien trachten etwas auszuwürcken.—

4./Soupponieren alle obige sachen wären paraht, worumb das Volck, da war Arbeit, könnten mit grösster Mühj kaum 300 Bewährte Männer ausmachen, und wahren viel darunter unwillig zu kriegen, meistens schlecht gekleit und versehen, hierüber war mir Commission gegeben, um Hülf in Virginien anzhalten, da entlich H: Goub: Spottswood, als in Nahmen der Königin, Ihnen solche zusagte, für restitution dess proviants und Sold, so wolten die Caroliner nicht, pretextierend, sie vermöchten solche Summen nicht zu restituieren, wann H: Goub: nicht Volck und die Nöhtige provision in der Königin Kosten senden wolte, welches absurd, worumb sollte die Königin die Kösten vor die Provinz haben, da doch das Einkommen, die Lord. propriet: beziechen, dies gabe Anlass dass etliche zu H: Goub: von Virginien giengen, um zu Sondieren, ob er die protectionen Caroliné auf sich nehmen wolte, welches aber H: Goub: aus guten Ursachen abgeschlagen.—

5./Proponiert dass man etwan ein ohrt in der Provinz befestigen solte, im fahl der Noht zu einer retraite zu gebrauchen, und sich da auch in Sicherheit zu halten, war aber nicht erheblich.—

Bey so bewannten Dingen, was zu thun: Indessen fuhren die Indianer fort, wurden von so schlechter gegenwehr übermühtig und bezwungen Eine Plantation nach der andern.—

Die letste ressource ware eilends nach Süd Carolinam um Hülf zu senden, welche auch erhielten, sonst wäre die ganze provintz zu grund gangen, so sandte das Gouver: Süd Carolina [43] 800 wilde Tributarys samt 50 englischen Süd Carolinern, under dem Commando Obrist Paravell, wohl montiert und versehen mit Pulver und bley, das Theatrum Belli wahre unweit Neuw Bern. Da diese angelangt, fieng der indianische Krieg erst recht an, und gerieten diese Süd Caroliner da sie nach zu den Tascarorus wilden kamen, dergestalten an Sie, dass grossen Schrecken unter ihnen erweckt, so dass die Nord Carolina Indianer gezwungen worden, sich zu verschanzen, unsere Fründ Indianer aber nachdeme Sie Ihre ordres zu Neu Bern Empfangen, miechen Sich gegen Cortown ein gross indianisch Torf, ungefehrt 30. Meil von Neuw Bern, jagten selben König sambt seinen Indianern aus, nachdeme Sie etliche nidergemacht ereifreten sie sich darüber, dass sie auch von einem erschossenen wilden Carolinisch Indianer das Fleisch gekocht und gefressen,: zu diesem Süd Carolinischen Soucours ordinierten wir 200 Nord Caroliner Engel: sambt etwelch wenig unser Indianern so fründ wahren, und bey 50 pfältzer und Schweizer unter Commando Obrist Boyd und H. Michel welchen wir auch zum Obrist gemacht.—

Dieses kleine HEr mieche sich weiters hinauf gen Catechna einem grossen Indianischen Dorf, wo ich und der General Feldmesser Lawson gefangen, und zum Tod verurtheilt wahren, wie in erster relation vermeldet. In diesem Dorf Catechna hatten sich unsre find, bestehet in Wetax, Bay, Revir Neuws, Cor Bamtego und theils Touscarorus Indianer versammlet und vast eingeschanzet und könnte man nichts ausrichten gegen Ihnen, ist zu wüssen, dass bey einem angestelten Sturm die Ordres nicht recht exequiert, der angrif solte an etlichen orten angehen, Es wahren aber des Bricens Leuth so hitzig dass sie vor der Zeit sturmten, wurden Ihrer viel plessiert, etliche tod geblieben, müssen also die unsrigen abweichen, da uns der Bericht im Raht ertheilt, wurden wir vast beschäftiget, wie die Find besser zu g'stellen, und bessere anstalten zu thun: Ungefehrt umsahe ich mich und erblickte 6 oder 8 Stück, in dem Hof, liederlich da ligen, ganz rostig und voller Sand, wahren meine Meinung, man solte 2 der kleinsten ausrüsten, übersenden und das fort mit beschiessen, hierauf wurde ich ausgelacht, mir representierend, dass solches unmöglich über die Möser, Wälder und graben zu bringen, mich aber erinnerd was mir H. Haubtmann Gallard von St. Croix erzellt, wie er es angeben, vor einer Festung in Flandern, welcher auch sein fortun gemacht, wurde jedes stückli als auf einem Prancour [44] zwischen zwey pferten ordentlich geferget, das übrige weiters angestelt, wie sich am besten geschickt, und ist wohl gelungen; dann da man die aprochen gemacht, und nur 2 Schüsz in der wilden fort gelassen, neben etlich wenig granaten so man getrachtet Einzubringen, erweckte dis eine solche Forcht unter den Wilden, die solches nie gehört und nicht gesehen, dass sie um einen Stillstand anhaltend, da wurde von unsren Obristen Officierern Kriegs Raht gehalten, was zu thun geschlossen, denn stillstand zu accordieren und trachten vortheilhaftigen Frieden zu machen, was dessen die Meiste Ursach wahren die gefangnen Christen, so sie noch von der ersten Massacre behalten, welche uns ruften dass so das fort in Sturm übergieng, sie alle erbärmlich um das Leben kämen, ist also hierauf capituliert worden, mit Condition, dass vor allem aus die gefangenen solten losgelassen werden, welches auch geschächen. Da nun dieses vorbey und die unsrigen nacher Neu Bern gerückt, umb sich ein wenig zu erlaben, dan die Lebens-Mittel genauw und sparsam, dem Obrist Barnwell nicht nach Vergnügen entsprochen, so wurde er ungeduldig, dass man ihme nicht mehr Ehr und guts erwiesen, auch sein Volck gar schlecht proviantiert, desswegen Er auf expedient bedacht, wie sich wiederumb mit provit nach Süd Carolinam zu begeben und unter dem Vorwandt eines guten friedens lockete er eine gute anzahl der fründlicher Indianer oder wilden Caroliner, nahme bey Cor Toone sie gefangen, darzu seine Indianer Tributari ganz genigt, weilen von jedem gefangenen ein Namhaftes sie zuzuhofen, miechen sich also mit Ihrem lebendigen Raub nacher Haus, was er hiemit zu vor loblich ausgerichtet, ist durch diese action verschertzt worden;—

Diese so unchristliche action habe die übrigen Tascaruros und Carolinisch Indianer obwohlen sie Heyden vast erbittret, wie billich, so dass sie den Christen nicht mehr getrauwet, desswegen Sie noch vester verschanzet, und viel ravage in Neus and Bamtego Grafschaft oder Distrikt gethan, ja das Lestere erger als das erstere wurd. Welches uns bewogen starcke Klägten wider den Obristen Barnwell zu thun, und schrieben widerumb nach Süd Carolina für Neuwe Hülf, welche aber nicht so starck als die Erstere erfolget, doch langt bald nach eine zimlich Anzahl unter dem Commando Capitain Moore welcher sich besser verhielt: Nach dem man zusammen gezogen, was man aufbringen könnte, ist man an dieses indianische Fort, bey Catechna oder Hancock Town gerahten, und ist solches endlich glücklich gestürmet in brandt gesteckt und erobret worden.—

Die Wilden hatten sich darinn unsäglich dapfer gehalten, so weit da man des forts meister, und Weib und Kind so unter der Erden, darin sambt Ihrer Provision verborgen, herausnemen wolten, die Plessierten wilden, am boden winselnd noch um sich schlugen, da wahren bey 200 so in einer redoute verbrant viel sonsten nidergemacht, so dass in allem bey 900 sambt Weib und Kindern Tod und gefangen. Von den unsrigen wahren auch viel plessierte, und etliche auf dem Platz geblieben.—

Auf dieses hin hatten wir ruh, doch streiften noch etliche überbliebene hin und her, wahre nun zu thun wie für das Könftige, von den überbliebenen benachbarten, uns in föllige Sicherheit zu setzen, cedierten unterschiedliche Könige. N.B.: die Könige sind Eigenlich nur die Cheff einer gewissen quantitet wilden Indianern, doch ist es erblich, und stelt auf die Posteritet, mit denen wir conferierten, und es entlich zu einem Erwünschtens Frieden brachten: Ist nun nicht das geringste mehr zu beförchten, weilen die Wilden, so hinder Virginien und selbiger Provinz Tributari sind, des Friedens garandt, die überbliebenen Carolinischen Indianer, sind nun auch der Lords Prop: Tributarj worden.—

Indessen obwohlen im Friden, so wahren unsre armen Colonisten nicht gar wohl, sondern hin und her bey englischen oder Carolinischen Planters verstossen, andre miechen sich widerumb nach Neu Bern, alwo sie etwas Landes zu ihrer Nohtdurft bauweten, und Erlaubt ich ihnen, für 2 jahr condition zu suchen, in Dienst zu eint und andern, vermöglichsten Caroll: Einwohnern zu gehen, um da ihr Subsistenz zu haben, und etwas für zu sparen, damit sie hernach wiederumb auf ihre Lächen, oder Plantationen gehen könnten; Für diese Zwey Jahr aber: Sollen sie von dem auferlegten Bodenzins frey seyn; H: Michel und den Bernern aber liess ich wüssen, dass ich nun nacher Virginien um die nöhtigen anstalten zu thun, der Hofnung sie dorten besser als in Carolina zu setzen, mich auch H: Michel gegebenes wort Tröstend, als gesinnt bey unserm vormahl gemachten Schluss zu verbleiben: zu mahlen mir unmöglich aus eigenen Kräften und Mittlen einer so delabierten Colloney aufzuhelfen, und von Bern aus nicht nur schlechter Prospect, sonder gar kein Hoffnung einiger Assistenz gemacht worden.—

Nahme hiermit meinen abscheid von H. Goub: und Raht; und mieche mich zu H: Goub: in Virginien, bey welchem ich erhielt, dass er wegen gefährlichen Krieg Zeiten inbesonder mir der Capitain nur ein Krieg Schiff, meine Leuth zu begleiten, vergönnt, welches ein grosse und sonderbahre Gunst, für einen particularen, hierauf wahre H: Michel avisiert, welcher dann bey einer Converentz auf den frontieren zwishen beyden H: Goub: H: Hide und Spotswood gehalten worden, sich auch einfunde, und da ward Zeit und Tag gesetzt, wann und wo Sie, in der Insul Caratuix in Carolina sich recontrieren solten: Ich indessen gienge weiter in Virginien gegen Potomaex und Marienland zu, um alles paraht zu halten mit quartieren, Lebensmitlen und Vich.—

Das ohrt [45] wahre ohnweit den fahl von Portomaec bey einem Civilischen, generosen und wohlhabenden H: Rosier genant auf mainen Landsitzen, alwo ein gewüsser H: Bart, neben andern H: von Pensilvania mir entgegen kammen um auch zu sehen, wie es mit dem von H: Michel angegebenen Silbermine worin sie auch interessiert, und dess wegen viel Kösten gehabt, Ein bewantnus. Nachdeme wir nun in erwartung H: Michels und der Berneren so mit kommend, halten, wegen so langer Verzögerung und keinen Berichts, ungeduldig wurden, auch in betrachtung H: Michels seltsamer Demarchen der Minen halber, gefassten gedanken, selbsten das ohrt laut gegebenen Plans zu besuchen, und die Wahrheit grundlich zu erfahren, rüsteten wir uns zu dieser Zwar gefährlichen Reis, doch weilen diss im Sinn hatte zu thun, wann schon die überigen H: nicht wären angelangt: hatte ich per precaution von H: Goub: in Virginien, als deme mein dessin communiciert, patenten erhalten, und war auch Ordre gegeben, dass auf erste avise ich von den nächst bestelten grenzenwächtern, so viel nöhtig erachtet, aufmannen könnte. Da wir nach Canarvest, ein überaus schönes ohrt, ungefehrt 4 Meilen oben führ dem fahl kamen, funden wir da einen Haufen Indianer und insbesonders Einen Frantzosen Martin Chartier genannt, welcher mit einer Indianerin verheurahtet und darbey den wilden Indianern der Nation so Hinter Pensilvania und Marien Land in grossem Credit, auch auf angeben H. Michels Pensilvania verlassend, und sich da gesetzt, welcher hier vor auch mit H. Michel die Minen aufzusuchen gegangen, viel Müh und Kösten gehabt, dieser warnet uns dass die Indianer selbiger gegne wo die Silber Minen zu seyn vermeinet, vast allarmiert von dem Krieg, so wir mit Tuscorussen Nation hatten, hiemit solten wir uns nicht ohne sonderbahre Noht, in solche gefahr zu setzen, welchem wir geglaubt, die Sach auf eine bequeme Zeit aufschiebend, indessen miechen wir einen Bund mit den Canavest Indianer als sehr nohtwendig, so wohl in ansehen der verhofenden Silber Mines, als auch unser kleinen Berner Colloney, so wir der Enden sezen wolten, besachen die trefliche Situation selbiger gegne Landes, wie auch insbesonders die Charmante Insul der Potomac Revier ob dem Fahl, auf diese Stund bedauerend, dass dies Schöne Land nicht bewohnen kann.—

Von danen giengen weiters zurück auf einen Berg den Höchsten der Enden, Sugarlowe genannt, als da hatte die Form eines Zucker Stocks, nahmen mit uns den Martin Chartier, einen Feltmesser hätten wir auch bey uns, und kamen noch Etliche Indianer mit uns, von dem Berg besahen wir eine überaus grosse Seite Landes, Ein Theil Virginien, Marienland, Pensilvanien und Carolina, bedienten uns des Compasses, miechen ein Plan, und observierten insbesonders den Berg, wo die Silber Minen sein solte, funden dass er hinder Virginien, vernahmen auch anbey von 2 Indianern, dass sie alles auf und um den Berg aufgesucht, nicht aber das minste Zeichen von Mineralien gefunden, und der Plan so uns gegeben worden, dem bericht nach ganz nicht respondiert, welches uns bestürtzt. Was weiters desswegen beschächen ohnnöhtig hier zu erzellen, endeckten da, noch viel schöner Landes, und drey Ketten Bergen, eine allzeit höcher als die andere, da wir vom Berg hinunter, blieben wir bei Martin Charitier übernacht, und kehrten den andern Tag wider nach H: Rosier quartier unter dem fahl, wo ich eine geraume Zeit verbleibe, der Hofnung da meine Leuth zu Empfahen, als denn abgeretet, die übrigen Verreisten widrum, aber nicht gar vernügt, wegen dem Confusen plan, nacher Pensilvanien.—

Kein schöneren Sitz [4 6] glaube in der Welt zu seyn als dieser, welchen wir in zwey kleine Colloneyen abtheilen wolten, die Erste grad unter dem fahl, wo eine überaus Lustige Insul von gutem Grund und gegenüber an Einem Eggen, zwischen der Potomax Rivier und einer kleineren Gold Crec genannt; alles was aber, für dem fahl hinunter oder hinauf willens zu empfahen. Und können die grössten Kauf Mann Schif dahinfahren, der andere Sitz, solte seyn bey Canarvest wie das Plan aufweist. Nach demme nun bey 2. Monath lang, nicht den minsten Bericht, aus Carolina empfangen, kame entlich der hinckende Bot mit bösen Zeitungen, da mich H. Michel nur mit wortenberichtet dass überbringer diss Zedelin, verlangte das Commando unserer Sloop zu haben, solte mit ihnen accordieren die Sloop nach deme Sie das Lang verlangte getreid entlich nacher Neus gebracht, Sie in der Zurückkunft auf einem Sand bank angefahren, seye in schlechter Condition sie bey heissem Wetter etwas wurmstichig worden:, Mangle Segel, Seil und anderst ausgerüstet zu werden, könne da nicht abkommen, solte mich Eilends nacher Carolinam begeben, und meldet nichts weiters, kein Meldung von Krieg Schif, so von Virginien uns entgegen geschickt, und was weiters in der langen Zeit vorgangen, dass ich halb vor ungedult verschmachtet und vergangen.—Solche widerwertige Zeitung und seltsamer bericht, bestürzte mich dergestalten, dass nicht wunder, wann ich von Sinnen kommen wäre, nachdeme alle Anstalten und provision gemacht, Nun alles vergebens, sandte den Capitain, nicht gar vernügt zu seyn, dennoch mit ordre die Schif so gut als möglich auszurüsten, und das Eillends, weilen es doch nur einen kleinen Traject auf den Meerküsten hätte, Schriebe auch an H. Obrist Pollock als der da am besten versehen, weilen das Schif in der Provinzen dienst, dass man für die Noht, das nohtwendigste verschafen solte, mit verdeuten, ich wolte durch Virginien schon das übrige machen, wurde aber alles auf den langen banck gezogen, wolt ich mein Sach befördret haben; Musst ich selbsten hingehen, da ich nun zu H: Goub: kame, funde ich ein ganz ander gesicht als vormahls, ganz Kalt, Indifrent und könnte dessen Ursach nicht errachten, Entlich half er mir aus meiner Bestürzung, mir dennoch Ernstlich vorhaltend, für wem wir ihne ansehen, hätte verhofet, wir wurden seine fründlichkeit und Diensten besser Erkennen, ja solche nahmhafte Dienst, die nicht einem jeden particularen bald erwiesen worden, anstatt unsre Schuldige Dankbarkeit wären wir sehr Cavalierisch gegen Ihne verfahren, wer im höchsten grad bestürtzt, der war ich, excusierte mich, ich wüsste noch nicht was das alles bedeuten Solte, bate doch um Erläuterung, so brache H: Goub: aus, Ja, ja, Euwer schöne, M: hat mich vast dargesetzt, Erzellet mir, wie das abgereter Maasen er, H. Goub: Ein Krieg Schif ausgesendt, unsres Sloop mit Volck abzuholen, und zu Convoieren, selbiges aber vor der Coratuex Insul bey 6. Tagen gewartet, entlich der Capitain ungetultig da er niemand sahe, sich herzumachen, sendte seinen kleinen Bargunen ans Land umb zu erfragen, ob von unsrer Slop mit Schweizeren nichts zu erfahren, wolt niemand das geringste darvon wissen, da er weiters zu einem Dörflin Little genandt, fuhr, vernahme er endlich dass M. M: zu Neu Bern und die Slop in einer schlechten Condition auf einem Sandbanck und nicht abkommen könnte. Nachdeme der Lieut: solche Zeitung vernommen, miech Er sich eilends zu seinem Haubtmann, welcher halb aus der Haut Sprung, dass er so amusiert und vergebens eine so gefährliche Reis gethan, dann wann ein Sturm sich hätte mercken lassen, Er in das weite Meer hinaus müssen, und so es gegen das Land geblasen hätte, wäre er in grosser gefahr gewesen, weilen der Enden das Wasser nicht Tief ist, also unmuhtig nacher Virginien gekehrt. Da nun dieses alles angehöret, ward mir halb ohnmächtig von Vertruss und Scham dass ein solcher H: von deme so viel fründlichkeit, Diensten, ja das Leben selbsten nechst Gott hätte, so dargesetzt: Fienge an mich bestends zu entschuldigen, respondierend, wie das ich selbsten vast dargesetzt, als alles schon auf Potomac bestelt, sey im grössten Kummer wie mich aus einem solchen Labirint zuschwingen. Nachdeme nun H. Goub: mich zu Erlaben Einen Trunck anpresentiert, fieng Er mich zu bedauren an, dass ich mit einem solchen wunderlichen Kopf zu thun hätte, Riehte er mir seiner zu müssgen.

Nachdeme nun fründlich Tractiert, da übernachtet, so mieche mich dess andern Tags, Eilends in Carolina, um die vorgemelte nöhtige Anstalten zu thun, hatte auch an einem ohrt, Sägel und Cartag: Bestelt, um im fahl der Noht die Slop zu Montieren: da ich nun bey H. Goub: Hide in Carolina ankam, vernahme Ich erst recht gründlich allen Handel, und weiss nicht was noch mehr unbeliebiges darzu, Schrieb alsbald H. M. zu, um mich der Bewantnus aller dingen zu berichten, wurde aber schlecht Satisfaciert, verlangte darauf er solte zu mir kommen, damit wir über Eint und anders die nöhtigen Mensuren nehmen könnten, war aber nicht zu erhalten, und möchte ich aus guten Ursachen nicht zu ihme gehen, so date anderwerts anstalten, hielte bey H: Goub: und Raht an, dass weilen die Sloop in der Provinz Diensten, so zugerichtet, seye nicht billichers als dass man mir sie im guten Stand widrum übergebe: Welches auch gut befunden so hat man Einen der Sachen Verständiger mann gesendet die Slop zu visitieren, und remitieren wurde aber mit Lebens-Mittlen und andrer Hülf so schlecht versehen, dass er widerum zurück kame, und zwar kranck weilen es im Heyssen Summer wahre, Er theilte auch den bericht dass die Schlop nicht lang halten könnte, weilen Sie durch den Sommer aus an der Hitz gelegen, von den Einwohnern beschädiget, und musste sie ganz Neuw Montiert werden, welches sie nicht wehrt. Hiemit übergabe ich der provintz die Schloop, und wolte sie geschetzt haben, in dem währt und preis, da sie in Diensten kommen, ist mir aber bey weitem nicht zugesprochen worden, was ich verlangt, so dass ich den halbigen Theil daran verlieren müssen, ist aber noch nichts entrichtet so wenig als von der Kleinren./

Indessen wo hinaus mit meinen Leuthen, schriebe widerum H: M. beweglich zu, und verlangte eine Converentz, bey so schlipfrigen Conjuncten, insbesonders, da die Creditoren verlangten bezahlt zu seyn, erfolgte kein Antwort, wohl aber vernahme dass der M. alles unter dem Vorwand Meine sachen zu salvieren, einpackten und nach Süd Carolina zu fahren gesinnet, auch etliche Pfelzer beret mit ihme dahin zu gehen, dieser nimmer Erwartete anschlag gefiel mir nicht, und ward ich gewarnet, meine Sachen in bessere Verwahrung zu thun, aber zu spaad, auf das hinweilen der Obrist Pollock, deme ich Eine Zimliche Summa zu thun Schuldig, für vorgestreckte Provision der Coloney, Etwas verdacht fassete, wie billich, so ersucht ich Ihne alles authorisiert durch geschworene Männer zu inventarisieren, so wohl der Pfälzer restierende Mittel als meine, und so wahren sie in verwahrung gethan, allein meine beste Sachen wahren fort.—

Da ich nun reflectierte auf H. M. Conduite wie er alles so seltsam angestelt, wie er alle Interessierten amusiert und nichts verfolget, so traute nichts gutes, Schriebe ihme noch zur Letze einen Brief, ime sehr per relation, verdeutend, was ich von eint und andren vernohmen, als aber verwis, und so man Ihne in einichen Verdacht, er wahrhaftig selbsten die Ursach darzu gegeben, durch seine Conduite, Tergiversationen und wanckelmuhtige VerEnderung wie dann solches besser ab apahrto mündlich zu erzellen, wie die Sachen nun seyn, in solcher extremitet müssten starke resolutions genommen werden, und seye apsolute nohtwendig das wir uns mündlich, gegen andren expectorieren und die letste Mensuren nehmen. Es seye perriculum Mora, anstatt einer zusammenkunft Erhielte nichts als das unverschandeste Schreiben, so könnte erdenckt werden, glaube wohl sey froh gewesen einen pretext zu finden, Seinen Tücken Eine Farb zu geben, und sich los zu machen. Von deme was er seinem angeben nach nicht ausführen könnte; hätte hier weitläufige Materj über sein unversprechliches Verfahren, zu klagen: Seinen ansehnlichen Verwanten aber mehr als ihme zu verschonen, will ich mit Seufzen und Stillschweigen übergehen.—

Es wahren in diesem Brief so viellerley Sachen, die klar zeigten, dass ich und andere mehr Dubiert insbesonders eine das ermelter M: von einer neuwen Entreprisen gemeldet, als welcher er fast zu gelten miech, nemlich eine Colloney der Rivier Mesesipy [47] nach zu setzen, an welcher 3 Cronen Spanien, Frankreich und Engelland Pret: der Meinung es werde der Stand von Bern als Neutral diss land grad von diesen 3 Cronen erhalten: Kann mann aber liecht betrachten 1. [48]/ die Jalousie solcher mächtiger Potentien, da keiner der andern Cedieren würde, 2./ die Unfähigkeit des standes von Bern als da kein Seemacht, Entfernht Land zu Colonieren, so siehet man liecht dass wahrhaftig H. M. Sein Calcul nicht wohl betrachtend, und dass solche Sprüng von Pensilvania in MarienLand von da in Virginien, weiters in Nord Carolina zu denen in Süd Carolina und Entlich auf Mesesipy, nicht passieren mögen. Der Schluss ist nun der Virginischen oder Marielandischen Silber Mines halben, bald gemacht, dann ist da Etwas realisches, warumb darvon Abstrahieren und nach dem Golfe von Mexico zu gehn; die Haar stehen mir zu berg, wann betrachte wie viel famillien, dargesetzt, insbesonders _ _ _ so viel famillien der Bergleuth die auf ein formalischen Tractat sich fondierend ihr Vaterland verlassen, mit grossen Kösten in Americam verreiset und nun dorten noch H. M. angetrofen, noch jemand der Ihnen angegebene Minen zeigte, ich muss nun von der vertriesslichen Matery aufhören zu reden, sonst wurde mich so darin Vertiefen, dass für die übrigen Sachen nicht Raum genug, dann Eigendlich diss nicht mein Vorhaben.

Komme wider auf meine Carolinische relation, nach deme nun aufgemeltes referirt wie wenig assistenz von Bern aus zu gewarten, Ein Wächselbrief über den andern, protestiert wahre mir obgelegen, was für experient in solcher dringender Noht zu ergreifen, dennoch hatte noch keine Gedancken in Europam zu gehen, weilen bey H: Goub: Hide noch Zwey Negers Sclaven, die mir zugehörten wahren, trachteten solche mit mir zu nemen, in gedanken mich derer zu bedienen bey Kanavest bey welchen Indianern, mich retirieren wolte, und nach und nach von den Collonisten, aus Carolina nach hier vorgemelten anschlag dahin zu ziechen welche auch ein grosses verlangen, darzu Erzeigten: allein H: Goub: Hide, hielte mich so lang auf, weilen der Frieden mit den Indianern noch nicht genzlich: rattificiert, welchen Schluss er auch absolute haben wolt, dass Einer meiner Creditoren Eine Invention erfunden, Subtiler weis auf diese Negers zu wachen, dass sie nicht fortkommen könnten.—

Indessen wurden wir von der grossen Hitz und ohne Zweifel weilen wir so viel Pfersich und apfel gegessen alle in H: Goub: krank, so dass auch Endlich H: Goub: In wenig Tagen gestorben, welches mir viel geschatt, da Er mein sehr guter Fründ, dieser Tod brachte seine ehl. Liebste Made: Hide schier in Desperation und hielte sie mit heissen Tränen bey mir an, ich solte sie in einer so traurigen Conjunctur nicht verlassen, sondern bey ihr bleiben, bis die Sachen, theils wegen des Gouv: in Richtigkeit, theils mit ihren wegen ihrer Verstorbenen H: Pretentionen und restanzen alles geschlichtet: mir weiters representieren dass dem rang und gesezen nach, als Landgrafen das Presidium mir gebührte, und dass sie lestlich zu Londen bey des Lord propriet: verspürt dass so vacants, sie mir das Gouvern: anvertrauwen wurden, bedankte mich dessen höflich, gab Ihr aber andre gründ vor, welche mich solches anzunehmen, abhielten, das bedeutete dass noch ein paar Wochen da verbleiben wolte, und mein bestes beytragen, Ihre Sachen richtig zu machen, da doch meine eben so pressierten.—

Nach der Begrabnus kame Obrist Pollock der Elteste des Rahts, sambt übrigen Richtern zu mir, und Ersuchten mich das Presidium anzunehmen, welches aber ausschlug, aus vielen wichtigen Gründen, vorgebend H: Obrist Pollock als der Elteste in Jahren und auch im Raht, solte solches annehmen, Seye ihme die Sachen der Provintz auch besser bekannt als mir der da ganz frembd in diesen Landen, welches nach vielen Complimenten Er Entlich angenommen.—

Indessen wurde von diesem Alles die Lord proprietet berichtet, gabe von weitem zu verstehn, dass so mir das Gouvern: angetragen, ich es nicht ausschlagen wurde: wolte aber darfür nicht anhalten, dieses wahr ohne einiches bedenken, wie schon berichtet, gut befunden weilen aber bekannt dass ich in Carolina vast in Schulden, und schon etliche Wexel protestiert, so wurde inngehalten, bericht von Bern aus erwartend,: da dann ich geschrieben, ob Hofnung einicher Bezahlung, denne ist auch bräuchlich, dass die Pretendenten persöhnlich sich in solchen Conjuncturen stellen, also wurde verzogen, 6 ganze Monath, bis ein Goub: bestelt wurde: Da doch zu Londen sich etliche hervorgethan, und grad dieser jetzige Goub: Eden wurde Entlich schier ungedultig, so da noch von Bern Bericht noch meiner persohn zu Londen angelanget, sind Endlich die Lord propriet: zu Wahl geschritten, und haben obigen H: Eden Erwehlt, welchen ich noch zu Londen angetrofen und besprochen, ja ihme mein Interesse so wohl als der Coloney bestends anrecommandiert, zu welchen Er seine officia Sinceriter versprochen, ist ihme auch von den Lord Propriet: selbsten anbefohlen worden, Intransiter vermelde, dass da ich zu Londen lestlich angelangt, und mich bey H: Collector Chevalier Baronet auch Lord Propriet: als meinen Special guten fründ aufgehalten, 8 Tag bey ihme auf seinem Landgute 8 Meil von Londen verbleiben, er mir beim ersten anblick, sein transport bezeuget, dass, wäre ich nur ein Monath Eher angelangt, ich nun Goub: Inn Carolina sein wurde, welches mich aber minder als Ihne verdrossen, weilen mir leyder wohl bewusst, dass zu Bern keine Disposition meine Schulden zu bezahlen, noch weder von den meinigen noch von den Propriet: die da von so vielen, widerwertigkeiten Deguragiert.—

Nun bin ich schier nach Londen anstatt nach Virginien kommen, fahre fort wo ich geblieben, wenig tag zuvor Eh ich von der Fr: Goub: Hide abscheid genommen, liess ich durch meinen Knecht in geheim der Negers anzeigen, sie solten sich in der Stille über die Rivier des Nachts machen, und drüben meiner Erwarten, mit mir in Virginien zu gehen, worzu sie ganz freudig, dann sie da hart tractiert, weis aber nicht wie sie es angestelt, jemand bekame Luft darvon, und wurden arrestiert, so musste ich Sie dahinden lassen, und wurde hierbey der Compass gantz verrückt, darauf nahme alsobald abscheid, mir selbsten nicht trauend, und kame zu H: Goub: Spotswood in Virginien welchem alle dise widerwertigkeiten Erzellet, Er mich heftig bedauerte, weillen aber an mein rendevous mit H. Bard auf der Potemack rivier gedachten, so hielte mich nicht lange zu Viliams Burg auf, sondren miech ich mich auf den weg Marienland, der Meinung ihne bey H. Rossier bey dem fahl anzutrefen, und da einen Schluss als Mitt Interesierten zu fassen, Eilte hiermit so stark ich könnte, da ich aber bey MarienLand point eine fahrt mit meinen Pferdten über die rivier wolte, hinderte mich Ein starker Wind, so bald der Wind nachliess fuhr ich hinüber und mieche mich dem fahl zu, wolte aber nicht das unglück dass wo ich bey H: Rosiers Haus angelangt, noch den H. noch die Fr: dess Hauses noch H. Bart antrefe, die zwey erstren wahren eine ganze Tag Reis weit zu ihren Verwandten Visits und H. Bart, wahre just den Tag zuvor verreisst, mich in Virginien vermeind anzutrefen,: ich alsobald obwohl müd von einer langen Reis, nahme nur Etwas Speis und einen Trunck in der Eyl, reisete im Sprung zurück, so dass meine Pferdt zu starck geritten wahren, gezwung en einen Tag Ehe wir zu Villiams Burg ankamen, zu Fuss zu gehen, so bald da angelangt befragten mich ob H: Bart vorhanden, Erfuhr aber dass er zu Hamton dem Ersten Virginichen Seeport wahre, sandte alsbald meinen Knecht mit einem lamen Pferdt dahin, welcher ihne auch nicht mehr antraf, dessen Ursach war, weilen H. Bart da ungefährt Ein Krieg Schif fertig nacher Neuw jorck zu seglen, antraf, und dessen Capitain sein guter Fründ sich gern dieser Gelegenheit zu seiner Rückreis bediente, nachdeme er sich meiner und der Colloney Sachen Innvormiert, vernommen, dass H. Goub: Hide gestorben, meine Sache alle denn Krebgang gewunnen, mir einen Brief hinderlassen, welchen auch Niemahlen Empfangen, ist er auf Neuw Yorck verreist, welches ohnweit von Bartington einem schönen Flecken, auf die Holendische Manier gebauwen, Ein Grenzohrt zwischen Neuwjork und Pensilvanien wo er sich meistends aufhielt, da war ich aber neben ab, dann dieser mein letste ressource war, weillen Er ein Verständiger Erfahrner und aufrichtiger Kaufmann wahre, Ein Gascon de Nation, welches mich verwundert, dass er als ein listiger Mann, M: M: soviel vertrauwet und fürgestreckt, gedachte es wäre noch etwas an der Sach der Silber Minen halben, und wäre die minste aparentz da gewesen Einicher realitet, hätte mich noch gelitten.—

Was nun zu thun, so ich liecht etwas gehabt, das mich zu Canavest hätte setzen können, so wir demnach zu weit gegangen, anstatt zu H: Goub: Spotswood, gienge zu einem bekannten particular fründ, wolt noch Einen Sach thun, [49] sandte meinen Knecht in Carolina, theils zu vernehmen er hätte sich anders besinnt, theils zu vernemen, was er eiggendlich für ein Routen genomen, Item [50] zu sehen ob villicht die Negers entrunen, in solchem fahl so ich Sie bekommen könnte, hätte noch zu Canavest etwas ausrichten Können, dan sie nur Korn pflanzen können, und zu etwas wenix Vich Achtung gegeben, Es kam aber mein Knecht unverrichteter Sachen zurück, doch wurde Ihme angesagt, dass wan ich meinen Berner Colonisten, und etwelchen Erlichen Pfälzern, eine Schlop oder grosse Barquen, mit Provision senden wolte, sie willens zu mir zu kommen, getröstete mich noch zu Erhalten mit den Bergwercken, so mit H: Goub: Spotswood hatte.—

Auf diesen bericht schriebe ich an Obrist Fitzhugh, ein richer mann Königlich. Rahts und mein bester fründ, welcher mit dieser Neuwen Colloney gern einstehen wolte mit officieren, des nohtwendigen proviant und andren Hülf Mittlen, da ich nun streng an dieser Arbeit, vermeinend ich hätte da ein loch gefunden, auszuschleuffen, wurde ich gewarnet. Ein Virginischer Kaufmann, der einen Carolinischen Einwohner auf meine Wexel Brief wahren verkauft, wolte auf den protestierten Wexel mich arretieren lassen, und ward der arrest würklich in dem Haus wo mich aufhielte angelegt, ich aber verbarg mich, hierauf gieng ich bey guten Fründen zu Raht, erfragte ob zu Canevest ich vor den Creditoren sicher wäre, oder an andren orten America wurde mir zur antwort an keinem ohrt, dann wann ich schon unter den Indianern ich vermittlest der Indianischen Händlern, oder Negocianten Entdeckt wurde, da stunde ich aber an, so dass keine ressource in america für mich zu finden, Es wäre dann sach, dass hofnung gelter von Bern aufzubekommen, oder funden Neuwe associerten, deren wohl zu finden gewessen, wolten aber mit den alten Schulden nicht zu thun haben./

Wann aber refectiert auf etliche Briefen die ich empfangen, welche mich wenig Satisfactierten, verfügte mich ganz vernünftig zu H: Goub: Spotswood, nacher Viliamsburg sein residentz ohrt, warf ihme meine Fatalitäten gleich einer Handvoll oblige oder mit diesen Worten, Mon. Le Gouv: Je suis tellement: Nachdeme nun die Zeit in acht genommen, dass er in guter Humor und müssig, fragte ob gelegenheit, mir audientz zu ertheilen, und das Zwar eine Lange, worauf er Ein wenig lachte, und bekame von diesem generosen H: ein gantz günstig Verhör, nach deme nun meine Unglückafftige avantiere erzellt, wie auch dass man mich arretieren wollen, so bezeugte H: Goub: hierüber ein hertzliches Mitleiden, sich verwundrend, dass man mich so im Stich liess, insbesonders die Societet, wusste nichts bessres zu rahten, als mich in Europam zu begeben, offerrierte mir eine recommandation an Einen guten Fründ, der procurieren solt, dass der Graf Orknay der Königin für mich ein Sublication presentieren wurde, dene solt ich nacher Bern meiner Societet alles kreftig vorstellen und die gelter zur Bezahlung der Wexelbrieffen Solicitieren. Diesen Raht communicierte etlichen meiner besten fründen, welche auch mitstimmten.—

Weilen aber der Winter anbrach, und zu diesen Zeiten keine Schif in Europam Segleten, hielte mich den Winter durch, welcher dorten nicht so lang währet, bey einem guten fründ, und weilen doch ungern in Europam widrum gieng, viel minder nacher Haus, so thäte ich alle diese Zeit unaufhörlich bitten, dass der allmächtige Gott, mir in Sinn geben wolte, was in einem so schlipfrigen geschäft thun solte, dass er es allés nach seinem heiligen Willen leiten wolle, damit inskönftig mehr segen in meinem Vornemen hätte, ich also eine solche resolution nemen möchte, welche meiner seelen am Erspriesslichsten seyn würde, dann wann nichts andres gesucht als nun mich die Zeit meines Lebens zur Nohtdurft durchzubringen, hätte noch wohl experient gefunden allein die Coloney zu verlassen, mieche mir auch Gedanken: wan betrachtet was ich Gott schuldig, insbesonders für eine sonderbahre erlösung und wie mir alles so fatal und widrig gienge so könnte ich schier errachten, dass es Gottes willen nicht währe, dass ich länger in diesen Landen verbliebe, und da kein guter Stern für mich schien, so nahm ich Endlich die resolution fortzureisen.

Mich tröstend dass meine Colonisten villicht besser unter diesen Carolineren vortkommen, als die inen zur Zeit besser helfen könnten als ich, hiemit desshalb keine grosse Versprechung auf mir hätte, dann was ich thäte wahre nicht der Meinung sie gentzlich zu verlassen, da doch mir ihrer ein grosser Theil Ursach gnug darzu gegeben, sondern im fahl bey Ihr Königlichen Mayesteht von Engelland günst: audientz, zu Bern auch mehrere assistenz, so könnte dann mit freuden und Nutzen widrum zu ihnen kommen.—

Wahre ich aber in dieser Negotiation auch unglückaftig so müsste ich wohl Gott diese Coloney und den Lord propr: anbefehlen, und mich in meinem Vaterland still halten, die übrige Zeit meines Lebens da Verschliessen in bereuwung der Verlohrnen Zeit, Einer wahren Demüthigung und aufrichtiger bekehrung in betrachtung, dass die Sünden meiner jugend mir diss unglück als zuwegen gebracht, obwohlen diese Züchtigung, alle der Menschlichen Natur hart, dennoch nicht so scharpf, wie ich es wohl verdient hätte: Solt mir nun obligen alle weltliche und Eitele Sorgen zu verlassen, hingegen mehrere Vorsorgend für meine arme Seel zu thun, darzu mir Gott die gnad geben wolle.—

NB. habe hiervor von dieser Coloney gemelt, wann ich sie schon verlassen, und sie so viel Unglück überfallen, haben Sie solches selbsten auf sie gezogen, 1./ wahren Sie, will sagen die meisten abtrünnig von Ihrer rechtmässigen Oberkeit, was sie gegen diesen gethan, thaten sie hernach auch mir, da der halbe Theil in der grossen Noht sich von mir gezogen: Item wahren Sie Gottloos Volck dass nicht zu verwundren, wann der allmächtige Sie mit Heyden hat heimgesucht, dann Sie Erger Lebten als die Heyden, und so ich gewusst, was diese Leuth währen, Berner so wohl als die Pfältzer, hätte mich Ihr wohl nicht angenommen; Von Pfältzeren gedachte das böste auszulassen, wie es der apparentz nach schiene, was die gewesen, so auf dem meer und eh ich in americam kommen, gestorben, ist mir unbewusst, von denen aber die ich noch angetrofen, darunter etliche Verloffene Schweitzer under Pfälzer nahmen, Erfund ich Sie meistends Gottlose aufrührische Leuth, darunter Mörder, Dieben, Ehebrecher, Flucher und Lesterer, was immer ich für Sorg und Mühj anwendte sie in gebühr zu halten, es hulfen noch kreftige Vermahnung noch treuwung, noch Strafen, was ich mit ihnen ausgestanden, das weiss Gott, unter den Bernern wahren Zwey Haushaltungen, welche wohl die excrementz dess ganzen Berngebiets, ein Gottloser Gesind hab ich nie gesehen noch erfahren, und da die Frommen sturben, blieben diese als das Unkraut über, so nicht bald verdirbt.—

Das schöne und gute Land durte mich mehr zu verlassen als so ein böses Volck,: doch wahren etlich wenig fromme Leuth, die sich wohl gehalten, mir lieb wahren, denen wünschet dass es ihnen wohl gehe, der H. bekehre die übrigen. Es wahre nun zu thun wie meine Reis fortzunehmen, per Wasser oder Land, per Wasser konnt es nicht geschächen, weilen kein Schif Capitain einiche persohn bey Verlusst einer Summa annehmen darf, die in Schulden und nicht im Vermögen mit den Creditoren abzuschafen, so musste es per Land geschächen, welches eine lange Reis, und worzu ich kein Gelt hatte, etwas Silbergeschirr, so ich noch behalten, musste ich zu gelte machen.—

Indessen schrieb ich briefen an die Coloney, ihnen mein und ihren kläglichen Zustand representierend, und wie nöhtig meine Reis, sendte zugleich auch Schreiben an die H. Presidenten des Rahts, ihnen auch meine Gründ vorstellend, und recommendierte bestends die Verlassene, und Delaprierte Coloney.—

Nachdeme nun meinen Abschied von H. Goub: Spootswood genommen, der mich zur Letze wohl regaliert, und für mein present, das ich ihme zu Einem kleinen Zeichen meiner schuldigen Dankbarkeit überreicht, mir an gold ein gegen present thate, welches meines gar weit übertraf, fing ich meine Reys mit des allerhöchsten beystand, grad auf ostren 1713 an, per Land durchzoge schier gantz Virginien, ganz Marienland, Pensilvaniam, Jersey, und kam entlich zu Neuw York, Gott sey Danck glücklich an, welches Eine auf die Holändische Manier wohl gebauwte schöne Statt auf einer Insul einer seits an einem schönen Seehafen, und Zwischen Zweyen Schifbahren rivieren die Situation überaus wohl gelegen, mit einem Vesten Schloss und ist die Landschaft daherum Charmant, in der Statt sind 3 Kirchen, ein Englische, ein frantzösische, und Holendische, in welcher auf teusch gebrediget wirdt, da ist aller überfluss und kann man da haben, was man begehrt, die besten Fisch, gut Fleisch, getreidt und allerley Erdgewächs, gut bier und allerley der köstlichsten Weine.—

In diesem so lustigen ohrt, blieb ich 10 oder 12 Tag, hernacher Seglete ich in einer Slopp nach Engelland, muss bekennen, dass anfangs mich förchtete, in einem so kleinen Schif, über den grossen Occeanum zu fahren, weilen ich aber vertröstet es wäre in so kleinem minder gefahr, indem Sie 1./der Seglen in Stürmen besser meister seyen, 2./ dass es besser und geschwinder fort kombt, 3./ waglet minder als die grossen, 4./bequemer Ein und auszuladen, und in der Handlung Nützlich, indem ein solch Schif Zwey Reysen thut, da der grossen nur Eine [51]./

Obwohlen wir das Unglück hatten, dass meistends Widerwind bliesen, und öfterns starcke Stürm, so langten wir dennoch Gott sey Dank zu End 6 Wochen zu Bristoll glücklich an: Diese Statt kann wegen bequemer zufuhr wegen ihrer grösse, grosser Handlung, Reichtum an Volck oder Einwohnern und gelt, wohl das kleine Londen genennt werden; Da Ruhete ich etliche tag aus und mieche mich zu Pferdt, weilen es in der Land-Gutschen unsicher wahre in guter Gesellschaft nach Londen, allwo ich mich etlich Monath aufgehalten, der Hofnung ich wurde etwan meine Suplication bey der Königin Anna durch den Hertzog Beaufort als meinem H: Patron, der der Erste Lord Propp: und Palatinus von Carolina war, eine kleine Zeit aber zuvor, da Er willig meine Suplication der Königin vorzutragen, hat ihne einsmahls der gehe Tod überfallen, aber ein streich meiner ungünstigen fortun, bald hernach sturbe die Königin selbst,: so geschache solche nahmhafte Endrung am Englischen Hoof, dass meine Suplication unter den Tisch gemust, wie ich für eine lange Zeit kein Hofnung sahe, zu Einicher favor an diesem Neuwen Hof; obwohlen doch zu seiner Zeit apparentz, es würde der Neuwe König als Teuscher Nation, diesem Geschäft geneigt seyn, weilen die Winters Zeit beschwerlich zum reisen, und ich zu Londen nichts ausrichten. Kann unterdessen nicht ubergehen zu erzellen, dass wie ich zu Londen angelanget mit Bestürtzung vernommen, wie dass der Berg Haubtmann J. Justus Allbrecht mit etlichen 40. Bergleuthen angelangt, welches mir nicht wenig Mühj, Sorg, Verdruss und Kosten verursachet: Indemme diese Leuth so blinderweis ohne ordre daherkommen vermeinend da alles Nohtwendige zu ihrer Erhaltung und Verschaffung nach den Americanischen Bergwercken zu finden. Es wahre aber nichts für sie vürhanden, und ward ich selbst so lehr an gelt, dass kaum ich für meine Nohtdurft bekommen könnte. Indeme aus America kein Gelt ver-

blieben und zu Londen kein wexel noch für mich Vermacht, so dass
mir unmöglich ein so menge Leuth zu assistieren: was dis mir für ein
unerträglicher last ist wohl zu dencken, in dem Sie Vermeinten, dass
Lauth habender Tractats ich schuldig sie zu versorgen, welche zwar also
auf meinen Befelch kommen währen, hätte aber aus America geschrieben, und das öfters sie etliche Briefen empfangen, dass nemlich der Berghaubtmann Justus Allbrecht mit seinem Gesind nicht
kommen solte bis auf meine ordres, mit verdeuten dass wegen en-
standenen Unruhen in Carolina und Indianischen Kriegs mit den
Bergwercken nichts zu thun, solche von H: Michel auch noch nicht
gezeigt, so aber H. Berghaubtmann, in einen weg kommen wolte nur
selbst ander oder dritt, um den Augenschein zu Nehmen. Dieser aber
ist unbedachter weis in Einen weg fortgefahren,—Was nun zu thun,
wusste nichts besser als diese Leuth wiederumb zurück nacher Haus
weisen, welches aber ihnen so unbeschwerlich viel dass sie lieber sich
für 4. jahr lang zu Knechten in America verdingen wolten, als zu-
rückgehen, indessen war kein Schif fertig in America zu Säglen, mussten
sie den ganzen Winter durch bis im Frühling zu Londen sich aufhalten,
woraus aber leben, diss mieche mir viel Mühj [52], Endlich lof ich zu
einem und andren grossen H: um ihnen Arbeit und Brodt zu procurieren: theilen fund ich platz andren nicht, unterdessen ward ich pressiert
nacher Haus zu gehen; fund zu Letst Zwey virginische vorneme Kauf
H: denen die Sachen bestends vorstellte, und recommandierte mich
hierbey berathen mit H: Obrist Blanckistone an welchem von H: Goub:
von Virginien recommandiert eben von wegen den Bergwerck, damit
seine Officien für mich bey hof leisten solten, ward hierüber resultat
dass diese Leuth Ihr Gelt zusammenschossen nach proportion dessen
Rechnung zu tragen, das übrige solte einiger obigen Kaufh: darschiessen, den Transport und Zehrung dieser Leuthen auszumachen, bey
Ihrer anländung solte H. Goub: von Virginien sie annehmen und
versorgen den Schif Capitain auszahlen, welcher dann den Londischen
Kaufh: ihr vorgestrecktes restituiren solte. darzu schrieb ich einen
umbständlichen Brief, an H. Goub: Spotswood, deme eint und anders
bestends representierten, mit verdeuten, dass sie die kleine Coloney/:
auf dem Land in Virginien so wir zusammen hatten:/ ohnweit dem
ohrt wo Mineralia gefunden, und anscheint Mines vermuhtet, solten
Destiniert seyn, wo sie sich durch die weisen anstalt und gutes fürsorg H: Goub; setzen könnten, indessen wo da nicht gnugsame Indicia
zu Silber Mine, anderwehrts zu sehen, und weilen doch in Virginien
noch Eisen, noch Kupfer Schmelze vorhanden, an solchen Mineralia
doch alle fülle, konnte man bey diesen anfangen, und brauchten wir
darzu kein Königliche Patenten wie zu den SilberMines, der Hofnung,
dieses wurde angehen, befahl ich diese guten Bergleuth der Obsorg

dess allerhöchsten, so verreisten sie anfangs Jahr 1714. Nun ist ein ganzes jar verflossen, dass noch von H. Goub: noch von Ihnen kein Bericht empfangen, desswegen in grossen Sorgen stehe.—

Es scheint dass nun meine americanische Traverses zu End gekommen, allein eben der Unglück stern so mich aus meinem Vaterland geführt, begleitete mich bis nacher Haus:—

Aus forcht es wurden meine americanischen Creditoren deme der allerschärsften einer zu allem Unglück zu Londen befunden, anstalten thun, dass man bey dem Meerport mich erfragen und arretieren sollte, nahm ich die resolution anstatt der gemeinen Routen Douvre oder Harwich zu nehmen, in einem kleinen Fährzeug so nacher St. Valerio destiniert, und meine Reis nacher Haus als kürzer und sicherer zu thun. Der Tag ward angesetzt: Weilen ich aber kein passport nemen dörfte aus forcht ich wurde entdeckt, rahtete mir der [53] welchem meine Sachen vertrauen musste, doch unter einem andren Nahmen in Einem kleinen Schiflein nacher Gravesand zu fahren, und er mieche sich auch fertig. Da ich ungefehrt halben wex wahre, Stürmte ein solcher starker Widerwind daher, dass ich gezwungen ans Land zu fahren und zu Fuess nacher Gravesand zu gehen, wo ich übernacht, und noch einen ganzen Tag, weilen köstlich zu zehren, nicht wüssend wie lange dieser Contrare Wind anhalten würde, neben das erst betrachtend, dass diss auch ein port, nahme den Weg wieder nach Londen, wo mein Schifpatron noch nicht fertig war, auf bessern Wind wartend, ich aber verbliebe in Southwick innerhalb der Tems bis auf ordre, da er abgestossen, ward ich gewarnet nachzufahren, und trate noch bey Greenwich ins Schif, zu Gravesand liesse mich der Schifpatron aussert der Statt jenseits aus und solte ich da warten, bis er angebend und visitiert, ohngeachtet dem visitatoren gesagt, meine Coffre gehörten einem Edelmann von St. Valerio, Er könne bezeugen, es wären nur Kleider und Hardes wolten Sie nicht daran kommen: So sendte er mir Eilends einen Jungen mir anzuzeigen, ich müsste meine Coffre aufthun, wurde mir aber bey diesem nicht geheim, doch hielte ich bonne Mine, Sprach frantzösisch, nahm allsobald mein Schlüssli sambt einer Englischen Cronen, und gabe die dem Commissarius, mit Bitt, er solte meine Kleider als die da gar wohl Eingepackt nicht vast vieggen, das passierte zu allem Glück, so sie meine Schriften erdauret, wäre ich entdeckt und in gefahr kommen.—

Nachdeme diss vorbey fuhren wir fort; da wir aber schier zu der embouchure der Rivier bey einem Seeport Margeth genannt, erwecket sich ein erschräcklicher Sturm, mit Donnern und blitzen, dass wir in grosser gefahr, und könnten wir die Nacht durch den ancker kaum behalten, den Tag hernach da sich der Windt gelegt, Segleten wir fort, und da wir auf dem Meere wahren, dass wir mit grosser Noth zurück an ein ander Seeport fahren, gezwungen, Ramsey genannt, wahren die Leuth aus dem Stettli und ein haufen Matrosen, so sich da befunden, uns nicht zu Hulf komen, wären wir zu grund gangen, da mussten wir 8 ganzer Tag wegen Widerwind und unsere verrissene Seegel und andre Sachen, zuzurüsten verbleiben, welches mir, der nur bloss gelt für meine Reys nacher Paris hatte, Schwär ankommen, da sich der Wind um etwas gelegt fuhren wir aus, wurden zum andren mahl zurückgetrieben. Entlich Endert sich der Wind Nordost, welcher uns günstig, da ruckten wir vor Dover, abermahl enderten sich die Wind, so dass diese Reys mir mehr überlegen als da ich zweymahl über den occeanum gefahren, brachten anstatt 3 Tagen die ganze wochen zu, nach St. Valerio zu kommen, und ist da eine so gefährliche Zufahrt, dass ohne guides die uns entgegen fahren, und fortgeholfen, wir niemahlen in selbigen hafen kommen wären, von dar kam ich die Rivier hinauf nacher aberville von wannen ich in der Land-Gutschen nacher Paris, von dar auf Lion bis zum fort de Cluse wo mich der Commandant aufgehalten, weilen kein passport hatte, da doch mir nach Eydmäss in gantz Frankreich, keines gefordret. Hätte ich nicht ungefehrt mein Amts Patenten von Yferten in meiner Coffre gehabt, und fürgewiesen, erzellend wie das sich mit H. Bernern gute Nahbahrschaft gehalten, dessen auch etliche nahmhafte Umständ geben, hätte ich da bleiben müssen, bis einen Schein von Bern bekommen, so reiste ich fort auf Genf, von da auf unser Reb Gut zu Salatz bey Vevay wo ich lauth geschriebenen berichts meine famillien gedachte anzutreffen, ja gar zu verbleiben, alles war zuvor 8 Tag nacher Bern gereist, so musste ich auch dahin, zwar mit grösstem unwillen, langte Gott sey Danck auf Martyny 1714 gesund an und trafe auch zu Haus alles in gutem Stand an.—

Aber ach was vor Enderung in der Statt wie ich alles gefunden, wie kalt die alten Fründ, was stolz und hochmüthig bey vielen, und was weiter ist Verdriesslich zu melden, dass böste war, dass wo ich vermeint Souccours zu finden, meine Delapierte Coloney zu restituiren theils abgewiesen, theils sonsten nicht zu recht kommen [54] kann, so dass gezwungen aus Mangel an assistenz insbesonders von meiner Societet, welche mich im Stich lasste die Coloney zu abandonieren, welches zu bedauren.—

Indeme nun andre im trüben Wasser fischen werden und profitieren von dem was mit grossen Kösten, gefahr, Mühj, Sorg und Vertruss zu wegen gebracht. Dann die Sachen nun in Carolina in einem guten Stand, das Gouvernement besser eingerichtet, die wilden Indianer ausgereutet, Ein guter frieden gemacht, fornembsten Dificulteten aus dem weg geraumbt, das bequemste ohrt der Coloney gesäubret, hiemit gesunder und mit Einwohnern besetzt: So dass die Nachkommen Es weit besser finden werden, als wie dann alle anfäng schwär sind, thut mir im Herzen weeh ein solch gut und schön Land zu verlassen, allwo in so schöner prospect mit der Zeit procurieren und die Coloney in Ein Nahmhaftes aufzubringen.,—

Weilen die fortun in dieser Welt mir nicht günstiger seyn wollen, nichts bessres ist als zu verlassen alles was der Welt ist, und die schätz suchen, die im Himmel, welche die Schaben noch der Rost fressen, und die Dieben nicht nachgraben können. ⁵⁵—

Hatte hierby ein ordentliche Beschreibung der Englischen provintzen, im Continuierten america welche durch reisen machen können: weilen aber hierüber unterschiedliche autous geschrieben, lass ich darbey bewenden, können hierüber gelesen werden. P. Henepin, Bloms Englisch America, Baron de la Honten Fischers gross Brittania Americe, und Von Carolina inspecié H: Ochsen Neustes Tacktätli Vishers Translation Lawsons Journal und Description Carolina.

Copey deren von H: Eduart Hide Goub: in Nord Carolina den 23. Oktober 1711 überschriebenen relation betrefend meine wunderbahre Errettung von den Wilden./.

Hochgeehrter Herr!
Durch die wunderbahre und gnädige Fürsehung und Hülf des Allerhöchsten, bin ich entlichen aus den barbarischen Henden dieser wilden Tuscoraro Nation Entrunnen, und in meiner kleinen Behausung zu New Bern angelanget, aber halb Tod, weilen Zwey ganzen Tag allein durch die Welder gegen Catechna aus zu fuess so starck und vast immer könnte marchieren musste, gezwungen mein Quartier bey Einem Erschröcklichen wilden graben, alwo ein tiefes Wasser, weilen die Nacht mich übernommen, und vor müde nicht weiters könnte, zu nehmen, wie ich diese Nacht zugebracht ist wohl zu denken, nicht in geringen forchten von den wilden oder fremden Indianeren, Erdappet zu werden, und von einer Menge Beren so die ganze Nacht ganz nach bey mir herumb brumelten, zerrissen zu werden: Zu deme wahre ganz lam von gehen, ohne Gewehr, ja nur nicht ein Messer bey mir etwas feur zu schlagen und weilen der Nordwind vast blies ward es ein Kalte Nacht. Des Morgens da der Tag anbrach und ich aufstehen wolte, von dem Kalten und harten liegn, waren meine beyn so steif und geschwollen, dass ich kein Drit gehen könnte, weilen es aber doch sein musste, suchte mir zwey Stöck aus, daran ich mit grosser Mühj und Schmerzen gehen, hätte genug zu thun, mich über diss Wasser zu machen, welches mit Schnagen, über einen langen ast aus geschache, Entlichen kame nacher Haus, da eine kleine Distanz darvon Eine Behausung Ins

G'sicht bekomen, befestiget und voller Leuth, wahre ich um Etwas getröstet, weilen vermeinte es wäre alles von den Indianern abgebrunnen und verderbt, so wohl als der Colonier Häuser, ja dass auch wenig meiner Leuthen antreffen wurde, indeme mir der wilden grausame expedition nur zu wohl bekannt, so sie den rivieren nach von Pamtego Neuws und Trent gebrandt, gemort und geblündret was sie angetrofen, auch resolviert das ganze Land zu verderben, da meine guten Leuth mich erblickt aussehend und schwarz wie ein Indianer, dennoch meine Statur und blauwen Rock betreffend, wussten sie nicht was zu gedencken, sondren der Meinung gentzlichen ich wäre Tod, Steiffe sie vielmehr ein Indianischer Späch der meinen Rock angethan, wolte dan etwas heraus Spächen, so dass die Mantschaff ins gewehr sich stelte, da ich aber nacher Haus kam, an Zweyen Stöcken ganz lam gehend, sahen sie bey meiner Continentz und postur dass ich kein Indianer oder Wilder wahre, doch kannten sie mich nicht, bis dass etliche voraus giengen, mich besser zu recognoscieren, da ich sie in ängsten sahe, finge von weitem zwar mit einer gantz brochnen Stimm an zu reden, welche so bestürzte, dass sie etliche schrit zuruck giengen, zu den übrigen Schreyend, sie solten nur hervorkommen, es seye ihr vermeinter Ermörter H: so kam alles übern haufen Mann und Weib und Kinder gelofen, mit Starcken exclamationen theils weinend, theils ganz stumm vor bestürzung, mich Salutierend, als ein wunderbahres Spectacul, da ward trauren, Freud und bestürzung vermischt, und gieng mir solches zu Hertzen, dass es mir gute tränen heraus presseten: Nachdeme mich nun, obwohlen sehr müd, mit diesem Volck, so mich umringte etwas verweilet, mieche mich entlichen in mein altes quartier, verschloss meine Kammer und thate mein Hertzliches Gebet der Danksagung, zu dem gütigen Gott für solche gnädige und wunderbahre Errettung; die dieser Zeiten wohl für ein Miractilum passieren mag./.

Den nechsten Tag fragte ich was in meiner abwesenheit sich zugetragen, kam aber so viel vertriessliches herfür, dass mir im Hertzen weh thut, das böste wahr, dass neben dem Verlust 60 oder 70. Pfeltzer so ermördet worden, die übrigen so sich Salvieren können, geblündert,: und von diesen restierenden Mein Haus, worin Ihre Eigne güter wahren, und das Stetli verlassen, welche ein gewüsser Viliam Brice undankbahrer mann deme viel gutes erwiesen, ja welchem mein und der armen Colonisten gelt und gut von der Armuht ausgesetzt von mir abgezogen, Sie durch allerley Verheissung und List auf die Trent Rivier zu sich gebracht, womit er sambt noch Etlichen Englischen planters oder Einwohnern, Eine garnison zu wegen gebracht, sein Haus zu defendieren, so musste ich zu frieden seyn, mit einem haufen Weib und Kindern, an bewehrter Mannschaft wahren nicht mehr dann 40

Dieses Musste ich alles Erhalten, Zwei und Zwanzig wochen lang, so ist all mein getreid so zu allem glück in Vorrath hatte, mein Vich gross und klein dahin, wann wir nicht fürderlich die Nohtwendigkeiten bekommen, müssten wir Nohtwendig verderben, oder den platz und posten verlassen: desswegen hochgeEhrter H. wir inständig bitten, verlangte provision, Munition und bewehrte Mannschahft so bald immer möglich und aller Eyl zu senden, damit wir diese Barbarische Mörder zurück treiben können sonsten wurd das übel je grösser und ist zu beförchten das ganze Land würde zu grunde gehen: Ist nicht genugsam zu verwundren, ja Ergerlich eine solche Kaltsinnigkeit und so wenig Liebe bey den Einwohnern der Grafschaft Albemarle zu sehen, dass sie so mit gebogenen Armen zusehen können, wie ihre nächste Brüder schröcklich von dieser Barbarischer Nation Ermordet werden,: ja sie selbsten nicht eines bessern zu erwarten, sollen sich wohl schämen und eines Immerwehrendes Verwisses wehrt. Ist sich auch nicht minder zu verwundern, über eine so schlechte Policey und ordres der Vorgesetzten, exceptieren aber hier in bester Vorm eure herlichkeit, Vergwüsseret dass meine HochwohlgeEhrteste H. alle Nohtwendige befelchen und anstalten gethan, solches aber schlecht oder gar nicht exequiert, welches zu bedauren.—

HochgeEhrter H. obiges nur zum bericht, wie ich nacher Haus kam, zu meiner entladnus und justification aber wird nötig sein zu vermelden, wie ich unter diese Barbarische Nation gerahten.—

Bey diesem Schönen und Scheinbahren beständigen Wetter kame der General Feldmesser Lauson mich zu Infitieren die Neusrivier hinaufzufahren, seyen da ein quantitet guter wilden Trauben, konnten uns ein wenig darmit ergetzen, das war aber nicht gnug, mich dahin zu persuadieren, so kam ermelter Mons: Lauson bald wider, gabe mir bessre gründ vor, namlich dass wir zugleich sehen könnten, wie weit hinauf die rivier Schifbaar, dass da ein kurzer weg nach Virginien einzurichten, anstatt dass der ordinari Weg weit und beschwerlich, Item zugleich zu sehen, was für Land dahinauf: dieses und wie weit es zu den bergen, hätte schon längst gern gewust, und selbsten gesehen. So resolvierte mich hiermit zu dieser kleinen reis, und nahme alles Nohtwendige sambt provision, für 14. Tag mit, fragte aber insbesonders H. Lauson ob gefahr wegen den Indianern sonderlich deren, mit welchen wir nicht bekannt, gabe mir zur antwort, hätte nichts zu bedeuten, Er habe diese reis schon gethan, und das ganz sicher, kannten auch an diesem arm der Rivier keine Wilden, sondern währen zimlich abgelegen, damit wir aber desto Sicherer gehen könnten, so nahme ich neben Zweyen Negers zum Rudern, noch Zwey bekannte nachtbahre Indianer, welchen viel guts erwiesen, und da einer die Englische Sprach verstund, gedachte wann wir diese Zwey Indianer mit uns hätten, wir von andern nichts zu beförchten; So fuhren wir ordentlich hinauf, hatte lang nicht geregnet, das Wasser wahre nicht dief, der Strohm oder Lauf des Wassers ward nicht starck, den ganzen Tag wahren wir auf der Rivier, des Nachts Spannten wir unsre Zelten auf dem Land nach beim Wasser, und Ruheten, dess Morgens früh fuhren wir wider fort.—

Es beliebe H. Goub: zu vernemen, dass ermelter Feldmesser Lauson, fast um meine pfert anhalten thäte, vorgebend, Er wolte ein wenig in die Wälder reiten, wann wir droben wären, um zu sehen wo der weg nacher Virginien am bequemsten könnte angefangen werden: wolte mich aber anfangs nicht darzu verstehen, doch entlichen hielte er nur um eines an, welches, ihme accordiert, der Einte Indianer Ritte per Land, musste aber an Einem Ohrt über die Rivier welches unser unglück, dann Er den Indianern, weiss nicht ob er Verirret oder verrähterischer weis, zu dem grossen Indianischen Dorf Catechna kam, wo allso bald gefragt was das Pferdt thäte, dann die Indianer der Enden keine gebrauchen, antwortete dass er das Pferdt uns führen müsste, wir aber fahrten indessen die rivier hinauf. diss allarmierte alsobald die Indianer insbesonders die Einwohner Catechna, so dass sie zusammen gerottet, in der ganzen Nachtbahrschaft, behielten das Pferdt, und sagten unsrem Indianer er solte alsbald zu uns gehen, und vermelden, sie wolten nicht gestatten, dass wir weiters hinauf durch Ihr Land fahren, aus befelche dess Königs der da residiere solten wir zurück, so gabe durch ein Schusz, den unser Indianer abliess, das Signal darmit wir still stunden, welches wir gethan, nachdem wir unsre flinten auch zum zeichen abgeschossen. Es ward schon Spaat, als er zu uns kam mit der bösen Zeitung, beim ersten Brunnen lendeten wir an unser nachquartier zu nemen, da trafen wir schon zwey bewehrte Indianer an, als Kamen sie vom Jagen, ich sagte hierauf diss gefiel mir nicht, wir wolten da nicht bleiben sonder zurückfahren, Er der Generalfeldmesser lachte meiner, aber Ehe wir uns umkehrten ward Ernst daraus, so dass ihme das Lachen Vergieng, augenblicklich kam aus allen Büschen und durch die rivier geschwummen eine solche menge Indianer und übernahmen uns, dass uns unmöglich zu Deffendieren: Wir wolten uns dann mutwilliger weis zu Tod schiessen lassen oder gar Erschröcklich Martren. wurden hiemit gefangen genommen, geblündret und weggeführt,: wir wahren schon 3 starcker Tagreisen hinauf gefahren, ohnweit von einem andren Indianischen Dorf, Zuruta genannt, die rivier ist da noch zimlich breit, aber nicht mehr als 2 oder 3 Schuh dief Wasser, und ist noch weit von den Bergen, wir verlangten dass man uns diese Nacht da lassen solte, mit einer wacht, wann sie an uns Zweifleten prextierend, ich könnt nicht so weit zu fuess gehen, wolte des Morgens früh per Wasser zum König nach

Catechna fahren, und uns da Versprechend, war aber nicht erheblich, eine so seltsame und Considerable Captur/: dann sie mich für den Goub: der ganzen Provintz hielten:/ Blaseten ihren barbahrischen Hochmuht dergestalten auf, dass wir gezwungen wurden die ganze Nacht durch Wälder gesteud und Morast mit ihnen zu laufen, bis dass wir gegen Morgen um 9. Uhr nacher Catechna kamen, wo der König Hencoex genannt in aller seiner Glori mit seinem Raht auf einem Erhabenen gerüst sassen, da sonsten die Heyden oder Wilden auf dem boden pflegen zu sitzen: Nach Einer Consultation und dess führers oder haubtmanns, unser Escorten gethaner scharfen red, brach der König mit seinem Raht auf, und kam mit dem Obrist Kriegshaubtmann zu uns ganz höflich, könnten aber mit uns nicht reden, wenig Zeit hernach gienge der König in sein Cabinet oder hütten, wir blieben bey einem feur mit 7 oder 8 Wilden bewachet, gegen 10 Uhr kam ein Wilder hier, der andere dort aus seiner Hütten heraus, da ward Raht gehalten, und ward fast disputiert ob wir solten als Criminalen gebunden werden oder nicht, ward geschlossen Neyn, weilen wir noch nicht Verhört wären. Gegen mitag brachte uns der König in einer Lausigen Pelzcappen, selbsten etwas Speis als ein gattung Brod von Indianischem Korn gemacht, pre um plins [5 6] genannt, und gekochtes kalltes Willdbret, darvon Zwar mit Widerwillen weilen mich fast hungerte, ass ich, wir hatten die Freyheit in dem Dorf herumb zu spatzieren, gegen Abend ward ein grosses Vest oder Zusammenkunft von allen benachtbahrten Ohrten, diss wahre bestimmbt aus Zweyen Ursachen. 1./weil sie das böse Tractament etlicher böser und unwirschen Englischen Carolinern rechen wolten, so vom Pamtego Neuw und Trent rivier 2./ umb zu erfahren, was sie für hülf zu gewarten von Ihren benachtbarten Indianern. NB: hierbey ist zu observieren dass noch weder wir noch unser Coloney die Ursach dieses Erschröcklichen Mords und Indianischen Kriegs, wie zu sehen und mit mehrerem zu berechnen.—

Dess abends kamen von aller ohrten her eine Menge Indianer, sambt den benachtbahrten Königen, um 10 Uhr nachts auf einem Schönen weiten Platz, insbesonders zu grossen Festiviteten oder executionen gerüstet und destiniert, wahre die Versammlung der grossen, wie sie es nennen, Verstehend in 40 aller Verständigster Indianer auf dem boden nach Ihrer art, und Manier Sitzend, in Einem Ring um ein grosses feur, König Hencox Presidiert, da war in dem Ring Platz für uns gelassen, wo Zwey Mats das ist gehürd von kleinen rohren geflochtene Bletzen, gelegt darauf zu sitzen, welches ein Zeichen grosser Defferentz und Ehr, so sassen wir nider, und unser Vorsprecher welches der Indianer ward, so mit uns gekommen, der gut Englisch konnte, an unsre linke Seiten, der König gab ein Zeichen dem Redner der Versammlung, welcher eine lange Red gantz grafitetischen thate, so wahre geordnet einer von den jüngsten der Versammlung dess Rahts oder Indianischer Nation interesse und sach zu representieren, und Defendieren, welches er so viel ich vermercken könnte in bester Form thäte, Sasse grad neben unsrem Dollmetscher und fürsprecher, der König formierte allezeit die questionen, das war dann pro et contra descutirt, hieruber alsobald consultiert und concludiert.—

Die erste Question war, was die Ursach unsrer reis, unser antwort ward dass wir für unser Lust, da hinaufgefahren, drüben zu gewunnen, zugleich um zu Erfahren, ob die rivier bequem dass per Wasser wir ihnen wahren zuführen könnten, mit ihnen zu Negotcieren und gute Correspondentz zu halten, so befragte uns der König warum wir uns bey ihme nicht angemelt und unser Vorhaben Communiciert. Hernacher kam in question eine generals Klag, dass sie die Indianer sehr übel von den Einwohnern der Pamtego Neuws und Trent Rivier Tacktieret und gehalten worden, welches nicht mehr zu dulden, und Namseten in Specié die autores, so war unter andren der Generalfeldmesser auch angeklagt, welcher aber als gegenwertig bestmöglichst sich Verantwortet: Nach Zimlichen Desputieren und erfolgter Deliberation ward geschlossen, dass wir wohl könnten Liberieret werden, und ward der nechste Tag zu unsrer heim Reis ernamset.—

Den andren Tag Verzug es sich zimlich, Eh wir konnten unser Canou oder Schiflein haben, Indessen kamen etliche ihrer Grandes und Zwey Könige, welche Curios zu wissen, was für Justificationsgründ wir hätten, so wahren wir noch einmal in dess Königs Hencok Cabinet Zwey Meyl vom Dorf examiniert, gaben gleiche Antwort zu allem unglück war da der König von Cartuca welcher Mons. Lauson etwas verwisse, so dass sie beyderseits in streit gerahten, und sich zimlich erhitzet, welches all unser sach verderbte,

Und wie ich immer den Lauson von seinem Disputieren abzuhalten trachtete, könnte nichts erhalten: die Examination endete sich endlich, wir stunden alle auf, wir Zwey spatzierten mit einander, und that ich ihme sein unbehutsamkeit in solcher geferlichen Conjunctur starck verweisen, in allem deme kamen Einsmahls 3 oder 4 Grandes gantz erzürnt, Ergrifen uns hart bey den armen, führeten und setzten uns in das alte ohrt hart darunder wahren keine Mattes für uns gelegt, nahmen uns Hütt und Baruque warfen sie ins feur, darauf hin kamen junge böse gesellen, thaten uns zum andren mahl blündren, unsere Seck visitierend, welches zu vor nicht geschächen, dass sie sich im ersten mahl nur an die grossren Sachen hielten.—

Hierauf wurde Kriegsraht gehalten und wahren wir beyde zum Tod verurtheilt, ohnwüssend was die ursach, so wahren wir die ganze nacht in gleicher postur auf dem Boden sitzend, bis am Morgen, da bey anbrechendem Tag wir von dannen weg, wiederum auf den grossen richt und Sammelplatz geführt wurden; böses Omen für uns kehrte mich umb gegen Mon. Lauson ihme bitter klagend wie dass seine Unfürsichtigkeit unser Ruin ein ursach, währe geschächen um uns, nichts bessres den frieden mit Gott zu machen, und uns zum Tod bezeiten zurüsten, welches ich in grösster Andacht thate, da wir an Gemelten ohrt angelanget, wahre der grosse Raht schon beysammen, ohngefehrt seche ich Ein Indianer wie ein Christ gekleidt, Ehe wir in den Ring beruefen, welcher Englisch reden könnte, befrieg ihn ob er nicht sagen könnte, was die Ursach unserer Condemnation welcher mir mit einem Sauren gesicht geantwortet, worum Lauson sich so mit Cortom gezankt und worumb wir getreut wir wolten uns an den Indianern rächen, auf das nahme ich den Indianer auf die Seiten Ihme alles was ich könnte versprächend, so Er mich anhören wolte und hernach meine Unschuld Etlichen der grandes erzellen, hatte genug zu thun, ihne nur dahin zu persuadieren, entlich gabe er mir gehör, so erzellt ich ihme, dass mir leid, dass Mon. Lauson so unfürsichtig mit Cortom Disputiert, es haben die Räht ja selbsten mögen sehen, dass ich dem Mon. Lauson mehrmahls abgemahnt, so dass ich hierzu kein Schuld, und was das bedräuwen währe, dessen nicht das minste nur gedenkt worden, were ein Missverstand oder Lauson sich über mein Negers beklagend dass sie ihne in der ersten Nacht von seiner Ruh verstört, hierüber Bedreute ich die Negers starck wegen ihrer Unverschandheit und diss wahre alles, nachdem mich der Indianer angehöret, gieng er von mir, ich hielte Ihme meine Versprächung: Ob nun dieser Sehr zu meinen gunsten geredt, kann ich nicht wissen, aber eine Viertelstund hernach kamen die alten grandes, führten uns auf den Richtplatz, und Bunden uns da an arm und beynen, darzu noch den grössern von meinen Negers, aldann finge an unser traurige Tragedie welche erzellen wolte, so Euer Lieb nicht zu lang und vertrüssig, dennoch weilen bereits schon angefangen will ich Continuieren.—

In der mite dieses grossen platzes sassen wir neben einander gebunden, auf dem Boden Sitzend, der Generalfeldmesser und ich, die Röck ausgezogen mit blossom haubt, hinder mir mein grosser Neger, vor uns ward ein grosses Feur umb das Feur herum miecht der Conjurer/: das ist ein alter grauwer Indianer als ein priester unter ihnen welcher insgemein Ein Schwarzkünstler ja der Teufel selbsten beschweret:/ Zwey weise Ring ob von Mehl oder gar weisen reinem Sand Kries weis ich nicht grad, vor unsren fuessen lag eine Wolfshaut, ein wenig besser vornen stunde ein Indianer in der allerhöflichsten und erschröcklichsten Postur, als könnte Erdenckt werden; Welcher nicht von dem Platz wiche, mit Einem Beil in der Hand, wahre dem Ansehen nach der Scharfrichter: Weiter vor uns jenseit dem feur wahre ein grosser Haufen Indianer Gesind durchmist mit jungen Gesellen, Weib und Kindern, diese Tanzeten alle in abscheulichen Posturen. In der Mitte war der Priester, oder Beschwerer./ Welcher wann im Tanzen Ein Pausen war, seine Beschwerung und Treuwungen mieche, um den Tantz oder Ring an vier Eggen, stunden ein Gattung officier, mit Flinten, welche mit den Fuessen Trapeten, und die übrigen Dänzer anjourierten, und wann ein Tanz aus ward, Ihre Flinten abschussen, in Einem Eggen des Rings wahren noch 2 Indianer am boden Sitzend, welche auf einem kleinen Trumlin Schlugen und sangen, und sangen darzu so wunderlich in eine solchen Melodey die Eher Zorn und Traurigkeit provizierte, als aber freud, ja den Indianern selbsten nach dem sie müd wurden, vom Danzen, Laufen Sie alle Einsmahls darvon in einen Wald, mit erschröcklichem Geschrey und Heulen, kamen bald wider aus dem Wald mit schwarz, weiss und Rohtangestrichenen gesichtern, theils noch mit aufgethanen haaren, voller Federflaum, theils in allerley Thier Bälgen, Summa in solchen ungeheuren Posturen, dass Sie mehr einer Truppen Teuflen gleichsahen, als aber andren Creaturen, wann man je den Teufel in der apscheulichstern Postur als kan Erdenk werden representierend, Laufend und Tanzend, aus dem Wald rangierten sie sich wiederum an den Alten Platz, und Tantzten um das Feur: Indessen wahren hinder uns 2 Reyen Bewehrter Indianer als Wacht, nicht von Ihrem Posten weichend, bis alles aus ward, hinder dieser Wacht wahre der Kriegs Raht in Einem Ring am Boden Sitzend, im Consultieren vast beschäftiget, gegen Abend da die Sonnen untergieng liess das vorrige gesind von Tanzen ab, und gienge in den Wald Holz zu holen, das Feur an Eint und andern ohrt zu erhalten insbesonders aber miechen sie Eines etwas weit im Wald so die gantze Nacht währte, und so gross dass ich vermeinte der ganze Wald wäre in einem feur.—

Es gedencke Mons: Goubernat. was Traurigen und Schröcklichen Spektacul mir das ward zu sterben, dennoch ward ich ganz resolviert, so wahre ich in einer Starcken Devotion den ganzen Tag und nacht, ach was hatte ich für allerly Gedancken, alles kam mir für was immer in Meinem Leben, sich mit mir zugetragen, so weit ich mich erinnern könnte, thäte mir alles aplicieren und zu Nutzen machen, was immer aus der Heiligen Schrift denn Psalmen und andren guten Büchern gelesen, kurz rüstete mich so gut ich könnte zu einem guten und Seligen End, ja der gütige Gott verliche mir so viel Gnad, dass unerschrocken gelassenlich alle augenblick Erwartete solte nach ausgestandener Seelen Angst mehr als Todesforcht, dennoch blieb in mir weiss nicht was für eine Hofnung, ungeachtet kein Zeichen Einicher Errettung Sahe, ob ich wie hievor meine Sünden vor mir Schwebten,

so funde hernacher grossen Trost in Betrachtung der Wunderbahren
so der H. Jesus in seinen Zeiten auf der Erden gethan, diss erweckt in
mir ein solches Zutrauwen, dass hierauf mein Einbrünstiges Gebett zu
meinem Heyland Rüstende, dess starcken Zutrauwens, Es wurd mein
Gebett erhört, und diese Wilde gemühter, steinerne und Barbarische
Hertzen etwan endren, so dass auf mein anhalten und representieren,
sie Gedancken Endren, zur Gnad geleitet und bewogen wurden, welches auch durch Gottes wunderbahre Fürsehung geschächen ist. Dann
da die Sonne vast undergieng, so versammlet sich der Raht noch
einmahl, ohne Zeifel ein End dieser vatalen, erschröcklichen und
traurigen Ceremoney zu machen, ich kehrte mich etwas hinderwehrts
ungeachtet gebunden, wüssend dass Einer unter Ihnen die Englische
Sprach zimlich wohl verstunde, und thate eine kurze Red, representierend meine unschuld, und wie so sie mir nicht verschonten, die
grosse und mächtige Königin von Engelland, mein Blut rechen würde:
Weillen aus Ihrem Befelch diese Coloney in dis Land gebracht, nicht
ihnen einichen Schaden zuzufügen, sondren mit ihnen wohl zu leben,
und was weitres gut funde zu sagen, sie zu einer Miltrung zu engag-
ieren, mit anerbieten meiner Diensten und allerley gutes so ich liberiert
wurd: Nachdeme nun ausgeret, observierte dass einer der fürnemsten,
der auch zuvor mir ganz genigt Schine, ja mir auch einmahls Speis
gebracht, und der des Königs Taylors/: deme das Land wo das Stettlin Neuw Bern abgekauf:/ Verwundert ganz ernsthaft rette, nicht
zweifelnd seye zu meinen gunsten, welches auch also wahre, dann
hierauf resolvieret worden, alsobald etliche ihrer Glieder zu denn benachtbarten Touscarusco Dörfern zu senden, und bey inhen der re-
sulat kam heraus dass ich solte bey leben bleiben, der Arme Generalfeldmesser Lauson aber exequiert werden: Zwüschen Leben und Tod
brachte die Nacht durch alle Zeit gebunden, an gleichem Ohrt in
Continuirlichem Gebet und Seufzen zu, Examinierte indessen auch
meinen armen Negers und Sprach Ihme zu, So gut ich könnte, welcher
mir mehr Satisfaction gab als Verhofete, H: General Feldmesser
aber als ein Mann von Verstamd nicht aber von Conduite liess ich
sein Devotion thun, dess Morgends ohngefehrt um 3. oder 4. Uhr
kamen die Precatierten von Ihrer Comission zurück, mit Bescheyd
von Ihrer Negotion aber sehr geheim, einer von ihnen kam Einsmahls
mich loszumachen, von meinen Banden nicht wüssend was das zu
bedeuten, Ergab ich mich gedultig in den Willen dess H: dess allerhöchsten, stunde auf und folgete: ach wie Bestürzt wann etlich Schrit
vom alten Ohrt, der Indianer mir ins Ohr auf ein gebrochen Englisch
sagte, ich solte mich nicht förchten, man wurde mich nicht töden,
wohl aber den General Lauson, welches mir sehr zu Herzen gieng,
ungefehr 20. Schritt von dem Platz wo ich gebunden wahre, brachte

mich der Indianer gegen dem Cabinett oder Hütten und gab mir
Speis zu essen, ich aber hatte kein apetit, Es kamen alsbald ein
grosser Haufen Indianisch Gesind um mich herr, welche insgesambt
grosse freudt erzeigten meiner Erlösung, eben derselbe Mann brachte
mich wieder auf den Platz aber ein wenig weiter hervor wo der ganze
Raht sich gelegret mir auf Ihre Manier gratulierend, Lächlend, indessen ward mir verboten Mon. Lauson das minste zu sagen, ja auch
kein Wort mit ihme zu reden, mein Neger Liessen sie auch loos, sahe
ihn aber nimmermehr, der amre Lauson im alten Platz bleibend,
könnte liechtlich Errahten, dass es aus und keine Gnad für ihne,
nahme Abschied von mir mich ersuchend in dieser gefahr zu sehen,
und nit dörfen mit ihme reden noch ihm den minsten Trost gebend,
bedeutete mein Mitleiden mit etwelchen Zeichen, so ich ihm gab.—
 Eine Kleine Zeit hernacher nahme mich der so im Raht für mich
gerett, und fürte mich in sein Gabinet wo ich mich still halten solte,
bis auf weitere Ordres: Indessen ward der Unglückhaftige Lauson
exequiert: was Todes weis ich nicht eigendtlich, wohl hatte ich hiervor von etlichen Wilden gehört, dass ihme gedreut worden Es Müsse
ihme die Gurgel mit dem rasierMesser so in seinem Sack gefunden
worden, abgehauwen werden, welches auch der kleinere Neger so bim
Leben bliebe, bezeuget, etliche aber sagten er wäre gehänckt worden,
andere er wahre verbränt die Wilden hielten es fast geheim wie er
getödet worden, Gott erbarme sich seiner Seele.—
 Den andren Tag nach des Feldmessers Lauson Execution kamen zu
mir der fürnimsten des Dorfs mich berichtend dass sie gesinnet Nord
Carolinam zu bekriegen: Insbesonders aber wollen sie hinder die von
Pam Tego Neus Trent rivier und Corsund, so dass sie aus guten ursachen mich nicht könnten gehen lassen, bis sie mit dieser expedition
fertig währen, was wolt ich thun: Musste gedult tragen, dann alle
meine gründ da nichts hulfen, Ein hartes, dass ich so böse Zeitung
anhören musste, und doch nicht helfen könnte, noch diese arme Leuth
das minste wüssen lassen, mir zwar versprachen sie, Es solte in Caduca/:
welches der alte Nahmen des stettlin Neu Bern/: kein Schaden geschächen, die von der Coloney aber solten alle hinunter in das Stettlin sonst
wolten sie nicht gut sprechen für den Schaaden, diss wahren gute Wort,
wie wolt ich es aber den armen Leuthen zu wissen thun, weillen kein
Wilder die Avisen bringen wolte, musste es also dem allerhöchsten
überlassen. Bey 500. Streitbahren und wohlbewehrten Mannschaft so
wahren, Ein zusammengerottetes Volck, theils Tuscaruscos doch wahren die Haubtflecken oder Dörfer dieser Nation nicht mitbegrifen die
andern Marmusiken Bay, Rivier Weitoc, Pamtego, Neuws und Cor
Indiens fiengen diss mörden und Blündern an auf einmahl zugleich
abgetheilt in kleine Plutons thäten diese Barbaren die armen Leuth

zu Pamtego Neus und Trent blündren und Ermorden, in wenig Tagen hernach kamen diese Mörder mit ihrer Beudte beladen, ach was trauriges Spectacul solches und die armen Weib und Kinder gefangen zu sehen, das Hertz möchte mir zerbrechen, könte zwar mit ihnen reden aber mit grosser Behutsamkeit: Die Ersten kamen, von Pamtego die andren von Neuws und Trent, grad eben der Indianer bey welchem Logierte, brachte mit sich ein jungen Knaben, Einer von meinen Lechen Leuthen, viel Kleyder und Hausrath, das ich kannte. ach wie gieng mir ein stich durchs Hertz in forchten meine Coloney wahre alle dahin: sonderlich wann da ich den jungen fragte, was da geschächen und Vorgangen were, Er mir bitter weinend erzellte dass von eben den Wilden wie obvermelt sein Vater, Mutter und Bruder ja ganze famillen ermördt, bey diesem allem dörfte nur nicht dergleichen thun, als thäte ich solches empfinden: bey 6. Wochen musste ich da gefangen bleiben in diesem beschwerlichen ohrt Catechna, Eh ich nacher Haus könnte, in was gefahr, schrecken, Schimpf und Vertruss ist liecht zu gedenken,: da Truge sich in der Zeit allerley zu, Einmahls war ich in grosser perplexitet, die Mannschaft wahre alle in dieser Mörder expedition die weiber alle zimlich weit vom Dorf Kirsen zu gewinnen andre Batatos, eine Gattung gelbe sehr gute und angeneme Wurzel zu graben, so dass ich mich ganz allein selbigen Tags im Dorf befund, da Stritte es mit mir, ob mich darvon und nach Haus machen wolte, studierte lang hierüber, in diesem Zweifel funde das beste meinen Gott um beystand anzurufen, dass er mir in Sinn geben wolte, was in solchen gefährlichen umstand zu thun, nach verrichtetem Gebett examinierte und betrachtete den Handel pro et contra befunde endlich das bessere zu bleiben, mich tröstend dass der mich aus erster gefahr Errettet mir noch ferners helfen würde. Dann wann mich Einicher Indianer angetrofen oder gesehen, ich des Todes, da dan kein Gnad ward zu hofen, zu demen wehren sie verbittret worden, dass sie Eheich zu Haus in deme die wägen nicht wohl wusste in das Stettlin kommen, wahre alles geblündret, verbrannt und ermordt, die erfahrung hat es hernach Erwiesen, dass ich das bessere erwehlte.—

Nachdeme nun diese Heiden das meiste von ihrer barbarischen expedition gethan, kamen sie nacher Haus und Ruheten aus für eine Zeit lang, da nahm ich die gelgenheit in acht, und wann ich die vornemsten des Dorfs in guter Humor antraf, fragte ob nun nicht bald nacher Haus könnte: Sie zu Einer günstigen Disposition zu bringen, proponiere ein particularfrieden mit ihnen zu machen, versprach zu gleich einem jeden grandes der 10 Dörfer ein Tuchener Rock, etwas noch für mein Rantzion, dem König 2. Buteillen Pulver, 500. Schrött, 2. Bouteille Raum, Prantenwein von Zucker gemacht: Die Indianer wolten aber vielmehr haben, als Flinten, mehr Pulver und bley oder Schrot, ich aber representierte dass dieses Contrebande, das ist wahre, welche Sie bey Häncken verboten, sie zu verkaufen zu geben, dass ich müsse aufs minst Neutral sein, und noch dem Eint, noch andren beystehen, sonsten gebe es nichts aus unsrem frieden, diese und mehrere Gründ nahmen sie an, so verglichen wir uns wie Euwer Herrlichkeit, Es im beyliegenden Tractat und articlen sehen wird.—

Aber obwohlen wir uns Verglichen so wolten diese Misstreuwige Gesellen, mich doch nicht lassen gehen, ohne Sichere und gewüssere precautionen wolten haben, dass ich mein Kleinern Neger hinunter sandte nacher Neuw Bern, dass alles was ich versprochen nacher Catechna hinauf geführt werden solte, doch wolte kein Wilder mitgehen, obwohlen ein passport oder sicher geleit mitgeben wolte, representierte dass von meinen Leuthen so noch übrig als erschrocken über die räubereyen und Mortthaten, wohl keiner hinauf fahren, und mein Neger allein nicht könnte gegen dem Strohm, mit einem geladnen Schif fahren, da wir uns nicht vergleichen könnten, remetierte ich dem Indianer wo ich logierte, welcher eine Vernünftige Decision unsres Streits herausgabe, so dass wir beyderseits zufrieden.—

Grad eben an dem Tag dass ich den Neger nacher Neu Bern senden wolte, mit einem Brief an den so zu meinem Haus sorg hatte, dass er halben wex die Obermelte Güter senden solte beyderseyts Sicherheit, kamen frömde Indianer zu Pferdt von H. Goub. von Virginien mit einem Brief wie beyliegende Copey ausweisst: Niemand könnte den Brief lesen als ich, der Brief wahre sehr scharpf, wusste nicht was für Continentz haltend, Endlich dachte die Boten wüssten dessen inhalt wohl, so las ich den Brief, denn Vornemsten des Dorfs vor, da ich ausgelesen observierte etwas In ihren Gesichteren, so nicht beliebig, dass sie mich angesicht des Briefs alsobald sicher solten nacher Haus liefern: Wo aber nicht und mir das minste Leyd von Ihnen wiederfuhre: Wolte und wahre er H. Goub: parat mich zu rächen, ja alles exterminieren noch weib und Kinder verschonen, hierauf hielten sie Raht, und ward geschlossen mich zu dem Dorf lassen gehen, bey den Touscaruscos wo der Indianische Negotiant von Virginien war, welcher grad zuvor da Mon. Lauson exequiert in selbigem Dorf sich aufhielte, und ihm zurückreissen H. Goub: unsere traurige avanture erzellet, worauf alsbald dieser generose H. Goub. Spotswood diesen Virginischen Kaufmann, der mit den Indianern handlete und Ihre Sprach ger wohl verstund und redete, mit obigem Brief zu den Touscaruscos gesendt, Er aber H. Goub. Selbstem im Ersten Indianischen Dorf Natoway genannt indessen mit einer starcken escorten wartend, mit ordres an die benachtbarten Militen sich parat zu halten, grad zu agieren, wann nicht beliebige antwort ankomme: So mieche mich des

Morgends früh zu Pferdt, Mit den Indianern Botten auf den weg, und kamen viel von den Vornemsten Indianern von Catechna mit mir gegen den Haubt Dorf genannt Tasky zu, welche so g'schwind Marchierten als ich zu Pferdt, des Abends zwischen Tag und Nacht langten wir an, wo sich der Virginische Kaufmann auch aufhielt, diss Dorf ward befestiget mit Balisaden, und wahren die Häuser oder Cabinet so artig von Binden allein gemacht, in einem Cirkel oder Ring herumb gesetzt: so dass ein grosses Feur, der Raht so von den Vornemsten des Touscarusco Nation bestund, auf dem Boden herum sitzend, da ward platz gelassen, für obgemelten Kaufmann, für mich und die Indianer so mit mir kamen, nachdem ich diese H. Salutiert sassen wir auch hernieder, bey diesem allem wahre ich schon in einer heimlichen Freud, der Hofnung nacher Natoway zu gehen, H: Goub: von Virginien auf mich wartete, und so dermahlen eins von dieser Wilden gefangenschaft, erlöset zu werden, gienge mir aber leyder nicht an. Der Redner der Versammlung fing eine lange Red an, befragte die 4. Indianer so mit mir kamen, was die ursach meiner Detention und Verbrechen nach Verhör, wahre unschuldig erfunden worden, und erkannt: dass H: Goub: von Virginien nach begehren solte entsprochen werden, bedeutend was für gefahr aus dem Abschlag entstehen würde.—

Der Virginische Kaufmann als Dollmetsch redte was er könnte zu meinen gunsten, die 4. Indianer von Catechna wolten sich aber darzu nicht verstehen, aus forcht es wurde alsdann keine rantion erfolgen, obwohlen der virginische Kaufmann sicherheit darfür versprache, pretexierend, sie därfen nicht ohne Consens der übrigen Vorgesetzten und des Königs thun, doch versprechend mich los zu lassen, sobald der König und Raht wurden bey einander sein, wolten aber mein Neger zur sicherheit behalten, bis die rantion ausgericht, den tag hernach gentzlichen meiner Hofnung frustriert, nahme von dem Virginischen Kaufmann mein Abschied, welchen dieser Wilden unfründl: Manier sehr vertross, so Marchierte ich ganz traurig wiederumb zurück, da wir 3. oder 4. Meilen nach bey Henecon Town oder Catechna kamen, hörten wir ein gross geschrey und rufens dort herumb, und kamen hier etliche dorten andre Wilden aus den Büschen hervor, welches mir nicht ohne ursach etwas Forcht einjagte, sondern wann sie gleichsam ganz aus dem atem und erschröcklichem _ _ _ die Englischen und Pfälzer wahren nächer bey Insbesonders aber deuten sie mit einem sauren gesicht die Pfelzer mit retirirenden ja, ja, verspotten, zu bedeuten darmit, dass eben auch meine Leuth als find sich da mercken liessen, und miechen mich ein abweg zu nemen, durch einen wüsten graben, da ich von ferne ein feur sache, da fieng es mir an lang zu werden, in forcht sie wolten mich da in geheim Ermorden: Studierte wie Sie zu bereden, dass die Pfelzer gar nicht mit den Englischen Conjugiert, bedeutet dass diese Wort ja, ja, nicht Teutsch wären, sondern ein Rauches Englisches Wort ay ay welches sonst in gut Englisch yess Heyst, das ist ja, behielte sie also in der Meinung so gut ich könnte: wann wir an das ohrt wo das feur ware kommen, sache mit bestürtzung alle das gesind, von Catechna wo ich gefangen ward, sambt ihrem Hausgeräht wenig Lebens Mittel in einem schönen kornfeld, wo ein Jed: Ind. mitten in einem Swamp, das ist einem Wilden Ohrt einem Stuck Waldes im Morast und Wasser einerseits, anderseits neben diesem Fluss: [57] alle nemlich die Alten ohnvermöglichen Menner, Weiber, Kinder, und Junges underjähriges Gesind vast erschrocken mich beliebt zu machen, und sie meinerseits in Sicherheit zu halten, ermanglete nicht Ihnen allen Trost zu geben, Sie versichernd so lang ich bey Ihnen, nichts Böses widerfahren wurde, representierte auf den Kriegs Leuthen, so kamen das Gesind aufzuMuntren, Sie solten mich Vornenherbey, und mit Ihrer Mannschaft gehen lassen, wolte trachten die Engellander zum frieden zu bereden, wolten mich aber nicht gehen lassen.—

Denn Tag hernach all die umliegende Indianer in der Zahl 300 Tapfere Kerl, kamen zusammen, stossten sich zu den übrigen, und suchten die Christen auf, welche nicht mehr als 60. an der Zahl, und nur 4. Meillen das ist 3. Viertel stund ohngefehrt, von unsrem Dorf wahren, die Pfelzer aber, so nicht wussten wie mit den wilden Indianern zu kriegen, als nur bloss sich zu zeigen, wahren meist alle verwündt, und ein Engelländer zu Tod geschossen, da sie von den Wilden übermeistret, kehrten den rücken, und Eylten nach Haus, welchen die Wilden nachjagten, thaten aber nicht grossen Schaden, als das sie etwas erbeuteten, so kamen die Wilden Zwey Tag hernach zurück nacher Catechna mit Pferdten, Lebens Mitteln mit hüten, stieflen, auch etwelchen Röcken, da ich dis alles sahe, insbesonders ein sauber Barboutine mit Silbernem Carniture, mir zugehörig, war ich ganz bestürzt und in grossen forchten, sie hätten mein Haus und Magazin geblündret, war aber kein schaaden gethan, worumb von meinen Sachen darunter ist weilen sie namlich meine Leuth sich der sachen bedienten, was sie zu dieser expedition vonnöhten wahren: So kamen diese Wilde Kriegs Leuth oder Mörder welcher in grosser glori und Triumph heim, und giengen wir also aus dem Verborgenen ohrt, alle wiederumb in unser altes Quartier nacher Catechna dess abends und die ganze Nacht durch, miechen sie grosse Freudenfeur, insbesonders eins in dem grossen Richtplatz, wobey sie 3. Wolfs Heut steckten, So viel protectores oder Götter vepresentierend, darbey die Weiber von Ihren Zierden oferten, als Halsbänder von Vampon, welches wie eine Gattung Corallen von Calinierten Muschlen, weiss, braun, und Goldfarb, in der Mitte des Rings, wahre ein Conjurer als ihr Priester,

welcher allerley seltsame posturen und bedeurungen miech, und die übrigen danzten in einem Ring umb das feur und obvermelte Hüet.—
Nachdeme dieses Indianische Vest verbey, fieng ich an ungedultig zu werden, fragte Etliche der grossen, ob sie mich jetzunder nicht wolten nacher Haus gehen lassen, in deme Sie Victorios villicht alle meine Leuth zu Tod geschlagen haben, einer aus den Truppen antworteten lachend, Sie wolten sehen was zu thun, den König und seine Räht berufend.—
Zwey Tag hernach Morgends früh brachten sie mir ein Pferdt, Zwey der Vornemsten begleiteten mich bewehrt aber zu fuess, bis ungefehrt 2. Stund weit vom Dorf Catechna da gaben sie mir ein stuck Indianisch Brodt und Verliessen mich, da ich einen langen weg vor mir sahe, Ersuchte ich Sie mir das Pferdt zu lassen, wolte es ohne fehlen zuruck senden, oder solten mit mir etwas näcker zu meinem Quartier gehen, könnte aber nichts erhalten, blieben an dem Ohrt wo ich sie verlassen, und miechen ein grosses feur mir bedeutend, es seyen in dem Wald främde Indianer, solte eilen und wacker gehen, ja für Zwey stund laufen so vast immer möglich, welches ich auch gethan, bis die Nacht mich übernahm, und ich zu meinem erschröcklichen wüsten Graben kam, uber welchen wegen diefen Wasser im Finstren nicht könnte, sondern da ich übernachtet bis Morgends. Das übrige von dieser Reis habe schon meinem H. Goub: Erzelt, ist Zeit abzubinden.
Etwelche Anotationes, dess was ich in meiner Touscarusco, und wehrender Gefangenschaft bey den Indianern observiert nur wie es mir in Sinn Kommen, ohne sonderbahre Ordnung, was unterzeichnet mit Littres a. b. c. zu finden./
Etlich Jalouse und indiscreten Einwohner Caroliné haben fürgeben als wär ich oder meine Leuth der Coloney die Ursach, dieses Indianischen Kriegs und Mördens. Zu meiner Justification konnte wohl viel Gründ dargeben, will aber desshalben nicht vast bemühen, weilen meine Unschuld gnugsam bekannt, doch kann ich mich nicht enthalten, diese Gründ hier anzubringen. 1./So ich die Ursach, worumb haben die Wilden mich nicht sowohl als den Generalfeldmesser Lauson hingerichtet und getödet, 2./hab ich das Land oder Stuck Erdtrich so die Wilden Catouca nennen dreyfach bezahlt den Lord proprietarys, dem Generalfeldmesser, dem Indianisch König Taylor.—Dieser Indianer König wohnte mit seinem Volck an solchem ohrt, wo jetzund mein Haus und das Stättlin Neu Bern angefangen worden, mit welchen Indianern ich und die Meinigen fründlich und wohl gelebt, das übrige Land, hate auch bezahlt so Etwas gefordret worden,. 3./wahre kein Klag, noch wieder mich noch die Coloney, Zeugen dessen die grosse Versammlung der Touscarouscos wo dis in Question kommen, in beysein dess Virginischen Kaufmanns, und da sind die autores dieser

Troublen mit Nahmen angegeben worden,: Will sie aber aus Christlicher Liebe nicht namsen, beyde H. Goub: von Virginien und Carolina sind in diesem berichtet.—

Habe viel Notable Versammlungen gesehen, auch etlichen selbsten beygewohnt, habe mich aber verwundert, über dieser Heyden gravitet und ordnung, Ihr Stillschweigen, gehorsam, Respect gegen den Vorgesetzten, keine Einred als in einem Kehr, und das nur einmahl mit grosser Decentz, keine passion könnte man nicht im geringsten Vermercken, und wahre Zeit gnug geben, zu replicieren, Summa alles in solcher anständigkeit zur überzeugung und beschämung vieler Christlichen Oberkeiten. Der Process wahre auch so ordentlich geführt, als immer bey Christl: Richtern seyen könnte, und habe ich solche schöne Vernünftige Gründ gehört, von diesen Wilden und Heyden die mich bestürzt.—

Da wahren Sieben Dörfer der Tuscoruscos Nation welche sich vast inocentieren wollen, als hatten sie mit diesem Indianischen Krieg und Massacre gantz nichts zu thun, und mit übrigen Indianern, deswegen kein Verständnuss, diese sind etwas weiter abgelegen, mehr hinter virginien, und auch in ihrer Devotion wegen der Handlung, diss noch haltend, diese 7. Townes oder Dörfer, die übrigen in dieser Gegend in gewüssen Schranken und Soumission dieser Tom Blount ist ein König oder Führer, eines Considerable Haufens Wilder Indianer, hat sehr guten Verstand, ist gantz wohl der Englischen Nation geneigt, und hat nicht wenig zu einem guten Frieden Contribuirt: ja es um mich zu thun, viel zu meinem besten gerett.—

Ich kann hier auch nicht vergessen, der generosität und Mitleydens Einer guten Wittfrauwen, welche mir grad anfangs meiner ankunft und Inwehrender meiner Gefangenschaft allezeit Speis gebracht, so dass mir an Nahrung nicht gefehlt, was aber das bedencklichste, so bald sie gesehen, dass da ich gegebunden wurd, Junge Gesellen mich geblündret under andren sachen meine Silbernen ringen, von den Schuhen genommen, und selbe nur mit einem kleinen Seil gebunden, hat sie von ihrer Saubren Mäschenen Schnallen dardurch ihr Harband an der Stirnen gezogen, genommen, und sie an meine Schuh gethan, hat keine Ruhj bis sie entdeckt, welcher Indianer meine Schnallen genommen, selbige von Ihme erhandlet, voller Freuden zurück gelofen kommen, und die Silbernen Schnallen an meine Schuh gethan: Diss wahre ja von einer Wilden Eine grosse gütigkeit, zur überzeugung manches Christen, muss hier zur Beschämung der Christen sagen, dass insgesambt die Indianer viel freygebiger, habe unter ihnen viel gute sachen observirt, als dass sie nicht Schweren, ihr Wort exact halten was sie versprechen, im Spielen nicht bald hadren, nicht so vast gizen, nicht so viel Hoch Muht unter jungen

Leuthen auch nichts ungebührliches observiert, obwohlen sie vast nackend, so halten sie sich Decenter als viele Christen. Das böse unter ihnen ist dass ihr Zorn furios.—

Hier ist zu observieren dass wan diese Barbarische Mörder nacher Haus kammen, So wüssen Ihre Weiber zuvor durch botten, Rüsten sie Sich zu Einem Fest in der Nacht, jede Haushaltung rüstet sich die besten Speise nach Ihrer Art, bringen dieselben auf ihren grossen Richtplatz wo sie auch Ihre Täntz halten, Jede Haushaltung miech eine kleine Brüge, vor deren im Feur so rings umbher und in der mitten dess grossen Platzes ein grosses feur wobey der Priester Stund, die Weiber nahmen sich alle Ihre Zierden, so bestunden in gehäncken dieser Wampan und gleserne Corallen, da nahmen sie weise Stöckli oder dicklächte Ruthen, Stückli, sie grad als ein opfer in der mitten im Ring, alwo auch drey Hirschen-Heut auf gesteckt, als eine Gattung abgötter die Sie verEhrten, die Königin oder die erste nach ihr in Abwesenheit fienge zuerst an, die andren alle nach Einander allezeit singend, wann der Ring voll ward, dann danzten sie alle umb dieses Feur, und die drey heut bis sie Müd wurden, deme gienge eine jede zu Ihrem Stand oder Brüge mit ihren Männern Mahlzeit zu halten,: wann sie fertig, nahmen sie weise Ruhten, Schwarz geringlet und miechen gleiche Ceremoney wie zuvor, nahmen die Ersten stöcklein oder Ruhten, Garniert mit Corallen wider, und steckten die Geringleten an Ihren Platz, so kehrten sie widrum zu Ihren Ständen, Indessen that der Priester sein officieren, die Finde betreuwend Ihn allerley der apscheuwlichsten posturen, hingegen seine Kriegs Leuth erhebend, und zur Dapferkeit ferners anstrengend, hernach gienge das junge gesind nahmen grüne Est von Laub, ferbten Ihre Gesichter mit Schwarz, weis und Roht, liessen ihre Haar hinunter mit Gensen Fläumen so sahen sie abscheuwlich mehr Teuflen als Menschen gleich und Lufen dem grossen Platz zu, mit einem abscheuwlichen geschrey und tantzten wie obgemelt, hier ist zu observieren, von obermelte Wilden Kriegs Leuth oder vielmehr Mörder, einkamen mit ihrer beut und den gefangenen, der Priester und die Vornemsten Frauwen nahmen die armen gefangenen, zwungen sie zum Tantz, und so sie nicht tanzen wolten, nahmen sie sie unter den armen und schlepten sie auf und Nider zum Zeichen, dass diese Christen nun nach Ihrer Music tantzten, und in ihrer Subjection wahren.—

Können also diese Heidnische Ceremoneyen für ihren Cantum Divinum: oder abgöttischen andachten passieren,: dess morgens habe bis weilen Observiert dass sie ein Serioses Kurzes Liedlein gesungen, anstatt dess gebets, und wann sie in gar grosser gefahr dess gleichen.—

Zu Neu Bern wo ich mich gesetzt und das Stettlin angefangen, hab ich unter den Indianern die zuvor da wohnten, eine andre Manier die da etwas nächer dem Christlichen Gottesdienst observiert: Da hatten sie eine gattung altar gar artig unt könstlich mit stecken geflochten und gewelbten Dome an einem ohrt, wahre eine öfnung als gerüst zu einer kleiner Thüren dardurch mann das opfer ein legt, in der Mitten dieser Heydnischen Cappellen, wahren kleine Hölen, worin sie dann hiengen Corallen und auch Wanpom opferten: gegen Sonnenaufgang wahre gesetzt ein Hölzernes Bild, zielmich wohl geschnitzt.— Der Figur wie neben verzeichnet, geferbt halb roht, halb weiss, vor deme gesteckt ein langer staab, oben Truf ein kleine Cron der Stab geringlet, Roht und weiss gegen Mitternacht oder viel Eher gegen Abend wahre oposité Ein ander Bild mit einem hässlichen gesicht, Schwarz und Roht geferbt, so representierten Sie durch das erste Bild, eine gute Divinitet und durch das ander der Teufel, welchen sie besser kennen.—

Hier kann ich nicht für über zu erzellen, was sich mit einem Meiner Lechen Leuth zugetragen, Ein starker lustiger Mann, da Er da vorbey gieng, diese Zwey Bilder betrachtend, mieche alsbald ein Unterscheid dessen, so den guten Gott und des andern so den bösen representierte, weilen dieses mit schwarz und Roht gefärbt welches Just die farb des cantons von Bern, ward er so erbittret, hierüber dass er mit seiner ax oder Biel dis wüste Bild Entzwey schnitte, da er wider nacher Haus kam Rühmete er es als eine wackere That, als hätte er den Teufel in einem Strich entzwey gespalten, welches zwar anfangs nur ein kleines Lachen provociert, aber die Sach dennoch nicht abrobiert. Bald hernach kam der Indianer König gantz vertrüssig dieses für ein Sacrilegium und grossen affront nemend, klagte, sich bitter, deme zwar ein Schertz bedeutete, nur ihr böser Abgott were beschädiget und dahin, Sey kein grosser schaden, wans aber der gute währe, so wolte ich es fast abstrafen: Werde aber hinfuhro solche anstalten thun, dass dergleichen Vertriesslichkeiten, Ihnen nicht mehr widerfahren solten. Obwohlen der Indianer König sache, dass ich diss wesen in Vexaats zog, so gefiel ihme solches nicht, sondern ward ganz serios: So bezeuget ich ihme auch im Ernst dass mir dieses Manns action ganz nicht gefiel, so Er mir den Mann Zeigen konnte, der solches gethan solte er dafür abgestraft werden: Mieche den König und die bey Ihm wahren Raum zu trincken, welches eine gattung Prantenwein so von distiliertem Zucker Truesse gemacht, der Enden ganz gemein und gesundt, so man es mit Moderation trinckt, wahre zu dem gantz fründl: mit ihnen, so dass sie ganz wohl zufrieden, und vergnügt von mir giengen, Bey ihren Begrebnussen miechen sie mehr Ceremoney als an Hochzeiten oder Heurathen, und hab ich in der Begrebnuss einer verstorbnen Witfrauen etwas sonderbahres observiert, will mich dennoch hier nicht fast extendieren, weilen Viellerley gedruckte relationes der Indianer Lebwesen und Manier betrefend, nur im fürbeygang was ich an wunderbahrstem gefunden, und vornemlich wann ein Indianer kranck oder sterbend, so kommen Ihre Priester ins Haus, machen allerley viguren und posturen thun allerley beschwerungen, und geben den Krancken auch allerley artzneyen, so das nicht hilft, blasen sie dem Krancken durch den Mund Ihren atem ein, mit einem Erschröcklichen Rurren, weiss nicht mit was Segnerey, kombt der Kranken auf, ist ein unbeschreibliches Frolocken, stirb er aber ist ein trauriges Heulen, ja sogar, dass es einem grauset: Sie machen Ihre Gräber mit grossem Fleiss, sind gewelbt mit rinden, wann der Verstorbene Ins Grab getragen wird, da standen zwey Priester die Lamentien und machen auf ihr ahrt ein Leichbredig, ist da etwas zu erholen, extollieren sie dess Verstorbemen Thaten, oder dessen Verwanten Trösten Sie, und machen weiss nicht was für allerley abenteurliche beschwerungen: Summa da ist viel Tuhns und Schwetzens, so dass sich die Conjurer, oder Priester ganz in Schweiss gesehen, aber diss geschicht ein gut present zu erwarten, wann alles vorbey, so geben die Erben etliche gehenck vom Wampon oder aus Calcimierten Muscheln gemacht, sind kleine Dinger als Corallen wie obgemelt weiss, purper und gelb, diesen Priestren und diss ist ihr Lohn: NB: Es pflegen die Indianer aus diesen Dingern Hosen und Halsband zu machen, und wüssens so artig und ingenios durch Einander zu Stricken und zu flechten, mit allerley viguren dass sich zu verwundren. Wann alles vorbey und das grab gedeckt, so hat sich etwas zu meiner Zeit wunderbahrs zugetragen, welches selbsten gesehen, Ein artiges feur oder Flammen ohngefehrt Zweyer Kerzen Liechter gross, fuhr grad auf von dem grab in die Höche, als wohl der Lengste und Höchste baum, fuhr wider in grader Lingien über der Verstorbenen Cabinet und so weiter über eine grosse Heyd wohl eine halbstund lang bis es in Einem Wald Verschwunden, da ich solches sahe und meine Verunderung bezeugte, lachten die Wilden mich aus, als wolt ich wüssen, dass dieses bey Ihnen nichts Neuwes, wolten mir doch nichts sagen, was es wäre, habe hernach etliche gefragt, Niemand könnte mir positive sagen, aber sie halten viel darauf, und wird für ein sonderbahr gut Zeichen für den Toden geachtet. Ein artivitial feur könnte es nicht seyn wegen der Lenge und weiten Distanz visicalisch könnte es wohl zugehen als Schweflechte Dunst aus der Erden, aber diese Lange regularitet übernimbt mich.—

Da ich einsmahls in H: Goub: Hidens Haus mich befand, presentz dess Rahts und Vielen andren, da wir wegen dess Friedens mit den Indianern beschäftiget nahm ich in acht eines alten Indianers der mir als ein Conjurer oder Priester vorkam, so fragt ich Ihne was das währe was ich hier oben erzelt, gesehen, unter 25 Indianern die da wahren könnte nur dieser alte neben noch einem andren bericht hierüber geben, welches mir aber als ein Fabel vorkam;.—

So sagten diese dass solches nur grosse Männer, alte erfahrene priester, sehen und thun könnten, da ich sie weiters befragte was das wäre, gaben sie mir zur antwort, dass dis feurlein die Seel dess Verstorbenen Seye, so In Ein andere gute Creatur fahre, so die persohn wohl gelebt, und sich wohl verhalten, habe sie sich nicht wohl verhalten, so fahr sie in einen wüsten rauchen und in ein Hässliche ungluckhaftige Creatur, diese Priester aber komen auf folgende Manier zu ihren kunst, nämlich es trage sich zu dass ein Subtiles Fuerlein oder Flämmlin von Einem Baum in den andren schiesse, aber gar selten, und wann ein Indianer solches sicht, muss er so vast möglich laufen solches zu fassen, und so er es fasset gehets grad an und wird zu einer kleinen Baum-spinnen, welche so Zableten und geschwind in und umb die Hand erwimslete, dass sie schier mit der andren Hand zu ergreifen, so ers aber Endlichen Ergreift, wascht diese Spinnen und wird wie ein Maus, also dass der wo solches wunderding ergreift, hernacher der beste Conjurer oder Schwarz-Künstler wird, und kann allerley Wunder thun,. NB: diese Künstler oder Beschwerer wie sie auf Englich genent werden, haben auch die facultet den Teufel hervorzubringen, und ihne wieder abzufergen;—

Es hat mir ein Schif Patron bedeuret dass er Einsmahls etliche Indianer in seinem Nachen oder kleinen Schifli geführt, und da in dem Caroliner Sund eine solche Stille ward, dass sie Nirgends hinkommen könnten, einer unter den Indianern gesagt, dass er wohl Einen guten Wind verschaffen könnte und wolte: Der Steur Mann so nicht viel proviant bey sich hatte, und gern weiter rucken möchte, liess es an den Indianer, bald hernach kam ein so Starcker Wind, dass ihme grausete, und hätte er gern minder Windes gehabt, allein es musste dadurch, So kamen Sie zu Einer gar kurzen Zeit an das Verlangte Ohrt: Ermelter Schif Patron aber bezeugte mir, dass Er desshalben in Eine so grosse forcht gerahten, dass er sein Lebtag sich solcher Hülf nicht mehr bedienen wolte.—

Diss und obiges mag glauben wer da will, ist gewüss, dass der Sathan viel Illusionen mit den armen Creaturen thut, doch wann solches unglaublich wäre es nicht in einer so ansehnlichen Gesellschaft repassieret und geredt worden: hätte mich auch nicht erkühnt solche fabulose sachen hier beyzubringen.—

Habe viellerley sachen mehr gehört und unter den Indianern observiert, weillen aber schon so viel autors hierüber geschrieben, dass meine remarque nur für repeditionen passierten, sonsten betrefend die Ruhe und Barbarische Manier der Heyden, Indianern und von hiervor Ermelten so sage, dass ja selbe furios wann sie erzürnt, aber so man sie im frieden lasst, ihnen nicht leidts thut, und sie nach Ihrer arth fründlich und gutthatig tractiert,—werden selten die Christen beleydigen, man habe ihnen dann die Ursach darzu gegeben: werden aber bissweillen hart und übel von den Christen, tractiert: habe mit manchem Indianer wegen Ihrer Grausamkeit geredt, es hat mir aber ein verständiger König geantwortet, und Ein artig exempel dargeben von einer Schlangen, so man sie in Ihrem Ring unbedastet ruhwig und unverletzt lasse, werde sie keiner Creatur Leids thun, aber wann man sie Distourbieren und verletze, so stech sie, sonderlich die Spanier seyen mit ihren Vor Eltern gar zu hart, ja vast unmenschlich umbgangen: betrefend ihr der Indianer Morden und hinderrucks fechten, müssten sie wohl sich Ihres Vortheils bedienen, sonsten könnten sie nicht bestehen, sie seyen nicht so starck an der Zahl, und seyen nicht so versehen, mit Stucken, Flinten, Schwertren und allerley andren Verrätherischen Inventionen von Pulver gemacht, die Menschen zu Destrouieren, Item haben sie noch Pulver noch Bley, oder sie bekommen solches von den Christen Selbsten, So dass unsere Weg viel betrieglicher Välscher und Schädlicher Seyen, sonst wir nicht mit ihnen so grausam umgehen würden, sonder unter uns selbsten die grösste Tiraney und grausamkeit verüben,: diss hab ich wohl selbsten erfahren.—

TRACTAT./.

So mit den Indianern gemacht Worden aus dem Englischen Translatiert.-/.

Zu wissen seye hiermit Mäniglichem, dass im Octob: 1711. Zwischen Baron und LandGrafen von Grafenried, Goubernatorem der Teutschen Coloney in Nord Carolina und denen Indianern der Touscarusco Nation Sambt Ihren Nachtbahren von Cor WilkilSons point, König Taylor denen von Pamtego und anderen der gegend Verglichen worden wie folget./.

1./Dass beyde Parteyen das Vergangene Vergessen, und fürrohin gute fründ sein sollend;.

2./Soll der unterschriebene Goubernator der Teuschen Coloney, in Zeiten die Engellender und Indianer im streit, findschaft und Krieg gegen Einander seyen werden, gantz Neutral seyn, Item soll er sich in seinem Haus und Stätlin still halten, Noch Engellander, noch Indianer, da passieren lassen noch keinem Indianer was Leids thun, dessgleichen Sie auch Versprächen gegen den unsrigen: Im fahl sich Etwas Streit ErEugnete unter Vermelten Partheyen, sollen sie sich selbsten nicht Recht schaffen, sonder an gebühreten Ohrt Erklagen, namlich wie Bey Beyderseits Vorgesetzten.

3./Verspricht Ermelter H: Goub: der Teuschen Coloney bey seinen Grenzen zuverbleiben, und kein Erdtrich mehr gegen ihnen hinauf zu nemen, den König und Nation unbegrüsst,./

4./Verspricht er ferners für vier Tag stillstand der Waafen zu procourieren, damit innert dieser Zeit Tüchtige persohnen, Erwehlt und Verornet wurden, heilsame Friedensprojecten zu proponieren, die da wo möglich bey den Streiteten Parteyen müssten angenem und gefällig seyn./.

5./Soll den Indianern Erlaubt seyn zu jagen, wo beliebig ohne Einiche Hindernuss, Es wäre dann sach, dass Sie So nach unsren Plantationen kamen, dass das fich verjagt oder beschädiget wurde, oder gefahr dess feurs zu beförchten.—

6./Soll Ihnen denn Indianern die Waahren und provision in einem raisonable und wohlfeillen preyss zu kommen Lassen,: weiters ist verglichen dass wo die hier unterzeichneten Marques seyn werden, an den Thoren unseren Häusern, dass da kein Leyd noch Schaden soll zugefügt werden.—

So sollen hiermit die hier gemelte Conditiones und Clausullen exacte Observiert werden.—Dessen zu wahrer Urkund wir beyderseits uns unterschreiben, die angewohnte Pittschaft und Zeichen Beygesetzt.—

Zeichen von Neuws. N. Graffenried Gouber: der Teuschen Coloney—

Touscoruscos Zeichen

Touscoruscos Ind:
und Nachtbahren.

Herren Gubernator Von Virginien Mandat Translatiert aus dem Englischem Orriginal—

Alexander Spootswood Goub: Staathalter und Commandant der Coloneyen und Provintz Virginien, als im Nahmen Ihr Königlichen Mayestet von Gross Britagnien;—an die Indianer Nation so H: B: von Grafenried gefangen halten./.

Nachdeme wir vernommen dass H. Baron von Grafenried Goub und das Haubt der Teuschen Coloney, in Nord Carolina unter Euch gefangen ist; Verlange und gebeute Euch, im Nahmen der Königin von Gross Brittanien deren Er ein Unthan ist, dass angesicht Ihr ihn frey und Losslassen sollend, und selbigen in unser Gouvernement senden.—

Und hier habt ihr zu vernemmen, dass wo Ihr Ihne Tödend, oder willends Schaaden zuzufuegen Im Sinn hättet, Ich Sein Blut rechen werde, und noch Mann noch Weibspersohnen, noch Kindern verschonen werde.

Gegeben unter meinem grossen Sigel,
d. 7. 8. bris 1711.   (L: S:)

A: Spootswood.

Carolina New Bern den 6. May 1711.

Messieurs:
Hier übersende nochmahlen Eine Copey in antwort dero vom 23. Aug. an mich und an F. Michel abgelassenen Schreibens den 11. Aprillio hier Empfangen, aus forcht mein Voriges möchte etwan verlohren gehen, verdeute, dass was hier vor an die H: als Hh. Schultheiss von Grafenried geschrieben worden, wir darzu genug Ursach hätten, Solche grosse Unterfangen müssen mit Kraft unterstützt werden, mit so wenigem ist ohnmöglich fortzukommen, were bessre solches bleiben zu lassen, als sich in Gefahr zu begeben, reputation und Ehr so zu exponieren und allen Credit zu verlihren, wann ich aber vorsechen könen, was ich jetzunder weyss, hätte ganz andere Mensuren genommen, forchtsame Negotianten machen selten grossen fortun, und sind H. Ritter und H. von Grafenried ausgestanden, kann ich nicht helfen, werden sich wohl andere an Ihren Platz finden. Wäre es nicht aus Consideration H. J. Ritters und deren, so hiervor Fr. Michel vorgeschossen und an die Hand gegangen, so hätten wir uns mit einem Reichen Engelländer associeren können, wollte aber allein mit uns seyn, so sind nun hier etliche brave Männer, die auch Sinnes einzustehen, aber nur in der Handlung, in dem Sie land genug für das gegenwertige, ist aber uns mit diesem Nicht bedient, dann diese grosse Schuld muss bezahlt seyn: Fr. Michel so in Pensilvania, hat mir zwar vermeldet, er wolle dorten genug H. für Associerte finden, zweifle aber daran, die traurige Erfahrung lehret mich nicht allzufest zu trauwen, ist besser das gewüssere zu spihlen.

Nimbt mich wunder, durch wen die 100£ Sterlin sollen zu Neuw-Castlen entrichtet worden seyn, weilen mir Monsr. Wrag nichts darvon Meldung thut./.

Sie vermelden dass wir in Carolina solten trachten auf Credit etwas zu thun, ist schon genug geschächen, müssten wohl unsern Credit allen anwenden, die Nothwendigen Lebensmittel und Vich für ein Jahr lang zu verschaffen, wann wir nicht mit dem gantzen Volk wolten vor hunger verderben, dann das Unglück wollen, dass wir das Gouvernement wegen absterben des Goubernatoren in höchster Confusion bey unsrer ankunft gefunden, da ich den General-Einzieher zu Haltung dessjenigen, was die Lords-Proprietarys versprochen, treiben wollen, hat Er resignirt indem der Lieut. Gouv. und Obrist Cary noch weder den Neuwen Gouv: Hide noch einichen der Lords Prop.: Neuwen Officieren annehmen wollen, hab' also nicht die mindste assistence auf seiten der Lords Prop: und Gouvernement gefunden, were uns nicht ein Ehrlicher wohlbemitleter Mann, Oberst Pollock und ein anderer an die Hand gangen, hätten wir wie obgemelt vor Hunger verderben müssen. So wahr ich gezwungen bey ihm und andern alles auf Billets de Change zu nehmen und diese Provision musste für ein jahr lang seyn, das ist bis künftigen December, dann die Benachtbarten Insuln, so in grossen Mangel an Victualien, kaufen das Korn auf, ehe es zeitig wird auf dem Felde, braucht also dis geschäft gut Hertz, gute Fründ, und Credit, und wäre ich nicht Landgraf gewesen, so dass ich in dem Raath und Oberen Haus des Parlaments können sitzen, welches mir Autorität und Credit geben, so häten wir alle verderben müssen.—

Sehet also Ihr H. per papant. dass die Jalousie in ansehen diesen Ehren Titlen, so zwar nichts ertragen, nicht wohl gegründet, sondern vielmehr der Colloney solch Ehrenstellen, Vortheil und Nutzen procourirt: Könnte villicht eingewendet werden, dass solches grosse Kosten und viel wesen verursachet, nichts minder, habe deshalb beim Train ja nicht einmahl ein Liverey Rock, halte mich so genauw als der minste Particular, wie Sie es dann von anderen wohl vernehmen werden.—

Betreffend die Mines, so ist Wahr, dass Sie Fr. Michel für die aufsuchung und Entdeckung deren verpflichtet sind, wann ich aber nicht bey der ersten Handlung gewest, wäre nichts daraus worden, und wolte H. Penn nichts thun noch schliessen, es seye dann von mir unterschrieben.—

Meine Beschwerlichkeiten und Mühwaltung betreffend, so ist darüber viel zu sagen, Melden von einer recompense, auch kann ich die Lebensgefahr, Verdruss, unsägliche Mühe und affrönte—die mir schon widerfahren, aus Mangel Erforderlicher assistence, und war ich wegen Protestation der wexel briefen zu gewarten, so ist wahrhaftig keine gross und gut genug für mich, thue besser keine zu Pretentiren, die beste recompense wird Seyn, mich aus diesem Schweren Labirinten förterlich zu ziechen, wird Ihr und mein Nutz seyn.—

In deme Sie melden, dass Sie Villicht alle in diese Land kommen werden, freuwet mich, möchte erwünschen, Sie weren von anfang Hier gewesen und weren noch Hier, So könten Sie Sehen, ob alles so liecht hergehet und mit so wenigem zu machen, hätten auch Ihre Part an diesem so grossen Beschwerden; Mühe Kummer und Verdruss haben müssen, anstatt dass alles auf mir ligt:—

Das Tage Buch von Begebenheiten zu machen wird nicht gar kurtzweilig seyn, weilen bis hieher wenig angehnemes, wohl aber viel Vertriessliches vorkombt; Ein Journal oder Verzeichnuss der Unkösten so Exact vom vergangenen, wird schwerlich zu machen seyn, Insbesonders wo Fr. Michel gehandlet, inskönftig aber wird mehr regularitet observiert werden, so Sie so bald nicht kämmen, were gut einen jungen treuwen Bürger, der die Buchhaltung versteht herzusenden, die Englischen sind gar zu thür, vordern 50£ Sterling zum

Jahr. was aber andere anlangt sey selbsten Lechen oder Handwerks-Leut, so wird man warten, bis der general frieden gemacht, Ein Pfarrer und Buchhalter aber thut noht, könten könftigen Herbst; das ist im Octob. oder 9. ber mit der Virginischen Flotten komen. Muss auch wohl in acht genohmen werden, alles dorten zu Schliessen und zu Handlen, dann wann Sie Einmahlen hier, werden Sie grad aufgeblasen, und wollen selbst H. seyn. So ich viel gelt geben wolte, könte ich nicht einen Knecht noch Magt von der Coloney in mein Dienst bekommen, Lechenleuthe und Bediente werden zu Bern müssen bestelt werden, wie auch allerley Handwerk Leuth.—

Hier ist nun die antwort über alle Articul des Schreibens, nun will ich ein wenig den Zustand Hiesiger Sachen, die Situation und Ertragenheit dess Lands mit wenigem berichten, das übrige referieren, bis mein Vertriessliches und Unruhwiges gemüht in einer Stilleren Situation. So übersende nun Ein Plan in der Eyl und Einfalt gemacht, die Situation der Stadt könte nicht Schöner, lustiger und bequemer seyn. So hanget auch die gantze Colloney daran alles beyeinander und am Wasser, von Einem Ort kann man von dem Mehr hinauf, und am anderen wider hinein, und nur 6. oder 8.— Meilen per Land, glaube nicht dass ein Schönere Colloney in der Welt gesetzet worden, nämlich die Situation betreffend, wird so Continuiert bis nach der Rivier Clarendon oder Cap. fare. ist sicher dass in wenig Jahren, unter dem Segen Gottes diese Colloney fast wird zunehmen. Das Land ist herrlich und gut. Korn, Reis, Hanf, Flachs, Rueben, Ruebli, Bonen, Erbs, allerey Gartengewechs und Baumfrücht, kombt alles wohl für, weyss wenig in unserem Land, das hier nicht auch man haben könne, Wilde Reben sind sehr viel und tragen überaus viel, zweifle nicht man köne sie auch zahm machen, und andere Pflantzen, wie dan schon angefangen, an getränk ob man schon zwar noch kein Wein hat, so macht man Generaliter ein sehr angenemes gesundes und wohlfeyles Bier, von Malasis, welches ein Saft von Zucker und Sasafras, ein wenig gederrtes Weitzen, Korn oder nur Krüsch, andere machen Bier aus Fygen, Quitten, Maul Beer,—Einer gatung rother Neschflen und ander Sachen mehr. GeWild und Fisch, alles im Ueberfluss, allerley gutes Fleisch per sée,—das klein Vich vermehrt sich, kostet gar nichts zu erhalten, Winter und Sommer, so dass wan Einer nur ein wenig hat einzusetzen in wenig Jahren, viel Hundert besitzen kann, und gehet auch die Handlung darvon gar wohl ab.—Die General Handlung dan ist überaus gut, geht aber alles Tauschweis, Gelt ist keines vorhanden, als in den Süd Inselen, und den Landen so die Spanier und Holländer besitzen, zu Landen aber bekombt man es für die Waaren, die Waaren so dorthin abgehen, sind Indigo etwelche Spetzereyen, Zucker, Ruhm, Malasis, diese beyde von

Zucker gemacht, macht uns ein köstlicher Brantenwein, Rysshut, und Fell,/: Weissgerber sehr vonnöhten:/Von wilden und zamen Thieren, Federn und Flum. NB. auf diesen Rivieren sind Schwanen, Gens und Enten Milionen weis, wilde welsche Hüner grosse menge.—

Das Climat betrefend ist ziemlich gut und gesund, nicht so gar warm wie vermeint, Junius, Jullius und august: sind heiss, dennoch geht bisweilen ein kühler Wind, die übrige Zeit des Jahres ist zimlich temperat, im anfang muss man den Tribut mit Einem Fieber zahlen.—

Die Indianer nun betrefend, so sind sie nicht zubeförchten, so man einen Bund mit Ihnen macht, welches schon Sollenisch, Sie wahren anfangs uns aufsetzig, weilen Sie von Jalousen Kaufleuthen dahin angestiftet worden, ist aber jetzund alles still.—

Das Gouvernement ist wohl angestelt, die guten Ordnungen und gesetz aber schlecht exequiert, wahre, wie gemelt, bey meiner ankunft alles in grosser Confusion zu meinem grössten Schaden, ist nun aber besser, allein die Einkünften, so ich pretentire sind hinweg, weilen der Lieut: Gouv: Cary, der sich des gantzen Gouvernements anmassen wollen, den ich aber durch den Neuwen Goubernatoren und Raht einsetzen lassen, aus der Gefangenschaft gerissen und flüchtig worden, zuvor alles verkauft und nun mitgenohmen: Dieser neben noch Zweyen andern haben eine solche rebellion angestelt, dass ich dem Gouvernement mit unsern Leuthen zu Hülf Kommen müssen. Aus diesem Anlass vermelde nochmahlen, dass ich in einer so grossen extremität gestanden, aus mangel exequierend guter Ordnung und Gesetzen, dene der Situation halben eines neuwen lands, dass es nur um den Kopf gestanden, wan ich anders Procediert, dan ich der Königlichen Comité müssen für 5000£ Sterlin Bürgschaft geben, wegen diesen Völkren, so ich nun anfangs, da ich gesehen, das alles fehlt, diss arme Volk im Stich gelassen, mich anderswo retiriert oder Sie vor Hunger lassen verderben: Wäre ich umb die 5000£ verwürkt und ohne gnad aufgehänckt worden, und wo wäre darbey noch mein Gewissen geblieben, könnte ich nun anderst thun als ich gethan: Ist noch viel dass in einem wilden Lande, wo ich sonderbahr keine Fründ noch Bekannten, so viel Credit, dass ich alles dasjenige so uns zur Nothdurft vonnöhten, bekommen hab; Ist aber jetzund zu thun wie mich aus diesem Labirint zu wiglen, dass ich nicht gar zu Schanden werde, und wir alles miteinander verlieren müssen, dan ich in forchten wegen der Protestation der Billets arrestiert zu werden; und dörfte sich Coll: Pollock als der Strengste Creditor alles Emparieren, welches uns allen ein unwiderbringlicher Schaden und grösste Schand verursachen würde, und die gantze Colloney verderben, dan Sie sicher alle darvonlaufen würden.—

So finde nun keine bessere Mittel als noch um 8. assossierte auf das minste zu sehen, wo möglich mehr per 300£ Einschuss ein jeder oder 4. und mehr per 600£, So wir in die Handlung etwas thun wollen, solten wir unsres auch verdoplen, dieses aber dörfte noch lang hergehen, und müssen diese Wechselbriefen, förderlichst bezahlt werden, kost was es wolle, so dunkte mich hierin noch ein experient gut, so die Companey zu meinem Vater gehen würde Ihne ansprechen auf eine Obligation und Einsetzung des gantzen Tractats, von seinen gelteren so er in der Banque zu London hat 2000£ zu geben, bliebe Ihme dennoch eine Considerable portion, und würde Ihn diss gantz nicht incommodieren, ist aber diss experient nicht erheblich, so wüsste ich nichts besseres als sich bei Mng: Herren anmelden Ihnen gleiche Sicherheit gebend.—

Ist hierbey diss zu merken, dass diss nicht verlohrne Schulden die verschwendt, und nicht widerzubringen, sondern alles nach Verfliessung 3. Jahren mit provit ersetzt wird, Die Spezial Rechnung werde diesen Sommer machen dismahlen nur en gros.—

RECHNUNG.

1./ Für Indianisch oder Türkisch Korn zur Nahrung der Colloney und anzuseyen 6000 Maas p. 2 Schillings thut __ 600£
2./ Weitzen 400 Maas p. 4 Schillings __ 80£
3./ Saltz 200 Maas p. 10 dit. __ 100£
4./ Früsch fleisch und gesaltzes für __ 250£
5./ Fuhrlohn aller dieser und andrer Sachen __ 100£
6./ Die Schlop oder Brigantin, welches Fr. Michel in meinem Abwesen gehandlet, da ich nicht so kine wagen dörfen __ 200£
7./ Ein Stoor oder Wirthshaus zu bauwen __ 60£
8./ Mülli und Sagi __ 70£
9./ Unser Losament so zugleich ein proviant Haus __ 70£
10./ Stück 10 Kühe und soviel Kelber 30£. 10 Schwein 10£. 4 Pferdt da zwey für den Lechenman 30£. 8 Schaaf 6£. noch 4 Küh für die Haushaltung 12£. Summa __ 88£
11./ Fournierte Schwein 2 p. familie __ 160£
12./ Provision für 150 Stück p. 3£. __ 450£

Summa Summarum __ 2228£

NB: das Brigantin müsste erkauft werden aus grosser Noth weilen die Fuhren überaus thür und schwerlich zu bekommen, nur eine Reis mit 600. Mass Korn und etwas kleiner zu führen kostete 20£. haben schon den halben Theil an führung gewonnen, ist _ _ _ gut zur Handlung zu gebrauchen, ohne das ist hier nicht zu leben, ist würklich jetzund auf der Reis in die Süd—Inselen, Saltz, Malasis, Corn, Zucker und andere Sachen zu holen./Das Wirtshaus auch nöhtig, diente anfangs für das Proviant haus, dan wir Schermen und Platz haben müssen, die Provisionen zu logieren, sonsten ware darzu noch dieser Grund, das theils wegen wanders theils Lebens Mittel herzubringen, alles daher kam solchen Kosten verursachet, dass in die Lenge nicht zubestehn, dan in diesem Land keine Wirthshäuser alles gastfrey, wan ich Ihnen nicht geben wollen, haben Sie gefordert, und könnte man die Leuth welche 10. 20. 50. bis 100 Meilen weit herkamen, nicht mit dem hungrigen Bauch lassen gehen, so bin ich nun desshalben ruhwig, muss aber provision gemacht werden, tragt aber ein Schönes ein. Mühli und Sagi sind auch sehr nohtwendig, waren darzu gleichsam gezwungen, dan die Leuth ihr Korn nicht mahlen könten, die Sagi tragt ein Namhaftes ein, so sie einmahlen recht im gang, man sägt in Engelland, so wohl als hier alles von hand, die laden kosten unsäglich viel, für 1. Laden will ich bey einer Sagi 6. bekommen, ja wohl 10. Ein Engelländer hat mir für das jährliche Einkommen von der Sagi 50£. Sterlin offeriert, wan aber die Stadt angeht wie sichs wohl anlasst ist 100£. werth Jährlich.—

Die Haushaltung ist Stark könnte wohl nicht seyn, wie sie H. Ritter und Isott zu Londen vermeint in particular zu leben, und in eine Kost zu gehen, Sie waren übel informiert, musste die Plantation zuerst gemacht werden, Losament wahre sehr schlecht, und in Eyl gebauwen, damit man auch im Grund arbeiten und darvon zu essen habe, und nicht gezwungen mit grossen Kosten die Nahrung zu verschafen, dene was nutz sonsten das Land und Leuth, ist noch für jemand in particular etwas aufgenommen worden, ich für mich selbsten, hab noch nichts, wird aber inskönftig für eint und anderer Vorsehung gethan werden

Uebrigens sind viel gute Sachen noch neben der Handlung und rentes zu verschafen, diss ist ein Neuwes Ohrt vor 5 Jahren noch wild und nicht bewohnt, haten die Leuth genug zu thun, mit ihren Plantationen, haben nicht Zeit nach der Industriam Sachen zu erfinden, und zu nutzen: Die Statt wird vest zunehmen, es kommen schier alle Tag Leuth die ein Lott, das ist ein Ackerland, um Haus, Kraut und baumgarten zu Bauwen, der Goubernator und die Fürnemsten dess Lands haben schon alle ihr Lott, ein Lott soll Jährlich ein englich Crone geben. Euch H. haben wir schon einen schönen Bezirk reserviert, und an dem gesundest Ohrt, aber was sage ich hier, diss ist alles schön und gut, die böse und unglückhaftige Bottschaft so von Londen angelanget, verderbt alles: Die Wechsel Briefe sind protestiert, meine Ehr, Credit und reputation dahin, und die Coloney leydet im höchsten grad, der Oberst Pollock so versprochen mich mit Vich zu versorgen, hat meine Leuth lehr zurück kommen lassen, nun habe für diss gantze Jahr/: Trachte demnach die aller Ernsten zu versehen, damit die Klag nicht gar zu gross:/Die Leuth haben keine Kühe, welches einen sehr grossen Schaaden verursachet, gibt so viel Murmlens, dass ich bald meines Lebens nicht sicher bin/: haben gedroht eine Klag Schrift an die Königlich Comité zu senden,:/In solcher Desperaten Condition was nun zu thun, mein gut, mein Ehr dahin, nichts als grösten Verdruss, affront, schand und Spott zu erwarten, würde das Kürzeste seyn mich zu absentieren in eine Insul oder in die Bergen oder gar in Canada zu den Frantzosen übergehen. Indessen wurde die Coloney verschwinden, Pollock sich dahin in possess setzen, so were alles dahin, und vergebens was bisher mit grosser müh und Kosten geschächen; doch thut es weh ein so schön Ort wo ein so schöner _ _ _ Ausblick guter Sachen zu verlassen, eben mit dieser bösen Zeitung, kamen auch Schlim Neuwes von Londen ein, betrefend Virginiam und Marienland wegen der Tabak Handlung: Ist alle verderbt weilen von anderen orten her, Tabac wohlfeiler gebracht, so sind nun diese arme Virginier schier ruiniert, welche all ihr Sach in Pflantzung des Tabakes gehabt, weilen nun Carolina die Einzige Provintz in Englisch America, wo das Vich sich ohne Kosten und Mühe wintern kann, so kombt alles Schwallweis daher, schlagt das land vast auf, so dass ich wohl versicheren, dass was man jetzund mit 10£. in fünf Jahren nicht mit 100 thun kan.—

Messieurs, Sie wollen diss nur wohl erdauren, den schönen provit, so in den 100000 ackers oder Morgen Landes, welches noch ausser lassen, zu machen, und was weiter mehr, Item die schon ergangenen Kösten, die er der Nation und Companey der schöne bevorstehende Nutzen und profit anderer sachen, so zweifle nicht, sie werden alles thun, was nur möglich, einen so grossen Schaaden abzuwenden, und diese so schöne Vorteille zu embrassieren: umb so viel desto eher, weilen nun alles an seinem Orth, keine grosse Kösten mehr als die 50 p. Cent und mehr eintragen, gehet von nun an das Einkommen schon an. H. Betschi ist vor 14. Tagen verreiset, sende Ihne express um die Leuth zu gstellen, dene damit ihr H. von Ihme, als persöhnlich und Zeugen, mündlich allen bericht der Sachen vernehmen könnet, ist gern gangen, und hat sich selbst offeriert./.

Will noch geduld haben, ja so ich den arrest erwehren kann, bis Antwort auf H: Betschis bericht kombt, kann ohngefehrt wohl ausrechnen, wann es sein kann, so aber die vorgemelte Güter bis darmit Einkommen, so werde sicher zu einer grossen Extremität gezwungen werden, und wird hernacher zu spat seyn, zu remedieren, ach wann ihr wüsstet und glauben köntet, was hier ein wenig zu thun, würdet Ihr

H. mich nicht so stecken lassen, sondern alles was nur möglich aufbringen, mich aus diesem Labirint zu ziechen, und diss Coloney-Geschäft mit Kraft fortzusetzen.—
Weilen wir von Londen kein Hausrecht noch Waaren bekommen, so waren wir froh H. Haubtmans Zechenders Sachen zu gebrauchen, wird hiemit vonnöthen seyn Ihne darfür zubefriedigen, und so er noch resolviert hieher zu kommen, Ihne dessen zu wahrnen, damit er sich demnach versehen könne.—
Fr. Michel hat die gewehr alle mit genommen aussert zweyen, hiemit in Holland provision zu machen, aber keine mit Möschern, Platinen./—
Hätte aber über eint und anders wohl noch viel zu schreiben, allein die Viele der geschäften, mein verdrossenes und verwirtes gemüht lasst mir dissmahlen nicht zu, wann ihr H: mich werdet aus diesem Labirint gezogen haben, durch übersendung schleuniger wexlen, so werde dann schon Exactern relation, oder gar keine mehr übersenden, dann an diesem hanget alles; wo nicht Efectuirt wird alles den Krebsgang gewinnen, und weiss Gott was aus mir werden wird. Thue Sie dess Allmächtigen Obhuet allerseits wohl Empfählen und verbleibe./.
Messieurs!

Dero bereitwilliger Diener
Von Grafenried.

P. S. Nach deme gantz verzagt nach diesem Geschriebenen Brief in meinen Gedanken herumb schweifende, nicht wüssend was weiters in dieser so vertrüssigen und gefährlichen Conjunctur zu thun, So gedachte an etwelche Psalm: so sich wohl auf meinen Zustand schickten, meine Zuflucht mit denem eifrigen Gebet bey meinem H: Jesu dem rechten Helfer und Erlöser nehmende, und munterte mich mit gewalt ein wenig auf. Zwey Tag hernach kam etwas daher so mich ein wenig tröstete, kann doch nicht vorbey selbiges zu erzellen, will doch nur die Substanz vermelden, da es wohl eine gantze Histori wäre, und dieser Brief schon ohne das lang genug.—
So kam zu mir ein altlecht Englisch Mänli vom Meer hinauf mir Uesters zu verkaufen, welches nach Fr. Michel fragte, weilen er aber nicht mehr vorhanden, fragte ich das Mänli, was es wolte, gab mir zur antwort, wünschte mit Fr. Michel zu reden, weilen er aber nicht vorhanden und verstehe dass wir gute Fründ, so woll er mir Etwas anzeigen, so mir villicht angenehm seyn werde. Sagte er seye mit Fr. Michel und Goubernator von Virginia _ _ _ Mines gereiset schon vor einer geraumen Zeit, Er wüsste aber wohl eine bessere und reichere, darbey konte er mir alle Umständ von Fr. Michel Reis vermelden,

stimbte wohl überein mit dem was ich schon wohl wusste, da ich Juncker Michel Sache schon gantz verschetz habe, sache hierbey dass doch realitaten, nun diesen Bericht nach, hab ich etwas Hofnung, der allerhöchste, der durch Seine unaussprechliche guete, dem Menschen so vielerley ding zu gutem erschafen, gebe seinen Segen darzu, und uns die Gnad dass wir seyne gutaten nicht missbrauchen, sondern Ihn ob allem preise.—

Diese Mine so das Mänli anzeigt ist ein golt Mine in Virginia da Fr. Michels ein Silber Mines in Pensilvania, und soll lauth aussag diese golt Mines 8 Tag von hier aus seyn, da die andere mehr als 14 Tag von Philadelphia aus ist.—Bey Erfindung dieser näheren und besseren Mines, war Fr. Michel nicht, sonder der Goubernator Nicholson aus Virginia, von der gold Matery wolte der Goub: noch weder ihme noch andern lassen, auch Ihnen verboten keinem Menschen nichts zu sagen, indessen sache sich der Goub: um einen in solchen Dingen verständigen Mann, auch funde er Einen welcher die Sach gantz reich und auf der prob befund. Thaten schon alle anstalten dieses zu éfectuiren, dieser Berg Meister oder Chimist starb aber bald hernach. etwas Zeit hierauf entstunde eine Aufruhr in Virginia, da wurde der Goub: in Neuw Engelland berufen, selbiges Gouvernement anzunehmen, und ist er würklich dissmahlen in einer nahmhaften Expedition gegen die Frantzosen in Canada begrifen, hat auch Fort Royal eingenommen, so ist bey ihm diese Mine verschwunden, und diss Minenwerk unterwegen blieben. Dieses Mänli gab mir noch diesen Bericht, dass einer von denen der mit Ihnen wahre, mit Namen Clärck, ein halber golt Schmid, gotloser mann, der einem andern sein Frau geraubet, und mit ihr sich in die Bergen hinaufgemacht, an diesem Ort Golt gefunden, daraus Müntz gebräget, aus Förcht, so er die Goltklompen verhandlete entdeckt zu werden, ist entlich seyn Gelt so gemein und etwas unterscheid darin gefunden worden, dass es an Tag kommen und ware er als ein falsch Müntzer aufgehängt: Fr. Michels Knecht, so in erwartung bis seyn H. widerkombt, nun bey mir, hat diesen Clerck sehen aufknüpfen./

Diese obvermelte Mines ist nicht mehr als 20 oder 30 Meilen von dem Land wo die Königin uns geben, so diss geheim, könnten wir ein Stück Land weiter hinauf nehmen, könnten wir also der Mine uns emperieren, verstehet sich der Königin Ihr portion vorbehalten, funde gut den jetzigen Goub. mit uns hierin auch zu interessieren, damit er uns an die Hand gehe, hätte auch bald das Mänlein mit 2. Bergleuthen so ich hier bey mir hab mitgenommen und wehren hinauf in die Bergen gereiset, um da den rechten Augenschein zu nehmen, und zugleich eine nahmhafte Curiostät zu sehen, ohnweit von diesem Ohrt soll eine steinene Tafel Seyn 40 Schuh lang und 10 breit auf 4 wohlgehauwenen und geschnitten Füssen. darauf Etwas geschrieben so aber diese Leuth nicht lesen könen, ohnweit darvon sind noch rudera von einer Mauren, und eine zerborstene Schantz./

Dissmahlen aber ist nicht Zeit wegen der dicke der Büschen, da man darvor die Schlangen nicht sehen kan, wird aber könftigen Herbst geschächen, so mir Gott die Gesundheit und das Leben lasst, von Bern auch Ein bessere Zeitung einlangt, dass ich auch ein wenig respirieren kann./

NB: Ueber diese Sum und noch etwelche Fr. Michels Schulden nicht bezahlt zu Londen, und etwas an Wahren, so wir mit ihrem eigenen Consens zu Londen genommen, Item wird von nöhten sein uns noch Etwas an güteren aufs minst für 300£. herzusenden, dan ohnmöglich ohne dem hier zu leben, weil kein gelt vorhanden, alles mit Gütern gemacht wird, muss also für alles zusammen wohl eine Sum von 3000£. aufgebracht werden. Das ist in unserem Land überaus viel, kombt aber alles hernacher auch mit grossem Nutzen Eyn.—

Was inskönftig verschrieben oder an gelteren vermacht wird, wollen sie dem Danson und Wrag nicht zusenden, dan Sie falsch an uns, hat ein schlimmer Berner, er sey wer er wolle, uns sehr übel zu Londen angeschrieben, nebem dem haben wir erst hier ersehen dass Ihre Sachen eben nicht bim besten, Danson als einer von den Propriet: haltet zwar Bona Mines_____Commission zu geben, könnte aber durch mein Vaters Conto_____geschächen, welcher ein ordentlicher Mann, von Ihme auch im Frantzösisch geschrieben werden, und blieben die Sachen in geheim. Diese Danson und Wrag haben meine Briefe aufgethan, welche H:_____mir im Nahmen der Societet geschrieben, welches einen sehr bösen Efect hier in Carolina gethan, dann alles hierher geschrieben worden.

NB. glaube nicht das H: Bötschi wider komme, und so er käme könnte ich Ihn zur Handlung nicht brauchen, weilen Er die Buchhaltung gar nicht versteht, aus vielen starken Gründen ist nöhtig, dass jemand von Euch H: harkomme aber nicht ohne wexel oder gelt, und das förderlich, dann wann ich sterben sollte, alles wunderlich herging;—

Die Reis ist nicht so beschwerlich und gefährlich, sonderlich in Friedens Zeiten, wie man sich einbildet, wir hatten das beste Wetter, und auf der gantzen Reis von Londen aus nur einen kleinen Sturm, ja so man über Schottland säglet und im Meyen ausfahrt:—Der Plan der Stadt und Colloney ist im vorigen Brief versendet und H: Bötschi bringt auch ein.—

NB: So Wexel vermacht werden, kann mann die Billets bey Monsieur Wrag zu Londen finden. Thomas der Balbierer und Chirurgus will nur seine zwey Jahr hier ausmachen, wird also gut seyn einen guten Chirurgum zu senden, kan hier gewinnen, was er will, H. Bötschi hat eines der kleinen Pistolets mitgenommen, wird gut seyn selbiges durch denn Buchhalter wider zusenden ist schaad das Paar zu verderben./.

HANDLUNGS—CONTRACT.

Unser Hilf und anfang seyn in der Kraft des H: der Himmel und Erden geschafen hat. Amen./.

Zuwissen seye hiermit, dass zwischen hernach unterschrieben H. und Fründen, als H. Frantz Ludwig Michel und Christofer von Grafenried an Einem und H. Georg Ritter und H. Peter Isot in ihrem und H. Allbrechts von Grafenriedts H: Johann Anthoni Järsing, H. Samuel Hopf, und H: Emanuel Kilchbergers Nahmen andern Theils mit einandern gegenwertigen Wahren, aufrichtigen Societet Contract aufgerichtet und beschlossen in folgenden puncten bestehend.—

1./Sollen zum fundament dienen diejenigen Hundert Siebenzechen Tausend und 500 Ackerland in Nord Carolina zwischen der Neuws Rivier und Cap fear gelegen, so in dieser Societet Nahmen von denn Lord proprietaris von Carolina sind erkauft worden, Lauth der derentwegen erhaltene Patenten, mit allen darzugehörigen priviligien und Vorrechten, was Sie auch für Nahmen haben mögen, auch derjenigen so noch inskönftig von Selbigen werden erhalten werden, und können gehören auch hierzu diejenigen 1200 und 50. Ackerlands so von H. Lawson gekauft, in dem Egen, bei Rivier News und Trent; gelegen.—

2./Ist auch zum Fundament gesetz die von der Königin von Grossbritanien erhaltene Concession in Virginia, auch was noch ferners von selbiger Königin oder von Ihren Nachkommen daselbsten für Freyheiten, gerechtigkeiten BergWerk, oder andere Concessionen, was nahmens sie immer seyn erhalten werden könnten, so alles zu gutem dieser Societet seyn soll.

3./Wir seyn unter dem Segen Gottes führende Handlung.—

4./Soll diese Societet unter dem Nahmen Georg Ritter, und Comp. Geführt werden, sollen auch alle acten und Schriften, Briefen und Obligationen in diesem Nahmen unterschrieben werden, wird auch darzu die Societet Ihr eigen Sigl haben, soll auch kein assossierter, als der, oder diejenigen so die Societet, darzu begwältigen wird, macht haben einige Acten noch Schriften in der Societet Nahmen zu unterschreiben noch zu versiglen.—

5./Das Capital dieser Societ soll bestehen in 7000 und 200£. Sterlin welche zur Bezahlung obbeschriebnen Lands, zu Unterstützung der schon dahin gesandten Pfältsischen und Schweitzerischen Coloneyen, und denen hernach volgenden wie auch zu führung vorhabender Handlungen, und Bergwerken sollen angewent werden.—

6./Zu formierung dieses Capitals sind gesetzt 24. portionen jede zu 300£. Sterlin, welche allhier zu Londen dem darzu bestelten H. sollen übermacht werden, der Ihme dann auch ein Récipissé darfür senden wird, wird Ihme auch in den Haubtbücheren darvon Credit gegeben werden.—

7./Soll keiner mehr als eine portion für sein persohn besitzen können, wohl aber könen Zwey oder aufs Höchste drey für eine portion conjungieren, wann aber nach Verfliessung dreyer Jahren diese 24. Portionen nicht complet, so soll es denen so schon eine portion haben, noch eine zu nehmen frey stehen.—

8./Bey Abhandlung vorfallender Haubsachen, als Erwehlung eines Directoren, eines oder mehr Deputierten bey dem Königlichen Hof, bey den Lordproprietaries oder anderstwo zu Negotcieren, bey Besatzung aller von der Societet Salarierten bedienten und Embteren, wie auch bey annehmung Eines oder mehr neu assossierten zu Bauwung, und Einkaufung, der zur Handlung dienlichen Schifen, und Eröfnung der Bergwerken, soll alles nach dem Mehr der Stimmen gemacht und erwehlt werden: mit dieser erleuterung dass wo mehr als einer zu einer gantzen Portion sie nur für eine Stimm solten gerechnet werden; soll auch keiner der kein gantze Portion hat, zu einem Directoren erwehlt werden;—

9./Bleibt einem jedweden frey sich in Carolina oder Virginia zubegeben, oder aber in seinem Vatterland zu verbleiben, da dann sein befehlhaber an seiner Statt gleiche Privilegia geniessen soll, Uessert dass er zu keinem Directoren kann erwehlt werden.

10./Stehet auch einem jeden frey seine portion einem anderen zu verkaufen, zu verhandelen und zu vergaben, und zu schalten und zu walten darmit, gleich wie mit andrem seinem hab und gut, und so er ab Intestato abstürbe, soll selbige gleich wie sein übriges gut seinem Nechsten Erben heim dienen, behalt sich allein die Societet vor bey Verkaufung das Zugrecht darzu zu haben, und dass nicht in Tode Hand falle, und Papisten verkauft oder vergabet werden solle.—

11./Wird einem jeden participanten ein Land an einem Ihme beliebigen Ort in der Aufbauwung einer Statt gezeichnet werden, wie auf ein freyes guth von 500 Jucherten in Virginia aber so viel ihme belieben wird, Zins und Zehnd Frey nur was den Lord proprietaris gebührt vorbehalten./.

12./Behaltet sich der H. Michel vor, weilen er das Pensilvanische Bergwerk der Societet zum besten einschiessen thäte, dass Ihme die drey ersten Jahr anzufangen, wann selbige Bergwerk werden eröfnet seyn und anfangen Nutzen zu bringen vorauszukommen sollen, im 4 Jahr dan wird der H. Ritter und H. von Grafenried, das Mehr der Kösten, so sie als der beläuf Ihrer Portion eingeschossen vor dem

Eingang desselben Bergwerk vorausnehmen, das übrige wie auch die noch restierenden 17 jahr soll der gantze sonsten zuhörende Theil der Societet zukommen, verspricht hierbey bey glücklichem Succes obgemelter Mine von diesen ersten Jahren der Societet des H: Ritters Capital zu vergütigen./.

13./So wird H. Michel für seine grosse gehabte Mühwaltung, und für die eingeschossenen Bergwerk zu gutem der Socitet, eine gantz portion gut geschrieben, doch soll er alles dasjenige so ihme von der Societet bis Dato vorgestreckt: und noch möchte vorgestreckt werden, so bald möglich wider vergüten.—

14./Dess H. Christoph von Grafenried aufgelegtes Gelt für 5000 Ackersland in Carolina, wie auch die wegen den Pfältzeren und anderen gehabten Kösten, lauth eingelegter Specification, soll Ihme für eine portion gut geschrieben werden, das mehrere aber soll er lauth des 13. artikuls von der Pensilvanischen Mines nehmen.—

15./Dessgleichen wird H. Georg Ritter für seine gehabte Kösten, eine gantze Portion gut geheissen und geschrieben, das mehrere aber soll er auch lauth 13. articuls von der Pensilvanischen Minen nehmen.—

16./Ist keinem erlaubt in Nord Carolina für sein eigen Conto land aufzunehmen, aussert der genamseten freyen Gütern, sondern alles Land daselbsten soll per Conto der Societet aufgenommen werden.—

17./Soll auch kein mitassossierter weder in Nord Carolina noch Virginia keine particularhandlung führen können, sondern soll dorten alles zum besten der Societet angewendt, denoch bleibt einem jeden frey sich mit anderen die nicht in dieser provintz handlen zu assossieren, und für sein eigen Conto Handlung zu treiben, alles in dem Verstand, dass es dieser Societet unschädlich seye.—

18./Sollen die übrigen hierobvernammseten, H. assossierten, so Ihr Capital noch nicht föllig eingeschossen, selbiges bis nächst könftigen Herbst Monath völlig einschiessen und an die in Engelland genamseten H. übermachen,—

19./Wird dieser Societet kein bestimbter Ausgang gesetzt, weilen ein jeder der nicht gern länger in der Societet verbleiben will, frey stehet seine portion zu verkaufen, im ansehen aber in dieser welt nichts steifes und unverenderliches kann gemacht werden so ist abgeret und beschlossen, dass diese Societet soll bestehen 20 Jahr lang ohne dass in dieser Zeit von Einicher Separation soll noch kan gered werden, nach Verfliessung aber dieser 20 Jahren kan auf gutbefinden dess 3 oder 4. Theils der H. assossierte, diese Societet aufgehoben werden, da sie dann nach dem Zustand, der dann zumahlen befindlichen Sachen, Ihre Theilung nach dem Mehr der Stimmen einrichten Können.—

20./Vor Verfliessung 4 Jahren soll kein separation gemacht werden, jedoch soll jährlich die Beschafenheit der Sachen berichtet, eine Rechnung der Bylantz gezogen, und jedem participanten eine Copey zugestelt werden, nach Verfliessung aber der 4. Jahren soll jährlichen jeder assossierter 10p. % von seinem eingeschossenen Capital beziechen, je nach gutbefinden der sämbtlichen Societet, was aber durch den Segen Gottes in den Mines solte gewonnen werden, das soll jährlich repartiert werden.

21./Bleibt der Societet frey mit dem Mehr der Stimmen diesen Tractat zu erleutern, und zu erklären, zu vermindern und zu vermehren, je nachdem es der Nutzen der Societet erfordert.

22./Versprechen die H. assossierten ein anderen Lieb und treuw und wahre fründschaft, und dass sie alles was zu dieser Societet nutzen und frommen dienen und gereichen mag, nach bestem Ihrem Vermögen wollen helfen befördern, und ihren schaden so viel an ihren wenden, alles ohngefehrt in Kraft dieses Tractats, dessen Zwey gleichförmig und gleichlautende exemplar verfertigt. Es gebe aber der Herr unser Gott seynen Segen darzu, demme allein gebührt das Lob, die Ehr und der Preis von Ewigkeit zu Ewigkeit Amen./.

Beschächen in Londen D. 18. Mey 1710./
Bezeugen William Edwards,
    Edward Woods./

                          Fr: Ludwig Michel.
                          Chr: von Grafenried.
                          Georg Ritter.
                          Petter Isoth.

MEMORIAL.

Ueber Eint und andre Puncten Carolina betrefend aus dem Englischen übersetzt.—

1./Das land in Süd Carolina ausmessen zu lassen kostet per Jucharten ein Pfennig Carolinisch Gelt, in Nord Carolina aber ein halber Pfennig, ein Certificat, die registrierung und Copey kostet 27 Schilling für jede Stück Land so erhandlet wird, es seye gross oder klein.—

2./Betreffend den Wechsel, so ist kein gesetz der Wechsel zwischen Carolina und Europa, aber nach dem Werth der stück von achten, ist der unterscheyd, ohngefährt 35 p. % mehr in Carolina als in Engelland.—

3./Die Wahren so mitzunehmen sind, betreffend, ist das Nützlichste, allerhand assortierte wahren, von englischen Manufacturen überzubringen, worüber wir ihnen berichtlich erteillen können, wann wir wissen werden, was für, und wie viel Volck hinüber kommen werde.—

4./Ein solches nach unsrer anweisung proportioniertes assortiment von Wahren kan in Carolina, wann es erhandlet wird, 200 bis 250 p.%, einiche sonderbahre Wahren aber bis 300 p.% profit geben.—
5./Eine jede Person, es seye Mann, Weib oder Kind, landseingebohrne oder fremde, so sich in Eigenen Kosten in Carolina transportieren lassen, haben das Privilegium für jeden Kopf 50 jucharten Lands für ewig aufzunehmen, und bezahlen jährlich den Lords proprietaris ein Pfennig per Jucharten Boden Zins,—
6./Das Land an Lehenleuthen auszuleichen. Es kan eine persohn welche eine gewüsse quantitet land erhandlet solches wieder in unterschiedliche Plantationes abteillen, deren jede Zwey, 3 4 bis in 500 Jucharten nach belieben halten thut, nach dem der Lechen H: mit dem Lechen Mann übereinkommen kann, worzu der Lechen H. seinem Lechen Mann, mit einer gewissen Quantität Werk Zeug, Negel, Schlösser, Rigel, Pfannen, Fenster Gleser. u. umb ein Haus zu bauwen, wie auch mit nothwendigen Vich als Pfert, Kühe, Schwein u. Wie auch mit nöthigem gewechs für Samen und unterhaltung bis zur ersten Ernd, für welches der Lechen Mann, oder Pflantzer dem Lechen H: zustellen soll, jährlich von allerhand aufwaxes des Vichs 2/3 neben einer gewissen Quantitet Rys, Weitzen u. jenach inhald Ihres accords.— Nachdem ich mich aller in dem land gebreuchlichen Conditionen halben wohl informiert und alles gegen einander ausgerechnet dass der Lehen H: vom aufwaxes des Vichs, und allem gewächs von Lehen Mann beziechen thäte.—
7./Die Productionen des Lands betreffend, ist gewiss, dass es hervorbringt, das beste Reyss, indianisch Korn, Weitzen, Haber Bohnen, Erbs. Insonderheit in Nord Carolina, sie säyen gemeinlich ein gleiches Stück Land ohne gebrauch des Bauws. Es mag aber rahtsam seyn, bisweilen mit dem Samen, nach Nothdurft abzuendern, welches die benachtbarten Pflantzer auch berichten können.—
8./Früsches und gutes Land, ist ohnzeifelbahr zum Reyss das beste, nehmlich dasjenige, so etwas fücht und nass ist, wann es aber zu nass ist, ist nohtwendig mit langen Fourren, und aufgeworfenen Fauschen zu tröchnen, und zum anbauw, bequemer zu machen.— Ist auch thunlich, eine gewisse Quantitet solch feuchten Lands, für die Pflantzung des Reyses aufzubehalten, das trockene Erdtreich aber für Weitzen und andere gewechs zu gebrauchen;—
9./Der Centner Reys/: Hundert und Zwölf £. haltet:/ wird verkauft zu 15 bis 16 Schilling, das indianisch Korn 2 1/2 Schilling die Buschel;/: zu 4 Mäss gerechnet:/ Weitzen 3 1/2 Schilling die Buschel. Was die gersten, haber, Erbs, bohnen, anlanget habe keinen gewissen Preyss gehört, weil solche weniger gebraucht werden, was die Vermehrung einer jeden gatung Gewächs betrift, kann mann solches, in

Lawsons Buch welcher Beschreibung für gantz bescheyden gehalten wird, und ist gewiss dass solche darin vermelte Vermehrung das Land gemeinlich produciert, in ansehen des Preises Vichs, die Pfert werden verkauft von 4 bis 6£. Eine Kuhe sambt dem Kalb umb 2 1/2 biss 3£. Ein Schwein mit ihrem Ferklein zu 12 Schilling, ein Ber 15 S: alles gerechnet nach Carolinischer Währung, so dass ungefähr 3/8. von abgesagdem Wehrt ausgelegt in englischen Wahren mag dieses Vich darfur erhandlet werden. Die Schaaf belangend, so sind dissmahl wenig, aber ihr anzahl mag durch sorg und fleiss liecht vermehrt werden, da man sie alle Nacht in absonderliche Schaaf Hürden eintreiben soll, umb vor den Wölfen sicher zu seyn. Die Form dieser Hürden kan hier nicht wohl vorgestelt werden, könte aber besser mündlichen Bericht ablegen, das Vich vermehrt sich eben so wie in Engelland. Die Kühe und Stuten einmahlen dess jahrs, die Schwein verjüngern sich 3 mahl, und jederzeit 12 14 bis 16 auf einmahl. Ihre Nahrung ist meistentheils das was sie in Wälderen finden, welches genennet wird Range für das Vich. So dass jede plantation bestehend in 500 Jucharten für Vich weyd behalten, dann sie haben nicht im brauch zu heuwen in ihren niederen Gründen oder matten, wie in Engelland, allwo das Vich den Winter durch damit gefütert wird, obschon die Winter in Carolina viel kürzer als in Engelland, so wird doch das Vich, in dieser kurzen Zeit mager und dünn, aber für die Schwein dienen die Wälder, welche allerhand Nuss und Euchlen hervorbringen, zu sonderbahrem Vortheil. Anfangs Winters und ein wenig vor der Zeit, da die Schwein gemetzget werden, nimbt man von der Härd so viel, alls man gesinnet zu töden, und futret solche noch zwey oder 3 Wochen mit indianischem Korn, Bohnen oder Erbs, sie können auch wohl unterhalten werden, in den Baumgerten deren einiche 2 3 bis 4 Jucharten inhalten, von allerhand gattung äpflen, Biren, Kirsen, Pfersich, Parillen u. Sie ernehren sich anfangs des jahrs von gras, hernach von denen abgefallenen Früchten, und wann sie für über, werden sie wider in die Wälder gejagt, damit sie aber nicht vollends erwilden, werden sie von 10 zu 10 Tagen durch das Horn blasen, nach Hause zu kehren gewohnt, da ihnen ein wenig indianisch Korn für geworfen wird; wann sie nun das Horn blasen hören, laufen sie stracks nacher Haus. Das Heuw für das Vich könnte zweifelsohn, aus den gründen, oder Savanas wohl zubekommen seyn, weillen an solchen Ohrten viel Gras wachset, es wird aber aus mangel abmäjend grob und unküstig, wann selbiges aber wie in Engelland gebräuchlich oft abgemähet wurde, könte frisches und zum Heuw bequemes Gras wachsen, Wan hiemit das Vich darmit gefüttert würde, könnte solches in gutem Stand erhalten werden, dann bey diesem Futter und dem Erbstroh, wird das Vich frisch und mastig.—

10./Der Transport kost für jede Persohn 6£. dass also 100 persohnen für den Transport allein Kosten werden 600£. Von Holland bis Engelland, kostets 5 Schilling von der persohn, welches sambt der Bagage kostet 20 Schilling oder 1£. Sterlin, welches in allem 100£. ausmacht.—

11./Derowegen ist rahtsam in Holland eine tüchtige Persohn zu bestellen, welche wir ihnen anrecommandieren können, umb ein englisch gefangenes Schif in einem frantzösischen Seehafen von ohngefährt 120 Tonen zu erhandlen, welches beyläufig 250£. kosten mag, die Wiederausrüstung dieses Schifs mit Säglen und anderen Nohtwendigkeiten zuversehen, kann zum besten und wohlfeilsten in Holland gemacht werden, die Lebensmittel und proviantierung aber in Engelland zu bekommen, welche zur Einladung könne fertig gehalten werden, bis zur ankonft des Schifs. welche Ausrüstung diss Schifs und Proviantierung der 100 Persohnen, bis nach Carolina sich allso belaufen würde, auf 450£. aufs vilste, so dass das Schif ausgerüstet und proviantiert Euer eigen wäre um 700.£. und hiemit umb etwas wenigs mehr als der Transport kosten würde. Es ist aber noch der Meister und die Sägler zu versorgen, von Welchen Sägleren 2/3 müssen Engelländer seyn, nemlich 9 Mann und ein jung, oder 8 Mann und 2 Jungen, welche wir auch verschafen können. Ihre gage belaufen sich 20 bis 24£. monathlich.—Die lenge ihrer Reys von Holland nach Engelland, die Wartezeit auf den Wind und andere Hindernüsse, bis sie von dem land ab, und in Carolina ankommen, mag sich aufs vilst auf 4 Monat belaufen. ich setze also, dass der Schifleuthen, sambt andern unerwarteten unkosten von der Zeit an, da das Schif von Holland nach Engelland, und nach Carolina fahret auf 100£. Sterlin sich belaufen mögen.—Ist das nicht ein wohlfeiles Schiff; und ist das nicht rahtsamer dan ein frachtschif zu mieten, und 700£. zu bezahlen, wormit man anders nichts ausrichten kann, als die Colloney bis an die Carolinisch Küsten transportieren und aussetzen, allwo sie vor sie selbsten Sorgen, und noch Schaloupen mieten muss, um sich und ihre Güter ins Land hineinzuführen.—

Ich setze nun ein solches Schif mit ausrüstung proviantierung würde kosten 800£. und 100£. Gages für die Schifleuth, für 4 Monath, thut zusammen 900.£. von solchen abgezogen 700.£. Transportgelt für obgemelte 100 persohnen, wie auch noch 50£. das Volk in Carolina von den Küsten ins Land hinaufzuführen, restiert 150£. So das Schiff noch kosten würde; Ich setze nun das Schif in Carolina für die Schifleuthe wider zu proviantieren kosten würde, 30 bis 40.£. Sterlin, ich setze ferners das Schif würde sich daselbsten bey 3 Monath, dem Volk mit dem Bood aufzuwarten, und widerumb Fracht nacher Engelland zubekommen, aufhalten. Innert diesen dreyen Monathen kann man sich darauf verlassen, in Nord oder Süd Carolina oder Virginien solche zu bekommen, und ist gläublich das selbige sich auf 550 bis 600.£. belaufen möchte, die ganze Versäumnüss, das Volk ins Land hinaufzubringen, und die völlige Ladung des Schifs anzuschafen, mag sich in 6 Monath verziehen. Der Schifsleuthen Sold für diese 6 Monath und andere zufällige ausgaben, sambt zu 150.£. sich belaufend, von obiger Fracht der wahren, abgezogen restieren 450£. wormit das Schif in Engelland wider mag ausgerüstet werden, und bleibt noch darvon übrig 150£. welches gelt für englische Waahren, für euren Conto kann ausgelegt werden, kann auch das Schif mit frischem Volck, wieder in Carolina versand, und dorten wider mit Wahren beladen werden, aus welchem allem liecht zu ersehen, dass es euwer Interesse wäre, ein solches Schif zu erhandlen.—

Ist allso wohl werth zu betrachten, wie dienlich Euch ein solches Schif sein würde, im fahl das Volk zu einer solchen Zeit in Carolina ankommen würde, da selbiges nicht genugsame Provision daselbsten zum Etablissement finden könnte, in Ermanglung derselbigen, könnte besagtes Schif einige andere englische Wahren nach Pensilvania oder andere benachbarte Küsten führen, und dargegen dasjenige, was zu der Coloney fernerer Subsistentz nötig ist dorten erhandlen. Ist auch rathsam einen Schif Zimmermann mit hinüber zu nehmen, welcher mit Hülf eines oder Zweyer Hauszimmermänner oder anderen von dem Volk in kurzer Zeit ein Schalouppen, ohngefähr 40 Tonen Ladung haltet bauwen möchten. Das Eysenwerk, Seylwerk, Segel muss von Engelland mit hinüber geführt werden, und mag ohngefehrt 80 oder 90£. kosten. Eine solche Schaloupen kann beständig zu gutem Nutzen gebraucht werden, in dem man an unterschiedlichen Orthen, englische Wahren kann erhandlen, wie auch Reys, gesaltzen Schwein und Rindfliesch, Blunder und Weinfass Tauben, Böden und Reisten an andere Ohrt zu Verhandlung transportieren, auch bisweilen eine Ladung Saltz in der Insul Tudos oder anderstwo zu holen, damit man solches nicht von anderer Hand desto theurer kaufen müsste. aus welchen Betrachtung noch viele andere, so da ferners könten vorgestelt werden, erhälet, dass es euch so wohl wegen eigener gemächlichkeit, als profits halber höchst nützlich seyn würde, ein solch Schif und Schaloupen zu halten. Inskönftig dan könnte zur gelegenen Zeit, widerum Holtz gefelt werden, daraus noch andere Schaloupen zu bauwen wären, umb die an banachbahrten flüssen, wohnende Plantationen zur gelegenen Zeit mit englischen Wahren zu besuchen, welches Sie zu allen Zeiten Nöhtig haben, wordurch Ihr grossen Nützen geniessen und zugleich dem Volk mit allerhand Nohtwendigkeit beyspringen könnet, welches hierdurch, je länger je mehr Fleiss und Arbeit anzuwenden bewogen wird; weilen selbiges auf solche weys des

Lands production gegen nöhtige Kleydung, Werkzeug, Hausgeräth etc: vertauschen kann, worüber wir euch particular Nachricht und exacte anweisung können geben, und sind unsres theils willig, solches in Engelland commissionsweis zu unternehmen./.

Neben dem werden Eure englischen Nachtbahren in Carolina froh seyn, ihre Wahren in euer Schif und Schaloupen, für Frachtgelt zuladen, oder ihr Reys, gewechs, Rind und Schweinen Fleisch, Heutte und Beltzwerk, wie auch lebendig Vich gegen eure englische Wahren auszuwexlen, welche ihr könnet an gelegene Ohrt, zu euren Schifen hinbringen, als Reys, Heutte, Fehl und Beltzwerk, Harz und Pech nach Engelland; Schwein und Rindfleisch in Tonnen eingesaltzen, Fasstauben Böden und Reisten, Mehl und Reys Jamaica Barbados, und Antheyoa, von dan kann man wider zurück bringen, so viel Zucker Rum, Zucker Rovalis:/Zucker mähl als ihr werdet nöhtig finden, und in Carolina kan überbracht und verkauft werden. der übrige dargegen erhandlete Zucker, dan kann auf englischen Schiffen, der in diesen Inseln allezeit anzutreffen, nacher Engelland versendt, und dorten versilbert werden, oder von uns nach Dortrecht oder Roterdamm und von dann in die Schweitz verschickt werden, wie dan euch anweisung können geben, wie ihr in Stand zu bringen wäret mit der Zeit, das gantze Schweitzerland mit Zucker zu versehn. Eine andere Schaloupen mag auch beladen werden mit Fasstauben, Reisten und Böden, und nach Maderas gesandt werden, diese Wahren gegen Wein auszuwechslen, und selbige in Carolina zu führen, woselbst wie auch in Virginia um einen guten Preys kann verkauft werden; können auch an besagten Ohrten, an gewisse Corespondenten recommandieren.—Wann ihr aber im anfang mehr als hundert personhen zu transportieren würdet nöhtig finden, könnten wir in solchem Fahl Euch andere Schif mieten, und den überrest sambt ihren Gütern zu transportieren, die Fracht aber des Schifs muss in Londen bezahlt werden.—

Wan ihr köntet mit etwan einer famillien versehen, welche verstunde mit Seyden Würmern und Seyden umbzugehen mit dieser Arbeit, könnte eine anzahl weiber und Kinder occupiert werden, diese Waahr würde von sehr grosser Ertragenheit und Nutzen seyn, welche sehr liecht und gemächtlich in Carolina produciert wird, wie die Erfahrung solches an wenigen erwiesen, wann nur der Hände genug währen, möchte ein grosses Wesen daraus werden, weilen eine grosse menge weyser und rother Maulbehr daselbst zu finden. Ist kaum gläublich wie grossen Nutzen hieraus zu hoffen währe, wann nur fleisige Arbeiter wie auch deren, die sich hierauf verstunden gnug verhanden, eine einige familie so dessen gute Wisenschaft hätte, könnte viele andere unterweisen.—

Der Endich ist auch in Carolina geplanzet worden, umb zu zeigen, was darmit zu thun seye, ist so gut befunden als einiger so von andern Ohrt ist gebracht worden. Es wird von grosser Nohtwendigkeit seyn, unterschiedliche Handwerksleuthe mit überzunehmen, als Küster allerhand, Gschirr zu machen, deren man eine grosse menge haben muss, Zimmerleuth die Häuser zu bauwen, welche gantz von Holtz gemacht werden, äussert dene Caminen von Ziegelsteinen, deswegen auch ein oder zwey Ziegler nöthig sein würden. Tischmacher Schäft, Stühle, Bettstatten, Tische und andere dergleichen Hausgerähte machen zu lassen: Schmieden sind von absoluter Nohtwendigkeit, nicht allein allerhand Eisenwerk zu Haus, Feld und Walte dienlich, sondern, die Flinten zu verbessern, und allerhand eisern Werkzeug zu verfertigen.—

Der Preys des Schwein und Rindfleischs, Mähl etc: Ist als volget— Rind fleisch in Fässlein eingesaltzen, haltend jedes 252lbs.: welches wir nennen 2 1/4 Centner, der Centner ist 112£. wird in Carolina verkauft von 30 bis 35 Schilling das Fässli in Barbados aber Jamaica und ander englischen Insuln, nach dem Solches, auf dem Markt in kleiner oder grosser Quantitet sich befindt, von 45 bis 60 Schilling das Fässli: Schwein Fleisch in Fässlin eingesaltzen haltend 2 1/4 Centner ist in Carolina wehrt von 40 bis 45 Schilling, und wird in gemelten Islen verkauft, von 50 zu 70 Sch. je nach dem der Markt darmit versehen.— Das Mehl wird in Carolina verkauft von 12 zu 16 Schilling der Centner; gilt auf Barbados 20 bis 24 Sch. Fassreifen, Tauben und Böden, der Preys in Carolina ist mir unbekannt, auf Barbados aber werden verkauft das tausend 8£. und bisweilen nur 4 oder 3 1/2.£. dessgleichen auch die Reifen, die Tauben und Böden werden ledig in die Schif gelegt, die Reifen aber werden in Bürden zusammen gebunden, ein 1000 Reifen sind für ein Tonen Fracht gerechnet, von weisen Eichen, werden die Besten Tauben gemacht, insonderheit für Maderas, allda keine andere käuflich sind, auf Barbados aber sind die Tauben von Roseichen und anderem Holtz, auch gebräuchlich für zucker Fesser, für Wein, Rum, Malases, und alle nasse Wahren müssen Fesser von weisen Eichen seyn, die unkösten Zucker von Barbados, Jamaica, antheyoa nach Londen zu, oder Wein von Maderas nach Carolina zu transportieren, können nicht specificiert werden, weilen die Fracht bisweilen mehr, bisweilen minder kostet, als in diesen Kriegszeiten, hat man bezahlt 8 bis 10 Sch. per Centner, zu friedens Zeiten aber kann mans zu 2 bis 2 1/2 p. % Cent Schilling haben.—

Der Wein auf Maderas gilt bisweilen 7£. auch 7 1/2. bis 8 1/2 p. Pipe, jede Pipe haltet 2. hoxheats, jeder Hoxheat haltet 63 Gallons, ein Gallon thut 4 Quart englisch Mass, so dass jede Pipe haltet 126

Gallons oder 504 Maas, eine solche Pipe wird in Carolina und Virginia verkauft zu 15 bis 16 £. etc.

Das Land wann es von den Proprietarys also Erhandlet wird, ist ohnzweifelbahr des Käufers eigen und freyes gut, und hat gewalt solches wieder zu verkaufen, oder nur einen Theil darvon zu vereussern, ohne Begrüsung des Eigenthums H: wann der Käufer des Lands, ein Untherthan von Gross Britanien entweders frey gebohren oder Naturalisiert ist, kann er wohl Land verkaufen, an wen er will, ist aber nicht rahtsam solches an fremde protestanten die nicht naturalisiert sind, damit nicht einige Disputes darüberentstehn, wann aber der Käufer naturalisiert ist, und andere Leuthe die nicht naturalisiert wären decliniert sind, einen Theil daran zu haben, mag es wohl geschächen, wann selbige ihr vertrauwen auf den naturalisiert setzen können, weilen aber ein act des parlaments zu naturalisierung aller fremden protestenten gemacht worden, auch die Unkösten nicht mehr als 3 oder 4 Schilling belaufen, so ist es rahtsamer für alle diejenige, so an dem Land theil haben wollen, sich naturalisiern zu lassen: Hernach dörfen sie wohnen, in Teutschland, Schweitzerland, oder wo es Ihnen beliebig ist.—

Im fahl Ihr ein kleines Schif erhandlen woltet, so können wir selbiges mit Meister und Schifleuth und andren Notwendigkeiten versehen, und nach Roterdam versenden, allwo das Volk kann eingeschifet werden, das gelt solches zu bewerkstelligen kann übermacht werden an Abraham Edens, Kaufmann in Amsterdam, oder Egbert Edens, Kaufmann in Rotterdam, welches so wohl wird versorget seyn, als wann Ihr solches, nach Londen remittieren würdet;: Besagte Abraham und Egbert Edens sind Brüder und Gemeiner wie auch sehr wohl bemitlete Leuthe, welche dem Volck bey dessen Ankunft in Roterdam konnten gute Hülfe leisten, im fahl Ihr das gelt in Ihre Hand remittieren würdet, welches Ihr mit grosser Sicherheit thun könnet.—

Es ist gewüsslich das rahtsamste solche Leuthe zu nemmen, welche ihren transport selbsten bezahlen können, und noch das Vermögen häten, bey ihrer Ankunft in Carolina sich selbsten zu setzen, mit Gewex, Vich u. sich zu versehen. Solchen kan man das Land lehensweys für 11 14 oder 24 jahr à 2. Stüber pro.—Jucharten jährlichen Bodenzins ausleichen, und die Freyheit ertheillen, selbige Lächen wider verflossener Zeit, auf Leydenliche Bedinge zu erneuwern; Es ist gewüss diesem Volk nützlicher, 2 oder wann es schon 3 Stüber wären, zu geben, für solches Land, welches bey oder in einer Colloney ligt, deren Vorsteher Ihnen mit Schifen und Schaloupen, zur verkaufung und Transportierung Ihrer Wahren von Ohrt zu Ohrt oder mit dero auswexlung gegen englische Wahren, als Werkzeug Kleydung p. c. accomodieren kann. Ich sage es ist viel besser für solche Leuth 2 oder 3 Stüber zu bezahlen, wo sie solche bequemlichkeit geniessen können, als Land von denen Lords proprietarys für einen Pfenning per Jucharten Land aufzunehmen: Dann so sie von denen Lords Land nehmen, müssen Sie in allen Dingen für sich selbsten sorgen, und können nicht diese obgemelte bequemlichkeiten geniessen, aus deren Mangel Ihre Lands production Beyweitem nicht so viel ertragen mag,./.

Die Unkösten Volk zu transportieren von Engelland in Carolina, werden sie Jedemnach sie mit Kleydung, Bettzeug, Zinigem und Kupfern Geschirr, Werkzeug zum Bauwen, und Feld Bauw werden versehen seyn, und wann das Volk, so hinüber fahrt, eine gewüsse Quantitet von diesen Dingen und gelt, Ihre Eigene überfahrt zu bezahlen hat, so habt Ihr weiters nichts zu thun, als auch mit einer gewissen Quantitet englischen Wahren, welche mit hinüber zu nehmen, das Rahtsamste sein wird, zu versehen, umb Vich und Lebens Mittel, und Sammen darmit zu Ertauschen, wie auch Vorraht zu haben, mit denn so wohl Englischen als Indianischen Nachtbahren zu handlen, welche für gewüss Euch besuchen werden; um gegen Eure Europeische Wahren, Ihre Landsproduction auszuwechseln; Die Indianer dann werden suchen, Ihre Hirsche und Rehe Heute, Beltzwerk u. gegen Wahren die Ihnen anstendig bey Euch austzutauschen,—: diese Gattung Trafic da Wahren gegen Wahren ausgewexlet werden, wird Euch ser Nützlich seyn, wesswegen wir Euch könen Instruction geben, so wohl welcherley gattung wahren mitzunehmen das Rahtsambste./, als auf was weis Ihr solche mit dem Volk im Land vertauschen könnt: Ein solches assortiment mit Wahren wird kosten 1500 bis 1600£. Sterlin welches mag gnugsam seyn, wir müssen aber 2 oder 3 Monath darvon bericht und gelt haben, alle diese Dinge anzuschafen, darüber wir auch den földigen bericht Schriftlich zustellen können, auf was biss jede Gattung dieser Wahren könnten in Carolina verkauft werden.. Was Euwer Volk anlangt, nehmlich die so nicht vermögen, sich selbsten zu setzen, denen müsset Ihr Credit geben, bis Sie der production des Lands geniessen, und euch wider billichen Ersatzung für diesen Vorschuss thun können, dardurch werdet in der Fehichkeit seyn, einen guten Theil von des Volks arbeit zu geniessen, darüber wir Euch nohtwendige Instructionen fertig halten und zustellen wollen; Es wird auch Rahtsam seyn, mit Euch einige dienliche Sachen hinüber zu nehmen, um den fürnemsten Indianern present zu thun, welche nicht viel gelt kosten mögen: könnet sie durch dis Mittel zu guten Nachtbahren machen, und Einen guten Willen verschafen mit euch zu handlen, worbey Euwere plantationen Ruhig und sicher seyn werden.;

Es wird auch ratsam seyn, allerhand Garten Samen mit Euch hinüber zu nehmen, als Cabiss, Rübli, Rüben, Sallath, Herdäpfel u.

welches das Volk mit aus der Schweitz nehmen wird, was aber da nicht zu finden, kann in Engelland gekauft werden.—

Sie können auch mitnehmen, einig grobleinig Tuch von geringem Preis aus der Schweitz, so da dienlich ist für den gemeinen Haus Brauch und wann solches der Mühe wert befunden wird, kann man Eine mehrere Quantitet verschreiben;—

Man könte auch mit ein paar Fässern Wein einen Versuch thun, ob er mit Nutzen in Londen könnte angebracht werden, in welchem fahl inskönftig ein meheres verhandlen könnte: dann was unser Vorhaben in diesem Unternehmen ist, kann zu beyder Theilen Nutzen gereichen, nicht nur für die allein, welche Land erhandlen und in Carolina gehn, sondern insgemein für die gantze Schweitz, welche Sie durch die handlung geniessen könte. Ein exempel welches dahin dienet, habe albereit angezogen, kann nehmlich die Production in Carolina gegen Zucker in Barbados und Jamaica auszuwexlen, welches nach Engelland, und von dann, nach Roterdam oder Dortrecht, und so fort nach dem Schweitzerland versandt werden, das Rys aber wurde zum grossen Vortheil der Mitassossierten in der Schweitz nach Holland, spanisch Niderland Bremen und Hamburg verhandlet werden, von welchen orten die Interessierten in der Schweitz das Gelt per wexel beziehen.

Wann Leinwand, Wein und einig ander Wahren mit etwas profit in Engelland könte angebracht werden, wann schon selbiger gering wäre, könte es doch zu grossem Vortheil dess Lands gereichen.—

Es wird auch nötig sein, 2 oder 3 Männer mitzunehmen, welche sich auf das Müllwerk verstehen, Wasserpferch oder Mühlen zu machen sowohl fur das Korn als für das Rys: worfür dennoch andere Mühlen erfordert werden, als nur gemeine Kohrn Mühlen, und wann man dieser Leuthen in der Schweitz nicht genug finden könte, müsste man solche aus Engelland oder anderstwoher anschafen und weil es von absoluter Nothwendigkeit ist, Schaloupen und Bood auf den Flüssen zu halten, welche dem Volck zu grosse bequemlichkeit dienen würden ja noch dienlicher als man sich einbildet und es so nutzlich für die, denen die Schaloupen zugehörte, wäre also nothwendig, das Gerüst darzu von Engelland mitzunehmen, da man dann in Carolina allwo das Holtz besser zu bekommen selbige Einwanden und ausfertigen könnte. Wann aber das Gerüst zu einer solchen Schaloupen aus Engelland könte angeschaft werden, wurde es inskönftich zu einem Muster dienen können, ein solch Gerüst mag in Londen ohngefehrt 30 à 35£. kosten, Segel, anker, Eisen und Seilwerck, zu einer Schaloupen müssen in Engelland gekauft werden, kostete 90 bis 100£. auf Meiste.—

Aus dergleichen Anmerkungen ist liecht zu sehen, wie viel kösten aufgehen würden, wann man 4 bis 500 persohnen transportieren und etablieren wolte. Wann ich die Zeit hätte, hätte ich diese Observationen in besserer Ordnung vorstellen können, muss aber solches dismahlen aufschieben, hofe doch, dass gegenwärtiges gnugsam sein werde, daraus schliessen zu können, was zu einem solchen Unternehmen nöthig seyn würde.—

Es ist auch mein Begehren, dass H. Ludwig Michel, solches lesen ja eine Copey hiervon nehmen möge, wann er solches der Mühe werth achtet.—

Wehre sehr nützlich, ein Schif von ungefähr 90 Last oder Tonen zu kaufen. Ein Schif mit 3 Mästen ist besser als ein Brigantin, und wann es geladen ist, muss es nicht über 8 Schuh tief im Wasser fahren, ja vielmehr einen halben Schuh weniger als mehr. Das Segel und Seylwerk könet ihr besser in Holland bekommen, und muss mit allem doplet versehen seyn, wie auch mit nohtwendigen ankern: damit es auch vor den Würmen gesichert seye muss es gefütret werden, diese Würmer setzen denen Schifen allezeit zu, von dem Meyen bis in den Herbst Monath, ihr könnet in diesem Schif etwas Volck von Holland in Engelland und von dannen in Carolina überführen;—Wann also das Schif beladen ist, und Sieben und ein halben, oder aufs höchst 8 Schuh tief fahrt, könnet ihr damit in den Land, und in die Neuss hinauf fahren, Ein so kleines Schif von gutem Holtz vest gebauwet, und wohl genaglet, kann allezeit gebraucht werden, um bisweilen Schwein, Rindfleisch, Mehl, Fasstauben, Reifen etc. nacher Barbados zu überführen, und von dannen wexelweiss Zucker, Baumwollen Rum, Malasis nacher Carolina mitzunehmen, Bisweilen Carolinische Wahren nacher Maderas überzuführen, und gegen Wein zu tauschen, bisweilen mit einer Ladung von Rys, Heuten, Beltzwerck, Hartz und Päch, nacher Engelland zu führen, das Hartz, Pech, heute und Peltzwerck in einem Hafen daselbst auszuladen, das reis aber in Holland zu bringen, und zu verhandlen, und so wider allerhand englische Wahren, als Eisenwerck, Wollenzeug, Tuch Dufils, Mentel für die Wilden, grober Leinwad, Heute, Strümpf, Schuh, Pulver, g'sröt, flinten und was mehr rahtsam seyn wird, in Carolina zu führen. Ihr könnet aber ein solches Schif nicht selbsten erkaufen, sondern müsset hier zu Egberd und Abraham Edens gebrauchen, mit welchem ihr sowohl der Zeit als Condition halber müsset accordieren zweifle nicht dass sie nicht werden bescheyden sein, und euch selbiges sowohlfeil anschafen als möglich seyn wird,: Sie müssen Euch selbiges verkaufen, und ein auf pergament geschriebenen, besigleten unterschriebenen Kauf Brief zustellen, damit wann solches in Engelland ankommet, Ihr erwiesen könnet selbiges von Holländern und nicht von Frantzosen gekauft zu haben, sonsten kan es nicht in Engelland frey gemacht werden.—Auf mehrere Nachforschung hab ich gefunden, dass es ein englisch gebauwen Schif muss seyn, sonsten kan es nicht frey gemacht werden: Ihr müsset auch wüssen, an welchem Ohrt es gebauwen und mit welchem Nahmen es in Engelland eingeschrieben seye, sonsten kan es nicht wieder registriert werden, das Schif muss inwendig 150 Schuh lang und 18 breit seyn.—

Wann das Volck im Vermögen stehet, seinen Transport zu bezahlen, und für sich selbsten eine gewüsse Quantitet Bettzeug, Werckzeug, provision, Vich und Samen zu kaufen, so habt ihr weiters nichts zu bezahlen, als das Land innert 4. jahren Termin, das Schif, das gestell für eine Schaloupen, Segel, Anker, Cabel und Seilwerk für 2 Schaloupen, und einen gnugsamen Vorraht allerhand englischer Wahren, welches alles mag kosten, überflüssig versehen zu seyn, auf höste 3000£. Sterlin, Wann dann Euwer Schif 100 persohnen zu Roterdam einladen, und nach Carolina transportieren, auch 2 oder 3 Monath daselbsten zu dessen Diensten gebraucht wurde, könnte es dardurch per Kopf 8£. verdienen thut 800.£

Restiert _____ 2200.£
Die erste Bezahlung für das Land _____ 200.£
Zufellige Ausgaben _____ 100.£
_____ S. a. _____ 2500.£

Das Schif und die Schaloupen werden Euch alle jahr provit bringen;— Wann ihr die Anzahl Eures mitbringenden Volckes, wissen werdet, könet mirs berichten, damit ich bezeiten Schif dingen möge für diejenige, die in Euwer Schif nicht können eingeladen werden.—

Nach dem ersten Transport werdet ihr nicht mehr vonnöthen haben, Schif zu mieten, sondren es wird euwer Schif alle jahr von Carolina nach Engelland mit Wahren beladen versend werden, und von dannen wider, mit frischem Volk zurück kehren./.

COPIA

UNTERSCHIEDLICHER BRIEFEN AUS NORD CAROLINA.

Neben fründlicher begrüssung thun ich Euch berichten, dass ich mit sambt meiner Haushaltung frisch und gesundt in Carolina ankommen, und das mit Glück, aber den 26. Hornung ist mir mein Sohn Hanss mit grossem Verlangen nach dem H. Jesu gestorben. Hingegen hat meine Tochter einen schönen jungen Sohn, dem letsten

Heumonath 1710 gebohren, wir sind gar auf einem guten und fetten
Land, ich bin der Hoffnung dass ich über Jahr über die 100 Stück
Ross, Rind Vich und Schwein haben werde. Wann man mir schon die
gantze Niederey schäncken wolte, dass ich wider ins Schweitzerland
solte, und die Vorigen Diensten annehmen, so wolte ich es nicht thun
wegen dess gwüssens Freyheit. Wann wein Sohn Uhli Es wurde
wagen sich auch auf die Reys wurde begeben, solte er zu Gelt machen
was er könne, und wann er sich nicht sind meiner Abreis verehlicht
hat, so solle er ein ehrlich redlich Mensch zur Ehe nehmen, wann sie
schon nicht viel zeitliche Mittel hat, wann er nur die Ueberfahrt bezahlen kann, wer herüber will, der kan sich beim H. Ritter in Bern
anmelden, wann du mein Sohn, die Reis wilt vor dich nehmen, so
halte allezeit Gott vor Augen, und auch wann du nicht kommen wilt,
dass wir einandren dermahleins droben im Himmel mit geistlichen
Augen mit Freuden können sehn,: wann du aber kommen wilt, so will
ich dich berichten, wie du sollest machen, kauf ein par hundert stehlene
Tabackpfeifen sambt den Röhrlenen und für 4 Thl. arrouwer Messer,
und etliche möscherne Messer, darvor kannst du schon zu Roterdam
2 mal die Helfte Kriegen, in Engelland und Carolina noch so viel, auf
dem Meer verseche dich etwan selbsten, aussert was auf dem Schif
gibet mit Speis und Trank, dann Hunger und Durst darf man nüt
zusparen, wann etwan mein Schwager Hans mit dir wolte, so kan ers
thun, Ich bin der Hoffnung wann ich gesund bleibe 5 oder 6 Haushaltungen mit Speis und Trank zu versehen, wohl auf ein Jahrlang,
Heissen will ich niemand, dass er sich auf die Reis begebe, wer nicht
die Anleitung von Gott hat, der kann im Schweitzerland bleiben:
wann meine Schwäger Peter Seemann und Uhli Küntzi Lust auf die
Reis hätten, so können sie es thun: unser H. Landgraf von Grafenried wile sie mit gutem Land versehen, hernach wile er ihm 4 jahr
lang Lehen geben, mit Vich und Hausrath versähen, dass sie hernach
ihr Leben lang wohl versehen seyen, wann sie glück haben, hernach
will ich euch wenig berichten wie es uns auf der Reis ergangen ist.
Den Rhyn hinab bis Rotherdam haben wir die grösste gefahr ausgestanden, zu Roterdam sind wir 6 Wochen stillgelegen, da sind 2
Kinder und ein Mann gestorben, von Rotterdam bis nach Neuw
Castlen, sind 2 Weiber gestorben, zu Neuw Castlen sind wir 4
Wochen stillgelegen da sind wir aufgebrochen, auf dem Meer gefahren
8 Tag still gelegen, hernach ist die Flotte aufgebrochen, da hat meine
Tochter einen jungen Sohn gebohren, da haben wir 8. Wochen gehabt
überzufahren, 6 Wochen haben wir neut gesehen, weder Himmel und
Wasser, da sind von 100 Persohnen niemand gestorben, so sind wir in
Virginia an das Land kommen, da sind wir noch 100 Meil zu Wasser
und Land gereiset, sind auf Michels Tag bey unsres H. Landgrafen

Haus angeländet, darzwischen ist ein Weib gestorben, hernach ist man still gelegen bis zum Neuwen jahr, So hat man angefangen ein jeder auf sein ausgetheilt land zu ziechen, bis jetzt sind von 100 persohnen 9 gestorben, ich und Tochtermann sind von einander gezogen, ohngefehrt eine halbe Meil, derhalben wurde ich meines Sohns vonnöthen seyn, darneben thun ich auch H. Pfarrer, und alle meine Verwante, wie auch mein Schwächer und die Seinen, auch Uhli Müllers Weib und Vogt; ja auch die gantze gemeind zu thausendmahlen grüssen mit dem Kuss der Liebe. Bendicht Kupfer Schmied, mein Tochtermann, lasst sein Vater und Brüder wie auch die Schwester fründlich grüssen, und möchte erwünschen, dass sie alle bey ihm wären, er wolte den Vater und die Seinen können mit Speis und trank versehen: Uhli Müller der Büchsenschmied solle mir recht bim H. Ritter schreiben, wie es um meine Mittel stande, wie auch umb die Nachtbauren und Sohn, für dissmahlen nicht mehr dan Gott befohlen; geben den 7. Aprilis aus Carolina 1711. Jahrs.

Von mir Hans Ruegsegger./.

Aus India oder America in d. Insel: Nord Carolina an dem Strohm gelegen an der Neuss.

d. 8. aprill 1711.

Neben Dienst und Gruss, lieber und getreuwer Vater, Mutter, Brüder und Schwester, Kinder und Verwandte, und alle gute fründ, was mich anbelangt wie ich gesund lebe, vergnügt, und wollte nicht dass ich zu Haus geblieben were. Bin auch verheurathet mit Margareth Pfund von Zweysimmen, das Land betreffend thät, ist sehr heiss, weil Wasserströhm, Waldung, die Einwohner oder Indianer sind schwartz, halb nacket, doch verständig und vertreglich, ungläubig, untüchtig zur Arbeit, ich will nicht viel rühmen noch schelten hat man gelt und gut, golt und Silber, so kann er herschen gleich wie in Europa, doch will ich sagen für ein Arbeiter oder armen Mann ist es besser dan hier. Er kann Land Kriegen, so viel er nöthig, Vich kann er halten, so viel er vermag, die Schwein kosten nichts zu erhalten, das Vich geht das ganze Jahr auf der Weyd, wird von sich selbsten fett, und gut zu schlachten, man macht kein Heuw, wahr ist es, dass mancher bis 1000 Stück und mehr Vich und Schwein hat, das Land ist ungebauwet, doch zu hoffen ziemlich fruchtbahr, doch ich keinen Menschen darzu will verursachet haben, noch rathen wegen der kostbahren und beschwerlichen Reis, über das grausame und wilde Meer, doch sind wir glücklich ankommen, und wenig Krankheit ausgestanden, und für mein part so gar saur nicht ankommen, für alte und Junge ist es beschwerlich, doch haben wir einen jungen Sohn bekommen auf dem Meer, der grosse Gott hat alles erhalten, wahr ist es viel hats gekostet

und langsam hergangen in diesen teuren schweren Kriegszeiten, 8.
Merz wie bekannt sind wir zu Bern abgereiset den 9. April kamen
wir zu Rotterdam an daselbst wir geblieben 7 Wochen 2 Tag auf
unsrem Kosten, den 30. Mey segleten wir ab zu Rotterdam, den 4.
Brachmonath sind wir zu Yarmut in Engelland ankommen, weiters
segleten wir fort bis 11 dito, kamen wir in Nord Engelland zu Neukastlen, an daselbst bleiben wir 5. Wochen, darnach d. 11. Heumonath
sind wir von dort abgereiset auf den Seen und Stunden an dem Anker
7 Tage lang auf die Flotten gewartet, alwo eine grosse Menge Schif
zusammen kommen, d. 24. ditto seglen wir ab, und fahren 8 Wochen
lang auf dem See und haben Sturmwind und andere gefahren ausgestanden, doch der grosse Gott bald zu Ende geführet hat, den 10.
Herbstmonath sahen wir Land, den 11. warfen wir den Anker aus zu
Virginia, darnach haben wir, noch eine grosse Reis gemacht bald über
Wasser, bald über Land, wohl bey 80 Stunden, allwo wir wohnen an
dem Strohm, die man heisset Neuss, hiemit so sind ihr noch einmahl
gegrüsst Vater und Mutter, Brüder, Schwestern, Kind und alle gute
Fründ, grüsset mir den Uhli Treut in der asseyten und seyn gantzes
Haus, Hans Klasner und sein geliebtes Ehweib, Rufascher und sein
gantzes Haus. wann ich jemand beleydiget oder zuwider gethan, so
bitte ich Ihr wollet es mir vergeben, wie uns Gott in Christo vergibt,
ich wünsche euch von Gott alles wohl Ergehen, er segne Eure Arbeit
und einkommen, von nun an bis in Ewigkeit Amen.

Euwer geliebter Samuel Jacob Gabley
und Margreth Pfund./.

Aus America oder India d. 9. Aprillis 1711.—

Neben meinem Dienst und Gruss lieber und getreuwer Vetter
Christen Egger, und euer gantzes Haus, könnt ich vernehmen dass ihr
gesundt wäret, so wurde es mich freuwen, was mein Zustand anbelangt, bin ich gesund und lebe vernügt, und wolt nicht dass ich zu
Haus blieben wäre, was das Land betrifft, ist so beschaffen, wer Richtum
hat, Gold und Silber, der kann ein H. seyn, gleich in Europa, doch
sag ich für einen armen Mann oder Arbeitsmann, ist es besser als
hier, will er im Taglohn arbeiten, so hat er alle Tag eine halbe Cronen
an Frucht oder Vich, Gold und Silber ist rar, Land kann er kriegen so
viel er vonnöthen Vich und Schwein kann er halten, so viel er vermag,
und die Schwein werden von sich selbsten fett und gut zu schlachten:
Das Vich geht das gantze Jahr auf die Weyd, ich sag mancher Mann
hat hier bis auf 1000 Stuck Vich und mehr: Das Land ist heiss, ungebauwen, viel Wasserström, grosse Waldungen, die Einwohner oder
Indianer sind schwartz halb nacket, doch vertreglich, doch zu hoffen

das Land sey ziemlich fruchtbar, doch ich keinem gerathen haben noch verursachen, daher zu ziechen wegen kostbahrer und beschwerlicher Reys, über das grausame und wilde Meer, doch vor mein part, ist es mir nüt saur ankommen aber alte und junge Kinder ist es beschwerlich, Langsam ist es mit uns hergangen von wegen der teuren und schweren Kriegszeit. d: 18. Mertz wie bekannt sind wir von Bern abgereyset d: 10. April kamen wir zu Roterdam an, daselbst blieben wir 7 Wochen und 2 Tag. d: 30. Mey segleten wir ab, d. 14. Brachmonath kamen wir in Nord Engelland an, daselbst blieben wir 5 Wochen, darnach traten wir auf das Schiff, und fuhren auf dem See, daselbst stunden wir 8 Tag am Ancker, und auf die Flotten gewartet, daselbst eine grosse Menge Schif zusammen kommen, darnach segleten wir ab, und fuhren über das grosse oceanische Meer, Eine Zeitlang fuhren etliche Schif mit uns, darnach so fuhren wir allein, und hatten Sturmwind und andre actionen ausgestanden, darnach hat der grosse Gott in 8 Wochen ein End mit uns gemacht, und auf das Land gesund gebracht, und Einer mehr ab dem Schif gebracht, als in Engelland draufgangen sind, darnach so haben wir noch eine grosse Reys gemacht, bald über Wasser bald über Land wohl bey 80 Stund weg an den ohrt wo wir wohnen, an den Fluss den man heisst die Neus. Was neuwes, die Krummen sind grad worden, und haben die Kranken auf die Seyten gethan, die Weibsleuth sind gar rar, die Monzua hat meinen grossen geheurathet, aber seine Unterthanen dienen Ihm zum Verderben, und trachten ihn aufzufressen, ein Knaupen auf dem Buggel, ein Knaupen im Bart, ein Knaupen an heimlichen Ohrten, das ich nicht melden will, und ein Schneider zum Handwerk, ein Graf zum Nahmen. Wann es sich solte zutragen, dass mehr leuth in dis land kommen solten; so bitte ich Euch, schicket mir ein 1/2 Dozet gemachte Hemder, ein paar Leinlachen, mehr 10 Ell Leinen Tuch und 10 Thlr. in gelt, ein halb Dozend Messer von Barbli, und ein Axt die probiert ist, und packets zusammen und gebets gewissen Leuthen dass sie mir sorg darzu haben, das mir neut erfaule auf dem See zu Rotterdam, oder in Engelland, kauft mir ein Camisohl und Hosen. Hiemit Gott wohl anbefohlen, grüsset mir den H. Pfarrer, und sein gantzes Haus, Schulvogt Zergen, H. Statthalter und seyn gantzes Haus, H. Seckelmeister Martge, beyde Kilchmeyer Trüwhart und Ihr gantzes Haus, Heinrich Egender von St. Stefan, des grichts und sein gantzes Haus, von wegen seines Sohns Jacobs und Peter Treuthart, Joseph Büllre von Wyssenbach, und sein Ehweib Wassle anna Mary, Jacob Goblei, und sin gantzes Haus oben im dorf: Grüsset mir meine geliebte Cameraden nemlich die frommen Saumer, ich wünsche Ihnen, dass sie mögen viel gewinnen, und reich werden in dieser Welt, dann in jener Welt säumet man Neuth, hiemit so wünsch ich Euch von Gott zeitliches und ewiges wohlergehen: Gott segne Eure Nahrung und einkommen, das wünsch ich zuletst meinem Vaterland amen.

Euwer geringer Jacob Währe von
Zweysimmen:

P. S. Es soll Euch nicht wunder nehmen, dass mein Bruder nüt schreibt; er hat die gelegenheit nit haben können wie ich./ Das zu berichten an Daniel Zant in Eriswyl, ich Johannes Zant in der Vogtey Trachselwald nunmehr zu begeben und gelegener Zeit mit meiner Hausfrauwen Anna Eva Zantin Witwen, so er hinder lassen mit einem Töchterli. So dass er mit Frauw und Kind mit dem H. Landgrafen von Riet in Nord Carolina gereiset, nunmehro aber die Frau Ana Eva Ihr fortun und Kind wider zu versehen angefangen, Eh wir uns auf die Reis zwar ungern aus forcht der so grossen gefahr, die auch mein Mann Johannes Zant wegen dess Todes nicht hat ausgestanden, dan er in dem Herrn Sel: entschlafen, er aber hinderlassen, und mir befohlen, dass ich solle nach Haus schreiben, Nunmehro weil ich gelegenheit hab zu berichten, dass ich widerum anfang zum Haushalten mache, dasselbe aber schwer fallt ohne Mittel, desswegen ich alle und jede fründ, Geschwisterte, Brüder und Schwestern und die 12. geschwornen, und der Weibel, der Landvogt und H. Pfarrer alle übrige gute Fründ, thun ich zu tausendmahlen grüssen und befehle Sie in all weg in Gottes Hut und Wacht, bitte darneben Ihr wollet doch so brüderlich und christlich seyn, und mit schicken was ich zu meinem häuslichen Niderlass gebrauche, nemlich ein benantliches Gelt, welches stehet bey meinem lieben und getreuwen Vetter, Daniel Zant, nemlich 100 Gulden, ist die Haubt Summ und. 15 Gulden ist Zins, dis Gelt könntet Ihr mir mit dem H. Landgrafen von Riet. seinem wexel zuschicken, der Ohrt und das Land, die Rivier wo wir jetzund leben und hausen ist ein guter Grund und Vich Zucht auch gute sichere und Freyheit in Nord Carolina um uns, was anlanget mein Zustand und Leben, so ist mein Tochter Catarina auch in dem H. entschlafen, Ehr und bevor ich an das Land vom See kommen bin zu Virginien und Nord Carolina. Hiemit in die Schutzhand Gottes befohlen und seyt nochmahlen zu tausendmahlen von mir gegrüsst Anna Eva Zantin in Nord Carolina.

A 1711. d: 15. aprillis.—

Ein fründlichen Gruss an meinen Grossvatter Bendicht Schetele von nider Linog und meines Vatters Brüder im Buche, Heinrich Simon und Andreass Krächig und mein Grossmutter im Buche,—So hat unser Vater Bendicht Simon in seinem Todbett hinderlassen, dass wir hinderlassene Kinder noch etwas zu suchen hetten, an meinem Grossvatter Bendicht Schettele: So haben wir ein fründliches Bitten an

Heinrich Simon und Andreas Krächig, wann wir Gelegenheit haben, auf dismahl wanns möglich zu verschicken in Carolina und in Neuw stadt Bern, mit des H. GrafenRitters Wexel. So ist Bendicht Simon seine Hausfrauw, und sein Kind Catarina Tod, und sein Tochtermann Joseph Stern von Riggisberg ist auch tod, so ist Madlena hinderlassene Wittib wider verheurathet, mit Jacob Himler von Madiswyl, und hat Madlena noch ein Kind Johannes Stern und Anna Margreta ist verheurathet mit Andreas Weinmann von Mentzingen, Johannes Simon dies drey geschwisterte sind in Carolina beim GrafenRitter.—

So ist Maria Magtalena zurück geblieben, mit ihrem Mann Johann Heinrich Hanss von Buchse, in Londen, so haben wir Kinder ein fründliches Bitten an unsere Vorgesetzten, sie wollen unsre annehmen als Väter, so seit nun 1000 mahl von uns gegrüsst alle guten fründ und bekannten, Jacob Himler und sein Hausfrouw Madlena, Andreas Weinmann und seine Hausfrouw Anna Margretha und Johannes Simon.

Dass dise hier vernameten persohnen verlangen und Begehren bezeuge von Grafenried.

Johann Jacob Bötschi
Landschreiber und Haubtmann
in Carolina./.

Neuw Bern in Carolina den 20. aprillis 1711.

Mein fründlicher Gruss und alles guts bevor an Euch, min hertzlieber Vater und Mutter, Bruder und geschwister, und Hanss und Bartlome und Bäsi wie auch den Gross Vatter alle guten Fründ und Nachtbauren. Es sey euch kund dass ich durch die Gnad Gottes früsch und gesund bin, solches von Euch zu vernehmen würd mir sehr erfreuwlich seyn, Es gehet mir wohl an Nahrung und Kleydung fehlet mir nicht, aber das gelt ist ziemlich rar im land, ich habe mich verdingt zu dem H. Christopp von Grafenried, Burger von Bern, gewesener Landvogt jetzt und Landgraf in Carolina: dess Lands beschafenheit ist sandächtig, aber doch zu allen Sachen was man pflantzet, doch gibts unterschiedlich strichen, es geratet ziemlich wohl, sonderlich das welsche Korn, wan schon jemand vordert, dass ihr mir schicket, so gebet Niemand nichts, ich bin niemand schuldig, wan es Gott gefelt, und er mir das Leben gönt, will ich noch mein Vaterland besuchen, hiemit lass ich Euch wie obgemelt allesambt zu tausendmahlen fründlich grüssen, ich befehle Euch Gott dem Wort und seiner Gnaden.

und verbleibe Euwer lieber Sohn
Benedict Zionien./.

Neben tausendfeltiger Begrüssung wünsche ich allen getreuwen
Fründen, Nachtbahren und Bekannten Gottes gnad und Segen, ich
und mein Weib 2 Kinder und mein alter Vater sind gottlob früsch
und gesund kommen, in Carolina, und wohnen 20. englische Millen
von Neuw Bern, ich hofe dieses Jahr Korn genug zu pflanzen, das
Land ist gut, danoch der Anfang beschwerlich, die Reis gefärlich,
meine 2 Kinder Maria und Hansli sind mir zu Rotterdam in Holland
gestorben, und an die gewohnliche Grab Stett begraben worden. Zu
hoch wird dis land in Europa gelopt, und zu viel geschulten, ich hofe
auch in kurzen Jahren Küh und Schwein zu haben so viel ich be-
gehre: Der H: von Grafenried ist unser Landgraf, unzifer, Schlangen
und dergleichen ist nicht so viel, wie man in Europa darvon ret, Croco-
tillen hab ich auch gesehen an den Wassern, sind aber bald geflohen,
mit g'wild soll man sich nicht trösten, zu erhalten, dan es sind keine
wilde Ochsen und Schwein, Hirschen und Reh, Enten und Schwanen,
und welsche Hüner sind viel; ich möchte wünschen, dass ich mein
Kind so ich bey meinem SchwächerVater gelassen hab, bey mir hätte,
sambt den 45.£. So ich hinder der gemeind Tofen gelassen und wann
mein Schwächer zu mir kommen wolt, so wollte ich ihn von meinem
Land geben, Schwein und Vich kann man haben, so viel man will ohne
Mühe und Kosten, Mich dauret sehr dass Christen Balsiger sein Uhli
zu Bern wider von mir genommen hat.—

    DIESER BRIEF ZUKOMMEN HANSS WICHTERMANN
        zu guten.   Brunen.—

P: S: Anna Wüll von Rümligen ist auch hier und reich genug—
hiermit Gott befohlen 1711./

Wer zu reisen Lust hat, der kann 100. eiserne Tabac Pfeifen,
Messer, Eiserne Häfen, und kupferne Kessel in Holland bringen,
daran kann er in America wohl 3. oder 4. Mahl so viel haben als sie
ihn kosten, 3. Küh und 4 Schwein ist mein Anfang in Nord Carolina,
der H. Jesus sei mit Euch allen. Amen./.

Unsern fründlichen Gruss alles guts bevor an Euch unsern Viel-
geliebten Vatter, Grossvatter und beyde Mütter, Brüder, Schwäger,
Schwästern, und Geschwey, es sey euch Kund und zuwüssen, dass wir
durch die Gnade Gottes, früsch und gesund sind, solches von Euch,
zu vernehmen wurde uns sehr erfreuwlich seyn, die Salomé ist lang
krank g'sin, aber durch die Gnad Gottes ist sie wider gesund worden, wir
haben noch keinen Predikanten, wir hofen aber bald einer zukommen, ich
hab noch kein Land angenommen, die Taglöhn sind gut, hat einer 1.
tag 18. Stüber macht 9. bz. und die Kost. Ich bin jetzt von meinen
Brüdern gezogen doch in Frieden, ich will bald ein plantage Land
annehmen, welches bis in die 300 Morgen begreift, dess Lands ist

genug, Arbeit braucht es im Anfang viel, wann man aber einmahl ein anfang mit Vich und Schweinen gemacht hat, so kann man sich mit geringer Arbeit fortbringen, es kann einer wohl bis auf 300 Stück ohne kosten haben, dass sie feyss genug werden, aber ziemlich wild, aber die Reys bis daher zu kommen ist kostbahr und beschwerlich eine persohn über Meer von Roterdam aus Holland 34 Thr. alwo wir 7 Wochen und 2 Tag auf unsere Kösten gelegen sind, den 30. Mey sind wir auf des Transport Schif getreten, und sind gefahren bis nach Brüll auf das Meer, den 4. Brachmonath sind wir bis nach Jarmouth kommen, den 11. in Neuw Castle, an ein ohrt in Engelland gelegen, allwo wir 5 Wochen still gelegen sind, den 17. Heuwmonath sind wir wieder auf das Schif getreten und zurück bis nach Schiel auf das Mehr gefahren, alwo wir 8 Tag stille gelegen, und auf die Flotten gewartet haben, welche 4 Tag mit uns gefahren ist welches über die 100 Schif gewessen sind, hernach sind wir allein gefahren, sind oft in grosser Gefahr gewesen, und sind durch die Güte Gottes glücklich allhier ankommen, ist Niemand unter uns gestorben, darum wir dem gütigen Gott nicht genug können danken, den 10. Herbst umb 9 Uhren haben wir Land gesehen, dess Nachts den Ancker geworfen, den 11. sind wir auf das Land getreten, welches uns sehr erfreulich gewesen ist, dann wir haben eine lange Zeit Nichts als Wasser und Luft gesehen, von Virginien ist es noch gar beschwerlich mit dem Bagage bald über Wasser bald über Land, wir wohnen in Nord Carolina am Strohm Neuss gennant, das Land betrefend ist ziemlich sandig, doch fruchtbar, zu allen Früchten ziemlich gut, sonderlich zum welschen Korn, Obs belangend wachst ohngepflantz nicht, weder schlecht noch gut, die gebohrene Einwohner dess Lands sind geschwind aber nackend, um die Heimlichkeit haben Sie Röck, und sonst Schürtz; für dissmahlen neut mehr, grüsset mir mein fründ Ziorien, und mein Mutter lasst Euch fürbefohlen seyn; grüsset uns alle guten Fründ und Nachtbahren, und ich befiehlen Euch Gott, dem Wort und seiner Gnad, und verbleibe eure liebe Kinder Michel Ziorien und Salomé von Mühlenen.

  An Christen von Mühlenen in der Schweitz im Bern Gebiet, im obern Simmenthal in der Kirchfäry Boltigen auf dem Flühli./.

 Min fründlicher Gruss und alles Guts zuvor Hans Aeschbacher, den Wirdt Uhli Bäche, dess Vetter auch alle meine g'fatter Leuth und gute Nachtbauren, Euch zu berichten, dass wir gottlob frisch und gesund sind, das Ani ist mir g'storben, es reuet mich sehr, Es ist Niemand gestorben als 3. Weiber, mein Ani ist die ganze Reys krank g'sin, wir haben kein Weibervolck das uns wäscht und flickt, ich bitte

Euch, wann das Erb g'fallen ist, so schicket mir es, ihr dörft es nur dem H. Ritter überliefern, schicket mir einen guten Knecht, 2 gute Mägt, 2 gute achsen, dann der Dietrich hat nicht Zeit zu schmieden, ich hab viel zu arbeiten, 250 Morgen Land angenommen, wann ich will kann ich 400 nehmen, ich hab Gelt von nöthen dass ich könnt Ross Vich und Schwein haben, ich könnt wohl 200 Stück haben Sommer und Winter ohne Mühe und Kösten, es ist hier miesch an den Bäumen, das den Winter so gut ist als das beste Embd und Eichlen auch sollen mir die Diensten ein Kistli machen lassen, und sollen 200 Ell flächsig Tuch, 100 Ell reistige Zwilchen, bey dem Schmied 4 sieben pfündige Leg Eisen, mit sambt den Lungen, Ein klein Naben Neyer, für Pflug reder zu bohren, 2.£. Pfeferkörner, 1/2.£. Nägeli 2 Möllstein die um das halb schwerer seyn, als ein Hand Mühli, aber die Spetzerey und Mühlisteinen müssen sie erst zu Rotterdam kaufen, auch kaufet mir ein Baar gegossene Tabackpfeifen, und ein 12 Von der andern 2 batzigen 2 Dotzen, etwas von Eysenpfannen von doppleten nur die Schalen ohne Fuess und ohne Stihl, dass in die kleinste ein Maass gehe, die andern aber grösser, und ein Dotzend harnige Röhrli, ich könnte für eine Pfeifen 5.£. kriegen, und auch ein paar Möschig Schuhringen, die Indianer kaufen solche Sachen so theür, als man will, Es ist der Grösste Fehler und Mangel hier in Carolina, dass zu wenig Leuth hier sind, und kein rechte Mühli, es wird aber von uns Leuthen, die hier in Carolina sind, kein Mensch Verlangen tragen noch einmahl ins Schweitzerland zu seyn oder zu bleiben, dann man kann in dem Schweitzerland gar wenig Fleisch essen, hier aber in Carolina darf ich nicht Kummer haben, für diss jahr hin, dass ich nicht alle Jahr 30 oder 40 bis 50 Schwein metzge, mehr wann ich will, und wann mir schon Vetter HaldMann den ganzen Hofacker wolte schencken, und alles was darzu ghört, so wollte ich nit, dan ich Weid und Waldungen für die Schwein und Ackerfeld alles genug an einandren, wann ich nur Gelt hätte, dass ich könnt ein halb dotzend Küh, und auch so viel Schwein, ein paar Ross kaufen, so verlangte ich hier zeitlich nicht mehr als die liebe Gesundheit nach dem das ewige Leben. Wie ich auch allen Menschen gönnen möchte, auch möchte ich erwünschen, dass die Nohtleidenden Nachtbauren bey uns wären, son dörften Sie nit Kummer haben, dass Sie müssten Hunger leyden, wann sie nur ein wenig arbeiten wollten, darum welcher Lust hat, der wage es nur käcklich unter dem Schutz des Allerhöchsten, Zwar man gibt eim nicht gebaute Häuser und gebutz Land, es mag darnach ein jeder selber arbeiten und Butzen, zwar die Reys ist schwer und hat mich am hertesten gehabt, aber nach dem Regen kombt Sonnenschein, aber jetzunder sind wir Gottlob so frisch als wir nie gewesen sind, und dess Wiebels Tochter hat ein Sohn gebohren auf dem Meer, und ist alles noch frisch und gesund. Sie sind des H. Gouverneurs Lehenleut und haben die beste sach, das Lechen aber wehrt 4. Jahr, und alle Wochen kann er ein Tag auf seinem Lechen arbeiten, und der halb aufwachs ist seyn an denn Pfannwärten, auch ist die Reys gar kostbahr gewesen, wir haben 8. Wochen zu Rotterdam ligen müssen, und ist gar theur gewesen, auch wie für 6. persohnen, den Schifmann von Bern, 31 Thr. zahlen, auch dem Schif Capitain über meer zu führen, 204 Thr. bezahlt, von dem Schif über Meer haben wir durch Virginien bis auf unsern Platz mehr als 100 Meil über Land müssen reisen, von wegen den Seeräubern, da wir zu spaad in Holland ankommen sind, und die Flotten versambelt haben, sind mit unserm Schif allein gefahren, und sind 8. Wochen auf dem Meer gefahren, aber jetzund haben wir gut fürtreflich Land. Schicket mir auch ein paar Dotzend ordentliche Messer, es ist grosser Mangel an teuschem Weiber Volck, grüsst mir mein SchwächerVatter, wann er noch lebt, meine Schwäger und g'sweyen, voraus aber den Christen Hausmann im Heybühl und seyn Frauw, ich und der Dietrich sein Knecht lassen den Schmied und Hanns zur Flüh fründlich grüssen, Es wär gut, wann die beyd hier währen, Sie könnten g'wunnen was sie wolten, was die Handwerk betrifft, so sind das die besten, Wafenschmied, Büchsenschmied, Zimmerleuth, Schneyder, Schuhmacher, Plattmacher und Seyler, wann diese kämen, so wäre es köstlich gut, auch Weber, wann ich für 30£. Messer und die obgemelten Wahren hier hätte, so könte ich mehr als 100 Englische £. g'winnen, ein Cronen ist mehr als in Teuschland ein Thlr. den 8. april 1711./ Der Casper Gerber solle dem H. Ritter in Bern übergeben, und verhofend wann mein Schwacher noch lebt, er werde mir auch noch ein Ehelich Reysgelt schicken, wann wider Volk solt hieher kommen, und ihr mir Diensten schicken könnt, so schickt mir doch die obgemelten Wahren, die aber gehen wollen, müssen sich bey H. Ritter anmelden, dass wann das ander Volck verreisen wolt, sie mit einander reisen, und wann das Erb gefallen ist, so gebet jedwederem Götti ein halber Thr. nemlich, dem Peter habegger, Helm Kupferschmied, Uhli Burger, und Niclaus Balts, wann sie noch bey Leben sind, hiermit nichts weiters, wir wünschen Euch gute Gesundheit und langes Leben, zeitliche und ewige Wohlfahrt an Seel und Leib: Lasst mir auch ein halb Dotzend deren Drucken kaufen, wie der Uhli Lerche mir eine geben, auch bezahlet dem H. Ritter den Brief. Es Wäre gut, wann einer oder 2. Kessler nemlich Flicker kämen, ich hab nicht Zeit mehr zu schreiben, sie ist mir zu kurtz./.

Christen Engel.

Copia eines Briefs geschrieben, von Christen Janzen aus Nord Carolina den letsten aprillis 1711.—

Gott zum Gruss liebste Seelen, Vatter, Mutter, Geschwisterte, Fründ und Nachtbauren, neben unser allerseits tausendfältigen Gruss und g'horsame Dienste, hat unsere G'sundheit zu dieser Stund zu vernehmen, und zu wüssen, dass ich mein Schreiben, so kurz als ich es fassen kann, geben muss; ich hofe ihr habet die Briefen die ich aus Hol-und Engel-Land geschrieben, der nohtwendigst Inhalt war, dass wir den 10. Brachmonath in Neuwcastle in Engelland glücklich ankommen, aber den 6t. war ich ein sehr betrübter Wittlig worden, in Castell lagen wir 5 Wochen, den 17. Heuwmonath kamen wir wieder in das Schif und lagen 8 Tag am Ancker, darnach fuhren wir in 8 Wochen unter Gottes allgewaltigen Schutz und Schirm in Virginia glücklich an das Land, haben auch nicht ein persohn verlohren ist auch ein junger Sohn auf dem Meere gebohren worden, sein Vatter heisst Bendicht Kupferschmied, hat bey unserm lieben Bruder Christen Bürki ein jahr gedienet, darnach sind wir noch ohngefährt 100 Stund zu Wasser und Land, doch alle Zeit gefürt und verproviantirt und haben die Leuth uns fast aller ohrten sehr gutes gethan und ist hier im Land kein wirdt, als von einem ohrt zum andern umsonst zu zehren, und halten es vor ein Schimpf, wann man nach der Werte fragen wolte, glücklich und gesund hierher gebracht: Der Schumacher Moritz ist erst hier auf sein Land gestorben, auf der gantzen Reys ist er früsch g'sin, sonst ist von uns Siebenthalern keins gestorben, der andern aber noch drey Pfelzer, aber unter welchen wir wohnen, sind sehr viel gestorben; Betreffend das Land insgemein, so ist fast lauter wald mit unbeschreiblich schönen Cedern Holtz, Papelen, Vohrlen, Eichlen, Buchen, Nuss und Kestenen Bäum, die Nuss aber sind gar hart und grüblig, und die Kestenen sehr klein doch gut; Item Sasafras, und sonsten so viel wohlriechende Bäum, dass ich das 100 ste nicht beschreiben kann; das Cedren Holtz ist roht wie der schönste eingebeizte Kirschbaum, und riecht noch besser als der schönste Wachholder, sind auch ins gemein wie auch andere Baum, 50 bis 60 Schuh lang unter der Esten; das Land insgemein, ist fast allerohrten schwartze Erden, und vetter Grund und kann ein jeder so viel kriegen als er haben will, sind 5 Jahre frey, darnach soll man ein Morgen, welches viel grösser als ein Jucharten bey uns, 2 Stüber geben, sonsten gantz frey, Eigenthumlich zu Nutzen und zu erben nach belieben: Aber diss ohrt ist noch gantz ohnbewohnt g'wesen, dann wir haben gar kein Merkzeichen gesehen, noch davon gehört, dass hier etwas anders solte gestanden seyn, als die sogenanten Wilden und Nakende: Sie sind aber nicht wild, dann sie kommen viel zu uns, und kleiden sich gern von uns, welches auch g'schicht, wann sie es mit wilt, fleisch und Leder, Speck, Bohnen, Korn, welches die Weiber pflantzen und Männer jagen, und die Christen Leuth, wie auch am allermeisten, und durch die Wälder führen, und Neuwe weg Zeichen, bezahlen, Sie haben Hütten von Cedrenrinden, können auch etliche gut englisch reden, haben auch ein Abgott, und halten Vest zu gewissen Zeiten,: Von dem wahren Gott aber wollen sie leider nichts wissen, die Vichzucht betrefend, so kostet die auferziehung schier nichts, wie das zu Franckfort getruckte Büchlin meldet, dann alles Vich ist den Winter so wohl an der weid als den Sommer, und weiss in diesem gemeldten Büchlin nichts zu tadlen für dieses zwey Stuck, wie wohl es von Süd Carolina schreibt, man schlachtet auch kein junges Thier, da kann man schon schliessen, wie bald sich die Zahl vermehren kann, die Küh geben kaum halb so viel bey Euch, dann die Kälber saugen so lang, bis sie andertalb jahr alt sind, so haben sie auch schon wider junge, Wir kaufen ein Kuh mit dem Kalb für 3£. Sterlin oder 12 Thr. Ein Schwein ein £. mit jungen oder Vett, ein Schaaf auch so viel, Geissen hat man noch wenig, doch hab ich g'sehen, der Juncker Michel hat mir gesagt, sie wollen uns herbringen, die wilde oder ungepflantzte Baumfrücht sind hier nicht so gut zu finden, als der Kocherthaler schreibt von Süd Carolina, Kirschen hab ich noch keine gesehen, Reben gibt es sehr viel, auch viel Trauben daran, deren etlich gut zu essen, und wohl zu glauben, wann man viel bey einander hätt, man wird aber trachten zu pflanzen dann es wachst alles sehr g'swind auf, und sind alle frücht von sehr gutem Geschmack, aber wir geniessen sie noch nicht viel, wir ligen an einem Strohm Neuss genannt, da haben vor 6. jahren die ersten, bis vor 2. jahren englische und Schweitzer Leuth ihnen angefangen zu Bauwen, dass die Meisten so arm wahren als wir sind, die sind wie mich bedunkt an Vich, an allerley Früchten, den schösten Baumfrüchten, alle reich genug, und das gantze Jahr etwa 2 Monath, wir haben uns der Natur nach hindenan setzen müssen, dass wir es noch nit haben, aber wir hofen es, durch Gottes Segen auch zu kriegen, wir sind kurtz vor Weinachten auf unser Gut kommen, und haben durch Gottes Beystand die Zioria mein Tochter Mann, Petter Reutiger und ich und noch andere, viel sterckere Häuser als die Englische, auch Land darzu gebutz, und haben die meisten schon eingezäunet, ist auch zu hofen, dass wir von nun an aus der Erden, und von dem Vich, durch Gottes Gnad, welcher seine mildreiche Hand, allezeit so hilfreich ausgestrecket hat, und uns für so vielen Finden, geistlichen und weltlichen, und über das grosse Meer, so sicher und ungehindert hindurch gebracht, auch zur gnüge Kriegen werden, aber eins ligt uns noch hart an, welches ich ohne Weinen nicht schrieben kann, nemlich der Mangel eines treuwen und eifrigen Seelsorgers, dann wir haben wohl Ursach mit Asaph zu klagen, unsre Zeichen sehen wir nicht mehr, kein Prophet predigt uns mehr, kein Lehrer lehrt uns mehr: Wir haben zwar alle Sonntag Betstunden in unsern Häusern, aber der Eifer umb unsrer alten Sünden Rost auszusfägen, ist so schlecht, dass zu förchten ist, er fresse noch alles bis auf den Grund, wann nicht der erbarmende Gott, zu Hilf kombt, wann es dem lieben Gott hätte gefallen wollen, von unsren Brüdern und Schwestern, oder doch aufs Wenigst Christen Bürki, zu einem Instrument, Leibs und Seelen Arzt mitzusenden, so hätte ich gute Hofnung gehabt, das Liecht wäre nicht zu einer stinkenden brächen worden, dann ich glaube nit, dass ein Mensch hier wär, weder englisch, noch teusch, noch frantzösisch, der ihn nicht hertzlich lieben solten, dann seyn Kunst ist hier überaus gut, dass er ein Hof nach Wunsch ohne Feldarbeit machen könnte: dann gut getränk, und solches arzneyMittel ist der grösste mangel im Land, darumb ich ein fründliche Bitt an dich lieben Bruder hab, nemlich also: Ich hab Christina Christeler ein Wittib von Sanen geheurahtet, ich bin ihr der dritte Ehmann, von dem Ersten hat sie 4 Kinder gehabt, 2 sind in Londen gestorben, der Mann und ein Kind auf dem Meer, das Eltest aber ein Knab von 13 Jahr heisst Bendicht plösch, er ist zu Mörigen, in der Vogtey Nidauw, bey seines Vaters sellig Kundschaft geblieben, und hat vor 4. Jahren noch g'lebt, ihr Vater hat Peter Christeler geheissen, so hat ihr Christen Walcker, welcher sambt dem Weib hier am Land gstorben und hat 8 Kind hinderlassen ihr gesagt, sie habe ein ziemlich gross Erb, von Ihres Vatters Seel. Bruder: Moritz Christeler gethan, dann er hab 100 Thr. dafür überkommen, wann nach Sannen geht, darnach zu fragen, ich hof, Heinrich Perret werde dir helfen können./. Dann sie sind die nächsten Nachtbahren g'wesen, und wann dem also ist, wie Walcker gesagt, so kannst zu deinen Handen nemen, weil mein Weib das Bräuen so wohl versteht und es viel jahr getrieben hat, und das getränk hier sehr rar ist, und hier weder gelt noch Bräuhafen zu bekommen ist, sonst wolte ich es dir nicht zumuthen, der Hafen aber muss 2 Rohr aber keine Schlange haben, wann nicht etwan vertrauhte Leuth kommen, so würde der H. Ritter noch wohl so gut seyn, dass er mir ihn hierher schafete, auch 4£. gewürtz, als Imber, Pfefer, Safran, Muscatnuss, Galgan, Nägeli, jedes nach Proportion dess gelts, dan hier ist noch nichts als Lorbehr, hab ich an den Bäumen in Wäldern gesehen, wann es aber zusammen nit wäre mit dem Erb so wolte ich doch dich und meinen Vatter, wann er noch lebt, fründlichst gebetten haben, etwan noch von den Minen helfen, dan mir sehr viel daran gelegen, und sonderlich den Weibs Leuthen, welche hier gar rar sind, wann noch mehr Leuth kommen wolten, so rathe ich dass sie Weiber mitnehmen, wann sie haben wolten, dann sind hier die brävsten die keine Weiber finden, weil sie nicht hie sind, die Reys ist wohl zu überwinden, wann man sich recht darauf versehen kann, mit altem Käs, dürrem Fleisch, dürr Obs, Essig, Wein, Bier,

Fesser, Butter, Zweyback in Summa was gut essen, und kumlich zu fergen ist, dann wan das Meer ungestühm so haltet sich das Schif auf eine Seiten, dass verschüttet wird, doch aber nüt gehört, dass ein Schif auf dem hohen Meer untergangen sey, wer sich mit obgemelten Mittel versehen könnt, und ein accord mit dem Schifshaubtmann machte, dass er freyheit liess zu kochen und ein guter platz zum ligen, so were mir die Reys nicht schwer, dann wir haben Junge und alte Leuth gehabt, sind alle früsch und gesund, was man an Wahren hieher bringt, ist alles zum Wenigsten noch einmahln so viel wehrt, sonderlich das leinig Tuch, und Glas wäre auch vonnöthen und ist in Holland gut kaufen. Es grüssen Euch Beter Röhtiger, und meine zwey Töchter, dan wir wohnen neben einandren, das Dichtli ist noch bey uns und leg ab den gruss von uns Allen, bey unsrer lieben und getreuwen Seelsorgern der gantzen Ehrbarkeit, sonderlich dem Gfatter Kilch-Meyer, Dreuthart, und Andreas Aescher, Christen Jantz. Ich hätte viel zu schreiben, ich muss abbrechen, habt gedult mit meinem schlechten Schreiben, dann wer mein Hand und Arbeit sicht, der wird wohl glauben, dass ich nit viel g'schreiben und g'studiert hab. Grüsset uns den Christen Bürki und ich wolt gern dass er den Inhalt dieses Briefs vernehmen könnte;

    Verbleibe euer genigtwilliger Diener, und meiner Eltern,
        gehorsamer Sohn bis in den Tod./.

Grüsset uns Anna Drus, Item Speismannsleuth und dein Schwester und Gschwey, auch meines Vatters Schwester, und voraus den Schulmeister./.

ENGLISH TRANSLATION OF THE GERMAN VERSION

ENGLISH TRANSLATION OF GERMAN VERSION

RELATION OF MY AMERICAN PROJECT

WRITTEN ON ACCOUNT OF CERTAIN PERSONS WHO COMPLAINED THAT I HAD UNDERTAKEN THIS COLONY IMPRUDENTLY, TO THE DISADVANTAGE AND RUIN OF MANY PEOPLE—A CHARGE WHICH IS EASILY CLEARED UP.

After I had, at the end of my travels, been living in England for two years, and had made such advantageous and eminent acquaintances in that country during the reign of Charles II that had I remained I might have made a considerable fortune, at that time I informed myself, partly from oral and partly from written accounts, and more recently, from a more accurate report, and especially after I had heard through a citizen of this city, who had lived in America five or six years, what fine lands there were and how cheap, what liberty, what great, good, and increasing trade, what rich mines and other advantages there were, and had been told what fine rich silver mines he had discovered and found, and when I considered that I was burdened with rather heavy debts which I had contracted even before my travels, due, in part, to a venture which turned out badly for me and for several other gentlemen, to sureties, to great expenses incurred during my candidacy, to hard times during the tenure of my office, (for I did not wish to flay the peasants); hard times due partly to the newly made reformation; and, in addition to all this, the troubles of Neufchatel and the attendant lack of prosperity coming on, the way to a better office was cut off. Moreover, on account of the newly made reformation it would be a long time before I could hope for even a small office. In the meantime having been blessed with a big and sturdy family, I was impelled to do something to satisfy the creditors and to help my family.

Since there was now in the Fatherland little hope of my being able to relieve such great distress, I took strongly into consideration the fine propositions of the above mentioned citizen, to whom out of consideration I shall here give no name, and consoling myself with my old and new friends of rank in England, and relying upon them, I finally took a firm resolution to leave my Fatherland and to see if fortune would be more favorable to me in England. Not to be detained by the creditors and my own people, I began my journey secretly, leaving to my father, who was financially able to do so to take charge of my debts and business.[1]

PREFACE [1]

This account was written in haste, without much thought, just as the things occurred to my weak memory, so that here no especial style is to be observed; and it has been arranged in 12 chapters or "misfortunes" for my society and for others who might have unfavorable ideas with regard to my American projects, thinking that I had undertaken them without consideration and foresight, and had passed my time in Carolina in splendor and luxury. So then I have shown the contrary. The beginning is also arranged to show that it was not merely carelessness which brought me to this distress, but serious reverses and unfortunate accidents. If ever I revise this in time of leisure, everything shall be better written and arranged.

NOTE:—The references are to the English Translation of the French Version and show wherein that version varies from the German.

When I arrived in Holland certain persons almost turned me aside from my plan, and other propositions were made me in which I was to be given my support and something as a profit, but I did not find enough in this to make good my losses, and continued my journey to England, where I immediately heard of my people, and was inspired by such a desire to continue in my undertaking, by persons of rank and others, who promised me all sorts of assistance, that I was brought into negotiations according to which very advantageous propositions, conditions, and privileges were made and given by the proprietors above mentioned which brought me also to my resolution.

At this very time there came over 10,000 souls from Germany to England, all under the name of Palatines, but among them were many Switzers and people brought together from other provinces of Germany. This caused the royal court as well as private individuals much concern and also unspeakable costs, so that they were embarrassed because of these people, and therefore there soon went out an edict by which it was allowed to many persons to take some of these people and care for them, and a good share of them had been sent into the three kingdoms, but partly because of their laziness, partly because of the jealousy of the poor subjects of the country, they did not do so well as it was supposed they would, and so they had begun to send a considerable number of these people to America and the Queen had had great sums distributed for that purpose.

At this juncture different persons of high and of middle rank, to whom my undertaking was known, advised me not to lose so favorable an opportunity; and at the same time gave me good hopes that, if I wished to take a considerable number of these people, the Queen would not only grant me the money for their passage, but in addition, would give me a good contribution for them. These hopes were realized and the sum reached almost 4,000£ sterling. Besides this, the Queen had granted to the royal council land upon the Potomac [2] River, as much as we immediately needed, and moreover had given strong recommendations to the governor of Virginia. [3] All this with the advantageous promises of the proprietors of Carolina gave to the undertaking a good appearance, and there was as much hope for a fortunate outcome as the beginning seemed good and prosperous.

To provide for and send this colony I took indescribable pains, 1. I tried to choose for this project healthy, industrious people and among them those of all sorts of trades necessary for this undertaking. 2. A supply of all kinds of necessary tools and things. 3. As also sufficient and good food. 4. Good ships and sailors, also certain over- and under-directors for this people, to keep every thing in good order. 5. In order that no negligence or lack of knowledge should be attributed to us, I have begun nothing without the knowledge, advice, and instruction of the royal committee.   6. Upon the ships, as afterwards upon the land, the over-directors were three of the most prominent persons from Carolina itself, who had already lived there many years and were acquainted with everything in those parts. These were the Chief Judge or Justice of the Peace, the Chief or General Surveyor, and the Receiver General, who were on business in London at this very time and were appointed by the royal committee, as well as by the Lords Proprietors, to have a close, faithful, and good watch over these people. The under-directors were composed of more than twelve of the most orderly and honorable men among the people—according to appearances.

So then, after everything had been adjusted, concluded, and ratified, by the royal committee as well as by the Lords Proprietors for me and the people, yet even before the departure, I begged the royal committee to be pleased to send some of their members, who were experienced in travel by ship, to examine whether everything was arranged as it should be, and to talk with the captain; this they did and the report was given in the committee. The day before the departure I went, with the pastor who remained in London after the company had gone to America, to Gravesend; to which place, because I was waiting for the little colony coming on from Berne, as well as for some of my associates, I could not go with them. I took my leave of them with a necessary exhortation, and then, when the German minister,[4] Mr. Caesar, had given the people a fine sermon, commending them to the protection of the Most High, I let them sail away, yet not without taking precaution on account of the dangerous war times, for I then obtained this favor from the chief admiral, Count Pembroke, that he ordered Vice Admiral Norris to accompany our people or ship with his squadron out upon the broad sea or towards Portugal.   This took place in the winter—in January—and then, because of the rough winds and storms, this ship was so driven about that it did not arrive in Virginia until after thirteen weeks. This, along with the salt food to which the people were not accustomed, and the fact that they were so closely confined, contributed very much to the sickness and death of many upon the sea. Others could not restrain their desires when they came to land, drank too much fresh water and overloaded themselves with raw fruit, so that they died of fever, and this colony therefore had half died off before it was well settled.[5]   N. B. The one ship which was filled with the best goods and on which those in best circumstances were traveling, had the misfortune, at the mouth of the James River, in sight of an English man-of-war, which however lay at anchor,⁶ to be attacked by a bold French privateer and plundered. This is the first misfortune.

After the surviving colony had regained health in Virginia where they were received very kindly, they betook themselves about twenty English miles towards Carolina, all of which, along with the goods cost a great deal.⁷ And now when they came into the county of Albemarle to the home of one Colonel Pollock upon the river called Chowan, a member of the council and one of the wealthiest in North Carolina, he provided these people, (but for money or the worth of it) with ships, so that they were conducted through the Sound into the County of Bath upon the River Neuse, with provision for only the most urgent necessity; and there the Surveyor General settled them on a point of land between the Neuse and the Trent River. This place called Chattoka is where the city of New Bern was afterwards founded.

Here begins the second fatality or misfortune. This surveyor general L_____ by name, who should have located the people immediately upon their allotted land and the plantations assigned to them, claimed that, in order to save time to enable them to clear their land, he had placed them on the south side of this point of land along the Trent River, in the very hottest and most unhealthy portion, instead of toward the north, on the Neuse River, where they could have been better placed and in a more healthy locality. But he did it for his own advantage, because this was his own land, in order that it might be cleared by these people for his benefit. But since he sold that same land⁸ and ours— and dear enough—yes wrongfully, (for he had no right to it), and moreover, since it was inhabited by Indians, (although he sold it to us for unencumbered land) the poor people had to live in great distress until fall, when I came. From lack of sufficient provisions they were soon compelled to give their clothes and whatever they possessed to the neighboring settlers for food.⁹ The misery and wretchedness were almost indescribable, for, on my arrival, I saw that almost all were sick, yes, even in extremity, and the well were all very feeble. In what a labyrinth and danger I then found myself, even my life not safe, the good Lord knows.

Consider how my Bern people, who in every other respect had had a favorable passage with me in a good and favorable time of year, with plenty of room, and not one sick on the way, looked on this tragedy, where sickness, despair, and lack of the most necessary things reigned supreme. The thing that caused this distress was in part, the bad conduct of the superior and inferior directors as well as their faithlessness; however, the principal cause of this whole disaster, out of which, for the most part, the rest arose, and from which came my ruin and that of the colony, was the great audacity and unfriendliness of Colonel Cary, who, at that time, on the death of the old governor, contrary to right and propriety and to the orders of the Lords Proprietors, tried to force his way into the government, and, as was found out, wished, even, to line his purse and to make off with the revenues taken in by him and to betake himself to Madagascar, a place inhabited by all sorts of pirates. When the newly elected Governor Hyde (though he was the representative of the Queen) and when I and the above mentioned three directors wished to introduce ourselves and show our patents and credentials before the council, this same Colonel Cary, disregarding the command of the Proprietors, boldly refused us all. Thus the promises of the Lords Proprietors, upon which I and my whole undertaking especially rested, came to nothing. I and the whole colony were shamelessly exposed to all those reverses which I have experienced up to this hour. And so this Cary finally became an actual rebel and made himself a following by spending money, so that Governor Hyde, for that reason, did not dare, at first, to take possession of the government by force; so much the less, because he really had no special patents in his hands. And since the governor of South Carolina had the order to install him, the time was already set for this purpose and letters were written to the council of North Carolina. Misfortune, however, would have it that the above mentioned governor of South Carolina, Colonel Tynte, died at this time. This death caused great confusion. In this interregnum I was not assisted, and because of the rebellion arising at this time, I was in great and pressing distress, since every one looked out for himself and kept what he had. The question arose whether I should risk my life and abandon this colony, yes, even let it die of hunger, or whether I should go into debt to save this people in such an extremity. As was only proper for a Christian-minded[10] man there could be no hesitation. Since at that time news of my arrival had gone abroad in America and I was in good credit, I sent immediately to Pennsylvania for flour, because fortunately, I had already made arrangements there, and in Virginia, and also here and there in the province, for the necessaries of life. Through notes which I gave the provisions eventually came, and slowly enough. Meanwhile our own goods and wares and those of the poor people were being used up for the necessaries which we managed to get from the neighboring inhabitants.

During this time I had the land surveyed and every family given its own plot of ground, so that they could clear it, build their cabins, and prepare their soil for planting and sowing. And so there arrived also with great expense and trouble, provision of corn, salt, lard in place of butter, and salt meat, also rum, and other products of the soil. But with the cattle there was difficulty. The people did not want to go where I showed them to get them, and I could not bring the animals right before their doors. But yet they accommodated themselves gradually, so that inside of 18 months these people were so well settled and had their affairs so well arranged that in this short time they had made more advancement than the English inhabitants in four years. Just one instance: for example, since there is in the whole province only one poor water mill, the people of means have hand mills, while the poor pound their corn in a hollow piece of oak and sift the cleanest through a basket. This takes much time. Our people on the contrary sought out convenient water brooks and in that way, according to the condition of the water and the strength of the current, made themselves regular stamping mills by which the corn was ground, and the good man-of-the-house had time to do other work. I had already commenced to build a grist and saw mill in a very convenient place, but what happened? When we were all hoping, after great effort and anxiety, to enjoy the fruits of our labor, aside from the reverses we had endured, and notwithstanding the fine prospect for a good establishment of the colony, there came the genuine storm of misfortune through the wild Indians, who were inspired by certain jealous and revengeful rebels of Cary's following, which overturned everything. The outcome of this tragedy is told in a separate account, and it is unnecessary to tell about it here. But, because from Colonel Cary's audacious, unfriendly, and hostile procedure arose all the trouble which came over the province, myself, and the colony, it will not be out of the way to tell something more of these confusions, and to continue what went on further after Governor Hyde's death.

As soon as I arrived from Virginia,[11] at the bordering colony and, in expectation of a comfortable rest for myself and for my people, was staying in the first village, there came a troop of the most prominent Quakers since there were many of them in those parts, and they presented the most persuasive reasons possible, saying that it befitted me as Landgrave who, after the governor had the first rank, as the one who always presided in an interregnum and at other times in the absence of the governor, to take the presidency. But I[12] politely refused the honor. We answered that Governor Hyde was actually in Virginia and that I was one of the witnesses, who had there seen how he was chosen governor by the Lords Proprietors and how they had congratulated him in their council room in London. Moreover he was a relative of the Queen and had been approved by Her Royal Majesty,[13] and although the gentleman in question had no patent at that time in hand, one would soon follow. So then the province ought to have no hesitancy in receiving him at once as governor, so much the more, since Governor Tynte had given the council of Carolina notice to that effect. But this did not please them[14] and they replied to me, but I did not refute them. After they were through with me they took their leave of me very politely and went away. Soon after this I came with my people farther into the province and arrived at the home of Colonel Pollock in Chowan, where a council was held by those who were inclined towards Governor Hyde, and I was very much urged to be present at the same. But in such a dangerous and delicate affair I did not go. And so there was soon given me a plan or report of the situation of things, and I can easily observe that because of my character as well as the number of my people, (since I could give the balance of power to whichever party I fell to), they looked on me with great respect. My ideas were in the direction of having a strong letter sent to Colonel Cary, representing one thing and another very well to him, and also finally threatening him, if he would not come to an agreement as he ought that I would throw myself with all my forces on the side of Governor Hyde. This brought him to the notion of taking other measures, but for all that he gave me a very haughty and shameless answer. He appeared to be sorry for it soon after, and we worked at it quietly to such good purpose that finally an agreement was reached and put into writing. According to this, Colonel Cary and his following were to agree to Governor Hyde's being president of the Council until new orders came from the Proprietors, but not to accept him as governor.

Meanwhile I hastily betook myself to New Bern, from where my Palatines, who, because of a great lack of food were in the last extremity,[15] had written to me. Since as a precaution, I had some provisions from Colonel Pollock, there was soon a good amount on hand for such a number of people.[16]

Shortly after this Governor Hyde came out of Virginia into Carolina and settled not far from Colonel Pollock on _____ Dyckenfield's plantation on Solomon Creek, where he received a rather fine dwelling.

And because Colonel Cary feared that his trick above mentioned, which he had in mind, would not work, he had tried in a cunning manner to get his hands on the agreement, in order to remove his name or signature which he well knew was on it. Hereupon he began to take up his old cause again. Some of his followers he got by spending money on them, for he brought all the vile rabble over on his side with rum and brandy. In this way he made himself a

very strong following and began an open rebellion against Governor
Hyde. In the meantime, the man was so crafty and sharp, that he
tried to lull me to sleep; he came to New Bern on pretense of a visit,
where I regaled him with the little which was then at hand. After
dinner,[17] when we had gotten into conversation over his improper
conduct towards Governor Hyde as well as towards myself, and when
I had spoken sharply to him about his disobedience towards those
in authority, the Lords Proprietors, and with threats had given him
to understand that I would take such measures as would make him
sorry, he promised me in the presence of four of his friends whom
he had brought with him, to send me within three weeks, grain and
other provision, as well as some cattle, to the value of 500£, or else
notes in place of the goods. As far as Governor Hyde was concerned,
he left that in statu quo. And so he took his departure. This was
only to blind me, which I also perceived, for I told him to his face
that I feared that the performance would not correspond to the
promises. This trip of Colonel Cary's was not in vain, for he attained
his end, because by instigating some of the English or Carolinian
inhabitants and people on the nearest plantations he so frightened
my people that no one dared venture to go out of his house or out of
the colony; for he had threatened that if they did not remain neutral,
the English and Indians would fall upon them and destroy them.

Not long after this Governor Hyde sent me expresses with a
whole package of patents, one of them for me, which made me
Colonel over the district of Bath County and gave to me the
appointing of the under officers, for their names were left blank, and
begged me earnestly to assist him against the rebels. Whereupon
I answered him how sorry I was that I could not yet respond to his
desire, reporting what I have remarked regarding Colonel Cary, that
my people were not disposed to go to either party, but were resolved
to remain neutral. This did not please the governor very well, and
there soon arrived a sharper command, that in case nothing occurred,
I should betake myself three good days journey from New Bern to
be present at the council. This I did, very much in fear, to be sure,
because I had also been threatened.[18]

When, now, I had reached the Governor, we were employed very
busily in the councel advising how to put ourselves in security against
this Cary faction, and it was ordered to get together, immediately,
a company of chosen men with which to protect ourselves, and to see,
further, how to compel different ones in some way or other to side with
us. At this same time there came from London a turbulent fellow[19]
with a ship full of goods belonging to a Quaker who was also one of the
proprietors, and wanted to trade in these parts. He was immediately

won over by the opposing party and this strengthened their courage, because he was well provided with shot, powder, and lead. This man libeled and defamed the Governor, giving out that he had different orders from the Lords Proprietors, but not in favor of Edward Hyde. This caused great doubt and confusion and made it hard for us.[20] He did me, in particular, great damage by making a note of 100£[21] sterling ineffectual, saying he had orders to this effect. Although this money had been deposited with Hanson & Co., my correspondents in London, yet because of this, I could get nothing of it in my great need. So then this Colonel Cary, R. Roach, and a Quaker, Em. Lowe, who, contrary to the foremost article of his own religion or sect, had himself made a Colonel, came well provisioned before the landing[22] on a night when we were lodging at Colonel Pollock's house where we for the most part held council, in a brigantine, well armed and provided with pieces. We put ourselves in the best position possible, and had only two pieces and not more than some 60 armed men with us. Along towards morning the rebels let fly a couple of balls from the brigantine at the house in which we were, but they were fired too high and merely grazed the ridge so that we were not harmed by it. Upon this we also shot off our pieces at the brigantine, and likewise did no damage. So the rebels began to send some of their best armed soldiery towards the land in two small barques. When we became aware of that, we drew up our force towards the landing[23] as a defense, among whom was my servant in a yellow livery. This frightened our opponents not a little, and the reason for it was they thought that my whole colony was holding itself there in the bushes. We immediately fired off our piece again. When the one shot merely grazed the mast and it fell over, it had such a good effect that the barques turned back, and as soon as the men had climbed into the ship, they hoisted up the sails and made off. Thereupon we ordered our most resolute men to follow in a sloop, but they could not overtake them. However, when they had gone down into the Sound the brigantine landed at a convenient place, and the most prominent ones got away through the woods. And so the small band won over the greater and the sloop brought the brigantine back, along with some provisions and the pieces. This scattered the opposing party and strengthened ours, so that we thereupon decided it would be well to announce a general pardon for all except the ringleaders, to which every one who desired to yield and submit to the Governor should subscribe. After this a parliamentary assembly was proclaimed in which, then, were treated the matters relating to these disturbers. The worst ones of the insurgents whom we could catch were taken into custody, but those who repented of their wrong and had been debauched only through instigation were accorded the amnesty. In this affair [24] I for the most part had to take the lead. This did not suit me very well because I feared it would make me enemies. After one thing and another had been arranged as well as possible and Governor Hyde and myself had been accepted and acknowledged, every one went home in the hope that all would quiet down. This calm did not last long; the authors of the revolt collected themselves together and the above mentioned Roach seated himself on an island, well provided with food, shot, and munitions, and stirred up as many as he could. We tried, indeed, to drive him out of his nest, but it was not to be done. This fire of sworn conspirators gradually took hold again and increased, so that the last was soon worse than the first.

Knowing how things were, it was thought best to make an effort to get other help. And so I was sent to Alexander Spotswood, Governor of Virginia, with two members of the Council, who were given to me, to beg assistance of him. [25] But before this we sent by expresses a writing to Governor Spotswood who appointed us a day in a village which lay between the two provinces, because, aside from seeing us, he wanted to muster his troops on the border. So I travelled by water in the captured brigantine because it was not quite safe by land, and in addition, we wanted to get provisions out of the neighborhood. After we had traveled several hours there arose such a contrary wind that we were driven back; and so we took the canoe, a little narrow boat made from a piece of tree trunk hollowed out, and continued our journey, now that the wind was somewhat quieted down. We came too late, however, for the muster was already past, but the Governor [26] directed further, that when I came an express should be sent immediately to him, and so I wrote a polite letter to the above mentioned gentleman, who came the next day with his secretary and two gentlemen to the appointed place where the conference was held, and the Governor received me in an exceedingly friendly manner. This business was more important than I supposed. After giving in my credentials I began my proposal, but there was immediately a strong objection made, namely, that the Virginians were not at all inclined to fight against their neighboring brethren, for they were all equally subjects of the Queen, and the cause was not so entirely just, for at least Governor Hyde had no patents. And so we had to try some other method. [27] And because Governor Spotswood wished to show himself somewhat more agreeable to me the first time he had seen me, since I had been introduced to him by the Queen herself, on account of the Virginia affairs, he finally considered that he should do Governor Hyde, myself, and the province the favor of sending us a man-of-war with the usual equipment of soldiers. Since they were likewise servants of the Queen, were in their red uniforms, and moreover, were good soldiers, they would accomplish much. This was granted, and we took our friendly leave of each other. With what expressions he invited me to him, and what proffers of service he made, and what marks of respects he showed me I can not sufficiently indicate. Meanwhile I made my way home very joyously. After such happy negotiations, as soon as I had made my report, I was received with a general applause of the whole people, and this increased my credit not a little.

Soon after this there arrived a valiant captain with his brave marines. When he had paid his respects and had delivered Governor Spotswood's letter, we besought him that he would show his commission before the assembly and speak as strongly as possible to the people, indicating that in case the revolters would not discontinue hostilities, as they were duty bound to do, we would proceed against them with the utmost severity. Upon this no one dared revolt any more, and the authors of the uprising got out of the province secretly, and they dared so much the less to stay because letters arrived from London reporting how the Lords Proprietors had chosen Mr. Edward Hyde to be governor of North Carolina and that the patents had therefore been sent by a trusty person. The often mentioned Colonel Cary, along with others of his associates, was arrested in Virginia and sent well guarded in a ship to London, and there suit was brought against him. The affair made a great stir in London; but this Cary was so fortunate in his base action as to have two of my Lords take his part and they saved his life. Hereupon he was let go on bail in order to defend himself, the Justice in Carolina was appointed to him, and so the affair still hangs to this hour.[28]

The confusion contributed not a little to the attack of the wild Indians, because several of the mutineers made Governor Hyde so hated among the Indians that they looked on him as their enemy, insomuch that when I was taken prisoner by the savages, thinking I was the Governor, they treated me rather severely until I had them informed through an Indian with whom I was acquainted, and who could speak English, that I was not Governor Hyde, upon which they treated me more kindly.

Now when this also was past I betook myself again to New Bern to my people. But soon after this Governor Hyde had received his patents, so he called a general assembly again in order that he might present himself to it, on which occasion I also was present. I did it the more willingly because I thereby had the opportunity, and used it, of seeking to get from the new governor what I could not obtain from Colonel

Cary. In this, Governor Hyde showed, indeed, all good will, but when
I urged him for something real, there was very little on hand, a circumstance which in itself was (not) without evil results. After this
I insistently urged upon the Parliament, that since I could not obtain
anything upon the account of the Lords Proprietors, seeing this was
the foundation of my enterprise, and since we could not subsist in this
way, and it would be a long time before information could come to
us out of Europe, and meanwhile we could not live on air, that the
provinces should assist us on the same terms as we had with the Lords
Proprietors; that is to say, they should supply us with the necessary
food, and expecially with cattle, upon two or three years' credit.
They refused me this, however, under pretext that this civil war had
made it impossible for them to do it. Upon this I went sadly home
to arrange my affairs as well as possible, as is to be seen in the preceding.[29]

Now Follows the Indian War

What caused the Indian war was firstly, the slanders and instiga-
tions of certain plotters against Governor Hyde, and secondly, against
me, in that they talked the Indians into believing that I had come to
take their land, and that then the Indians would have to go back towards the mountains. I talked them out of this and it was proven
by the friendliness I had shown them, as also by the payment for the
land where I settled at the beginning (namely that upon which the
little city of New Bern was begun), regardless of the fact that the
seller was to have given it over to me free. I had also made peace
with the same Indian inhabitants so that they were entirely satisfied
with me. Thirdly, it was the great carelessness of the colony.[30]
Fourthly, the harsh treatment of certain surly and rough English inhabitants who deceived them in trade, would not let them hunt
about their plantations, and under this excuse took away from them
their arms, munitions, pelts or hides, yes, even beat an Indian to
death. This alarmed them very much and with reason.

The Indians kept their design very secret, and they were even then
about to take counsel in an appointed place at the time that I happened
to travel up the river.

I thought I was so much the more in safety, since only ten days
before, when I was coming home from surveying and had lost my
way in the forest, just as night overtook me I had fallen into the hands
of the Indians, who before my coming had lived in Chatalognia, at
present New Bern. They had now settled in this place and received
me very kindly and in the morning accompanied me as far as the right
way. They gave me two Indians who went with me as far as my

home, and out of thankfulness I gave them something and sent some rum and brandy to the king. This very king, together with the help of the Most High, contributed not a little to my rescue when I was captured by the Indians, condemned to death, and saved in a marvelous manner. What took place among the Indians and how I finally came home and got to New Bern again is to be seen in the account sent to Governor Hyde. Right on the end of this account I had begun to tell what adverse and disagreeable things happened to me immediately on my return, and so there appears to be no end of my ill fortune. But since I could not foresee the future, I shall tell as briefly as possible, what took place further, up to my departure to Europe and my journey home. Firstly, How this Indian war was renewed and ended: Secondly, For what motives I left the colony and went to Europe, yes, clear to Berne. What happened to me after my arrival among the Christians was almost more dangerous and vexatious than when I was among the heathens. Before the heathen tribunal I had my accusers before me, everything was done in good order, nothing behind my back and under cover nor in a rebellious and turbulent manner; but when I came home, thinking to be among friends and Christians and hoping to rest a little, it became worse.

There were a number of rough, jealous, and morose planters or inhabitants. And because I would not immediately accede to their notion of killing or of giving over to their discretion, an Indian to whom I had promised safe conduct because he had come to get my ransom, this sort of evil Christians, worse than the heathen, secretly got information against me, and there was much talk, and threats of nothing less than that I must be hanged. I had not considered it feasible for those to go to war with the Indians before the fifteen Palatine prisoners had been freed and delivered over, who did not have enough provisions nor munitions nor soldiers, since in addition, half of the Palatines had left my quarters in my absence. So now from a heathen tribunal I had to appear before a Christian judge's bench, yes, to a trial worse than the heathen, if it had gone according to the will of certain godless fellows. To this a Palatine blacksmith who wished to revenge himself because I had punished[31] him for frightful execrations, disobedience, stealing, and horrible threats, contributed not a little, and this he did in a very treacherous manner. He went immediately over to the Indians, and made them very suspicious of me, as though my promise was of no value, as though I were deceiving them, since, instead of keeping peace and neutrality with them, I was entirely on the side of the English, whom I was supplying with firearms and munitions of war.[32] But as soon as I

learned of his treachery, and for that cause wanted to punish him,
he had gotten wind of it and had betaken himself to William Brice, a
common man, who because of his audacity had been chosen captain,
and who was very much opposed to me. There, where a garrison
composed of rowdies collected together and of disloyal Palatines were
guarding his house, the above mentioned blacksmith had said the
same things of me as before to the Indians, and more yet, so that I
passed for a traitor. Very soon there was a list of 20 articles written
up, of which not a point was true. As soon as I had heard of this, I
wrote, nevertheless without fear, since I had a good conscience, to
the governors of Virginia and of Carolina, informing them circumstantially of all that had happened; and they approved of my conduct, as did all other persons of understanding and reason.

Along with this it happened that since I had caused the effects of
the smith as a criminal and a fugitive, who was, moreover, much in
debt to me, to be inventoried and put into safe keeping,[35] this
abovementioned Brice wanted very much to have the smith and the
detained goods given out. His intention was to do this by force in
addition to bringing me bound to Governor Hyde, as one guilty of
treason, and so he took counsel in secret with some of the most prominent of his crew, and the conclusion was to the effect that if I should
refuse to give out the smith's goods, they would take them by force,
giving as pretext that they needed them for defense,[34] and because I
would doubtless resist, they would then take possession of my person,
and so bring me to the Governor. But there was, by chance, a little
Palatine boy in the room of whom they took no notice, who understood English. Hearing this he got out of the room as quietly
as he could, and told his mother, one of those who were still my
subjects. She got quickly into a little boat and came over to me.
When she told me this conspiracy I immediately had the drum beat,
the gate locked, and my people placed in a good position. I could
scarcely get this done when Brice came with 30 or 40 neighboring men, among them that same godless smith and probably 20
of the disloyal Palatines. Not knowing that I was informed of the
affair, they thought to go right into the yard[35] and take possession
of me. But they found everything in a position that they did not
expect, and when they asked our people what that was to signify,
the corporal answered that we were well on our guard because of
the wild Indians and the wild Christians. It was asked in reply
whether we took them for enemies, then, and again it was answered
that friends are not in the habit of visiting their neighbors in such
a manner, that it seemed as though they were our enemies, especially
since such traitors and deserters were among them, yet if Colonel

Brice and one other wanted to come in he thought this would not be refused. When this was represented to me I allowed them to come in under good guard. When Colonel Brice complained of my actions I gave as answer that a fine design was known to me, but that I would know how to make his shameless and audacious procedure known in the proper place. I asked him if it was the proper manner towards his superiors to thus raise a mutiny. I told him that I, as a member of the upper house, landgrave, and commandant of this district would be in the right to send him away bound.[36] So I let these false, designing fellows go with short courtesy and severe threats until the next parliament. What other insults were done me and my people by this captain and the disloyal Palatines would be too lengthy and too disagreeable to write in detail, and so I have for the sake of brevity not cared to tell more. But yet a little more in passing.

It is to observed that the agreement here below made and signed with the Indians, was entered into while I was still in bonds and to save my life, and so I could not be compelled to keep my word. But according to this, since I was not of the view quod hereticis non habenda fides (faith need not be kept towards heretics), I was resolved to keep as much as I could conscientiously, with regard also to the duty which I owed to the crown of England. And if they had left me alone afterwards it would have been well for the entire country and much murder and misfortune would have been avoided.

But this Captain Brice along with his gang was so heated, that, without having the wisdom to take counsel, following their blind passion, without reflecting upon any measures nor upon the smaller number of people nor the small amount of food and munitions nor upon the danger to the poor captured women and children, he rejected the proposed truce and immediately began hostilities, and so through his unreasonable caprices exposed the whole province to danger and interrupted all my measures. But if they had let me manage, we should, in the first place, have gained time by this truce, so that the whole province and I could have put ourselves into a good position and we could in this time provide ourselves with soldiers, war and food supplies. Secondly, I was actually already at work during this truce to save the poor captive women and children, for I was not going to give over my ransom, except they had given the prisoners over to me. This had been agreed upon in the first conference, with great danger and difficulty. N. B. It has been very well shown, of how much importance it was and afterwards related in the history of the Indian war how this captured Holtzmann (woodsman?) had to manage the

Indians, unless one can make an end of them at the very first. Now while I was doing my best with the Indians in this good work, and thirdly, through my alleged neutrality and the delay, wished to gain time so that the English, as well as the Carolinians, and especially the colony, might get again what they had left buried in their plantations and houses, and likewise be able to catch as much of their cattle as possible in the forests, there came this Brice's mob, wilder and more unreasonable than the Indians, and spoiled all my negotiations for me, by an attack unbeknown to the rest. This whole bad business, the before mentioned treachery of the smith, and this action took all confidence of the Indians in me away. So that from that time on they made attack upon my colony also, since until then their houses and goods had been spared according to the agreement made. But following the untimely procedure of the Carolinians, the Indians have gone on to destroy everything, and my poor people's houses although the doors were marked with a sign,[37] had to be burned. The rest of the household furniture, although concealed and buried, was hunted up, taken away, and the cattle in the forests shot down. From there the Indians have beset one plantation after another, plundered, slaughtered, and done much harm here and there in the province, especially on the Neuse, Trent, and Pamtego Rivers. What caused worse retaliation by the Indians was the harsh procedure of Brice, for when he got some of the Indians of Bay River,[38] their chief, the king, was used most terribly, yes, severely roasted, tormented with all sorts of unchristian tortures, and so killed. This so embittered the Indians that it is not to be wondered at that they also treated the Christians cruelly. What grieved me most in this was that a disloyal Palatine did the most in this torturing and took pleasure in it. It was this same man who was the author of the disloyalty of the Palatines. There were indeed in Brice's following, bold and courageous people, but wholly inconsiderate. If the other Carolinians had behaved better and had not been so faint-hearted we should have become master of the Indians sooner and things would not have gone so badly.

And now, since it was of so much concern to me to justify my conduct and to show the godless and impudent behavior of Brice's rabble, I went in when the general assembly[39] was held and asked where these false accusers were, and demanded that they should bring these slanderers before my eyes, and give me copies of the complaints in order that I might defend and justify myself in a fitting manner, but no one dared to appear against me, and no one here wanted to tell the articles of complaint, and so there was an end of it. During this time I had much trouble and was in great danger, suffering not a little in my honor and reputation and demanded satisfaction because the complainants and the slanderers were well known to me. I named them out, but the authors did not appear, and in such a confused government and in the midst of the Indian war I could not get any satisfaction. The Governor and the upper house, which consisted of the seven councilors and representatives of the Lords Proprietors, two landgraves, several colonels, and the secretary, made, indeed, their excuses and paid me a compliment in regard to this affair, and with this I had to be satisfied. I sent many memorials and letters to the Governor about this matter, in which these disagreeable stories and proceedings are to be seen in detail, especially in the register of my letters of the years 1711 and 1712. But O, if all the adverse and grievous things which happened to me in Carolina and Virginia should be told it would make a big book.

To give here as was done above, only a few of the causes of the Indian war:

The carelessness of the Carolinians contributed not a little to the audacity and bold actions of these Indians, because they trusted them too much, and for safety there was not a fortified place in the whole province to which one could retire; also in case of any eruption or hostility no arrangements were made and much less were there the necessary provisions of food and war supplies. This was carried so far that in these times of unrest, whole shiploads of corn and meat were carried away and exchanged for sugar, molasses, brandy, and other less necessary things. In short, everything was carelessly managed. Instead of drawing together into one or two bodies of well ordered soldiery in order to drive the enemy from the boundaries of the settlements, every one wanted to save his own house and defend himself. This was the cause that finally the Indians or savages overpowered one plantation after another, and soon brought the whole province under them. My idea was that in case the savages would not act in accordance with the agreement made with them, and could not be brought to a good treaty, to divert them with the peace I had made, to procure a truce, and meanwhile, with the help of my people to establish myself in some place and, provided with all necessary munitions and food, by this means to make a greater and more vigorous resistance, or else entirely to destroy the savages. But there was nothing to be done with these wrong-headed Carolinians, who, even if some were more courageous than the others, took the matter up so heedlessly and clumsily, got around behind the Indians who were much stronger in numbers, good shots, and well provided with everything, so that this small handful of Christians immediately had to get the worst of it. Yes, without the help of the

Palatines and Switzers they would have been destroyed, as is to be seen in the first account. N. B. In the same account there is to be seen from a letter with the date and salutation, how the troops who were in Bath Town, a little village on the Pamtego River, about 150 in number, would not go according to their word and the sign which they had given to them, and did not have the heart to cross the river to help their neighbors, in such urgent need; but rather, after they had eaten up the corn and meat of the inhabitants of this district, leaving us on the other side along the Neuse River in the lurch, they went home again.

How I fortified myself and New Bern for 22 weeks long and supported myself and the colony with my own means, and finally had to leave my post from lack of anything to eat, in order to go to the Governor, is partly to be seen in the first account. Yet I can not pass over without telling how it went with me on this journey into Albemarle County.

So then after I had experienced and seen how miserably everything was going; what poor, yes, absolute lack of assistance; the impossibility of holding out so, for in the long run, indeed, we were reduced to the very extremity; how that through the invasion of the savages the whole colony had been destroyed, since, as has been said, about 70 had been murdered and captured, the houses of all the colonists burned, their household furniture and whatever they owned carried off, most of the cattle shot down, and our own used for food. So upon the representations of Mr. Michel and other gentlemen from Virginia and Maryland, I resolved to take other measures and because the colony was divided, half of the Palatines having turned from me, to betake myself with the rest, along with the Switzers, to the above mentioned places. Hereupon I packed a part of my things, had my little sloop fitted out with the intention, that when I had reached Governor Hyde I should succeed in getting better assistance in the parliament or general assembly, failing which, I would continue in my design to go to Virginia and Maryland.

So I departed in great perplexity, because my people were in the greatest straits,[40] yes, so much that there was no longer a measure of corn left, but we had to make shift with pork, and that very sparingly. This journey was also unfortunate. I departed with good weather and wind, after I had collected my people and addressed them as best I could, comforting them with hope of speedy help. In the evening when we were almost at the mouth of the river and were about to sail out into the Sound, there occurred a noteworthy sign. On the tip of the mast there suddenly came a small fire and it whistled rather loudly for about a quarter of an hour, and finally it ceased. When I asked the captain of the ship what that was, he told me nothing very good, that directly a great storm would follow and that was certain. I laughed at this and desired to continue my journey. But an hour did not pass, before the wind began to blow harder, and because it was toward night we did not venture, but looked about where we might drop anchor by the land. We were scarcely able to approach the land before the wind struck us so hard that a little later we should have come into the greatest danger. So we stayed over night with a planter, a good man,[41] who had settled there upon an estate. In the morning when the storm was past, we went on, and so came in the evening of the second day into the middle of the Sound, which is a sea much bigger than Lake Geneva, since in the middle one could not see land; but we struck against a sand bank, so that the ship gave such a loud crack that we thought it broken in two, and if it had not been very strong we should have had to suffer shipwreck there. We were, then, in the greatest anxiety, and took all imaginable means to get away from this dangerous place. The greatest fear was that even if the ship were finally freed it would have a crack, so that we should have been sent down without fail. But God was so gracious, that after the sea had risen and the wind had become better, we happily got away with spread sails. When we saw that no water came into the boat, we thanked God and started out. On the third day we had such a strong contrary wind that in one place we had to sail towards land. There, where there was a broad expanse grown up to reeds, we dropped anchor, and were compelled to remain several days, until the wind calmed down somewhat, so that we could sail with a side wind through a canal which flows through the reeds. We were scarcely out of the reeds when ill luck would have it that we remained sticking upon a solid rock, so that for half a day we had enough to do before we were free, and again the sea had to help us. Finally the wind increased and we came off all right and reached the appointed place, and it was time we did, for all our meager provisions of food and drink were used up. Instead of arriving in twice twenty-four hours as we hoped to with good winds we used over ten days. Thus one sees what the weather sign upon the tip of the mast means. It seems to be a superstition, to be sure, but experience knows differently.

After I had spent six whole weeks at Governor Hyde's, partly in waiting the termination of the council and the other affairs of the province, partly in providing my people at New Bern with the necessaries of life and military stores, after the expenditure of great pains and much time, my sloop was filled with corn, powder, lead, and tobacco, and sent to New Bern. But oh, what a misfortune. The good people in their extreme distress waited in vain for it. For when the sloop was clear past the Sound and far from the mouth of the river, the people on the ship drank too much brandy, so that they all went to sleep, thinking they were now out of danger; but because they had not entirely put out the fire in the kitchen, a spark sprang from a stick of wood and got into the tobacco leaves, which were not far from there. These caught more and more, until a fire started, and at length the smoke wakened the shipmen, who, out of fear that the powder cask would catch, tried to save themselves, got into the canoe, that is, a little round-bottomed boat, and left. Before they came clear to land the fire got into the powder, and the sloop went up in flames.

Imagine what sad news for the half-starved colonists to hear a thing like that, instead of the assistance waited for so long and with such great desire, and how that went to their hearts. By the time I had learned this sad news, which had delayed a good while, I had worked with all my might to have them provision a larger sloop or brigantine, but this went forward so slowly that I became very angry, seeing well that such tergiversations in such critical times would not do. For this reason I disposed my affairs with this in view that as soon as my people should have received these provisions, they should sail immediately in the same ship with Mr. Michel to Virginia. This was very much delayed. After I had stayed a long time at Governor Hyde's, as has been said before, waiting for the affairs relating to the war and the province where there was much to do, I went into Virginia in order to make the best arrangements possible. But before I go on to this journey, I can not omit to tell what in the meantime was done for the safety of the country.

After I had strongly represented to Governor Hyde and the General Assembly that we should make better arrangements than had previously been made, otherwise we were in danger of all being killed by the Indians, we got to work, and never in my life should I have thought to meet such awkward and faint-hearted people.

First of all it was of importance to find where provisions were to be obtained, for it was impossible to go to war, and yet these improvident Carolinians were so foolish as to sell grain and meat out of the country. For this reason I urged Governor Hyde immediately, to publish a sharp command forbidding the exportation of certain things.

Secondly, to find out what grain there was in the country, and to take measures accordingly. It was found that there was not enough by far, to carry on such a tedious war. Hereupon arrangements were made with the neighboring provinces which had plenty, to procure some.

Thirdly, to provide powder, lead, and firearms, with which the province was not at all supplied, and of which the individuals had very little. Hereupon it was decided to send for it among those from other places. But no one wanted to give the money for this purpose, nor did the province which was then in bad credit, find means, and so I had to try to effect something with the Governor in Virginia.

Fourthly, Suppose that all the above things of which the people had need were ready, there was still labor. We could with the greatest difficulty make out scarcely 300 armed men, and there were among them many who were unwilling to fight. They were mostly badly clad and equipped. With reference to this, commission was given to me to seek for help in Virginia. When, finally, Governor Spotswood, acting in the Queen's name, promised them this with the stipulation that the provisions and soldiers' pay should be returned, they did not want it, unless the Governor would send the soldiers and the provisions at the expense of the Queen, asserting that they could not pay back such sums, which was absurd. Why should the Queen have the expenses of the colony since the Lords Proprietors draw the revenue? This gave occasion for several to go to the Governor of Virginia to sound him to see whether he would take upon himself the protection of Carolina. But this the Governor refused, for good reasons.

Fifthly, it was proposed that we fortify some place in the province to be used in case of need as a retreat, in which to keep ourselves in safety. But this did not succeed.

With things as we knew they were, what was to be done? Meantime the Indians continued their depredations, became bold with such poor defense, and overcame one plantation after another.

The last resource was to send hastily to South Carolina for help, which we also obtained, otherwise the province would have been destroyed. So the Governor of South Carolina[42] sent 800 savage tributaries with 50 English South Carolinians, under the command of Colonel Barnwell, well equipped and provided with powder and lead. The theatrum belli was not far from New Bern. Only when these arrived did the Indian war begin in earnest, and these South Carolinians went at it, when they came to the Tuscarora savages, in such a manner that they awakened great terror among them, so that the North Carolina Indians were forced to fortify themselves. But our friendly Indians, after they had received their orders at New Bern went against Core Town, a great Indian village about 30 miles from New Bern, drove the King and his Indians out of the same after they had slain several, got into such a frenzy over it that they cooked and ate the flesh of one of the Carolinian Indians that had

been shot down. To this assistance from South Carolina we detailed
200 North Carolina English with some few of our Indians who were
friendly to us, and about 50 Palatines and Swiss under command
of Colonel Boyd and Mr. Michel, whom we made Colonel. This
small army went further up, to Catechna, a large Indian village,
where I and Surveyor General Lawson were captured and condemned
to death as has been told in the first account. In this village Catechna,
our enemy consisting of Indians of Weetox, Bay River, Neuse, Core,
Pamtego, and partly of Tuscaroras, had collected and strongly fortified themselves, and we could accomplish nothing against them; that
is to say, in the storm planned against them, the orders were not
properly executed, the attack should have been made in certain
places. But Brice's people were so hot-headed that they stormed
before the time, many of them were wounded, some were left dead,
and so our forces had to withdraw. When the report of this was
given to us in the council we were very much busied considering how
better to subdue the enemy and how to make better arrangements.
By chance I was looking about and saw six or eight pieces in the
yard, lying there uncared for, all rusty and full of sand. My notion
was that two of the smallest should be refitted, sent over, and the
fort bombarded with it. At this I was laughed at heartily, and it
was represented to me as impossible to take them through morasses,
forests, and ravines. But I remembered what Captain Jaccard of
St. Croix had told me. Just as he said he had done it before a
fortress in Flanders (which made his fortune), each small piece was
carried very nicely, as though upon a litter,[43] between two horses,
the rest disposed further as suited best, and the scheme succeeded
well. For when the approaches were made and only two shots had
been fired into the fort of the savages along with some grenades which
we tried to send in, such a fear was awakened among the savages
who had never heard nor seen such things before, that they asked
for a truce. Then a council of war was held by our highest officers
to decide what to do, and it was decided to accord a truce and to try
to make an advantageous peace. The principal cause of this was the
Christian prisoners which they still held from the first massacre, who
called to us that if the fort fell to us in a storm they would all miserably perish without mercy. Hereupon they surrendered under condition that first of all the captives should be set free. And this was
done.

Now when this was past and our troops had marched to New Bern
to refresh themselves a little, for the food was getting scarce and
scanty, and the response to Colonel Barnwell had not been to his satisfaction, he became impatient that he had not received more honor

and kindness. His soldiers also were very badly provisioned. For these reasons, he thought of a means of going back to South Carolina with profit, and under the pretense of a good peace he enticed a goodly number of the friendly Indians or savage Carolinians, took them prisoner at Core Town (to this his tributary Indians were entirely inclined because they hoped to get a considerable sum from each prisoner) and made his way home with his living plunder. Whatever before this he did worthy of praise, was flung away by this action.

This so unchristian act very properly embittered the rest of the Tuscarora and Carolina Indians very much, although heathens, so that they no longer trusted the Christians. Therefore they fortified themselves still more securely and did much damage in Neuse and Pamtego County, yes, the last became worse than the first. This induced us to lay strong complaint against Colonel Barnwell and to write to South Carolina for new help, which followed, but not so strong as the first. But soon after there arrived a goodly number under the command of Captain Moore, who behaved better. After what could be raised had been brought together they went to this Indian fort at Catechna or Hancock Town and at last this was successfully stormed, set fire, and overcome. The savages showed themselves unspeakably brave, so much so that when our soldiers had become master of the fort and wanted to take out the women and children who were under the ground, where they were hidden along with their provisions, the wounded savages who were groaning on the ground still continued to fight. There were about 200 who were burned up in a redoubt and many others slain so that in all about 900, including women and children were dead and captured. Of ours there were also many wounded and some remained on the field. From this time we had rest, although some survivors still wandered here and there. It was now a question of providing for the future, for putting ourselves in complete security against the surviving neighbors. Certain of the kings with whom we conferred yielded. N. B. The kings are really only the chiefs of a certain number of wild Indians, but still, it is hereditary and is passed on to posterity. We conferred with them and finally brought about a wished-for peace.

At present there is not the slightest thing to fear, for the savages who live beyond Virginia and this same province are tributary, a guarantee of peace; and the surviving Carolina Indians have also become tributaries of the Lords Proprietors.

Meanwhile, although in peace, it did not go well with our poor colonists; but they were dispersed here and there among the English or Carolina planters; others made their way back to New Bern where they tilled a little land to supply their most pressing need. I allowed

them to try to take service for two years and to go into the service
of one or another of the wealthiest of the inhabitants of Carolina
in order to have their living there and to save up something so that
they could afterwards go back upon their fees or plantations. But
for these two years they should be free from the quitrent imposed
upon them. To Mr. Michel and the people from Berne I let it be
known that I was going to Virginia to make the necessary arrangements there in the hope that they might settle there better than in
Carolina, trusting myself upon the Mr. Michel's word which he had
given, that he was minded to stay by the agreement which we had
made before. At the same time it was impossible with my own
strength and means to restore a colony so ruined, and from Berne the
prospects were not only poor, but no hopes of any assistance whatever had been given.

With this I took my departure from the Governor and council
and went to the Governor of Virginia, from whom I obtained this
that he granted me, particularly because of the dangerous war times
the captain of only one warship to accompany my people. This
was a great and peculiar favor for an individual. Hereupon Mr.
Michel, who was then at a conference held upon the frontiers between
Governors Hyde and Spotswood, was advised and at that time the
day was set when and where they should assemble themselves on the
island Currituck in Carolina. While this was going on I went further
into Virginia towards the Potomac and Maryland in order to have
everything ready with lodging, food, and cattle.

The place [44] was not far from the falls of the Potomac, with a civil,
generous, and well-to-do man named Rosier, settled upon the mainland. There a certain baronet and other gentlemen from Pennsylvania came to meet me in order also to see how it was with the silver
mine of which Mr. Michel had told and in which they were interested,
and on this account had been to much expense. After we had waited
there in expectation of Mr. Michel and the Bern people who were
coming with him, after such a long delay and no news coming from
him we became impatient, and in consideration also of Mr. Michel's
strange actions with regard to the mines, we got the idea of visiting
the place ourselves following the plans given us to ascertain the truth.
We equipped ourselves for this truly dangerous journey, yet because
I had had it in mind to do this even when the other gentlemen had
not yet arrived, I had as a precaution, received patents from the
Governor of Virginia, to whom I communicated my design, and
orders had been given that at the first notice I could summon as
many of the rangers stationed nearest as I considered necessary.

When we came to Canavest, a remarkably beautiful spot, about four miles above, before the falls, we found there a band of Indians and in particular a Frenchman named Martin Chartier, who had married an Indian woman, and thereby was in great credit with the wild Indians of the nations which live beyond Pennsylvania and Maryland. He also, leaving Pennsylvania on the representations of Mr. Michel, had settled himself there. Before this he had also gone with Mr. Michel to look for the mines and had been to much labor and expense. He warned us that the Indians of this same region where the silver mines were supposed to be, were very much alarmed at the war which we had had with the Tuscarora Nation, and therefore we ought not to expose ourselves to such danger without especial necessity. We believed him and postponed the matter to a convenient time. Meantime we made a league with the Canavest Indians, a very necessary thing, as well in respect to the hoped-for mines as for our little Bern Colony which we wanted to settle there. We also examined the admirable situation of the same region of country and in particular the charming island of the Potomac River above the falls, to this hour regretting that I can not live in this beautiful land.

From there we went further back upon a mountain of the highest in those parts, called Sugar Loaf, for it has the form of a loaf of sugar. We took with us Martin Chartier, a surveyor we also had with us, and there came with us several Indians. From the mountain we viewed an exceedingly broad extent of country, a part of Virginia, Maryland, Pennsylvania, and Carolina, used the compass, made us a map, and observed especially the mountain where the silver mines were said to be, found that they were beyond Virginia, and incidentally from the two Indians that they had looked up and down the mountain but had found not the slightest sign of minerals, and that the map that had been given us did not correspond to the report at all. This disturbed us greatly. What else happened on this account is not necessary to relate here. We discovered still finer land and three broad mountains each higher than the other. When we came down from the mountain we stayed overnight with Martin Chartier, and returned the next day to Mr. Rosier's quarters below the falls, where I stayed a considerable time in hopes of receiving my people there, as had been agreed. The other travelers returned to Pennsylvania, but not very well satisfied on account of the confused plan.

I believe there is no more beautiful site [4,5] in the world than this which we intended to divide into two small colonies; the first directly below the falls where there was a very cheerful island of good soil and opposite, in a corner between the Potomac River and a smaller

one called Gold Creek, suited to receive everything which comes up
or down before the falls, and the greatest merchant ships can sail
there. The other site was to be at Canavest as the map shows.
Now after there had not been received the least news for about two
months long from Carolina, the limping messenger finally came
with bad tidings. Since Mr. Michel, so the bearer of this note
reported to me in words only, demanded to have the command of our
sloop, I should come to an agreement with them. He said the sloop,
after it had finally brought the long desired grain to Neuse, on its
return had gone upon a sand bank, was in bad condition and had
become somewhat worm-eaten during the hot weather; that it needed
to be fitted out with sails, cable, and with other things; that it could
not get off; that I should betake myself quickly to Carolina, and told
me nothing further; nothing of the warship which had been sent to us
from Virginia, and of the other things which had gone on in the long
interval, so that I almost pined away and died of impatience. Such unfavorable news and so strange a report overcame me so that it would
be no wonder if I had lost my senses. After all the arrangements in
the way of provisions had been made, now everything was in vain.
Nevertheless I sent the captain who did not seem to be entirely satisfied,
with orders to fit out the ship as well as possible, and that quickly,
because it had to make only a small passage along the coasts, and
wrote to Colonel Pollock since he was in the best circumstances that
since the ship was in the service of the province, it should provide
the most essential things for this need, indicating that I would do
the rest through Virginia. But everything was postponed, and if
I wanted to have my affair advanced I should have to go there myself. When, now, I came to the Governor I found an entirely different
face than formerly, cold, indifferent, and I could not guess the cause
of it. Finally he helped me out of my consternation, nevertheless
earnestly expostulating with me and asking what I took him for,
saying that he had hoped that I would have been more grateful for
his friendliness and services, yes, such noteworthy services which
would not have been shown very soon to every individual; instead
of our due thankfulness we had acted very haughtily towards him.
The one who was in the highest degree astounded was I. I excused
myself. I said that I did not know as yet what that all meant, and
yet begged for enlightenment. So the Governor broke out, "Yes,
yes, your fine gentleman has used me very badly." He told how
that, as had been agreed, he, the governor, had sent out a warship
to bring our sloop with the people and to convoy it; that the ship
had waited about six days before Currituck Island; that the captain
had at last become impatient since he saw no one coming, sent his

small barque to the land in order to find out whether any thing was to be learned of our sloop of Switzers. No one pretended to know the least thing of it. When he traveled further to a little village called Litta (Little River), he finally learned that Mr. M. was at New Bern and the sloop was in bad condition on a sand bank and could not get off. When the lieutenant heard such news he went quickly back to his captain, who nearly jumped out of his skin to think that he had been so played with and had made such a dangerous voyage for nothing; for if a storm had been seen he would have been compelled to go out upon the high sea, and if the wind had blown towards the land he would have been in great danger because in these parts the water is not deep. So he turned angrily back to Virginia. Now when I had heard all this I half fainted away with vexation and shame that such a gentleman, from whom I had received so much friendliness, so many services, yes, after God, my life itself, had been so mocked. I began to excuse myself as best I could, telling him in answer how I had been exposed, since everything was arranged on the Potomac, that I was in the greatest anxiety how I was to work myself out of such a labyrinth. After the governor had offered me a drink to refresh me he began to express his sympathy for me that I had to deal with such a strange fellow. He advised me to get along without him.

Now after he had treated me in a friendly manner, and I had passed the night there, I went hastily into Carolina the next day, in order to make the above mentioned necessary arrangements. I had also ordered in one place sails and cordage, in order to equip the sloop in case of need. Now when I came to Governor Hyde's in Carolina I heard the whole affair for the first time really in detail, and I know not what more unpleasant things in addition. I wrote immediately to Mr M. requesting him to report to me the condition of everything; but was badly satisfied. Thereupon I demanded that he come to me in order that we might take the needed measures over one thing and another, but this was not to be obtained; and for good reasons I could not go to him, so I made arrangements elsewhere, obtained from the governor and the council that since the sloop was put into such a condition while it was in the service of the province, nothing was more fitting than that it should be given back to me in good condition again. This seemed good to me and so there was sent a man experienced in such affairs to visit the sloop, but he was so badly provided with food and other assistance that he came back again and indeed, sick, because it was in the heat of the summer. He gave us the report that the sloop could not hold together long because it had lain through the summer exposed to the heat and had been damaged by the inhabitants, and would have to be equipped anew, and it was not worth it. With this I gave the sloop over to the province and wanted to have its worth estimated, at its value and price when it came into the service. But the response was by far not what I demanded, so that I had to lose the half part in it and there is nothing yet paid any more than in the case of the small one.

In the meanwhile where was I to go with my people? I wrote again pathetically to Mr. M. and desired a conference in such a slippery conjuncture, especially since the creditors demanded to be paid. Not a word followed. But I learned that the gentleman had it in mind to pack all my things, under pretense of saving them, and to take them to South Carolina, and that he had persuaded several Palatines to go there with him. This never suspected scheme did not please me and I was warned to put my things into better keeping, but too late. In consequence of this, because Colonel Pollock, to whom I owed a tolerably large sum for provisions advanced to the colony, became somewhat suspicious, as was proper, I asked him to inventorize through chosen men everything authorized, as well the remaining property of the Palatines as mine, and so they were put into safe keeping, but my best things were gone.

Now when I reflected on the conduct of Mr. M. how he had ordered everything so strangely, how he had played with all those interested and nothing had resulted, I had no confidence in it. At last I wrote him a letter, as related, indicating what I had heard from one and another, but as a reproof, I said that if he was found to be under any suspicion he had truly given the cause for it himself, through his actions, tergiversations, and fickle minded changes, such as were better related apart by word of mouth; as affairs then were in such an extremity, strong resolutions would have to be taken, and it was absolutely necessary that we should talk out our hearts to each other in a personal conversation and take the last measures, that there was peril in delay. Instead of any meeting I received the most shameless writing that could be thought of. Indeed I believe he would have been glad to find a pretext to lend color to his tricks and to get himself free from that which, according to the information he had given, he could not carry out. I could have here a great matter for complaint over his inexpressible behavior. But to protect his eminent relatives more than him I will pass on with sighs and say nothing.

There were in this letter so many things which showed clearly that I and others besides were duped, especially one thing that the aforementioned gentleman said about a new enterprise which he almost made effective, namely, to found a colony upon the Mississippi River [46] to which three crowns, Spain, France, and England lay claim, under the opinion that the state of Berne, as neutral, would be supported in this land. One can easily observe: first, [47]the jealousy of such mighty powers, since none of them would give way to the others: second, the unsuitablity of Berne to colonize distant lands, since it is no sea power. Thus one easily sees that Mr. M. in fact did not look carefully at his calculations, and that such leaps from Pennsylvania into Maryland, from there into Virginia, further into North Carolina along with that into South Carolina, and finally to the Mississippi can not pass muster.

The conclusion, as regards the silver mines of Virginia or Maryland, is soon made. For if there is anything real there, why withdraw from it and go to the Gulf of Mexico? My hair raises when I think how many families were deceived, especially so many families of miners, who, building upon a formal contract, left their Fatherland, traveled at great expense to America and now met neither Mr. M. nor any one else there who showed them the reported mines. I must now cease to speak of the disagreeable matter, otherwise I should bury myself so deeply in it that there would not be room enough for the other things, for this is really not my purpose.

I come again to my Carolina account. After I had reflected upon the above mentioned circumstances, how little assistance was to be expected from Berne, one note after the other protested, it was incumbent upon me to consider what means to seize in such urgent need; and nevertheless I had as yet no idea of going to Europe. Because there were still two Negro slaves at Governor Hyde's, which belonged to me, I tried to take them with me, thinking to make use of them at Canavest; to which Indians I wished to retire, and gradually draw there some of the colonists out of Carolina according to the plan before announced, and they showed a great desire for it. But Governor Hyde kept me so long because the peace was not yet entirely ratified with the Indians, which conclusion he absolutely would have, that one of my creditors found a scheme to slyly keep watch of these Negroes, so that they could not get away.

Meanwhile we all became sick at the Governor's with the great heat and without doubt because we ate so many peaches and apples, so that eventually, in a few days the Governor died, which caused me much business, since he was a very good friend of mine. This death brought his very dear Madame Hyde almost to despair and she implored me with hot tears that I should not leave her in such a sad circumstance, but should remain with her, partly until the affairs, with reference to the governorship, were arranged, partly until her own affairs, relating to the deceased's claims and the debts of those owing him, were straightened out; representing to me further that according to my rank and the law, as landgrave, the presidency was due me, and that lastly, she had observed at London with the Lords Proprietors, that if the place were vacant they would entrust me with the government. I thanked her politely for it, but gave her other reasons which kept me from accepting it. I signified to her, that I would remain there a few weeks more and contribute my best to settle her affairs although my own were right then pressing so much.

After the burial Colonel Pollock, the oldest of the council, with the other justices came to me, and begged me to take the presidency. But I refused it for many weighty reasons, saying that Colonel Pollock as the oldest in years and in the council should assume it; that the affairs of the province were also better known to him than to me for I was entirely strange in this land; and after many compliments he finally accepted.

In the meantime the Lords Proprietors were informed of all this. I gave them remotely to understand, that if the government were delegated to me I should not refuse it, but that I should not solicit them for it. This was without any hesitation. As already related it seemed good to me, because it was well known that I was very much in debt in Carolina, and already several notes had been protested, so I refrained, waiting for news from Berne since I had written there to know if there was hope of any payment, for it is the custom that the candidates present themselves in person in such circumstances. So then it was postponed six whole months until a governor was appointed. Yet since several persons had put themselves forward in London and among them this same Eden, now Governor, they became impatient because neither from Bern nor from me did any one arrive in London. The Lords Proprietors finally came to an election and elected the above mentioned Mr. Eden, whom I met in London and spoke with, yes, recommended to him, as well as I could, my interests as well as those of the colony. He sincerely promised his offices, and a command to the same effect was given him by the Lords Proprietors. In passing I will say that I finally reached London and stayed with a gentleman, Chevalier Colleton, a Baronet and also a Lord Proprietor, a man who was my special friend. I was eight days upon his estate eight miles from London. At the first sight of me he evidenced his joy saying (besides) that if I had arrived only a month earlier I should now be Governor in South Carolina, a thing which grieved me less than it did him because I, unfortunately knew very well that at Bern there was no disposition to pay my debts, either on the part of my own people or on the part of the Lords Proprietors who were discouraged by so many adversities.

Now I have gotten clear to London instead of Virginia. I will continue where I left off. A few days before I took my leave of Mrs. Hyde, I had the two Negroes secretly informed through my servant that they should quietly get across the river in the night, and wait for me on the other side to go with me to Virginia. They were quite happy to do this, for they were harshly treated there, but I do not know how they managed it. Some one got wind of it and they were arrested so I had to leave them behind and by this my compass was entirely disarranged. Upon that I took my departure not trusting myself, and came to Governor Spotswood in Virginia to whom I told all these vexations. He felt very sorry for me, but because I was thinking about making my rendevous with the Baronet upon the Potomac River, I did not stay long at Williamsburg, but set forth upon my way to Maryland intending to find him at Mr. Rosier's at the falls and there to make an agreement with him as one interested. So then I hastened as fast as I could. But when, at the point of Maryland, I wanted to make the passage of the river with my horses, a strong wind hindered me. As soon as the wind left off I rode over and took my way to the falls, but would ill luck not have it that when I arrived at Mr. Rosier's house I should find neither him nor the wife nor the Baronet. The first two were distant a whole day's journey on a visit to their relatives, and the Baronet had departed just the day before, thinking to find me in Virginia. Although tired from my long journey, I took some food and a drink in haste and journeyed so quickly back that my horses were overridden, and I was compelled a day before we came to Williamsburg to go afoot. As soon as I arrived there I inquired whether the Baronet were there, but I learned that he was at Hampton, the first seaport of Virginia. I sent my servant there immediately with a lame horse, who also did not find him any more, the reason of which was that the Baronet having there by chance found a war ship ready to sail to New York and the captain of it being a very good friend of his, he had gladly availed himself of this opportunity for his return. After he had informed himself regarding the affairs of the colony and of myself, and had heard that Governor Hyde had died, and that my affairs were getting worse, he left me a letter which I never received and went to New York which is not far from Bartington, a beautiful village, built in the Holland manner, a place on the boundary between New York and Pennsylvania where he mostly stayed. But there was I left off one side, for this man was my last resource, because he was a prudent, experienced, and upright merchant, a Gascon in nationality That which amazed me was that he as a cunning man trusted and advanced Mr. M. so much. I thought there was something in the business relative to the silver mines, and if there had been the least appearance there of any reality, might still have held out.

What was I now to do? If I could easily have gotten something, so that I could have settled myself at Canavest. But because we had gone too far for that, instead of to Governor Spotswood, I went to a well known and particular friend, wished him to make another trial,[48] sent my servant into Carolina, in part to find out if he had changed his mind, in part to find out what route he had actually taken,[49] likewise to see whether possibly the Negroes had escaped, and in that case if I could get them I could yet have done something at Canavest, for they could, at least, plant corn and attend to some cattle. But my my servant came back without having accomplished anything, but it was told to him that if I wished to send a sloop or barque with provisions to my Bern colonists and a few honorable Palatines, they were disposed to come to me. I trusted to still maintain myself with the mines which I had in company with Governor Spotswood.

On this report I wrote to Colonel Fitzhugh, a rich man of the royal council and my very good friend, who would gladly have backed me in this new colony with the offer of the necessary provisions and other means. When I was now hard at work trying to open up a way, thinking I had found a loophole there, I was warned that an English merchant, to whom a resident of Carolina had also sold one of my notes, wished to have me arrested on the protested note and that the arrest was actually laid in the house where I was staying, but I hid myself. After this I took counsel with good friends, asked whether I should be safe from the creditors at Canavest or in any other place in America and the answer was in no place, for even if I were among the Indians I should be discovered by the Indian traders or merchants. So I delayed until there was no resource to be found for me in America. It was of importance to me that I should get hope of money from Bern or should find new associates. Of the latter there were, to be sure, some to be found, but they would have nothing to do with my old debts.

When I reflected upon several letters that I had received which gave me little satisfaction, I very wisely went to Governor Spotswood, at Williamsburg, his place of residence, threw my misfortunes like a handful of necessities, or in these words, "Governor, I am so very," etc. When I had observed the time that he was in good humor and at leisure I asked if he could give me an opportunity for an audience, and that a long one. At which he laughed a little and I had from this generous gentleman an entirely favorable hearing. After I had told my unfortunate adventures, as also how they wanted to arrest me, the Governor evidenced at this a hearty sympathy, wondered that they should leave me so in the lurch, especially the society; knew nothing better to advise me than that I should betake myself to Europe; offered me a recommendation to a good friend who was to procure it that the Count Orkney should present to the Queen a supplication. Then I should go to Bern, vigorously represent everything to my society, and solicit the moneys for payment of the notes. This counsel several of my best friends communicated to me. They also agreed with it.

But because winter was coming on and at these times no ships sailed to Europe, I stayed with a good friend through the winter, which there does not last so long, and because I was going to Europe again only unwillingly, much less willingly home, I prayed unceasingly all this time that the almighty God should put into my mind what I should do in such a precarious affair, that he would conduct everything according to His holy will, in order that in the future I might have more blessing in my undertaking, that thus I might take such a resolution as would be most profitable to my soul, for if I had sought barely to pass my own life I should likely have found expedients; but I had scruples about abandoning the colony. When I considered how much I owed to God, especially for such a marvelous rescue, and how disastrously and adversely everything had gone with me, I could well guess that it was not God's will that I should remain longer in this land. And since no good star shone for me I finally took the resolution to go away, comforting myself that my colonists would probably get along better among these Carolinians who could help them better at the time than I. Herewith, and because I had no great hopes in myself, I departed, for what I did was not with the intention of entirely abandoning them, although a greater part had given me cause to, but in case I received favor of an audience with her Royal Majesty the Queen of England, also more assistance at Bern, I could with joy and profit come to them again.

But I was unfortunate in these negotiations also, and so I had to commend this colony to God and the Lords Proprietors and hold myself quietly in my Fatherland, to pass the remainder of my life there in sorrowing for the time lost, in a true humility and sincere conversion, in consideration that the sins of my youth brought all this upon me. Although all this chastisement is hard for human nature still it is not so sharp as I probably deserved. It should now be for me to leave all worldly and vain cares; on the contrary, take more care for my poor soul, to which may God give me grace.

N. B. I have before this, said of this colony, when I was leaving them and so much misfortune was coming upon them, that they brought it upon themselves. Firstly, I mean to say of them that most of them were recreant to their lawful authority. What they did to it, they did afterwards to me, since the half part went from me in my great need. Also they were a godless people so that it was not to be wondered at if the Almighty has scourged them with the heathen, for they lived worse than the heathen, and if I had known what these people were, those from Bern as well as the Palatines, I should not have taken up with them.

Of the Palatines I thought to exclude the worst, as it did seem from appearances. What those were who died upon the sea and before I came to America is not known to me. But of those whom I still met, among them several escaped Switzers under Palatine names, I found them for the most part godless, rebellious people; among them murderers, thieves, adulterers, cursers, and swearers. Whatever care and pains I bestowed to keep them in order, there helped neither strong warning, nor threat, nor punishment. God knows what I endured with them. Among the Bern people there were two households which were undoubtedly the excrement of the whole Canton of Bern, a more godless rabble have I never seen nor heard of, and when the pious ones died these remained as the weeds which do not quickly die out.

I was sorrier to leave the beautiful and good land than such a bad people, and yet there were a few pious people who behaved themselves well, who were dear to me, with whom I wish it may go well; the good Lord convert the rest.

It was now a question of how to continue my journey, by water or by land. It could not be done by water because no ship captain, under penalty of losing a sum, might accept any person who was in debt and had not the power to get rid of his debtors. So it had to be by land, which is a long trip, and for which I had no money. I had to turn silverware, which I still kept, into money. Meanwhile I wrote letters to the colony representing to them my pitiful condition and how necessary my journey was. At the same time I sent also a writing to the president of the council showing them my reasons and recommended as best I could the abandoned and wrecked colony.

Now after I had taken my leave of Governor Spotswood who at the last regaled me well; and in return for my present which I gave as a small token of the gratitude due him, he made me a return present in gold which far exceeded mine. I began my journey with the help of the Most High, right at Easter 1713. Went by land clear through Virginia, clear through Maryland, Pennsylvania, Jersey, and came, the Lord be thanked, at length to New York, which is a pretty city well built in the Holland style upon an island, along by a fine sea harbor, and between two navigable rivers. The situation is especially convenient. It has a strong castle and the landscape round about it is charming. In the city are three churches, an English, a French, and a

Hollandish in which there is preaching also in German. There is all abundance and one can have whatever he wants, the best fish, good meat, grain, and all kinds of vegetable products, good beer and all sorts of the most expensive wines.

In this so pleasant a place I stayed ten or twelve days. After this I sailed in a sloop to England. I must confess that in the beginning I feared to travel over the great ocean in such a small vessel. But because I was comforted with the information that there was less danger in such a little ship since, first, they are better masters of the sails in storms; second, that it goes better and faster; third, it rocks less than the big ones; fourth, it is easier to load and unload, and is useful in trade since such a ship makes two trips while the large one is making one, I ventured to travel on it.[50] Although we had the misfortune that for the most part contrary winds blew and very often there were heavy storms, yet we arrived, God be thanked, at the end of six weeks at Bristol. This city can, because of its convenience of importation, its size, great trade, multitude of people or inhabitants, and wealth, be called the little London. There I rested several days and because the stagecoach was not safe, I went horseback in good company, to London, where I stayed several months in hopes that I might possibly get my supplication to Queen Anne through the Duke of Beaufort as my patron, who was the first Lord Proprietor and Palatine of North Carolina. But a little while before when he was minded to bring my supplication before the Queen, swift death suddenly overtook him. Again a stroke of my unfavorable fortune, for soon after the Queen herself died. So there came so many noteworthy changes in the English court that I knew my supplication was laid on the table. Although I saw no hopes of any favor at this new court for a long time, yet there was appearance that in time the new king being of the German nation would feel inclined towards this business.

Because the winter time is troublesome to travel in and I could not accomplish anything in London I was in a hurry to go home.

Meanwhile I cannot omit to relate that when I reached London I was shocked to learn that Mr. J. Justus Albrecht with some forty miners had arrived. This caused me not a little pains, worry, vexation and expense, since this people had come there so blindly, thinking to find everything necessary for their support and their transportation to the American mines. But there was nothing on hands for them, and I was myself so lacking of money that I could scarcely get enough for my needs. Meanwhile no money remained from America and at London no note had been made for me, so that it was impossible for me to assist such a number of people. What an unendurable load this was for me can well be imagined, because they thought that on account of the treaty I was under obligations to look out for them, and they had come, thus, at my command. But I had written to them from America, and that often, and they had received several letters to the effect that the chief miner Justus Albrecht with his company should not come without my orders, saying that on account of the disturbances in Carolina and the Indian wars there was nothing to be done with the mines; that they had not been shown by Mr. Michel, but if the chief miner wanted to come immediately with one or two others to take a look, very well. But he went right about it in this thoughtless way.

What was now to be done? I knew nothing better than to direct these people back home again, but this seemed so hard for them they preferred to hire themselves out for four years as servants in America than to return. In the meantime no ship was ready to sail to America, and they had to stay through the whole winter till spring in London. But what were they to live on? This question caused me much trouble.[51] Finally I ran to one great man and another in order to procure work and bread for them. For some I found places, for others not. Meantime I was pressed to go home. At last I found two merchants of Virginia to whom I represented the matter as best I could, and recommended myself to Colonel Blankistore and was advised by him. I had been recommended to him by the Governor of Virginia with reference to the mines in order that his officers should help me at the court. The result was that these people were to put their money together and keep account according to the proportion of it. The rest of it certain above mentioned merchants advanced to make up the transportation and living charges of these people. At their landing the Governor was to accept them and look out for paying the ship captain, who should pay back then, to the merchants of that country, the money they had advanced. For this purpose I wrote a circumstantial letter to Governor Spotswood to whom I represented one thing and another as well as I could, telling him that the little colony should be appointed to the land which we had together in Virginia not far from the place where minerals were found and, as supposed, the traces of the mine, where they could settle themselves according to the wise arrangements and under the helpful supervision of the Governor.

Meantime if there were not sufficient indications for a silver mine they were to look elsewhere, and because in Virginia there were, at any rate, neither iron nor copper smelters but yet plenty of such minerals they could begin on these. And for these we needed no royal patents as we did for the silver mines. In the hopes that they would succeed, I commended these good miners to the protection of the Most

High, and so they departed at the beginning of the year 1714. A whole year has now passed that I have received no report either from the Governor or from them, and for this reason I am in great anxiety.

It appears that my American misfortunes have come to an end, but the very same ill luck which led me from my country, accompanied me clear back home. Out of fear that my American creditors, of whom unfortunately the sharpest of all was in London, would make arrangements that I should be inquired for and arrested, I took the resolution, instead of taking the common routes to Dover or Harwich, to make my journey home in a small vessel which was bound for St. Valery, as being shorter and safer. The day was set but, because I dared take no passport for fear I should be discovered, he,[52] to whom I had to entrust my affairs advised me nevertheless to travel to Gravesend under another name, in a small boat, and he himself got ready. When I was half way there, such a contrary wind raged that I was compelled to go to land and to walk to Gravesend, where I stayed over night, and a whole day besides. But since it was costly to live, not knowing how long this contrary wind would last, and besides this, now considering that this also was a port, I took my way back to London, where my ship captain was not yet ready, waiting for better wind; but I remained at Southwick in the neighborhood of the Thames, waiting for orders. When he had cast off, I was warned to follow after, and I got aboard the ship at Greenwich. At Gravesend the captain let me go ashore outside the city on the further side, and there I was to wait until he had made his declaration and the ship had been inspected. Despite the fact that he said to the inspectors that my chest belonged to a nobleman of St. Valery, that he could bear witness that they contained only clothes and personal effects, they did not want to believe it. So he sent a sailor boy quickly to me to indicate to me that I would have to open up my chest. At this I did not feel easy, but yet I put a good face on it, spoke French, immediately took out my little key together with some English crowns and gave them to the inspector with the request that he would not disturb my clothes much, as they were well packed in. Fortunately this worked. If they had discovered my writings, I should have been found out and should have come into danger.

After this was past we went on, but when we were at the very mouth of the river at a seaport named Margate, there awoke such a frightful storm with thunder and lightning that we were in the greatest danger and through the night we could scarcely keep our anchor. The day after, when the wind had calmed down we sailed away, and when we were upon the sea we were driven back with great danger to another seaport called Ramsay. If the people and a number of sailors who were there had not come to our help should have gone to the bottom. There we had to remain eight whole days on account of contrary winds and to fix our torn sails and other things, which came very hard to me who had only money enough for my journey to Paris. When the wind had died down somewhat we sailed out but were driven back again a second time. Finally the wind changed to the northeast, this was favorable to us and then we advanced before Dover; again the wind changed so that this journey caused me more difficulty than when I went twice across the ocean. We passed instead of three days the entire week getting to St. Valery, and it is so dangerous that without pilots who sailed to meet us we should never have gotten into this same harbor. From there I went up the river to Abbeville, from where I took the stagecoach to Paris; from there to Lyons and as far as the Fort of Cluses where the commandant detained me because I had no passport. But yet, according to the agreement of the two countries, I did not need any and had not asked for one for myself in France. If I had not chanced to have the patents of my office in Yverdon in my chest and had not shown them, telling how that there had been good friendship kept with the people of Bern, and had not given several noteworthy circumstances, I should have been obliged to remain there until I should receive a document from Bern. So I traveled on to Geneva, from there to our vineyard in Vaud near Vevay, where, according to written reports I had thought to find my family, yes, also, to stay. All had gone to Bern eight days before, so I had to go there also, with the greatest unwillingness, to be sure. I arrived, God be thanked, upon St. Martin's day 1714 in good health and found everything in good state at home.

But O what a change I found in the city, how cold the old friends, what haughtiness and arrogance among many; and of the things which further are grievous to tell, the worst was that where I hoped to find help to restore my ruined colony I was part of the time refused and partly in other respects can not succeed,[53] so that I was compelled by lack of assistance, especially from my society which left me in the lurch, to abandon the colony, which is to be regretted, since others will fish in the troubled waters and will benefit by what I have accomplished with great cost, danger, pains, anxiety, and vexation; for affairs in North Carolina are now in good condition, the government better arranged, the savages rooted out, a good peace made, the greatest difficulties taken out of the way, the most convenient situation for the colony cleared up, and thereby made more healthy, and settled with inhabitants; so that those who come after will find it far better than we, since all beginnings are difficult. It grieves me to the heart to leave such a good and beautiful land where there was prospect of doing well in time and of bringing the colony to something considerable.

Since fortune does not wish to be more favorable to me in this world, there is nothing better than to abandon everything which is of this world and to seek the treasures which are in Heaven, where neither moth nor rust doth corrupt and where thieves do not break through nor steal.[54]

I might have made a regular description of the English provinces on the American continent through which I journeyed, but because different authors have written about them I let it rest here. On this subject one can read P. Hennepin, Blome's English America, Baron de la Hontan, Vischer's (translation of Oldmixon's), *The British Empire in America*, and of Carolina in special the latest treatise of Mr. Ochs, Vischer's translation of Lawson's Journal and Description of Carolina.

COPY OF THE ACCOUNT WRITTEN MR. EDWARD HYDE, GOVERNOR IN NORTH CAROLINA, THE 23D OF OCTOBER, 1711, WITH REFERENCE TO MY MIRACULOS DELIVERANCE FROM THE SAVAGES:

Honored Sir:

Through the wonderful and gracious providence of the Most High, I have at last escaped out of the barbarous hands of the wild Tuscarora Nation, and have arrived at my little dwelling at New Bern; but yet half dead, because for two whole days I had to travel afoot, as fast as ever I could, out alone through the forests which lie towards Catechna, compelled to take up my quarters by a frightful wild ditch in which there was deep water, because the night overtook me and I could not go farther from weariness. How I passed this night can well be imagined, in no small fear of being caught by the savage or strange Indians, and of being torn to pieces by a number of bears which growled the whole night close about me. In addition I was very lame from walking, without a gun, yes, I did not have a knife with me with which to strike a fire, and because the north wind blew very hard it was a cold night. In the morning when I tried to arise my limbs were so stiff and swollen by the cold and hard lying that I could not go a step. But because it had to be I looked me up two sticks upon which I could walk, but with great difficulty and pain. I had enough to do to get myself over this water, which was full of snakes. I did it by climbing over on a long limb.

At last I reached home. When, I at a little distance from home, came within sight of a dwelling, fortified and full of people, I was somewhat comforted, because I thought that everything there had been burned out and destroyed by the Indians, as well as the houses of the other colonists; yes, also that I should find few of my people, because the terrible expedition of the savages was only too well known to me, when they burned, murdered, and plundered whatever they found along the rivers Pamtego, Neuse and Trent. When my good people got sight of me, black and looking like an Indian, and yet looking like myself as far as my size and blue coat were concerned, they did not know what to think. But thinking, all of them, that I was dead, they were firm in the opinion that it was, rather, an Indian spy who had put on my coat and wanted to spy out something there; and so the men folks put themselves into an attitude of defense. But when I came toward the house walking very lame on two sticks, they saw by my countenance and posture that I was no Indian or savage. Yet they did not recognize me till several came out in advance to look at me better. When I saw that they were in anxiety I began to speak from a distance, with a very broken voice, to be sure. This shocked them so that they retreated several paces, crying to the rest to come forward, that it was their master, whom they supposed murdered. So they all came running pell-mell, men, women, and children, with loud exclamations, some weeping, some completely dumb with amazement, saluting me as a marvelous spectacle. There was mourning, joy, and bewilderment mixed, and this went to my heart, so that it forced out abundant tears.

After I had stayed some time with these people who surrounded me, although I was very tired I finally went to my old quarters, closed my door, and made a hearty prayer of thanksgiving to the good God for such a merciful and wonderful rescue, which for these times, indeed, may pass for a miracle.

The next day I asked what had happened in my absence, but so many vexatious things came out that it makes my heart heavy. The worst was that, besides sixty or seventy Palatines who were murdered, the rest who could save themselves were plundered, and the survivors of these Palatines had left my house, in which were their own goods, and the little city. A certain William Brice, an unthankful man to whom I had shown much kindness, yes, whom the money and goods belonging to myself and the poor colonists had brought out of poverty, had drawn them away from me with all sorts of promises and cunning and had brought them to himself upon the Trent River, by means of whom, with some English Planters or inhabitants in addition, he had succeeded in getting together a garrison to defend his house. So I had to be satisfied with a number of women and children. In armed soldiery there were no more than forty. These all I had to support for twenty-two weeks. So all my grain, which luckily I had in store, my cattle great and small, were all gone. If we do not soon receive the necessaries, we shall have to starve to death or give up the post. Therefore, Honored sir, we urgently beg you to send as soon as possible and in all haste the needed provisions, military stores, and armed troops, in order that we may drive back these barbarian murderers, otherwise the evil will become greater, and it is to be feared that the whole land will be destroyed.

One cannot wonder enough, yes, it is provoking to see such coolness and so little love among the inhabitants of Albemarle County that with folded arms they can see how their nearest brothers are frightfully murdered by this barbarous nation. Indeed, they themselves need not expect a better fate. They ought to be ashamed of themselves and are worthy of a continuous rebuke. This is also no less to be wondered at, a policy so bad and wrong orders of those in authority, but I except your Excellency here in the best form, assured that you, Most Honorable Sir, had given all necessary commands and made all needful arrangements, but they were badly executed or not executed at all, which is a thing to be mourned.

Honored Sir, the above only as a report how I came home. But to free and justify myself it will be necessary for me to tell how I came into this barbarous nation.

Because of the fine and apparently settled weather, the Surveyor-General Lawson came to invite me to travel up the Neuse River, saying that there was a quantity of good wild grapes, that we could enjoy ourselves a little with them. But that was not enough to persuade me to go there. So the above mentioned Monsieur Lawson came again soon, pled better reasons, namely that we could at the same time see how far up the river was navigable; whether a shorter way might be made to Virginia, in place of the ordinary way which is long and difficult, and in like manner see what kind of land is up there. This, and how far it is to the mountains, I had been for a long time desirous to know and to have seen for myself. So at this I resolved upon a small journey and took everything that was necessary, including provisions for fourteen days. I asked Mr. Lawson in particular whether there was danger from the Indians, especially with those with whom we were not acquainted. He gave me for an answer that this was of no consequence, that he had already made the trip and it was entirely safe, that he knew of no wild Indians on this arm of the river, but that they were tolerably distant. But that we might go the more securely, I took besides two negroes to row, two neighboring Indians whom we knew, to whom I had shown much kindness. And since one understood the English language, I thought if we had these

two Indians with us we should have nothing to fear from the others.
and so we traveled right on up. It had not rained for a long time;
the water was not deep; the stream or current of the water was not
strong. The whole day we were upon the river; at night we spread
our tent upon the land by the water and rested; in the morning we
proceeded again.

May it please the Governor to learn that the above mentioned
Surveyor-General Lawson urged me very much for my horses, pleading that he wanted to ride a little into the forest when we were up
above, in order to see where the way to Virginia could be most conveniently commenced. At first I did not wish to agree to it. But
finally he begged for only one. This I granted him. The one Indian
rode by land, but at one place he had to go over the river, which
was our misfortune, for he went first to the Indians. I do not know
whether he lost his way or did it treacherously. He came to the great
Indian village Catechna, where he was immediately asked what the
horse was doing, for the Indians use none. He answered that he had
to drive the horse for us, while we traveled up the river. This immediately alarmed the Indians, especially the inhabitants of Catchena,
so that they ran together from the whole neighborhood. They kept
the horse and said to our Indian that he should go immediately to us
and announce to us that they would not allow us to go further up
through their country. At the command of the king who resides there
we should come back, and so the signal that we should stand still was
given by a shot which our Indian fired. This we did after we also
had fired off our guns as a signal. It was already late when he came
to us with the bad news. We were landing at the first spring to take
up our quarters for the night. We met already two armed Indians
there, who looked as though they were coming from hunting. Upon
this I said it did not please me, that we would not remain there, but
would go back. He, the Surveyor-General, laughed at me, but before we turned around it became serious so that his laughter disappeared. In a moment there came out of all the bushes and swimming through the river such a number of Indians and overpowered us
that it was impossible to defend ourselves, unless we wanted to have
ourselves wantonly shot dead or frightfully tortured. We were forthwith taken prisoners, plundered, and led away.

By this time we had gone three good days journey up the river, not
far from another Indian village, called Zurutha.

The river is there still rather broad, but the water not more than
two or three feet deep, and it is still far from the mountains.

We asked that they should leave us there this night, with a guard
if they doubted us, giving as reason that I could not go so far afoot,

that early in the morning we would go by water to the king at Catechna, promising that we would be there. But it was not to be done since I was such a rare and important capture; for they took me for the Governor of the whole province. Their barbarous pride swelled them up so that we were compelled to run with them the whole night, through forests, bushes, and swamps, until the next morning about three o'clock when we came to Catechna where the king, Hancock by name, was sitting in all his glory upon a raised platform; although the Indians are accustomed at other times to sit upon the ground. After a consultation and a sharp speech by the leader or captain of our escort the king with his council left and came to us very politely with his chief warrior. But he could not speak with us. After a short time the king went into his cabin or hut; we remained by a fire guarded by seven or eight savages. Toward ten o'clock there came a savage here, another there out of his hut; council was held, and it was disputed vigorously whether we should be bound as criminals or not. It was decided no, because we had not been heard yet. Toward noon the king himself brought us some food in a lousy fur cap. This was a kind of bread made of Indian corn, called dumplins,[55] and cold boiled venison. I ate of this, with repugnance indeed, because I was very hungry.

We had the liberty of walking about the village. Toward evening there was a great festival or assembly of all the neighboring villages. This was appointed for two reasons: first, they wanted to revenge themselves of the evil treatment of certain bad and surly English Carolinians who were of Pamtego, Neuse, and Trent Rivers; and second, to find out what help they might expect from their neighboring Indians.

N. B. Hereby it is to be observed that neither we nor our colony were the cause of this terrible slaughter and Indian war, as is to be seen and concluded from several circumstances.

In the evening there came hither from all the villages a great number of Indians with the neighboring kings, upon a fine, broad, open space, especially prepared for the festivities or executions. And there was appointed an assembly of the chiefs as they call them, consisting of the most prudent, sitting after their fashion in a ring around a great fire. King Hancock presided. There was a place left in the ring for us, where were two mats, that is to say pieces of wickerwork woven of small canes or reeds, laid down to sit on, which is a sign of great deference and honor. So we sat down, and our spokesman, the Indian that had come with us, who could speak English well, sat at our left. The king gave a sign to the orator of the assembly, who made a long speech with much gravity. And it was ordered that one of the youngest of the assembly should represent and defend the interests of the council or of the Indian nation. He, so far as I could discern, did it in due form. He sat right next to our interpreter and spokesman. The king always formed the question, and then it was debated pro et contra. Immediately after that came a consultation and decision.

The first question was, what was the cause of our journey? Our answer was, that we had come up there for our pleasure, to get grapes and at the same time to see if the river were convenient so that we could bring goods to them by water; to have good business and correspondence with them. So the king asked us why we had not paid our respects to him and communicated our project to him. After this there came into question a general complaint, that they, the Indians, had been very badly treated and detained by the inhabitants of the Pamtego, Neuse, and Trent Rivers, a thing which was not to be longer endured. And they named the authors of it in particular, and among others, the Surveyor-General was accused. He being present excused himself the best he could. After considerable disputing and after a deliberation which followed, it was decided that we should be set free, and the next day was appointed for our journey home.

The next day there was a considerable delay before we could get our canoe or small boat. Meantime there came some of their chiefs and two kings who were curious to know what grounds of justification we had. And so we were examined again in King Hancock's hut two miles from the village, and gave the same answer. Unfortunately the king of Cartuca was there, who reproached Lawson with something, so that they got into a quarrel on both sides and became rather angry. This spoiled everything for us.

However much I tried to keep Lawson from disputing, I could not succeed at all. The examination finally ended, we all rose up, we two walked together and I reproached him very strongly for his unguardedness in such a critical condition. Immediately thereafter there came suddenly three or four of the chiefs very angrily, seized us roughly by the arms, led us back and forcibly set us down in the old place. There were no mats laid for us, they took our hats and wigs away from us and threw them into the fire. After that some malicious young fellows came and plundered us the second time, searching our pockets, which they had not done before when they confined themselves to the larger things.

Hereupon a council of war was held and we were both condemned to death, without knowing the cause of it. And so we remained the whole night, sitting in the same position upon the ground till morning. At the break of day we were taken away from there and again led to the great judgment and assembling place, a bad omen for us, and I turned toward Mr. Lawson bitterly upbraiding him, saying that his lack of foresight was the cause of our ruin; that it was all over with us; that there was nothing better to do than to make peace with God and prepare ourselves betimes for death; which I did with the greatest devotion.

When we arrived at the place mentioned, the great council was already together. By chance I saw an Indian dressed like a Christian before we were called into the ring. He could speak English. I asked him if he could not tell us what was the cause of our condemnation. He answered me with a very disagreeable face, why had Lawson quarreled with Core Tom and why had we threatened that we would get revenge on the Indians? At that I took the Indian aside, promising everything I could if he would listen to me and afterward tell of my innocence to some of the chiefs. I had enough to do to persuade him to do it. Finally he paid attention to me. And so I told him I was sorry that Monsieur Lawson was so imprudent as to quarrel with Core Tom; that the councilors could themselves see very well that I was not to blame for that; and about the threatening, there was not the least thought of that, it was a misunderstanding or else Monsieur Lawson complaining at my negroes for disturbing his rest the first night. At this I threatened the negroes sharply because of their impudence, and this was all. After the Indian had heard me he left me, I repeating my promises to him.

Whether he spoke very much in my favor I do not know, but a quarter of an hour after the old chief came, led us out upon the place of judgment and bound us there hand and foot, and the larger of my two negroes as well. And there began our sad tragedy which I would like to relate with your leave, if it would not be too long and sad. Yet since I have begun I will continue.

In the middle of this great space we sat bound side by side, sitting upon the ground, the Surveyor-General and I, coats off and bare headed; behind me the larger of my negroes; before us was a great fire and around about the fire the conjurer, that is, an old gray Indian, a priest among them, who is commonly a magician, yes, even conjures up the devil himself. He made two rings either of meal or very white sand, I do not know which. Right before our feet lay a wolf skin. A little farther in front stood an Indian in the most dignified and terrible posture that can be imagined. He did not leave the place. Ax in hand, he looked to be the executioner. Farther away, before us and beyond the fire, was a numerous Indian rabble, young fellows, women, and children. These all danced in the most abominable postures. In the middle was the priest or conjurer, who, whenever there was a pause in the dance, made his conjurations and threats. About the dance or ring at each of the four corners stood a sort of officer with a gun. They beat time with their feet and urged on the other dancers and when a dance was over shot off their guns. Besides this, in a corner of the ring, were two Indians sitting on the ground, who beat upon a little drum and sang, and sang so strangely to it, in such a melody, that it would provoke anger and sadness rather than joy. Yes, the Indians themselves, when tired of dancing, would all run suddenly away into a forest with frightful cries and howling, but would soon come back out of the forest with faces striped black, white, and red. Part of them, besides this, would have their hair hanging loose, full of feathers, down, and some in the skins of all sorts of animals: In short in such monsterous shapes that they looked more like a troop of devils than like other creatures; if one represents the devil in the most terrible shape that can be thought of, running and dancing out of the forest. They arranged themselves in the old places and danced about the fire. Meanwhile there were two rows of armed Indians behind us as a guard, who never left their post until all was over: Back of this watch was the council of war sitting in a ring on the ground very busy in consultation.

Toward evening when the sun went down, the rabble above mentioned left off dancing and went into the woods to fetch wood to maintain the fires in different places; but especially they made one at some distance in the forest which lasted the whole night and was so great that I thought the whole forest was afire.

Let the Governor consider what a mournful and terrifying sight that was for me to die, yet I had my mind made up for it. I was, thus, the whole day and night in ardent devotion. Oh what thoughts I had! Everything that happened to me so far back as I could remember occurred to me. I applied and made use of everything that I had read from the scriptures and the Psalms and other good books. In short, I prepared myself as well as I could for a good and blessed end; yes, the merciful God gave me so much grace that fearlessly, calmly, I waited what my end might be. After the anguish of soul I had endured, worse than the fear of death, nevertheless there remained in me I hardly know what kind of hope, despite the fact that I saw no sign of any rescue. Although, as I said before, my sins hovered before me, still I afterwards found great consolation in considering the miracles which the Lord Jesus did in His times on the earth. This awakened such a confidence in me, that upon this I made my ardent prayer to my Saviour, in the strong confidence that my prayer was heard, and that these savage minds and stony barbarian hearts would perhaps turn, so that at my pleading and explanation they would change their minds and be led and moved to mercy; which also happened through God's wonderful providence. For as the sun was going down the council assembled once more, without doubt, to make an end of this fatal, terrible, and sad ceremony. I turned myself somewhat around, although bound, knowing that one of them understood the English language rather well, and made a short speech, telling my innocence, and how if they did not spare me the great and mighty Queen of England would avenge my blood, because I had brought the colony to this land at her command, not to do them any harm but to live on good terms with them; and what else seemed to me good to say to engage them to kindness; with the offer of my services and all sorts of favors if I were liberated.

Now after I had finished talking, I noticed that one of the leading Indians, who before this seemed entirely inclined to me, the one, indeed, who had once brought me food, and who belonged to King Taylor, from whom I had purchased the land where New Bern now stands, was amazed and spoke very earnestly; I had no doubt in my favor; which turned out to be the case, for it was hereupon decided to send some of their members immediately to the neighboring Tuscarora villages; and with them the result was that I should have my life, but the poor Surveyor General would be executed. I passed the night between life and death, bound all the time in the same place, in continual prayer and sighs. I examined my poor negro and spoke as well as I could to him, and he gave me more satisfaction than I hoped. But Surveyor General Lawson, being a man of understanding though not of good life, I allowed to do his own devotions. In the morning about three or four o'clock the deputies came back from their mission bringing the decision regarding their errand, but very secretly. One of them came after a while to loose me from my bonds. Not knowing what that might mean, I submitted patiently to the will of the Lord, the Most High, arose and followed. Oh how dumb-founded I was, when, some paces from the old place, the Indian said to me in my ear, in broken English, that I should not fear, they would not kill me, but they would kill General Lawson. This went to my heart.

About twenty paces from the place where I was bound the Indian brought me to the cabin or hut and gave me food to eat, but I had no appetite. Soon there came a great number of the Indian rabble about me, who all evidenced great joy at my deliverance. The very same man brought me again to the clear space, but a little further in advance, where the whole council sat, and they congratulated me in their way and smiled. Meantime I was forbidden to say the least thing to Monsieur Lawson, not even to speak a single word to him.

They let my negro loose also, but I never saw him again. Poor
Lawson remaining in the same place could easily guess that it was all
over and no mercy for him. He took his leave of me striving to see
me in his danger; and I, not daring to speak with him or give him
the least consolation, indicated my sympathy by some signs which I
gave him.

A little while after this, the man who had spoken for me in the
council led me to his hut, where I was to remain quietly until further
orders, and in this interval the unfortunate Lawson was executed;
with what sort of death I really do not know. To be sure I had
heard before from several savages that the threat had been made that
he was to have his throat cut with a razor which was found in his
sack. The smaller negro, who was left alive, also testified to this; but
some say he was hanged; others that he was burned. The savages
keep it very secret how he was killed. May God have pity on his
soul.

The day after the execution of Surveyor General Lawson the chief
men of the village came to me with the report that they had it in mind
to make war on North Carolina. Especially did they wish to surprise
the people of Pamtego, Neuse, and Trent Rivers, and Core Sound. So
that for good reasons they could not let me go until they were through
with this expedition. What was I to do? I had to have patience, for
none of my reasons helped. A hard thing about it was that I had
to hear such sad news and yet could not help nor let these poor people
know the least thing of it. It is true, they promised that Caduca,
which is the old name of the little city of New Bern, should receive no
harm; but the people of the colony should come down into the little
city, otherwise they could not promise much for the damage. These
were good words, but how was I to let the poor people know? Since
no savage would take the warning to them, I had to leave this also to
the Most High. There were about five hundred fighting men collected
together, partly Tuscaroras, although the principal villages of this
nation were not involved with them. The other Indians, the Mar-
muskits, those of Bay River, Weetock, Pamtego, Neuse, and Core
began this massacring and plundering at the same time. Divided
into small platoons these barbarians plundered and massacred the
poor people at Pamtego, Neuse, and Trent. A few days after, these
murderers came back loaded with their booty. Oh what a sad sight to
see this and the poor women and children captives. My heart almost
broke. To be sure I could speak with them, but very guardedly.
The first came from Pamtego, the others from Neuse and Trent.
The very same Indian with whom I lodged brought a young boy with
him, one of my tenants, and many garments and house utensils that I

recognized. Oh how it went through my heart like a knife thrust, in the fear that my colony was all gone, and especially when I asked the little fellow what had happened and taken place. Weeping bitterly he told me that his father, mother, brother, yes, the whole family had been massacred by the very same Indian above mentioned. With all this I dared not act in any way as though I felt it. For about six weeks I had to remain a prisoner in this disagreeable place, Catechna, before I could go home. In what danger, terror, disgrace, and vexation is easily to be thought.

All sorts of things happened in this time. Once I was in great perplexity. The men folks were all on this massacring expedition, the women all somewhat distant to get cherries, others to dig sweet potatoes, a species of yellow roots, very good and pleasant. And so I found myself entirely alone that same day in the village. A struggle arose in me whether I should get away from there and go home or not. I studied long over it, considered it best to call upon my God for help in this doubt, so that he would put it into my mind what I should do in such a critical circumstance. After I had made my prayer, examined and treated the matter pro et contra, I finally considered the better way would be to stay; comforting myself with this that He who had saved me from the first extreme peril would still help me further. Again, if any Indian met or saw me I should be a dead man, for there would be no hope of mercy. In addition they would be so embittered that before I could get home, since I did not know the way, everything would be plundered, burned, and murdered. Experience proved afterwards that I chose the better way.

After these heathens had made their barbarous expedition they came home and rested for a time. Then I watched the opportunity and when I found the chiefs of the village in good humor I asked whether I might not soon go home. To bring them to a favorable disposition I proposed to make a separate peace with them, promised at the same time each chief of the ten villages a cloth coat, something in addition for my ransom; to the king, two flasks of powder, five hundred bullets, two bottles of rum, a brandy made of sugar. But the Indians wanted to have much more, such as guns, more powder, and lead or bullets; but I told them this was contraband, that is, ware which was forbidden to offer for sale under penalty of hanging; that I would, at least, have to be neutral and help neither one side nor the other: Otherwise there would nothing come of our peace. They accepted these and other reasons, and so we made an agreement as your Highness will see in the enclosed articles of the treaty.

But although we made our treaty, still these suspicious fellows did not want to let me go without more secure and certain guarantee.

They wanted that I should send my smaller negro to New Bern, so that everything that I had promised should be brought up to Catechna; but yet not a savage would go with him although I wanted to give him a passport or safe conduct. I told him that none of my people who survived would come back with him, because they were so frightened at the robberies and murders, and my negro could not come alone against the current with a loaded boat. Since we could not come to an agreement, I referred it to the Indian with whom I lodged, who gave a sensible decision about our strife so that we were satisfied on both sides.

On the very day that I wanted to send the negro to New Bern with a letter to the man who had charge of my house that he should send the above mentioned goods half way, for the security of both sides, strange Indians came on horseback from the Governor of Virginia with a letter as enclosed copy will show. Nobody besides myself could read the letter. The letter was very sharp. I did not know what it contained. Finally I thought the messenger might know the contents of it, so I read the letter to the chiefs of the villages. When I had finished reading the letter I observed something in their faces which showed that it was not acceptable to them, that on receipt of the letter they should send me immediately to my home, failing which, if the least injury came to me, he, the Governor, was prepared to avenge me, yes, to exterminate every one and spare neither women or children. Upon this they had a council, and it was decided to let me go to the village among the Tuscaroras where the Indian trader from Virginia was, who before, at the very time that Monsieur Lawson was executed, was staying in the same village; and on his, the Governor's return, had told him our sad adventure. Upon which this generous Governor Spotswood had immediately sent this Virginia trader, who dealt with the Indians and understood and spoke their language very well, with the above letter to the Tuscaroras. But he, the Governor, was waiting in the first Indian village called Natoway, with a strong escort, with orders to the neighboring militia to hold itself in readiness to act at once if the desired word did not come.

So the next morning early, I set out on horseback with the Indian messengers; and many of the chief Indians of Catechna came with me towards the principal village called Tasky. They marched as swiftly as I on horseback, and in the evening between day and night, we arrived at the place where the Virginia merchant was also staying. This village was fortified with palisades, and the houses or cabins were very artfully made of withes, mere pieces of bark, placed around in a circle or ring, so that a great fire was placed in the center. The council which consisted of the chiefs of the Tuscarora Nation was sitting around on the ground. There was a place left for me and a place for the Indian trader above and the Indians who came with me. After I had greeted this gentleman we sat down. In all this I had a secret joy, having the hope of going to Natoway to the Governor of Virginia, who was waiting for me; and so at length of being free from this savage captivity. But unfortunately it did not succeed. The orator of the assembly began a long speech and asked the four Indians who came with me what was the cause of my detention and my crime. After a hearing I was found and declared innocent, and it was decided to comply with the desires of the Governor of Virginia, when it was represented to them what danger would arise from a refusal.

The Virginia trader, as interpreter, spoke what he could in my favor; the four Indians of Catechna would not agree to that for fear that the ransom would not follow although the Virginia trader promised them surety for it; they pretending that they dare not do it without the consent of the other kings and chiefs, yet promising to let me loose as soon as the king and council should be together; but they wanted to keep my negro as security until the ransom should be paid.

The next day my hopes were entirely frustrated. I took my leave of the Virginia trader, who was much vexed at the unfriendly manner of these savages. So I marched back again very sadly. When we had gone three or four miles and were near Hancock Town or Catechna, we heard a great outcry and yelling around in that direction, and here some and yonder other savages came out of the bushes. This inspired fear in me, and not without cause; especially when they came right up to me, all out of breath and frightened, saying that the English and the Palatines were close by. In particular they signified the Palatines with a disagreeable expression, mocking the Palatines by the repetition of ja, ja, to signify that even some of my own people were seen there. In order to have me take a roundabout way they made me go through a desolate ravine. When from a distance I saw a fire time began to hang heavy on my hands, fearing they wished to murder me in secret. I studied how to persuade them that the Palatines had not joined with the English at all; that these words ja, ja, were not German but a rough English word, aye, aye, which is otherwise a good English word meaning yes, that is, ja. I kept them in this opinion as well as I could. When we came to the place where the fire was I saw with perturbation the whole rabble of Catechna where I was captured, together with their household goods and a little food, in a fine corn field where every Indian had placed his own family in the midst of a swamp, that is, in a wild place, a portion of forest in the morass, and water on one side and the other it is next to the river.⁵⁷ All, that is to say, the old decrepit men, women, children, and young men under age were there, very much frightened. In order to make myself acceptable to them, and for my part to keep them in security, I did not fail to give them every comfort; assuring them, that as long as I was with them, nothing evil would happen to them. I represented to the warriors who came to encourage the throng, that they ought to have let me go before, and with their warriors; that I would treat with the English and persuade them to peace. They would not let me go however.

The day following, all the Indians round about to the number of three hundred brave fellows came together, joined themselves together with the others, and went to look for the Christians who were no more than sixty in number, and who were only four miles, that is, about three quarters of an hour distant from our village. But the Palatines who did not know how to fight with the Indians any other way than merely to show themselves, were mostly wounded and one Englishman was shot to death. Since they were overpowered by the Indians they turned their backs and hurried home. The Indians pursued them but did no great damage except for what they got in the way of booty. So the savages came back two days afterwards to Catechna with horses, food, hats, boots, also some coats. When I saw all this, especially a neat pair of boots with silver trimmings belonging to me, I was much dismayed and greatly feared that they had plundered my house and store, but there was no damage done. Why my things were among them is this. My people used the things of which they had need for this expedition.

So these wild warriors or murderers who were in great glory came in triumph home; and we also went out of our place of concealment in the evening, and traveled the whole night through, back again to our old quarters in Catechna. They made great fires of rejoicing, especially in the place of execution, on which occasion they hung up three wolf hides, representing as many protectors or gods. At the same time the women made offering of their ornaments, such as necklaces of wampum, which is a kind of coral of calcined mussels, white, brown, and gold colored.

In the midst of the ring was a conjurer acting as their priest, who made all sorts of strange motions and adjurations; and the rest danced in a ring about the fire and the above mentioned skins.

After the Indian celebration was over I began to become impatient, asked certain of the chiefs whether now they would not let me go home, because they were victorious and possibly all of my people had been slain. One of the troop answered laughing, that they would see what to do, and he called the king and his council.

Two days after, early in the morning, they brought me a horse. Two of the chiefs accompanied me, armed, but afoot, until about two hours distant from Catechna. There they gave me a piece of Indian bread and left me. Because I saw a long way before me I begged them to leave me the horse, saying that I would send it back without fail, or they should go somewhat nearer to my quarters with me. But I could not prevail upon them. They remained at the place where I left them and made a big fire, to signify to me that there were strange Indians in the woods, and I should hasten and walk swiftly; yes, for two hours run as fast as ever I could, which I also did, until night overtook me and I came to my frightful, desolate ravine, over which I could not go in the dark on account of deep water; but on the contrary I had to stay over night there until morning. The rest of the journey I have already told to the Governor.

Some notes of what I observed among the Indians and during my Tuscarora captivity, merely as they come to my mind, without especial arrangement; which are to be found designated with a, b, c.

Certain jealous and indiscreet inhabitants of Carolina have asserted that I or my colony was the cause of this Indian war and massacre. To my justification I could, indeed, present many reasons; but for this reason will not trouble myself much, because my innocence is sufficiently known; yet I cannot refrain from adducing here the following proofs:

(1) If I were the cause why did not the Indians execute me as well as Lawson?

(2) I paid for the land or piece of ground which the savages called Cartouca, three times. To the Lords Proprietors, to the Surveyor-General, and to the Indian King Taylor. This Indian King lived with his people in that place where my house now stands and the little city of New Bern was begun; with which Indians, I and my people lived on friendly terms. For the rest of the land I had also paid whatever was demanded of me.

(3) There was no complaint against me or the colony; witness which the great assembly of the Tuscaroras where this had come into question in the presence of the Virginia trader, and there the authors of these troubles were indicated by name. But out of Christian love I will not name them. Both the Governor of Virginia and of Carolina are herewith informed of it.

I have seen many notable assemblies, have myself been present at some; but I have wondered at the gravity and good order of these heathen, their silence, obedience, respect towards those in authority; no contradiction except by turn, and that only once and with great decency. One could not in the least observe any passion, and there was time enough given for reply. In fine everything was done with a propriety which would bring conviction and put many Christian magistrates to shame. The trial was conducted also in as orderly a manner as could ever be with Christian judges, and I have heard such sensible reasons given by these savages and heathens that I was amazed.

There were seven villages of the Tuscarora Nation, which very much wanted to pretend that they had nothing to do with this Indian war and massacre, and for this reason had no understanding with the other Indians. These were somewhat farther distant, more beyond Virginia, and are loyal yet, keeping their loyalty on the account of trade. These seven towns or villages hold the others in this region in certain bounds and submission. This Tom Blount is a king or leader of a considerable number of wild Indians, has very good understanding, is very well inclined towards the English nation, and contributed not a little to a good peace; yes, when it was argued with regard to me, spoke as best he could for my rescue.

I can here also not forget the generosity and sympathy of a good widow, who, immediately at my arrival and during my captivity, always brought me food, so that there was never any lack of food with me. But the most remarkable thing was, as soon as she had seen that when I was bound young fellows plundered me (among other things, my silver rings were taken from my shoes and these were held on by a small cord only), she took some of her pretty brass buckles through which she had drawn her hair bands on her forehead and fastened them upon my shoes, and had no rest until she discovered what Indian had taken my buckles, and had traded with him and gotten them. She came running back full of joy and put the silver buckles on my shoes. This was indeed a great kindness from a savage, enough to bring conviction to many Christians. I must say here to the shame of Christians, that all in all, the Indians are much more generous. I have observed many good things from them, such as—they do not swear, keep their word exactly whatever they promise, do not quickly quarrel in their games, are not so avaricious, there is not so much haughtiness; among their young people also, I have not noticed anything improper; Altho they are almost naked they act more decently than many Christians. The bad thing about them is that their rage is furious.

It is here to be observed that when these barbarous murderers come home, their wives know before hand through messengers. They prepare themselves for a feast in the night. Each household prepares the best food, after their fashion, brings the same out upon the great execution place where they also hold their dances. Each family makes a small scaffold, before which is a fire. These scaffolds are round-about, and in the middle of the great space is a big fire, beside which the priest stands. The women took off all their ornaments, which consisted of pendents of wampum and glass corals; then they took white wands or rather thick whips as an offering into the midst of the ring where there were also stuck up three deer skins as a sort of an idol which they honored. The Queen, or in her absence, the first after her, began; the rest, the one after the other, followed singing. When the ring was full they danced about the fire and the three hides till they were tired, and then each went to her place or scaffold to eat with her husband. When they were through they took white wands with black rings about them and went through the same ceremony as before; took the first little sticks or whips adorned with the corals, stuck the ringed ones in their place, and so turned again to their places. In the meantime the priest did his office, cursing the enemy in the most horrible motions, on the other hand exalting his warriors and urging them on to further bravery. After this the young people took the green limbs covered with foliage, colored their faces with black, white, and red; let their hair hang loose covered with goose down, so that they looked terrible, more like devils than men, and ran to the great open space with a terrible outcry, and danced as described above.

Here is to be observed, that when the above mentioned savage warriors or rather murderers came in with their booty and prisoners, the priest and the leading women seized the poor prisoners, compelled them to go into the dance, and if they did not wish to dance they caught them under the arms and dragged them up and down, as a sign that these Christians were now dancing to their music and were subject to them.

And so these heathenish ceremonies may be considered a sort of sacred litany or divine worship. In the morning I observed at times that they sang a serious little song instead of a prayer; and when they are in great danger, the same.

At New Bern where I settled and started the little city, I observed another custom among the Indians who lived there before, which was somewhat nearer the Christian worship. There they had constructed a sort of altar, very cleverly and artistically, out of woven twigs and having an arched dome. In one place there was an opening as though made for a little door, through which they laid the offering inside. In the middle of this heathen chapel were little holes in which they hung corals and also offered wampum. Towards sunrise there was set up a wooden image tolerably well carved, the figure as herewith sketched, half red, half white, before which was stuck up a long staff upon which was a crown. The staff had rings around it, red and white. Toward the north or rather towards the west, there was placed opposite to it another image with an ugly face, colored black and red. They represented thus by the first image a good divinity, and by the other the devil, with whom they are better acquainted.

I cannot omit to tell here what happened to one of my tenants, a sturdy, droll man. When he was coming past, observing these two images, he immediately made a distinction between the one which represented the good God and the other which represented the bad; and because this one was colored with black and red, which were the very colors of the Canton of Bern, he was so embittered at it that he cut the ugly image in two with his ax. Then when he came home again he boasted of it as a brave deed, as though he had split the devil in two at one blow. This in the beginning provoked a small laughter; but yet I did not approve of the deed. Soon after there came an Indian king very angry, taking this for a sacrilege and a great affront, and complaining bitterly. I treated it indeed as a joke, saying that only a bad idol was injured and destroyed, that it was of no great harm, but if it had been the good one, I would inflict severe punishment; but I would thenceforth take such measures that such vexations should not happen to them any more. Although the Indian king saw that I made a joke of the matter it did not please him, but he became serious. So I gave evidence to him in earnest that this man's action also did not please me entirely; and if he could point out the man who did it, he should be punished for it. I gave the king and those who were with him rum to drink, which is a kind of brandy made of distilled sugar waste, in those parts very common and healthful if one drinks it with moderation. In addition I was very friendly with them, so that they went from me well contented and satisfied.

In their burials they make more ceremony than in their weddings or marriages. And I have observed something strange at the burial of a deceased widow. I will not expand much on it here because there are many printed accounts of the life and customs of the Indians; only in passing, what I found most strange.

And principally; when an Indian is sick or dying their priests come into the house, go all through all sorts of figures and antics, make all sorts of conjurations and give to the sick also all sorts of medicines. If that does not help they blow their breath into the mouth of the sick with a frightful roaring, and I do not know what all conjurations. If the sick one arises there is an indescribable rejoicing, but if he dies a sad howling, enough to frighten one.

They make their graves with great care, and arch them over with bark. When the deceased is carried to the grave two priests stand there and lament and make a funeral sermon after their fashion. If there is anything to be gained thy extol the deeds of the departed or comfort his relatives and make, I do not know what all strange conjurations. In short there is much action and chattering so that I have seen the priest or conjurer all in a sweat, but this happens if a good present is to be expected. When this is all over the heirs give to the priest pendants of wampum or made of calcined mussels. These are little things like corals, as has been mentioned above, white, purple, yellow; and this is their pay. N. B. The Indians are accustomed to make out of these things trousers and necklaces, and they know how to knit and to weave them so skillfully and ingeniously through one another, with all sorts of figures, that it is to be wondered at.

When it was done and the grave covered over, in my time something marvellous took place which I myself saw. A pretty fire or flame of about two candle light size went straight up into the air, as high probably, as the longest and tallest tree, traveled again in a straight line over the hut of the deceased and so farther over a great heath, probably half an hour long until it disappeared in a forest.

When I saw this and evidenced my astonishment, the savages laughed at me, as though I ought to know that this was nothing new to them, but did not want to say what it was. After this I ask several about it. No one could say positively, but they set much store by it and it is considered an especially good sign for the deceased. An artificial fire it cannot be because of the duration and great distance it traveled. Physically it might be considered a sulphurous vapor out of the earth; but this long regularity is too much for me.

Once when I was at Governor Hyde's in the presence of the council and many others while we were busied with the Indians about the peace, I took notice of an old Indian who looked to me like a conjurer or priest. So I asked him what that was which I have just related to have seen. Among twenty-five Indians that were there only this old one besides one other could give me an account of it. But it seemed to me like a fable.

They said that only great men, old experienced priests, could see and do such things. When I questioned them further, they gave me for an answer that this little fire is the soul of the departed, which goes into another good creature, if the person has lived well and behaved himself; if he has not behaved well it goes into a villainous smoke and into an ugly and miserable creature. The priests come to their art in the following manner; namely, it happens that a subtile little fire or flame shoots from one tree into another, but very sel-

dom; and when an Indian sees that he must run as fast as possible
to catch it, and if he catches it, it goes right on and becomes a small
wood spider which jumps and runs so quickly in and over his hand
that it has to be seized quickly by the other hand. But if he finally
catches it, this spider grows and becomes like a mouse; and so who
ever catches this wonderful thing afterwards becomes the best conjurer or magician and can do all sorts of wonders. N. B. These
artists or conjurers as they are called in English, have the faculty of
invoking the devil and sending him away again.

A ship captain has asserted to me that he once carried several
Indians in his boat or small ship and in the Carolina Sound there
came such a calm that they could get nowhere. One among the
Indians said that probably he could procure a good wind, and was
willing to do it. The steersman who did not have much provisions with
him and wished very much to advance farther, left it to the Indian.
Soon after this there came such a strong wind that he became frightened and would gladly have had less wind, but he had to go through
with it, and so they came in a very short time to the desired place.
But the above mentioned captain assured me that he received such a
great fright on this account that as long as he lived he would no more
use such help.

Whoever will may believe this and the above. It is certain that
Satan practices many delusions with these poor creatures; yet if such
things seem incredible, I would not have made bold to tell such fab-
ulous things here if it had not gone about and been talked of in such
eminent company.

I have heard and observed many more such things among the Indians. But because so many authors have written about them that
my remarks would only pass for repetition I will not relate more,
except to say concerning the cruel and barbarous manner of the Indians, that they are indeed furious when one angers them; but if one
leaves them in peace, does them no harm, and treats them according
to their ways in a friendly and goodhearted manner, they will seldom injure a Christian, except if given cause for it. They have occasionally been treated cruelly and badly by the Christians. I have
spoken to many of the Indians about their cruelty, but a sensible
king answered me and gave a nice example of a snake. If one leaves
it in its coil untouched, quiet, and uninjured, it will do no creature
harm; but if one disturbs and wounds it, it will bite and wound. And
the Spaniards had used their forefathers too cruelly, yes, very in-
humanly. Concerning their, the Indians' massacres and fighting
treacherously: They had to use their advantage or else they could
not hold their own; they were not so strong in numbers, and were

not provided with pieces, muskets, swords, and all sorts of other treacherous inventions made with powder to destroy men; likewise they had neither powder nor lead or else they got them from the Christians themselves; so that our ways were much more treacherous, false, and harmful; otherwise, we would not use them so cruelly. Moreover we practiced among ourselves the greatest tyranny and cruelty. Indeed I have experienced this myself.

TREATY.

Which was made with the Indians and translated from the English.

It is hereby made known to all and sundry that in October 1711, it was agreed as follows between Baron, Count von Graffenried, Governor of the German Colony in North Carolina, and the Indians of the Tuscarora Nation with their neighbors of Core, Wilkinsons Point, King Taylor, those of Pamtego, and others of the region.

1. That both parties shall forget the past and henceforth be good friends.

2. The subscribed Governor of the German colonies, in times when the English and the Indians are in strife, enmity, and war against each other, shall be entirely neutral; in like manner he shall remain quietly in his house and city, allowing neither English nor Indians to pass there, nor do any Indian injury. They promise the same toward our people. In case strife occurs between the parties named, they shall not get justice for themselves, but shall make their accusation at the proper place; namely with the authorities of both sides.

3. The above named Governor of the German colony promises to stay within his boundaries and to take no more territory, up toward them, without the consent of the king and nation.

4. He promises further, to procure a truce of arms for four days, in order that within this time able persons may be chosen and commissioned to propose salutary plans of peace, which, as far as possible, would have to be acceptable and pleasing to the parties in strife.

5. It shall be allowed to the Indians to hunt where they wish without any hinderance, except in case they come so close to our plantation that the cattle would be driven away or injured or danger of fire might be feared.

6. To them, the Indians, wares and provisions shall be allowed to come at a reasonable and cheap price. Further it is agreed, that where the marks written below shall be on the doors of our houses, hat there no injury or damage shall be done. So shall, herewith,

the conditions and clauses be exactly observed. As a genuine voucher of which we on both sides, subscribe ourselves and there is affixed the ordinary signs.

    The sign of Neuse, N. Graffenried, Governor of the
                   German Colony.
    Tuscaroras' Sign, MM Tuscarora Indians and
                   Neighbors.

Mandate of the Governor of Virginia, translated out of the English original.

Alexander Spotswood, Governor, Regent, and Commandant of the Colonies and Provinces of Virginia, in the name of Her Royal Majesty of Great Britain, to the Indian Nation which holds Baron von Graffenried prisoner.

Having heard that Baron Von Graffenried, Governor, and the head of the German Colony in North Carolina is captive among you, I request and command you, in the name of the Queen of Great Britain of whom he is a subject, that on receipt of this you let him go free and send him to our government.

And here you are given to know that if you should have it in mind to kill or willfully inflict any injury upon him, I will revenge his blood, and will spare neither men, women, nor children.

    Given under my great seal,
     the 7th of October, 1711.

              A. Spotswood. <L. S.>

            Carolina, Newburn, May 6, 1711.
Gentlemen:

I send you once more a copy in answer to the letter of August 23, sent to me and F. Michel, received here April 11th., for fear that my previous one had gone lost, to indicate what before this was written to the old Schultheiss von Graffenried, as I had cause enough, to the effect that such great enterprises must be strongly supported. It is impossible to succeed with so little. It would have been better to let it rest than to put one's self into danger and to so expose one's reputation and honor and lose all credit. Or if I could have foreseen all that I know, I should have taken entirely different measures. Timid business men seldom make great fortunes, and if Messrs. Ritter and Von Graffenried stay out of it; if I cannot help; others will probably be found in place of them. If it were not out of consideration for H. J. Ritter, and those who before this advanced money to one F. Michel and assisted him, we could have associated ourselves with a rich Englishman. But he wanted to be alone with us. Thus there are here only a few good men who are of a mind to stay in, but only in the trade. Since they have land enough for the present, we are not served with this, for these great debts must be paid. Fr. Michael, indeed, when in Pennsylvania, told me he would there find enough associates. But I doubt it. Sad experience teaches me not to trust too firmly. It is better to make a more certain play.

I wonder through whom the 100£ sterling shall be paid at New Castle, because Mr. Wray gives me no notice of it.

You tell us that we in Carolina should try to do something on credit. Enough has already been done. Indeed we had to use all our credit to get the necessaries of life and stock for a year, if we did not want to die of hunger with the whole colony; for ill-fortune will have it that we found the government at our arrival in the greatest confusion because of the death of the Governor. When I wished to bring the Receiver-General to keep that which the Lords Proprietors had promised he resigned. Since the Lieutenant Governor, and Colonel Cary will accept neither the new Governor Hyde nor any of the Lords Proprietors' new officers, I have not found the slightest assistance upon the side of the Lords Proprietors and of the government. If an honorable well-to-do man, Colonel Pollock, and another, had not assisted us, we should have been compelled, as said before, to die of hunger. So I was compelled to get everything from him and others upon notes, and these provisions had to be for a year long, that is, until the coming December; for the neighboring islands which are in great want of food buy the corn before it is ripe in the field. So then this business needs a good heart, good friends, and good credit; and if I had not been a land-grave so that I could sit in the Court and Upper House of Parliament, which give me authority and credit, we should have had to die.

Thus you see Gentlemen, in passing, that the jealousy in regard to these titles of honor, which indeed bring in nothing, is not well founded; but rather this position of honor procures the colony advantage and benefit. It might be objected that it causes great expenses and ceremony. For this reason I have not even a livery coat in the procession. I live as poorly as the least private individual, as you can well hear from others.

Regarding the mines; It is true that you are under obligation to Fr. Michel for looking for and discovering them. But if I had not been present at the first negotiation nothing would have come of it, and Mr. Penn would do and conclude nothing, unless it were signed by me.

Regarding my difficulties and pains, there is much to be said about them. Speaking of recompence, even if I can be recompenced for the danger to my life, unspeakable cares, and affronts which have already come to me because of the lack of needed assistance, and if I were, on account of the protestation of my notes to expect it, there is, in truth, none big enough and none good enough for me. I should do better to claim none. The best recompense would be to pull me forthwith out of this difficult labyrinth; it will be to your advantage and my own.

Since you announce that probably all of you will come to this country, I am glad. I could wish that you had been here from the beginning, and were here still. Then you could see whether everything goes so easily, and with so little to do with. You would also have been compelled to take your share in this great complaint, toil, anxiety, and vexation, instead of all this resting upon me.

To make a day-book of occurrences will not be entirely a pastime because until now little of anything pleasant, but many vexations have occurred.

A journal or table of the expenses of the past is hardly to be made so very exactly, especially where Fr. Michael has acted. But in the future more regularity will be observed.

If you should not come so very soon, it will be well to send here a young honest burgher who understands book-keeping. The English are entirely too expensive. They ask 50£ sterling a year. As far as the others are concerned, whether they are tenants or artisans, we will wait until the general peace is made, but there is need of a pastor and a book-keeper. They could come this next autumn, that is, in October or November, with the Virginia Fleet. Care must be taken to conclude and negotiate everything there, for when they get here they immediately become puffed up, want to be masters themselves. But if I would give high wages I could not get a man- or woman-servant into my service. Tenants and servants must be hired at Bern, as also all sorts of artisans. Here is the answer to all the articles of the letter.

Now I will report upon the condition of affairs here, upon the situation and productiveness of the land, in a few words; deferring the rest till my vexed and disturbed mind is in a quieter frame. And so I send to you only a map made in haste and quite plain. The situation of the city could not be finer, more cheerful, and convenient. So also the whole colony touches upon it; and all the settlements ie side by side, and all lie along the water in such a way that at one place one can come up from the sea and on the other back into it again and go only six or eight miles by land. I do not believe that there has been a finer colony planted in the world, that is regarding the situation. It continues thus as far as the River Clarendon or

Cape Fear. It is certain that in a few years, under the blessing of God, this colony will greatly increase. The land is excellent and good; corn, rice, hemp, flax, turnips, beets, beans, peas, all sorts of garden produce, and tree-fruits grow well. I know of few in our country that one cannot have here. Wild grapes are very abundant and yield especially well. I do not doubt that one could make them tame and plant others, just as has been commenced already.

In the way of drink, even if one does not yet have wine, they generally make a very pleasant, healthful, and cheap beer of molasses, which is a juice of sugar, and sassafras, a little dried wheat, corn, or only cherries. Others make beer of figs, quinces, mulberries, a kind of red medlar, and other things beside.

Wild game and fish are all in abundance. All sorts of good meat can be gotten by the way of the sea. Small cattle increases, costs nothing to keep winter or summer; so that if one has only a little to invest, he can, in a few years, own many hundreds, and the trade in them goes well.

The general trade is exceedingly good, but everything goes by barter. Of money there is none at hand, except in the South Island and the lands which the Spaniards and Dutch possess. But in these countries one receives it for wares. The wares which are disposed of there are indigo, certain spices, sugar, rum, molasses, (both of these made from sugar afford us a delicious brandy), rice, hides, and skins. Tanners of furs are much needed for the skins of the wild and tame animals, feathers and down. N. B. Upon these rivers are swans, geese, and ducks by the millions. Wild turkeys are in great numbers.

Regarding the climate; it is tolerably good and healthy, not so exceedingly warm as supposed. June, July, and August are hot, yet there blows occasionally a cool wind. The rest of the time of the year is tolerably temperate. In the beginning one must pay the tribute of a fever.

Regarding the Indians, they are not to be feared if one makes a league with them, which we have already solemnly done. At first they were hostile to us because they were incited to it by jealous traders, but everything is now quiet.

The government is well appointed, but the good ordinances and laws are badly executed. Everything, as I said, at my coming was in great confusion, to my great harm. But it is now better; only the revenues to which I had claims are gone because the Lieutenant Governor Cary wanted to assume the whole government. But he, whom I had put into jail through the new governor and council, broke out of his confinement and has become a fugitive. Before this he sold everything and took the proceeds with him. This man with two more has made such a rebellion that I had to come to the aid of the government with our people. For this cause I repeat that I was in great extremity from the failure in the execution of good ordinances and laws; for because of the situation, on account of its being in a new land, it would have been all topsy-turvy if I had proceeded differently, since I had to give the Royal Committee security for 5000£ sterling on account of these people. If in the beginning when I saw that everything was failing, I had left these poor people in the lurch and had retired elsewhere, or had let them die of hunger, I should have lost the five thousand pounds and should have been hanged without mercy; and where would my conscience have been as I did it? Could I do differently than I did? It is still a great thing that in a wild country, where, strange to say, I have no friends or acquaintances, I have so much credit that I have received everything which was really necessary. Now it is a question of how to work myself out of this labyrinth that I may not come to disgrace, and we all be compelled to lose together; for I am fearful of being arrested because of the protestation of the notes, and Colonel Pollock, as the strictest creditor, could take possession of everything, a procedure which would do us all irreparable damage and cause the greatest disgrace and destroy the whole country, for they would certainly run away from it.

So I find no better means than to look for eight more associates at the least, if possible more, at 300£ each to be paid in, or four or more at 600£ each. If we wanted to do something in trade we should double our money, but this might be postponed for a good while. But these notes must be paid directly, cost whatever it will. So it seems to me on this point, that one more experiment would be good; that is, if the Company would go to my father, speak to him about an obligation and the investment of the whole amount from his money which he has in the bank in London, 2000£. There will still remain to him a considerable portion, and this would not discommode him at all. But if this trial is not successful, I should know nothing better than to call upon my Lords, giving them the same security. N. B. This is to be remarked along with it, that these are not lost debts, which have been squandered and are not to be gotten back, but at the end of three years all will be replaced with profits. The especial account I will make this summer; this time only in general.

ACCOUNT.

1. For Indian or Turkish Corn for feeding the colony and for sowing, 6000 measures p. two shillings make.......... 600£
2. Wheat, 400 measures, p. 4 shillings.... 80-
3. Salt, 200 measures, p. 10 dit.......... 100-
4. Fresh meat and salted for............ 250-
5. Carriage of all these and other things.. 100-
6. The shallop or brigantine which in my absence Fr. Michel bought, since I would not dare to venture so much.. 200-
7. To build a store or proprietor's house.. 60-
8. Grist and saw mill................... 70-
9. Our lodging which was at the same time a provision house.............. 70-
10. Stock, ten cows and as many calves, 30£, ten swine 10£, four horses, since two were for the tenants, 30£, eight sheep, 6£, four more cows for my household, 12£. Sum.............. 88-
11. Furnished swine 2 p. family.......... 160-
12. Food for 150 head p. 3£............. 450-

Summa Summarum...............2228-

N. B. The brigantine had to be purchased because of a great necessity, since transportation is excessively dear and hard to get. Only a small journey, with six hundred measures of corn and some small things, costs 20£ to transport. Have saved already half in the transportation. It is a good thing to use in trade, and without it, it is impossible to live here. It is now on a voyage to the South Islands to get salt, molasses, corn, sugar, and other things. The proprietor's house is also necessary. It served first as the provision house, for we must have shelters and a place to store the provisions. Besides, there was this reason; it was in part on account of travellers and in part to use as a place to bring food to. All came there and caused such expense that in the long run it could not be endured. For in this country there are no inns. Everything is free. When I did not wish to give, they demanded, and one could not let people who had come twenty, fifty, to a hundred miles, go with hungry bellies. So I am now easy on this score; but provision must be made, but yet it will bring in a pretty income.

Grist and saw-mills are also necessary. We were, as it were, forced to it, for the people could not grind their corn. The saw-mill will bring in a considerable amount when it is well in operation. They saw ever thing, in England as well as here, by hand. Planks are incredibly dear. For one plank I will, at a saw mill, get 6, yes indeed, 10. An Englishman has offered me for the yearly revenue of the saw-mill, fifty pound sterling; but if the city progresses as it appears probable that it will do, it is worth 100£ yearly.

House-keeping is hard. It would not be possible as they, Ritter and Isot, thought at London, to live individually and to have one common expense. They were ill-informed. The plantations had first to be made. Lodgings were very poor and constructed in haste, so that one could also work his ground and have something to eat from it and not be compelled to get food at great expense; otherwise what good would the land do the people? Land has been taken up for each one in particular. I have not taken up any for myself yet, but in the future provision will be made for everything.

Moreover there are still a good many things to get besides trade and income. This is a new place, only five years ago still wild and not inhabited. The people have enough to do with their plantations. They have not the time to invent things and get the good of them.

The city will increase rapidly. Almost every day there come people who want a lot, that is an arable field on which to build a house and cultivate a garden and an orchard. The Governor and the most prominent people of the country already have each their lot. A lot is to yield an English crown yearly. For you gentlemen, we have already reserved a fine section, and in the healthiest locality. But what am I saying here. It is all fine and good.

The sad and unfortunate message which arrived from London spoils all. The notes are protested, my honor, credit, and reputation gone, and the colony suffers in the highest degree. Colonel Pollock, who promised to supply me with cattle, has let my people come back empty handed. I now have enough for this whole year. I shall try accordingly to supply the most seriously needed things, in order that the complaint may not be too great. The people have no cows, and this occasions great loss; there is so much murmuring that soon I shall not be sure of my life; they have threatened to send a letter to the Royal Committee. In such a desperate condition what is to be done? My property, my honor gone; nothing but the greatest vexation, insult, disgrace, and scorn, to be expected; the shortest way out would be to withdraw into some island or into the mountains, or even go over into Canada to the French. Meantime the colony would disappear,

Pollock would put himself into possession of it, so that everything would be gone, and everything which had hitherto been done with great labor and expense would be in vain.

Yet it pains me to leave such a beautiful place where there is such fine prospect of good conditions.

Right with this bad tidings came bad news also from London relating to Virginia and Maryland about the Tobacco trade. Everything is destroyed there, because from other places tobacco is brought more cheaply. And so these poor Virginians, who had all their capital in the planting of tobacco, are completely ruined. Because now, Carolina is the only province in English America where cattle can winter without expense or labor, so all are coming there like a wave. The land increases in value so that I can well assure you that what one can do now with 10£, in five years he cannot do with 100£.

Gentlemen, you will indeed consider well this fine profit which is to be made on the 100,000 acres of land that you still have, and whatever else there is; likewise the loss of the costs already incurred, which the nation and the company has had before, and the fine future returns and profits of other things. So I doubt not you will do all possible to avert such a great loss, and to embrace these splendid advantages; and so much the more, because everything is now in its place, no more great expenses, except those which will bring in fifty per cent or more. From now on the revenue begins.

Fourteen days ago Mr. Bötschi sailed away. I sent him expressly to recruit people, for he went gladly and offered himself, so that you might hear the whole account of the matter by word of mouth from him, as one personally present and an eye witness.

I will continue to be patient; indeed, if I can avoid arrest until answer to Mr. Botschi's report comes. I can just about calculate when it can be. But if the goods mentioned do (not) come then, I shall certainly be driven to great extremity and afterwards it will be too late to remedy it. Oh if you only knew and could believe a little of what there is to do here you would not leave me in the lurch so, but you would raise as much as you possibly can to pull me out of this labyrinth and to advance this colonization business vigorously.

Because we have received no house-hold utensils nor wares from London we were glad to use Captain Zechender's things. It will therefore be necessary to satisfy him for it, and if he is still resolved to come here, to advise him of this, so that he can supply himself accordingly.

Fr. Michel has taken with him the firearms of all except two. Therefore provision is to be made in Holland, but none with brass plates.

I would have much still to write on various matters but the multitude of occupations, my vexed and confused mind do not permit me to at this time. If you, gentlemen, shall have pulled me out of this labyrinth by speedily sending the notes to me, there will be a more detailed account or else I will send no more at all, for all depends upon this. If nothing is effected everything will go backwards, and God knows what will become of me.

I commend you to the protection of the Almighty and remain, Gentlemen,

Your most obedient servant,

von Graffenried.

P. S. After I had been very despondent following the writing of this letter, and had been going over things in my mind, not knowing what to do further in this so vexatious and critical position, I remembered certain Psalms which fitted my condition very well, with ardent prayer taking my refuge in the Lord Jesus, the true helper and Redeemer, and encouraged myself a little by an effort. Two days afterwards there came something which comforted me a little, and I cannot pass on without telling it. Yet I will tell only the substance, since it would be a whole tale in fact, and this letter is already long enough without that.

There came up to me from the sea a little old Englishman, to sell me oysters. He inquired for Fr. Michel, but since he was not present any more and understanding that we were good friends he wanted to show me something that probably would be acceptable to me. He said he had, sometime ago, traveled with Fr. Michel and the Governor of Virginia, to look for mines; but he knew of a better and richer one, and in that connection, he could tell me all the circumstances of Fr. Michel's trip. It agreed well with what I already knew very well. Although before this I had entirely discounted Squire Michel's affairs, I saw by this there were nevertheless realities. Now according to this report I have some hope. May the Most High, who through his inexpressible kindness has created so many things for the good of man, give his blessing to it, and give to us the grace not to misuse his benefits, but to praise him for all.

This mine which the little man indicated to me is a gold mine in Virginia, while Fr. Michel's is a silver mine in Pennsylvania; and this gold mine is said by report to be eight days out from here, while the other is more than fourteen days from Philadelphia. At the discovery of this nearer and better mine Fr. Michel was not present, but Governor Nicholson of Virginia was. In the matter of the gold, the Governor would let neither him nor any one else know and also forbade him to tell anyone of it. In the meantime the Governor looked about for a man expert in such things. He found one also, who, on test, found it very rich. They were already making arrangements to put it into operation, but soon after, the mining master or chemist died. Some time after this a disturbance rose in Virginia, the Governor was called to New England to take the government of the same, and he is actually at this time in a notable expedition against the French in Canada, has also taken Fort Royal, and so this mine has disappeared with him and this mining operation is suspended.

This little man gave me in addition, this report that one of those who was with him, one named Clark, a sort of goldsmith, a godless man who had robbed another man of his wife and had gone up into the mountains with her, had found gold in this place, had coined pieces of money out of it. He feared he would be discovered if he sold the lumps of gold. Finally his money got so common and some difference was found in it so that it came to light, and he was hanged as a counterfeiter. Fr. Michel's servant who is with me now waiting for his master's return, saw this Clark hanged.

The mine referred to is not more than twenty or thirty miles from the land which the Queen gave us. This in secret; we could take a piece of land further up, and so we could also take possession of the mine, reserving of course the Queen's share for her. I considered it advisable to interest the present Governor in this in order that he might help us. I was on the point of taking the little old man and two miners that I have here, immediately with me, and we should have gone up into the mountains in order to get a good view of it, and at the same time to see a notable curiosity. Not far from this place is said to be a stone table forty feet long and ten feet wide, upon four well-hewn and carved feet; upon it something written which these people cannot read. Not far from that there are still fragments of a wall and a broken intrenchment. But this is not the time because on account of the thickness of the bushes, one cannot see the snakes. It will be done the coming autumn, if God gives me health and life, and also if better news arrives from Bern so that I can breathe a little.

N. B. Regarding these amounts and some more debts still, of Fr. Michel's not paid at London, and something in wares which we took at London with your consent; it will likewise be necessary to still send us something, at least 300£ worth of goods, for it is impossible to live here without them. Because there is no money here everything is done with goods. And so there must be altogether a sum of 3000£ raised. That is a great deal in our country, but it all comes in afterwards with great profit.

Whatever in the future is subscribed or made over in monies you will not send to Danson and Wray, for they are false to us. A malicious Berner, let him be who he will, has written to London very badly about us. Besides this we have seen only after coming here, that their affairs are not at the best. Danson as one of the proprietors, to be sure, keeps a good appearance . . . to give commission,[1] but it could be done through my father's correspondent who is a good man. From him the writing could be in French, and the affairs would remain secret. This Danson and Wray have opened up my letters which Mr. . . . . wrote to me in the name of the society, which had a very bad effect here in Carolina for everything was written to persons here.

N. B. I do not believe that Mr. Bötschi will come back, and if he came back I could not use him in the business, because he does not understand book-keeping at all. For many good reasons it is necessary that some one of you come, but not without money or notes, and that speedily; for if I should die everything would go badly.

The voyage is not so troublesome and dangerous especially in time of peace, as one imagines: We had the best of weather and on the whole voyage out from London only one small storm; that is, if one sails around Scotland and starts away in May. The map of the city and colony was sent in the previous letter and Mr. Bötschi is bringing one also.

N. B. If notes are made out one can find the bills of exchange with Mr. Wray at London. Thomas the barber and surgeon wishes to finish out only his two years here. It will, therefore, be well to send a good surgeon. He can make as much here as he wishes too. Mr. Bötschi has taken one of the small pistols with him. It will be well to send the same by the book-keeper again; it is too bad to spoil the pair.

BUSINESS CONTRACT.

May our help and beginning be in the might of the Lord who created Heaven and earth. Amen.

Know herewith that between the hereafter subscribed gentlemen and friends, Mr. Frantz Ludwig Michel and Christoph von Graffenried on the one part, and Mr. Georg Ritter and Mr. Peter Isot in their own and Mr. Albrecht von Graffenried's, Mr. Johann Anthoni Järsing's, Mr. Samuel Hopf's and Mr. Emanuel Kilchberger's names on

---

[1] It is impossible to conjecture what the writer was trying to say, as the passage is defective, several words having become illegible in the original MS.   V. H. T.

the other part, there has been made and concluded with another present, true, and bona fide society, a contract consisting of the following points.

1. There shall serve as the foundation the one hundred seventeen thousand five hundred acres of land lying in North Carolina, between the Neuse River and Cape Fear, which in the name of this society have been purchased from the Proprietors of Carolina according to the patents obtained for that purpose, with all the privileges and rights thereto pertaining, whatever name they may have, and with all those that shall or can be obtained in the future. And there also belong to this the twelve hundred and fifty acres of land which were purchased from Mr. Lawson, situated in the angle, between the Rivers Neuse and Trent.

2. There is also placed as foundations the concession in Virginia obtained from the Queen of Great Britain; also whatever further liberties, rights, mines, or other concessions, whatever name they may bear, which shall be obtained from the same queen or her successors, so that all shall be for the good of this society.

3. We under the blessing of God shall constitute the board of directors.

4. Mr. Frantz L. Michel promises that of all minerals which he has already found and shall yet find, he will put in all the portion coming to him therefrom to the good of the society.

5. This society shall be conducted under the name, Georg Ritter and Company. All the papers, writings, letters, and obligations shall be signed by this name; and the Society shall have its own seal; also no member, except the one or the ones whom the Society shall empower so to do, shall have power to sign or to seal any document or writing in the name of the society.

6. The capital of this society shall consist of seven thousand two hundred pounds sterling which shall be employed for the payment of the above described lands, to the support of the Palatine and Swiss colonies already sent there and those following after, and also for the conduct of proposed trade and mining operations.

7. To the formation of this capital there are set twenty-four shares, each at three hundred pounds sterling, which shall be made over to the gentleman here at London appointed therefor, who shall also send a receipt for it, and credit shall also be given him in the books.

8. No one shall be able to possess more than one share for himself, but two or at most three can combine for one share; but if, after the lapse of three years, these twenty-four shares are not complete, it shall be free to those who already have a share to take another.

9. In the transaction of matters of importance which may occur, such as the election of a director, one or more deputies to the Royal Court, to negotiate with the Lords Proprietors or elsewhere, at the nomination of the society's salaried servants and officers, as also the acceptance of one or more new associates, the building and the purchasing of the ships useful for trade, and the opening of mines, everything shall be done and election made according to the majority of votes, with this in explanation, that where there are more than one to a whole share they shall count as one vote only and also, no one who has not a whole share shall be elected director.

10. It is free to each to go to Carolina or Virginia, or to remain in his Fatherland; and then his deputy shall enjoy similar privileges in his stead, except that he cannot be elected director.

11. It is free to everyone to sell his share to another, to trade it off or to give it away, to use and control it just as his other goods and property; and if he dies intestate the same shall fall to his nearest heir, just as his other goods. But the Society reserves to itself, at the sale of it, to have the preference, and ordains that it shall not fall into mortmain and be sold or given to Papists.

12. To every participant there shall be designated a piece of land in an acceptable place at the building up of the city, as well as a free estate of five hundred acres in Virginia; but as much as he shall desire shall be free from interest and tithes, with the exception of what is due to the Lords Proprietors.

13. Mr. Michel reserves this to himself, because he contributes the mines in Pennsylvania to the good of the Society, that the first three years, when these mines shall be open and begin to produce the profits, shall come to him in advance. In the fourth year Mr. Ritter and Mr. von Graffenried, since they have more of the expenses, shall take out according to the amount of their shares contributed before the beginning of this same mine. What is left (for that year), as well as the whole profits on the other portion belonging to the Society, shall go to the Society for the remaining seventeen years. He hereby promises, with good success of the above-mentioned mine, to repay Mr. Ritter's principal from these first years of the Society.

14. So there is put to the credit of Mr. Michel, for his labor and for the mine contributed to the benefit of the company, an entire share; but he shall, as soon as possible, pay back all that the Society to-date has advanced and may still advance.

15. Mr. Christoph von Graffenried's money laid out for five thousand acres of land in Carolina, as well as the expenses incurred through the Palatines and others, according to the enclosed specifi-

cations, shall be credited to him for a share; but anything more than that he shall, according to the thirteenth article, take from the Pennsylvania mines.

16. In like manner an entire share shall be given and credited to Mr. Georg Ritter for the expenses he has incurred; but anything more than that he shall, according to the thirteenth article, take from the Pennsylvania mines.

17. It is not allowed to anyone to take up land in North Carolina on his own account, except the named free lands; but all land shall be taken up on the account of the Society.

18. No member shall be allowed to carry on private trade, either in North Carolina or Virginia, but everything shall be done there for the benefit of the society; and yet it is free to every one to associate himself with others not trading in this province, and to carry on a trade on his own account, always understood that it shall not be to the detriment of this Society.

19. The other above named gentlemen, associates, who have not entirely paid in their capital, shall pay it in before the next approaching September and make it over to the gentleman in England, already named.

20. There shall be no definite end set for the Society, because each one who does not wish to remain longer in the Society has liberty to sell his share. But in view of the fact that nothing in this world can be made fixed or immutable, it is agreed and resolved that this Society shall exist twenty years, and that in this time, neither shall or can there be talk of any separation. But after the lapse of these twenty years the Society can, at the discretion of three-fourths of the associates, be abolished; when they can make their division of the effects then existing, according to the majority of the votes.

21. Before the expiration of four years shall no separation be made, but a report shall be made yearly of the state of things, a reckoning of the balance shall be made, and for each share-holder a copy be prepared; but after the expiration of the four years each stock-holder shall draw ten per cent of his invested capital, according to the judgment of the whole Society. But whatever, by the blessing of God, is gained in the mines, that shall be divided yearly.

22. It is free to the Society to elucidate this contract by the majority of votes, to explain, to diminish, to increase, according as the advantage of the Society demands it.

23. The associates promise each other love, faith, and true friendship, and that they will help to further, to best of their ability, whatever may serve and promote the good of this Society; and, as much

as in them lies ward off injury and do everything which is in any way within the meaning of this contract, two copies of which, uniform and of the same tenor, shall be prepared. And may the Lord our God give his blessing to it, to whom alone belongs the praise, honor, and glory, from eternity to eternity, Amen.

Done in London, the 18th of May, 1710.

Witnesses,
> William Edwards.
> Edward Woods.
>> Fr. Ludwig Michel.
>> Chr. Von Graffenried.
>> Georg Ritter.
>> Petter Isoth.

MEMORIAL.

Various matters relating to Carolina translated from the English.

1. To have land surveyed in South Carolina costs one penny, Carolinian money, per acre, but in North Carolina a half penny. A certificate, registration, and copy, costs twenty-seven shillings for every piece of land which is bought, whether it be great or small.

2. Regarding exchange: There is no law of exchange between Carolina except by the piece of eight. The difference is about thirty-five per cent more in Carolina than in England.

3. Regarding the wares which are to be taken: The most useful is to bring over all kinds of assorted wares of English manufacture; about which we can inform you in a report, when we shall know what kind of people and how many shall come over.

4. An assortment of wares proportioned according to our direction can give in Carolina a profit of two hundred to two hundred fifty per cent when it is bought, but certain special wares give a profit up to three hundred per cent.

5. Every person whether man, woman or child, native or foreign, who has himself transported to Carolina at his own cost, has the privilege to take up forever for each person, fifty acres of land and to pay to the Lords Proprietors one penny quit-rent per acre.

6. Renting out land to tenants: A person who purchases a certain amount of land can divide it off again into different plantations, of which each can contain as desired, two, three, four, to five hundred acres. Afterwards the land-owner can make an agreement with the tenant, whereby the owner obligates himself to give his tenant a certain quantity of tools, nails, locks, bolts, pans, window-glasses, etc.,

in order to build a house; also to supply him with the necessary animals, as horses, cows, swine, etc., and likewise necessary crops for seed and subsistence, until the first harvest; in return for which the tenant gives to the planter or owner yearly, of all the increase of the cattle two thirds, together with a certain amount of rice, wheat, etc., according to the tenor of their agreement. On which subjects I informed myself well regarding the usual conditions, and reckoned up what the owner takes of the increase of all the crops from the tenant.

7. Regarding the production of the lands. It is certain that it produces the best rice, Indian corn, wheat, oats, beans, peas, etc., especially in North Carolina. They sow, ordinarily, a level piece of land without plowing. It may be advisable to change the seed occasionally, as need may require, as the neighboring planters can also testify.

8. Fresh and good land is without doubt the best for rice, namely that which is somewhat damp and wet; but if it is too wet it is necessary to dry it with long furrows and the constructing of fascines makes it more convenient for cultivation. It is also feasible to keep a certain amount of such damp land for the planting of rice, but to use the dry soil for wheat and other crops.

9. The centner of rice contains one hundred and twelve pounds. It is sold at from fifteen to sixteen shillings, the Indian corn at two and one half shillings a bushel, reckoned at four pecks; wheat at three and one half shillings a bushel. As far as barley, oats, peas, beans, are concerned, I have heard of no certain price, as these are less used. Regarding the increase of each kind of crop, one can read in Lawson's book, which description I consider very modest and it is certain that the land produces that increase. In respect to the price of animals: Horses are sold at from four to six pounds, a cow with its calf at about two and a half to three pounds, a sow with its pigs at twelve shillings, a boar at fifteen shillings, all reckoned according to the Carolina standard; so that these animals may be bought for about three-eighths of the above mentioned value laid out in English wares. With respect to the sheep: These are at this time scarce, but their number may be easily increased with attention and industry, since one can drive them at night into an especial sheepfold in order to be safe from the wolves. The form of this fold cannot be represented here, but can be reported better by word of mouth. Animals increase just as in England. Cows and mares breed once a year, hogs three times, and each time twelve, fourteen, to sixteen at a time. Their food for the most part is what they find in the forests, which are called ranges for the cattle. And so every plantation consisting of five hundred acres has pasture for cattle, for they have no need of cutting hay in their lowland or meadows, as they do in England where the cattle are fed through the winter. Al-

though the winters are much shorter in Carolina than in England, the stock in this time becomes lean and thin. But the forests, which produce all sorts of nuts and acorns to our especial advantage, serve for the swine. At the beginning of winter and a little before the time when the swine are butchered one takes from the herd as many as one intends to kill and feeds these two or three weeks longer with Indian corn, beans, or peas. They can also be very well kept in the orchards, some of which contain two, three, to four acres of all sorts of apples, pears, cherries, peaches, apricots, etc. They feed themselves in the beginning of the year with grass, afterwards with the fallen fruit; and when this is past they are again driven into the forest. In order that they may not become entirely wild, they are, every ten days, gotten into the habit of coming to the house by the blowing of a horn, and then a little Indian corn is thrown down before them. Now when they hear the horn blow they run straight for home. Hay for the stock could without doubt be gotten very well from the lowlands or savannas because a great deal of grass grows in such places. From lack of mowing it becomes coarse and inedible. But if, as is the custom in England, it were mowed often, new fresh grass suitable for hay could grow. If the cattle were fed with that they could be kept in good condition, for with this fodder and the pea vines the cattle become vigorous and fat.

10. The passage for each person costs six pounds, so that accordingly, a hundred persons, for passage alone, will cost six hundred pounds. From Holland to England costs five shillings per person, which, with baggage, costs twenty shillings or one pound sterling, which in all makes a hundred pounds.

11. For this reason it is advisable to appoint an able person whom we can recommend to them, in order to purchase an English captured ship of about one hundred and twenty tons in a French seaport; which, by the way, may cost two hundred and fifty pounds. The refitting of this ship with sails and other essentials can be done best and cheapest in Holland. But the food and the provisions are to be gotten in England. These can be held ready for putting on board until the arrival of the ship. This fitting out of the ship and provisioning of the hundred persons to last as far as Carolina would thus amount, at most, to four hundred and fifty pounds. So that the ship equipped and provisioned would be your own for seven hundred pounds, and hereby would cost some little more than the cost of passage. But there are still the captain and sailors to be provided for, of which sailors two thirds must be Englishmen, that is to say, nine men and a boy or eight men and two boys, whom we can also procure. Their wages amount to from twenty to twenty-four pounds monthly.

The length of their journey from Holland to England, the wait for wind and other hinderances until they are away from shore and until they arrive in Carolina cannot amount to four months at most. I assume, then, that the crew along with unexpected expenses from the time the ship sails from Holland to England and Carolina may amount to a hundred pounds sterling. Is that not a cheap ship? And is that not more advisable than to rent a freight ship and pay seven hundred pounds, with which one can do nothing else besides transport the colony to the Carolina coast, and unload them where they have to look out for themselves and rent shallops in order to transport themselves and their goods into the country?

I assume, now, that such a ship, with fitting out and provisioning would cost eight hundred pounds, plus one hundred pounds for the crew for four months, making altogether nine hundred pounds. Subtracted from this the seven hundred pounds for the above mentioned one hundred persons, as well as fifty pounds additional for carrying people in Carolina from the coast into the country, there remains one hundred fifty pounds which the ship would still cost. I assume now, that to reprovision the ship in Carolina for the crew would cost thirty to forty pounds sterling. I assume further that the ship would stay there about three months to wait upon the people with the boat, and to get freight again for England. Within these three months one can rely upon getting this in North or South Carolina or Virginia, and it is easy to believe that the same might amount to from five hundred and fifty to six hundred pounds. The entire delay of bringing the people into the country and procuring a complete cargo for the ship may be prolonged into six months. The pay for the crew for this six months and other incidental expenditures amounting altogether to one hundred fifty pounds, subtracted from the above freight of the goods, there remains four hundred and fifty pounds with which the ship may be refitted in England and of this there will still be left one hundred and fifty pounds; which money can be laid out in English wares for your own account. The ship can also be sent again into Carolina with a fresh supply of people, and there be loaded with goods. From which it is easy to be seen that it would be to your interest to purchase such a ship.

It is also worth while to consider how serviceable such a ship would be to you, in case the people should come to Carolina in a time when they could not find sufficient supplies there for the establishment. In case of a lack of the same, the above mentioned ship could carry some other English goods to Pennsylvania or other neighboring coasts, and in return, buy there that which is necessary to the further subsistence of the colony. It is also advisable to take a ship carpenter with you, who, with the help of one or two house carpenters or others of the people, could in a short time build a shallop which would hold about forty tons of cargo. The iron materials, cordage, sails, must be brought over with you from England, and may cost about eighty or ninety pounds. Such a shallop can continually be put to good use, by purchasing English goods in different places, such as rice, salt, pork and beef, household goods, wine-cask staves, heads, and hoops, and carrying them to another place to sell; also to get occasionally, a cargo of salt in Tortuga, or elsewhere, so that we shall not have to buy it from another hand so much the dearer. For which considerations and many others still it is plain that it would be eminently useful to you, as well for your own convenience as because of the profits, to have such a ship and shallop. In the future, trees could be felled out of which other shallops might be built, in order to visit the planters living on the neighboring rivers, at the opportune time, with English goods, of which they have need at all times, and through which you could enjoy great profits and at the same time assist the people with all sorts of necessaries, who thereby are induced to use more industry and to labor the longer, because they can exchange in such a manner the productions of the country for the necessary clothing, tools, household utensils; upon which I can give you special reports and exact direction. And for my part I am willing to undertake it on commission in England.

Besides this your English neighbors in Carolina will be happy to embark their goods in your ship and shallops for freight money, or to exchange their rice, crops, beef and pork, hides, pelts, as well as live stock for your English goods, which you can bring to your ships at convenient places; for instance rice, hides, pelts and skins, rosin and pitch to England; pork and beef salted down in barrels, cask staves, heads and hoops, meal and rice, to Jamaica, Barbadoes, Antigua. From there one can bring back as much sugar, rum, royal sugar, grain sugar, as you will find necessary, and it can be brought over into Carolina and sold. The rest of the sugar bought there can then be sent to England in English ships, which are always to be found in these islands, and there turned to silver or sent by us to Dortrecht or Rotterdam, and from there into Switzerland. I can give you directions then how you could in time be brought into a condition to provide all Switzerland with sugar. Another shallop may also be loaded with cask staves, hoops, and heads, and sent to the Madeiras, to exchange these wares for wine and to bring the same into Carolina, where, as also in Virginia, it can be sold for a good price. We can also recommend them to certain correspondents in the places named. But if you should find it necessary in the beginning to transport more than a hundred persons, we could in such a case, rent another ship for you and transport the remainder with their goods, but the freight of the ship must be paid in London.

If you could provide yourself with possibly one family which understood how to handle silk worms and silk, a number of women and children could be occupied with this work. This commodity, which is produced easily and with little labor in Carolina would be of great benefit and profit, as experience has demonstrated in a few instances. If there were only hands enough a big business might come from it, because an abundance of red and white mulberries is to be found there. It is scarcely credible what great benefit might be expected from it, if only there were present enough industrious workers, as well as some of those who understood the business. A single family on hand which had a good knowledge of it could teach many others.

The indigo has also been planted in Carolina in order to show what may be done with it. It is found as good as any brought from other places. It will be of great necessity to take various working people with you, woodworkers of all sorts, to make utensils, of which one must have a great many; carpenters to build houses, which are entirely of wood, except the chimneys of brick, for which reason one or two brick-makers will be necessary; cabinet makers in order to have gunstocks, chairs, bedsteads, tables and other such like household furniture made. Smiths are also of absolute necessity, not alone to repair all kinds of iron work useful in the house, field, and forest, but also to repair muskets and to manufacture all kinds of iron tools.

The price of pork and beef, meal, etc., is as follows: Beef salted down in casks, each holding two hundred and fifty-two pounds, which we call two and a quarter centners, the centner being a hundred and twelve pounds, is sold in Carolina for from thirty to thirty five shillings a cask, in the Barbados or Jamaica and other English islands, according as it is on the market in less or greater quantity, for from forty to forty-five shillings a cask; pork salted down in casks holding two and quarter centners is worth in Carolina from forty to forty-five shillings, and is sold in the islands mentioned for from fifty to seventy shillings, according to how the market is supplied with it. Flour is sold in Carolina for from twelve to sixteen shillings a centner. It is worth in the Barbados twenty to twenty-four shillings.

Of barrel hoops, staves, and heads, the price in Carolina is not known to me; but in the Barbados they are sold for eight pounds per thousand, and occasionally for only four, or three and one half pounds. Such things also, as the hoops, staves, and heads, are merely laid in the ship, but the hoops are bound together in bundles. One thousand hoops are reckoned as a ton of freight. The best staves are made of white oak, expecially for the Madeiras. There, no others are saleable. But in the Barbados staves from red oak and other woods can also be used for sugar. Casks for wine, rum, molasses, and all wet goods must be of white oak. The cost of transporting sugar from the Barbados, Jamaica, Antigua to London, or wine from the Madeiras to Carolina cannot be specified because the freight costs sometimes more, sometimes less than in these war times. Eight to ten shillings per centner has been paid. But in times of peace one can get it for from two, to two and one half shillings per hundred.

Wine in the Madeiras is worth sometimes from seven, to seven and a half, to eight pounds per pipe. Each pipe holds two hogsheads. Each hogshead holds sixty-three gallon. A gallon makes four quarts English measure. So that a pipe holds a hundred and twenty-six gallons or five hundred four measures. Such a pipe is sold in Carolina and Virginia at fifteen to sixteen pounds, etc.

The land when it is purchased from the proprietors, is without question the purchaser's own private possession, and he has power to dispose and sell it again, or only a part of it, without the consent of the lords of the property. If the purchaser of the land is a subject of Great Britain, either free born or naturalized, he can sell the land, indeed, to whomsoever he will, but it is not advisable to sell it to foreign Protestants who are not naturalized, in order that disputes may not arise over it. But if the purchaser is naturalized, and other people who are not naturalized should be inclined to have a part of it, sale may very well be made if they can put their confidence in the naturalized person. But because an act of Parliament was made for the naturalization of all foreign Protestants, and the cost also does not amount to more than three or four shillings, it is more advisable for all those who wish to have a share in the land to have themselves naturalized. After this they may live in Germany, Switzerland, or wheresoever they please.

In case you should wish to purchase a small ship we can provide it with master and crew and other things needed, and send it to Rotterdam, where the people can be embarked. The money for carrying this into effect can be given over to Abraham Edens, a merchant in Amsterdam, or to Egbert Edens, merchant in Rotterdam, and it will be as well cared for as though you should remit to London. The Abraham and Egbert Edens mentioned, are brothers, and common as well as very well-to-do people, who can give the settlers valuable assistance on their arrival in Rotterdam, in case you should remit the money into their hands, a thing which you can do with the greatest safety.

It is certainly the most advisable course to take people such as can pay their transportation themselves, and who would still have the ability, on their arrival in Carolina, to make their settlement, by themselves, to provide themselves with grain and stock, etc. To such, one can rent out his land in leases of eleven, fourteen, or twenty-four years at two pennies sterling per acre yearly, quit-rent, and grant the liberty of renewing the same lease on fair conditions after the expiration of the time. It is certainly more useful for these people to give two or even three pennies for such land as lies near or in a colony, whose leader can accommodate them with ships and shallops for the sale and transportation of their wares from place to place, or with the exchange of the same for English wares, as tools, clothing p. c. I say it is much better for such people to pay two or three pennies where they can enjoy such conveniences, than to take up land from the Lords Proprietors, at one penny per acre for land. For if they take up farms from the Lords' land they have to look out for themselves in everything, and they cannot enjoy these above mentioned conveniences, from the lack of which the products of their land cannot yield them so much by far.

The expenses of transporting people from England into Carolina will be according to how they are provided with clothes, bed-clothes, tin and copper utensils, tools for building and for cultivation of the soil. And if the people which come over have a certain amount of these things, and money to pay their own passage, you have nothing further to do than to provide yourselves also with a certain quantity of these English goods which will be the most advisable to take over with you so as to have cattle, food, and seed, with which to barter; as well as a store of goods with which to trade with the English, and with the Indian neighbors, who will certainly visit you in order to exchange the products of their country for your European goods. The Indians will then seek to trade their stag and deer hides, pelts, etc., with you, for wares which are suitable to them. This kind of traffic, where wares are exchanged for wares, will be very useful to you; wherefore we can give you instructions regarding the best kind of goods to bring, as well as how you can exchange them with the people in the country. Such an assortment of goods will cost fifteen to sixteen hundred pounds sterling, which may be sufficient; but we must have two or three months notice, and money to get all these things together. About this we can prepare the complete report in writing; namely for what amount every sort of these goods could be sold in Carolina. As regards your people, namely those who do not have the ability to settle themselves, to them you will have to give credit until they enjoy the productions of the country and can give you due reimbursement for this advance. Through this you will be in a capacity to enjoy a good portion of the people's labor. On this point we have the necessary instructions ready for you and are delivering them. It will also be advisable to take over with you some serviceable things, in order to make a present to the chief Indians. These need not cost much. By this means you can make them good neighbors to you and create a good will to trade with you, whereby your plantations will be quiet and secure.

It will also be advisable to take over with you all sorts of garden seeds, as cabbage, turnip, beet, salad, potatoes, etc., which the people will take out of Switzerland. But what is not to be found there can be bought in England.

They can also take with them some coarse linen cloth of small price, from Switzerland, which is serviceable for the common household use; and if it is found worth while, one can order a greater quantity. One could also make a trial with a few casks of wine, whether it could be disposed of with profit in London, in which case more could be disposed of; for what we purpose in this undertaking can be to the advantage of both sides; not only for those who purchase land and go into Carolina, but also in general for all Switzerland, which advantage it could enjoy through commerce. An example which serves as an illustration I have already adduced, namely, the productions in Carolina can be exchanged for sugar in the Barbados and Jamaica. This can be sent to England, and from there to Rotterdam or Dortrecht, and so on to Switzerland; but the rice will be disposed of to the great advantage of the associates in Switzerland, after that in Holland, Spanish Netherlands, Bremen, and Hamburg; from which places those interested in Switzerland get their money by note. If linen, wine, and certain other commodities can be disposed of with some profit in England, even if it were small, it could be to the great advantage of the country.

It will also be necessary to take two or three men with you, who understand the construction of mills, in order to make water wheels or mills, for corn as well as for rice. For which nevertheless, other mills are demanded than merely common corn mills; and if one cannot find enough of these people in Switzerland you will have to secure them from England or elsewhere. And while it is of absolute necessity to keep shallops and boats upon the rivers, which would serve as a great convenience to the people, indeed, they are more serviceable than one would imagine, and it is so profitable for those to whom shallops belong; it would be necessary to take the equipment for them from England with you; while one could construct the ship in Carolina where the wood could be found more easily. But if the equipment for such a shallop could be secured from England it could serve in the future as a pattern, Such an equipment may cost in England about thirty to thirty-five pounds. Sails, anchors, iron, and cordage for a shallop must be purchased in England. It would cost ninety to a hundred pounds at the most.

From such observations it is easily to be seen how much the costs would run up too, if one should wish to transport and establish four or five hundred persons. If I had had the time I should have been able to bring these observations before you in better order, but must postpone it this time; yet I hope the present report will be sufficient to enable you to conclude what would be necessary for such an undertaking. It is also my desire that Mr. Ludwig Michel should read it, and that he might take a copy of it, if he considers it worth the effort.

It would be very useful to purchase a ship of about ninety tons burden. A ship with three masts is better than a brigantine, and when it is loaded it must not go deeper than eight feet in the water; in fact, a half foot less rather than more. You can get the sails and cordage in Holland, and it must be supplied with everything double, as well as the necessary anchors. It must be sheathed in order to be assured against worms. These worms attack ships at all times from May to September. You could bring over some people from Holland in this ship, and from there into North Carolina.

So then, when the ship is loaded and draws seven and a half, or at most, eight feet, you can travel with it into the country and up into the Neuse. A little ship such as that strongly built of good wood and well nailed can always be used; sometimes to transport pork, beef, flour, cask staves, hoops, etc., to the Barbados; and from there by barter, to take sugar, cotton, rum, molasses to Carolina; occasionally to carry Carolina goods to the Madeiras to exchange for wine; to go occasionally, with a load of rice, hides, peltry, tar and pitch to England, to unload the tar, pitch, hides and peltry in a harbor in that country, but to bring the rice to Holland and sell it; and so bring into Carolina all sorts of English goods, as iron ware, woolen stuff, duffles cloth, blankets for the savages, coarse linen, hats, stockings, shoes, powder, shot, muskets and whatever else would be advisable.

But you could not purchase such a ship yourselves. On the contrary you would have to use Egbert and Abraham Edens for this; with whom you would have to agree regarding the time, as well as the terms. I have no doubt that they will be modest and get it as cheaply as possible. They must sell it to you and deliver a bill of sale written on parchment, sealed and signed, so that when it comes to England you can show that you have purchased it from the Dutch and not from the French. Otherwise it cannot have entry. On further investigation I have found that it must be an English built ship, otherwise it cannot have free entry. You must also know at what place it was built and under what name it was registered in England, otherwise it cannot be registered again. The ship must be within one hundred and fifty feet long and eighteen broad.

If the people are able to pay their own passage and to purchase themselves a certain quantity of bed-stuff, tools, provisions, stock, and seed, you would have nothing more to pay for than the land within a four years term; the ship, the hull for a shallop, sails, anchors, cables, and cordage for two shallops and a sufficient provision of all kinds of English goods. This all may cost at the most three thousand pounds sterling, and we should be supplied with more than enough. If then your ship should embark one hundred persons at Rotterdam and transport them to Carolina, and should be used there two or three months in their service, it could earn thereby eight pounds per person, which makes 800-£

>   Remaining............................2200-
>   The first payment for the land.......... 200-
>   Incidental expenditures.................. 100-
>
>   S. a............................2500-£

The ship and the shallop will bring a profit every year. When you shall know the number of your people you are bringing with you, you can inform me, in order that I can rent a ship in time for those who cannot be loaded into your ship. After the first passage you will have no need to rent a ship, but your ship will be sent every year from Carolina to England loaded with goods, and from there it will return again with fresh people.

COPIES OF VARIOUS LETTERS FROM NORTH CAROLINA.

With friendly greeting I inform you that I with my household arrived safe and sound in Carolina, and that with happiness. But on the twenty-sixth of February, my son Hans, with a great longing for the Lord Jesus, died. On the contrary my daughter has a fine young son, born the last of July, 1710. We are in a very good and fat land. I am in hopes that within a year I shall have over a hundred head of horses, cattle, swine. If one would present me with the whole lowland, in order that I should go back again to Switzerland and take up the former service I would not do it on account of the freedom of conscience. If my son Uhli would venture to go upon the journey, he should turn whatever he can into money, and if he has not married since my departure, let him take an honorable honest girl to wife, even if she has not much temporal means, if only he can pay the passage over. Whoever desires to come over here, he can call upon Mr. Ritter in Bern. If you, my son, wish to undertake this journey, keep God always before your eyes, and also if you do not wish to come, so that we may enjoy and see one another sometime up above with spiritual eyes in Heaven.

But if you will come, I will inform you how you shall do. Buy a few hundred steel tobacco pipes with the stems and four thalers worth of Arau knives and several brass knives. From these you can get twice the price of the half in Rotterdam. In England and Carolina as much again. On the sea provide yourself with something besides what there is upon the ship in the way of food and drink, for one must not save, by hunger or thirst. If my brother-in-law Hans should want to go with you he can do it. I am in hopes if I stay well to provide five or six households with food and drink for possibly a year long. I will not tell anyone he should go upon the journey. Whoever has not the leading from God, he may stay in Switzerland. If my brother-in-law, Peter Seeman, and Uhli Küntzi should have a desire for the journey, they can make it. Our Count Von Graffenried will supply them with good land; after this he will give them a four-year lease, supply them with stock and furniture, so that they can thenceforth be well supplied their life long, if they have luck.

After this I will report to you a little how it went with us upon the voyage. Down the Rhine to Rotterdam we passed through the greatest danger. At Rotterdam we lay quietly for six weeks. There two children and one man died. From Rotterdam to Newcastle two women died. At New Castle we lay quietly for four weeks. Then we started away, went out on the sea, lay still for eight days. After this the fleet started. At that time my daughter gave birth to a little son. Then we took six weeks to cross. For six weeks we saw nothing but sky and water. Out of the hundred persons no one died. So we came to land in Virginia. Then we traveled a hundred miles by water and land, landed at our Landgrave's house on Michael's day. Meanwhile a woman died. After this we lay quietly till New Years; then they began, everyone, to move upon his own land alloted to him. Until now of a hundred persons, nine have died.

I and my daughter's husband have gone from one another about half a mile, for this reason I would have need of my son.

Besides this I send also to the pastor, and all my relatives, as also my father-in-law and his family, also Uhli Müller's wife and the Mayor, yes, also, the whole community, a thousand greetings with a kiss of love. Benedict Kupferschmied my son-in-law sends his father and brothers, as also his sister, friendly greeting, and could wish that they were all with him. He would like to be able to provide his father and his household with food and drink.

Let Uhli Müller, the gunsmith, write me accurately, through Mr. Ritter, how it stands with my property, and also about my neighbors and my son. For this time nothing more than to commend you to God. Given this seventh day of April, from Carolina, 1711.

By me Hans Ruegsegger.

Out of India or America, in the Island of North Carolina, on the river Neuse.

April 8, 1711.

With service, duty and greeting, dear and faithful father, mother, brothers and sisters, children and relatives, and all good friends. With regard to myself, I live well and happy and would not wish to have remained at home. I am also married to Margaret Pfund of Zweysimmen. As far as the land is concerned it is very hot, many brooks, and much forest. The natives or Indians are black, half naked, yet clever and sociable, unbelievers, unsuited for work. I will not praise much nor complain. If one has money and property, gold and silver, he can be master just as in Europe, but I will say that for a workman or a poor man it is better there than here. He can get land as much as he needs. He can keep as much stock as he is able. Swine cost nothing to keep. Cattle go the whole year on pasture, become fat and good to butcher by themselves. They make no hay. It is true that many a one has up to a thousand head or more of cattle and hogs.

The land is uncultivated, yet is to be hoped tolerably fruitful; but yet I would not cause any one to come here, nor would I advise it, because of the costly and difficult journey over the fearful and wild sea. Yet we arrived safely and suffered little sickness, and for my part, did not get here so badly. For old and young it is hard, nevertheless we got a young son on the sea. The great God has kept all. To be sure it has cost much and gone slowly in these expensive, hard, war times.

On the 8th of March, as you know, we departed from Bern; the 9th of April we came to Rotterdam; there we remained seven weeks and two days at our own expense; the 30th of May we set sail at Rotterdam; the 4th of June we arrived at Yarmouth in England; we sailed on farther, until the 11th ditto we arrived at New Castle in north England; there we remained five weeks. After that on the 11th of July we sailed from there upon the sea and stood at anchor for seven days waiting for the fleet, whither a great number of ships came together. On the 24th ditto we sailed away, and sailed eight weeks long upon the sea and went through storm-wind and other dangers. Yet the great God brought it quickly to an end. On the 10th of September we saw land. The 11th we cast anchor in Virginia. After that we made another long journey, now by water, now by land, probably about eighty hours, to where we live on the river, which is called Neuse.

Herewith you are again greeted father and mother, brothers, sisters, children, and all good friends. Greet for me Uhli Treut especially, and his whole house, Hans Klasner, and his dear wife, Rufascher and his whole house. If I have injured anyone or done anything to anyone please forgive me for it, as God, in Christ forgives us. I wish you all prosperity from God. May he bless your work and the fruit of your labor from now on till into eternity. Amen.

Your beloved Samuel Jacob Gabley
and Margreth Pfund.

Out of America or India the 9th of April, 1711.

With my duty and greeting dear and faithful Cousin, Christen Eggen; and your whole house. If I could hear that you were well it would rejoice me. As far as my condition is concerned I am well and live contented, and do not wish that I had remained at home. As far as the land is concerned, it stands like this. Whoever has riches, gold and silver, can be master just as in Europe, but I will say that for a poor man or workman it is better there than here. If he wishes to work for day wages he gets a half crown for every day, in produce or stock. Gold and silver are rare. He can get as much land as he has need of. He can keep as much cattle and swine as he is able, and the swine become, of themselves, fat and good to butcher. Cattle go on pasture the whole year. I say that many a one here has up to a thousand head of cattle or more. The country is hot, uncultivated, many streams of water, great forests. The natives or Indians are black, half naked, yet sociable; but it is to be hoped that the land is tolerably fruitful. Still I would not advise nor cause any one to come here on account of the costly and difficult voyage over the terrible and wild sea. But yet, for my part, it has not gone badly with me; but for old people and young children it is difficult. It has gone slowly with us here because of the expensive and hard war times.

The 18th of March, as you know, we left Bern. The 10th of April we came to Rotterdam; there we remained seven weeks and two days. The 31st of May we sailed away. The 14th of June we came to the north of England. There we stayed five weeks. After that we boarded the ship and put out to sea. There we stood at anchor eight days waiting for the fleet, whither came a great number of ships together. After that we sailed away and traveled over the great oceanic sea. For a while several ships sailed with us. After that we traveled alone and endured storm-winds and other actions. After that, in eight weeks, the great God made an end of it for us, and brought us safe to land, and one more from the ship than embarked in England. After that we made a great journey farther, now by water, now by land, for about eighty hours, away to the place where we lived by the River which is called the Neuse.

Something new: The crooked have become straight and the sick have recovered. Women folks are very rare.

Monzua has married my big son; but the people under him serve him to his destruction and try to eat him out. There is a pinching of his back, a pinching in the beard, a pinching in the private parts that I will not name, and a tailor for business, a count in name.

If it should come about that more people should come into this country, I beg you send me a half dozen readymade shirts, a few sheets plus ten ells of linen cloth and ten thalers in money, a half dozen knives of Barbli and an axe that has been tested, and pack it together and give it to certain people that they may have care of it, so that nothing may spoil for me on the sea. Buy me at Rotterdam or in England a jacket and trousers. With this I commend you to God. Greet the pastor for me and his whole house, Magistrate Zergen, the Mayor and his whole house, Treasurer Martge, both Kilchmeyers, Truwhart and their whole house, Heinrich Egender of St. Stephan's Court and his whole house for his sons Jacob and Peter Treuthart, Joseph Bullre of Wyssenbach and his wife Wassle, Anna Maria, Jacob Gobli and his whole house up in the village. Greet for me my dear Comrades namely the good Säumers. I wish for them that they may earn much and become rich in this world, for into the other world one takes nothing. With this I wish you all temporal and eternal prosperity from God. God bless your food and income. Finally I wish the same for my fatherland. Amen.

           Your humble Jacob Währe of
                Zweysimmen.

P. S. Do not think it strange that my brother is not writing, he did not have the chance as I did.

This is to be reported to Daniel Zant in Eriswyl.

[Owing to the corrupt text in the original of the two sentences which should follow here, no attempt has been made at a translation.—EDITOR.]

Before we went upon the journey, unwillingly to be sure, for fear of such great danger, my husband, Johannes Zant, who did not stand it but fell asleep in the blessed Lord, left word and commanded me that I should write home; and at the present time because I have opportunity, I announce that I am making a beginning of housekeeping again. But this comes hard without means, wherefore I greet a thousand times each and every friend, relatives, brothers and sisters, and the twelve sworn friends, and the Usher of the Court, the Mayor, and the Pastor, and all other good friends, and commend them always to the protection and care of God, and with it beg that you would be so brotherly and Christianlike as to send what I need for my domestic settlement. Namely a specified some of money, which lies with my dear and faithful cousin, Daniel Zant. The principle is, namely, a hundred guldens and the interest is fifteen guldens. You can send me this money with Graffenried's draft. The place and the country, the rivers where we now live and dwell is a good soil, and cattle raising also good and safe, and there is freedom in North Carolina.

Now concerning ourselves, my condition and life. My daughter Katherine also desired to go to the Lord before I came from the sea to land in Virginia and North Carolina. You are herewith commended to the protecting hand of God, and again greeted a thousand times by me.

Anna Eva Zant, in North Carolina.
Anno 1711. the 15th of April.

A friendly greeting to my grandfather, Benedict Schetele, of Nider Linog and my father's brother in Buch, Heinrich Simon, Andreas Krächig, and my grandmother in Buch.

Our father, Benedict Simon, willed on his deathbed that we surviving children should still have something on demand from my grandfather, Benedict Schettele; and so we have a friendly request for Heinrich Simon and Andreas Krächig, while we have opportunity, at this time if possible to send it into Carolina, to the city of New Bern, with Mr. Graffenried's draft. Benedict Simon's wife and child Katherine are dead. His daughter's husband Joseph Stern of Riggisberg is also dead. Madlena, the surviving widow is married again to Jacob Himler of Madiswyl and Madlena has another child, Johannes Stern, and Anna Margreta is married to Andreas Weinmann of Mentzingen. Johannes Simon, these three relatives are in Carolina with Graffenried.

Maria Magdalena remained behind with her husband Johann Heinrich, Hans von Buchse in London.

We brothers have a friendly request to make to our magistrates that they would take an interest in us like fathers. And so a thousand greetings from us to all good friends and acquaintances. Jacob

Himler and his wife Madlena, Andreas Weinmann and his wife Anna Margretha, and Johannes Simon. That these here named persons desire and request, witnesseth von Graffenried.

Johann Jacob Bötschi,
Clerk of Court
And Captain in Carolina.

New Bern in Carolina, the 20th of April 1711.

My friendly greetings and all good, first to you my dearly beloved father and mother, brother and sister-in-law, and Hans and Bartlome and Bäsi, as also grandfather, all good friends and neighbors. Be it known to you that through the grace of God, I am well and healthy. To hear the same from you would be very pleasant, to me. It goes well with me. I do not lack food nor clothes, but money is rather scarce in this country. I have hired myself out to Christoph von Graffenried, citizen of Bern, formerly mayor, now landgrave in Carolina. The quality of the country is sandy, but yet suitable for everything one plants, still there are different streaks. It produces fairly well especially Indian corn.

If any one should demand that you send me something, do not give any one anything. I owe no one anything. If it please God and he grants me life, I want to visit my Fatherland again. With this I send you all a thousand friendly greetings. I commend you to God, the Word, and his mercy, and remain, your dear son

Benedict Zionien.

With a thousandfold greeting, I wish all true friends, neighbors, and acquaintances God's grace and blessing. I and my wife, two children, and my old father have, the Lord be praised, arrived safe and sound in Carolina, and live twenty English miles from New Bern. I hope to plant corn enough this year. The land is good, but the beginning is hard, the journey dangerous. My two children, Maria and Hansli died at Rotterdam in Holland and were buried in the common burial place.

This country is praised too highly in Europe and condemned too much. I hope also in a few years to have cows and swine as much as I desire. Mr. Graffenried is our landgrave. Of vermin, snakes, and such like, there is not so much as they tell of in Europe. I have seen crocodiles by the water, but they soon fled. One should not trust to supporting himself with game, for there are no wild oxen or swine. Stags and deer, ducks and geese and turkeys are numerous.

I wish that I had my child with me, which I left with my father-in-law, together with forty-five pounds which I left behind me in the parish of Tofen. And if my father-in-law wishes to come to me I will give to him from my land. One can have as much swine and cattle as he wants without labor and expense. I am very sorry that Christian Balsiger took away his Uhli from me again at Bern.

This letter to Hanss Wichtermann,
Bränen.

P. S. Anna Wüll of Rümligen is also here and rather rich. With this you are commended to God.

Who ever has a desire to travel, he can get in Holland one hundred iron tobacco pipes, knives, iron pots, and copper kettels. He can make on them in America about three or four times the cost. Three cows and four swine are my beginnings in North Carolina. The Lord Jesus be with you all. Amen.

With our friendly greeting, all good first to you and to your and our beloved father, grandfather, and both mothers, brothers, brothers-in-law, sisters, and sisters-in-law. Be it known to you that we, by the grace of God, are hale and hearty. To hear the same from you would be very pleasant to us. Salome has been sick, but, by the grace of God, she has become well again. We still have no minister but we hope soon to get one. I have as yet taken no land. The day wages are good. One gets eighteen Stüber, this makes nine Batzen, and board. I have now separated from my brothers but yet in peace. I will soon take up a plantation which comprises toward three hundred acres. There is land enough. It requires considerable labor at the beginning, but if one has once made a beginning with cattle and swine he can prosper with small labor. He can have indeed up to three hundred head without cost, so that they become fat enough but rather wild. But the journey coming here is costly and difficult. One person over sea from Rotterdam in Holland thirty-four Thaler, where we lay seven weeks and two days, at our own expense. The thirtieth of May we went aboard the transport ship, and went upon the sea to Brüll. The 4th of June we came to Yarmouth, the 11th to Newcastle, a place situated in England. The 17th of July we went aboard the ship again, travelled as far as Shields upon the sea, where we lay quietly eight days and waited for the fleet, which traveled four days with us and which consisted of over one hundred ships. After this we sailed alone, and often in great danger, and arrived here safely through the goodness of God. No one among us died. For that we cannot thank the good God enough. The 10th of September about nine o'clock we saw land. At night we cast anchor. The 11th we stepped upon land, which was very joyful for us, since, for a long time we had seen nothing but water and sky. From Virginia it is very difficult with baggage, now by water, now by land.

We live in North Carolina on the stream called Neuse. Regarding the land: It is tolerable sandy and productive, fairly good for all crops, especially for Indian Corn. Regarding fruit; It does not grow unplanted, either good or bad. The native born inhabitants are quick but naked; for the covering of their nakedness they have coats or else shirts. For this time nothing more. Greet for me my friends Ziorien, and my mother wishes to be remembered to you. Greet for us all good friends and neighbors, and I commend you to God, the Word, and his grace, and remain your affectionate children Michael Ziorien and Salome von Mühlenen.

       To Christian von Mühlenen in Switzerland,
        in the Canton of Bern, in upper Simmenthal,
         in the parish of Bottigen of the Flühli.

My friendly greeting and all good first of all to Hans Aeschbacher, the inn-keeper Uhli Bache, cousins, also all my godparents and good neighbors. This is to inform you that, the Lord be praised, we are hale and hearty. Anni died. I am deeply grieved. No one has died except three women. My Anni was ill the whole journey. We have no women folks that wash and mend for us. I beg you if the inheritance has been decided send me it; you need only to deliver it over to Mr. Ritter. Send me a good servant, two good servant girls, two good axes, for Dietrich has not time to do blacksmithing. I have a great deal of work to do. I have taken up two hundred and fifty acres of land. If I wish I can take up four hundred acres. I have need of money so that I can have horses, cattle, and swine. I could likely keep two hundred head summer and winter without labor and expense. Here there is moss on the trees, that is good as the best aftermath hay and also acorns.

I wish you would do me the favor of having a chest made and of purchasing two hundred ells of linen cloth, one hundred ells of flax ticking; from the blacksmith, four seven pound skeins with the linchpins, a small hub auger to bore plow wheels, two pounds of whole pepper, one half pound cloves, two mill stones that are a half heavier than those of a hand mill; but you must not buy the spices or the mill stones till you are in Rotterdam; also buy me a few cast tobacco pipes, about a dozen; of the others at two batzen, two dozen; some iron pans in duplicate, only the dish part without feet and handles, in the smallest of which a quart would go, but the others larger; and a dozen little horn pipe stems. I could get five pounds for a pipe and also a few brass shoe rings. The Indians buy such things for as much as one desires. The greatest failing and lack here in Carolina is that too few people are here, and no good mills. There is one being built by us people who are in Carolina. No one has any desire to be back in Switzerland, for one can eat but little meat in Switzerland, but here in Carolina I need have no anxiety from this year on, that every year I should not butcher thirty or forty to fifty swine, more if I wish. And if Cousin Haldmann would give me the whole meadow of the estate with everything belonging to it, I should not want it for I have meadow and forest enough for the swine and arable soil, one adjoining the other. If I only had money so that I could buy a half dozen cows, and also as many swine, a few horses, I would ask nothing more of temporal blessing than good health and afterwards eternal life, as I wish for all mankind. I would also wish that the poor neighbors were with us and then they would not need to suffer hunger if they would only be willing to work a little. Therefore whoever has a desire for it, let him just venture boldly under the protection of the Most High. To be sure they do not give one a ready built house and cleared land. Each one can labor for it and clear it himself. The journey is certainly hard and was hardest for me. But after the rain comes sunshine. And now we are, the Lord be praised, all as well as we have never been before. And the Usher's daughter has borne a son upon the sea and all are hale and hearty. They are tenants of the Governor and have the best conditions. But the lease runs four years, and every week he can work one day upon his lease and half the product from tending to the (salt) pan is his. The journey has been very expensive. We had to lie eight weeks at Rotterdam and it was very dear. Also for six persons we had to pay the boatman thirty-one Thaler from Bern, also paid the ship captain to take us over the sea, two hundred and four thalers. From the ship over the sea we had to travel through Virginia to our place, more than a hundred miles over land because of sea-robbers. Since we arrived in Holland too late and the fleet had assembled, we went alone and traveled eight weeks upon the sea with our ships. But now we have good fine land. Send me also a few dozen good knives. There is a great lack of German women folks. Greet for me my father-in-law if he is still alive, my brothers and sisters-in-law, but first, Christian Hausmann in Heybühl and his wife. I and Dietrich his servant send friendly greetings to the blacksmith and Hans at Flüh. It would be well if they both were here. They could make as much as they wished to. As far as trades are concerned the best are armorers, gunsmiths, carpenters, tailors, shoemakers, potters, and ropemakers. If these came it would be exceedingly fine. Also weavers. If I had thirty pounds worth of knives and the wares mentioned above I could gain more than an hundred English pounds. A crown is worth more than a thaler in Germany. April 8th, 1711.

Let Casper Gerber give this over to Mr. Ritter in Bern, and I hope that if my father-in-law is still alive he will send me a respectable amount of money for my journey. If people wish to come here and you could do me the favor just send me the wares mentioned above. But those who intend to go must call upon Mr. Ritter, so that when the other people wish to go they may travel together. And if the inheritance has been settled let my godfather give to each a half thaler, namely to Peter Habegger, Helm Kupferschmied, Uhli Burger and Nicholas Balts, if they are still alive. Herewith nothing more. We wish you good health and long life, temporal and eternal wellfare in soul and body. Have some one buy for me a half dozen of those books like those of which Uhli Lerche gave me one, and also pay Mr. Ritter for the letter. It would be well if one or two pot makers, that is to say tinkers, should come. I have not time to write more, it is too short for me.   Christen Engel.

Copy of a letter written by Christen Janzen, out of North Carolina, the last of April 1711.

God greet you most beloved souls, father, mother, related friends, and neighbors, always with our thousandfold greetings and obedient service. I wish you at this time to learn of my health, and to know that I must make my writing as short as I can compose it. I hope that you have the letters that I wrote from Holland and England. The most essential contents are that we came the 10th of June to New Castle in England, but the 6th I became a very sad widower.

In New Castle we lay five weeks. The 17th of July went aboard the ship and lay eight days at anchor. After that we sailed, under the all-powerful protection of God, safely to land in Virginia. Also did not lose a person. A young son was born on the sea. His father's name is Benedict Kupferschmied. He worked a year for our dear brother, Christian Bürki. After that we went about a hundred hours by water and land, yet always guided and fed, and the people everywhere have done us much kindness and there is in this country no innkeeper. All go from one place to another for nothing and consider it an insult if one should wish to ask the price.

Brought here hale and hearty, the shoemaker Moritz did not die till he was on his farm. He was well on the whole journey. No one else of us Siebentaler people has died, but of the others though, three Palatines. Of the people among whom we live, however, a good many have died.

Regarding the land in general. It is almost wholly forest, with indescribably beautiful cedar wood, poplars, oaks, beech, walnut and chestnut trees. But the walnuts are very hard and full of indentations and the chestnuts very small but good. There is sassafras also, and so many other fragrant trees that I cannot describe the hundredth part. Cedar is red like the most beautiful veined cherry and smells better than the finest juniper. They are, commonly, as well as the other trees, fifty to sixty feet below the limbs.

The land in general is almost everywhere black dirt and rich soil, and everyone can get as much as he will. There are five free years. After that one is to give for an acre, which is much greater than a Juchart with us, two pennies. Otherwise it is entirely free, one's own to use and to leave to his heirs as he wishes. But this place has been entirely uninhabited, for we have not seen any signs nor heard that anything else ever was here except the so-called wild and naked Indians. But they are not wild, for they come to us often and like to get clothes of us. This is done when they pay with wild meat and leather, bacon, beans, corn, which the women plant and the men hunt; and when they, as most frequently happens, guide the Christians through the forest and show new ways. They have huts of cedar bark. Some also can speak English well. They have an idol and hold festivals at certain times. But I am sorry to say, of the true God they do not want to know anything.

With regard to the rearing of cattle. It costs almost nothing for the raising, as the booklet printed at Frankfort says, for all stock pastures in the winter as well as in the summer. And I know of nothing to find fault with in the booklet mentioned regarding these two items, although it writes of South Carolina.

They butcher also no young animals, so one can conclude how quickly the number can increase. The cows give scarcely half so much as with you for the calves suck so long; until they are a year and a half old and in turn have young. We buy a cow with a calf for three pounds sterling or twelve thalers, a hog for one pound, with young or fat; a sheep also for as much. They have but few goats, but I have seen some. Squire Michel told me they wished to bring some here to us. Wild and unplanted tree-fruits are not to be found here so good as Kocherthal writes of South Carolina. I have seen no cherries yet. There are many grape-vines and many

grapes on them, of which some are good to eat; and it can well be
believed, if one had many together (they would do well). We are
going to try to plant them for everything grows up very quickly and
all fruit is of very good taste, but we do not enjoy them much yet.

We lie along a stream called Neuse. There six years ago the first
(people), English, until two years ago (when) the Swiss people (came),
began the cultivation. They are, as it seems to me, rather rich in
cattle, all sorts of crops, the finest tree-fruit, and that, the whole
year (except for) two months. From the nature of things we were
behind in that regard, so that we do not have it yet; but we hope,
through God's blessings to get it. We came shortly before Christ-
mas and we have by God's blessing, Zioria, my son-in-law Peter
Reutiger, and I, and others besides, much stronger houses than the
English; have also cleared land in addition, and the most have put
fences around.

It is to be hoped that now from the ground and the cattle we will
get enough, through the grace of God who has always stretched out
his hand helpfully and has brought us safely and unhindered through
so many enemies, spiritual and worldly, and over the great sea. But
one thing lies heavy on us which I cannot write without weeping,
namely the lack of a true and zealous pastor. For we have indeed
cause to complain with Asaph, our sign we see no more, no prophet
preaches to us any more, no teacher teaches us any more. We
have, indeed, prayers in our houses every Sunday, but the zeal
to cleanse away the canker of our old sins is so small that it is to be
feared it will consume everything to the foundation, if the pitying
God does not come to our help.

If it had pleased the good God to send some of our brethren and
sisters or at least Christian Bürki as an instrument, as a physician of
body and soul, I should have had good hopes that the light among us
would not become an evil smelling lamp, for I do not believe there
is a person here, either English, German, or French who would not
have loved him heartily; I believe that his profession is especially
good here and that he could have an estate according to his wish without doing work in the fields. For of good liquor and such medicine
there is the greatest lack in this country, therefore I have a friendly
request to make of you, dear brother; namely, as follows. I have married Christina Christeler, a widow of Sannen. I am her third husband.
By the first she has four children. Two died in London. Her husband and one child upon the sea. But the eldest, a boy of thirteen,
named Benedict Plösch, is at Mörigen in the baliwick Nidauw, staying with his deceased father's clientage. And he was alive four years
ago. Her father was named Peter Christeler. Christen Walcker,

who, with his wife died here in this country and left eight children, said to her that she has a rather large inheritance from her late father, left with her brother Moritz Christeler, for he has received a hundred pounds of it. When you go to Sannen to ask about it, I hope Heinrich Perret will be able to help you; for they have been nearest neighbors. And if it is as Walcker says you can take it into your hands.

Because my wife understands brewing so well and has done it for years, and the drink is very scarce here and neither money nor brewing pots are to be obtained here, otherwise I would not think of such a thing for you to do. But the pot must have two pipes but no worm; and if some reliable people should not be coming, would Mr. Ritter still be so good as to get it to me here; also four pounds worth of spice, such as ginger, pepper, safron, nutmegs, galangale, cloves, each according to the proportion of the money? For here there is nothing but laurel. I have seen it on trees in the forest. But if there should be nothing to be got from the inheritance, I would most kindly beg you and my father, if he is still alive, to still help me somewhat from my own, for it is very important to me and especially to the women folks, who are very scarce here.

If only more people should wish to come, I advise that they take women with them if they want to have any, for here some of the very best men find no wives, because they are not here.

The journey is easily to be made if one can supply himself properly with old cheese, dried meat, and dried fruit, vinegar, wine, beer, and casks, butter, biscuits, in fine whatever is good to eat and feasible to transport, also a pan or kettle that is narrow at the top and broad below; for when the sea is violent the ship lies over on one side so that things are spilt. Yet I have never heard that a ship has sunk upon the high sea.

Whoever could provide himself with the things named above and should make an agreement with the ship captain that he give him liberty to cook and a good place to lie the voyage would not be hard. For we had young and old people, all are hale and hearty. Whatever one brings here in the way of wares is worth at least as much again. Linen cloth and glass would be especially needed, and is to be purchased very well in Holland.

Peter Röhtiger and my two daughters greet you, for we live beside each other. Dichtli is still with me, and I am delivering the greeting of us all to our dear and faithful pastor, to the whole number of honored persons, especially Godfather Kilchmeyer Dreuthart, and Andreas Aescher, Christen Jantz.

I would have much to write. I must break off. Have patience with my bad writing, for whoever sees my hand and labor will believe that I have not written and studied much. Greet for us Christien Bürki and I should be glad if he could hear the contents of this letter.

I remain your well affectioned servant, and my parents' obedient son until death.

Greet for us Anna Drus, item Speismann's people, and your sister and relatives, also my father's sister, and first of all the school-master.

FRENCH VERSION

FRENCH VERSION

1. Relation du Voyage d'Amerique que le B. de Graffenried a fait en y amenent une Colonie Palatine et Suisse, et Son Retour en Europe.

PREFACE

Quoique plusieurs Persones m'ayent demandé la Relation de mes tristes adventures d'Amerique, je ne me Serois pas disposé a cela, n'estoit que j'estoit bien dise de me justifier tant aupres de ma Societé aussi bien qu'a d'autres persones lesquelles auroient peutestre pu avoir des pensées Sinistres de ma Conduite. Come Si j'avois entrepris cette Colonie legerement et imprudement, et que j'aurois passé mon tems en Carolina en Luxe et oisivité, en quoy on ce Seroit bien trompé, et ma Relation en fait bien voir le Contraire. On y trouvera aussi des particularitez quon auroit bien pu laisser, mais accause des desmarches irregulieres de certaines persones qui ont agis de mauvaise foy, tant a legard des pauvres Colonistes qu'envers ma persone, en estants meme venus jusques a des actions noires et inéxcusables, Je nay pu de moins que d'en faire mention, (quoi que bien charitablement puis que ie nomme persone) affin qu'on ne m'en impute pas, et que mon innocence Soit au jour.

Sans doute quelques Curieux voudroient Scavoir les raisons d'une Entreprise Si grande et eloigneé de mon Pays et Patrie. Quelques uns les Scavent, les autres ce contenteront de Scavoir que des le tems que jeu l'honneur de faire quelque Sejour chez feu le Duc d'Albemarle a Londre qui fust alors establis du Roy Charle II. vice Roy de Jamaique, par la Relation qu'on me fist de la beauté, bonté, et richesses de L'Amerique Angloise, J'en conclus une Ideé si advantageuse, que Sur les fortes invitations de ce Seigneur je l'aurois Suivis en ce Voyage avec empressement, si je n'eusse esté detourné par les fortes remonstrances de mes parents qui voulloient que je m'etablisse dans ma Patrie, et nonobstant touttes les douceurs que j'y pouvois avoir, il me resta pourtant toujours quelque amorce et quelque chose d'attirant pour les pays Susdits. Et la Fortune ne me regardant pas d'un oeuil Si favorable come je l'aurois Souhaitté, apres avoir finis mon Bailliage d'Yverdon, grand et important a Contentement de mon Souverain, des Estats voisins, et des Ressortissants, Dieu Soit loué, avec une Conscience bone et nette, mais n'y ayant pas profité pour y avoir eu des Contretems, d'autre Coté n'ayant pas esté homme a m'enrichir au depends des pauvres Ressortissants, outre les troubles de Neuffchatel qui me causerent beaucoup de perte, Voyant encore que la

Reforme nouvelle me privoit de pouvoir obtenir quelque charge profitable pour bien longtems; dans l'esperence de faire une fortune plus considerable dans ces Pays eloigné de L'Amerique Angloise, Affin de mieux Soutenir une Famille nombreuse Selon mon Caractere et qualité: Je pris dont une forte resolution pour ce Voyage important pas moins dangereux que long et penible, d'autant avec plus de Courage que ie fus invité fortement par diverses lettres des Pays susdits, aussi bien que de Londre. Je hesitois longtems si ie communiquerois mon dessein a quelque amy ou Parent, mais prevoyant qu'ils m'en disuaderoient, je n'en dis rien pas meme a ceux qui me touchoient de plus pres, et partis Secrettement. Cependant avant que de quitter le Pays, je m'arrestay aux frontieres chez un amy, et fis une disposition de mes affaires que je n'avois pu entierement regler avant mon depart, et l'envoyay a un de mes Parents, en comuniquant mon dessein, mais le malheur voulust que ce pacquet de papiers fust intercepté ou perdu, ce qui causa beaucoup d'embarass et de confusion. Ne recevant aucune reponce pendant 8 ou 10. jours, Je partis dont dans une ferme resolution de ne plus retourner, mais L'home propose et Dieu dispose.

2. A marginal note says Potomak (von neuer Hand) _ _ _ The French has Potomack.

3. Mons. le Gouverneur de Virginie:

4. L'un estoit le Receveur General lautre L'Arpenteur General, le 3e. Un Juge de Paix, qui touts trois ont paru pour cett effect devant le Comité Royal, ou ils ont recu leurs instructions et ont esté confirmé pour avoir la direction de ce Peuple, en mon absence, tant sur Mer que Sur Terre, n'ayant pu partir alors accause d'une petite Colonie de Berne qui devait Suivre bientost outre d'autres affaires que J'avois encore a regler.

5. Monsieur Cesar ministre de l'Eglise Refformée Allemande de Londre a Gravesand

6. il en mourut plus de la moitié Sur Mer

7. et en partie dematé

8. n'ayant oséz ce commetre en mer accause des Capres outre que les Eaux estant basses aux Embouchures des Rivieres de Caroline les gros Vaisseaux n'auroient pu passer ny entrer _ _ _

9. Consistent en environ 1000 arpents de Terre.

10. Il faut que j'arest icy le cours de ma Relation, affin que ie puisse aussi dire quelque chose de ce que j'ay negotié plus particulierement a Londre, item de mon depart, de ce qui s'est passé et ce que j'ay remarqué dans mon voyage, et de mon arivée en Nord Caroline ce meme mois de 7bre 1710 apres on continuera en ordre.

Nayant touché qu'en passant ce que j'avois negotié a Londre, ie diray quelque chose de plus particulier icy, pourtant le plus Succincte-

When I arrived in Holland certain persons almost turned me aside
from my plan, and other propositions were made me in which I was
to be given my support and something as a profit, but I did not
find enough in this to make good my losses, and continued my journey
to England, where I immediately heard of my people, and was inspired
by such a desire to continue in my undertaking, by persons of rank
and others, who promised me all sorts of assistance, that I was brought
into negotiations according to which very advantageous propositions,
conditions, and privileges were made and given by the proprietors
above mentioned which brought me also to my resolution.

At this very time there came over 10,000 souls from Germany to
England, all under the name of Palatines, but among them were many
Switzers and people brought together from other provinces of Germany. This caused the royal court as well as private individuals
much concern and also unspeakable costs, so that they were embarrassed because of these people, and therefore there soon went out
an edict by which it was allowed to many persons to take some of
these people and care for them, and a good share of them had been
sent into the three kingdoms, but partly because of their laziness,
partly because of the jealousy of the poor subjects of the country,
they did not do so well as it was supposed they would, and so they
had begun to send a considerable number of these people to America
and the Queen had had great sums distributed for that purpose.

At this juncture different persons of high and of middle rank, to
whom my undertaking was known, advised me not to lose so favorable an opportunity; and at the same time gave me good hopes that,
if I wished to take a considerable number of these people, the Queen
would not only grant me the money for their passage, but in addition,
would give me a good contribution for them. These hopes were
realized and the sum reached almost 4,000£ sterling. Besides this,
the Queen had granted to the royal council land upon the Potomac [2]
River, as much as we immediately needed, and moreover had given
strong recommendations to the governor of Virginia. [3] All this with
the advantageous promises of the proprietors of Carolina gave to
the undertaking a good appearance, and there was as much hope
for a fortunate outcome as the beginning seemed good and prosperous.

To provide for and send this colony I took indescribable pains,
1. I tried to choose for this project healthy, industrious people and
among them those of all sorts of trades necessary for this undertaking.
2. A supply of all kinds of necessary tools and things. 3. As also sufficient and good food. 4. Good ships and sailors, also certain over- and
under-directors for this people, to keep every thing in good order.
5. In order that no negligence or lack of knowledge should be at-

Reforme nouvelle me privoit de pouvoir obtenir quelque charge profitable pour bien longtems; dans l'esperence de faire une fortune plus considerable dans ces Pays eloigné de L'Amerique Angloise, Affin de mieux Soutenir une Famille nombreuse Selon mon Caractere et qualité: Je pris dont une forte resolution pour ce Voyage important pas moins dangereux que long et penible, d'autant avec plus de Courage que ie fus invité fortement par diverses lettres des Pays susdits, aussi bien que de Londre. Je hesitois longtems si ie communiquerois mon dessein a quelque amy ou Parent, mais prevoyant qu'ils m'en disuaderoient, je n'en dis rien pas meme a ceux qui me touchoient de plus pres, et partis Secrettement. Cependant avant que de quitter le Pays, je m'arrestay aux frontieres chez un amy, et fis une disposition de mes affaires que je n'avois pu entierement regler avant mon depart, et l'envoyay a un de mes Parents, en comuniquant mon dessein, mais le malheur voulust que ce pacquet de papiers fust intercepté ou perdu, ce qui causa beaucoup d'embarass et de confusion. Ne recevant aucune reponce pendant 8 ou 10. jours, Je partis dont dans une ferme resolution de ne plus retourner, mais L'home propose et Dieu dispose.

2. A marginal note says Potomak (von neuer Hand) _ _ _ The French has Potomack.

3. Mons. le Gouverneur de Virginie:

4. L'un estoit le Receveur General lautre L'Arpenteur General, le 3e. Un Juge de Paix, qui touts trois ont paru pour cett effect devant le Comité Royal, ou ils ont recu leurs instructions et ont esté confirmé pour avoir la direction de ce Peuple, en mon absence, tant sur Mer que Sur Terre, n'ayant pu partir alors accause d'une petite Colonie de Berne qui devait Suivre bientost outre d'autres affaires que J'avois encore a regler.

5. Monsieur Cesar ministre de l'Eglise Refformée Allemande de Londre a Gravesand

6. il en mourut plus de la moitié Sur Mer

7. et en partie dematé

8. n'ayant oséz ce commetre en mer accàuse des Capres outre que les Eaux estant basses aux Embouchures des Rivieres de Caroline les gros Vaisseaux n'auroient pu passer ny entrer _ _ _

9. Consistent en environ 1000 arpents de Terre.

10. Il faut que j'arest icy le cours de ma Relation, affin que ie puisse aussi dire quelque chose de ce que j'ay negotié plus particulierement a Londre, item de mon depart, de ce qui s'est passé et ce que j'ay remarqué dans mon voyage, et de mon ariveé en Nord Caroline ce meme mois de 7bre 1710 apres on continuera en ordre.

Nayant touché qu'en passant ce que j'avois negotié a Londre, ie diray quelque chose de plus particulier icy, pourtant le plus Succinctement que ie pourray: Il séra bon de distinguer un peu les deux viseés des Colonies proposées de celle de Virginie, et Celle de la Nord Caroline.

Pour Celle de Virginie nous avions des ordres de L.L.E.E. de Berne notre Souverain Magistrat (marginal note: Proposition de l'Etat de Berne pour un district de Pays en Virg:) de sonder aupres de sa Maj: La Reine de la Grande Bretagne, Si Elle seroit disposée d'accorder a L'Etat de Berne un district de Terres pour la Colonie proposée avec Jurisdiction Sous certaine Clauses et sans dependre d'aucun Gouverneur mais directement de la Reine ou Son Conseil; mais la Couronne ne Voulant rien deroger de Son Authorité et Grandeur ne voulust S'entendre a cette Proposition pretendant que tout ce devoit conformer aux Loix et Reglement du Royaume, ce qui fesant aussi de la péine a un Etat Souv: de sabaisser d'autant, rien ne fust fait.

Cependant nous en particulier ma Societé et moy, Sous la recomandation ou par assistance de Monsieur Stanion Envoyé extr: de Sa Maj: Brit: obtimes de la Reine la permission de prendre des Terres en Virginie au dessus de la Chutte de la Rivier de Potomack Sous les memes Conditions que les autres Ressortissants de sa Majesté, dans le dessein de partager notre Colonie pour des bones raisons, mais Come on nous fist esperer plus d'avantage de la Nord Caroline, et que ces Terres estoient a beaucoup meilleur marché, outre que nous y avions quelque jurisdictions et privileges particuliers, nous Commencames par la et l'issue fatale fait voir que nous aurions mieux fait de comencer par Virginie d'autant que nous y aurions esté plus en Sureté et mieux Soutenus en cass de danger par la Couronne que par des particuliers en Caroline, meme la Situation suivant le plan que j'en ay fait, ne cedoit rien a celle de Caroline ny en beauté ny en bonté. Cependant touttes ces desmarches que dessus, me cousterent bien des pas inutiles de la peine et des frais, pour a la fin n'obtenir qu'un ombre de faveur, car lors que nous voullions faire asseurer et arpenter les Terres Sus mentionées il ce trouva qu'elles estoient desia prises par Mylord Coulpeper: tellement qu'il en faloit chercher la plus grand partie en Maryland Pays appartenant en proprieté a Mylord Baltimore: Il est vray que nous en fismes encore marquer et assurer en d'autres endroits assez bons en Virginie mais eloignéz des Plantations Chrestiennes. A l'egard de la Colonie pour la Carolina ie n'eus pas moins d'embarass de peines et de frais, quoy que pourtant les Lord Proprietaires ayent esté bien disposéz a me favoriser. Je crois qu'avant que dentamer cette negociation, il ne seroit pas hors de propos de dire quelque chose de leur Pouvoir et Priviliges cest ce qu'on voit amplement dans la Relation ou journal imprimé de larpenteur general Lawson, ou est copiée la Charter, ou acte accordé par le Roy Charles

II. Cette grande faveur et haute Jurisdiction qu'aucun particulier ny Seigneur des 3. Royamues n'a a esté accordé a ces Mylords et Seigneurs qui ont rappellé ce Roy de Son exile, et ont favorisé Son Retour dans le Royaume. Ce Roy n'ayant voulu etre ingrat envers ses bienfaiteurs n'a Sceu coment les mieux reccompenser que par une faveur si Singuliere en donant et remettant la Province de Caroline a ces Seigneurs en pleine possession, Authorité et pouvoir absolu come le Roy meme l'avoit possedée, aussi ont ils le Titre, Come s'en suit.

A Son Excellence N.N. Palatin, et aux autres Veritables et absoluts Seigneurs Proprietaires de la Province de Caroline. (Marginal note: dont il y a 2 Gouvernement du Sud et du Nord.)

L'un des Chefs de ces Siegneurs Prop: estoit au Comencement, Le General Monck Duc d'Albemarle, C'estoit luy qui presenta la Courone qu'il avoit fait faire au Roy a Son Entrée au Royamue la quelle on garde a la Tour de Londre aupres de la veritable du Royaume et que j'ay veue, on les montre toujours touttes deux aux Etrangers curieux.

Entre d'autres Privileges que ces Seigrs. Prop: ont est le pouvoir de creer des Cassiques, des Comtes, Barons, Chevalliers, et Gentilshomes en ces Provinces et Ceux qu'ils veulent bien favoriser ils les font corroborer et registrer dans la Heroldrie Royale, Come ils ont fait a mon egard, lors que pour me procurer plus d'Authorité, aupres de mon Peuple, ils m'honorerent des titres de Landgrave de Caroline, Baron de Bernbery, et Chevallier du Cordon pourpre avec la Medaille, come mes Patentes en font foy: mais le mall est qu'avec ces Titres il n'y a pas un Revenu proportioné: tout le bien qui m'en est provenu est qu'ils m'ont doné le premier rang apres le Gouverneur dans la maison haute des Parlements de la Province et m'a conserve du Respect aupres des Ressortissants; Car ayant au comencement paru au Parlement sans Cordon, j'y fus bien receus, mais en certaines occasions ie ne fus pas obeis come cela ce devoit, C'est pourquoi on m'advisa de porter le Cordon et la medialle quand ie paroitray dans les assemblées ce que ie fis, et j'apperceus incontinant leffect, car certaines gens qui n'avoient asséz respectéz mes ordres vinrent apres pour m'en demander pardon a genoux. C'est assez de L'Authorité et pouvoir de ces Seigrs. Propr: Je diray succinctement quelque chose de ce qu'ils m'ont accordé notre Traitté estant trop ample pour l'inserrer icy.

1. Ils m'ont vendu 15000 arpents terre choisie que j'ay fait arpenter Sur la Riviere de News et Trent et 2500 acres Sur Weetock River, a 10 livres Sterlins le 1000, ou une livre Sterl: p cent acres, et 6 Sols par 100 arpendts. cence fonciere, ce qui fait la Somme de 175£. Sterl: ce que j'ay d'abord payé content. 2. Il y a eu une reserve de 100 mille acres a choisir entre ces Rivieres cy nomées et Clarendon R. pour le meme prix, et pour cela j'ay eu 7 ans de terme pour faire le premier

payment et des la 7e: jusques a la 12e: tout devoit etre payé. 3e Les differents qu'auroient mon Peuple avec les Anglois ce devoient terminer devant les juges Anglois mais ce que mes Colonistes auroient de dificulté entre Eux cela ce termineroit entre Eux ou par devant moy: La haute Jurisdiction au faits criminels a mort reservéz aux Seigrs. Prop: 4e. Liberté de Religion, et d'avoir un ministre de notre Pays qui pourroit prescher en notre langue. 5e. Droit de Ville et marché ou faire a Neuberne. 6e. francs de toutte taille et impots dimes et Cences hormi les 6 Sols p. 100 acres annullement come susdit. 7e. Les Seigrs Prop: ou la Province par leurs ordres me devoient fournir pour 2 ou 3 ans de provision de vivres et betail pour moy et toutte la Colonie moyenant restitution apres le terme prescript.

J'avois aussi un Traitté particular et bien exact avec les Palatins lequell fust projecté examiné & arreté, devant & par la Comission Royale trop ample a inserrer icy, seulement en Substance ce qui suit 1e. mes Colonistes me devoient fidelité obeysance et Respect, et moy la Protection aug 2e. Je devois fournir chaque famille de provision pour la premiere année, d'une Vache de deux Cochons et de quelques utensils, moyenant restitution apres 3 ans. 3e. Je devois doner a chaque famille 300 arp: de Terre et ils devoient me livrer pour Cence fonciere 2 Sols par acre, en contre ie devois Supporter les 6 sols p. 100 acres de reconnoissance envers les Sigrs. Prop. come desia Susdit; pour ce qui est du transport et nouriture de ma Colonie iusques en Caroline la Reine l'a gratifié et 30 shellings pour habits a chaque psne gros et petits.

Apres cela il s'agissoit de ce pourvoir de bon Vaisseaux, et il ce presente une persone de ma Connoissance, le Chevallier Fyper qui entreprist de fournir deux Vaisseaux bien equipez avec la provision de vivres necessaires, mais tout cecy ne pust etre executé avec telle regularité come on lauroit Souhaité. Come ces Seigrs. les Directeurs ou providirecteurs de cette foule de monde qui ce trouva alors a Londre avoient asséz affaire a pourvoir tant de 1000 ames, L'argent comenca a devenir rare, tellement que notre bon Chevallier qui fist ces provisions a Credit dans la ferme psuasion que l'argent luy seroit livré a tout tems qu'il le demanderoit, fust bien Surpris de ce voir renvoyé tant de fois, ce qui dura meme plusieurs mois, tellement que ces Crediteurs luy firent denoncer les arrets ce qui fust meme executé pour 24 heures, Le Chevallier tout allarmé de ce pcedé vient un mattin pour m'en faire de meme ce tennant a moy pour touts ces inconvenients, ce qui me mist bien en peine. Come alors ie me trouvay a la Campagne pour prendre l'air et me reposer un peu de mes fatigues, je me hastay pour aller a Londre pour representer a la Commission Royale mes griefs Sur le retard du payement de cett argent: on me dona des bones paroles, mais ils ce passerent encore plusieures Semaines avant que l'argent promist fust livré au Chevallier Fyper qui ne manqua pas de jour a autre de presser les Tresoriers, a la fin le tout fust bien conduit et a Souhait.

Apres que ma Colonie fust partie dans les vaisseaux mentionez ie me preparay aussi pour les Suivre, apres avoir disposé mes affaires particulieres et pris Congé d'une partie des Seigneurs de la Comission Royale et des Seigrs. Proprietaires de Carolina.

Je passe icy Sous Silence un Traitt fait avec William Penn Proprietaire de Pensilvanie pour des Terres et des mines; Et du Traitté particulier que j'ay eu avec une Societé de Berne sur la quelle ie me reposois pour en avoir lassistance necessaire dans une Entreprise laquelle ie me trouverois trop faible de Soutenir, mais il auroit esté bien mieux pour moy de massocier, pour un fait de cette importance avec quelque persone moyennée et entendue d'Angleterre laquelle ne ce Seroit peut etre pas laisser epouvanter si viste de mes Contretems, come ces Messieurs.

Mes Colonistes Palatins estant partis au mois de Janvier 1710 je les Suivis et partis de Londre a la fin du mois de May meme je me Servis pour cela d'une voiture tres comode, presque de meme que celle de Paris a Lyon. Je ne puis de moins que de parler icy quelque chose de ce que j'ay observé en ce petit Voyage. Un Dimanche qu'il falust rester a une petite Ville nomée Harford ou pres de la il y a la maison de Campagne du Comte d'Essex fort antique que ie fus curieux de voir et jy fus venu civilement. dans ce Palais magnifique i'observay dans un grand dome des peintures grandes et extraordinaires dans le Cabinet du Comte quantitéz de pieces rares et antiquitéz tres Curieuses; et dans une grande Sale ie crus voir sur une table de marbre un lutt des fluttes et autres instruments, avec des livres deployéz de musique, item un jeu de carts deployé, une bourse de jettons plusieurs pieces d'argent et plusieurs autres gentillesses tres bien faittes et quand ie viens plus pres de la table ie fus bien surpris de voir la ouvrage d'un Second Appelles, que ces pieces que ie croyois effective n'estoient que contrefaittes en peinture ce qui fust ou me Sembloit le plus curieux est que la Superficie de Cette table de marbre estoit si bien polie qu'on auroit cru que c'estoit des peintures dessous un verre ou une glace, et on y pouvoit verser de leau Sans gaster la table ny la peinture, assurement il faloit que cela fust peint d'un vernis merveilleux. Apres avoir veu le reste du Palais, et esté raffreschis d'une belle Colation et de bones liquers ie fis mes Compliments et pris Congé pour Suivre ma routte.

Apres quelque journées nous vinmes a Yorck Ville antique assez grande et bien peuplée, ou j'eus Seulement le tems de voir la Cathedrale d'une tres belle Structure ou j'attendis justement une tres belle Symphonie ou Vepre et Messieurs les Chanoines my firent Civilité. de la nous vinmes a Durham assez jolie Ville la Cathedrale est assez belle, L'Eveque de ce lieu a le titre Seul d'un Prince hormis celuy de Galle en Angleterre aussi a-il la pcdence Sur touts les Eveques Hormis celuy de Londre: apres il ny eust rien de remarquable jusques a Neucastle.

Neu Castle est une Ville grande bien peuplée Riche, marchande, bien Située au bord de la Riviere de Tyne qui S'egorge dans la Mer, toutt abonde en cette ville on y fait bone chere et a bon marché le Saumon y est en abondance, cett Ville est remarquable par la houille ou Charbon de piere qu'on y trouve il en part des flottes entieres pour fournir la Ville de Londre et voisinage de ce charbon, et les Charboniers y sont en si grand nombre quil faloit alors y tenir garnison pour les tenir en bride il y a des concavitéz si terribles par lá qu'on disoit que c'est l'antichambre des Enfers, et il faut qu'un Etranger aye bon courage d'y aller bien avant, on y fait aussi quantité de Sell marin et il y a plusieurs verriers, et d'autres fabriques outre les marchands il y a aussi des persones d'un autre rang bien Civiles, et honestes, avec lesquelles on passe agreablement son tems, de 15 jours que j'y ay esté, ie ne Saurois asséz me louer des Civilitéz qu'on m'y temoigna, Un des Chefs de la Ville Alderman Fenwich me regala magnifiquement d'une belle Symphonie de Musiciens persones de qualité. il y a aussi un tres beau boul en gren, une tres belle promenade ou il y a un jeu de boule entouree de plusieurs rangs de tilliots, et cela Sur la hauteur de la Ville, ou il y a une tres belle vue. Cependant ie n'y ay pas esté Sans Chagrin que me causast le Capite. du Vaisseau qui transportoit mes Colonistes Suisses, il en estoit aussi le proprietaire bourgois de Boston Capitale de la Nouvelle Angleterre, sans la mediation de ce galant home Mr. Fenwich j'etois pour my ruiner en process avec ce Capte. on avoit desia composé et conclu avec luy qu'il fourniroit touttes les provisions necessaires, depuis Roterdam jusques en Amerique, Cependant lors qu'il aborde a Neuw Castle pour ces propres affaires tant pour y decharger des marchandises que pour en prendre d'autres pour Boston et partie de provisions de vivres qu'il aymoit mieux y prendre qu'en Hollande y estant en effect meilleurs et a meilleur marché ayant esté obligé de sy arrester pres de 4 Semaines, Il pretendoit que nous y fussions a nos propres frais avec toutte notre Colonie Suisse, ce qui me causa bien de L'embarass.

A la fin nous estants accomodéz tellement quellement nous partimes au Commencement de Juillet pour l'Amerique a l'embouchure de la Riviere de Tyne nous nous arrestames quelques heures pour faire provision de Saumons tant verds que Secs en un bourg situé au bord de cette Riviere ou il y eust une si grande quantité de Saumon que tout le bourg en estoit tapissé les sechant au Soleil devant les maisons aussi bien que pour exposer a la vent.

Nous sortimes de L'embouchure environ les 3 heures du soir par un Vent favorable et un tres beau jour, quand nous fumes sur la hauteur de la Mer nous vimes quelques Vaisseaux tant plus que nous les approchions tant plus nous en decouvrimes a la fin passant plus outre nous nous trouvames entre 3 flottes, celle de Hollande qui estoit en ligne assez nombreuse qui venoit aux Costes d'Angleterre pour prendre du harang, entremelée de Batiments de pecheurs et de distance de Vaisseaux de Guerre d'un autre Costé estoit celle des Charbonier qui revenoit a viude de Londre: Et d'un Coté celle de Moscovie Le Sole qui s'en alloit coucher y donant a plein et le vente ayant cessé, c'estoit le plus beau spectacle qu'on put voir, ces grands vaisseaux de Guerre parmy ces autres batiments paroissoient come autant de Superbe Chatteaux parmis des maisons mediocres et le tout ensemble paroissoit come 3 belles Villes, basties Sur mer, le lendemain qui estoit un dimanche d'un beau Calme, le Commandeur Anglois de la flotte de Moscovie dona le Signal et touts les voisseaux deployerent leurs Pavillions come de coutume a ce jour apres la devotion Les trompettes, haubois, et tambours ce firent entendre, on ce visita les uns et les autres, come si on auroit esté en ville on passa le tems si agreablement que j'aurois alors souhaitte d'etre toujours en mer: Mais Contre le Soir il s'eleva Soudain un Vent impetueux que ceux qui estoient en visite eurent assez de peine de ce Sauver dans leur barquets pour ce rendre dans leurs Navires, et meme un bon biberon qui avoit de la peine de quitter sa bone liquer pour avoir trop tardé, fust d'obligation de rester dans le bastiment ou il estoit en visite et fust contraint de prendre un autre routte malgré luy. Pour nous qui estions en dessein de faire voile Nord about, cest adire contre le nord au dessus des Isles de Shettland primes partis pour notre Seurete de nous mettre parmis la flotte de Moscovie la quelle pour eviter les Francois avec qui on estoit en Guerre alors au lieu de passer la Mer Baltique prist son tour aussi par le Nord, nous estions 7 Bastiments destinéz pour l'Amerique qui Fimes voile de compagnie avec ceux qui estoient destinéz pour Danemark, Suede, et Moscovie; A la hauteur du Nord d'Ecosse nous nous separames apres avour Salué le Comandeur de la flotte marchande, de nos Cannons qui est lordre usité, Eux prirent contre Nordoest et nous au Nord et Nordwest, cependant come le Vent ce changea en oest il nous fust si favorable, quau lieu de prendre notre routte par dessus les Isles de Shettland nous coupames et passames entre ces Isles et celles des orcades, pourtant la nuit, mais heureusement, Dieu en soit loué.

Quand nous fumes sur une Certaine hauteur au dessus d'Irlande, nous vismes de loin paroitre quelque Vaisseaux faisant 5. voiles contre nous, cela nous mist en allarme ne Sachant sils etoient Ennemis ou amys, nous primes d'abord nos licts et matelats pour border notre Vaisseau ce qui nous devoit servir de rempart, et nous nous mimes en aussi bone posture qu'il ce pust pour nous deffendre, nous en eumes une petite peur accause que de 3 Vaisseaux que nous vismes, il y en eust avec les banderoles blanches, Couleur de France, quand nous fumes a portée d'un Canon, Le Commendeur de cette flottile tira un coup perdu pour Signal que nous devions le recconnoitre, mais ny repondant pas, il tira le second en Serieux et nous brisa presque le grand mas, alors il faloit ce Soumettre et nous repondimes de nos canons, arborant notre pavilion Anglois, et tendant le contrevoile; dans un moment le Commandeur nous joignist si pres qu'on pust S'entreparler, et come il ne fist pas grand Vent pour faire Civilité au Commandnous l'invitames de monter notre vaisseau, ce qu'il ne refusa pas estant bien aise de ce regaler de notre bon biere freche, angloise, et d'une piece de Saumon a la marinade pendant ce petit intervalle ie pris mon tems pour ecrire en Europe et remis ma lettre a ce petit Comandeur (qui accompagnoit 4 ou 5 autres Vaisseaux Ecossais et anglois venants de Jamaique, Barbados, et autres endroits) et ma lettre fust bien remise a la poste et parvenue a Berne. Contre le Soir nous nous quittames et chacun prist Sa routte.

J'avois fait beaucoup de remarques de ce que ie vis sur Mesr et de ce qui s'etoit passé, en ayant fait un journal assez curieux mais le malheur voulust, que une petite masle ou coffre et dans lequell il y avoit encore plusieurs raretéz d'Amerique avec des autres papiers et quelques hardes, S'est perdu quoy qu'il fust bien reccomandé a un capite. d'un Vaisseau qui partis de Virginie ne layant pu prendre avec moy accause que j'avois un grand voyage a faire depuis Williamsbourg Capitale de Virginie iusque a la Nouvelle York, par terre, estant desia Surcharge de hardes tant que mes deux chevaux purent porter. Ainsi ie ne ferai mention que de quelque peu de choses dont ie men Souviens bien et que ie crois assez dignes de la Curiosité du lecteur, au rest il y a tant d'autheurs de la Mer qui ont ecrit des Merveille de la Mesr, que iy renvoye le lecteur.

Seulement diray ie a ceux qui nont pas lu ces Autheurs que quand nous Sommes venu Sous la ligne Tropique du Cancer, ou Sur une certaine hauteur de la Mer entre cette ligne et celle du pole Arctique, nous y vismes des oiseaux blancs de la grandeur d'un Corbeau qui memes ce vinrent poser Sur notre mas, les mattelots les tiennent pour oiseaux de bon augure et ne Souffrent qu'on tire dessus, ce qui est le plus remarquable et qu'on ne voit ces oiseaux que sur cette hauteur de la Mesr et non pas autrepart.

Mais pour oiseaux de mauvois augure il y en a d'autre plus petits noirs avec un peu de blanc qui Volent ca et la sur la mesr, et autant de fois qu'on les voit voler a l'entour du Vaisseau et principalement Sus le devant on observe qu'ils presagent rien de bon, mais du mauvais tems, ou tempeste ou terribles orages, ie pris cela au commencement pour des fables mais l'ayant remarqué moy meme diverses fois, ie Suis presque oblige d'y adjuster foy, ie crois au fond, si on voulloit philosopher la dessus qu'on trouverait des raisons naturelles, de ces Sortes d'evenements.

J'ay encore observé une chose remarquable en un poisson nomé Dauphin, le poisson est tres beau dans leau ayant la Couleur de l'Iris, quand il Suit un Vaisseau il ne ce tient qu'a deux pieds de la Superficie de leau, C'est un Charme de le voir nager, il est toujours accompagné de quelques petits poissons qui ce tienent toujours pres du gouvernail et ne quittent pas ce poste que le Dauphin S'en alle ou qu'il Soit tué. Nous en primes un avec un trident, et voicy come on les prends, le baton ou perche ou est affiché le trident est attaché a une longue Corde, et lors que le Dauphin nage assez pres du Vaisseau, un mattelot, ou qui voudra pour veu qu'il aye l'addresse, jette le trident contre le Dauphin, quelque fois on l'attrappe du premier coup, assez souvent on y manque, quand on la piqué, on retire la Corde et on le leve, aussi beau que ce poisson est dans l'eau aussi villain est il hors de leau, mais bien bon aprestéz nous en fimes bone chere, tant plus jeunes tant meilleurs et plus delicats. on y voit aussi des poissons volants, et tant d'autres sortes et choses merveilleuses a observer Sur Mesr qu'on en feroit un Volume; quand il y avoit du calme ou Seulement quelques petit air ie me plaisois a regarder et examiner tant de Sortes d'insectes et autres choses provenantes de l'ecume de la Mesr; En certaines endroits on voit des herbes et fleurs extraordinaires, il est Surprenant ou ces herbes prenent racine au millieu de L'ocean ou il y a de si terribles profondeurs. on apercoit en plusieurs endroits des Courrents si forts que des habiles maitres de Vaisseaux ce detournent quelque fois de leur routte s'ils ne prenent bien garde, mais le plus curieux Seroit de Scavoir d'ou vienent ces courrents. Il y a un qui vient du Golfe de Mexique, mais pour dautre on y peut encore penetrer d'ou ils viennent.

R'envoyant les Curieux aux Autheurs qui ont ecrit amplement des raretéz de la Mesr, je continue ma routte. Quand nous vinmes a la hauteur de Terre Neuve, on me montra a peu pres les grands bancs de cette Isle, ou il se prend une si grande quantité de Morucs dont la France et l'Angleterre ce pourvoient.

Par la un Capre Francois nous Suivist une journée entiere mais n'ayant eu le Vent favorable, il ne nous pust atteindre Cependant nous apprehendions beaucoup, C'est pour quoy nous Consultames par ensemble et la Conclusion fust qu'aussitot que le Soliel Seroit couché nous baisserions peu a peu et insensiblement les voiles, affin que contre la nuict le Capre nous perdist de vue, et come sans doute il nous Suiveroit toujours contre le Continant il faloit changer de routte: aussitost qu'il fust abscur nous tendimes touts nos voiles et rebroussames chemin pour 3 or 4 lieux et prenant le haut de la mesr nous fimes nos efforts pour gagner la gauche du Capre, et prenant en droiture contre Virginie nous echapames de ses mains; car nous aurions eu le dessous n'ayant eu que 4 Canons dans notre Vaisseaux.

Peu de jours apres nous decouvrimes le Courent, des herbes des hyrondelles de Mesr, et bientost apres des Canars et d'autres Sortes d'oiseaux deau, qui est une marque Seure qu'on n'est pas loin de Terre ferme, ausse fimes nous monter un petit garcon tout au haut du mas qui ne pust rien decouvrir encore, mais quelques tems apres montant pour la Seconde fois il remarqua du Terrein qui sembloit etre une petite nuée, bientost apres reconnasissant mieux que c'estoit du Terrein il cria "Ou Rée" qui est le mot de joye ou d'aplaudissement des Anglais, et demande pour boire un etreine. Nous nous aprochames du Continant et cotoyames les Provinces de Pensilvanie Jersey, et Maryland, iusqu'a ce que nous decouvrimes Cap Henry en Virginie a la gauche de L'embouchure de James River, Un Vent de Nordoest nous favorisant nous entrames fort bien en cette Riviere et arrivames heureusement a *Guiguetan* presentement nomé Hampton un bourg assez joly le premier a lentrée de Virginie, apres un Voyage ou passage de deux mois, fort heureux n'ayant eu qu'un Seul orage qui n'a duré qu'une couple d'heures, et n'ayant point eu de maladies. nous y restames une nuict et un jour pour nous raffrechir.

Apres avoir fait Scavoir au Lieut: Gouverneur de Virginie notre arrivée et luy remis la lettre de la Reine, le Gouverneur ayant été absent nous descendimes la Riviere et entrames dans celle de Nunscimund cest la ou nous dechargames le Vaisseau de nos provisions et hardes et ou le Capite. du Vaisseau prist congé de nous prenant la routte de la Nouvelle Angleterre pour ce rendre au Lieu de Sa Naissance a Boston Capitale de cette Province. Et nous louames des barques pour charger nos hardes et provisions pour les faire mener avec notre monde a une maison qu'on nous indiqua etre la plus proche chez un Nomé Hamstead galant home qui nous receust fort bien et nous accomoda tres bien tant pour les Vivres que les Voitures pour de la prendre notre Chemin par Terre en Caroline.

"A un honest homme il n'y avoit pas la matiere de hesiter et come par bonheur ma Reputation estoit assez bien etablie en Amerique et que mon dessein fist grand bruit, j'envoyay d'abord en Pensilvanie pour Provisions de farine ou par bonheur j'avois desia doné ordre depuis Londre par precaution et aprehension que peut etre les choses ne Seroient pas si bien etablies en Nord Caroline come on m'en faisoit croire: Je n'ay pas manqué d'envoyer aussi en Virginie et dans la Province meme pour me procurer les Provisions necessaires, mais tout cela traina si longtems que pendant ce tems ces nouveaux Colonistes furent obligé de vendre encore partis des hardes et marchandises (qu'ils avoient acheptée a Londre pour faire profiter le peu d'argent qu'ils avoient) pour ce procurer les vivres necessaires des habitants voisins pour ne pas mourir de faim.

12. Aussitot que nous fumes arrivéz a Sommertowne un Village aux frontieres de Virginie et Caroline une petite bande d'habitants de Nord Carolina me vinrent Saluer et moffrirent le Gouvernement _ _ _

13. Je repliquay, que quand bien j'estois revetus de cette dignité de Landgrave, que ie ne voullois pas me prevalloir presentement de ce Titre, Leurs remerciant civilement _ _ _

14. que ce seroit de mauvoise grace a moy de m'ingerer dans une affaire de semblable matiere;

15. Mais come ces gens qui estoient la plus grand partie des Noncomformistes, n'aymoient pas d'avoir un Si grand Toris pour Gouverneur ma reponce ne leur plust pas _ _ _

16. Je ne Scaurois assez exprimer l'Etat triste et deplorable dans laquell j'ay trouvé ces pauvres gens a mon arrivée, presque touts malades et dans l'extremité et le peu qui resterent bien portants desesperéz. Dieu le scait dans quell Labyrinthe voire danger de ma Vie, ie me suis trouvé alors; Je laisse a pencer le lecteur de quelle maniere ma petite Colonie Bernoise regarda dans ce jeu, qui jusques alors ne manquerent de rien leur Voyage ou passage ayant este heureux des le Commencement jusques a leurs arivée en Caroline: la Saison bone et belle, bien fournis de toutte provisions, bien ecquipes, bien placee au large sus le Vaisseau presentement de voir un Si triste Spectacle devant Eux ou maladies, disette et désespoir estoient dans l'extremite. Ce qui augmenta encore le mall est que ces pauvres Pallatins ayant employé le plus grand partie de leurs habits pour S'achepter de vivres dans la plus grande necessité, furent bien deconcertéz lors qu'ils virent que les directeurs Sus noméz, ayant la plus grand partie de leurs effects encore en mains, les retenoient, mais principalement un N. R. Sous pretexte de ce reserver une bone partie pour ces peines et frais, et quand ie demanday a faire Conte il me renvoya Si Souvant qu'a l'heure qu'il est le Conte n'est pas encore regelé, et cela luy fust bien facile accause des troubles survenus, il faut qu'il ce Soit bien accomode de ces fournitures des Palatins puis qu'avant qu'il eust ses Effects en main il vivoit petitement et quapres

il fist le gros Monsieur: Il garda Ses effects jusques a mon arivée at quand ie les voulu faire ammener a notre lieu de residence ie ne les pus avoir partie Seulement qu'a main armée et par force, meme ne les pus avoit touts quelle plainte que i'en fis au Gouvernement accause qu'il estoit de la Magistrature.

Ce qui fust cause de touts ces malheurs fust la mechante Conduite et infidelité dune partie des *Inspecteurs Superieurs* et inferieurs _ _ _

A marginal note to the words in italics is as follows—Dont le N. R. en fust aussi un que ie nomme pas accause de Son Parantage considerable.

17. Pendant que de mon Coté ie fis touts mes efforts pour etablir ma Colonie, come ie vien de dire, d'autre Coté on ecrivit a Monsieur Hyde en Virginie ou il avoit fait quelque sejours en attendent une meilleurs issue de Sa pretention, qui ne manqua pas de se rendre avec Sa Famille au plutost en Caroline Sur la Riviere de Chouan pres du Colonel Pollock, _ _ _

18. apres le repas aupres d'une bouteille de Vin de Madere nous vinmes a des discours bien Serieux, et come c'estoit luy qui (en vertu de mes Patentes et ordres des Lords Prop: me devoit pourvoir de touts les necessaires des revenus de la Province) me refusa tout, j'estois bien aise de luy en faire des reproches et luy repsenter aussi l'enormite de son procede Criminel, ce voyant convaincu, par tant de bones raisons, d'autre coté pour m'endormir affin que ie ne travaille pas trop contre luy il me promit, etc.

19. A quoy ie me resolus non Sans prendre, bien mes precautions, d'autant que iay eté menacé de meme que mes Colonistes, et le chemin n'estoit pas trop assuré estant eloigné de deux journées, ou il faloit descendre et passer des grandes Rivieres et des forests assez dangereuses.

20. Le malheur voulust que justement alors un Certain Personage mutin et turbulent nomé Richard Roach, ariva de Londre qui causa bien du desordre, Celuy estoit facteur d'un des Seigr. Prop: mais de la Secte des Trembleurs qui devoit venir en ces pays pour negotier,

21. ce qui fomenta la Rebellion et augumenta le troubles et nous fist bien da la peine:

22. 200

23. équipé et arméz d'environ 60 ou 80 homes,

24. quand nous observames ce manege nous mimes aussi en posture et descendimes dernier une haye vers le bord de la Riviere.

25. Parmy tout cela je fus obligé de prendre le presidial contre mon gré car la matiere etoit delicate et dangereuse

26. Et par advance on luy ecrivit une lettre pour luy comuniquer notre dessein qui par honesteté nous marqua un endroit et jour aux

frontieres de Virginie et Caroline, ayant Sans cela eu envie d'excercer Ses trouppes dans ce Voisinage.

27. Monsieur le Gouv de Virginie laissa ordre qu'on le luy feroit Scavoir a Williamsbourg lieu de la Residence, aussi tost que ie Serois arivé.

28. Il faloit dont chercher d'autres expedients, Et Mr. le Gouv: Spotswood pour luy avoir esté reccomande de la Reine et pour la premiere fois qu'il m'avoit vu auroit pourtant bien Souhaitté de me faire quelque plaisir et de ne me pas renvoyer Sans m'accorder quelque faveur: Il me demanda dont si j'avois quelque autre chose a luy proposer ou quelque expedient qui fust plus facile pour m'accorder. Voyant dont que ces Virginiens n'estoient pas disposé a notre Secours, peutetre tenant Eux memes un peu de cett Esprit libre et democratique, je m'advisay Si on ne trouveroit pas quelque Soldats de trouppe reglées, Je demanday dont Mr. le Gouv: puis qu'il estoit vice Admiral des Cotes de Virginie qu'il eust la bonté de nous envoyer un Vaisseau de Guerre bien cequipé, ce qu'il nous accorda:

29. Dans la Suitte du tems il fut relegé Sur une Isle eloignée pour Sa vie et y mourut.

30. A mon retour a News je fus bien Surpris de trouver tant de malades etmeme plusieurs de morts dont deux de mes Domestiques qu'on m'avoit ammené de Berne en estoit du nombre, c'estoit Sans doute la grande Chaleur quil fist ces 3 mois de Juin Juillet et ougst qui en furent cause nos gens venant d'un pays froid et de montagne n'ayant pas esté encore accoutumé a ces pays plats et cett air chaud; ils ne manquerent pourtant pas de Medecins et Chirurgiens qui en eurent soin, qui apres devinrent aussi Malades: mais la principale cause en estoit, qu'ils avoient negligé en mon absence mes ordres de Regime, les quells j'avois doné d'abord a mon arivée en Amerique lors que ie trouvay desia les Palatins Si malades, C'estoit par bon advis de persones qui avoient fait long Sejours en Caroline que ie leurs avois indiqué de ne pas trop boire d'eau crue et froide, mais de la cuire avec du Sasafras dont les bois en Sont touts plains et apres la laisser raffroidir et en boire tant quon voudra, ie m'en Servis le mattin avec un peu de Sucre a place de Thée ce qui me fist beaucoup de bien; J'ay observé aussi que ceux qui ce mettoient dabord au lict quand ils ce trouvaient malades S'en trouvoient bien mall et beaucoup en moururent: Il y regne en ce pays une certaine fievre, cett un tribut general qu'il faut que les Etranger payent au Comencement, et la guerison en est fort particuliere, Quand cette fiévre vous prend, le meilleur remede est au lieu de ce mettre au lict d'abord, il faut courir jusqua ce qu'on Sue de grosse goutte et qu'on tombe de lassitude meme il n'en faut pas rester la, mais ce relever et continuer jusqua ce qu'on n'en puisse

plus, j'en parle par experience, aussi ne l'ay ie eu que 3 Semaines au lieu que dautres ont trainé des années entieres, ce Sont enflés a la fin et en Sont mort: j'advertis icy les paresseux ce nest pas une maladie qui les accomode, les gens oisifs et paresseux y Sont presque toujours maladies, il y faut de l'exercice preuve qu'il est necessaire et bon, C'est que je fus atteint beaucoup de la goutte en Europe, et en ce pays j'en fus quitte p. quelques petites atteintes.

En ces Pays Les Chesnes rouges y Sont Si Savoureux, qu'en y faisant une petite ouverture d'une hasche il en Sort quantité de jus qui est un Vinaigre, mais il est pernicieux a la Santé, nos gens S'en servirent dans les grandes Chaleurs pour manger de la Salade et ne S'en trouverent pas bien. Il y avoit encore deux inconvenients lesquels il estoit necessaire de ce precautionier. Ce sont les Serpents et les ticks en francais Sourons. Il y croit un si merveilleux contrepoison et en assez grands abondance duquel il ne faut pas manquer de ce pourvoir il y en 3 Sortes, il en a d'une sorte qui a une vertu particuliere si on porte la racine avec Soy on peut dormir librement Sous un arbre aucun Serpent ne Saprochera, les Indiens Sen Servent d'ordinaire, Si on pile cette racine et qu'on en done dans une tasse ou pot d'eau fresche a l'animal qui est mordu d'un Serpent il en revient et se guerit en peu de tems; j'en ay fait l'epreuve Sur un de mes chevaux et sur mon Chien qui en ont esté gueris. Les Surons incomodent les gens jusques a doner la fievre, on croit que c'est une rosée corrompues qui Sattache a l'herbe cependant on n'en appercoit que la ou il y a du betail, pour les femmes elles ont plus de peine a s'en garantir, les homes en portant de bas de peau en Sont quittes, les paysants qui ont la peau plus dure ne s'en Sentent pas tant cela ne dure que certain mois de lannée.

Chacun de mes Colonistes s'accomodant le mieux posible et selon Sa capacité et adresse, Il sagissoit de n'en pas faire moins en Ville, Suivant la permission que j'avois et les privileges ie choises dont une pointe de Terre entre Trent et Neuws River, Endroit ou il y avoit un Roytelet Indien avec ses gens en une 20e. de familles le lieu S'appeloit Chatouka. Il en est fait mention pag. 6. Nous l'avons acheté Si cher accause de la Situation advantageuse, Il sagissoit dont d'avoir ma place libre L'arpenteur gen: Lawson qui L'avoit vendue voulloit que j'en dechassasse les Sauvages mais ie n'en voulus rien faire, bien loin de cela je me Suis mis aux Eux acheptant d'un de ses Indiens une petite etendue de Terre ou je bastis, ma Cabane en attendant mieux, et fis meme une espece d'aillance avec ce Roitelet nomé Taylor et Son monde, cela ce fist Solennellemt. quelque peu de tems apres voyant que ces Sauvages ne pouvoient s'accorder avec mes gens ny les miens avec les Sauvages ie m'advisay de leur proposer d'achepter encore une fois cette terre d'Eux et de leur assigner un autre endroit ou ils pourroient demeurer aussi comodement et sur la meme Riviere pas loin de ce lieu, ils commencerent de gouter mes raisons et on tient pour cela une assemblee Solenelle. Puis que je Suis en mattiere de ces Sauvages avant que parler du plan et fondation de la Villette de Neuberne Je continue ou j'en Suis resté avec les Indiens et diray aussi quelque chose de leur Culte et de ce qui s'est passé.

Nous convinmes dont d'un jour pour faire notre accord le Roitelet ce mist sur Son propre mais d'une maniere Si crotesque qu'il aproissoit plutost en Singe, qu'un home il vint avec 17 Peres de famille on ce mist en pleine campagne en rond a Terre, Moy is mis aussi tout ce qui pust briller le plus me fist apporter une chaise, et prenant a mon Costé un truchement un Sauvage qui parlait bon anglais, i'entamy la matiere et le Sujet de cette assemblée apres leurs avoir repsenté mes raisons ils dirent aussi les leurs, et a parler sans partialité ils avoient dans leurs oppositions des meilleures raisons que moy: Cependant on en vint en une bone conclusion. Je leurs fis quelque petits presants de petite valeur, et pour pris d'achapt ie livray pour ce Terrain de question au Roy deux bouteilles de poudre soit 4 livre, une bouteille contenant 2 liv: de poudre et avec cela 1000 gros graines de dragée de plomb; a Chacun des assesseurs une bouteille de poudre et 500 grains de plomb. (marginal note. de la dragée un peu grosse.) apres ie les fis bien boire de Rum, eaux de vie distilée de La lie de Sucre liquer ordinaire de ces pays: et voicy la pacte faitte.

Cette Feste fust pourtant troublée par la brutalité de M. M: qui pour avoir bu copieusement avec quelques Anglais qui vinrent disner avec moy, perdit le Respect et vint insulter ces pauvres Indiens, prist le Chappeau du Roy et le jetta Si loin qu'il pust, et entra dans le Cercle prenant l'un de leurs orateurs qui parla un peu trop contre notre procedé par le bras et le Sortit du Cercle luy donant quelque coup. Je fis d'abord prendre ce Mr. si touffus par quelques uns de mes Domestiques pour le mener a la maison ou ces anglois invitéz luy tinrent compagnie l'amusant le mieux qu'ils purent. Le lecteur ce peut aisement imaginer quell effect aura produit un procedé Semblable, aussi le Roy s'en plaignant me dit si les Chréstiens faisoient la paix et leur alliance de cette maniere qu'il ne voulloit rien avoir affaire avec Eux: Je ne manquay pas de luy repliquer qu'il ne faloit pas faire attention a ce qu'un brutal gouverné par la force des liquers avoit fait, que ie l'en reprimanderois fortement, memement que ie l'envoyeray loin d'icy, qu'il ne les insultera plus, et, qu'ils ce devoient tenir a moy, qu'ils pouvoient Sassurer que jamais je ne leur ferois aucun mal pendant qu'ils voissineroient bien avec moy: Content de ma reponce et de mon meilleur traitemt. ils S'en retournerent chez Eux. Ce M: quoy que depuis un peu de Someil qui devoit luy faire passer les vapeurs, il se fust tranquilisé ie ne Scay quelle mouche le piqua, apres les 10. heures du Soir que ie fus couché croyant tout en repos, il ce leva et sen allast vers les Cabines des Indiens trouvant encore L'orateur Ind: debout il le traitta fort mall, mais d'abord le Roy avec quelque Indiens mirent le hola: et j'admire la patience et discretion de Ces Sauvages, de n'avoir a leur tour rossé le barbare Chretien. Le Lendemain le Roy avec Ses Conseilliers ne manquerent pas de ce plaindre aupres de moy, du mauvais traittement reitere de ce brutal pis qu'un Sauvage avec menaces qui Sils estoient insultéz plus outre qu'ils payeroient de meme monoye; J'eus assez de peine a les apaiser, les fis encore bien boire et les renvoyay avec assurance que ie ferois partir cett home turbulent, et qu'ils ne Seroient plus insultéz.

Apres le depart de ces Indiens, trouvant mon home dans Son meilleur Sens ie luy parlay Serieusement d'affaires, Il sera parlé de ce personage bien Souvent dans cette Relation mais accause de Ces Parents qui sont de distinction de qualité et de merité j'en ay de la Consideration, et ie ne le nome pas ne le denotant que par deux M. M: de 8 associez que nous estions il estoit l'un mais a notre perte a ma Ruine et plusieurs autre: Le Bon Dieu le Convertisse et luy donc a Connaitre tant de mall qu'il a Causé. L'arpenteur gener: a esté punis par une terrible execution des Sauvages p. ses Crimes et mauvaise foy: Si celuy ne ce convertit il pourroit lui bien arriver la meme Chose, ne vivant pas mieux quun barbare il pourrait bien etre chatié par les barbares. (marginal note. est mort parmis les Indiens.) Mall Content de luy, j'ay cherché des expedients pour L'envoyer autrepart, Il ce mist dont en chemin pour arpenter les Terres le long de la Riviere de Weetock et pour cela ie luy fournis tout le necessaire a Son retour il ariva un de ses vieux Camerades de Pensilvanie dans une Chaloupe et un autre bon drole avec luy, Entre Eux 3 le partis fust pris de faire un tour vers Cap Fear et d'arpenter des Terres le long de cette Riviere nomée autrement Clarendon River: Et pour cela ils firent des provisions de bouche et des marchandises tant qu'ils ne m'en resta presque plus rien cependant ils firent une vie de couchant, et des debauches outrées, ce manege ne me plaisant pas jy fis mes Reflexions, et un mattin avant qu'ils eussent dejeunéz je leurs repsentay que de la maniere qu'ils s'y prennoient ie voyais qu'ils avoient plutost envie de ce bien divertir que pour faire une besogne necessaire et profitable que j'avois besoin de ses marchandises pour Subvenir a ma nécessité et celle de la Colonie, que nous avions pour le psent asséz de Terres, qu'ils faloit voir pmierement coment reussiroient Nos Colonistes, que puis qu'il falait des grandes Sommes pour Soutenir une Enterprise de cette importance il faloit plutost songer a ce procurer de quoy pour Subsister, que de faire des depenses inutiles et pas encore necessaires, etc. ma proposition deconcerta ces bons debauchéz, et ils firent tout leur possible pour me desbuser mais ma resolution fust ferme, et ie representay a M. M: Quayant tant fait de bruit de ses mines d'argent que meme on en estoit venue a des Traittés authentiques tant avec Mons. Penn Proprietaire de Pensilvanie qu'avec J: Justus Albrecht Chef des Mineurs d'Allemagne, qui n'attendoit que nos ordres pour les faire venir, que cestoit la ou il faloit travailler, qu'ils devoient dont aller a Philadelphia (Cap: de Pensilvanie) pour notifier a M. le Gouverneur mon arivée en ces Pays, luy remettre notre Patente de M. le Prop: Penn et luy denoncer qu'estions en dessein daller visiter les mines de questions puis quelles devoient etre Situées sur Sa Jurisdiction, et que pour cela il nous donne l'assistance necessaire, qu'apres que le tout seroit prest et en bonne ordre assuré contre les Indiens, que ie my transporterois, etc. Ces deux droles cy devant Compagnions de M. M: lors qu'ils allast avec plusieurs autres a la decouverte de la mine de question gouterent me proposition et encouragerent M. M: a cette expedition, il y dona a la fin la main, et partirent fournis des memes provisiones qu'ils avoient prises pour ce petit voyage de Clarendon R. Quelques iours apres leur depart Le Roy avec quelques de ces Ind: me vint trouver, ne Sachant pas que pour d'autres Sujets i'avois fait partir M. M.: temoigna bien de la joye de ce que je les avois delivré de cett home dangereux, Et cett affaire me fist beaucoup de bien dans ma Captivité de Cathechna ou ce Roitelet parla en ma faveur.

La dessus nous nous promimes reciproquement bon Voisinage, et les Indiens quitterent bientost apres cett endroit pour ce placer au lieu assigné pas loin dela. Quelque tems apres je fis un tour a Cor Towne a 10 milles de Chatouka, ou ie fis assembler les Sauvages pour leur proposer que me trouvant dans leur Voisinage que ie pretendois de vivre bien avec Eux avec offre de mes Services cela fust bien receu, mais Come il y avoit deux Chefs dans le Vilage l'un nomé Cor Tom et l'autre Sam, le premier Enemy des Anglois et L'autre Amy, qui fust absent, ie ny pus pas tout a fait regler ce que j'aurois bien Souhaitté, Cependant assez content de leur acceuil ie m'en retournay le meme jour chez moy, Ce village de Cor est tres bien Situé, il y a un air plus frais, borde de la Riviere de Neuws. Si ces Indiens auroient voulu changer de place j'en aurois eu bien envie.

Ayant eu jusques icy des occupations plus pressantes Je n'avois pas fait encore grand chose pour l'Etablissment de la Ville, me trouvant un peu desoeuvré je pris l'arpenteur general avec moy et son Clerc pour faire le Plan de cette nouvelle Ville. Come en Amerique on n'ayme pas etre logéz a letroit affin de jouir d'un air plus pur j'ordonay dont les rues bien larges et les maisons bien Separées l'une de l'autre, ie marquay 3 arpents de Terre pour chaque famille, pour maison grange, Jardin, Verger, chenevier bassecour et autres places, je partagay la Ville en Croix et au millieu ie destinay l'Eglise, l'une des rues principales tendoit des le bord de la Neuws droit avant dans les bois et l'autre rue principale croisoit depuis la Riviere de Trent jusques a la Riviere de Neuws: apres cela nous plantames des picquets pour marquer les maisons et faire les deux premieres rues Capitales le long et au bord des deux Rivieres et la miene estoit Située a la pointe. Et come les artisans Sont mieux en Ville quaux Plantations, le leurs donay quelques privileges au lieu que les habitants ou nouveau bourgois estoient obligéz de me payer annuellement pour mon droit et les 3 arpents de Terre un Escublanc, les gens de mettier estoient francs pour 10 Ans les autres Seullement pour 3. J'eus d'abord un bon nombre qui Comencerent a coupper du bois pour faire leurs maisons, Il y eust deux Charpentiers un masson, deux menuisiers un Serrurier, un mareshal Un ou deux Cordoniers, un tailleur, un munier, un armurier, un boucher, un tisseran, un tourneur un Sellier, un vitrier, un potier et tuiller, faiseurs de moulin deux, Un medecin, un chirurgien un maitre d'ecole. il y avoit encore ça et la aux Plantations encore quelques artisans, Il ne manquoit encore qu'un ministre et en attendant celuy que ie faisois venir d'Allemagne, ie fis la *fonction* (marginal note. lisant a la maniere Angloise les Sermons.) ayant meme pmission de Mr. l'Eveque de Londre de marier et babtiser, pour Comunier j'en fis venir un ministre l'an une fois de Virginie. Il vint de Virginie un ministre qui preschoit en Anglois et Francois et je l'avois engagé pour ma Colonie estant tres Content de venir moyennant 50£ St. que la Chambre de Londre de propagande Fide, ordone en Semblable cas, et une discretion raisonable que la Colonie en general feroit.

Apres qu'une partie de ses artisants eurent leurs Charpante preste et qu'ils s'etoient au moins mis a Couvert en attendant mieux et que jeus aussi accomodé un peu mieux le mienne. Il S'agissoit de doner un nom a la Ville ce que nous fimes en grande Solennité, et nous joignimes au nom de Neuws celuy de Berne, ainsi la Ville fust babtisée Neuberne. Pour le Comencement il ce devoit etablir Seulement dun mois une fois un marcher et une fois L'an une foire. Enfin il y eut plusieurs autres reglements; Quand Mr. le Gouverneur le Conseil et beaucoup de Planteurs de Caroline eurent advis de notre etablissement ils prirent non Seulement touts envie de Sy loger mais effectivement ce firent marquer des lots, cela veu dire des places limitées.

Et ils avoient raison, Car dans toutte la Province il n'y avoit pas un Seul endroit de Seureté, ils n'avoient ny provision general de bouche ny de munitions de Guere, ny d'armes chacun estoit pour ainsi dire abandoné a la geule du loup Si les Sauvages estoient des gens un peu mieux faits a la guere ils auroient pu detruire les habitants de cette Province quand ils auroient voulu. Si le Bon Dieu n'auroit pas mieux veilléz ces Carolins legers, il n'en Seroit pas resté un ame.

Il y eust beaucoup de psones de Pensilvanie et plusieurs de Virginie qui prirent de lots, tellement qu'en peu d'anées on auroit une jolie Ville j'en y auroit transferé le Gouvernement d'autant que Little River, ou La Grande assemblée ce tenoit, il n'y avoit que quelque peu de maisons dispersees on estoit fort Mall et point en Seureté.

Pendant que je m'occupois a etablir de mon possible les affaires de ma Colonie, ayant meme pour la Seureté de la Colonie d'en haut vers mellcreeck fait construire une redoute pour tenir les Indiens en bride de ce Coté: Jai fait aussi plusieurs reglements et ordonances tant pour le militaire que pour le Civil, mes provisions de Vivres comencerent a diminuer et les marchandises qui Sont en ces pays come de l'argent Content aussi; tellement que ie comencois a faire de reflexions bien Serieuses Sur mon entreprises, bien loin de recevoir aucune assistance et Secours soit de la Province ou des Lords Prop: Soit de mon Pays et de ma Société au contraire il arivoit des billets de change protestéz. dans cette mauvise Situation d'affaires, ie ni Scavez plus ou me tourner, ayant desia ecrit plusieurs fois au pays et a la Societé pour du Secours n'estant Suivis aucune reponce, et de crainte quon ne prenne mes informations que pour des Contes, ie m'advisay de Sonder Si ie ne trouverois pas quelqu'un de la Colonie qui degouté de Ses miseres eust envie d'aller au pays, j'en trouvay un, qui estoit justement un psonage que deux membres de la Societé avoient choisis pour Soigner leur Plantation, mais qui voyant que ces Messieurs ne fournissaient pas de quoy pour Soutenir prist la resolution de S'en retourner chez luy me promettant meme qu'il ne m'en couteroit que les frais iusques en Pensilvanie je luy livray pour cela 5 Guines, et un petit billet de change pour en recevoir autant a Philadelphia, Mais le drille quand il fust arivé a Philadelphia ne ce Contenta pas de ci peu, et trouva un marchant assez facile qui Sans mes ordres, Sur mon Credit luy advanca plus qu'il ne faloit a Londre il en fis de meme, et a Amsterdam aussi ainsi plus outre jusques a Berne, et nos Messieurs assossiez bien Surpris de voir ce visage et bien plus de Son effronterie et grand Conte. Cependant avant le depart de ce mechant Pellerin, j'avois fait et remis un plan du Terrein et des Rivieres ou j'avois placé ma Colonie et un memoire de ce que j'avois fait pour cett etablissement aussi bien que les frais que j'ay eu a ce Sujet avec un Conte de tout, avec une lettre preparée pour les encourager a me Soutenir en cette Enterprise la quelle quoique tres difficile au Comencement mais en ayant Surmonté le plus dangereux il y avoit belle apparence de reussir remettant le reste a La relation qu'il feroit de bouche principalement concernant la beaute et bonté du pays: Ce qu'il a bien remis, et Suivant que j'en Suis informé il avoit rien obmis de ce qui pouvoit tendre a ladvantage de cett Etablissement, et Sans doute j'aurois obtenu le Secours necessaire Sans le malheur qui m'est arivé peu de tems apres, come il est a voir Si apres dans ma Relation.

Dans cett esperance d'un prompt Secours: et Suffisant voyant que les vivres pour la Colonie me coutoient plus de voiture que d'achapt par advis de bons amis et psones entendues j'acheptay une Sloop, un batiment propre pour S'en Servir sur mers et dans les rivieres, avec une barque qui ne put Servir que dans les Rivieres, cecy pour lettres de change; Ces batiments me firent grand Service aussi bien qu'a la Province, comme on verra cy apres et ie fus meme contraint a cett expedient accause qu'il y avoit fort peu de ces batiments dans la Province et pendant cette guere Civile ils furent touts engagéz ne pouvant en avoir ny pour or ny pour argent, cependant il faloit vivre. Il y avoit en ce tems une Si grande disette de Sell accause que les estrangers n'osient se hazarder pendant ces troubles, pour en amener, que ie fus d'obligation d'envoyer ma Sloop aux Isles de Barmuides pour querir du Sell, et come il falut quelques chose pour echanger j'obtins de Mr. le Gouverneur Hyde pmission d'amasser des *graines* (marginal note. cet icy du blé Lambard) ca et la dans la Province Sur le Comte des Lords prop: et le Sien, mais le malheur voulust que par un grand orage ces bleds furent moulléz, ce qui gasta mon marché et le profit de ce voyage fust fort petit, cependant le Sell que j'eus de Barmuides me fist beaucoup de bien et a mes voisins, et fus bien content que pour la premiere fois mon batiment fust Sauvé et de retour en bon etat hormis les voiles qui estoient bien dechirez et quelques cordages gatéz, il avoit esté absent si longtems que je croyois tout perdu, cela me devoit bien mettre en peine mayant couté 300 £. Sterlins; mais le plus qui me mettoit en peine c'est l'equipage, j'y avois de tres bon mattelots. Dans l'incertitude de ce que dessus pour me desennuyer, je suis allé quelque fois arpenter des Terres et ie ne peu de moins que de raconter icy une advanture assez particuliere qui preceda celle de Catechna ou ie fus pris captif par les Sauvages.

Un jour que j'alois arpenter des Terres, Le tems estant changé froyant une grande tempéte, n'aymant pas coucher dans les bois, ie laissay mes arpenteurs et pris le chemin de la maison avec mon Valet, la grande haste fist que ie pris un Sentier pour l'autre, qui fust si long que la nuict me Surprist, et ie tombay justemt. parmy les Indiens qui delogerent de lendroit ou ie mestois placez a Chatoucka psentemt. Neuberne. Je laisse a pencer le lecteur dans quelle apprehension j'estois et si les Sauvages n'avoient pas beau jeu de ce venger contre moy Si ie les avois maltraitté et que je n'eus pas bien vecu avec Eux; n'ayant rien eu a me reprocher a cett egard, ie me rassuray un peu et par bonheur ils me receurent tres bien; Ce qui devoit augmenter mon apprehension estoit, qu'un des Chefs des Sauvages de Core qui n'estoit pas bien porté pour les Anglois ce trouva justement en Visite aupres du Roy Taylor, Cependant j'en fus quitte pour une petite peur: Come j'estoit fort alteré pour avoir parcouru les bois toutte la journeé, de crainte que buvant d'eau elle ne me fist du mall, par surcroy d'honesteté ils envoyerent aupres d'une femme malade qui avoit du Cidre pour m'en faire avoir, ie ne l'apris que quelques jours apres sans cela ie n'en aurois pas tant bu et ie me Serois fait de la peine de priver cette pauvre malade d'une boisson dont elle en Servoit plutost pour un cordial, que pour contenter Son palais. Pour mon Souper le Roy me fist present d'une quartier de Venaison, mais ie me passay ce Soir de Soupper, fatigue de ma Course ie fus bien aise de me reposer, ie fis dont tendre par mon Valet Ma petite tente pour y coucher mais ie ne dormis guere: Ils firent toutte la nuict des feus de joye dansant et chantant a l'entour faisent quelque fois des Corus et des cris qu'on auroit chassés les loups du bois, musique different de celle d'orphée qui apprivoisoit les bestes les plus farouches. Le Lendemain de bon mattin le Roy me dona pour convoy deux Sauvages qui me mirent en bon chemin et m'accompagnerent a la maison apres leurs avoir doné bien a manger et a boire ie leurs remis un petit present, pour le Roy Taylor, et au place de Son Sydre ie luy envoyay deux bouteilles de Rum ou brantevin de Sucre pour en faire part aussi a la pauvre Malade cordial bien meilleur, ce qui fust tres bien receu a ce que j'ay apris. Ce meme Roy ne contribua pas peu a mon elargissement apres l'assistance Divine, lors que ie fus condamné a mort par les Sauvages a Catechna.

31. n'ayant ny lieu de retraitte, ny de provisions soit de vivres Soit d'armes Soit de munitions, ne les encouraga pas peu au dessein projecté.

32. Celuy dabord apres la Soufferte qui ne consistoit qua Sier des tronces d'arbres pour la Scurté publique durant un Seul jour dont la peine n'aprochoit pas le Crime, passa la riviere pour rencontrer les Indiens, etc.

33. Les Indiens qui avoient de la peine a croire une Semblable pfidie de moy, ce doutterent de ce que le drole avoit rapporté, hazarderent un de leur trouppe qui Sceut bien l'anglois ce fust meme mon

interprete de Catechna, pour l'envoyer aupres de nous quoy qu'avec beaucoup d'apprehension d'etre pris et en danger de vie. Sur quoy il ariva une assez plaisante advanture; C'est Indien ayant passé deça la riviere, veilla l'occasion de parler a quelqu'un de mes gens, pour Scavoir la realité de ce fait, quand l'Indien voulust aprocher un de mes Colonistes le pauvre home fust tellement epouvanté qu'il vient tout essouflé mettre l'allarme dans mon quartier et m'advertit qu'il avoit vu un Sauvage qui avoit voullu S'approcher, que Sans doute les autres n'estoient pas loin, ce qui en effect m'allarma un peu et ie mis mon monde en posture. Cependant ie m'imaginay pourtant que les Indiens impatients d'avoir leur Rantion pouvoient avoir envoyé quelqu'un pour voir a quoy on en estoit: J'ordonay dont au meme home qui avoit pris l'epouvante de ce remettre au meme endroit Seul, que de loin ie posteray des gens pour le deffendre en cas de danger, ce qu'on fist, peu de tems apres, le Sauvage ne manqua pas de ce montrer et S'approchant luy fist Signe, qu'il ne devoit rien craindre, notre home faisant le meme Signe a L'autre ils S'approcherent a la fin et s'aboucherent: Ils vinrent dont sur le Chapitre du marschal qui avoit parle contre moy, Sans pourtant que jamais le Sauvage voullut le nomer, mais il en parla bien d'une maniere qu'on pouvoit diviner qui s'etoit: Notre home qui avoit Son Instruction representa que les Sauvages estoient mall informé, et que S'estoit un malhonest home qui avoit fait ses Scinistres rapports, que ie gardois une exacte Neutralité bien loin, que les Anglois n'estoient pas contents de moy, en ce que ie n'avois voulu me joindre a Eux, me contentant de garder mon poste, insinuant plus outre que les Sauvages devoient ramener les Palatins prisoniers S'ils voulloient avoir leur Rantion, et plusieurs autres choses que notre home eust ordre de dire: apres Sans faire beaucoup de bruit il laissa aller L'Indien luy insinuant qua l'advenir aucun des Sauvages ne devoit plus venir par icy, que S'ils avoient a dire quelque chose, qu'ils devoient faire un feu vis a vis de notre quartier, qu'apres i'envoyeray quelqu'un a batteau pour leur parler, mais qu'on leur parleroit que Sur l'eau, et Eux les Indiens devoient venir en contre et pas plus de deux a la fois.

34. Le Susnomé Brice qui auroit bien eu envie d'avoir ses utensils principalement ceux qui Servoient pour raccommoder les fusils, s'advisa de les ravoir par finesse, S'il ne les pourroit avoir autrement, resolu meme de les prendre par force,

35. (pretextant que S'est pour la defence et service de la Patrie)

36. petit fort

37. Ce qui auroit esté fait si j'avois eu des temoins Suffisants contre luy.

38. marquées d'une marque —: ce qui Signifie News

39. (qui proprement ne furent pas en action contre Eux mais Soubconéz d'etre du partis de leurs Ennemys)

40. Quand l'Assemblée Generale fust convoquée ie ne manquay pas de my transporter: Premiermt. ie me presentay dans la maison haute consistant de Monsr. Le Gouverneur des Representants des Lords Proprietaires des Conseillers, et Cassiques ou Gentilshomes de la Province. Apres que j'eus fait mes plaintes et m'etre justifié de ma Conduite ie me transportay a la maison Basse, Consistant en Deputéz des Communes, apres un petit discours au Sujet de question, ie demanday apres Ses Calomniateurs qui avoit pris information Secrette Sans aucun ordre de Magistrature, Voulus qu'on me les nommast et qu'on me produisit, ou l'original ou copie des 20 ou 23 articuls qu'on avoit formé contre moy, Je voullois absolument que L'accusateur ce produisit, affin que ie le puisse convaincre de fausseté, m'innocenter et justifier en due forme, mais psone n'osa ny ce produire ny Seulement ouvrir la bouche au Sujet de ces fausses accusations.

Sans doute Ses faux accusateurs eurent vent et aprirent de quelle maniere ie m'estois justifie aupres de Mrs. les Gouverns. de Virginie et Caroline, et voyant que ma conduite fust aprouvée ils n'oserent poursuivre leurs accusations de crainte de Succomber. Cependant parmy tout cela mon honner et Reputation Souffrit beaucoup et meme ie fus en danger de ma vie, d'autant que parmy les Palatins de mes Ressortissants meme il s'estoit trouvé de faux temoins que faire dont dans cette malheureux Situation d'affaires? Voyant que psone ne voulust parler, je commencay moy meme a nomer les accusateurs fulminant contre Eux, et demandant Justice; Mais helas! dans un Gouvernment Si confus ou le premier feu de Sedition ne fust pas encore tout a fait eteint, une bone partie des membres de ce Parlement gardant encore des rancunes Secrettes et qui estoient bons amis de ce Brice qui en fust aussi, et qui aurroient eté bien aise que quelque affront m'ariva, pour avoir tenu le partis de Mons. le Gouverneur: d'autre coté embarassés de cette Guerre Indiene, ie ne pus avoir auccune autre Satisfaction, Si non que de voir un profond Silence. Sur ma representation et defence. Il est vray que Mr. le Gouvern: et la maison Haute me firent des excuses et un compliment, me r'envoyant au reste a demander Justice Selon les formalitéz usiteés en tems de Paix contre mes Calomniateurs: Songées mon cher lecteur combien de tems il auroit falu attendre pour avoir ma due Satisfaction, puis qu'a l'heure qu'il est la Guerre Indiene n'est pas finie. Marginal note A. 1716—.

41. Ces pauvres gens qui ne Sentoient que trop les effets de l'extremité dans la quelle nous fimes alors, (n'estant resté de nos provisions qu'une mesure de bled, ayant soutenu 22 Semaines sans aucun Secours

de quoy que ce Soit du Gouvernement ou de la Province) n'eurent pas de la peine de consentir a ce que ie leurs proposoit.

42. Un Planteur Anglois de la Secte des trembleurs,

43. Le Gouvernement de Sud Caroline envoya dont 800 Sauvages tributaires, avec 50 Anglois Carolins, sous Comendement de Colonel Barnwell

44. brancar.

45. L'endroit de notre Rendevous fust chez un tres galant home le Sieur Rosier, pres de la chutte de Potomack ou quelques messieurs de Pensilvanie qui estoient aussi interesséz avec nous, m'estoient venus a rencontre, dans l'esperance de voir une fois ce qu'en Seroit de cette belle et riche mine d'argent dont le Sieur M: en fist tant bruit, et a quelle recherche ils avoient desia fournis tant d'argent. Nous estant tenu assez longtems a cett endroit Sans aprendre aucune nouvelle ny du Sr. M. ny de la Colonie qu'attendions de jour a autre avec impatience; Les demarches si etranges de ce M. nous firent presque douter et pas Sans raison de la realité de ses advances. C'est pourquoy nous primes la resolution d'aller nous memes visiter l'endroit des mines, dont il nous avoit doné un plan: Nous preparames dont en meilleure forme pour ce Voyage quoy que bien dangereux; Et come j'avois formé ce dessein desia avant que j'eusse eté advertis de ce rendevous, ie pris mes precautions, communiquant mon dessein a Mons: le Gouver. de Virginie qui me dona des Patentes, mememant publia des Mandats par lesquels il ordona qu'a ma premiere recherche ou Sur les premiers advis des gardes frontieres devoient me Suivre et m'accompagner. Quand nous vinmes a un petit village nomé Canavest endroit enchanté et bien plaisant, environ 40 miles au dessus la Chute de Potomack nous trouvames la un trouppeau de Sauvages etablis, et principalement un francois de Canada, nomé Martin Charetier qui avoit epousé une Indienne ou Sauvage, qui etoit en grand Credit parmy les Sauvages riere Pensilvanie et Maryland, et Sur les beaux advancéz du Sr. M. sy estoit placé, quittant pour ce Suject son endroit ou il fust bien etablis en Pensilvanie. Ce meme Martin Charetier avoit aussi fait le Voyage de Senantona pour la recherche des Mines avec le Sr. M. et y contribua une bone Some d'argent; Cett home nous advertit que les Indiens qui estoient dans le Voisinage de cette Montagne de S: ou devoient etre les mines, estoient fort allarméz de cette Guerre qu'avions avec les Tuscoruros, que nous ne devions pas nous hazarder dans un Voyage Si dangereux Sans necessité, a quoy nous fimes attention remettant ce partis pour une occasion et tems plus assuré. Cependant nous fimes une alliance avec ses Indiens de Canavest come tres necessaire, tant par raport des Mines qu'esperions trouver par la aussi bien qu'accause de l'Etablissement qu'avions resolu de faire en

Ses endroits de notre petite Colonie Bernoise qu'attendions. Apres cela nous visitames ses beaux endroits du Pays, ses Isles enchantées Sur la Riviere de Potomack au dessus la Chutte: Et dela a notre retour nous allames sur une montagne haute seule au millieu d'un vaste pays plat, nomé accause de sa forme Sugarlove qui veut dire en francais pain de Sucre, prenant avec nous un arpenteur: Le susdit Martin Charetier et quelques Sauvages. Des cette montagne nous vimes une grande etendue de Pays partie de Virginie, Maryland, Pensylvanie, et Caroline, nous Servant du compas, nous fimes un plan, et observames particulierement la montagne de Senantona ou devoient etre les mines, trouvames que cette montagne etoit située riere Virginie et non riere Pensilvanie come on nous en avoit doné le Plan, et par hazard deux de ces Sauvages connaissant la Situation de cette Montagne, nous dirent qu'ils avaient desia rodé par la, qu'ils avaient presque visité touts les coins de cette Montagne mais qu'ils navoient trouvé aucun Mineral et que notre plan n'estoit pas juste de quoy nous fumes bien Surpris. Nous decouvrimes de cette hauteur trois chenes de Montagnes toujours une plus haute que l'autre, un peu eloignées, et des tres beau Valons entre les premieres; Apres que fumes redescendus de cette Montagne ou il y eust au bas une tres belle et bone fontaine et bon terrein, nous allames coucher chez ce Martin Charetier ou nous fumes logéz et traittéz a l'indiene: Le jour apres nous partimes pour nous en retourner, nous descendimes la Riviere a quell sujet Les Indiens nous firent un petit batteau d'ecorce d'arbre a moins d'une demie journée d'une adresse merveilleuse, nous y entrames 5 de nous et deux Sauvages, qui conduisoient le navet, nous y mimes encore notre bagage c'estoit un charme de voir en descendant le beau pays a cotés et les jolies isles, mais quand nous vinmes aupres d'un grand Roc au meilleu de la Riviere guere loin de la chutte come est a voir dans le plan No. 6. nous trouvames le passage dangereux (car a lentour de ce roc qui est presque une petite montagne ou il y a une jolie plaine dessus ou meme il y demeuroit un Indien) il y a encore quantité de petit rocs et grosses pieres ce qu'il fait que les passages sont rapides etroits et mechants; Je ne voulus pas y descendre et sortimes touts, hormis Mr. Rosier qui connoissant l'adresse des Indiens l'hazarda, quand nous vimes de loin quels tours quil falut faire, de quelle adresse inexprimable il falut conduire ce canon ou navet, nous crumes quasi qu'il y avait de la magie dans le fait, et nous fumes bien aise detre dehors, principalemt. quand nous entendimes chanter les Indiens lors qu'ils passerent d'une grande rapidité, hurtant presque a une grosse piere ou roche, cela fist pourtant prier mon bon Sr. Rosier tant hardis qu'il put etre: A une 4d. de lieu de dela ce mechant passages ils s'arreterent et nous rentrames au batteau, le bon home

Rosier encore tout pasle de peur nous assura bien qu'il ne Seroit plus si temeraire, Nous descendimes de la fort bien et doucement la Riviere, jusques a la Chutte, a un 4d de lieu de ça nous Sortimes les valets ayant amené la nos cheveaux. cependant avant que de monter a cheval nous regardames come les Indiens portoient leur navet Sur les epaules dans le bois pour le raccommoder, s'estant bien gardé de nous dire que le bout avoit esté gaté en hurtant contre une roche, il falut raccourcir le navet en coupant ce bout, apres l'avoir bien r'accomodé les Indiens le rapporterent a la Riviere, et furent assez temeraires que de descendre le Saut ou la grande chutte de Potomack, ils passerent a leur dire heureusement, mais pourtant ils nous mirent bien en peine en ce quils tarderent beaucoup avant que de nous joindre chez Mons. Rosier ou nous logames: Je restay encore quelque tems chez ce mons. y attendant toujours mon Peuple de Caroline, le reste de la Compagnie reprirent le Chemin de Pensilvanie, mal Satisfait des tergiversations de M. M. et de Son etrange conduite.

Il est a remarquer icy que le Sr. M. que ie nomme pas icy par des bones considerations, bien a dupé du monde par ses belles Relations et psuasions d'avoir trouvé des mines si riches, et Si jay doné aussi dans le panneau, il estoit facile de m'atraper estant etranger dan ces Pays, mon fondement fust 1. que ie croyais un home de sa qualité et encore compatriot, incapable de Semblables tours. 2. le mineral qu'il avoit montré, ayant esté prouvé fust trouvé bien bon. 3. Les serments quil fist. 4. Les Patents qu'il demandoit a la Reine d'Angleterre pour ce fait, un trait bien hardis. 5. puis que tant de psones de Pensilvanie et d'autre Provinces avait fait le voyage tout ouvertement avec pmission des Gouverneurs voisins pour la decouverte de ses mines il paraissoit quelque chose de reel dans le fait. 6. Entre autres il sy etoient interessé, un marchand de Pensilvanie bien rusé et pas jeune, encore un habile orfeuvre et d'autres psone qui devoient bien connoitre le Terrein par la, Voyant que ceux cy habiles gens habitants dans ces Pays des leurs jeunesse meme, quelques uns natifs dans ces Lieux y hazardoient des Somes considerables, ie ne pouvois m'imaginer qu'ils n'eussent pas pris touttes leurs Scuretéz et pcautions. 7. Nous fimes un traitté formel avec des mineurs d'Allemagne, pour acheminer le tout le Sr. M. fist un Voyage en Hollande pour s'entreparler avec le Chef des mineurs qui devoit preparer touts les ustensils et choses necessaires pour cette Entreprise, qui coustaient pres de 1000 Escubl. 8. Monsieur Penn Proprietaire de Pensilvanie fist un Traitté avec nous, ayant connoissance de tout ce fait a fond, qui nous favorisa beaucoup a cett egard, meme etablist le Sr. M. Directeur general de touts les minéraux de La Province. Qui apres tant d'autres Semblables demarches, douteroit plus de la realité du fait. De cette farce il y auroit une histoire entiere a faire, et assez crotesque, mais ie plains les pauvres mineurs qui ont quitté le Certain qu'ils avoient en Allemagne pour aller chercher l'incertain en Amerique, pour une bone vocation qu'ils avoient, ils ont psentement rien que ce qu'ils peuvent profiter de quelque terrein defriché ou ils Sont obligé de vivre bien petitemt. Le Maitre Mineur meme fust arreté avec touts Ses hardes et utensils par l'Ambassadeur de L'Empereur et en danger d'une grande peine, Meme de Sa vie, si l'Ambassadeur d'Angleterre n'eust trouvé le moyen de le liberer.

46. Je reviens a la petite nouvelle Colonie que Voullions etablir, Je crois qu'il y a guere d'endroits dans le monde, plus beau et mieux Situé que celuy cy de Potomack et de Canavest lequell nous voulions partager en deux petites Colonies. La premiere Justement dessus le Saut ou Chutte, ou il y a une tres jolie Isle de tres bon terrain et vis a vis un Coin entre la grand Riviere de Potomack et une autre petite Riviere nomé Gold Creeck, en francois ruisseau d'or, comode pour recevoir tout ce qui vient d'enhaut la Riviere les plus gros navires marchands, y pouvant faire voile, aussi bien que ce qui vient en bas de dessus le Saut ou d'alentour, L'autre Colonie devoit etre etablie pres de Canavest come est a voir par le Plan.

Marginal note says: Belle Situation des Terres dessus et dessous le Saut de Potomack ou nous voullions etablir aussi une Colonie vide le plan.

47. C'estoit de pousser outre contre Mexique, il voulloit que ie transferasse la Colonie le long de la Riviere de Mesesipy, par la il a fait voir ou qu'il avoit perdu le bon Sens ou qu'il etoit un fourbe, ie crois l'un et l'autre ensemble: Sans doute il avoit bu quand il ecrivit cette lettre.

48. 1. Cette Riviere de Mesesipy est bien eloignée de l'endroit ou nous estions en Nord Caroline, ou prendre les vivres pour tant de monde, et la voiture. 2. Quelle Scureté contre les capres et les Nations Ennemies estant alors en guere avec la France, 3. Coment passer parmy tant de Sortes de Sauvages inconnus, terrible danger et quelque chose de bien temeraire. 4. Il y a 3 Nations qui y ptendent L'Espagne, La France, et L'Angleterre, il croyoit que Berne come Neutre obtiendroit ce Pays facilement, quelle pensée! cela s'apelle batir des Chatteaux en Hispagne. 5. Considerez l'incapacité de L'Etat de Berne qui pour n'avoir pas des forces maritimes ne Scauroit Soutenir un Pays si eloigné 6. ce Pays est desia marqué par les deux Puissances L'Espagne et la France, La premiere possedant les Pays delà de la Riviere contre le Mexique, La Seconde ce qui est de ça la Riviere le prenant pour une dependance ou plutost une bienseance

a la Canada, en ayant pris desia possession et y batis plusieurs forts come est a voir a la petite Mappe de Mexique et La Nouvelle France;

49. voulant faire encore un essay.

50. item s'il n'avoit rien laissé de mes linges et meubles

51. En ce traject il ne se passa rien d'extraordinaire, hormis que nous fumes une fois bien en danger, par la negligence de notre Captaine qui dans un tres grand orage dormoit bien a Son aise, quoy que les mattelots l'advertissassent plusieurs fois il ne s'en pressa pas de regarder ce qui pourroit manquer tellement que le petit voile de dessus le beaupré fust engloutis par les ondes, les cordes rompirent, alors notre vaisseau passa au dessous les ondes tellement que nous fumes dans leau et touts mouillèz, bientot apres le Beaupré rompist qui est la pointe du Vaisseau, et nous crumes de perir, il fallust attacher les mattelots a des cordes et les plonger dans la mer fort agitée pour pecher les cordes, voile, et principalment le beaupré, lequell on eust bien de la peine de lever, ces pauvres mattelots furent bien mouillèz et battus des vagues il falut avaler quelque fois de leau Salée, a la fin nous eumes les Choses les plus necessaires, on ce tremoussa beaucoup et on travailla a raccomoder le Beaupré le mieux qu'on put le vent cessa un peu et on put r'accomoder ce qu'il faloit plus a l'aise, mais apres accause que le beaupré fust r'accourcis, notre Navire, n'alast plus avec cette vitesse come auparavant.

Quelques jours apres nous decouvrimes une chose asséz curieuse. La premiere fois nous crumes de voir de loin un voile, ce qui nous obliga d'ordonner au petit garcon de monter au haut du Mas, la il apperceut que ce qui paroissoit blanc estoit trop gros pour des voiles, a la fin il cria que c'estoit Sans doute du terrein et nous bien en peine nous croyons au milliou de L'ocean, nous examinames dabord la Carte ou mappe geographique, fimes le conte des heures ou miles qu'avions fait, et trouvames qu'en cette latitude il n'y avoit point d'Isles; affin que nous ne hurtions a cett endroit inconnu, nous trouvames a la droite, a la fin nous decouvrimes que cestoit un monceau de glace qui Sans doute par un vent chaud s'estoit defait de ces glaciers du Nord, nous en aprochames de bien pres et nous fumes surpris de voir une petite montagne de glace flottant au milliou de L'ocean. La forme et la figure en etoit Come une forteresse de hauteur, on y voyoit une espece de rempart, des maisons, tournelets, etc. l'etendue en etoit meme assez grande tellement qu'on eust cru que ce fust un fort si cela avoit paru en terre ferme en hyver: La glaciere flottante Contre le Sudwest, et nous faisants Voile contre Nordost, nous la perdimes de vue.

52. Ce qui me fist une peine inconcevable; a la fin ie me tremoussay beaucoup aupres de quelque gros Seigneur pour procurer a ces gens du travail et du pain, on les employa a faire ou raccomoder une grande dique, mais une pluye forte survient et tout fust renversé, il falut dont regarder pour des nouveaux expedients pour les faire subsister, ie trouvay place a une partie mais pas a touts Cependant j'estois pressé d'aller chez moi, craignant de Voyager en hyver Sentant desia une atteinte de goute qui ne S'accomode pas du froid: Je trouvay a la fin deux Puissants marchands negotients pour la Virginie, aux quels ie proposay et recomanday le mieux cette affaire, avec cela ie Consultay un Seigneur de Consideration a qui ie fus reccomandé, par Mr. le Gouv. de Virginie justement concernant les mines affin qu'il me put Servir et rendre des bons offices en Cour. Nous conclumes, que Ses gens devoient, etc.

53. Le Capite. du batiment, a qui il falut confier la chose (marginal note: que j'avois dans mon coffret quelque chose de contrebande.), pourtant Sous un autre nom, me conseilla d'aller dans un petit batteau a Gravesand, pour ly attendre, lorsque ie fus a moitié chemin il s'eleva un Si gros Vent Contraire, que ie fus contraint d'aborder et rebrousser un peu et de marcher a pied a Gravesand, ou ie couchay et restay un jour entier, mais y faisant cher vivre et ne Sachant pas si ce vent contraire dura encore Longtems, considerant avec cela que cecy estoit aussi un port, ie repris le chemin de Londre ou mon Capt. du vaisseau n'etoit pas encore prest, attendant un Vent plus favorable, cependant ie restay a Southrick de dela la Tamise, jusques a nouvel ordre; Lorsqu'il eust debarque ie fus advertis de le Suivre, et a Greenwich ie suis entre dans le Vaisseau, et un peu hors de la Ville de Gravesand me laissa Sortir me disant que ie devois attendre jusquace qu'il eust accuse tout ce qu'il y avoit dans le batiment: Nonobstant qu'il eust dit aux Visitateurs que mon Coffret apartenoit a un Gentilhome de St. Valeris, qu'il pouvoit temoigner que ce n'estoit que des habits et hardes, ils ne voulurent pas ce contenter de cela; il m'envoya dont promptement un garcon pour m'advertir qu'il me falust ouvrir mon coffret, ce qui me mist en peine pourtant ie tiens bone mine et parlay francais, ie pris d'abord ma Clef avec un demy Eccu d'angleterre et le donay au Comis le priant de ne pas chifoner mes habits qui etoient si bien ployez, ce qui passa par bonheur, car S'ils avoient examine tout j'aurois etédecouvert et en danger.

Apres cela nous passames outre, Lorsque nous fumes presque vers L'Embouchure de la Tamise aupres d'un Port nomé Marguet il seleva un Si terrible orage accompagné de tonere et declairs que nous fumes en grand danger, qu'a peine nous pumes retenir l'ancre durant la nuict. Le jour Suivant lors que le vent fust un peu appaisé, nous fimes voile plus outre, et lorsque nous fumes sur le haut de la mer, un gros vent contraire nous poussa en un endroit plain de bancs de Sable, tellement que nous fumes obligé de rebrousser et d'aborder a un autre Port nomé Ramsey, si les gens de cette Vilette et grand nombre de Mattelots n'etoient venus a notre Secours, nous serions peris infailliblement. C'est la ou nous fumes obligé de rester 8 jours accause du vent contraire et affin de pouvoir rapatasser nos voiles dechiréz et accomoder dautres affaires, ce qui me fust bien incomode, accause que ie n'avois pas beaucoup d'argent pour mon Voyage de Paris, n'ayant pas fait mon Conte de faire de la depense hors du Vaisseau. Lorsque le vent fust un peu apaise nous sortimes, mais fumes repoussé pour la Seconde fois: A la fin le Vent ce changea a Nordost qui nous fust favorable, ainsi nous passames pres de Douvre, apres cela le Vent ce changea encore une fois. Le Voyage ou traject me fist plus de peine que celuy ou ie passay deux fois L'ocean, au lieu de 3 jours nous eumes 3 Semaines pour St. Valeris et ou il y a un entreé Si dangereuse qu'il falust que des guides nous vinrent a la rencontre pour nous mener, car il fist un grand vent on ne put voir les marques. Je faillis encore detre arresté a St. Valeris pour n'avoir pas engraissé la patte des Comis du Port qui d'une maniere fort brusque me demanderent le passeport, Sans doute pour m'epouvanter affin d'avoir la piece, mais come si ie Savois que les Suisses avoient le passage libre dans touttes la France ie ne fis pas grand facon avec Eux et come il me citerent devant le Gouverneur, j'y allay d'abord, et luy montray un petit billet de change pour Paris par lequell il pouvoit voir que j'estois Suisse et Bernois, Luy disant que ie n'avois pas demandé un passeport puisque les Suisses etoient en alliance avec la France, et que meme une bone partie etoient au Service du Roy, que moi meme avois passé et repassé en France que iamais on ne m'en avoit demandé, Mr. le Gouverneur fust Satisfait de ma reponce et ie Suivis outre a mon Voyage montant en haut la Riviere pour Abeville ou, j'entray dans la diligence pour Paris, ou ie ne fis qu'une couchée et partis dans la diligence pour Lion, dela j'allay a cheval avec la chasse maré, mais au Fort d'Eccluse il falust encore monter au Chatteau pour parler a Mr. le Commandant qui prist plus de facon que le Gouv: de St. Valeris et ne voulust me laisser la dessus j'ouvris ma Valise pour y prendre ma Patente que Mon Souverain m'avoit donée pour le Gouverneur d'Yverdon, la quelle ie montray a Mr. le Commandant luy disant que ie n'avois pas dessein de passer par icy, mais par Pontarlier connaissant particulierement Mr. le Gouverneur come ayant vescu en bon Voisin avec luy pendant ma Prefecture, que ie n'avois pas besoin de passeport et d'autres raisons que ie luy dit, il me laissa dont passer et ie continuay mon chemin a Geneve de la vers notre Vignoble a la Vaut pres de

Vevay, ou ie crus rencontre ma famille selon l'advis doné, meme dans l'intention dy faire quelque Sejour, mais j'y trouvay visage de bois, puis qu'elle etoit partie 8 jours auparavant, il falust dont Suivre quoy qu'avec regret, j'arrivay le jour de la St. Martin 1714 a Berne en bone Santé Dieu soit loué, trouvant aussi tout en bon Etat a la maison.

54. Et je ne pus pas venir a bout aupres des autres, les moyens me manquoient de faire un process contre ma Societé quoy que bien fondé en vertu d'un Traitté authentique que j'ay en main j'avois presenté en Senat une Supplication par la quelle ie demanday Seulement une Commission pour m'entendre a ce que j'avois a proposer, mais ie fus econduit, ce qui me m'encouragay guere de playder:

55. Come ie viens de dire cy dessus, ie n'ay pas Seulment faits touts mes efforts, aupres de mes Parents amys, de la Societé, et de la Magistrature de Berne, j'ay encore ecrit en Allemagne, et ay fait encore un essay aupres d'une Republique voisiné, mais ie nay pu reussir quelles raisons psuasives j'ay doné. Apres cela iay prié Mr. Stanion qui a eté Envoyé Extraordinaire de Sa Majesté Britanique aupres de Corp Helvetique, luy ayant remis une Suplication pour Sa Majesté avec une Relation Succincte et un memoire mais ce Monsieur ayant eté choisis pour L'ambassade de Vienne et partis pour ce Sujet, toutte ma besogne est restée la et en un Coin: J'avois fait encore une autre tentative, ma reponce fust que les troubles d'Angleterre n'estant pas encore calmées, il n'y avoit rien affaire pour moy psentemt.

Au Retour du Roy George, de Hanover, croyant que tout etoit dissipé et que la nouvelle alliance avec la France et la Hollande affermiroit tellement la tranquillité au Royaume qu'il n'y auroit plus rien a craindre, pour le Pretendant, j'aurois fait encore un dernier effort mais me voicy encore renvoyé par la nouvelle conspiration decouverte: Voyant dont qu'autant de fois qu'il me Semble paroitre une bone etoile pour favoriser mon dessein, et cependant il est toujours ou traversé ou empeché, il paroit qu'absolumt. La Fortune ne m'en veut pas. C'est pourquoy il n'y a rien de meilleur que de quitter mes Projets, et de chercher les tresors d'enhaut, etc.

56. dumplins.

57. Cette Endroit, quoy que dans un terrible desert, avoit encore Son agreement, Cestoit un beau Champ de bled Lombard ou il y avoit une grosse Cabine Indiene, cette place estoit entourée d'une petite Riviere profonde ce qui fist une petite Isle tellement que la nature avoit fait la un petit fort presque imprenable par le marest et les buissons epais qu'il y avoit tout alentour. Toutte cette Populace Susdite consistoit en vieux homes infirmes, femes, Enfants et de la jeunesse Sous l'age pour porter les armes.

(See English translation.)

A. Au bas de cette chutte ou Saut, a coté nous voulions bastir une maison et etablir une Plantation, pour de la charier les marchandises jusques a une demy 4d. lieu a ce Saut les plus gros Vaisseaux marchands peuvent voiler ce qui est bien comode pour le negoce.

B. Justement au dessous du Saut on y prend une prodigieuse quantité de meilleurs poissons, au mois de may ils y Sont tant en foule qu'on les tue avec le baton.

C. Cette Isle est toutte escarpée du Roc au dessus de tres belle et bonne terre assez pour entretenir une famille entiere il y demeure des Indiens on en feroit un fort imprenable: Cest pres de cett Isle que nous mimes pied a Terre en descendant cette Riviere depuis Canavest.

D. Plantation du Col: Bell de 800 pause de Terre a vendre pour 168 liv. Sterlin tres propre et comode pour notre dessein, de la on prend la route de Canavest ou a pied.

E. Au pied de cette Montagne il y a une tres bone Source chaude, les Indiens l'estiment beaucoup et se guerissent de plusieurs incomoditéz.

F. Au milieu de cette Montagne il y a une tres belle Source d'eau

G. On peut monter cette montagne a cheval comodement jusques a un coup de fusil du Sommet, au dessus il y a une jolie plaine, ou il y a une etendue passable il y a des chesnes chattagnests et noyers Sauvages. Cest des la ou nous avons decouvert bien du Pays partie de Virginie, Maryland, Caroline et Pensilvanie.

H. Isle de Canavest Terre haute tres bone, ou les Indiens ou Sauvages avoient planté du tres beau bled Lombard, C'est sur cette Isle ou nous avions fait dessein au comencement de nous etablir, come tres bien Située pour negocier en Virginie Maryland et Pensilvanie et a ce Sujet nous avions fait arpenter presque tout ce qu'il y avoit de bonne terre cottoyant la Riviere.

I. Etang fort curieux a deux pieds de profondeur l'eau est toutte chaude, pour avoir de leau fresche, bone a boire il y faut plonger une bouteille de verre attachée a une fiselle bien bas, soit a 4 ou 5 pied profond et on aura de leau tres excellente freche come glace.

K. Par icy nous avions fait marquer 6000 pauses de arpends de Terre choisie abondante et pleine d'arbres de Sucre ses arbres sont tres beau et gros come des chesnes, ne vienent que Sur des Terres tres grasses. quand on y fait un coup de hasché ou tronc de larbre il en sort un Suc a 3 ou 4 pots de ce Suc ou liqueur bouillie dans une mermite il rests au fond une matiere douce et c'est du Sucre, on en fait des petits pains, ce Sucre est un peu grisatre et a un petit goust different de celuy des roseaux mais bon ie m'en Suis servis dans du Thé et café ie l'ay trouvé bon.

L. De canavest nous Sommes venu embas la Riviere jusques cett endroit dans un batteau ou navet que les Indiens nous avoient fait expres d'ecorce.

M. La Plantation de Mr. Rosier Gentilhome honeste genereux et civil tres bien logé, ou iay Sejournay quelque tems.

N. Endroit ou devoient etre les mines d'argent que M. M. nous avoit proposée.

O. Partie de Pensilvanie.

P. Salines Un endroit ou on a decouvert des eaux Salées.

Q. Charmant Isle de tres bone terre et d'arbres, d'un coté escarpée de Rocher de l'autre d'un abord comode pour les bateaux cett endroit avec la Plant: du Col: Bell nous auroit accomodé.

Si L'Arpenteur General Lawson ne nous avoit detourné de notre premier dessein qui fust de nous etablir au comencement icy, ou nous aurions eté plus en Scureté, mieux assisté et mieux soutenue a toutte aparence nous n'aurions pas echoué en notre Entreprise mais le Mr. n'auroit pas eu le benefice de l'arpantage, cependant il auroit mieux valu detre privé de ce benefice que de la vie qu'il a perdu miserablemt. come est a voir. Il est vray qu'outre les belles paroles de Lawson c'estoient les belles promesses des Lords Prop: qui nous avoient tanté de nous etablir pmierement en Nord Caroline.

ENGLISH TRANSLATION OF THE FRENCH VERSION

ENGLISH TRANSLATION OF FRENCH VERSION

1. Account of the voyage to America which the Baron Graffenried made when he brought a colony of Palatines and Swiss; and his return to Europe.

PREFACE

Although several persons have asked me for the account of my sad adventures in America I should not have been disposed to give it if I had not said to myself that I could justify myself before my society as well as before other persons who might possibly have unfavorable thoughts concerning my conduct, as though I had undertaken this colony thoughtlessly and imprudently and had passed my time in Carolina in luxury and idleness, in which they would have been very much deceived, my account showing the contrary. One will find in it also some particulars which could very well be omitted, but because of the vagaries of certain persons who have acted in bad faith, as well in regard to the poor colonists as towards me personally, having come even to black and inexcusable actions, I can do no less than make mention of them (although very charitably since I name no one) in order that people may impute nothing to me and that my innocence may come to light.

Doubtless certain curious people would like to know the reasons for an enterprise so large and so distant from my country and fatherland. Some know them, and the others will be content to learn that from the time that I had the honor of making some stay with the late Duke of Albemarle in London who was then made viceroy of Jamaica, from the accounts which were made of the beauty, wealth, and richness of English America I conceived such a favorable idea of it, that at the urgent invitations of this lord I should have followed him on his voyage with eagerness, if I had not been turned aside by the strong remonstrances of my relatives who wished that I should establish myself in my fatherland. And not withstanding all the pleasantness that I might have there, there nevertheless always remained some enticement and some attraction in the aforementioned country. Fortune, also, did not look upon me with so favorable an eye as I could have wished, but I had finished my mayorship of Yverdon, a great and important office, to the contentment of my sovereign, the neighboring states and the subjects, the Lord be praised, with a good and clean conscience; I did not make any profit, however, because of

---

NOTE:—Only so much of the French Version is published as is necessary to show wherein it varies from the German Version.

adversities, and on the other hand I was not a man to enrich myself at the expense of the poor subjects. Besides this, the troubles in Neufchatel brought me heavy loss. Seeing again that the new reform deprived me of the ability of obtaining any profitable office for a long time, hoping to make a more considerable fortune in these distant countries of English America in order better to support a numerous family according to my rank and station, I took a firm resolution for this important voyage, no less dangerous than long and difficult, with so much the more courage that I was strongly invited by different letters from the country above mentioned as well as from London. I hesitated a long time considering whether I should communicate my design to some friend or relative, but seeing in advance that they would dissuade me from it, I said nothing of it even to those who were nearest to me, and left secretly. Nevertheless before leaving the country, I stopped at the frontier at the home of a friend, and made a disposition of my affairs which I had not been able entirely to arrange before my departure, and sent it to one of my relatives, communicating to him my design; but ill luck would have it that this packet of papers was intercepted or lost, causing me much embarassment and confusion. And so receiving no answer during eight or ten days, I departed in the firm resolution of returning no more. But man proposes and God disposes.

2. Potomac [by a different hand].

3. The Governor of Virginia:

4. The one was the Receiver-General, the other the Surveyor-General, the third a justice of the peace. These three appeared for this purpose before the Royal Committee, where they received their instructions and were officially given the direction of this people in my absence, as well upon the sea as upon land, because I was not able to leave at that time on account of a little colony from Bern which was to follow shortly, as well as other matters which I had to look after.

5. Mr. Caesar, minister of the German Reformed Church of London at Gravesend.

6. More than half of them died on the sea.

7. And partly dismasted.

8. Not daring to commit itself to the sea because of the privateers, and besides, the water at the mouths of the rivers of Carolina being low, large vessels were not able to go out nor enter.

9. Consisting of about 1,000 acres of land.

10. It is necessary for me here to stop the course of my account, in order that I may also say something of what I transacted more particularly at London, item of my departure, what passed and what

I noticed on my journey, and of my arrival in North Carolina this same month of September 1710. After that I will continue in order.

Having touched only incidentally upon what I transacted at London I shall say something more in detail here, nevertheless as succintly as possible. It will be well to distinguish somewhat the two plans of the proposed colonies, that of Virginia and that of North Carolina.

For that of Virginia we had the orders of L. L. E. E. of Berne, our sovereign magistrate [marginal note: Proposition of the state of Bern for a district of country in Virginia] to sound Her Majesty, the Queen of Great Britain, to see if she would be disposed to accord the state of Berne a district of country for the proposed colony, with jurisdiction under certain clauses, without depending upon any governor, but directly of the Queen or her Council; but the Crown not wishing to diminish its authority and grandeur, would not listen to this proposition, asserting that everything ought to conform to the laws and regulations of the realm. Since it caused some embarrasment also to a sovereign state to abase itself so much, nothing was done.

Nevertheless we, in particular my society and I, on the recommendation of Monsieur Stanion, Envoy Extraordianry from her Britannic Majesty, or by his assistance obtained from the Queen the permission to take land in Virginia above the falls of the Potomac River, under the same conditions as other subjects of Her Majesty, with the intention of dividing our colony, for good reasons. But as they gave me hope of more advantages in North Carolina, since the lands were much cheaper, and since we had certain jurisdictions and special privileges besides, we began there, and the fatal issue makes it plain that we should have done better to commence with Virginia; so much the more that we should have been more in security and better supported in case of danger, by the Crown than by individuals in Carolina. Moreover the situation according to the map that I have made of it, was not at all inferior to that of Carolina either in beauty or richness, nevertheless all these overtures before mentioned cost me many useless steps, pains, and expenses, in order to obtain only a shadow of favor; for when we wished to have the lands above mentioned secured and surveyed, it was found that they were already taken by Mylord Culpeper, so that it was necessary for us to look for the greater part in Maryland, a country belonging as an estate to Mylord Baltimore. It is true that we still had other places in Virginia marked out and secured, rather good but distant from Christian plantations. With regard to the colony for Carolina I had no less embarassment, pains, and expense, nevertheless, although, the Lords Proprietors were disposed to favor me. I think that before broaching this negotiation, it would not be out of the way to say something of their power and privileges. That is something we can see fully in the account or journal printed by the Surveyor-General Lawson, wherein is copied the charter or act accorded by the King, Charles II. This great favor and high jurisdiction which no private person or lord of the Three Kingdoms has, was accorded to these lords who recalled the King from his exile and have favored his return into the kingdom. This King, not wishing to be an ingrate towards his benefactors, did not know how to recompense them better than by such a signal favor, giving and handing the provice of North Carolina to these lords in full possession, authority, and absolute power, just as the King had possessed. So then they have the title as follows: To His Excellency, N. N. Palatine and to the other real and absolute Lords Proprietors of the Province of Carolina. One of the chiefs of these Lords Proprietors was at the beginning General Monk, Duke of Albemarle. It was he who presented the crown which he had made, to the king at his entry into the kingdom; which crown they keep in the Tower of London beside the veritable crown of the realm, which I have seen. They always show them both to curious strangers.

Among the other privileges which these Lords Proprietors have is the power of creating Casiques, Counts, Barons, Knights and Gentlemen in these provinces. And those whom they wish to favor they cause to be corroborated and registered in the royal heraldry; just as they did with me, when, in order to procure me more authority with my people they honored me with the title of Landgrave of Carolina, Baron of Bernburg and Knight of the purple ribbon, with a medal, as my patents give proof. But the bad part of it is that with these titles there is not a proportionate revenue. All the good that has accrued to me of it is that they gave me the first rank after the governor in the upper house of parliament of the province, and preserved me the respect of the subjects. In the beginning, appearing in the parliament without the ribbon, I was well received, to be sure, but on certain occasions I was not obeyed as I should have been. That is why I was advised to wear the ribbon and the medal when I appeared in the assembly. This I did, and I perceived the effect immediately, for certain people who had not sufficiently respected my orders came afterwards to beg my pardon for it on their knees. This is sufficient concerning the authority and power of these Lords Proprietors.

I shall tell in a few words something of what they granted me, our treaty being too long to insert here. Firstly: They sold me 15,000 acres of choice land which I had surveyed upon the rivers Neuse and Trent and 25,000 acres upon the Weetock River at 10.£. sterling per thousand, or 1£ per hundred acres, and 6 pence per hundred acres quit-rent, which makes the sum of 175£ sterling, which I paid at the beginning in cash. Secondly: There was a reserve of 100,000 acres to choose between the rivers here named and Clarendon River, at the same price, and for that I had seven years time in which to make the first payment and between the seventh and the twelfth the whole was to be paid. Thirdly: The differences which my people might have with the English should be settled before the English judges, but the difficulties which my colonists might have among themselves should be settled among themselves or before me, the final jurisdiction in capital offenses reserved to the Lords Proprietors. Fourthly: Liberty of religion and the right to have a minister from our country who might preach in our language. Fifthly: Right of city and market or fair at New Bern. Sixthly: Freedom from all tax, imposts, tithes and hundredths, aside from the six pence per hundred acres annually as mentioned above. Seventhly: The Lords Proprietors or the province by their orders were to furnish me with two or three years provision of food and stock for myself and all the colony, to be paid back after the prescribed term.

I also had a special and very exact treaty with the Palatines which was planned, examined, and agreed upon before and by the Royal Commission, too large to insert here. Merely the substance as follows. Firstly: My colonists owed me fidelity, obedience, and respect; and I owed them protection. Secondly; I was to furnish each family provisions for the first year, a cow, two swine and some tools, to be repaid in three years. Thirdly: I was to give each family 300 acres of land and they were to give me as quit-rent two pence per acre. On the other hand I was to pay the six pence per hundred acres, the fee to the Lords Proprietors as already mentioned. As for the expenses of transportation and food for my colony to Carolina, the Queen granted that and in addition thirty shillings for clothes to each person large and small.

After that it was a question of providing good vessels, and there presented himself a person of my acquaintance, Chevalier Fyper, who undertook to furnish two vessels well equipped with the necessary provisions of food. But all this was not to be executed with such regularity as one could have wished. Since these lords, the directors or sub-directors of this swarm of people which was then at London, had considerable difficulty providing for so many thousands of souls, money began to become scarce, so much so that our good Chevalier, who procured these provisions on credit in the firm persuasion that the money would be delivered over at any time that he should demand it, was much surprised to see himself turned away so many times. This went on for several months even, so that the creditors had an attachment executed upon his person for 24 hours. The Chevalier much alarmed at this procedure came one morning to inform me of it, charging me with all these evil consequences, which accusation troubled me greatly. As I was then in the country to get some air and to rest a little from my fatigue, I hastened to go to London to represent my griefs to the Royal Commission regarding the delay in the payment of this money. They gave me good words but several weeks more passed before the money promised was given over to Chevalier Fyper who did not fail from day to day to press the treasurers. In the end everything was done as desired.

After my colony had left in the vessels mentioned I proposed to follow them as soon as I had disposed of my private affairs and taken leave of a part of the lords of the royal commission and the Lords Proprietors of Carolina.

I pass over in silence a treaty made with William Penn, proprietor of Pennsylvania, for lands and mines, and a private treaty which I had with a society in Bern, upon which I was relying in order to have necessary assistance in an enterprise which I would find myself too weak to support; but it would have been better for me to associate myself, for an affair of this importance, with some wealthy and well known person in England who would possibly not have let himself be so quickly frightened by my reverses as these gentlemen.

My Palatine colonists having departed in the month of January 1710, I followed them and left London the last of May. I made use of a very comfortable carriage, almost the same as that from Paris to Lyons. I can do no less than speak here of something which I observed on this small journey. One Sunday I had to stop at a small village called Hartford, near which is the country house of the Count of Essex, a very ancient building which I was curious to see. And so I went there with due courtesy. In this magnificent palace I observed in a great dome some large and extraordinary paintings, in the Count's cabinet a quantity of rare pieces and very curious antiquities, and in a large hall I thought I saw upon a table a lute, some flutes and other instruments, with open music books, item a deck of cards scattered about, a purse of counters, several pieces of money, and several other pretty things very well made; but coming closer to the table I was much surprised to see the work of a second Apelles, for these pieces which I believed actual were only counterfeits in painting. That which seemed the most curious to see was that the surface of this marble table was so well polished that one would have thought they were paintings under glass or ice. One could even pour water on it without injuring the table or the painting. Certainly that must have been painted with a marvelous varnish. After having seen the rest of the palace and been refreshed with a fine collation and good liquors, I paid my respects and took my leave in order to go on my way.

After some days we came to York, an ancient city rather large and well populated, where I had time to see merely the Cathedral, a very beautiful structure. There I heard a very beautiful symphony or vespers and the canons used me courteously. From there we came to Durham, a rather pretty city. The Cathedral is rather fine. The Bishop of this place alone aside from the Prince of Wales, has the title of a prince in England. He also has the precedence over all the bishops except the bishop of London. After that there was nothing remarkable clear to New Castle.

New Castle is a large city, well populated, rich, commercial, well situated beside the River Tyne which empties into the sea. Everything abounds in that city. One lives well there and at a low price. There is salmon in abundance. The city is remarkable for the coal which is found there. Whole fleets leave in order to furnish the great city of London and the neighborhood with coal, and the miners are in such a great number that it is necessary to have a garrison to keep them in check. There are excavations so terrible thereabouts that they say they are the antichamber of Hell, and a stranger must have good courage to go far into them. There is made also a quantity of sea salt and there are several glassworks and other factories. Besides the merchants there are also very civil and honorable persons of another rank, with whom one passes his time very agreeably. From the fifteen days that I have been there, I could not sufficiently praise the kindness that they showed me. One of the chief men of the city, Alderman Fenwick, treated me magnificently to a fine symphony of musicians, persons of rank. There is also a very fine bowling green, a very beautiful prominade where there is a bowling green surrounded by several rows of Lindens, and this upon the eminence of the city where there is a fine view. Nevertheless, while I was there I had trouble which the captain of the vessel that was carrying my Swiss colonists caused. He was the master of it, a citizen of Boston, the capital of New England. Had it not been for the mediation of this gallant man Mr. Fenwick I should have ruined myself in a suit against the captain. We had agreed and concluded with him that he should furnish all the provisions necessary from Rotterdam to America. Nevertheless when he approached New Castle for his own private affairs to unload merchandise as well as to take on some for Boston, a part being provisions which he preferred to get there rather than in Holland, since they were cheaper, and actually better; having been obliged to stop there almost four weeks, he asserted that we were at our own expense with all our Swiss colony, which caused me much embarassment.

At last having agreed after a fashion, we left at the beginning of July for America. At the mouth of the River Tyne we stayed several hours to get a provision of salmon, fresh as well as dry, in a town situated on the bank of this river where there was such a great quantity of salmon that all the town was carpeted with them, drying in the sun before the houses as well as exposed for sale.

We left the mouth about three o'clock in the afternoon with a favorable wind and a fine day. When we were upon the high sea we saw several vessels. The nearer we approached them the more of them we discovered. At length passing out farther we found ourselves among three fleets; that of Holland which was rather numerous in ships of the line, was coming to the coasts of England to catch herring, mingled with the barques of the fishers and in the distance war vessels; on another side was that of the coalships which returned empty from London; and on another side that of Muscovy; the sun which was going down making them plain to be seen. These great vessels of war appeared among the other vessels like so many superb castles among mediocre houses and the whole appeared like three pretty cities built upon the sea. The next day which was a beautifully calm Sunday, the commander of the Muscovy fleet gave the signal and all the vessels unfurled their flags. As is the custom on this day, after the devotions, the trumpets, hautbois, and drums made themselves heard. Visits were made from one to another as though we were in a city. We passed the time so agreeably that I could then have wished to be always on the sea. But along toward evening there arose suddenly an impetuous wind so that those who were on visits had a great deal of difficulty getting into their boats to return to their vessels; and indeed, one good toper who had difficulty leaving such good liquor, from having delayed too long, was obliged to remain on the vessel where he was visiting and was constrained to take a different route in spite of himself. As for us who were planning to make sail northabout, that is to say towards the north above the Shetland Isles, for our security, we took the plan of putting ourselves among the fleet of Muscovy, which in order to avoid the French with whom we were having war, in place of going by the Baltic Sea took its turn also to the north. We were seven vessels bound for America which made sail in company with those which were bound for Denmark, Sweden and Muscovy. At the latitude of the north of Scotland we separated after having saluted the commander of the merchant fleet, which is the usual order. They went toward the northeast and we toward the north and northwest. Nevertheless when the wind changed to the east it was so favorable to us that in place of taking our route above the Shetland Islands we cut and passed between these islands and those of Orkney, but safely, the Lord be praised, although it was night.

When we were at a certain latitude above Ireland, we saw several vessels appear at a distance making five sails coming toward us. This threw us into an alarm, not knowing whether they were enemies or friends. We took first of all our beds and mattresses in order to put them along the sides of our vessel to serve as a rampart, putting ourselves into as good position as possible to defend ourselves. We had a little fear, because of the three vessels that we saw, there was one with the white banner, the color of France. When we were a cannon shot distant the commander of this flotilla fired a blank shot as a signal that we should recognize him, but no response following, he fired the second in earnest and almost broke our main mast for us. So then it was necessary to submit and we answered with our little cannon, hoisted our English flag, and spreading the middle stay sail, in a moment the commander joined us so closely that we could speak together, and in order to act courteously to the commander, since there was not much wind, we invited him to board our vessel, which he did not refuse, being very glad to regale himself with some of our fresh English beer and a piece of pickled salmon. During this brief interval I took my opportunity to write to Europe and gave my letter to this little commander (who was accompanying four or five other Scotch and English vessels coming from Jamaica, Barbados and other places) and my letter was given to the post and arrived at Bern. Towards evening we separated and each took his way.

I have made many remarks about what I saw upon the sea and of what took place, having made a rather curious journal, but ill luck willed that a small trunk or coffer in which there were some more rarities of America with other papers and some clothes was lost, although it was well recommended to a captain of a vessel which left Virginia, I not being able to take it with me because I had a long journey to make by land from Williamsburg, the capital of Virginia to New York, being already overloaded with clothes, for I had as much as my two horses could carry. So then I shall make mention of only some few things which I remember well and which I believe sufficiently worthy of the curiosity of the reader. Moreover there are so many authors who have written about the marvels of the sea that I refer the reader to them. I shall merely say to those who have not read these authors that when we came under the tropical line of Cancer, or at a certain latitude of the sea between this line and the Artic pole, we saw there white birds of the size of a crow which even came to sit upon our masts. The sailors take them for birds of good omen and do not allow anyone to shoot them. The thing that is most remarkable is that we see these birds only at this latitude of the sea and not elsewhere.

But for birds of bad omen there are others, smaller, black with a little white, which fly about here and there upon the sea, and as often as one sees them fly about the vessel and principally about the bow it is observed that they presage nothing good, but bad weather, either tempest or terrible storms. I took that at first for a fable, but having myself noticed it at different times, I am almost obliged to believe in it. I really believe if one wished to philosophize upon it one would find natural reasons for such occurrences.

I have observed also a remarkable thing in a fish called the dolphin. This fish is very pretty in the water, having the color of the rainbow. When it follows a vessel it stays only two feet below the surface of the water. It is charming to see it swim. It is always accompanied with several small fish which keep always near the tail and never leave this post unless the dolphin goes away or is killed. We took one of them with a trident and this is the way they are caught. The shaft or pole to which the trident is fixed is attached to a long cord and when the dolphin is swimming sufficiently close to the vessel, a sailor or whoever wishes to, provided he has skill, throws the trident at the dolphin. Sometimes they catch it at the first throw, rather often they fail. When they have speared it, they draw in the cord and raise the fish out. As pretty as the fish is in the water just so ugly it is out of the water; but when well dressed we made good cheer of it. The younger they are the better and more delicate. One sees also flying fish and there are so many other sorts of marvelous things to be seen on the sea that one would make a volume of them. When there is a calm or merely some small breeze, I enjoyed looking at and examining so many kinds of insects and other things coming from the sea foam. In certain localities one sees plants and extraordinary flowers. It is surprising where these plants take root in the midst of the ocean where there are such terrible depths. One sees in many places currents so strong that skillful masters of vessels are sometimes turned out of their course if they do not take good care. But the most curious thing would be to know where these currents come from. There is one which comes from the Gulf of Mexico; but for the rest, one has yet to penetrate to where they do originate.

Referring the curious to authors who have written amply about the rarities of the sea, I continue my way. When we came to the latitude of Newfoundland, some one pointed out to me approximately the grand banks of this island, where such a great quantity of cod is taken, with which France and England supply themselves. At this place a French privateer followed us a whole day, but not having a favorable wind it could not overtake us. Nevertheless we feared greatly. That is why we consulted together and the conclusion was that as soon as the sun should have set we would lower our sails gradually and unnoticeably in order that the privateer should lose sight of us against the night, and since it would doubtless keep following us towards the continent, it would be necessary to change the route. As soon as it was dark we stretched our sails and went back the way we had come for three or four leagues, and taking to the high seas we made our efforts to gain the left of the privateer, and going straight towards Virginia we escaped his hands, for we should have had the worst of it, having only four cannons in our vessels.

A few days after, we discovered the Gulf Stream, sea plants, sea gulls, and presently ducks and other sorts of sea fowl; a sure sign that one is not far from terra firma. And so we had a lad climb to the top of the mast. As yet, however, he could not see anything. But going up for the second time, awhile after this, he saw land which looked like a low cloud bank. But recognizing directly that it was land, he cried out "hooray" which is the English exclamation of joy or applause, and asked for some drink money. We approached the continent and skirted the provinces of Pennsylvania, Jersey and Maryland until we discovered Cape Henry in Virginia, at the mouth of the James River. A north-west wind favoring us, we entered easily into this river and arrived safely at Guiguetan, now called Hampton, a rather pretty town, the first (one comes to) at the entrance to Virginia, after a voyage or passage of two months. We were very happy in having had but one storm and that lasting but a couple of hours, and in having had no sickness. We remained a night and one day in order to refresh ourselves.

Having made our arrival known to the Lieutenant Governor and given him the Queen's letter, the Governor being absent, we went down the river and entered into the Nunscimund River. There it was that we unloaded the vessel of our provisions and clothing and the captain of the vessel bade us goodbye, taking the route to New England in order to go to Boston, the capital of this province, which was his birth place. We hired some boats to load with our clothing and provisions in order to have them taken along with our people to a house which was described to us as being the nearest (for us), the home of one Hamstead, a fine man who welcomed us and accommodated us effectually both with food and wagons for our journey by land from there into Carolina.

11. For an honest man there could be no hesitation and since, by good fortune, my reputation was pretty well established in America and my design made a great stir, I sent at first into Pennsylvania for provisions of flour, where, fortunately, I had already given order from London as a precaution, fearing that possibly things might not be so well established in North Carolina as they made me believe. I also did not fail to send into Virginia and into the Province even, in order to procure for myself the necessary provisions. But all this dragged out so long that in the meantime these new colonists were obliged to sell even a part of their clothes and merchandise (which they had bought at London to make some gain from the little money which they had) to procure the necessaries from the neighboring inhabitants in order not to die of hunger.

12. As soon as we had arrived at Summertown, a village on the frontier of Virginia and Carolina, a small band of inhabitants of North Carolina came to greet me and offered me the government . . .

13. I replied that although I was indeed invested with this dignity of Landgrave, I did not at present wish to take advantage of this title, thanking them civilly . . .

14. That it would be in bad taste for me to meddle in a dispute concerning such a matter;

15. But as these people, who were, the majority of them, Nonconformists, did not want to have such a great tory for governor, my answer did not please them . . .

16. I could not sufficiently express the sad and deplorable state in which I found these poor people at my arrival; almost all sick and in great extremities and the few who remained well, in despair. God knows in what a labyrinth, yes, even danger of my life I found myself then. I leave to the reader to think how my little Bernese colony looked upon this play, who until then lacked for nothing, their voyage and passage having been fortunate from the commencement until their arrival in Carolina, the season good and fine, well furnished with all provisions, well equipped with sailors, well quartered with plenty of room on the vessel, now to see such a sad spectacle before them where disease, poverty, and despair were at their height. That which increased the evil more yet is that these poor Palatines having used the greater part of their clothes in order to purchase food for themselves in the greatest necessity, were very much disconcerted when they saw that the directors above mentioned, having the greater part of their effects still in their hands, retained them; but principally one, N. R., under pretext of reserving a good part for his pains and expenses. And when I asked him to make an account, he put me off so often that to the present time the account is not yet settled; and that was

very easy for him because of the trouble which followed. He must have found these furnishings of the Palatines very convenient for himself because before he had their effects in his hands he lived humbly and afterwards he played the great gentleman. He kept their things until my arrival and when I wished to have them brought to our place of residence I could not get even a part except with arms and by force, indeed could not have all notwithstanding the complaints I made of it to the government because he belonged to the magistracy.

That which was the cause of all these misfortunes was the bad conduct and unscrupulousness of a part of the *superior* and inferior *inspectors.*

A marginal note to the *italicized* words is as follows: Of whom N. R. was one also, whom I do not name because of his eminent connections.

17. While on my part I made all my efforts to establish my colony, as I have just said, on the other hand we wrote to Mr. Hyde in Virginia where he had made some stay waiting a better outcome of his candidacy, who did not fail to come as soon as possible, with his family into Carolina upon the Chowan near Colonel Pollock.

18. After the repast, over a bottle of Maderia wine we came to very serious discourse, and since it was he who refused me everything (by virtue of my patents and the orders of the Lords Proprietors he was to furnish me with all the necessaries from the revenues of the province), I was very glad to reproach him and to represent to him also the enormity of his criminal proceedings. Seeing himself convinced by so many good reasons and moreover in order to lull me to sleep so that I would not work against him too much, he promised me _ _ _ _ etc.

19. To which I resolved, not without taking good precautions, the more so that I had been threatened by some of my colonists even, and the road was none too well secured, being two days journey distant, where I had to descend and cross great rivers and rather dangerous forests.

20. Bad luck would have it that just then a certain mutinous and turbulent personage named Richard Roach arrived from London. This caused much disorder. He was an agent for one of the Lords Proprietors but of the sect of Quakers, who was said to come into this country to trade.

21. Which fomented the rebellion and augmented the troubles and made us a great deal of inconvenience.

22. 200.

23. Equipped and armed with about 60 or 80 men.

24. When we observed this manoeuvre we also put ourselves into position and went down behind a hedge towards the bank of the river.

25. During all this I was obliged against my will to take the presidency, for the matter was delicate and dangerous.

26. And in advance a letter was written to communicate our design to him, and he courteously marked out a day and a place for us on the frontier of Virginia and Carolina, having aside from that the desire to exercise his troops in that vicinity.

27. The Governor of Virginia left orders that they should let him know at Williamsburg, the place of his residence, as soon as I should have arrived.

28. It was necessary then to look for other expedients. Now, because I had been recommended by the Queen and because the first time Governor Spotswood saw me he wished to do me a pleasure and not send me away without granting me some favor, he asked me if I had something else to propose or some expedient which was easier to grant me. Seeing then that these Virginians were not disposed to help us, perhaps themselves having a little of that free and democratic spirit, I considered whether some soldiers of regular troops might be found. Accordingly I asked the Governor, since he was the vice-admiral of the Virginia coasts, to have the kindness to send us a warship well manned. This he granted us.

29. In the course of time he was banished to a distant island for life and died there.

30. At my return to Neuse I was much surprised to find so many ill and even several dead, among the number of whom were two servants who had been brought to me from Bern. Without doubt it was the great heat which came the three months of June, July and August, that was the cause of it; our people coming from a cold and mountainous country were not yet accustomed to this flat country and this hot air. Yet there was no lack of physicians and surgeons who took care of them. These afterwards also became sick. But the principal cause of it was that in my absence they had neglected my orders for diet which I had given at first on my arrival in America when I found the Palatines already so ill. It was by the good advice of persons who had made a long stay in Carolina that I had instructed them not to drink too much fresh and cold water, but to boil it with some sassafras, of which the woods are full, and afterwards to let it cool off and to drink as much of it as they wished. I used it in the morning with a little sugar in place of tea and it did me much good. I have noticed also that those who went right to bed when they felt bad became very sick and many died. There prevails in this country a certain fever. It is a general tribute which strangers have to pay at the beginning, and the

cure for it is very peculiar. When this fever attacks you the best remedy is, in place of going first of all to bed, to run until you sweat in great drops and even fall over from weariness. You must not stop there but arise and continue until you can go no farther. I am speaking from experience. And so I had it only three weeks whereas others have dragged out whole years, at last become swollen and died of it. I here warn the lazy that it is not a disease which suits them. Idle and lazy people are almost always sick there. Exercise is needed. A proof that it is necessary and good is that I was very much afflicted with gout in Europe, and in this country I escaped with a few small attacks.

In this country the red oaks are so juicy that by making a small opening with an ax, there comes out a quantity of sap which is vinegar. But it is bad for the health. Our people used it during the great heat in order to eat some salad and did not feel well from it. There are two more inconveniences against which we had to guard ourselves. These are serpents and ticks, in French surons. There grows a marvellous antidote and in great abundance with which one must not fail to provide himself. There are three sorts of it. There is one kind which has a peculiar virtue. If one carries the root with him he can sleep freely under a tree; no serpent will approach. The Indians ordinarily use it. If one bruises this root and gives some of it in a cup or pot of fresh water to the animal which is bitten by a serpent, it recovers and gets well in a short time. I have made proof of it upon my horses and my dog and they got well. The ticks trouble people to the point of causing fever. It is believed to be corrupt dew which fastens to the grass, nevertheless one sees it only where there are animals. As for the women they have more difficulty protecting themselves, the men wearing stockings of leather are free. The peasants who have tougher skin do not feel it so much. It lasts only certain months of the year.

Each of my colonists adapting himself as best he could and according to his capacity and skill, it was a question of doing no less in the city. Following the permission and the privileges I had, I accordingly chose a point of land between the Trent and Neuse Rivers, a place where there was an Indian kinglet with his people, about a score of families. The place was called Chatouka. Mention has been made of it on page six (of the original manuscript). We purchased it so dearly because of the advantageous situation. It was a matter of importance then to have my place free. Surveyor General Lawson, who had sold it wanted me to drive off the savages. But I did not want to do anything like that; far from it. I set about purchasing from one of these Indians a small extent of land where I built my cabin, while waiting for something better, and I even made a sort of alliance with this kinglet, named Taylor, and his people. This was done formally. Some little time afterwards, seeing that these savages could not agree with my people nor mine with the savages, the idea occurred to me to propose to them to buy this land also of them, and to assign them another place where they could live just as comfortably and upon the same river not far from this place. They began to appreciate my reasons, and we held a solemn council regarding it. Since I am on the matter of these savages, before speaking of the plan and foundation of the little city of New Bern, I shall continue where I left off with the Indians and also say something about their religion and what took place.

And so we decided upon a day to make our agreement. The kinglet dressed himself in his best, but in such a grotesque fashion that he seemed more like an ape than a man. He came with seventeen fathers of families. They went out into an open field and placed themselves in a circle on the ground. I also put on whatever would glitter most, had a chair brought for me, and taking to my side an interpreter, a savage who spoke English well, I broached the matter and the object of this assembly. After having represented my reasons to them they also told their own, and to speak without partiality they had better reasons in their opposition than I. Nevertheless we came to an agreement. I made them several small presents of little value, and as purchase price for this land in question I gave to the king two flasks of powder holding four pounds, a flask holding two pounds, and with that 1,000 coarse grains of buckshot; to each of the chiefs a flask of powder and 500 lead shots (a marginal note says some rather coarse shot). After that I had them drink well on rum, brandy distilled of the settlings of sugar, the ordinary liquor in this country, and the agreement was made.

This occasion was nevertheless troubled by the rudeness of Mr. M. who, having drunk too copiously with some Englishmen who came to dine with me, lost his sense of duty and coming to insult these poor Indians, took the head dress from the king and threw it as far as he could. He entered into the circle and taking by the arm, one of their orators who spoke a little too much against our proceedings, he pulled him out of the circle giving him several blows. I first had this gentleman who was so intoxicated, seized by some of my servants in order to take him to the house, where these invited English kept him company, diverting him as best they could. The reader can easily imagine what effect a procedure like that produced. And so the king making his complaint said that if the Christians made peace and their alliances after that fashion he did not want to have anything to do with them. I did not fail to answer him that he ought not to pay attention to what a brute, controlled by the power of liquor, had done, that I would reprimand him vigorously for it and I would even send him far away, that he should not insult them more, that they should rely on me assuring themselves that I would never do them injury so long as they were good neighbors with me. Satisfied with my answer and with my better treatment they returned home. This gentleman, after a little sleep which ought to have made the vapors pass from him, became quiet. I do not know what fly bit him, but after ten o'clock in the evening when I had gone to bed believing all were at rest, he arose and went toward the Indian lodges. Finding the Indian orator still up, he treated him very badly. But immediately the king with some Indians gave the halloo and I admire the patience and discretion of these savages, in not having beaten the barbarous Christian in their turn. The next day the king with his concillors did not fail to complain of the reiterated bad treatment of this brute worse than a savage, with threats that if they were insulted any more they would pay him in the same coin. I had considerable difficulty appeasing them. I had them drink freely again and sent them away with assurance that I would have this turbulent man leave and that they would not be insulted any more.

After the departure of these Indians, finding my man in his better senses, I talked to him seriously about some things. This person will be spoken of very often in this account; but because of his relatives who are people of distinction, rank and merit, I have consideration for him and do not name him, denoting him only by Mr. M. He was one of the eight associates, to our loss and my ruin and that of several others. May the Good God convert him and give him to know how much evil he has caused. The Surveyor-General has been punished with a terrible execution by the savages for his crimes and bad faith. If this man does not change, the same thing may very well come to him. Living no better than a barbarian he might well be chastized by the barbarians. (The marginal note says, He died among the Indians'. This appears to have been put in later).

Being badly satisfied with him I sought an expedient for sending him elsewhere. And so he set out to survey the lands along the Weetock River, and for that purpose I furnished him all the necessaries. On his return there arrived one of his old comrades from Pennsylvania in a shallop and another worthless fellow with him. Among the three the plan was made to take a trip towards Cape Fear and to survey the lands along this river, otherwise called Clarendon River; and for this they made such provisions of food and merchandise that there remained to me almost nothing more. Nevertheless they idled away their time in outrageous debaucheries. This trick did not please me and making my reflections upon it one morning before they had eaten breakfast I told them that from the way they were going about it I saw that they preferred to disport themselves than to do a necessary and profitable piece of work, that I had need of this merchandise in order to relieve my necessity and that of the colony, that we had land enough for the present, that we needed first to see how our colonists would succeed, that since great sums were needed to sustain an enterprise of this importance there was more need to think how to procure for ourselves the wherewithal to subsist, than to go to useless and as yet unnecessary expenses, etc. My proposition disconcerted these fine debauchees and they did all they could to argue with me but my resolution was firm and I told Mr. M. that having made so much noise about his silver mines that we had come to genuine treaties, as well with Mr. Penn, Proprietor of Pennsylvania, as with J. Justus Albrecht, chief of the miners from Germany, who was waiting only our orders in order to have them come, it was there that he ought to labor. Accordingly they ought to go to Philadelphia, Capital of Pennsylvania, to notify the governor of my arrival in this country, give our patent to Proprietor Penn and announce to him that we had the design to go visit the mines in question, since they appeared to be situated in the rear of his jurisdiction, and that he should give us the necessary assistance. And then after everything should be ready and in good order and assured against the Indians I would transport myself there, etc. These two rascals, the above mentioned companions of Mr. M. when he was going with several others to the discovery of the mine in question, approved of my proposition and encouraged Mr. M. to this expedition. At last he gave his hand upon it, and they left, provided with the same provisions that they had taken for the little journey to Clarendon River. Several days after their departure, the king with some of his Indians came to find me. Not knowing that for other reasons I had had this Mr. M. leave, he evidenced much joy that I had delivered them from the dangerous man, and this affair did me a great deal of good in my captivity at Catechna where the kinglet spoke in my favor.

Thereupon we promised each other reciprocally to be good neighbors and the Indians left the place shortly after to settle themselves in the place assigned to them, not far from there. Some time afterwards I made a trip to Core Town ten miles from Chatouka, where I had the savages assembled to propose to them that finding myself in their vicinity I intended to live on good terms with them, making offer of my services. This was well received, but as there were two chiefs in the village, one named Core Tom and the other Sam, the first an enemy of the English and the other who was absent, a friend, I could not entirely arrange some things which I should have wished very much to arrange. Nevertheless, rather satisfied with the reception, I returned home the same day. This village of Core is very well situated. There is a cooler atmosphere, and is bordered by the Neuse River. If these Indians had wished to change places I should have liked very much to do so.

Having had until now more pressing occupations, I had not as yet done very much for the establishment of the city. Finding myself a little disengaged I took the Surveyor-General and his clerk with me to make a plan of this new city. Since in America they do not like to live crowded, in order to enjoy a purer air, I accordingly ordered the streets to be very broad and the houses well separated one from the other. I marked three acres of land for each family, for house, barn, garden, orchard, hemp field, poultry yard and other purposes. I divided the village like a cross and in the middle I intended the church. One of the principle streets extended from the bank of the rivier Neuse straight on into the forest and the other principle street crossed it, running from the Trent River clear to the Neuse River. After that we planted stakes to mark the houses and to make the first two principal streets along and on the banks of the two rivers, mine being situated at the point. And since artisans are better off in a city than on plantations, I gave them some privileges. In place of the inhabitants or new citizens being obliged to pay me annually as my fee and for the three acres of ground a silver crown, the people with trades were free for ten years, the other for three only. At the first I had a good number who began to fell timber in order to build their houses. There were two carpenters, a mason, two carpenters and joiners, a locksmith, a blacksmith, one or two shoemakers, a tailor, a miller, an armourer, a butcher, a weaver, a turner, a saddler, a glazier, a potter and tilemaker, one or two millwrights, a physician, a surgeon, a schoolmaster. There were here and there on the plantations still other artisans. There was lacking as yet only a minister, and while waiting the one I was having come from Germany I performed the function. (Marginal note. Reading sermons after the English fashion) having permission of the Bishop of London to marry and baptize. For the Communion I had a minister come once a year from Virginia. There came a minister from Virginia who preached in English and French and I had engaged him for my colony, he being very well satisfied to come for the 50£ sterling which the Chamber of London for the propogation of the faith orders in such cases, and a reasonable offering which the colony in general made.

After a part of these artisans had their timber work ready and had at least put themselves under cover, while waiting something better, and when I had also fitted up my own dwelling a little better, we were concerned to give a name to the city, which we did in great solemnity; and we joined to Neuse that of Bern. Thus the city was christened New Bern. At the commencement there was to be established a market once a month and once a year a fair. Finally there were several other regulations. When the governor, the council, and many planters of Carolina had advice of our establishment they not only all had a desire to live there but actually had lots, that is to say, limited plots, marked out for them.

They were right; for in all the province there was not a single place of security. There was neither a general provision of food nor munitions of war nor arms. Each was, so to speak, abandoned to the jaws of the wolf. If the savages were a people better adapted for war they could have destroyed the people of that province whenever they had wished. If the good God had not watched over these fickle Carolinians better (than they themselves did), there would not have remained one soul.

There were many persons of Pennsylvania and several for Virginia who took lots, so that in a few years we should have had a fine city. I should have transferred the seat of government there, the rather, than at Little River, where the large assembly stayed, there were only a few scattered houses, where we were badly lodged and had no security.

While I was busying myself in establishing the affairs of the colony to the best of my ability, having even caused a redoubt to be built up above towards Mill Creek for the safety of the colony and to hold the Indians in check from this side, I also made several regulations and ordinances, as well for the military as for the civil affairs. My provisions of food began to diminish and the merchandise also, which in this country is used as cash. And so I began to reflect very seriously upon my enterprises. Far from receiving any assistance and help, whether from the province or the Lords Proprietors, or of my own country and my society; there arrived, on the contrary, protested bills of exchange. In this bad state of affairs, I no longer knew where to turn, having already written several times to the (old) country and to the society for help. No response having followed, and fearing that they would take my information for tales, I conceived the notion of inquiring whether I might not find some one of the colony, who, tired of his troubles would have a desire to go back to the old country. I found one who was the very person, a man whom two members of the society had chosen to take care of their plantation, but who, seeing that these gentlemen were not furnishing anything for him to live on, resolved to go back home. On his promising me that it would cost me only the expense to Philadelphia, I gave him five guineas for that and a small bill of exchange for him to collect as much at Philadelphia. But the rascal was not satisfied with so little when he came to Philadelphia and found a merchant who was so easy that, without my orders, on my credit, he advanced him more than he needed. At London he did the same, and at Amsterdam also and so on clear to Bern. And our friends, the associates, were much surprised to see his face and more at his boldness and the big bill. Nevertheless before the departure of this rascally pilgrim, I had made and given to him a map of the land and rivers where I had placed my colony and a memorandum of what I had done for this establishment, as well as of the expenses I had incurred on this account, with the bill of everything and a letter prepared to encourage them to support me in this enterprise, to the effect that although it was very difficult and dangerous at the commencement, still, having surmounted the most dangerous obstacles, there was good appearance of success; leaving the rest to the account which he would make by word of mouth, principally concerning the beauty and wealth of the country. This letter he delivered and according to the information I have received of it, he omitted nothing which could tend to the advantage of the establishment, and doubtless I should have obtained the help needed except for the misfortune which came to me a short time after, as is to be seen in my account.

In this hope of a prompt and sufficient assistance, seeing that food for the colony was costing me more for carriage than the purchase price, at the advice of friends and persons of understanding, I purchased a sloop, a vessel suited to be used upon the sea and on the rivers, with a barque which could serve only in the rivers; this for bills of exchange. These vessels did me as well as the province great service, as will be seen later. I was constrained to this expedient because there were very few of these vessels in the province, and during this civil war they were all engaged and one could not get them for love or money, and yet we had to live. There was at this time such a scarcity of salt, because strangers did not dare to bring any during these troubles, that I was obliged to send my sloop to the Bermuda Islands to look for it; and since there had to be something to exchange, I obtained permission of Governor Hyde to gather up grain (marginal note, in this case Indian corn) here and there in the province upon his account and the account of the Lords Proprietors. But ill luck would have it that this corn was wet by a great storm, which spoiled my market, and the profit of this voyage was very small. Nevertheless the salt which I got from the Bermudas did me and my neighbors much good, and I was very glad that for the first time my vessel was saved and returned in good shape except for the sails which were much torn and for some cordage ruined. It had been absent so long that I thought all lost. This might well disturb me very much, having cost me 300£ Sterling. But what disturbed me most was the crew: I had some very good sailors on it. In the uncertainty of the above I went sometimes to survey lands in order to find relief, and I can do no less than relate here a rather peculiar adventure which preceded that of Catechna, when I was taken captive by the savages.

On day when I was going to survey lands, the weather having changed, fearing a great tempest and not wishing to sleep in the woods, I left my surveyors, and took my way home with my valet. My great haste caused me to mistake one path for the other. In this way so much time was lost that night surprised me and I fell among the very Indians who moved from the place where I had settled at Chatouka, now called New Bern. I leave the reader to think in what apprehension I was, and whether the Indians would not have had a fine chance to revenge themselves on me if I had misused them and had not lived peaceably with them. Having had nothing with which to reproach myself in this regard, I reassured myself a little and luckily they received me well. The thing that should have increased my apprehension was that one of the chiefs of the Core savages, who was not favorable to the English, was at that very time on a visit to King Taylor. Nevertheless I got off with a little fear. As I was very thirsty from having traveled all day through the woods, fearing that drinking water would make me sick, in their excess of politeness they sent to a sick woman who had some cider in order to let me have some of it. I did not learn that until several days after or I should not have drunk so much, and I should have had scruples against depriving this poor sick woman of a drink which she used for a cordial rather than to satisfy her palate. For my supper the king made me a present of a quarter of venison, but this evening I did without supper. Tired with my traveling I was very glad to rest, and so I had my valet stretch my little tent for me to lie under, but I scarcely slept. All night they made fires of joy, dancing and singing about them, making sometimes choruses and cries such as might have chased the wolves from the forest; music different from that of Orpheus who tamed the most savage animals. The next day early, the king gave me as escort two savages who put me on the right road and accompanied me home. After having given them something good to eat and drink I gave them a little present for King Taylor and in place of his cider I sent him two bottles of rum or brandy of sugar to divide also with the poor sick woman, a much better cordial. This was very well received as I have learned. This same king contributed not a little to my release, next to the Divine assistance, when I was condemned to death by the savages at Catechna.

31. Having neither place of retreat nor provision, whether of food, arms, or amunition, encouraged them not a little in the project.

32. He first of all, after the punishment, which consisted only in sawing logs for the public safety during a single day, a punishment which did not approach the crime, crossed over the river to meet the Indians.

33. The Indians who had difficulty believing such perfidiousness of me doubting what the rascal had reported, risked sending to us one of their troop who knew English well, this was, indeed, my interpreter of Catechna, although he was in great apprehension of being taken and his life endangered. Upon which there happened a rather amusing adventure. This Indian, having passed across to this side of the river, watched for an occasion of talking to some of my people, in order to know the reality of the matter. When the Indian wished to approach one of my colonists the poor man was so frightened that he came all out of breath to give the alarm in my quarter and informed me that he had seen a savage who had wanted to approach; that doubtless the others were not far distant, which in fact alarmed me a little and I put my people into position. Nevertheless I imagined that the Indians, impatient to get their ransom, might have sent some one to see where we stood about it. And so I ordered the same man who had taken fright to betake himself again alone to that same place, telling him that I would post people at a distance to defend him in case of danger, which we did. The savage did not fail to show himself a little while after, and approaching made signs to him that he need fear nothing. Our man making the same sign to the other, they eventually approached and came face to face. They came thus upon the chapter of the blacksmith who had talked against me, nevertheless without the savage ever being willing to name him, but he talked of him in such a way that one could guess who it was. Our man who had his instructions represented to him that the savages were badly informed and that it was a dishonest man who had made these invidious reports; that I was keeping an exact neutrality, so far from the contrary that the English were not satisfied with me because I did not wish to join with them, contenting myself in keeping my post. He insinuated, moreover that the savage ought to bring back their Palatine prisoners if they wished to have their ransom, and several other things that he had orders to say. After this he let the Indian go quietly, telling him that in the future none of the savages should come here any more,

but if they had anything to say they should make a fire opposite to our quarters, that afterwards I would send someone in a boat to talk to them, that we would talk to them only on the water; and they, the Indians, should come to meet us and not more than two at a time.

34. The above mentioned Brice, who would gladly have had his tools, especially those which were used for repairing guns, took it into his head to get them back by cunning. If he could not have them otherwise, resolved, even, to take them by force.

35. (Pretending that it is for the defence and service of the country.)

36. Small fort.

37. Which would have been done if I had had enough witnesses against him.

38. Marked with a mark N: which signifies Neuse.

39. (Who really were not in action against them, but suspected of being on the side of the enemies.)

40. When the general assembly was convoked I did not fail to betake myself to it. First of all I presented myself in the upper house, consisting of the governor, the representatives of the Lords Proprietors, the councillors, and caciques or gentlemen of the province. After I had made my complaints and had justified myself for my conduct I went to the lower house, consisting of the deputies of the communes. After a small discourse on the subject in question, I asked about these caluminators, who had made secret inquiries without any order of the authorities. I wanted to have them named to me and to have brought before me the original copy of the 20 or 23 articles which had been formed against me. I absolutely wished that the accuser should produce himself, in order that I might convince him of falseness, prove my innocence and justify myself in due form, but no one dared show himself nor even open his mouth on the subject of these false accusations.

Doubtless these false accusers got wind of it and learned how I had justified myself before the governor of Virginia and Carolina, and seeing that my conduct was approved they did not dare to pursue their accusations for fear of being beaten. Nevertheless my honor and reputation suffered much in all this and I was even in danger of my life; so much the more, since among the Palatines, my subjects even, there were false witnesses. What should I do then in this wretched situation of things? Seeing that no one wished to speak I myself began to name the accusers, fulminating against them and demanding justice. But alas! In a government so confused, where the first fire of sedition was not yet entirely extinguished, because a good part of the members of Parliament were still holding secret grudges, men who were good friends of this Brice who was also a member of it, and who all would have been glad if some affront should come to me for having taken the side of the Governor; and because of the embarassment of this Indian war, as well, I could get no other satisfaction than to see a profound silence at my explanation and defence. It is true that the governor and the upper house made excuses and paid their respects to me, advising me for the rest, to seek justice according to the forms usual in the time of peace against slanderers. Think, my dear reader, how much time it would have been necessary to wait to have my due satisfaction, since until now the Indian war is not finished. A marginal note says, A. 1716.

41. These poor people who felt only too keely the effects of the extremity to which we were then reduced (nothing of our provisions having remained except a measure of wheat, having endured 22 weeks without any help whatsoever from the government or the province) had no difficulty in consenting to what I proposed to them.

42. An English planter of the sect of Quakers.

43. So then the government of South Carolina sent 800 savage tributaries with 50 English Carolinians, under the command of Colonel Barnwell.

44. Shaft or litter.

45. The place of our rendezvous was at the home of a very gallant man. Mr. Rosier, near the falls of the Potomac, where several gentlemen from Pennsylvania who were also interested with us had come to meet me, in the hopes of seeing what there was of this fine and rich silver mine of which Mr. M. had made so much noise and for the find- of which they had already furnished so much money. Having staid a rather long time at this place without learning any news either of Mr. M. or of the colony which we were awaiting for daily with impatience, the strange vagaries of this M. made us almost doubt, and not without reason, of the reality of his advances. That is why we took the resolution to go ourselves to visit the place of the mines, of which he had given us a map. And so we prepared in a rather good manner to make this journey, although it was very dangerous. And as I had formed the design before I had been given notice of this rendezvous, I took my precautions, communicating my design to the Governor of Virginia who gave me patents, even published commands by which he ordered that at my first request or at the first notification, rangers should follow and accompany me. When we came to a small village called Canavest, a very pleasant and enchanting spot about 40 miles above the falls of the Potomac, we found a troop of savages established there, and in particular a Frenchman from Canada, named Martin Charetier, who had married an Indian woman or savage. He was in great credit among the savages beyond Pennsylvania and

Maryland, and at the fine advances of Mr. M. had settled himself there, leaving for this his place where he was well established in Pennsylvania. This same Martin Charetier had also made the journey to Senantona to look for mines with Mr. M. and contributed a good sum of money to it. This man warned us that the Indians, who were in the vicinity of this mountain of S. where the mines were said to be, were much alarmed by the war which we were having with the Tuscaroras, and told us that not to risk ourselves on so dangerous a journey without necessity. We gave heed to this, postponing the plan for a more secure occasion and time. We made an alliance, however, with these Indians of Canavest, a very necessary thing, in connection with the mines which he hoped to find there as well as on account of the establishment which we had resolved to make in these parts of our small Bernese colony which we were waiting for. After that we visited those beautiful spots of the country, those enchanted islands in the Potomac River above the falls. And from there, on our return, we ascended a high mountain standing alone in the midst of a vast flat stretch of country, called because of its form Sugar Loaf which means in French pain de sucre, taking with us a surveyor, the above named Martin Charetier, and some savages. From this mountain we saw a great extent of country, a part of Virginia, Maryland, Pennsylvania and Carolina. By use of the compass we made a map, and observed particularly the mountain Senantona where our mines were said to be. We found that this mine was situated beyond Virginia, and not beyond Pennsylvania as the map of it had been given to us.

And two of the savages by chance knowing the situation of this mountain, told us that they had already roamed about the locality having visited almost all parts of this mountain, but that they had found no mineral and that our map was not correct, at which we were much surprised. We discovered from this height three chains of mountains, the last higher than the one before, somewhat distant and a very fine valley between the first ranges. After we had come down again from this mountain to a place at the foot where there was a very fine spring and good soil, we went to Martin Charetier's where we were lodged and treated after the Indian fashion. The day after, we departed in order to return home. We went down the river. For the purpose of the descent the Indians with marvelous skill made us in less than a half day a small boat of the bark of trees. We got into it, five of us, besides two savages, who managed the boat. We even put in our baggage. It was charming going down the river to see the beautiful country on the sides and the pretty islands, but when we came close to a great rock in the middle of the river, not far from the falls, as is to be seen on the map (number 6), we found the passage dangerous, for about this rock which is almost a little mountain with a pretty plain up on top where an Indian lived, there are still a number of small rocks and great stones, which make the passages swift, narrow, and bad. I did not want to go down it, and we all got out except Mr. Rosier, who, knowing the skill of the Indians, risked it. When we saw from a distance the turns they had to make, what inexpressible skill it needed to steer this canoe or boat, we almost thought there was some magic in the act, and we were very glad to be out of it, especially when we heard the Indians singing as they passed at great speed, almost striking against a great stone or rock. But this made my good Mr. Rosier pray, bold as he might be. At a quarter of a league beyond this bad passage they stopped and we got into the boat again. Good Rosier, still very pale with fear, assured us that he would never be so rash again. We went down the river very nicely and easily from there to the falls. At a quarter of a league from them we got out, the valets having brought our horses to that place. Nevertheless before mounting our horses we saw how the Indians carried the boat upon their shoulders into the forest to repair it, they taking good care not to tell us that the end was damaged by striking against a rock. It was necessary to shorten the boat by cutting off the end. After having it well repaired, the Indians brought it back to the river and were rash enough to go down the rapids or great falls of the Potomac. They passed down very nicely, according to their story, but yet they caused us considerable anxiety because they delayed very much before they joined us at Mr. Rosier's where we lodged. I staid some time longer with this gentleman, waiting for my people from Carolina. The rest of the company took their way to Pennsylvania, badly satisfied with the tergiversations and strange conduct of Mr. M.

It is to be remarked here that Mr. M., whom for good reasons I do not name, has thoroughly duped people by his fine and persuasive accounts of having found such rich mines; and if I have also gone into the snare it was easy to entrap me, being a stranger in these parts. My foundation was this: First, I hardly thought a man of his rank and a fellow countryman besides, capable of such tricks. Second, the mineral which he had shown, having been tested, was found very good. Third, the oaths that he took. Fourth, the patents which he asked of the Queen of England for this purpose, a very bold trick. Fifth, since so many persons from Pennsylvania and other provinces having made the journey openly, with the permission of the neighboring governors for the discovery of these mines, there appeared something real in the affair. Sixth, among others who had interested themselves in it, were a merchant of Pennsylvania a very shrewd man and no longer young, a skillful goldsmith and other persons who ought to know the country thereabouts well. Seeing that these persons of ability living in these parts from their youth even, some of them natives of these places, risked considerable sums, I could not think that they had not taken all security and precaution. Seventh, we made a formal agreement with some German miners to carry on the whole thing. Mr. M. made a voyage to Holland to confer with the chief of the miners who was to prepare all the tools and supplies necessary for this enterprise, the cost of which was nearly one thousand ecus in silver. Eighth, Mr. Penn, Proprietor of Pennsylvania made a contract with us, having thorough knowledge of all. He favored us very much in this regard, even made Mr. M. director-general of all the minerals in the province. Who after so many such proceedings would doubt the reality of the thing? There could be made a whole history of this farce, and a rather funny one; but I am sorry for the poor miners who have left the certain thing they had in Germany to go to find the uncertain in America. In place of a good vocation that they had, they have nothing at present except what they can gain from some cleared land where they are obliged to live very modestly. The mining master was even arrested with all his clothes and tools by the ambassador of the Emperor and would have been in danger of a grave punishment, even of his life, if the English ambassador had not found means to liberate him.

46. I return to the little new colony which we wished to establish. I believe that there are scarcely any places in the world, more beautiful and better situated than this of the Potomac and of Canavest, which we wished to divide into two little colonies, the first just below the falls. There is a very pretty island of very good ground, and facing it, an angle between the great Potomac River and an other little river named Gold Creek, in French Ruisseau d'Or, suited to receive everything which comes up the river, the greatest merchant vessels being able to sail there, as well as that which comes down from above the falls or from the surrounding country. The other colony was to be established near Canavest as is to be seen by the map.

Marginal note. Fine situation of land above and below the falls of the Potomac, where we wished also to establish a colony. See map.

47. It was to push further, towards Mexico. He wanted me to transfer the colony along the Mississippi. By this he has made it clear that he had either lost his good sense or that he was a rascal. I believe both together. Without any doubt he had been drinking when he wrote this letter.

48. First: This Mississippi River is very far from the place where we were in North Carolina. Where get the food for so many people,

and the transportation? Second: What security against the privateers and the hostile nations then in war with France? Third: How were we to pass through so many tribes of unknown savages, a terrible danger and something very rash? Fourth: There are three nations which lay claim to it, Spain, France and England. He thought that Bern, as neutral, would easily obtain this country. What an idea! This is what they call building castles in Spain. Fifth: Consider the incapacity of the state of Bern, which, having no maritime forces would not be able to maintain a country so far away. Sixth: This country is already marked by the two great powers, Spain and France, the first possessing the country from the river towards Mexico, the second taking whatever is this side of the river for a dependency or rather as territory belonging properly to Canada, having already taken possession and built several forts there, as is to be seen on the small map of Mexico and New France.

49. Wishing to make one more attempt.

50. Likewise whether he had left anything of my linen and furniture.

51. On this crossing nothing extraordinary took place except that we were once in danger by the negligence of our captain, who in a great storm was sleeping at his ease. Althought the sailors warned him several times he did not hurry himself to see what might be wrong, so that the small sail above the bowsprit was submerged by the waves, the ropes broke, and then our vessel went down under the waves so that we were in the water and all were wet. Shortly after the bowsprit broke, that is the point of the vessel, and we expected to perish. We had to fasten sailors to lines and plunge them into the troubled sea to fish up the ropes, sail, and especially the bowsprit, which we had great difficulty in raising. These poor sailors were well soaked and beaten by the waves, and more than once they had to swallow salt water. Finally we secured the most necessary things. We stirred around a great deal and endeavored to repair the bowsprit as best we could. The wind ceased a little and we were able to repair what was needed more at our ease; but after that because the bowsprit was shortened our boat did not travel with such speed as before.

Several days after this we discovered a rather curious thing. The first time we saw it we thought it a sail at a distance, which obliged us to order the small boy to mount to the top of the mast. There he perceived that this which looked white was too big for sails. At length he thought that it was doubtless land, and we were much troubled supposing ourselves in midocean. We first examined the chart or geographic map, counted the hours or miles we had made, and found that in this latitude there were no islands. In order not to strike against this unknown place we turned more to the right. At length we discovered that it was a mass of ice which, without doubt, had been detached from the glaciers of the north by a warm wind. We approached it closely and were surprised to see a little mountain of ice floating in the middle of the ocean. The form and figure of it were like a fortress of some height. One could see a sort of rampart, houses, turrets, etc., upon it. The breadth of it was also rather great so that one might have thought it a fort if it had appeared on terra firma in winter. The glacier floating towards the southwest and we making sail towards the northeast, we lost it from view.

52. Which caused me inconceivable pains. At length I bestirred myself very much with some great lords in order to procure work and bread for these people. They employed them to make or repair a great dike. But a heavy rain came on and all was overturned. So then we had to look about for new expedients to enable them to subsist. I found place for a part, but not for all. Nevertheless I was anxious to go home, fearing a voyage in winter, feeling already an attack of the gout which does not suit well with cold. At last I found two powerful merchants, traders of Virginia. To them I proposed and recommended this affair as best I could. Along with that I consulted a lord of distinction to whom I was recommended by the Governor of Virginia regarding these very mines, in order that he might serve me and do his good offices at the court. We concluded that these people, etc.

53. The captain of the vessel, to whom I had to entrust the matter, (marginal note: because I had something contreband in my chest,) nevertheless under another name, advised me to go to Gravesend in a little boat in order to wait for him there. When I was half way, there arose such a heavy contrary wind that I was constrained to go ashore, turn back a little and go to Gravesend afoot, where I went to bed and remained a whole day. But since living was high there and I did not know whether the contrary wind would last a long time yet; considering besides, that this was also a port, I took the way for London again, where the captain of my vessel was not yet ready, waiting for a more favorable wind. In the meantine I remained at Southwick on this side the Thames for later orders. When we had come to land I was given notice to follow him, and at Greenwich I entered the vessel, and a little outside the city of Gravesend he let me go ashore, telling me that I was to wait until he had declared everything there was on the vessel. Notwithstanding that he had said to the customs officers that my chest belonged to a gentleman of St. Valery, that he could testify that there was only coats and clothing in it, they would not be content with that. Accordingly he

promptly sent a boy to notify me that I had to open my chest, which caused me some anxiety, nevertheless I put a good face on it and spoke French. I immediately took my key with an English half sovereign and gave it to the clerk, begging him not to disturb my coats which were so nicely folded. Fortunately this worked; for if they had examined everything I should have been discovered and in danger.

After that we passed out. When we were almost at the mouth of the Thames, near a port named Margate, there arose such a terrible storm, accompanied with thunder and lightning, that we were in great danger, being scarcely able to hold the anchor during the night. The following day when the wind had quieted down a little we made sail farther out, and when we were upon the high sea a great contrary wind drove us into a place full of sand banks, so that we were obliged to turn back and approach another port named Ramsey. If the people of this little city and a great number of sailors had not come to our help we should have perished without fail. There is where we were obliged to stay eight days because of contrary wind and in order to be able to mend our torn sails and repair other damages. This was very inconvenient for me because I did not have very much money for my journey to Paris, not having counted on incurring expense off the vessel. When the wind had quieted a little we went out, but were driven back for the second time. At last the wind changed to the northeast, which was favorable to us, and so we passed close to Dover. After that the wind changed again. The voyage or crossing gave me more trouble than I had when I crossed the ocean twice; in place of three days we took three weeks to reach St. Valery. And at this place there is such a dangerous entrance that we had to have pilots, who came to meet us in order to guide us, for there was a great wind and one could not see the marks. I came near being arrested again at St. Valery, because of not having greased the palms of the officers of the port, who in a very brusk manner asked for the passport, doubtless intending to frighten me in order to get the coin. But just as though I knew that the Swiss had free passage in all parts of France, I did not spend much time with them and when they haled me before the Governor I went immediately and showed him a little bill of exchange for Paris, by which he could see that I was Swiss and a Bernese, saying to him that I had not asked for a passport because the Swiss were in alliance with France, and that a good part even, were in the service of the King, that I myself had passed and repassed into France, and never had anyone ask me for one.

The Governor was satisfied with my answer and I continued my journey, going up the river towards Abbeville, where I entered into the diligence for Paris, where I stayed only one night and departed in the diligence for Lyons. From there I went on horseback with the driver of the fish cart, but at the fort of Ecluse I again had to go up to the castle to talk with the Commandant, who had more scruples than the Governor of St. Valery and did not wish to let me pass. Thereupon I opened my valise to take out my patent which my sovereign had given me for the governorship of Yverdon. This I showed to the Commandant, saying to him that I had not had the design of passing this way, but by way of Pontperlier since I knew the Governor particularly, having lived neighbor to him during my prefectureship, and that I had not had need of a passport for this and other reasons which I gave him. So then he let me pass, and I continued my way to Geneva; from there towards our vineyard in Vaud near Vevay, where I expected to meet my family according to the advice given, intending, indeed, to make some stay there. But I found no one since they had left eight days before. So then it was necessary to follow them, although with regret. I arrived in Bern on St. Martin's Day, 1714, in good health, the Lord be praised, finding everything in good condition at home.

54. And I cannot succeed with the others. Means failed me to bring suit against my society although it would be well founded in virtue of a bona fide contract which I have in hand. I have presented a supplication in the Senate, in which I merely demanded a commission to hear what I had to propose, but I was not heard, a thing which hardly encouraged me to go to law.

55. As I have just said above I not only made all efforts, with my relatives, friends, the society and the magistracy of Bern, I having written moreover to Germany, but I made a further attempt with a neighboring republic. Nevertheless I could not succeed, whatever persuasive arguments I gave. After that I tried Mr. Stanyon, who has been envoy-extraordinary from Her Britannic Majesty to the Helvetian Corps, having given him a petition for Her Majesty with a succinct account and a memorandum. But this gentleman, having been chosen for the embassy to Vienna and having departed for this purpose, all my labor has been for nothing and things are at a standstill. I made one more attempt. The answer was that the troubles of England having not yet calmed down, there was nothing to be done for me at present.

On the return of King George of Hannover, thinking that all was dissipated and that the new alliance with France and Holland would so confirm the tranquility to the realm there would be nothing more to fear for the claimant, I should have made one last effort, but at this point I was put off again by the discovery of the new conspiracy. Seeing then that as often as a good star arose apparently to favor my design, and yet that it was always crossed or hindered, it appears that fortune absolutely will have nothing to do with me. That is why there is left nothing better than to leave my projects and seek the treasures above, etc.

56. Dumplings. (?)

57. This place, although in a terrible desert, still had its charm. It was a fine field of corn where there was a great Indian cabin. This place was surrounded by a deep little river which made a small island, nature having made of it a small, but almost impregnable fort by the morass and the thick bushes which surrounded it. All this populace above mentioned consisted of old, decrepit men, women, children, and young men under age to bear arms.

A. At the foot of this fall, to the side we wished to build a house and establish a plantation in order to cart merchandise from there. The greatest merchant vessels can sail up to within a half of a quarter of a league of this fall, which is very convenient for commerce.

B. Just below the falls there is caught a prodigious quantity of the best fish. In the month of May they come there in such numbers that they kill them with a stick.

C. This island is all cut out of rock. Above it is a very fine and good soil, sufficient to support a whole family. Indians live there. One could make an impregnable fort of it. It is near this island that we set foot on land when we came down this river from Canavest.

D. Plantation of Colonel Bell, eight hundred acres of land to sell for 168£ Sterling. Very suitable and convenient for our design. From there one goes to Canavest horseback or on foot.

E. At the foot of this mountain there is a fine hot spring. The Indians esteem it highly and cure themselves of several complaints.

F. Half way up this mountain there is a very fine spring of cold water.

G. One can ascend this mountain on horseback very conveniently to within a gunshot of the summit. On the top there is a pretty plain of considerable extent. There are oaks, chestnuts and wild nuts. It is there that we discovered a big extent of country, a part of Virginia, Maryland, Carolina and Pennsylvania.

H. Island of Canavest, elevated country and very good, where the Indians or savages had planted some fine Indian corn. It is upon this island that we had made the design to establish ourselves at the commencement, as being very well situated to carry on trade in Virginia, Maryland and Pennsylvania. For this reason we had had almost all the good land bordering the river surveyed.

1. A very curious pond. At a depth of two feet the water is very hot. To get cold water, good to drink, one has to plunge a glass bottle attached to a string down deep, probably four or five feet and then one will get very excellent water cold as ice.

K. Here we had caused to be marked out six thousand (pauses or) acres of choice land, abounding in and full of sugar trees. These trees are very handsome and are as tall as oaks. They grow only on rich soil. When one makes a blow with an ax into the trunk of the tree there comes out a juice. From three or four pots of this juice boiled in a kettle there remains a sweet substance in the bottom and this is sugar. They make little cakes of it. This sugar is a little grayish and has a taste a little different from that of cane, but good. I used it in tea and coffee and found it excellent.

L. From Canavest we came down the river to this point in a boat or canoe which the Indians had made of bark, expressly for us.

M. The Plantation of Mr. Rosier, a good, generous, and polite gentleman, very well settled, where I stayed for some time.

N. The place where the silver mines were supposed to be, which Mr. M. had proposed to us.

O. Part of Pennsylvania.

P. Salt springs, a place where salt water has been discovered.

Q. Charming island of very fine land and trees, on one side steep rocks, on the other an approach suitable for boats.

This place with the plantation of Colonel Bell would have suited us well.

If the Surveyor-General Lawson had not turned us aside from our first design, which was to establish ourselves here at the commencement, where we should have been more in security, better assisted and better supported, to all appearances we should not have failed in our enterprise. But the gentleman would not have had the profits of the surveying. But yet it would have been better to be deprived of this profit than of his life which he miserably lost, as is seen (in the account). It is true that besides the fine speeches of Lawson, it was the fine promises of the Lords Proprietors which tempted us to establish ourselves at first in North Carolina.

SHORT VOCABULARY

SHORT VOCABULARY

The appended small glossary is intended to be of some assistance to readers of the German account of Graffenried's adventures, the arbitrary spelling and crude syntactical structures of which show that, its author was no literary adept, at least in German, which he wrote as he spoke and heard it. It was not thought necessary to include all the words of the story, but only such as seemed likely to cause trouble to the average reader. In preparing this section of the work use has been made of the following:

G. A. Seiler. Die Basler Mundart. Basel. 1879.

J. Hunziker. Aargauer Wörterbuch. Aarau. 1877.

Josua Maaler. Die Teutsch Spraach, etc. Zürich. 1561.

Johann Christoph v. Schmid. Schwäbisches Wörterbuch, etc. Stuttgart. 1844.

Johann Hübner. Natur-Kunst-Berg-Gewerck-und Handlungs-Lexikon. Leipzig. 1722.

Fr. Staub und Ludwig Tobler. Schweizerisches Idiotikon. Frauenfeld. 1881.

Franz Joseph Stalder. Versuch eines Schweizerischen Idiotikons, etc. Basel und Arau. 1806.

Allgemeines Oeconomisches Lexicon. Leipzig. 1731.

Weisthümer, Gesammelt von Jacob Grimm.

Neu-gefundenes Eden; oder, Ausführlicher bericht von Süd & Nord-Carolina, Pensilphania, Mary Land & Virginia. 1737.

Lawson's Journal, etc. John Lawson. 1709.

(Josua von) Kocherthaler Ausführlich, und umständlicher bericht von der berühmten landschafft Carolina, in dem engellandischen America gelegen. Franckfurt am Mayn. 1709.

Virginia Historical Magazine, Vol. VI.

The plan has been to give, first the form as found in the accounts, then in italics the form which Graffenried probably intended in case the word is badly spelled, or if it is an unusual word, the form which might have been expected, and finally the translation in italics. Where the word or a similar word occurred in any of the works consulted the name of the work is then indicated, usually by the name of the author and the form there found is given in italics. In many cases enough of the Graffenried text is given to enable the reader to locate the sentence where it belongs, and in a few instances a translation of the passage follows in italics.

A

abgebrunnen: *abgebrannt, burned.*
abgeret: *abgeredet, agreed;* abgereter Massen, *abgeredetermassen, as agreed.*
abgereyset: *abgereist, departed, sailed away.*
abgesagdem: for *obgesagtem,* i. e., *obgesagtem, abovementioned.*
abmäjend: *abmähend, mowing off.*
abrobiert: *approbiert, approved.*
Abscheid: *Abschied, departure.*
abbinden: *abbrechen, to close* (a letter).
abendern: *abändern, to change off.*
abfergen: *to send away.* Maaler, *fergken.*
albo (in), (Latin): *in blank.*
allemaus (vor): *vor allem, before all.*
alls: *als, as, since, because.*
als: *alles, all.* diss Unglück, als etc.
altlecht: *ältlich, rather old.* Stalder *-lech for-lich.*
ambouchinen: for French *embouchure, mouth.*
Ambtli: *Aemtlein, Aemtchen, small office.*
amnith: for French *amnestie, amnesty.*
anbefählend: *anbefehlend, commending.*
anderstwoh: *anderswo, elsewhere.*
anderwehrts: *anderwärts, elsewhere.*
anfiengen: old for *anfingen, began.*
angebend (hatte): *angegeben, declared.*
angewent: *angewendet, employed.* Stalder, introduction to the dictionary, gives this and similar forms.
ängsten: *Aengstigung, anxiety, fear.*
ankonft: *Ankunft, arrival.*
anlasst: *anlasst, promises:* wie sichs wohl anlasst, *as it promises well to do.*
anlenden: *anlanden, to land.*
anmassgen: *anmassen, assume.*
Ansechen: *Ansehen, consideration.*
anscheint: perhaps for *Anschein liklihood:* und anscheint Mines vernichtet.
antrefe: *antraf, met.*
aparentz: French *apparence, appearance.*
apharto: Latin *a parte, apart, aside, privately.*
aplausu: Latin *applausus, applause.*
apparentz: see *aparentz.*
artivitial: *artificiel, artificial.* French version gives *artificial.*
asseyten (in der) *im äussersten,* for *besonders, especially.*

aufmanen: *aufmahnen, summon.*
Aufwaxes: *Aufwuchses, increase.*
ausfägen: *ausfegen, cleanse.*
ausgeret: *ausgeredet dissuaded.*
ausgesezt: *ausgezogen:* von der Armuht ausgesetzt, *taken out of poverty.*
ausleichen: *ausleihen, to loan out, rent out.*
ausschleuffen: *ausschlüpfen, to slip out.*
äusser: *auser, except.*
aussret: see *äusser.*
auswexlung: *Auswechselung, exchange.*
Autous: *Autoren, authors.*
avantiere: *Abenteuer, adventure.*

B

Baar: *Paar, pair.*
Balbierer: *Barbier, barber:* Hunziker, balbier.
Balisaden: *Pallisaden, palisades.*
Barbantine: possibly intended for Paar Bottines, *pair of half boots:* French version, une pair de bottines.
Bard: *Baron, baron:* Bard de la Hontan.
Bargunen: French, *barque, small boat.*
Baruque: *Perücke,* French, *perruque; wig.*
Batatas: *Bataten, sweet potatoes.*
bate: *bat,* from bitten, *begged.*
Batz Tone: *Bath Town.* Eden spells *Charleston, Charlestone.*
Bauws: *Baues (Bau), cultivation.*
Bay Revir Neuws: *Bay River, Neuse.*
beace (Justice of): *Justice of the peace.*
bedenchens: *Bedenken* (pl.), *thought, care.*
bedeurungen: *Beteuerungen, protestations, threats.*
bedrauwen: *bedrohen, threaten.*
Bedreute: *bedrohte, threatened.*
Befelchen: *Befehle, commands.*
befrieg: *befrug, befragte, asked, questioned.*
Begrabnus: *Begräbnis, burial.*
begwältigen: *bevollmächtigen, empower.*
behürzter: *beherzter, more courageously, boldly.*
bekame: *bekam, got, received.*
belagret: *belagert, beleaguered, overcome.*
Beltzen: *Pelzen, pelts;* Beltz werk, *peltry.* Maaler, *Belz.*
bemitlete: *bemittelte, well-to-do.*
benantliches: *benanntliches, specified.*
Benöhtigte: *nötige, needed, necessary.*
Ber: *Eber, boar;* Stalder, Ber, *Zahmer Eber, tame boar.*

Beren: *Bären, bears.*
beret: *beredet, persuaded.*
beruefen: *berufen, called.*
besachen: *besahen, saw, examined.*
Besatzung: *Besetzung, nomination.*
beschächen: *geschehen, happen;* Maaler, *beschähen.*
beschwärt: *beschwert, offended;* Maaler, *beschwären.*
beschweret: *beschwört, conjures.*
beschwerungen: *Beschwörungen, incantations.*
besser: *weiter, farther;* Seiler, *besser.*
besten: *bösesten, worst;* die besten Aufrührer.
betreuwet: *bedräuet, bedroht, threaten.*
betrieglicher: *betrüglicher, deceptive, treacherous.*
Beudte: *Beute, booty.*
bewehrte: *bewährte, proven genuine,* also *armed.*
bey: *Beine, legs:* waren meine bey so steif.
beynachen: *beinahe, almost.*
bezeiten: *beizeiten, in good time.*
beziechen, *beziehen, to draw revenues.*
Biel: *Beil, ax:* Stalder, under *bielen to peel, Biel, an ax.*
bim: *beim, by the:* bim wasser, *by the water.*
Biren: *Birne, pears:* Schmid, *bir,* plural *biren* or *birn.*
bishar: *bisher, until now.*
Bitt: *Bitte, request:* mitt Bitt.
Blaseten . . . auf: *bliessen* . . . *auf, puffed up:* Blaseten ihren Barbarischen Hochmuht dergestalten auf.
blauwen: *blauen, blue.*
Bletz: *Lappen, piece of cloth.* Tobler, *Blatz* or *Blätz.*
Blunder: *Hausgeräth, household goods:* Stalder, *Blunder.*
Bodenzins: *quit-rent.*
Bona Mines: *good appearance.*
Bonen: *Bohnen, beans.*
Bood: *Boot, boat.*
böste: *böseste, the worst.*
Botten: *Boten, messengers.*
bredt: *beredet, to be convinced, talked into.*
Bredig: *Predigt, sermon.*
Brüge: *Brücke, scaffold:* Stalder, *Brüge.*
Buch: *Bauch, belly:* mit dem hungrigen Buch.
Büchlin: *Büchlein, little book.*
Buggel: *Buckel, back:* used here as a term of great contempt.
bulver: *Pulver, powder.*
Bouteillen: *bouteilles* (French), *flasks.*
bz: *Batzen, a coin worth about one penny.*

C

Cabis, *Kohl, cabbage:* Stalder, *Kabis.*
Calinierten: the French version shows it must have been intended for *calcinierten, calcined.*
Callons: *gallons.*
Camisohl: *Kamisol, jacket.*
canon: *canot,* French *canoe.*
cap, fare: *Cape Fear.*
Carniture: *Garnitur, trimmings.*
Cartag: *cordage.*
Cartuca: spelled also Chatoka, Chattoka, Chatalognia, caduca, chatouia, Catouca, Chatouka. The original name of the New Bern settlement.
Castel: *New Castle.*
Chaloupen: *chaloupe* (French), *shallop, sloop.*
Chirurgum: *Chirurgus, surgeon.*
Chirurguo; see *chirurgum.*
Clausullen: *Klauseln, clauses.*
Conclusum (Latin): *conclusion.*
conjugiert: *konjugiert, united.*
conjuncten: *conjunctures.*
conjurierten: *conjures* (French), *conspirators.*
conti: *county,* borrowed from the English.
Continentz: *contenance* (French), *countenance.*
Continuierten: *continent (?).*
Contum Divisio: *part of the account.* Können also diese Heidnische Ceremoneyen für ihrem Contum Divisio:
Convaieren: *to convoy.*
Convention: *agreement.*
Converenz: *conference.*
Coro . . . : *Korrespondent (?), agent (?).*
Corruption: *Irruption (?), attack.*
Couv.: *Gouverneur, governor.*
Couvern: *Gouvernement, government.*
Credidif: *Kreditiv, credentials.*

D

dan: *als, than:* dan ein frachtschif zu mieten.
dantwas: *da etwas, since something.*
Danz: *Tanz, dance.*
Dänzer: *Tänzer, dancers.*
dapfer: *tapfer, brave.*
dargeben: *darbieten, offer.*

dargesetzt: *ausgesetzt (?), exposed.* Perhaps combined from *aussetzen* and *darstellen.*
darschiessen: *vorschiessen, advance (money).*
date: *tat, did, made,* and for French *daté, dated.*
debochiert: *debauched.*
Decentz: *decency.*
Decenter: *more decently.*
decliniert: *incliniert (?), inclined.*
Deguragiert: *decouragé* (French), *discouraged.*
delabierten: *délabrer* (French), *delapidated.*
delaprierten: see *delabierten.*
deme: *dem,* Stalder, *deme.*
den: *denn* for *als, than:* Nichts bessres den Frieden mit Gott zu machen.
dene: *dem,* Stalder, *dene.*
denn: *unless:* wir wolten uns denn mutwilliger weis zu Tod schiessen lassen, *unless we wanted to have ourselves wantonly shot.*
depectiert: *debattierte, debated.*
Depitis: *Debet, debt.*
dergestalten: *dergestalt* for *derart, so that.*
dermaleneins: *dermaleinst, sometime.*
derowegen: *deswegen, for which reasons.*
desieren: *desierenden, desiring.*
Desoriert: *in disorder.*
dess: *des,* genitive singular of the masculine or neuter article.
desshalben: *deshalb, for this reason.*
Dessin: *design.*
Destrouieren: *destruieren, destroy.*
deuren: *teuren, dear.*
Devension: *Defension, defence.*
dicklächte: *dickliche, rather thick:* Stalder, *lech* or *lach* for the ending *lich.*
dief: *tief, deep.*
dis: *das* or *dieses, this.*
diss: see *dis.*
Distourbieren: *disturb.*
doubliciert: *dupliziert, rejoined.*
dörfte: *dürfte, might, dared.*
Dozet: *Dutzend, dozen.*
drachteten: *trachteten, tried.*
Drit: *Tritt, step.*
dritt: *dritte, third:* selbst ander oder dritt. *One or two others besides onesself.*

drüben: *Trauben, grapes:* drüben zu gewinnen. Hunziker and Seiler, *drüben.*
Drucken: *prints (?),* Hunziker and Seiler, *Buch* and *Tuch* for *Druck.*
drung: *drang, urged.*
Dubiert: *dupiert, duped.*
Dufils: *duffels cloth.*
durchmist: *durchmischt, mingled.*
durte: *dauerte, grieved.* Seiler, *Dure* for *Mitleid.*

E

Egen: *Ecke, corner.* Stalder, *Egge.*
Eggen: see *Egen.*
Ehelich: *ehrlich (?), respectable:* ein Ehelich Reysgelt.
eiggendlich: *eigentlich, really.*
eim: *einem, to one:* man gibt eim.
Einbrunstiges: *inbrünstiges, ardent.*
einich: *irgend ein, any, some:* ohne einich mensur.
Einstung: *Einsetzung, investment, contribution.*
Einte: *eine, one:* das einte Schif.
eintringen: *eindringen, penetrate.*
Einwanden: *einwenden, to object:* selbige Einwanden.
Embd: *aftermath hay:* Schmid, *Embd.*
embouchure (French): *mouth.*
Embousse: see *embouchure.*
Emparieren: *emparer* (French), *to take possession.*
emperieren: see *emparieren.*
Empfahen: *empfangen, receive:* Maaler, *empfahen.*
Enden: *parts:* der Enden, *in those parts.*
Endich: *Indigo.* Eden, *Endich.*
Endrung: *Aenderung, change.*
en gros (French): *in sum.*
entladnus: *Entladung, exoneration.*
entrunen: *entronnen, escaped.*
er: *eher, before.*
erdauret: *discovered (?).*
erdappen: *ertappen, capture.*
erdappet: see *erdappen.*
Erdenck: *erdacht, thought of.*
Erdenckt: see *Erdenck.*
Erdrich: *Erdreich, soil.* Hunziker, *rich* for *reich.*
ereignet: *erigiert, promoted.* The French version has *érige:* zu einem Obrist ereignet, *made himself a colonel.*
Ereugnete: *ereignete, occurred.*

Erfahrner: *erfahrener, experienced.*
Erfund: *erfand, found.*
Ergangenheit: *Ergebnis, outcome.*
erger: *ärger, worse.*
ergetzen: *ergötzen, enjoy.*
erhälet: *erhellt, is evident.*
erheb: *erhebe* (subjunctive), *arise.*
erheblich (nicht): *(not) to be done.* A Swiss gentleman confirmed this meaning.
erhub: *erhob, arose.*
erinnerd: *erinnerend, remembering.*
erleuterung: *Erläuterung, explanation.*
ermelter: *ermeldeter, above mentioned.*
ermört: *ermordet, murdered.*
Ernd: *Ernte, harvest.*
erobret: *erobert, overcome, conquered.*
errachten: *erachten, consider.*
ers: *er es:* so ers aber endlichen Ergreift, so kan ers thun, *if he finally takes hold of it he can do it.*
erschräcklicher: *erschrecklicher, frightful.*
erschröcklich: see *erschräcklicher.*
Erwehlt: *erwählt, chosen.*
erwimslete: *wriggled:* Maaler, *erwimseln.*
erzellend: *erzählend, telling.*
Escadre: *Escadron* (French), *squadron.*
Est: *Äste, branches:* Est von Laub.
etwan: *etwa, possibly.*
Euchlen: *Eicheln, acorns.*
eussersten: *äussersten, most extreme.*
Evidia: *evidentia* (Latin), *traces.*
excipieren: *excipere* (Latin), *to except.*
excrationen: *execrations.*
exequiert: *exekutiert, executed.*
exparient: *expedient* or *experiment (?), expedient:* the French version has *expédient.*
experient: see *exparient.*
extendieren: *dilate:* nicht fast extendieren.
Ey: see *Nider.*
Eydmäss (dem Eydmäss): dem Eid gemäss, *according to the oath or treaty.*
Eyenwerk: *Eisenwerk, iron articles.*
Eyl: *Eile, haste.*
Eyn: *ein,* separable prefix.

F

Fässli: *Fässlein, casks.*
Fassreifen: *hoops.*
Fauschen: *Faschinen, facines.* French, *facines.* Colonel More in his report says that the Germans were skillful in making *faschines.* Vir. Hist. Mag., Vol. VI, p. 44.
Fehichkeit: *Fähigkeit, ability.*
Fecker: for *Flicker, tinker:* Kessler nämlich Fecker.
Fel: *viel, very.* Fel: liebste Made. Hide.
fergen: *fortbringen, transport:* Maaler, *fergken.*
Fesser: *Fässer, casks.*
feyss: *feist, fat.*
ff: *Pfunde, pounds:* 252 ff.
Fich: *Vieh, cattle:* Tobler, in note to *Vech,* gives *Vich.*
find: *Feinde, enemies.*
Flum: *Flaum, down.*
föllig: *völlig, completely.*
förchte: *fürchtete, feared.*
forcht: *Furcht, fear.*
founierte: *fournir* (French), *furnished.*
Fourren: *Furchen, furrows:* Stalder, *Furre.*
främde: *fremde, strange.*
freudt: *Freude, joy.*
Fr. Goub: Hyde: *Frau Gubernator Hyde, wife of Governor Hyde.*
frömde: *fremde, strange.*
fründ: *Freunde, friends.*
früsch: *frisch, fresh:* Seiler, *früsch.*
fücht: *feucht, damp:* Stalder, *fücht.*
fuess (zu): *Fuss (zu), afoot.*
fun: *von, from.*
fürnimsten: *Vornehmsten, most prominent people:* Hunziker, *für* for *vor.*
fürohin: *hinfüro, henceforth.*
fürrohin: see *fürohin.*
Fürsten: *Fersen, heels.* Trapeten mit den Fürsten.
für über: *vorüber:* hier kann ich nicht für über zu erzellen: *Here I cannot omit to tell.*
fürtrefflich: *vortrefflich, fine.*
fütret: *füttert, feed.*

G

Gabinet: *Kabinett, hut, cabin.*
galgan: *Galgant, galangate:* Hübner, 1722, *Galgant.*
gebeute: *gebietet, commands.*
geblagt: *geplagt, tormented.*

geblünderet: *geplündert, plundered.*
gebräget: *geprägt, coined:* Stalder, *gebraget.*
gebühreten: *gebührenden, fitting.*
gederrtes: *gedörrtes, dried:* gederrtes Weitzen: Maaler, *derren* for *dürr machen:*
Gedreit: *Getreide, grain.*
geführet: *gefüttert, fed:* darmit geführet wurde.
gefütret: *gefüttert sheathed* (of a ship).
gehe: *jähe, sudden:* der gehe Tod. Seiler, *geech.*
geheim: *ungeheim, uncomfortable:* wurde mir bei diesem nicht geheim.
Gehürd: *Hürde, wattles, wickerwork.*
gelegret: *gelagert, rested, camped.*
gelofen: *gelaufen, ran:* Stalder, *geloffe.*
Generalfeltmesser: *Surveyor General.*
genigt: *geneigt, inclined.*
gered: *geredet, spoken.*
geredt: see *gered.*
gerett: see *gered.*
geschächen: *geschehen, all over:* um uns geschächen.
Geschatt: *geschadet, damaged.*
geschärft: *geschürft, grazed.*
g'sin: *gewesen, been.*
Geschwei: *Schwägerin, sister-in-law.* Tobler and Schmid, *G'schwei.*
Gewahrsame: *Gewährschein, credentials.*
gewechs: *Gewächs, crops.*
gewelten: *gewölbten, arched.*
gieng: *ging, went:* Stalder, *gienge.*
gizen: *geizen, envy.*
Göti: *Taufpate, godfather:* Hunziker, *Göti.*
Gleit: *Geleit, safe conduct.*
Glust: *Gelüst, desires.*
graumt: *geräumt, removed.*
greuwlich: *greulich, horrible.*
g'stellen: *bestellen, order.*
G'sweyen: see *Gewchwei.*
gulte: *gülte,* (subjunctive mood) *is worth.*
gutaten: *Guttaten, benefactions.*

H

habender (dass Lauth habender Tractats): *according to the tenor of an existing agreement.*
Haber: *Hafer, oats:* Seiler, *Haber.*
hadren: *hadern, quarrel.*

han: *haben, have.*
Häncken: *hängen, hang.*
Hardes (French): *clothing.*
Häuflin: *Häuflein, small number.*
Hausraht: *Hausgerät, household utensils.*
Hausrecht: see *Hausraht.*
H: B: *Herr Baron, the Baron:* an die Indianer Nation so H: B: von Grafenried gefangen halten.
Hehr: *Herr, man:* ob nun dieser Hehr.
Her: *Heer, army.*
Herdöpfel: *Erdäpfel, potatoes:* Hunziker, Kocherthal, Eden, *Herdäpfel.*
Heurath: *Heirath, marriage:* Stieler, *Heurath.*
Hierobvernamseten: *above mentioned.* Maaler, *namsen.*
hindenan (setzen): *hintenan (setzen), to put at a disadvantage.*
Hindansetzung: *Hintansetzung, disregard.*
hochem: *hohem, high:* Maaler gives inflection to *hoch.*
höste: *höchste, highest, most.*
Hoxheat: *hogshead.*
Huet: *Häute, hides.*
Huete: *Hüte, hats.*
Hüner (Welsche): *wild turkeys.*
hütten: *hätten, had* (subjunctive mood)*:* das Vermögen hütten.

I

Imber: *Ingwer, ginger:* Tobler, *Imber.*
infitieren: *invitieren, invite.*
inspecié: *speciell, especially.*
Intransiter (Latin): *in passing.*
inventieren: *inventer* (French), *invent, pretend.*
Inwehrender: *während, during.*
Islen: *Inseln, islands.*
Itam: *item, likewise.*

J

jar: *Jahr, year.*
Jed. Ind (ein Jed. Ind): perhaps from *ein jeder* and *jeder Indianer:* each Indian.
jedemnach: *je nachdem, according to:* jedemnach sie mit Kleidung.
jit: *jetzt, now.*
justifidicieren: *justifizieren, justify.*

K

Käcklich: *kecklich, boldly.*
Kehr: *Reihe, turn:* Stalder, *Kehr:* Keine Einred als in einen Kehr.
kestenen: *Kastanie, chestnut:* Seiler, *g'Chestene,* Hunziker, *Chestene.*
kine: *kühn, boldly.*
Kirchfäry: *Kirchpfarre, parish.*
Kirsen: *Kirschen, cherries:* Maaler, *Kirsen.*
Kistli: *Kistlein* or *Kistchen, small chest.*
Klägten: *Klagen,* Kläger, *complaints, plaintiffs.*
kleinet: *Kleinigkeiten, trifles.*
Knaupen: *Knaupeln, gnawing.*
könftige: *künftig, future.*
könstlich: *künstlich, artistically.*
Kries: *Kies, gravel.*
Krüsch: *Kirschen, cherries:* Schmid, *Kries.*
Kuchli: *Küchlein,* small *kitchen.*
kum: *kaum, scarcely:* Hunziker, *chum.*
Kumlich: *bequem, easy:* Hunziker, *kommlich.*
Küster: *Kistner, Kistler, cabinet-maker.*

L

Lächen: *Lehen, fee, estate.*
Laden: *Brett, board.* Eden, *Laden.*
Lamentien: *lament.*
LandGutschen: *Landkütschen, stagecoach.*
Langgraf: *Landgraf, landgrave.*
Lechen: see *Lächen.*
Leg Eisen: *Achsenblech (?), skeins.* Hübner describes Legeisen as the irons put upon the timbers of mining machinery to resist the wear of ropes passing over them. Another definition makes them to be the pieces of iron put into the cleft of rock on each side of the wedge with which the rock is to be split. In either case the name is applied to an iron used to resist wear. Achsenblech is a piece of iron nailed to an axel to keep it from being worn by the hub of the wheel. The word meaning to fasten on such pieces of iron is *auflegen.* The ordering of linch pins would seem to indicate the same thing. See *Lungen.*
lehr: *leer, empty:* Maaler, *lehr.*
leinag: *leinig (?),* for *leinen* or *Leinwand, linen.*
Leinlachen: *Leilachen, sheets:* Seiler, *Leilaken.*
Leinwad: *Leinwand, linen:* Stieler, *Leinwad.*
Lenge: *Länge, length.*
Lengste: see *Lenge, longest.*

Lente: *Landung,* landing.
lestlich: *letztlich,* lately.
Leuth: *laut,* according to the tenor. See *Habender.*
Lingien: *Linie,* French *ligne,* line.
lof: *lief, ran:* Stalder, *luff, geloffe;* Stieler, *geloffen.*
loos: *los,* loose.
Lott: *lot.*
L. S.: *large seal.*
lufen: *liefen, ran.*
Luffen: see *lufen.*
lügen: *liegen,* to lie.
Lungen: *Lünse, Nabennagel, linch pin:* Seiler, *Lung,* a variant form under *Lone* for *Lünse.*
Lntz (des): abbreviation for Landes, of the land, country.

M

Mägt: *Mägde,* maids.
mähl (Zucker mähl): *fine sugar:* Maaler, *Zuckermehl.*
mainen: *mainland.*
Malasio: *Malasse, molasses.*
Mänli: *Männlein,* little man.
Mantschaff: *Mannschaft, soldiery.*
Marens: *Marinen, marines.*
Margues: *Marken, marks.*
Martyny: *Martini, Martinmas.*
Mäschenen: *Möschernen,* Swiss for *messingern, brass;* Maaler, *möschern;* Tobler, *Mösch,* for *Messing.*
mäser: *Moraste, swamps:* Tobler: *Mos;* from Middle High German, *möser* for *Moore;* English *moor,* swamp.
Mäss: *Mass, peck* when used as a dry measure: Tobler, *Mass* or *Mess.*
Materj: *Materie, cause:* Maaler, *Materi.*
Matey: *Materie, cause.*
Matronen: *Matrosen, sailors.*
Mattes: *Matten, mats.*
Maulbehr: *Maulbeeren, mulberries.*
Mayesteht: *Majestät, majesty.*
mensuren: *measures.*
Mentel: *Mäntel, mantels.*
mepesi per: *Mississippi.*
Meutinierer: *Meuterer, mutineers.*
Meyen: *Mai, May.* von dem Meyen bis in den Herbst Monath.
mieche: *mache, macht, make, makes:* Seiler, *miecht.*
miecht: see *mieche.*

Miesch: *Moos, moss.* Stalder, *Miesch.*
Mill: *Meile, mile.* Hunziker, *mil.*
Miltrung: *Milderung, kindness.*
min: *mein, mine, my.* Stalder, *min.*
Mine: *Miene, mien.* doch hielte ich bonne Mine.
minste: *mindesten, at least.*
Misstreurige: *misstrauische, suspicious.*
Mitternacht: *north.*
Mng: Herren (bei): *bei meinen gnädigen Herren, with my gracious Sirs.*
Mn H: *mein Herr, Sir:* Es gedenke Mn H: Goubernat:
Möllstein: *Mühlsteine, millstones.* Possibly from *mole,* given in Seiler for *mahlen,* to grind.
Mon.: *Monsieur;* Mon: LeGouv: Je suis tellement, *Governor, I am so.*
Monzua: *a female proper name.*
Morgen: *acre.* Any unit of land measure.
Motifa: *Motiv, motives.*
Mst: *Meister(?), captain.*
Mühj: *Mühe, pains.*
Mühli: *Mühllein, small mill:* Hunziker, *Müli.*
Mühwaltung: *pains, effort.*
Mülli: see *Mühli.*
Murmlens: *Murmelns, murmuring.*

N

Naben Neyer: *Nabeneisen(?)* or *Nabenei(?),* literally perhaps *hub iron* or an article having to do with hubs. The evident meaning is an *auger.*
nacher: *nach, after.*
nächer: *näher, nearer.*
Nägeli: *Nägelein, Nelke, cloves.*
Naht: *Nacht, night.*
namsen: *nennen, to name.* Maaler, *namsen.*
Narrung: *Nahrung, food.*
nemmen: *nehmen, to take.*
Neschflen *néfle,* French: *Mispel medlar,* Hunziker: *Nesple medlar.*
Neuenburgischen: *of Neuchatel.*
neut: *nicht, not:* Schmid, *neut.*
Neuw: *neu, new:* Maaler, *neuw.*
Nider Ey: *Niderei* for *Niederung(?) lowland.*
Niderlass: *Niederlassung, settlements.*
Niemahleneins: *niemals, never.*
Norost: *Nordost, northeast.*
nüt: *nicht,* Schmid, *nüt.*

O

ob: *ober, above:* ob den Fahl, *above the falls.*
obentruf: *oben darauf, on the top of it.*
Oberkeit: *Obrigkeit, authority.*
obgemelt: *obgemeldet, above mentioned.*
oblige: perhaps for *Obligationen* or *Obliegen, requests, matters of importance.*
Obrist: *Oberst, colonel.* Stalder, *andrist* for *anderst.* Shows same interchange of letters.
Obsorg: *Obsorge* for *Obhut, care, protection.*
odre: *orders.*
officia: *Officium-a* (Latin), *offices.*
ohn: in composition is *un.*
ohngeacht: *ungeachtet, notwithstanding.*
ohngefehrt: *ungefähr, about.*
öpflen: *Aepfel, apples.*
oposité: *opposite.*
ordinari: *ordinär, ordinarily.*

P

Päch: *Pech, pitch:* Maaler, *Päch.*
Panque: *Bank, banque* (French), *bank.*
Parillen: *Barillen, Aprikosen, apricots:* Maaler, *Barille.*
Particulatoren: *particuliers* (French), *individuals.*
p. c.: *per conto* for *Konto, on account.*
perfallieren: *fallieren, fail.*
Pfannwärten: *taking charge of the pan.* This seems to indicate that Graffenried had started a manufactory of salt. In the first place he had been acquainted with the industry from boyhood; then there was the great difficulty in obtaining salt from the Bermudas (for which see the French text), and lastly, one common German word for salt making is Pfannewerken, a term quite similar fo Pfannwärten.
Pfarher: *Pfarrer, minister:* Maaler, *Pfarrher.*
Pfersich: *Pfirsich, peach:* Maaler, *Pfersich.*
Pflugredre: *Pflugräder, plow wheels:* Maaler, under Rad *Pflugrad;* Seiler, plural of *Rad* is *Reder.*
Pittschaft: *Petschaft, seals.*
Platinen: *platine* (French). One definition meaning lockplates for guns may be what was intended.
Plattmacher: *Geschirrmacher, potters:* Seiler, *Blatt* for *Geschirr.*
plessiert: *blessiert, wounded.*
Ploät: *Blount* or *Blunt,* an Indian chief.

Plutons: *Pelotons, platoons.*
Presidium: *Präsidium, presidency.*
Pretendenten: *Prätendenten, candidates.*
preyss: *Preis, price.*
pricé: *Brice,* one of Hyde's opponents.
Procedieren: *to produce, bring forward(?).*

Q

quarquer: *Quakers.*

R

rahren: *Rohre, reeds.*
Raht: *Rat, council, counsel, advice.*
rahtete: *riet, advised.*
ranges: *ranges,* Lawson's Journal.
Rauchen: *rauhes, rough.* ein Rauchen Englischen Wort.
Raum: *rum.*
rauwen: *rohen, rauh, rough.*
Reb Gut: *Rebgut, vineyard.*
recanstrieren: impossible to translate with certainty, evidently means *to collect together.*
rechen: *rächen, to avenge* or *get revenge.*
Rechtschaffen: *Recht schaffen, to get justice;* recht schaffen: just, honest.
Récipissé: *récépissé* (French), *receipt.*
recontrieren: rencontrer (French), *to meet.*
recusiert: *recusare* (Latin), *refused.*
red: *Rede, speech.*
Redlisführer: *Rädelsführer, ringleaders.*
Reept: *Representative,* Reept und obern Haus.
refidieren: *revidieren, revise.*
Reiften: *Reifen, hoope.* Hunziker, *Reifte.*
reistige: *hanfen, hempen.* Seiler, *ristig* from *Reiste, ristig Duech, ausgehechelter Hanf.*
rention: *Ranzion, ransom.*
restanzen: *Restanten, those in arrears.*
ret: *redet, relates.*
reterieren: *to retire.*
retierierenden: from *réitérer* (French), *repeating. retierierenden, ja ja.*
retressieren: *redressieren, redress.*
rette: *see ret.*
Reys: *Reise, journey.*
Reyss: see *Reys.*
Rhyn: *Rhein.*

Richtum: *Reichtum, wealth:* Hunziker, *Richtum.*
rieggen: *rücken, to move, disturb.*
Riehte: *riet, advised.*
Riett: Land Graff von Riett. To the unlettered colonists, a syllable or two more or less makes little difference and Landgrave von Graffenried easily becomes Land Graff von Riett, Graffen Ritter and Graff Ritter. Perhaps the fact that the principal member of the company in Bern was named Ritter helped in the confusion of names by which the baron was called. Certainly the context would not allow of any other than Graffenried's having been the one meant.
Rigel: *Riegel, bolts.*
Ris: *Reis, rice:* Seiler, *Ris.*
Ritter: see *Riett.*
Roseichen: *Roteichen, red oak.* Eden, *Roteichen.*
Rost: *rust.*
Roum: *rum.*
Routen: *route.*
Rovalis: *royal* (French), *royal.* Sucre Royal; c'est en terme de Confiserie, ce qu'il y a de plus dure & de plus fin en fait de sucre: on le clarifie in Hollande où l'on a l'art de le faire meilleur qu'ailleurs. Encyclopédie, Ou Dictionnaire raisonné des sciences, Des Arts Et Des Métiers. Found under *Sucre.* *Royal sugar; that is, a confectioner's term for the hardest and purest variety of sugar. It is clarified in Holland where they have the art of making it better than elsewhere.*
Rübli: *Möhre, carrots:* Stalder, *Rübli.*
rudera: *rudus, eris* (Latin), *ruins, fragments.*
Ruebli: see *Rübli.*
ruften: *riefen, called out.*
Ruhe: *rauhe, rough:* betrefend die Ruhe, etc.
Ruhj: *Ruhe, rest.*
Ruhten: *Ruthen* or *Ruten, wands, whips.*
ruhwig: *ruhig, quiet:* Stalder, *ruw.*
Rurren: *schnurren, roaring, buzzing:* Seiler, *Rure* for *Schnurre.*
Rysshut: *Ryss, Hut* for *Reis, Häute; rice, hides.*

S

sach: *Sache(?), case:* es wäre denn sach, *except in case* . . .
sache: *sah, saw.*
Sagi: *Säglein, Sawmill:* Hunziker, *Sagi* for *Sägemühle.*
Säglen: *Segeln, sails:* Maaler, *Sägeln.*
sagt: *sägt, saws:* man sagt in Engelland.
Salafra: *Sasafras, sassafras.*

sammen: *Samen, seed.*
Sänckten: *senkten, sunk.*
Santen: *sandten, sent.*
säumet: from *säumen,* to convey with pack animals, *to take.*
säyen: *säen, to sow.*
schaad: *schade, too bad.*
Schaaden: *Schaden, damage.*
Schaben: *Motten, moths:* Reference to: Ihr sollt euch nicht Schätze sammeln auf Erden, da sie die Motten und der Rost fressen, und da die Diebe nachgraben und stehlen. *Luther's Bible, Mat. 6:19.*
Schäft: perhaps to be joined to the preceding word, making *Tischmacherschäft* for *Tischmacherei, things made by a cabinetmaker.* The ordinary expression is *Tischlerarbeit.*
schäncken: *schenken, to present.*
Scheil: *Schields(?), North and South Shields,* towns near New Castle on the Tyne River, closer to the mouth.
Scheitzer: *Schweitzer, Swiss.*
Schermen: *Schirmen, shelters:* Tobler, *Scherm.*
schiene: *schien, appeared.*
schier: *entirely:* Maaler, *schier,* for *ganz.*
Schifli: *Schifflein, small boat.*
Schifwahren: *schiffbaren, navigable.*
schindten: *schinden, to flay.*
schinen: *schienen, to seem, appear.*
schine: see *schinen.*
schlifrigen: *schlüpfrigen, slippery, percarious.*
Schlop(p): *sloop or shallop.*
Schlüssli: *Schlüssellein, small key.*
Schnagen: *Schlangen, snakes:* Grimm, *Schnake* or *Schnacke.*
Schott: *Schiff, sloop:* In *Pennsylvanien im 17. Jahrhundert* Schute is given as a Dutch word for barque. The word appears there to be well known.
Schrött: *Schrot, shot.*
Schwächer: *Schwiegervater, father-in-law.* Hunziker, *Schwäher.*
schwär: *schwer, hard, with difficulty.*
Schwefliechte: *schweflich* for *schwefelartig, sulphurous.*
Schweren: *schwören,* swear.
Schwertren: *Schwertern, swords.*
seche: *sehe, see.*
Seck: *Säcke, sacks.*
Seckel: *Säckel (machen), to line one's purse.*
sée: *See, sea.*
Segl: *Segli(?)* for *Segen, blessing.*

Segnerey: coined from *Segen(?), pronouncing of all sorts of blessings(?), incantations.*
Seylwerk: *Seilwerk, cordage.*
Seyten: *Seiten, to one side.*
sezen: *setzen, settle, place.*
sicht: *sieht, sees.*
Siebenzechen: *siebzehn, seventeen.*
sinth: *sint,* old form for *seit, since.*
so: *if, who, which, when.*
Sollath: *Salat, salad:* Hunziker, *Sollath.*
son: *sonst, otherwise:* son dörften Sie nit Kummer haben.
Sond: *Sund, sound.* Here used of the Albemarle Sound.
sondrest: *besonders, especially.*
Soucours: *assistance.*
souponieren: *suppose.*
sous: French for *unter.* Sous pretense.
spaad: *spät, late:* Stieler, *spat.*
spaat: see *spaad.*
Späch: *Späher, spy.* Maaler, *Späch* for *spying,* but *Späher, a spy.*
Spat: see *spaad.*
Specié: *speciell, especially, in particular.*
speren: *sperren, resist.*
speter: *später, later.*
spihl: *spiel, play.* Maaler, *Spil.*
Stählen: *stehlen, stealing.*
Steiffe: *steifen,* persist.
Stettli: *Städtlein, small city.*
Stettlin: *Städtlein, small city.*
stif: *steif, stiff, firm.*
Stihl: *Stiel, handle.* Seiler, *Stil.*
Stilus (Latin): *style.*
Stöckli: *Stöcklein* for *Stöckchen, small stick.*
Stoor: *store.*
Stückli: *Stücklein, small pieces, small cannon.*
stunde: *stand, stood.*
sturben: *starben, died.*

T

Tauwen: *Dauben, staves.*
Tems: *Thames.*
Terres (French): in the expression Terres land, *acres(?).*
thäte: *tät* for *tat,* with anhalten, *begged.*
thür: *teuer, expensive.*

thuür: see *thür.*
Tischmacher: *Tischler, cabinetmaker.* Tobler, *Tischmacher.*
Töchterli: *Töchterlein, little daughter.*
Todne (Hand): *tote (Hand), mortmain.*
Tofen: sambt den 45 K. So ich hinder der Gemeind Tofen gelassen perhaps meant for *der Gemeinde Tofen*). *Which I left behind with the Tofen congregation.*
Tonen: *Tonnen, tons, tuns.*
Torf: *Dorf, village.*
Tractatieren: *traktieren, treat.*
Train (French): *procession.*
tresilieren: *tressaillir* (French), *tremble.*
treuwen: *drauen, drohen, threaten.*
tringender *dringender, urgent:* tringender Noth.
trüber: *drüber, darüber, up above.*
truf: *drauf, darauf, thereon:* Stalder, *druff.*
Truessen: *Druse, dregs.* French version speaking of rum calls it eau de vie distilée de la lie de sucre: *brandy distilled from the residue of sugar.*
trumlin: *Trommellein, small drum.*
Tudos: *Tortugas(?).*
Turgisch (Korn): *Indian corn:* Stalder, *Türkenkorn.*

U

übelzellung: *übele Erzählung, unhappy circumstance,* occurrence.
überlass: *überliess, left.*
überlegen: *lästig, troublesome* (Maaler): So dass diess Reys mir mehr überlegen als da ich zweymahl über den oceanum gefahren.
übernacht: *übernachtete, passed the night.*
Uerte: *Wert, worth.*
Uessert: *ausser, except:* Seiler, *usse* for *aus.*
Uesters: *Austern, oysters.*
unbedastet: *unbetastet, untouched.*
Unbeschwerlich: *beschwerlich(?), troublesome.*
ungefehrt: *ungefähr, about.*
ungereimbt: *ungereimt, preposterous.*
Ungetultig: *ungeduldig, impatient.*
Unterscheyd: *Unterschied, difference.*
unterwex: *unterwegs, on the way.*
Unthan: *Unterthan, subject.*
Unverschandheit: *Unverschämtheit, insolence.*
unzifer: *Ungeziefer, vermin.*
unversichtig: *unvorsichtig, without foresight.*
Unwüssenheit: *Unwissenheit, lack of knowledge.*

V

Vampan: *wampum.*
vast: *fast, nearly, very much;* an old usage.
verbränt: *verbrennt* for *verbrannt, burned.*
verderbten: *verdarben, verdorben, destroyed.*
verdeuten: *to indicate that,* mit verdeuten.
vereblen: *verreblen, to die.* Schmid, *verreblen,* used of animals.
vereschafen: *verschaffen, procure.*
Verglich: *Vergleich, agreement.*
vergwüsseret: *vergewissert, assured.*
verheurathete: *verheiratete, married:* Stieler, *verheurathen.*
verliche: *verlieh, granted, gave.*
Verlümdungen: *verleumdungen, slanders.*
vermeind: *vermeinend, believing.*
vermeinet: see *vermeind.*
vermitten: *vermieden, avoided.*
vernamsete: *named, appointed.* Maaler, *namsen.*
Verornet: *verordnete, ordained.*
verissene: *zerrissene, torn.*
Versäumnüss: *Versäumnis, delay.*
Verschandtes: *unverschämtes, shameless.*
verschätz: *verschätzt, lose confidence* guess wrongly. Perhaps related to schätzen with adversative signification to the prefix.
verseche: *versehe* (subjunctive mood), *provide.*
versend: *versendet, sent.*
versendt: see *versend.*
verspürte: seems to mean *gave evidence.*
vertreglich: *verträglich, affable.*
vertrieslich: *verdriesslich, vexatious.*
vertruss: *Verdruss, vexation.*
vertrüssig: *verdriesslich, vexatious.*
Verwierung: *Verwirrung, confusion.*
verwis: *Verweis, reproof.*
verwürkt: *verwirkt, forfeited:* Maaler, *würcken:* ware ich umb die 5,000 verwürkt.
Verzug: *verzog, delayed.*
vest: *fast, firmly.*
vest: *fest, festival.*
vetter: *fetter, fat, rich:* vetter Grund.
Vexaats: *jest,* from vexieren (?). Obwohlen der Indianer König sache dass ich diss wesen in vexaats zog.
Vich: *Vieh, cattle;* Tobler, Vech.
viel: *fiel, came, befell:* so unbeschwerlich viel.

viguren: *Figuren,* faces, figures.
villicht: *vielleicht, possibly:* Hunziker, *filicht.*
vilste: *vielste, most:* Seiler, *vill:* Hunziker, *vil.*
visicalisch: *physikalisch, physically.*
Vohrlen: Lawson's Journal mentions a Sower-Wood Tree. Possibly Graffenried intended to write *Sohrlen.*
vollnutz: *völlig, completely.*
von: *wann (?), when:* von obermelte Wilden Kriegs Leuth oder vielmehr Mörder, einkamen.
vor: *für, for.*
vorsechen: *vorsehen, foresee.*
vortgieng: *fortging, went on:* Stalder, *gieng.*
vürhanden: *vorhanden, at hand.*

W

Wächselbrief: *Wechselbrief, bill of exchange:* Maaler, *Wächsel.*
wägen: *Wege, ways.*
Währe: *wäre, were.*
Wahre: *Waren, wares.*
wans: *wenn es, if it.*
Wasserpferch: *dam (?).* Pferch, fold or pen.
weg (in einen): *immediately, any way.*
weger: *wegen, on account of.*
Wehrender: *während der, during the:* wehrender Gefangenschaft.
wehrten: *wendeten, turned:* wehrten den Rücken.
wenix: *wenigs, a little.*
wex: *wegs,* in *halbwegs, halfway.*
wexel: *Wechsel, note.*
weyd: *Weide, meadow, pasture.*
weyss: *weiss, know.*
widrum: *wiederum, again.*
wiglen: *wickeln, disentangle.* Solothurn, *wiglen:* mich aus diesem labirint zu wiglen.
wiglete . . . auf: *wiegelte . . . auf, stirr up.*
Willdbret: *Wildpret, venison.*
wilt: *willst, will:* die Reis wilt vor dich nehmen.
wis: *weis,* millionen wis, *by millions.*
Wittlig: *Witwer, widower:* Stalder, *Witling.*
wo: for *wenn, if.* wo ihr Ihne Todend . . . Im Sinn hatet.
wüssend: *wissend, knowing.*
Wys: *Weise, manner:* Maaler, *Wys.*

Z

Zableten: *zappeln, ran about:* Schmid, *zabeln.*
Zedelin: *Zetteln, notes:* Stalder, *Zedel.*
Zedlen: see *Zedelen.*
Zehnd: *Zehnt, tithe, tenth.*
Zeifel: *Zweifel, doubt.*
Zellung: *Zählung, calculation.*
zechen: *ziehen, to go, draw.*
Zufähl: *Zufälle, accidents.*
Zugrecth: *option, preference.* Hübner makes it equivalent to *Näher recht*, that is *preference.* Hunziker defined it: Das Recht zum Miterben zugestanden wird, ein Stück der Erbmasse, das verkauft wird den Verkaufspreis sich anzueignen. *The law on joint inheritance (which is) acknowledged (is) that one (is allowed) to appropriate a portion of the inheritance which is sold, (that is, a portion) of the sale price to his own uses.*
zukönftig: *zukünftig, in the future.*
Zwüschen: *zwischen, between:* Maaler, *zwüschen.*

INDEX

TO THE INTRODUCTION AND TRANSLATIONS

In order to avoid making the index too complicated the items in German and French have not been included. It is believed that if desired they can without excessive difficulty be found from the passages in the translations.

V. H. Todd.

INDEX

Adams, 57.
Abbeville, 260, 389.
Aeschbacher, Hans, 314.
Aescher, Andreas, 319.
Albemarle, 226; Assembly of, 65; County, 36, 240, 263; Duke of, 54, 359, 362; Chancellor of Cambridge University, 28; Sound, 75; Settlements near, 53.
Albrecht, Justus, 92, 104, 257, 258, 376.
Allemande, 93.
America, 13, 21, 31, 38, 42, 65; advantages of, 223; evidences of Graffenried's return to lacking, 96, 97; Palatines sent to, 9, 16, 24, 224.
Amsterdam, 104, 379.
Anabaptists, 62; convicts, 46; Dutch, 47; in Switzerland, 11; persecutions of, 30.
Angleterre, see England.
Antigua, cost of transportation to London from, 302; trade with, 300.
Arau, knives of, 307.
Archdale, 31.
Arctic pole, 367.
Ashe, Thomas, 31.
Ashley, Lord Anthony, 54.
Assistance for the colony expected from Hyde, 72; from the Lords Proprietors, 48, 49, 70, 363, 371; failure of Graffenried to obtain, 49, 73, 75, 92, 93, 94, 234, 240, 251, 254, 255, 257, 283, 378, 390; granted, 46, 73, 283, 363.

Bache, Uhli, 314.
Balsiger, Christian, 313.
Baltic Sea, 366.
Baltimore, 361.
Balts, Nicholas, 316.
Barbadoes, 367; cost of transportation to London from, 302; prices in, 301; supplies required in, 302; trade with, 300, 305.
Barnwell, Colonel, 86, 87, 243, 244, 245, 383.
Barony, 64, 65, 66.
Bartington, 253.
Bartlome, 312.
Bath, 81, 226; County, 82, 98; Town, 240.

Bayley, John, 65.
Bay River, 240, 270; Indian chief of tortured, 238.
Beaufort, Duke of, 45, 93; death, 94, 98, 257.
Beaumont, 15, 21.
Bell, Colonel, 391, 392.
Bellinger, Captain Edmund, 65.
Bericht, Kocherthal's, 31, 32.
Berkeley, Governor of Virginia, 53; Lord John, 54; Sir William, 54.
Bermudas, 104; salt obtained from, 379, 380.
Bern, 27, 28, 46, 47, 71, 91, 93, 94, 96, 97, 102, 104, 109, 110, 252, 255, 256, 278, 284, 291, 307, 314, 315, 367, 372, 378, 379, 387; arrival of Graffenried in, 260, 390; colony from, 23, 360; colonists from willing to settle at Canavest, 254; departure of colonists from, 308, 309; expense to Rotterdam from, 315; not qualified to colonize, 251; proposition of for a tract in Virginia, 361; treaty with a society in, 364; Canton of makes negotiations for land, 33.
Bishop of Durham, 53, 365; of London, 62, 377.
Blackheath, 21.
Blankistore, Colonel, 258.
Blome, 31, 261.
Blount, Tom, 276.
Boehme, Anton Wilhelm, 14.
Booklet, printed at Frankfort, 317.
Boston, 365, 369.
Bötschi, 104, 107, 292, 312; report of, 289.
Bottigen, 314.
Boyd, Colonel, 244.
Boyle, 17, 18.
Brünen, 313.
Brice, 71, 86, 382; campaign of, 85, 86, 237, 238, 244; charges against Graffenried preferred by, 84; opposition to Graffenried, 85, 236; plot of, 85, 236; settlers enticed by, 262.
Brigantine, see also under vessel, 74, 231.
Brill, the, 18.
Bristol, 92, 94, 257.
British America, 13.
Buch, 311.

Buchse, Hans von, 311.
Bullre, Joseph, 310.
Burger, Uhli, 316.
Bürki, Christian, 316, 318; Christen, 320.
Byrd, William, 24, 42, 97, 110; memoirs showing that the Indians had cause for resentment, 77, 78, 79; Lawson's death described by, 80; reference of to Madame de Graffenried, 96.

Caduca, also Cartouca, Cartuca, Chatalognia, Chatoka, Chatouka, Chattoka, Indian village where New Bern was afterward built, 34, 226, 234, 266, 270, 275, 373, 380.
Caesar, Mr., 225, 360.
Camberwell, 21.
Canaan, das verlangte, nicht erlangte, 14.
Canada, 288, 291, 383, 387.
Canary Islands, 44.
Canavest, 91, 104, 247, 248, 251, 254, 383, 392; alliance with Indians of, 384; description of country near, 390; site of proposed settlement near, 89, 386; treaty with Indians of, 247.
Cancer, Tropic of, 367.
Cape Fear, also Fair, 38, 43, 53, 77, 285, 293; surveying expedition along, 375.
Cape Henry, 369.
Carlyle, Duke of, 28.
Carolina, 14, 25, 33, 34, 45, 49, 51, 62, 79, 221, 226, 229, 236, 239, 247, 248, 249, 252, 294, 315, 359, 369, 371, 382, 384, 391; advantages of, 36, 42, 284, 285; arrival of colonists in, 306; characteristics of settlers of, 39; climate of, 298; cost of transportation to, 299; described by Hennepin, 31; early settlers not religious refugees, 53; foreign trade of, 305; freedom of from bloodshed, 39, 40, 41, 42; governed by concessions, 54; government of, 41; governor of, 275; inaccessibility of to large vessels, 360; increase of settlers in, 289; incursion of Indians into, 82; indigo planted in, 301; mining rights of the colony in, 47; prices of provisions in, 301; profits on trade in, 307; requirement of oaths of allegiance a dead letter in, 56;

Carolina—*Continued*.
silk industry in, 301; trade of with the Madeiras, 300.
Carolinians, carelessness of, 239.
Cartaret, Sir George, 54, 55.
Cary, Thomas, 56, 57, 58, 70, 72, 73, 106, 231, 234, 283; arrest of, 233; attack of on Hyde, 74; banishment and death of, 372; believed to have incited the Indians, 76, 81, 82, 228; capture of, 75; death of, 102; deception of Graffenried by, 230; defeat of, 231; disorders occasioned by, 227-233; evades assisting Graffenried, 62, 285; flight of, 74; opposed by Graffenried, 62; rebellion of, 229; renewed rebellion of, 74, 75, 232; rivalry of with Glover, 57; threatened by Graffenried, 229; visit of to New Bern, 230.
Casique, also cassique, cacique, 64, 65, 67, 69, 362; number of, 66; title sold, 65.
Catawbas, 78.
Catechna, 83, 261, 264, 271, 272, 273, 275, 376, 379, 380, 381; attack on, 244, 245; return of the Indians to, 274.
Catholic cantons, 30.
Catholicism in the Palatinate and Switzerland, 9-11.
Chamber of London for the Propagation of the Faith, 377.
Channing, Edward, appreciative notice of Germans in history by, 5.
Charles II, 9, 28, 44, 53, 103, 223, 362.
Charleston, also Charlestown, 33, 35.
Chartier, also Charetier, 247, 383, 384.
Chief Justice, 225.
Chowan River, also Chuwon, 52, 226, 371; precinct, 36.
Christeler, Christina, 318; Moritz, 319; Peter, 318.
Church of England established by law, 56; given the preference, 54, 55; missionaries, 57.
Clarendon, Edward, Earl of, 54; River, 77, 284, 363, 376; surveying expedition along, 375.
Clark, counterfeiter, 291.
Cluses, Fort of, 260.
Colleton, Sir John, 54, 74; Chevalier, 252.

INDEX 423

Colonial Records, showing that the Indians had cause for resentment, 79.
Colonists, arrival of in Carolina, 316; in Virginia, 49, 51, 309, 310, 369; contentment of, 306, 308, 309, 310, 316, 317, 318; death of, 49, 51, 225, 306, 307, 318, 360; defrauded by the surveyor-general, 59, 226; deplorable condition of, 59, 73, 86, 370, 372, 383; duties of, 363; letters of criticised, 73; need of keeping away from the Indians, 61; permission given to leave the colony, 87; prosperity of, 72, 228, 370; wages earned by, 309, 313.
Commissioner for the Palatines, 73.
Committee of council, proposals of, 44, 45.
Community of expense, 288.
Concessions, 54.
Congaree River, 34.
Connecticut, 5; silver in, 6.
Constitution, revised, 64.
Contentment of the colonists, 306, 308-318.
Contract of the Ritter Company, 107, 292.
Constantinople, 28.
Copper, 258.
Core, Indians, 244, 270, 281; kindness of to Graffenried, 76, 380, 381; sold as slaves, 87; Sam, 377; Sound, attack on, 270; Tom, 267, 377; Town, 104, 243, 245, 376.
Counter Reformation, 9, 10.
Counts, 362.
Court Leet, see Leet Court.
Craven County, 99; House, 43, 45, 48; William, Earl of, 54.
Cromwell, plans of, 9; work of taken up by Queen Anne, 9.
Crown, share of in mines, 47, 48.
Culpeper, 88, 103, 361.
Currituck, 246, 248.

Daniel, Governor, 56; Major Robert, 65.
Danson, 73, 292.
Dauphin, 29.
Davenant, 17.
Dayralle, 19.
Deerfield, 25.
Denmark, 366.
Departure of the colony for America, 46, 308.

Dictli, 319.
Dietrich, 314, 315.
Directors, 59, 363; faithless conduct of, 59, 226, 370, 371.
Dissenters, 9.
Dortrecht, trade with, 300.
Dover, 259, 260, 389.
Drummond, 54.
Drus, Anna, 320.
Duckenfield, 229.
Duplin County, 99.
Durham, Bishop of, 53, 365.
Dutch Anabaptists, 47.

Ecclesiastical Council, 11.
Eden, Governor, 92, 94, 252; land of, 24.
Edens, Abraham, 305; Egbert, 305.
Edmundson, 55.
Edwards, William, 296.
Eggen, Christen, 309.
Egender, Heinrich, 310.
Elector Palatinate, also Palatine, 17, 18, 44.
Elector of Saxony, 28.
Elizabeth, 9; daughter of James I, 10.
Emigration to New York, poor management of, 50; to Pennsylvania, causes of, 13.
Emigrants, see under Palatines.
Engel, 28; Christen, 316.
England, 12, 15, 17, 19, 21, 28, 29, 42, 43, 46, 47, 56, 59, 66, 91, 92, 93, 94, 223, 250, 305, 310, 316, 387; arrival of colonists in, 309; cost of transportation from, 299; emigration from Germany to, 9, 44, 224; profits on trade in, 307; protector of Protestantism, 9; Reformation in, 9; return of Graffenried to, 257; trade with, 300; visited by Graffenried, 33.
English, attack of on the Indians, 83, 86, 273; colonies, 22; element, percentage of in the United States, 5; Government, employment of Indians by, 81; massacred, 82; reformers, 9; relations with the Indians, 22; settlers, 318; vessels, 367.
Eriswyl, 310.
Essex, Count of, 364.
Exchange, 296.

Farwel, 28.
Faust, Professor A. B., 102.
Fenwick, Alderman, 365.

424 INDEX

Feudal, acknowledgment, 67; relationship acknowledged by the colonists, 69; system, 67.
Fitzhugh, Colonel, 254.
Flanders, 244.
Florida, 22.
Flüh, 315.
Flühli, 314.
Fort Royal, 291.
Foster, 57.
Fox, 55.
France, 29, 93, 250, 387, 389, 390.
Frankfort, 15, 17; Booklet printed at, 317.
Frankfurt, 34.
Frankreich, see France.
Frederick, Elector, 10.
Freedom, see also under Liberty, 311; of conscience or religious liberty, 42, 54, 55, 57, 62, 68, 71, 103, 306, 363; provided for especially, 62.
French, colonists, 67; menace to the English colonies, 22; privateer, 369; relations with the Indians, 22.
Frontiers, protected by foreign protestants, 22-25.
Fundamental Constitutions, also Fundamentals, 62, 63, 65; extracts from, 64; impracticability of, 67; requirements of regarding land not observed, 65, 66; revision of, 64, 67.
Fyper, Chevalier, 363.

Gabley, Samuel Jacob, 309.
Gale, Receiver-General, 49; Christopher, extract from a letter of, regarding the death of Lawson, 80.
Galliar, Mons, 36.
General Assembly, also Assembly, 242; a democratic body, 54.
Geneva, 28, 260, 390; Lake, 241.
George I, 94, 390.
Gerber, Casper, 316.
German, colony, 282; edition of Lawson's Journal, 34; miners, 25; element, percentage of in the United States, 5; protestant situation, interest of England in, 10; Reformed Church, 360; women, lack of, 315.
Germanna, 25.
Germans, 13; discrimination against by historians, 5; emigration of to England, 44; to New York, 9; to North Carolina, 9; to Pennsylvania, 9; induced to come to England, 17; in Maine, 25; measures for the re-

Germans—*Continued*.
lief of, 16; number of in the migration to England, 16; official help given to, 19, 20; relation of to freedom of conscience, 6; relation of to freedom of the press, 6; relation of to the Indians, 6; settlements of, 5; to be sent to America, 44; used as frontiers against the French and Indians, 22-25.
Germantown, 5, 13.
Germany, 13, 17, 18, 90, 390; emigration from, 9, 224; reformation in, 9; refuge, for the persecuted, 9, 15.
Glebe, in Parish of S. Thomas, 42.
Glover, William, 58, 70; administration of, 57; rivalry of with Cary, 57.
Gobli, Jacob, 310.
Goebel, Professor Julius, 93, 101, 102, 105.
Gold, 290.
Gold Creek, 248, 386.
Golden Book, 14, 17.
Gordon, 57.
Graffenried, also Graffenriedt, Albrecht von, 48, 292; Anton von, 27, 28, 93; Barbara, also Madame de, and Baronne de, 96; Baron Christoph von, 6, 14, 24, 25, 27, 28, 29, 42, 50, 52, 61, 64, 71, 72, 73, 97, 111, 282, 294, 296, 311, 312; abandonment of by the Georg Ritter Company, 110, 260, 390; accusation of against Cary, 81; advice of regarding defense of the Province, 88, 242; agent of colonists in dealing with the Proprietors, 69, 362; agreement of with the Commissioners, 68; agreement of with the Indians regarding a ransom, 83, 271; alliance with the Canavest Indians, 384; amount expended by, 72; amount of livestock supplied by 106, 107; amount of money and goods needed by, 291; amount of provisions to be furnished by, 363; appeal of for assistance, 263; arrangement of with the Proprietors, 45; arrival of in America, 49, 57, 226, 369; arrival of in Bern, 390; arrival of in Virginia, 51, 369; available funds of at the beginning of the colonization project, 48; attempt of to obtain his slaves, 91, 253; attempt of to settle in Vir-

INDEX 425

Graffenried—*Continued.*
ginia, 88-91, 242; belief of that Cary instigated the Indians against him, 76, 81, 228, 234; bailiff of Iferton, 29; bond given by, 46; called into the council against Cary, 74, 230; called into court, 85, 235; cannon used by, 87, 244; capture of by the Indians, 76, 80, 264; care of for the colony, 46, 224; care of for the miners, 92, 257, 388; clause against extortion in the treaty of neutrality of, 83, 281; colonists criticized by, 107, 255, 256; commissioned to solicit military help, 88, 243; condemned to death, 80, 266; confidence of the Indians in lost, 86, 234, 238; consideration for the peasants shown by, 30, 359; contract of with the Georg Ritter Company, 48, 107, 292; contract of with the Lords Proprietors for assistance, 363; contribution of 5,000 acres of land by, 109; courtship of, 29; critical position of, 59, 73, 74, 86, 286, 371; criticised for mortgaging the colonists' lands, 109; deceived by Michel, 89; defense of against calumnies, 236, 238, 382; defense of New Bern by, 87, 262; defrauded by Bötschi, 104; delayed at Governor Hyde's, 88, 241; delay of in giving ransom, 84, 237; departure of from London for Bern, 93, 259, 364; deserted by the Palatines, 85, 240; difficulties with Brice, 85, 236-240, 382; discrepancy in statements of regarding the part the settlers played in the Cary troubles, 72; disposal of Palatines' lands by, 70; dissatisfaction of the colonists with, 288; duties of towards the colonists, 363; efforts of to provide for the colony, 87, 88, 388; employer of Benedict Zionien, 312; empowered to marry and baptize, 46, 377; entrance of into the Swiss colonization company, 44, 45; entrance of into the Ritter Company, 47; espousal of Hyde's cause by, 62, 227; exercise of seignorial rights by, 69, 87, 246; exploring expedition of, 75, 76, 80, 81, 82, 83, 263; expedition of in search of silver, 383; failure of in obtaining assistance for the colony, 75, 94,

Graffenried—*Continued.*
97, 230, 234, 240, 242, 248, 254, 255, 257, 260, 283, 370, 378, 390; failure of to make settlement at Canavest, 88-91, 254; failure of to make settlements on the Potomac, 88-91, 247-251; fairness of in dealing with the Indians, 59, 374; feudal system planned for, 67, 68; financial difficulties of, 251, 252, 254, 259; fortification of New Bern by, 63, 240, 262, 378, 383; fortitude of, 268; friendship of the Indians for, 76, 80, 82, 234, 275; friendliness of towards the Indians, 60, 61, 234, 275, 376, 380; governorship refused by, 57, 90, 228, 252, 370; grant of land to, 45, 362; granted degree by Cambridge University, 29; hygienic instructions given by, 75, 372; inability of to take slaves to Canavest, 91, 251; in a position of authority, 372; incidents of voyage to America, 367, 368, 369; incidents of voyage to Europe, 387, 388; Indian protected by, 235; Indians made suspicious of, 235; influence of with the Indians, 60; influential personage, 59; in London, 43, 92, 257-259, 388; in peril from his subjects, 382; in Switzerland, 33, 93-95, 260, 390; interview with Cary, 62, 371; in war with the Indians, 86, 87, 243-245, 372; irregularities in the appointment as landgrave, 66; journey to obtain assistance from Governor Hyde, 87, 240; journey to Maryland, 88-90, 253, 254, 383-385; judge of the colony, 68, 69, 235, 381; jurisdiction of, 363; justification of, 221, 359; lack of democratic feeling of, 70; lack of evidence of a return to America, 96, 97; last years and death of, 95; led to expect substantial assistance, 49; letter of to Anton von Graffenried, 95; life of spared, 80, 269; loss of papers belonging to, 97, 367; made colonel, 230; made landgrave, 45, 102, 283, 362; means taken by to keep peace with the Indians, 103, 375; meeting with Michel, 33; mill built by, 63, 228, 287, 288, 315; mining rights defined, 47, 48; misrepresented in London, 292; mistaken for Governor Hyde, 81, 233, 265; negotia-

Graffenried—*Continued.*
tions with the Indians hampered by Brice's attack, 83, 237; neutrality of, 82-84, 238, 271; not a member of the Swiss colonization company on April 28th, 44; not in England at the time of the death of Beaufort and Queen Anne and the accession of George I, 94; offered the presidency of the council, 57, 90, 228, 252, 370; opposition of to Cary, 62, 227; original plans of, 33; part taken by in the Hyde and Cary troubles, 74; part played by in the Indian War, 84, 87; partnership of with Michel, 33, 43; permission granted by for colonists to enter the service of the English planters, 69, 87, 246; persistency of in the search for silver, 6; petition of to Queen Anne, 97, 257, 390; plans of for the city of New Bern, 63, 288, 377, 378; plan of to settle in Maryland and Virginia, 88, 240, 361; plea of for a new attempt to finance the company, 94, 286, 390; prisoner among the Indians, 80, 82, 83, 261-275; provision made by for the welfare of the colony, 73, 106, 227, 228, 307, 377-380; provision made for the German miners, 92, 258, 388; provisions supplied by, 59, 62, 229, 287, 370; purchase of land by, 45; purchase of sloops by, 379; ransom given to the Indians by, 83, 84, 237; reasons why Graffenried was easily deceived regarding silver, 385; released by the Indians, 83, 262, 275; relief brought to the first settlers by, 59, 226; religious services conducted by, 73, 377; report of, 72, 282, 379; resolution of to go to America, 30, 223, 360; responsible for 17,500 acres of land, 45; return of to England, 92-94, 255-257, 387-388; return of to North Carolina from the exploring trip to the Potomac River, 90, 249; return of to Switzerland, 93, 260, 388; satisfaction given by the administration of, 70, 306-320; security given by, 286; signature of required by Penn, 283; support of the colony for 22 weeks by, 87, 240; sent to Virginia for help, 74, 75, 232; settlers' lands mortgaged by, 97, 98, 109; share in the Georg

Graffenried—*Continued.*
Ritter Company, 48, 294; son of in America, 96; suggestion of to use cannon against the Indians, 87, 344; titles of, 362; treaty of with the Indians, 82-87, 237, 281; treaty with the proprietors, 68, 362; trouble of with the captain of a vessel, 365; unable to warn the settlers, 82, 270; unable to collect a note for £100, 231; vindication of, 101; visit of to the Core Indians, 76, 380; visit of to Holland and England, 33; wife of, 96.
Granville, Lord, 56, 57.
Graves, 97.
Gravesend, 225, 259, 360, 388.
Great Deed, 54.
Grenwich, 259, 388.
Grist mill, 63, 287, 288, 315.
Guiguetan, 369.
Gulf of Mexico, 22, 251, 368.
Gulf Stream, 369.

Habegger, Peter, 316.
Hague also Haag, 18, 19.
Haldmann, 315.
Hamburg, 34.
Hampton, 253, 369.
Hamstead, 369.
Hancock, King, 76, 265, 266; town, 245, 273.
Hanover, 390.
Hanson & Co., 231.
Hartford, 364.
Harwich, 19, 259.
Hausmann, Christian, 315.
Heath, Robert, grant made by Charles II to, 53.
Heidelberg, 28.
Hellevotschluiss, 19.
Helvetian Corps, 390.
Hennepin, 31, 33, 261.
Herteln, Zacharias, 34.
Heybühl, 315.
Himmler, Jacob, 311, 312.
Hoen, Moritz Wilhelm, 51.
Holland, 12, 16, 17, 46, 47, 289, 305, 313, 315, 316, 319, 365, 366, 386, 390; arrival of Graffenried in, 224; cost of transportation from, 299; refuge for the persecuted, 9; trade with, 305; visited by Graffenried, 33.
Hontan, Baron de la, 261.
Hopf, Samuel, 292.

Horne, 31.
Horneg, chaplain to the Duke of Marlborough, 28.
House of Commons, investigation of the naturalization bill conducted by, 17.
Hunter, Governor, 22.
Hyde, Governor, 51, 58, 70, 72, 75, 88, 92, 103, 227, 228, 230, 232, 235, 236, 240, 241, 242, 246, 249, 253, 279, 371, 379; death of, 90, 251; entrance of into North Carolina, 72, 229; favored by Graffenried, 62, 229; Graffenried's slaves kept by, 251; hostility of the Indians, 81, 233, 234; libeled by Richard Roach, 231; Madame, 251, 253; recognized as governor, 74, 233; resistance of to the Indian invasion, 82, 242; to be deputized by Governor Tynte, 57.

Iferton, also Ifferton, Iverton, Yverdon, 29, 93, 95, 101, 260, 359, 390.
Immigrants, bill to naturalize, 16.
Immigration, Germans to New York, 9; to North Carolina, 9; to Pennsylvania, 9.
India, 308, 309.
Indian, protected by Graffenried, 235.
Indians, absence of danger from, 32, 39, 42, 263, 285; angered by Barnwell's treachery, 87, 245; attack made on the colonists by, 81, 228; attacked by Brice, 85, 238; at Core Town, 104; capture of Graffenried and Lawson by, 76, 264; causes for resentment of, 77-79; ceremonies of, 267, 274, 276; character of, 308, 309, 314, 317; cruelty of, 80, 280; danger from, 387; desire for revenge, 265; employed by the English Government, 81; fort of attacked, 86-87, 244-245; friendship of for Graffenried, 76, 276; frightened by cannon shots, 87, 244; Graffenried tract encumbered by, 59, 226; hostility of to the colony, 74, 81; idol belonging to destroyed by a colonist, 61, 278; ill treatment of by the English, 77-79, 234, 265-266; loss of confidence of in Graffenried, 86, 235, 238; messenger sent by to investigate Graffenried's neutrality, 381; need of keeping the settlers away from, 61, 374; plan of the General Assembly for

Indians—*Continued.*
defense against, 88, 242-243; ravages of, 86, 243, 262, 270; satisfaction of with Graffenried's treatment, 275, 376; skill with the canoe, 384; secure themselves against extortion, 83, 281; sold into slavery, 77, 87, 245; solemn league with, 285; subdued, 91, 245; torture of chief of, 86, 238; treaty of with Graffenried, 82-84, 86, 281, 374; trial of Graffenried and Lawson by, 80, 265; trade with, 40, 315, 317; used as guides, 75, 317; war, 86, 233, 383; causes of 234; Graffenried's part in, 87.
Indigo, 301.
Ireland, 65, 367; settlement of Germans in, 16.
Iron mined by Spottswood using Graffenried's miners, 110.
Iroquois, friendly to the English, 22.
Isot, 47, 288, 292, 296.

Jaccard, Captain, 244.
Jamaica, 44, 359, 367; cost of transportation to London from, 302; prices of provisions in, 301; trade with, 300.
James I, 10; James II, 9.
James River, colonists plundered at the mouth of, 51, 225.
Jantz, Christen, 319.
Janzen, Christen, 316.
Järsing, Johann Anthoni, 292.
Jerseys, 44, 256, 369.
Johann Heinrich, 311.
Johnston, Governor, 98.
John William, religious toleration announced by, 11.
Jones County, 99.

Ketelby, Abel, 65.
Kilchberger, Emanuel, 292.
Kilchmeyer, 310; Dreuthart, 319.
Klasner, Hans, 309.
Kocherthal, Joshua, 13, 17, 22, 317; Bericht of, 19, 31; date of appearance of the Bericht, 14; passages from, 14-15; settlement in New York, 11.
Krächig, Andreas, 311.
Kupferschmied, Benedict, 307, 316; Helm, 316.

Land, amount of secured for the colony, 43 47, 362-363; price of, 43-47, 362-363.
Landgrave, 43, 45, 57, 59, 61, 64, 65, 67, 69, 103, 362, 370; advantage of the office to the colony, 283; title of sold, 65; irregularities in the appointment of, 64-65; number of, 66.
Laws, popular assent to required, 54.
Lawson, John, also Surveyor-General, 33, 49, 104, 225, 244, 261, 267, 275, 293, 297, 360, 362, 373, 375, 392; accused by the Indians, 80, 266; captured by the Indians, 76, 264; condemned to death, 80, 266; death of, 80, 269-270; expedition of, 75, 263; journal of, 23, 33, 35-42, 60, 77, 80; fraud practised by, 59, 226; prisoner among the Indians, 76, 80; settlement of colonists by, 59, 226.
Leet Court, also Court Leet, 63-64, 67.
Leet man, 64, 67, 69, 71, 87.
Leipzig, 34.
Lerche, Uhli, 316.
Leyden, 28.
Liberty, 223; of conscience or religion, 11, 62, 103, 363; resistance to invasions of, 55; tradition of in Switzerland, 71.
Lieutenant Governor of Virginia, 369.
Litta, see Little River.
Little River, 249, 379.
Live stock, 36, 38, 86, 228, 238, 287, 308, 309, 312, 313, 314, 317, 327.
L. L. E. E. of Bern, 361.
Locke, John, 6, 55, 65; ideal of approached in the New Bern colony, 69.
London, 21, 43, 44, 48, 92, 94, 105, 225, 228, 230, 231, 233, 252, 258, 286, 288, 301, 311, 359, 360, 363 364, 370, 371, 379, 388; arrival of miners in 257; death of two children in, 318; duration of Graffenried's stay in, 93, 94; fleet of coal ships from, 366; return of Graffenried to, 257; return of settlers in Ireland to, 16.
Lord Palatine, 257.
Lord of a signiory, barony, manor, 64.
Lords, Commissioners of Trade, 24, 25, 77.
Lords Proprietors, also Lords or Proprietors, 13, 33, 42, 43, 44, 51, 54, 55, 56, 57, 58, 61, 62, 64, 65, 66, 98, 225, 227, 228, 230, 245, 275, 392; arrangement of with Graffenried

Lords Proprietors—*Continued.*
and Michel, 45; arrangement of with Graffenried, 362, 363; assistance of to the colonization project, 48, 68, 70, 371; confirmation of Hyde as governor by, 233; discouraged by the disasters, 104; failure of to give assistance, 49, 378; favorable to Graffenried, 252, 361; permission of required for obtaining large tracts of land, 65; plans of with reference to the Palatines, 45; privileges of, 362; promises of unfulfilled, 227; rights of, 53; share of in the mines, 47.
Lots, sale of in New Bern, 72, 288, 378.
Louis XIV, 10, 29.
Louisburg, 23.
Lowe, Em, 231.
Ludwell, Colonel Philip, 67.
Luther, 10.
Luttrell, 44, 50.
Lyons, 260, 264, 390.

Madagascar, 227.
Madeiras, cooperage required in, 302; price of wine in, 302; trade with, 300, 305.
Madiswyl, 311.
Magdeburg, 16.
Maherine Indians, 78.
Maintenon, Madame de, 10.
Margate, 259, 389.
Maria, death of, 312; Magdalena, 311.
Marlborough, Duke of, 16, 18, 19, 20, 28.
Marmuskit Indians, 270.
Martge, 310.
Mary, 9, 15.
Maryland, 44, 103, 240, 246, 247, 256, 289, 369, 384, 391; attempt of Graffenried to settle in, 88, 90, 253; mining rights of the colony in, 47; price of land per acre in, 38; proprietors of, 88; silver mines in, 6, 251.
Massachusetts, 5, 22.
Mayor, 307, 310, 311.
Mentzingen, 311.
Mexico, 91, 251, 386-387.
Michel, also Mitchel and M. M., 23, 34, 44, 65, 90, 92, 97, 104, 106, 247, 249, 251, 253, 282, 283, 284, 287, 289, 293, 294, 296, 305, 317, 376,

INDEX 429

Michel—*Continued.*
383, 384, 385, 392; agreement of with the Commissioners, 68; contract of with the Ritter Company, 47, 107, 292; contribution of 2,500 acres of land by, 45, 109; death of, 102, 375; debts of, 291; directed to bring colonists to Virginia, 89, 242; director-general of mines, 386; entrance of into the Ritter Company, 47; exploring expedition of, 290; failure of to bring settlers to the Potomac River, 89, 246, 248, 249; duplicity of, 89, 250; in command of the Palatine forces, 86, 244; Indian orator misused by, 61, 374, 375; made colonel, 244; mining rights of defined, 47, 292-295; negotiations of for land in Carolina and Virginia, 33; negotiations of for the Ritter Company, 45; new arrangement of with the Proprietors, 45; partnership of with Graffenried, 33; reached Nimwegen with convicts, 47; reliance of Graffenried upon reports of, 33, 88, 240, 290; share of in the Ritter Company, 48, 294.
Mill Creek, 98, 378.
Mill, built by the colonists, 63, 287, 288, 315.
Miners, agreement with, 386; arrival of in London, 257, 258; cared for by Graffenried, 92, 258; departure of 259; distress of, 386, 388; employed to work Spotswood's mines, 92; from Germany, 33; in England, 92; treaty with, 104, 376.
Mines, 40, 89, 90, 107, 247, 251, 254, 283, 290, 364, 376, 383, 385, 392.
Mining rights, 47.
Minister, function of performed by Graffenried, 46, 73, 377; from Virginia, 377; lack of, 313.
Mississippi River, proposal to settle along, 91, 250, 251, 386.
Mohawk chiefs, 21, 23.
Monk, General, 362.
Monzua, 310.
Moore, Colonel, 91, 245.
Mörigen, 318.
Moritz, death of, 317.
Morotok River, 34.
Morton, Landgrave, 65.
Mühlinen, Christian von, 314; Salome von, 314.

Müller, Uhli, 308; wife of, 307.
Müntzi, Uhli, 307.
Murton, 95.
Muscovy, 366.

N. sign of Neuse, 83, 282, 382.
Natoway, 83, 272, 273.
Naturalization, 302; bill investigated, 17, 18.
Navigation laws resisted, 55.
Negroes, 40; attempt of Graffenried's to reach him, 91, 253; captured with Graffenried, 75, 263, 267, 269, 270; property of Graffenried, 251, 254.
Netherlands, 15.
Neuchatel, 29, 30, 223, 360.
Neujahrsblatt, 93, 96.
Neuse, also News, 43, 45, 52, 59, 63, 68, 82, 87, 98, 226, 240, 244, 245, 248, 262, 266, 293, 305, 308, 309, 310, 314, 318, 362, 372, 373, 377, 378, 382; Indian attacks on, 238, 262, 270; sign of, 282.
New Bern, 33, 34, 71, 81, 86, 90, 99, 110, 229, 233, 235, 243, 244, 249, 272, 277, 282, 311, 312, 380; attacked by the Indians, 82, 238; capital of the province, 111; form of government of, 63, 70, 71; Graffenried's return from captivity to, 83, 261; immunity from Indian attacks, 82, 270; location of, 59, 63, 226, 373; location bought from the Indians, 60, 234, 269; naming of the city, 63, 71, 378; payments for the site of, 275; price paid the Indians for the site of, 374; plans for, 377, 378; precarious position of, 73, 87, 240; prosperity of, 63, 228, 377, 378; re-inhabited, 245; rights of, 363; relief for destroyed, 88, 241; unhealthful location of, 59, 226; visit of Cary to, 230.
Newcastle, 103, 283, 307, 308, 313, 316, 365.
New England, 44, 291, 365, 369; historians, 5.
New Englanders, 53.
Newfoundland, 368, 387.
New York, 25, 50, 92, 94, 253, 367; description of, 256; German emigrants to, 9.
Nicholson, Governor, gold discovered by, 290.
Nidauw, 318.

Nider Linog, 311.
Nimwegen, 47.
Noncomformists, 370.
Norris, Vice-Admiral, 225.
Northern Neck, 88.
North Carolina, 33, 41, 42, 43, 48, 51, 57, 96, 97, 102, 111, 226, 227, 251, 293, 295, 311, 313, 316 361, 370, 386, 392; Colonial Records of, 93, 101, 102; cost of surveying in, 296; favorable conditions in, 260, 361; German emigrants to, 9; grant of to the Proprietors, 362; Indian war on, 270; Island of, 308; not a frontier, 40; plan of a colony for, 361.
N. R. one of the directors, 370, 371.
Nunscimund River, 369.

Oath of office required, 56, 57.
Ochs, Joh. Rudolff, 261.
Old mixon, 261.
Onslow County, 99.
Orkney, Count, 255; Islands, 367.
Orpheus, 380.

Palatinate, 12, 15, 46, 47; devastation of by Louis XIV, 10; Lower, 10; Reformation in, 10; religious toleration in, 11.
Palatine blacksmith, punished by Graffenried, 69, 235, 381.
Palatines, 15, 16, 17, 48, 62, 68, 71, 72, 96, 109, 110, 240, 244, 294, 359, 381; abandonment of New Bern by, 235; among Brice's following, 85, 238; attack of on the Indians, 83, 86, 273, 274; boy discloses Brice's plot, 85, 236; character of criticized by Graffenried, 107, 255, 256; departure of from England, 364; disloyalty of, 69, 236, 237, 238, 240; dispersal of among the English colonists, 87, 245; emigration of to England, 9, 13, 16, 18, 224; disposal of, 21; implicated in torturing an Indian, 86, 238; induced to come to England, 17; massacred, 82, 240, 262; mortality of, 49, 50, 74, 225, 317, 372; number of taken by Graffenried, 45, 46, 47; persuaded to go to South Carolina, 250; petition of, 98; prisoners among the Indians, 82, 84, 235; proposals for transporting of to America, 44; provision made for in England, 12,

Palatines—*Continued*.
16, 20, 21, 224; sent to America, 22, 45, 224; settlement of in New York, 22; settlement of at Schoharie, 23; defrauded by Lawson and the directors, 59, 226; sufferings of, 51, 86, 229, 370, 371; transportation of, 50, 51; Graffenried's treaty with, 69, 363; used as a frontier against the Indians, 22, 23, 88, 98; willingness of to settle at Canavest, 254.
Pamlico River, 82.
Pamtego also Pampticough, 42, 240, 244, 245, 262, 266, 281; Indians attack on, 238, 262, 270.
Paris, 260, 364, 389, 390.
Parish of S. Thomas, 42.
Passage, price per hundred persons, 298.
Pastor, 310, 311; lack of 318.
Pastorius, settlement in Pennsylvania, 11.
Pembroke, 225.
Penn, William, 13, 68, 103, 104, 283, 364; contract with, 104, 376, 386.
Pennsylvania, also Pennsilvanie, 11, 44, 63, 68, 72, 103, 104, 246, 247, 251, 253, 256, 295, 369, 370, 375, 378, 383, 384, 385, 391, 392; conference with gentlemen from Pennsylvania regarding mines, 89, 247, 383, 385; expedition to discover silver in, 89, 246, 376, 383; mining rights in, 47; provisions obtained in, 227, 370; German immigrants into, 9; trade with, 299.
Pennsylvanische Berichte, 19.
Perret, Heinrich, 319.
Pfund, Margaret, 308, 309.
Philadelphia, 5, 104, 290, 376, 379.
Plösch, Benedict, 318.
Pollock, Colonel or Governor Thomas, 57, 70, 91, 98, 103, 106, 226, 248, 252, 286, 289, 371; Council of war at the home of, 74, 229; disapointed in receiving money due from Graffenried, 98; house of attacked, 74, 231; Indians misused by, 79; Palatines' land taken over by, 97; letter of Graffenried to, 93; letters of to Graffenried, 97; refusal of to grant supplies, 288; supplies obtained from, 229, 283; suspicious of Graffenried, 250.
Pollock, Cullen, 98.
Pontarlier, 390.

Popular assemblies in Switzerland, 71.
Porter, 55, 57, 81.
Portsmouth, 51.
Portugal, 225.
Potomac, 89, 102, 105, 246, 253, 360, 361, 384; falls of, 47, 89, 383, 384, 385; description of country near, 391; sites for settlements on, 89, 247, 386; intention of Graffenried to settle on, 88; land granted along, 224.
Presbyterians, 56.
Price, John, Landgrave, 65.
Price paid for land in Carolina, 43.
Proposals for transporting Palatines to America, 44-46.
Prince of Wales, 365.
Proprietorship, rights of in Carolina, 302.
Protestant, Cantons, 30; protestants, bill to naturalize, 16; protestantism, protected by England, 9; relation to Catholicism, in the Palatinate and Switzerland, 9-11; restored by Elizabeth and William of Orange, 9.
Provision, made by Graffenried for the colonists, 307; to be made for the voyage from Switzerland, 319; made for transporting the colonists, 363; prices of, 301.

Quakers, 13, 55, 56, 57, 74, 228, 230, 371, 383; excluded from the Assembly, 56; Quaker Proprietor, 74.
Queen Anne, also Queen or Anne, 13, 16, 19, 20, 47, 56, 58, 93, 98, 228, 229, 269, 282, 291, 293, 361; assistance granted to the colonists by, 46, 224; Cromwell's work taken up by, 9; death of, 94, 257; diplomatic methods of, 15; interviews of with Graffenried, 255; patents granted by for mining, 385; transportation for the colonists granted by, 46, 363.
Quit-rent, 43, 68, 296; amount of per acre, 54, 363; colonists relieved of 87, 246; higher in New Bern than elsewhere in the colonies, 69; raise in protested against, 55; reduced by the Great Deed, 54.

Ramsey, 389.
Rangers, 24, 93,
Rappahannock, 24.
Receiver-General, 48, 225, 283, 360.
Reformation, in England, 9; in Germany, 9; pamphlets on, 10.
Reformers, in England, 9; in Germany, 9.
Reformed Church, relation of to the Anabaptists, 11.
Religious convicts, 43, 46; become free on reaching Holland, 46; religious disturbances, 55.
Rents, 296, 317.
Resistance to governors and collectors in Carolina, 55.
Reutiger, Peter, 318.
Revolution, beginnings of in Carolina, 55.
Reya de la Plata, 44.
Rhode Island, 5.
Rhine, 46, 307.
Riggisberg, 311.
Ritter, Georg, 47, 70, 282, 288, 294, 295, 296, 307, 308, 314, 316, 319; contract of, 48, 292; share of in the Georg Ritter Company, 48, 295; Company, 33, 45, 72, 104, 107, 109, 110, 293; contract of, 106; discouragement of, 104; foundation of 47; Michel's contract with, 47, 48, 294; purchase of 10,000 acres of land by, 109; stock of, 48, 293.
Roach, Richard, 74, 231, 232, 371.
Roanoke River, 34.
Roche, 27.
Röhtiger, Peter, 319.
Rome, 9.
Rosier, 246, 247, 253, 383, 385, 392.
Rotterdam, 17, 18, 19, 307, 310, 312, 313, 315, 365; arrival of colonists in, 308, 309; goods to be purchased in, 314; trade with, 300.
Roux, secretary to the Duke of Carlyle, 28.
Royal Commissioners, also Committee, inspection of ships by, 49, 286, 288, 360, 364.
Ruegsegger, Hans, 308.
Rufascher, 309.
Ruisseau d'Or, 386.
Rümligen, 313.

Salome, 313 .
Salt pan, 315.
Sannen, 318, 319.

Santee River, 33, 35.
Sauer, Christoph, printer and publisher, 19.
Säumers, 310.
Schenectady, 25.
Schetele, Benedict, 311.
Schoolmaster, 73, 377.
Schoharie, German settlers at, 6, 23.
Scotch vessels, 367.
Scotland, 366.
Secretary, London Royal Society, 6.
Seeman, Peter, 307.
Sewee Indian, 35.
Shaftesbury, 55.
Sheets, Jacob, 98.
Shenandoah, also Senantona, 89, 384.
Shetland Isles, 366, 367.
Shields, 313.
Siebentaler people, death of, 317.
Silk industry in Carolina, 301.
Silver and silver mines, 6, 89, 90, 110. 223, 247, 251, 254, 258, 290.
Simmenthal, 314.
Simon Benedict, 311; Heinrich, 311; Johannes, 311, 312.
Smith, 31.
Society for the Propagation of the Gospel, 55, 73.
Soil, quality of in North Carolina, 38, 308, 309, 312, 314, 317, 318.
Solomon Creek, 229.
Somerton, 57, 370.
South Carolina, 77, 86, 227, 245, 250, 251, 252, 383; booklet on, 317; cost of surveying in, 296; Governor of, 75; Kocherthal's description of, 13, 317; military assistance supplied by, 88, 243, 244, 245.
South Islands, 287.
Southwick, 259, 388.
Spain, 250, 387.
Spanish, settlements, 22; succession, war of, 30.
Speismann, 320.
Spotswood, Governor, 42, 48, 51, 70, 75, 83, 233, 243, 253, 254, 256, 258; accusation of Cary by, 81; appeal of Graffenried to, 254; assistance given by, 88, 232, 372; attitude of towards Graffenried, 89; convoy granted, 89, 246; description of condition in New Bern, 86; description of the Indian massacre, 82; iron industry founded by, 110; letter of regarding the settlements along the Potomac River, 88;

Spotswood—*Continued.*
letter of regarding Graffenried's neutrality, 84; letter of showing that the Indians had cause for resentment, 77, 79; letter of regarding Graffenried's part in the Indian war, 87; letter of to the Indians, 272, 282; letter of to the Lords Commissioners of Trade, 24.
Stanian, also Stanyon, 102, 361, 390.
States General, 18, 46.
Stern, Joseph, 311; Johannes, 311.
St. Lawrence River, 22.
St. Saphorin, 46.
St. Stephen's Court, 310.
St. Valery, 259, 260, 388, 389, 390.
Sugar Islands, 44.
Sugar Loaf, 247, 384.
Sunderland, Duke of, 16; Earl of, 19.
Surveying, cost of, 296.
Sweden, 366.
Swiss, Swiss settlers, Switzers, 46, 47, 49, 68, 71, 96, 109, 224, 240, 244, 359, 389; Ambassador, 46; arrival of in America, 51, 57, 226; character of criticized, 256; colony to be used as a frontier against the Indians, 24; colonies, 293, 366; colonists, 318, 365; desperate situation of, 86; letters written by, 106, 306-320; massacred, 82, 237, 270; mentioned by Lawson, 23; settlement intended along the Potomac River mentioned by Spotswood, 88.
Switzerland, 13, 15, 33, 71, 90, 94, 306, 315; Anabaptists in, 11; refuge for the persecuted, 9; trade with, 300.

T. A. (Thomas Ashe), see Ashe.
Tasqui, also Tasky, 83, 272.
Taylor, 59, 269, 275, 281, 374, 380.
Thames, 259, 388, 389.
Thirty Years' War, 10.
Tofen, 313.
Torne, Henry, 18.
Tortuga, 300.
Townshend, English Ambassador, 46.
Trade, 223; between Carolina and other countries, 305; in tobacco ruined, 289; profits in, 296, 307, 313, 316; with the Indians, 78, 83, 317.

INDEX 433

Traders, dishonesty of, 78.
Trades in demand, 316.
Transportation, cost of between the Barbadoes, Jamaica, Antigua and London, 302; between Eurpoe and Carolina, 299; of Palatines criticized, 50.
Treaty of neutrality of Graffenried with the Indians, also truce, 82, 84, 87, 237, 238, 239, 271, 381.
Trent River, 45, 52, 59, 63, 68, 226, 266, 362, 373, 377; Indian attacks on, 238, 262, 270.
Truce, see treaty of neutrality.
Tscharner, Regine, wife of Christoph von Graffenried, 29, 96.
Treut, Uhli, 309.
Treuthart, Jacob, 310, Peter, 310.
Truwhart, 310.
Turenne, 10.
Tuscarrora Indians, also Tuscaro, Tuscaruru and Tuskuru, 25, 77, 243, 244, 245, 247, 269, 270, 272, 281, 282, 384; defeat of, 91; escape of Graffenried from, 261; incited by Porter 81; incursion of 82.
Tyne River, 365, 366.
Tynte, Governor of South Carolina, 57, 62, 229; death of, 227, 383.
Typhoid fever, 75.

Uhli, 306, 313.
Urmstone, 49, 73.
Usher of the Court, 311; daughter of, 315.

Vaud, 260, 390.
Versailles, taken as a model by the petty German princes, 11.
Vessel, also boat, brigantine, ship, sloop, 74, 106, 231; advisability of purchasing, 298, 300; destruction of, 90, 241; loss of when bringing relief, 88, 250; formalities for the purchase of, 305; outfitting of in England, 298; outfitting of in Holland, 305; profits to be made on, 306; purchase of by Graffenried, 73, 287, 379.
Vevay, 260, 390.
Vienna, 390.
Virginia, 25, 33, 34, 36, 40, 44, 51, 57, 58, 62, 63, 74, 75, 79, 91, 92, 94, 103, 109, 110, 226, 233, 236, 239, 240, 246, 247, 248, 253, 256, 264, 289, 291, 293, 294, 295, 311, 315, 367, 369, 370, 371, 372, 378, 382, 384;

Virginia—*Continued*.
391; arrival of colonists in, 225, 307, 309, 314, 316; copper ore in, 258; flour purchased in, 62, 227; Gazette, 96; Governor of, 33, 47, 97, 273, 275, 290, 360, 372, 383, 388; convoy granted by the Governor of, 89, 246, 248; Graffenried recommended to the Governor of 224; Indian trader from, 272; iron ore found in, 258; letter to the Indians from the Governor of, 272; Magazine, 96; Military help granted by the governor of, 88, 243; mining rights of the colony in, 47; Minister from, 377; price of land per acre in, 38; quit-rents in, 53; return of the ship captain to, 249; settlement of Graffenried in, 86, 88, 90, 242, 246, 251, 254, 361; silver mines in, 6, 89, 90, 110, 223, 247, 251, 254, 258, 290; trade of with the Madeiras, 300; traders from entrusted with the care of the miners, 388.
Virginians, 70; democratic spirit of, 372.
Vischer, M., 261; translation of Lawson's Journal by, 34.

Währe, Jacob, 310.
Walcker, Christian, 318, 319.
Waldo, German colony of, 25.
Walker, Governor, 56.
Waller, Lady, 28.
Waller, Sir William, 27, 28.
Walloons, 13.
Wassle, 310.
Wateree River, 34.
Weeks, 81.
Weetock River, 45, 68, 103, 244, 270, 362, 375.
Weinmann, Andreas, 311, 312.
Weiser, Conrad, Indians kept loyal to the English by, 23.
West Indies, 22.
Westphalia, Peace of, 11.
White Oak River, 98.
Wichtermann, 313.
Wiering, Thomas von, 34.
Wilkinsons Point, 281.
William of Orange, 9.
Williamsburg, 75, 96, 97, 253, 254, 367.
Winthrop, John, 6.
Woods, Edward, 296.

Worb, 29, 95; Graffenried memorial in the church at, 96.
Wray, 283, 292.
Wüll, Anna, 313.
Wyssenbach, 310.
Washington, 89, 105.

Yadkin River, 34.
Yarmouth, arrival of colonists in, 308, 313.
York, 365.

Zant, Anna Eva, 311; Daniel, 310, 311; Johannes, death of, 310.
Zechender, 289.
Zergen, Magistrate, 310.
Zioria, 318.
Zionien, Benedict, employed by Graffenried, 312.
Ziorien, 314; Michael, 314.
Zurutha, 264.
Zweysimmen, 310.

www.ingramcontent.com/pod-product-compliance
Lightning Source LLC
Chambersburg PA
CBHW051623230426
43669CB00013B/2157